AF782265

Real World
Macroeconomics

Second Revised First Edition

Edited by David Moglen

cognella
San Diego, CA

Bassim Hamadeh, CEO and Publisher
Christopher Foster, General Vice President
Michael Simpson, Vice President of Acquisitions
Jessica Knott, Managing Editor
Kevin Fahey, Cognella Marketing Manager
Jess Busch, Senior Graphic Designer
Stephanie Sandler, Licensing Associate

First published in the United States of America in 2012 by Cognella, Inc.

Printed in the United States of America

ISBN: 978-1-62131-163-8

cognella™

www.cognella.com 800.200.3908

CONTENTS

Introduction

By David Moglen

Economics. The economy. An economist. These words provoke images of factories churning out merchandise, money changing hands, or financial people on Wall Street, all of which is perfectly accurate. The idea of what is economics may seem somehow distant when you start, but it is all around you. You may well find as you go on that you have long ago internalized most concepts in economics. For example, most people make choices in life in an ongoing effort to make themselves as happy as possible. Businesses try to make as much money in profit as they can. Microeconomics formalizes these and other intuitive concepts into a toolbox of standard graphs, formulas, and reasoning to interpret, apply, and predict reality.

Major decisions are based on economics. How much should a company charge for their goods? How much output should they produce? How many workers should they hire? Microeconomics provides the tools to most profitably answer these questions, vital if you plan to have a role in running a company. Microeconomics explains the full implications of what happens when an industry is competitive, versus when it is monopolized, as well as market structures which fall in between those extremes.

This book contains several special features to enhance your learning and link the theory the real world.

In-Class Project

Numerous activities designed for small groups (up to five students per group) to apply concepts in a real-world context. Any of the in-class projects can be assigned as homework.

Unlocking the Mysteries

Discover the hidden answers to make your understanding of the model on a real-world level much more concrete; the story behind the graph. If rent control hurts some renters, why might they still support it? How exactly can minimum wage be modeled as causing unemployment when a doctor or a lawyer, or even someone making twenty dollars an hour, is not directly affected by an eight dollar minimum hourly wage? Why did mortgage lenders provide home loans if their professional expertise ensured them that the borrowers would default?

Discussion Questions

Open-ended inquiries to illuminate topics which can initiate discussion for the whole class, or be assigned for short-answer responses. Many of these question sets will follow incisive articles or excerpts on issues that profoundly resonate for people in their everyday lives.

Experiments

Economic experiences which involve everyone's simultaneous participation to simulate a real market. Thus, experiments must be held in class.

These frequently interspersed features will reinforce your knowledge, as will the contributing authors' question sets available for your practice at the end of each chapter.

The * ("star" or "asterisk") symbol indicates that particular question is somewhat more difficult or requires deeper analysis. It is up to the teacher whether starred questions will be required along with non-starred questions in a given problem set, offered as bonus questions, or discussion topics for the class as a whole.

You will cultivate a skill in reading between the lines when analyzing news stories, current events, and important real-world situations. You will develop the tools to work with the economic forces behind the choices and conflicts faced by yourself and your community.

CHAPTER 1
Modern Economics

1 Modern Economics

By Joseph E. Stiglitz and Carl E. Walsh

The past decade has seen tremendous changes in the world economy. Many of these changes are linked to new technological advances that have transformed what the global economy produces, the ways in which many goods and services are produced, where they are produced, and how goods and services are transferred from the firms that produce them to the households, governments, and other firms that buy them. New technologies are transforming everything, from how airlines sell tickets to how automobiles are produced, from how we buy books to how we communicate with one another.

Like the industrial revolution of the eighteenth and nineteenth centuries that transformed first Britain and then other countries from agricultural to manufacturing based economies, the information revolution of the late twentieth and early twenty first centuries promises to transform almost all aspects of our daily lives. In 1999, in recognition of the growing importance of new, high-tech firms, Microsoft and Intel the producer of the Windows computer operating system and the major producer of the microprocessors at the heart of personal computers, respectively, were added to the Dow-Jones Industrial Average, the most widely followed index of prices on U.S. stock markets. Though the booming stock market of the late 1990s that was driven in part by enthusiasm for new technologies came to an end in 2000, innovation continues to be a critical force in the economy.

But the old economy is still alive and kicking. Four of the five largest United States corporations in *Fortune* magazine's top 500 list for 2003 were traditional industrial firms—General Motors, Exxon, Ford, and General Electric. IBM at number 8 and Verizon Communications at number 10 were the only information or "tech" firms in the top 10. Hewlett-Packard was number 14 and Dell Computers was 36, but Microsoft managed to make it no higher than number 47.

So the old economy and the new economy coexist side by side. But it is not just the emergence of new software and Internet companies that represents the effects of new technologies. The way all firms do business is being changed, and their customers are being affected too. Assembly lines now rely on robots aided and controlled by computers. Car repair shops with grease-stained floors have been replaced by clean, quiet garages where computers diagnose a car's problems. The way we buy things is also changing. Whether an individual purchases a car, book, or CD over the Web; books a hotel or plane reservation; or even applies to a college through the Internet, the relationship between people and firms is evolving. New technologies are changing the way courses are taught, too—textbooks like this one have Web sites that provide students with help, with interactive exercises, and with links to news, policy debates, and the latest economic information. The address of the home page for this text is www.wwnorton.com/stiglitzwalsh4.

With such far-reaching changes, what insights and understanding does the study of economics have to offer? After all, the field usually looks to Adam Smith, an eighteenth-century Scottish professor of moral philosophy, as its founder. Smith published his most famous book, *The Wealth of Nations*, in 1776, a time when today's industrial economies were still overwhelmingly agriculture-based. It might seem unlikely that a theory developed to understand the factors that determine the price of wheat would have much to say about today's modern economy.

But, in fact, study of economics continues to provide a critical understanding of today's global economy. As Carl Shapiro and Hal Varian of the University of California, Berkeley, put it, "Technology changes. Economic laws do not."[1] The way we produce things, what we produce, and how goods are exchanged have altered tremendously since Smith wrote. Yet the same fundamental laws of economics that explained agricultural prices in the eighteenth century can help us understand how economies function in the twenty-first century The foundation laid by Adam Smith and built upon by generations of economists has yielded insights that will continue to offer guidance to anyone wishing to make sense of the modern economy.

Over the past two hundred years, economists have refined and expanded our understanding of economic behavior. By incorporating the role of information and technological change, they are now able to explain much more than was possible just twenty years ago, offering new insights into topics that range from why car dealers build fancy showrooms to how the factors important for encouraging the production of new ideas differ from those that encourage the production of new cars.

But what are these insights? What do economists study? And what can we learn from looking at things from the perspective of economics? How can economics help us understand why we need to worry about the extinction of salmon but not of sheep, why auto manufacturers advertise but wheat farmers don't, why countries that rely on uncoordinated markets have done better than countries that rely on government planners, and why letting a single firm dominate an industry is bad?

The headlines from some recent news stories involving the computer industry and the Internet illustrate some of the key issues that a study of economics can help illuminate.

[1]Carl Shapiro and Hal R. Varian, *Information Rules: A Strategic Guide to the Network Economy* (Boston: Harvard Business School Press, 1999), p. 2.

- **"Bill to Curb Online Piracy Is Challenged as Too Broad,"** *New York Times,* June 24, 2004. A bill recently introduced in the U.S. Senate aims to restrict the illegal online sharing of music and other files. This proposed legislation represents just the latest development in the running battle between the companies that own the rights to the music and consumers who want to freely share music files. After all, it doesn't cost the music company any more to have a file shared by a thousand people than it does to have it shared by two. So why, many ask, should they have to pay for music files? The advent of digital music has made it possible for listeners to exchange copies indistinguishable from the originals. But if the producers of the music cannot earn a profit, they have less incentive to seek out and record new artists. Property rights in this case, the legal right of the music company to charge for the use of its property, play an important role in market economics, and disputes over property rights aren't new. But the new information technologies have made trading this property much easier and raised new questions. As we will see, economics can tell us a great deal about the issues involved in these disputes.

- "**Internet Drug Trade Proves Bitter Pill for Canada**," *Financial Times,* April 21, 2004. The Internet has changed the nature of the market for goods such as prescription drugs. Buyers in Florida can as easily have their prescriptions filled by a pharmacy based in California, or Canada, as by one in Florida. But why has this led to shortages of some popular prescription drugs in Canada? What will be the likely consequences for drug prices in Canada and the United States?

- **"Intel Cancels 2 Chip Projects,"** *San Jose Mercury News,* May 8, 2004. After spending as much as $2 billion on a new line of computer chips called the Itanium, Intel pulled the plug on the project. As the company decided whether to go ahead with the project, was the money already invested a factor? Firms are always concerned about costs, but economics gives critical insights that help us understand which costs are important and whether some costs, such as the $2 billion Intel had already sunk into the Itanium project, aren't.

- **"EBay Bids and Buys Baazee,"** *The Economic Times,* June 23, 2004. According to a story on economictimes.indiatimes.com, the online auction company eBay purchased Baazee.com, an Indian online shopping company, for $50 million. The purchase extends eBay's network throughout Asia, adding to its current ventures in Hong Kong, Singapore, and China. By linking online buyers and sellers globally, eBay will enable a consumer in Sioux City, Iowa, to trade with someone in Bangalore, India.

- **"Oracle's Bid for PeopleSoft to Be Tested in Court,"** *New York Times,* June 7, 2004. In early 2004, the software giant Oracle announced that it was making a hostile bid to buy PeopleSoft, another software company. The U.S. Justice Department initially filed a lawsuit to block this takeover, arguing that it would reduce competition in the market for business software. Oracle was eventually allowed to take over PeopleSoft, but why does the government try to ensure that there is competition? What are the advantages of competition? What tools does the government use to promote competition?

- **"FASB Holds Meeting on Expensing Stock Options,"** *San Jose Mercury News,* June 24, 2004. Many tech companies, particularly those located in California's Silicon Valley, have used stock options to reward their employees.

This mechanism grants the employee the opportunity to purchase shares in the company at a set price. If the company does well and its shares go up in value, the employee can sell the stock for a profit—a prospect that creates an incentive to work hard and help the company succeed. The Federal Accounting Standards Board (FASB) proposed new accounting rules requiring firms that offer stock options to report these as an expense, thereby reducing the firm's reported profits. The FASB argues that to do so would present investors with a more accurate picture of the firm's profits, enabling investors to make better decisions about buying stock in the company.

News headlines frequently focus on economic issues, and these six point to some of the key topics that economists study: the role of incentives and information, globalization and exchange, competition and government regulation, costs and business decisions. The study of economics will give you new insights into the news stories you see in the paper, it will give you insights into the world of business, and it will help you understand the world of economics you participate in every day.

> **Internet Connection**
>
> TRACKING THE DIGITAL ECONOMY
>
> Since 1998 the U.S. department of Commerce has issued an annual report on the digital economy. You can find the latest, report at www.esa.doc.gov/reports.cfm.

What Is Economics?

Headlines can illustrate many of the important issues with which economics deals, but now a definition of our subject is in order. *Economics* studies how individuals, firms, government, and other organizations within our society make *choices,* and how these choices determine society's use of its resources. Why did consumers choose to buy small, energy-efficient cars in the 1970s and large sports utility vehicles in the 1990s? What determines how many individuals work in health care industries and how many work in the computer industry? Why did the income gap between rich and poor rise in the 1980s? To understand how choices are made and how these choices affect the use of society's resources, we must examine five concepts that play an important role: trade-offs, incentives, exchange, information, and distribution.

1. Choice involves **trade-offs**—deciding to spend more on one thing leaves less to spend on something else; devoting more time to studying economics leaves less time to study physics.
2. In making choices, individuals respond to **incentives**. If the price of Zen MP3 players falls relative to the price of iPods, there is a greater incentive to buy a Zen. If the salaries for engineers rise relative to the salaries of people with an MBA, there is an increased incentive to choose to study for an engineering degree rather than a business degree.
3. When we **exchange** with others, our range of choices becomes larger.
4. Making intelligent choices requires that we have, and utilize, **information**.
5. Finally, the choices we make, about how much education to get, what occupation to enter, and what goods and service to buy, determine the **distribution** of wealth and income in our society.

These five concepts define the core ideas that are critical to understanding economics. They also guide the way economists think about issues and problems. Learning to "think like an economist" means learning how to discover the trade-offs and incentives faced, the implications of exchange, the role of information, and the consequences for distribution. These key concepts are emphasized throughout the text in "Thinking Like an Economist" boxes.

TRADE-OFFS

Each of us is constantly making choices—students decide to study at the library rather than in the dorm, to have pizza rather than sushi, to go to college rather than work full-time. Societies, too, make choices—to preserve open spaces rather than provide more housing, to produce computers and import televisions rather than produce televisions and import computers, to cut taxes rather than increase government expenditures. In some cases, individuals or governments explicitly make these choices. You decided to study economics rather than some other subject. The government decides each year whether to cut taxes or to increase spending. In other cases, however, the choices were the result of the uncoordinated actions of millions of individuals. Neither the government nor any one individual decided that the United States would import cars from Japan and export wheat to India. But in each case, choice involves trade-offs—to get more of one thing involves having less of something else. We are forced to make trade-offs because of **scarcity.**

Scarcity figures prominently in economics; choices matter because resources are scarce. For most of us, our limited income forces us to make choices. We cannot afford everything we might want. Spending more on rent leaves less available for clothes and entertainment. Getting a sunroof on a new car may mean forgoing leather seats to stay within a fixed budget. Limited income is not the only reason we are forced to make trade-offs. Time is also a scarce resource, and even the wealthiest individual must decide what expensive toy to play with each day. When we take time into account, we realize scarcity is a fact of life for everyone.

One of the most important points on which economists agree concerns the critical role of scarcity. We can summarize this point as follows:

There is no free lunch. Having more of one thing requires giving up something else. Scarcity means that trade-offs *are a basic, fact of life.*

INCENTIVES

It is one thing to say we all face trade-offs in the choices we make. It is quite another to understand how individuals and firms make choices and how those choices might change as economic circumstances change. If new technologies are developed, will firms decide to increase or decrease the amount of labor they employ? If the price of gasoline rises, will individuals decide to buy different types of automobiles?

When faced with a choice, people evaluate the pros and cons of the different options. In deciding what to eat for dinner tonight, you and your roommates might weigh the advantages and disadvantages of having a frozen pizza again over going out for sushi. Similarly, a firm evaluates the pros and cons of its alternatives in terms of the effects different choices will have on its profits. For example, a retail chain deciding on the location for a new store must weigh the relative advantages of different locations. One location might have more foot traffic but also higher rent. Another location might be less desirable but have lower rent.

When decision makers systematically weigh the pros and cons of the alternatives they face, we can predict how they will respond to changing economic conditions. Higher gas prices raise the cost of driving, but the cost of driving a fuel-efficient car rises less than the cost of driving a sports utility vehicle. Therefore, households weighing a car purchase have a greater incentive to choose the fuel-efficient car. If a firm starts selling more of its goods through the Internet, it will rely less on foot traffic into its retail store. This shift reduces its incentive to pay a high rent for a good location.

Economists analyze choices by focusing on incentives. In an economic context, incentives are benefits (including reduced costs) that motivate a decision maker in favor of a particular choice. Many things can affect incentives, but among the most important are *prices.* If the price of gasoline rises, people have a greater incentive to drive less. If the price of MP3 players falls, people have a greater incentive to buy one. When the price of a good rises, firms are induced to produce more of that good, in order to increase their profits. If a resource used in production, such as labor or equipment, becomes more expensive, firms have an incentive to find new methods of production that economize on that resource. Incentives also are affected by the return people expect to earn from different activities. If the income of college graduates rises relative to that of people with only a high school diploma, people have a greater incentive to attend college.

When economists study the behavior of people or firms, they look at the incentives being faced. Sometimes these incentives are straightforward. Increasing the number of courses required to major in biology reduces the incentive to pick that major. In other circumstances, they may not be so obvious. For example, building safer cars may create incentives to drive faster. Identifying the incentives, and disincentives, to take different actions is one of the first things economists do when they want to understand the choices individuals or firms make.

Decision makers respond to incentives; for understanding choices, incentives matter.

Trade-offs and Incentives in Practice: Online Music Sharing

Since 1999, when Napster introduced the first file-sharing program that allowed users to swap music files over the Internet, the practice has been embroiled in controversy. On one side is the music industry, which views the sharing of music files as an illegal activity, and on the other side are the companies producing the software that allows file sharing and the millions of music lovers who do not want to pay for music. The debates now also encompass the movie industry, as digitized movies can be shared as easily as music files. The legal battle between MGM and Grokster, a distributor of peer-to-peer file-sharing software, reached the United States Supreme Court in 2005.

Incentives are at the heart of the case against file sharing. Record companies make money by selling CDs. They, or the artists who create the music, hold copyrights that give them the right to charge others for its use. Copyrighted material, which includes books like this text as well as music, cannot be distributed or sold without the permission of the copyright holder. In that way, the holder of the copyright—the book publisher, author, artist, composer, or record company—is able to limit access to the material and charge a fee for its use. When music could only be copied by physically duplicating a tape recording or burning a CD, it was costly to make illegal copies. While people might burn a CD to use in the car or give to a friend, this type of sharing was relatively minor, and something the music industry tolerated.

The advent of digital music changed the situation dramatically. Now, a music file can be shared with millions of other listeners. In 1999, Napster introduced a filesharing service that focused exclusively on music. In the process, Napster helped to popularize the MP3 format; by February 2001 the service had over 26 million users worldwide. Napster also quickly attracted the attention of the record companies, who sued Napster for distributing copyrighted music without paying royalties to the copyright holders. In 2001, Napster settled the lawsuit, agreeing to pay $26 million to the music copyright holders. Faced with paying this huge fee, Napster declared bankruptcy in 2002. It has recently converted itself to a subscription service for downloading music legally.

Napster's place has been taken by services such as Grokster and Morpheus that offer peer-to-peer (p2p) file sharing. In their legal battles with the music industry, these services have argued that they should not be held liable simply becuse their products might be used to duplicate copyrighted materials illegally. However, in July 2005, the U.S. Supreme Court ruled that the services could be found liable because they knowingly promoted products that were designed to infringe on the rights of copyright holders and did nothing to disourage this illegal activity.

So how does all this relate to the concept of incentives? First, free music clearly creates an incentive for music lovers to download songs rather than pay for them by buying a CD. This is at the heart of the music industry's opposition to p2p file sharing. Second, if record companies cannot charge for their music because it can be downloaded for free, they have less of an incentive to record new music. According to the record industry, by reducing the incentive to produce new music, file sharing will ultimately reduce the opportunities for new musicians to record with major record labels.

While the effects of free, online file sharing on incentives are clear, the magnitude of those effects is open to debate. The music industry points to a decline in CD sales, from 942.5 million CDs in 2000 to 766.9 in 2004, as evidence that the availability of free downloads has hurt their business. However, critics of the music industry argue that this decline in sales is simply a reflection of the economic slowdown and rise in unemployment that began in 2001. Some studies have argued that the availability of free music downloads might actually increase CD sales. Listening to music online can actually increase interest in new music and individuals who are able to listen to music online before buying an album may actually be more likely to purchase CDs. A study by economists at the University of North Carolina and the Harvard Business School was unable to find any effect of online access to music on subsequent CD sales.

Whatever the ultimate outcome of this battle might be, incentives are essential to understanding the issues. The incentive to avoid paying

Thinking Like an Economist

INCENTIVES AND THE PRICE OF AOL

Today, most online services such as AOL charge their customers a fixed monthly fee for Internet access. In the earlier days of the Internet, the access charge was commonly based on how many minutes the member was connected to the Internet. In 1997, AOL announced that it would change its pricing policy and move to a flat monthly fee with unlimited minutes of connect time. AOL's servers were quickly overwhelmed and members found it almost impossible to log on.

Why? Because charges were no longer based on the number of minutes a member was logged on, many customers never logged off. Once connected, they simply left AOL running, typing up its modem capacity. When members had to pay on a per-minute basis, they had an incentive to log off when the service was not being used. The flat fee left no incentive to economize on connect time. The flat fee left no incentive would have shown AOL that it need to greatly increase its modem capacity before announcing the new pricing plan.

for music provided by low-cost or free access reduces the incentive of record companies to discover, record, and promote new musical talents.

EXCHANGE

Somehow, decisions that are made by individuals, households, firms, and government as they face trade-offs and respond to incentives, together determine how the economy's limited resources, including its land, labor, machines, oil, and other natural resources, are used. The key to understanding how this happens lies in the role of *voluntary* exchange in *markets*.

Long before the rise of modern industrial societies, the benefits of exchange were well understood. Coastal societies with access to fishing resources, for example, would trade some of their fish to inland societies in return for meat and furs. The coastal group sought meat and furs that were worth more to them than the fish they gave up; the inland group likewise exchanged meat and furs for fish. Both groups benefited from voluntary exchange.

In modern societies, millions of exchanges take place. Few individuals produce any of the goods and services they themselves want to consume. Instead, teachers, police officers, lawyers, and construction workers sell their labor services to a school district, a city, a client, or a homebuilder and then exchange the income they earn for all the various goods and services they wish to consume that are produced by others. An important insight in economics is the recognition that *both* parties in a voluntary exchange gain. Whether it takes place between two individuals, between an individual and a firm, or between residents of two different countries, exchange can improve the well-being of both parties.

Economists describe any situation in which exchange takes place as *a market*. For thousands of years, societies have established physical locations such as village markets or periodic trading fairs where people have brought their products, haggled over terms of exchange, and reaped the benefits of trade. The economic concept of markets covers any situation in which exchange takes place, though this exchange may not necessarily resemble a traditional village market or a modern stock exchange. In department stores and shopping malls, customers rarely haggle over the price. When manufacturers purchase the materials they need for production, they give in exchange money, not other goods. Most goods, from cameras to clothes, are not sold directly from producers to consumers. Instead they are sold from producers to distributors, from distributors to retailers, and from retailers to consumers. All of these transactions are embraced by the concept of markets and a **market economy**.

In a market economy like that of the United States, most exchanges take place through markets, and these exchanges are guided by the prices of the goods and services involved. The goods and services that are scarcer, or require more resources for their production, come at a higher price. Automobiles are more expensive than paper cups; lawyers charge more than janitors. As a result, markets enable consumers and firms to make choices that reflect scarcity, and therefore lead to efficient uses of resources.

Internet Connection

AUCTION SITES

An auction is one form of market that used to require potential buyers to be physically present in a single location. Now, auctions are held over the Internet and can involve participants from around the world. Some sites, such as eBay (www.ebay.com), offer just about everything for sale. Other sites specialize. For instance, Heritage Coins (www.heritagecoins.com) provides an auction site for rare coins. Even the U.S. government has gotten into the act. The U.S. Treasury does not actually auction items online, but it uses the Web to publicize the locations at which confiscated property will be auctioned (www.treas.gov/auctions/customs.)

Market economies thus rely primarily on market exchanges to resolve the most basic economic questions: What and how much is produced? How is it produced? For whom is it produced? And who makes the economic decisions? Individuals and firms make the decisions. Individuals make decisions that reflect their own desires as they respond to the incentives they face. Firms make decisions that maximize their profits, and to do so they strive to produce the goods that consumers want at the lowest possible cost. This process determines what is produced, how it is produced, and for whom. As firms compete in the quest for profits, consumers benefit, both from the kinds of goods produced and from the prices at which they are supplied. On the whole, markets ensure that society's resources are used efficiently.

In some areas, however, markets lead to outcomes that society may find inadequate. There may be too much pollution, too much inequality, and too little concern about education, health, and safety. When the market is not perceived to be working well, people often turn to government. An economy such as in the United States is often called *a mixed economy*—one that relies primarily but not exclusively on the free interaction of producers and consumers to determine what is produced, how, and for whom. In some areas, the government makes the decisions, in others it imposes regulations that affect the incentives firms and households face; and in many areas, both the *private sector* (households and businesses) and the *public sector* (local, state, and federal governments) are involved (education is a good example).

Governments play a critical role in all market economies. For example, governments provide the legal structure within which private firms and individuals operate. No one would open a store if others could simply steal things off the shelf with impunity; the store owner needs to know there is a legal system that he can use to prosecute theft. No bank would lend money to a family to buy a home if it could not legally require the family to repay the loan. Governments also regulate businesses in many ways. There are regulations to ensure firms do not discriminate by race or sex, do not mislead consumers, and are careful about the safety of their workers. In some industries, such as education and mail service, the government is a major supplier of services. In other industries, such as the defense industry, government is the major purchaser. The government also supplies goods and services that the private sector does not, such as the national defense, roads, and currency. Government programs provide for the elderly through Social Security (which pays income to retired individuals) and Medicare (which funds the medical needs of the aged). The government helps those who have suffered economic dislocation, through unemployment insurance for those temporarily unemployed and disability insurance for those who are no longer able to work. The government also provides a safety net of support for the poor, particularly children, through various welfare programs.

One can easily imagine the government controlling the economy more directly. In countries where decision making is centralized and concentrated in the government, government bureaucrats might decide what and how much a factory should produce and set the wages that should be paid. At least until recently, governments in countries such as the former Soviet Union and China attempted to control practically all major decisions regarding resource allocation. Even in Europe, not long ago many governments ran oil companies, coal mines, and the telephone system. Increasingly, however, governments have sold these enterprises to the private sector, a process called *privatization.*

Market economies in which individuals and firms make the decisions about what to produce and how much to pay have proven adept at developing new technologies and products. It is hard to imagine government bureaucrats developing MP3 players or iMacs in neon colors. Markets also generally ensure that resources are used efficiently.

Exchange in markets is *a key to understanding how resources are allocated, what is produced, and who earns what.*

INFORMATION

Making informed choices requires information. After all, it is hard to weigh the costs and benefits of alternative choices if you do not know what they are! A firm that is contemplating the purchase of a new software system needs to know not only the costs of the various alternatives but also the capabilities and limitations of each. Information is, in many ways, like other goods and services. Firms and individuals are willing to purchase information, and specialized institutions develop to sell it. In many areas, separate organizations are designed solely to provide information to consumers. *Consumer Reports* is a prime example. The Internet also now serves as a major source of independent information for buyers. But there are some fundamental ways in which information differs from other goods. A car seller will let you test-drive a vehicle, but a seller of information cannot let you see the information before you buy. Once you have seen the information, you have no incentive to pay for it. Another way information differs from other goods is that unlike a can of soda or a bagel, information can be freely shared. When I tell you something, it does not subtract from what I know (though it may subtract from the profits I might earn from that information).

In some key areas of the economy, the role of information is so critical that it affects the nature of the market. In the used-car market, buyers and sellers negotiating over the price of a vehicle may have quite different information about its quality. The seller may have better information about the quality of the car but also has an incentive to misrepresent its condition, since better-quality cars command higher prices. As a result, the buyer will be reluctant to trust claims that the car is in perfect shape.

When consumers lack adequate information to make informed choices, governments frequently intervene to require that firms provide information. In the United States, we are all familiar with the mandatory nutritional information placed on food products. The Securities and Exchange Commission (SEC) that oversees American stock markets compels firms to meet certain reporting requirements before their stock can be listed on exchanges such as the New York Stock Exchange. Such reporting helps ensure that private investors have reliable information on which to base their investment decisions. Often, however, these regulations do not work adequately, as the Enron scandal in 2001 clearly illustrates. The oil trading company Enron had cooked its books to overstate its profitability in its mandated reports. One outcome of Enron's subsequent financial collapse was the introduction of new regulations designed to improve the reliability of the information that companies must provide to the public. Governments also regulate the safety of products. In the United States, the Food and Drug Administration (FDA) must approve new pharmaceuticals before they can be sold. The need for such oversight was driven home in 2005 when the drug manufacturer Merck had to pull its pain relief drug Vioxx off the market after studies suggested it increased the risk of heart attacks and strokes. Critics of the FDA argued that the agency is not adequately monitoring the safety of drugs once they are approved, and proposals have been made to establish a new government review board whose job it will be to decide when new information warrants removing a drug from the market.

Even in the absence of regulation, firms have incentives to signal to buyers that their products are of high quality. One way they do this is to offer guarantees that a producer of low-quality goods could not afford to offer.

Imperfect information also can interfere with incentives. Employers want to create incentives for employees to work hard. One way to do this is to base pay on a measure of how productive each worker is. Often, however, it is difficult to measure a worker's productivity. Under such conditions, it is difficult to link pay to performance. For example, a major debate in the United States concerns tying teacher salaries to performance. Because it is hard to measure teaching performance, the pay of most teachers is based primarily on how long they have been teaching.

Information, or its absence, plays a key role in determining the shape of markets and the ability of private markets to ensure that the economy's scarce resources are used efficiently.

DISTRIBUTION

The market economy determines not only what goods are produced and how they are produced but also for whom they are produced. Many people find unacceptable the way the market distributes goods among households. "While recognizing the efficacy of capitalism to produce wealth, there remains considerable unease among some segments about the way markets distribute that wealth and about the effects of raw competition on society."[2] Like bidders at an auction, what market participants are willing and able to pay depends on their income. Incomes differ markedly across occupations. Some groups of individuals—including those without skills that are valued by the market—may receive such a low income that they cannot feed and educate their children without outside assistance. Government provides the assistance by taking steps to increase income equality.

[2]Alan Greenspan, speech at the Federal Reserve Bank of Kansas City Jackson Hole Conference, August 25, 2000.

Steps that soften the distributional impact of markets may blunt economic incentives. While welfare payments provide an important safety net for the poor, the taxation required to finance them may discourage people from working and saving. If the government takes one out of every two or three dollars that an individual earns, that individual may not be inclined to work as much. And if the government takes one out of every two or three dollars a person earns from interest on savings, the person may decide to spend more and save less. Thus, efforts by the government to redistribute income may come at the cost of reduced economic efficiency.

The primary reliance on private decision making in the United States reflects economists' beliefs that this reliance is appropriate and necessary for economic efficiency. However, economists also believe that certain interventions by government are desirable. Like the appropriate balance between public and private sectors, the appropriate balance between concerns about equality (often referred to as *equity concerns)* and efficiency is a central issue of modern economies. As elsewhere, trade-offs must be made.

Wrap-up

FIVE CORE IDEAS

1. *Trade-offs:* resources are scarce, so trade-offs are a basic fact of life.
2. *Incentives:* in making choices, decision makers respond to incentives.
3. *Exchange:* people benefit from voluntary exchange, and in market economies, market exchanges lead to the efficient use of resources.
4. *Information:* the structure that markets take and how well they can function depend critically on the information available to decision makers.
5. *Distribution:* markets determine how the goods and services produced by the economy are allocated to members of society.

The Three Major Markets

The market economy revolves around exchange between individuals (or households) who buy goods and services from firms, and firms, which take *inputs,* the various materials of production, and produce *outputs,* the goods and services that they sell. In thinking about a market economy, economists focus their attention on three broad categories of markets in which individuals and firms interact. The markets in which firms sell their outputs to households are referred to collectively as the **product market**. Many firms also sell goods to other firms; the output of the first firm becomes the input of the second. These transactions too are said to occur in the product market.

On the input side, firms need (besides the materials they buy in the product market) some combination of labor and machinery to produce their output. They purchase the services of workers in the **labor market**. They raise funds to buy inputs in the **capital market**. Traditionally, economists also have highlighted the importance of a third input, land, but in modern industrial economies land is of secondary importance. For most purposes, it suffices to focus attention on the three major markets—products, labor, and capital—and this text will follow that pattern.

As Figure 1.1 shows, individuals participate in all three markets. When individuals buy goods and services, they act as *consumers* in the product market. When people act as *workers,* economists say they "sell their labor services" in the labor market. When people buy shares of stock in a firm, deposit money in a savings account, or lend money to a business, they are participating in the capital market as *investors.*

KEEPING TRACK OF TRICKY TERMS

Terms in economics often are similar to terms in ordinary usage, but they can have special meanings. The terms *markets* and *capital* illustrate this problem.

Though the term *market* is used to conjure up an image of a busy *marketplace,* there is no formal marketplace for most goods and services. There are buyers and sellers, and economists analyze the outcomes *as if* there were a single marketplace in which all transactions occur. For example, economists analyze the "market for books," even though the buyers and sellers in the market for books interact in thousands of individual bookstores and online selling locations.

Moreover, economists often talk about the "market for labor" as if all workers were identical. But workers differ in countless ways. In some cases, these differences are important. We might then talk about the "market for skilled workers" or the "market for computer engineers." In other cases—such as when we are talking about the overall state of the

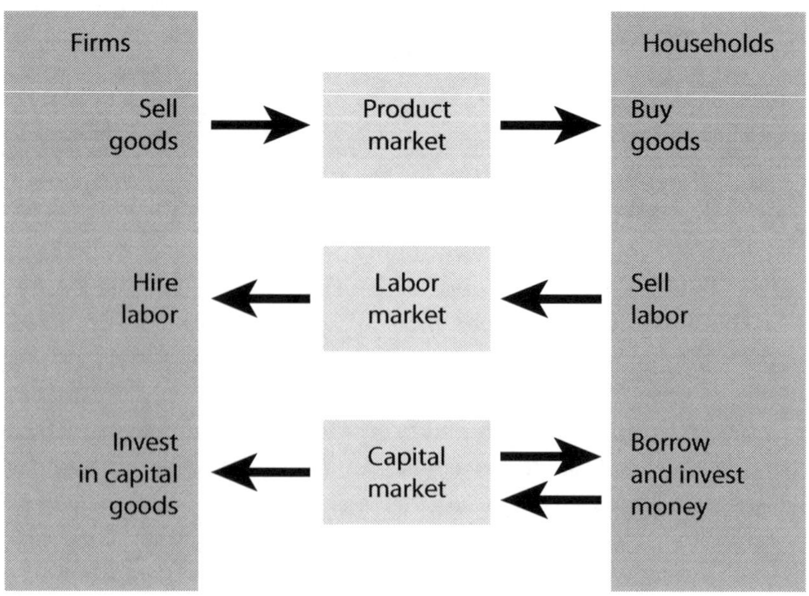

FIGURE 1.1
The Three Markets
To economists, people wear different hats. They are usually consumers in the product market, workers in the labor market, and borrowers or lenders in the capital market.

economy and focusing on the overall unemployment rate (the proportion of workers who are looking for jobs but cannot find them)-these differences can be ignored.

When newspapers refer to the *capital market,* they mean the bond traders and stockbrokers and the companies they work for on Wall Street and in other financial districts. When economists use the term *capital market,* they have in mind, a broader concept that includes all the institutions concerned with raising funds (and, as we will see later, sharing and insuring risk), including banks and insurance companies.

The term *capital* is used in still another way—to refer to the machines and buildings used in production. To distinguish this particular usage, in this book we refer to machines and buildings as **capital goods**. The term *capital markets* thus refers to the markets in which funds are raised, borrowed, and lent. *Capital goods markets* refers to the markets in which capital goods are bought and sold.

Wrap-up

THE THREE MAJOR MARKETS

1. *The product market:* the markets in which firms sell the goods they produce.
2. *The labor market:* the market in which households sell labor services and firms buy labor services.
3. *The capital market:* the market in which funds are borrowed and lent.

Microeconomics and Macroeconomics: The Two Branches of Economics

Economists have developed two different ways to look at the economy. The detailed study of the decisions of firms and households, and of prices and production in specific industries is called **microeconomics**. Microeconomics *(micro* is derived from the Greek word meaning "small") focuses on the behavior of the units—the firms, households, and individuals—that make up the economy. It is concerned with how the individual units make decisions and what affects those decisions.

By contrast, **macroeconomics** *(macro* is derived from the Greek word meaning "large") looks at the behavior of the economy as a whole, in particular the behavior of such aggregate measures as the overall rates of unemployment, inflation, and economic growth and the balance of trade. The aggregate numbers do not tell us what any one firm or household is doing. They tell us what is happening in total, or on average. In a dynamic economy, there are always some industries expanding and others contracting. For instance, the economic expansion of the late 1990s saw rapid growth in Internet-related industries, while oil firms in Texas contracted. But there are times when overall growth in an economy slows and times when the level of economic activity actually declines, not just in an isolated industry but seemingly across all or almost all industries.

In macroeconomics, we also look at the behavior of the general level of prices, interest rates, and exchange rates. Why do prices of almost all goods and services seem to rise at rapid rates during some periods, while at other times they remain stable? Why do interest rates fluctuate? And what determines the value of the dollar relative to other currencies?

In approaching these questions, it is important to remember that the behavior of the economy as a whole is dependent on the decisions made by the millions of households and firms in the economy, as well as the decisions made by the government. Micro and macro perspectives are simply two ways of looking at the same thing. Microeconomics is the bottom-up view of the economy; macroeconomics is the top-down view.

Wrap-up

THE BRANCHES OF ECONOMICS

- **Microeconomics**: focuses on the decisions of households and firms and the detailed study of prices and production in specific industries.
- **Macroeconomics**: focuses on the behavior of the economy as a whole and the behavior of aggregate variables such as overall employment, output, economic growth, the price level, and inflation.

The Science of Economics

Economics is *a social science.* It studies the social problem of choice from a scientific viewpoint, which means that it is built on a systematic exploration of the problem of choice. This systematic exploration involves both the formulation of theories and the examination of data.

A **theory** consists of a set of assumptions (or hypotheses) and conclusions derived from those assumptions. Theories are logical exercises: *if* the assumptions are correct, *then* the results follow. If all college graduates have a better chance of getting jobs and Ellen is a college graduate, then Ellen has a better chance of getting a job than a nongraduate. Economists make predictions with their theories. They might use their theory to predict what would happen if a tax is increased or if imports of foreign cars are limited. The predictions of a theory are of the form, "If a tax is increased and if the market is competitive, then output will decrease and prices will increase."

In developing their theories, economists use *models.* To understand how models are used in economics, consider a modern car manufacturer trying to design a new automobile. It is extremely expensive to construct a new car. Rather than creating a separate, fully developed car for every conception of what engineers or designers would like the new car to be, the company uses models. The designers might use a plastic model to study the general shape of the vehicle and to assess reactions to the car's aesthetics. The engineers might use a computer model to study air resistance, from which they can calculate fuel consumption.

Just as engineers construct different models to study particular features of a car, economists construct different models of the economy—in words or equonations—to depict particular features of the economy. An economic model might describe a general relationship ("When incomes rise, the number of cars purchased increases"), describe a quantitative relationship ("When incomes rise by 10 percent, the number of cars purchased rises, on average, by 12 percent"), or make a general prediction ("An increase in the tax on gasoline will decrease the demand for cars").

DISCOVERING AND INTERPRETING RELATIONSHIPS

A variable is any item that can be measured and that changes. Prices, wages, interest rates, and quantities bought and sold are variables. What interests economists is the connection between variables. When economists see what appears to be a systematic relationship among variables, they ask, could it have arisen by chance or is there indeed a relationship? This is the question of *correlation*.

Economists use statistical tests to measure and test correlations. Consider the problem of deciding whether a coin is biased. If you flip the coin 10 times and get 6 heads and 4 tails, is the coin a fair one? Or is it weighted toward heads? Statistical tests will show that the result of 6 heads and 4 tails easily could have happened by chance, so the evidence does not prove that the coin is weighted. It also does not prove that the coin is *not* weighted. The evidence is not strong enough for either conclusion. But if you flip the coin 100 times and get 80 heads, statistical tests will tell you that the possibility of this happening by blind chance with a fair coin is extremely small. The evidence supports the assertion that the coin is weighted.

A similar logic can be used on correlations among economic variables. People with more education tend to earn higher wages. Is the connection merely chance? Statistical tests support the existence of a systematic relationship between education and wages.

CAUSATION AND CORRELATION

Economists want to accomplish more than just asserting that different variables are indeed correlated. They would like to conclude that changes in one variable *cause* the changes in another variable. This distinction between correlation and causation is important. If one variable "causes" the other, then changing the first variable necessarily will change the other. If the relationship is just a correlation, this may not be true.

During the 1970s, imports of Japanese cars into the United States increased while sales of U.S.-produced cars decreased. The two variables were negatively correlated. But did increased Japanese car sales *cause* the decrease in sales of American-made cars? Perhaps both were responding to a common factor that was the true cause of both the rise in Japanese car sales and the decline in sales of American cars. In fact, that is what was happening—the huge increase in oil prices after 1973 caused consumers to shift their purchases away from gas-guzzling American cars and toward more fuel-efficient Japanese cars.

Why Economists Disagree

Economists are frequently called on to make judgments on matters of public policy. Should the government cut taxes? How should Social Security be reformed? Should Internet commerce be taxed? In these public policy discussions, economists often disagree. These disagreements arise for two reasons. First, economists can differ in their views on the consequences of a proposed policy. Second, they can differ in how they evaluate those consequences.

When economists describe the economy and construct models that predict how the economy will be affected by different policies, they are engaged in what is called **positive economics**. When they evaluate alternative policies, weighing the various benefits and costs, they are engaged in **normative economics**.

Consider the positive and normative aspects of a proposal to restrict imports of textiles produced in developing countries. Positive economics would describe the consequences: the increased prices American consumers would have to pay for clothes, the increased sales of American textiles, the increased employment and profits of U.S. textile manufacturers, and the reduced employment among textile workers in developing countries. Economists might disagree over the consequences of restricting imports because they disagree over the magnitude of the effects, perhaps agreeing that prices to consumers would rise but disagreeing over the size of that rise.

In the end, though, the policy question is, *Should there be restraints on textile imports?* This is a normative question. Normative economics would weigh these various effects—the losses to consumers, the gains to U.S. textile workers, the increased profits—to reach an overall judgment. Normative economics develops frameworks within which these complicated judgments can be systematically made. Good normative economics also tries to be explicit about precisely which values or objectives it is incorporating. It tries to couch its statements in the form "If these are your values, then this is the best policy."

Economists, like members of any other profession, often have different values. Two economists might agree that a particular tax change would increase saving but would benefit the wealthy more than the poor. However, they might reach different conclusions about the desirability of that tax change. One might oppose it because it increases income inequality; the other might support it because it promotes saving. They differ in the values they place on the effects of the policy change, so they reach different conclusions even when they agree on the positive analysis of the proposed policy.

While economists may often seem to differ greatly among themselves, in fact they agree more than they disagree. When they do disagree, economists try to be clear about the source of their disagreement: (1) to what extent does it arise out of differences in models, (2) to what extent does it arise out of differences in estimates of quantitative relationships, and (3) to what extent does it arise out of differences in values? Clarifying the source of and reasons for disagreement can be a very productive way of learning more about an issue.

IN-CLASS PROJECT

Graduating Into a Recession

By David Moglen

This article illustrates how the personal decisions you make as an individual are connected to economic forces. It also provides practice writing good responses for all written work in this economics class and in your future academic career. Just like any written response, a good answer should go back and forth between quotes (using "quote marks") and your own analysis/ interpretation—in your own words.

Directions

As a group activity, each group (as always, up to five students per group) is given a number from one to four, and answers that number below after reading the article. As a set of Discussion Questions, the whole class has read the article and is ready to respond to all four questions collectively.

For all these questions: Imagine the economy is clearly in a deep recession.

1. If you are about to graduate with a bachelor's degree (BA), how should the economic situation influence your decision of what to do next as an individual in this economy? Start by asking yourself, what are the main options people have when they are about to complete or just finished with their BA?
2. What does the research by Columbia University economist Mr. von Wachter mean for your decisions about where you should apply to college, what your major should be, and the type of job you should try to get as a recent graduate?
3. If the economy is not in a recession, would that guarantee that average real wages would rise? What do you think are the major factors that explain this?
4. Which aspects of this article and the issues it raises macroeconomic, and in which way are they microeconomic?

THE CURSE OF THE CLASS OF 2009

For college grads lucky enough to get work this year, low wages are likely to haunt them for a decade or more

By Sara Murray

The bad news for this spring's college graduates is that they're entering the toughest labor market in at least 25 years.

The worse news: Even those who land jobs will likely suffer lower wages for a decade or more compared to those lucky enough to graduate in better times, studies show.

Andrew Friedson graduated last year from the University of Maryland with a degree in government and politics and a stint as student-body president on his résumé. After working on Barack Obama's presidential campaign for a few months, Mr. Friedson hoped to get a position in the new administration. When that didn't pan out he looked for jobs on Capitol Hill. No luck there, either.

So now, instead of learning about policymaking and legislation, he's earning about

$1,250 a month as a high school tutor and a part-time fundraiser for Hillel, a Jewish campus organization. To save money, he's living with his parents.

If asked a year ago whether he'd be tutoring now, Mr. Friedson says, "I would have laughed in your face."

Trading down to a lower-skilled job isn't just a hit to Mr. Friedson's ego. It could also hurt his bank account for years to come. Economic research shows that the consequences of graduating in a downturn are long-lasting. They include lower earnings, a slower climb up the occupational ladder and a widening gap between the least-and most-successful grads.

In short, luck matters. The damage can linger up to 15 years, says Lisa Kahn, a Yale School of Management economist. She used the National Longitudinal Survey of Youth, a government data base, to track wages of white men who graduated before, during and after the deep 1980s recession.

Ms. Kahn found that for each percentage-point increase in the unemployment rate, those with the misfortune to graduate during the recession earned 7% to 8% less in their first year out than comparable workers who graduated in better times. The effect persisted over many years, with recession-era grads earning 4% to 5% less by their 12th year out of college, and 2% less by their 18th year out.

For example, a man who graduated in December 1982 when unemployment was at 10.8% made, on average, 23% less his first year out of college and 6.6% less 18 years out than one who graduated in May 1981 when the unemployment rate was 7.5%. For a typical worker, that would mean earning $100,000 less over the 18-year period.

The impact on wages could be just as severe this time around, says Ms. Kahn. That's because of the depth of this recession and the possibility that the unemployment rate may approach the 10.8% level not seen since the early 1980s. The rate hit 8.9% in April, the Labor Department reported Friday.

One reason behind declining wage potential, economists say: The caliber of jobs available in a recession, and their accompanying wages, tend to suffer. High-end firms hire fewer people and drive down salaries because jobs are in such demand.

That means many graduates end up with lower-wage, lower-skill jobs at less-prestigious firms or in firms outside their field of interest. Once the economy picks up and they try for better jobs, these workers have to learn skills they should have been developing immediately out of college. In the meantime, colleagues who graduated in a better economy have already developed these skills and progressed much further.

For Brad Dechter, a 24-year-old who majored in graphic design, this could mean starting at the bottom when and if he gets a job at an advertising agency. He studied at the Art Institute of Colorado partly because the Denver school advertises that 86% of alumni get a job within six months of graduation. So far, no dice.

Eight months after graduation, Mr. Dechter is making just $500 a month freelancing for bands, designing flyers and album covers. When he runs short of cash, he borrows from his friends. He spends his days on Craigslist searching for job openings instead of learning the marketing and design skills he would have picked up in his first year at an agency.

"I've pretty much given up on trying to find my dream job," says Mr. Dechter.

Christine Pacheco, director of career services at the Art Institute, acknowledges that graduates face a struggle now. "They may need to take two part-time jobs and do some freelance rather than get a full-time job," she says.

College graduates remain better off than those with only high-school diplomas, in good times and bad. The unemployment rate in April among four-year college graduates between 20 and 24 years old was 6.1%; among those the same age with only high-school diplomas, it was 19.6%.

But a college degree isn't an automatic ticket to upward mobility, either. Even before the recession began, graduates were seeing their wages shrink. Between 2002 and 2007, according to government data, the inflation-adjusted hourly wage for men ages 25 to 35 with bachelor's degrees (and no graduate degrees) fell 4.5%. For the typical woman, inflation-adjusted wages fell 4.8%.

This year, employers say they'll hire 22% fewer college graduates than last year, according to the National Association of Colleges and Employers, an organization of career counselors. At the same time, colleges are expected to see the highest number of graduates in a decade. The average starting salary for graduates who do get jobs, meanwhile, dropped to $48,515 this spring, down 2.2% from the same time last year, according to NACE.

Plenty of recent graduates are making far less than the average. Between her business marketing degree and numerous New York City contacts, Nicole Buckley, 21, figured she would find a marketing job after graduating in December from Siena College, a small Catholic liberal arts college near Albany, N.Y. She didn't expect to be working the jobs she has now, five months after graduation: As a full-time receptionist with a part-time gig as a model, promoting Bacardi rum and Grey Goose vodka to patrons at bars. But after doing two interviews a day and applying to more than 50 jobs, she had to do something to pay the bills.

"I don't think anyone went to college and said, 'I want to graduate and make $25,000 a year,' " says Ms. Buckley. She estimates her earnings at a little less than $30,000 between the two jobs.

Sarah Veilleux, 22, one of Ms. Buckley's two roommates in a $1,125-a-month Brooklyn apartment, graduated in May 2008 from the University of New Hampshire with a communications degree. For a few months, she worked selling band merchandise at a music venue. Then she found her ideal job: doing promotions for Sirius Satellite Radio. But they need her only 20 hours a week.

"As soon as I saw the offer for Sirius," she says, "it didn't matter how many hours a week." She spends the other half of her week doing administrative tasks for a staffing company, earning $1,500 a month—$18,000 a year—between the two jobs.

Still, Ms. Veilleux probably will be better off than those who take low-wage jobs outside their fields, says Till Marco von Wachter, a Columbia University economist. Mr. von Wachter, with a couple of colleagues, has looked at wage data covering 70% of all Canadians who graduated from college between 1976 and 1995, a span encompassing two recessions. His work indicates that graduates who get jobs in their fields—even low-paying jobs—are able to learn the right skills, and thus have an edge when the economy rebounds.

Mr. von Wachter also found that what recession-era graduates studied, and where they went to school, made a big difference in how quickly they caught up to workers who graduated in boom times. People who majored in fields that lead to high-paying jobs, such as chemistry, biology, physics and engineering, tended to catch up to other graduates more quickly, primarily by switching jobs during the economic recovery and landing at better firms. In contrast, says Mr. von Wachter, the wages of humanities majors at less prestigious schools were less likely to catch up to the wages of their peers who graduated in healthier times.

For some graduates, the recession has had an unintended upside: a career path they never thought they wanted.

Diane Hempe, 24, planned to be a teacher. But after graduating from the University of Maryland last year with an elementary education degree, she failed to find a job at a school. So she settled for working at a day-care center, where the $12 an hour she brought in felt like an affront.

In December, Ms. Hempe went in an entirely new direction. She took a job in the customer-service department at a Wells Fargo call center in Frederick, Md. "I definitely know

I can move up," she says. "I can be in customer service; I can be in collections; I can be in so many different departments."

And in the meantime she's shifting her long-term goals. Instead of getting a master's degree in education like she once thought she would, Ms. Hempe says eventually she plans to get her master's in business.

Others are opting to ride out the slump doing public service. At AmeriCorps, a nationwide community-service network, applications more than tripled to about 48,500 between November 2008 and March 2009 compared to the same time period a year earlier. Teach for America received 35,000 applications this year—42% more than last year. About 70% of those were recent college graduates. Among the most common reasons people cited for applying, according to Teach for America, were poor job conditions and President Barack Obama's call to public service.

Another alternative to unemployment or a low-paying job: Stay in school.

Graduate applications for 2007–2008 were up 8% nationwide compared to the year before, according to the most recent numbers from the Council of Graduate Schools. Schools such as Northwestern University and Harvard are already tracking double-digit increases this year.

College grads who went to graduate school instead of the job market during the early '80s recession didn't suffer the same wage losses, says Ms. Kahn, the Yale economist.

That's the approach John Bence is taking. A 2008 graduate of Kenyon College in Ohio, the history major worked with a temp agency and did a six-month stint at an international consulting company. After repeatedly losing out on jobs—at museums, universities, consulting firms—to more-qualified candidates with master's degrees, he'll head to New York University to get a master's degree in history, specializing in archival management.

"I wasn't surprised I didn't get those jobs in, like, museums," Mr. Bence says. "But I was surprised that no one was willing to hire me to do anything."

SUMMARY —

1. Economics is the study of how individuals, firms, and governments within our society make choices. Choices, and therefore trade-offs are unavoidable because desired goods, services, and resources are inevitably scarce.
2. Economists study how individuals, firms, and governments within our society make choices by focusing on incentives. People respond to changes in incentives by altering the decisions they make.
3. Exchange occurs in markets. Voluntary exchange can cause the other party to change. Additional outside factors may be influencing both.
4. Making choices requires information. Limited or imperfect information can interfere with incentives and affect the ability of the private market to ensure an efficient use of society's scarce resources.
5. The incomes people receive are determined by the market economy. Concerns over the equitable distribution of wealth and income in

the economy lead to government programs that increase income equality.

6. The United States has a mixed economy, one in which there is a mix of public and private decision making. The economy relies primarily on the private interaction of individuals and firms to determine how resources are allocated, but government plays a large role as well. A central question for any mixed economy is the balance between the private and public sectors.
7. The term *market* is used to describe any situation where exchange takes place. In the U.S. market economy, individuals, firms, and government interact in product markets, labor markets, and capital markets.
8. The two major branches of economics are microeconomics and macroeconomics. Microeconomics focuses on the behaviour of the firms, households, and individuals that make up the economy. Macroeconomics focuses on the behaviour of the economy as a whole.
9. Economists use models to study how the economy works and to make predictions about what will happen if something is changed. A model can be expressed in words or equations and is designed to mirror the essential characteristics of the particular phenomena under study.
10. A correlation exists when two variables tend to change together in a predictable way. However, the simple existence of a correlation does not prove that one factor causes the other to change. Additional outside factors may be influencing both.
11. Positive economics is the study of how the economy works. Disagreements in positive economics center on the appropriate model of the economy or market and the quantitative magnitudes characterizing the models.
12. Normative economics deals with the desirability of various actions. Disagreements in normative economics center on differences in the values placed on the various costs and benefits of different actions.

KEY TERMS

trade-offs
incentives
exchange
information
distribution
scarcity
market economy
product market
labor market
capital market
capital goods
microeconomics

macroeconomics
theory
correlation
causation
positive economics
normative economics

REVIEW QUESTIONS

1. Why are trade-offs unavoidable? Why are incentives important in understanding choices?
2. After a voluntary exchange, why are both parties better off?
3. As a commodity, how does information differ from standard goods? How do information imperfections affect markets?
4. Why might there be a trade-off between equity and efficiency?
5. What is a mixed, economy? Describe some of the roles government might play, or not play, in a mixed economy.
6. Name the three main economic markets, and describe how an individual might participate in each one as a buyer or a seller.
7. Give two examples of economic issues that are primarily microeconomic and two examples that are primarily macroeconomic. What is the general difference between microeconomics and macroeconomics?
8. What is a model? Why do economists use models?
9. Give two examples of variables that you would expect to be positively correlated. For each example, explain whether a causal relationship exists between the two variables.

PROBLEMS

1. How does each of the following affect the incentive to go to college?
    a. An increase in tuition costs
    b. A fall in the interest rate on student loans
    c. A rise in wages for unskilled jobs
    d. An increase in incomes of college graduates
2. Characterize the following events as microeconomic, macroeconomic, or both.
    a. Unemployment increases this month.
    b. A drug company invents and begins to market a new medicine.
    c. A bank lends money to a large company but turns down a small business.
    d. Interest rates decline for all borrowers.
    e. A union negotiates for higher pay and better health insurance.
    f. The price of oil increases.
3. Characterize the following events as part of the labor market, the capital market, or the product market.

a. An investor tries to decide which company to invest in.
b. With practice, the workers on an assembly line become more efficient.
c. The opening up of economies in Eastern Europe offers new markets for American products.
d. A big company that is losing money decides to offer its workers special incentives to retire early, hoping to reduce its costs.
e. A consumer roams around a shopping mall looking for birthday gifts.
f. The federal government uses a surplus uses a surplus to pay off some of its debt.

4. The back of a bag of cat litter claims, "cats that use cat litter live three years longer than cats that don't." Do you think that cat litter actually causes an increased life expectancy for cats, or can you think of some other factors to explain this correlation? What evidence might you collect to test your explanation?
5. Life expectancy in Sweden is almost eighty years. Does this prove that if an Indian moved to Sweden, he would live longer? That is, does this prove that living in Sweden causes an increase in life expectancy, or can you think of some other factors to explain these faces? What evidence might you collect to test your explanation?
6. During 2004, some economists argued that the federal Reserve should undertake policies to slow the economic expansion in the United States in order to ensure low inflation. Other economists opposed such policies, arguing that the dangers of inflation were exaggerated and attempts by the Federal Reserve to slow the economy would lead to higher unemployment. Is this a disagreement about positive economics, or about normative economics? Explain.

CHAPTER 2
Tradeoffs, Efficiency and Global Trade

2 Tradeoffs, Efficiency and Global Trade

By Timothy Taylor

In November 1968, the Rolling Stones recorded a song called: "You Can't Always Get What You Want." But economists had already been singing a similar tune for many years. For example, an English economist named Lionel Robbins (1898–1984) wrote *An Essay on the Nature and Significance of Economic Science* in 1932, in which he described the problem of not always getting what you want in this way:

> The time at our disposal is limited. There are only twenty-four hours in the day. We have to choose between the different uses to which they may be put. The services which others put at our disposal are limited. The material means of achieving ends are limited. We have been turned out of Paradise. We have neither eternal life nor unlimited means of gratification. Everywhere we turn, if we choose one thing we must relinquish others which, in different circumstances, we would wish not to have relinquished. Scarcity of means to satisfy given ends is an almost ubiquitous condition of human nature. Here then, is the unity of subject of Economic Science, the forms assumed by human behavior in disposing of scarce means.

Economics studies how every person, every firm, and every society must make choices, because none of them can have everything that they desire.

This chapter begins with a discussion of three broad categories of choices made by individuals and households: choices about which goods to consume, how many hours to work, and how much to borrow or save. Not coincidentally, these three categories of choices match the three main markets of microeconomics discussed in the circular flow diagram in Chapter 1: the markets for goods, labor, and financial capital. The discussion then introduces a framework for thinking about society's choices. Finally, the chapter discusses some concerns over whether the economic approach to facing scarcity and making choices describes accurately either how choices *are* actually made or how choices *should* be made.

Choosing What to Consume

People live in a world of scarcity: that is, they can't have all the time, money, possessions, and experiences they wish. Since people must choose, they inevitably face trade-offs, in which they have to give up things that they desire to get other things that they desire more. When economists analyze how individuals make these choices, they divide the decision process into two steps. The first step is to consider what choices are possible for individuals. The second step is to think about which choices individuals actually make, based on their individual preferences. The model that economists use for illustrating the process of individual choice in a situation of scarcity is the **budget constraint**, sometimes also called the **opportunity set**, a diagram which shows what choices are possible.

budget constraint:

A diagram which shows what choices are possible, given the prices.

opportunity set:

Another name for the budget constraint.

A CONSUMPTION CHOICE BUDGET CONSTRAINT

To illustrate how the budget constraint model applies to choices about how much of each good to consume, consider the case of Alphonso, illustrated in Exhibit 2-1. Each graph in Exhibit 2-1 shows a different combination of Alphonso's income and the prices for two goods, burgers and bus tickets. In Exhibit 2-1a, Alphonso has $10 in spending money each week that he can allocate between bus tickets for getting to work and the burgers that he eats for lunch. Burgers cost $2 each, and bus tickets in Alphonso's town are 50 cents. Different combinations of choices that are possible for Alphonso are shown in the table and also depicted graphically in the accompanying budget constraint. Each combination of burgers and bus tickets shown in the table and the budget constraint adds up to exactly $10. Thus, the points along the budget constraint represent what consumption opportunities are possible for Alphonso.

HOW CHANGES IN INCOME AND PRICES AFFECT THE BUDGET CONSTRAINT

Changes in income will alter the budget constraint. For example, say that Alphonso's spending money increases to $12 per week. Exhibit 2-1b shows both his original budget constraint and his new budget constraint. In the new budget constraint, each combination of burgers and bus tickets at the given prices now adds up to $12. A higher income level means that the budget constraint will be to the right of the original budget constraint; conversely, a lower income level means that the budget constraint will lie to the left of the original budget constraint.

Now suppose Alphonso's income remains the same, but the price of one of the goods increases. Changes in the price of goods will affect Alphonso's budget constraint. In other words, his income level stays at $10 per week, but the price of bus tickets rises to $1 each, while the price of burgers remains at $2. Exhibit 2-1c shows how this change in price alters the budget constraint. A higher price for one good causes the budget constraint to shift inward; more specifically, the budget constraint swings inward as if on a hinge attached to the vertical axis or the horizontal axis—depending on which good's price has risen. Conversely, a lower price for one good would lead to an outward shift of the budget constraint.

Exhibit 2-1 Alphonso's Consumption Choice Opportunity Set

(a) Each point on the opportunity set represents a combination of burgers and bus tickets whose total cost adds up to Alphonso's income of $10. The slope of the budget line is determined by the relative price of burgers and bus tickets. All along the budget set, giving up a burger means gaining four bus tickets.

(b) If Alphonso's income increases from $10 to $12, his opportunity set shifts to the right of the original budget set. The lower line is the original budget set, and the upper line is the new budget set. On the new budget set, each combination of burgers and bus tickets now adds up to a total cost of $12. However, because the trade-off of burgers for bus tickets is unchanged—still one burger for every four bus tickets—the slope of the budget line is unchanged.

(c) Alphonso's income remains at $10, as in *(a)*, but the cost of bus tickets rises from 50 cents to $1. This change causes the budget set to swing inward, as if on a hinge at the upper left. If Alphonso wishes to purchase only burgers, the change in price of bus tickets doesn't alter how many he can buy. However, giving up a burger now adds only two bus tickets, not four. The budget line slopes more steeply as a result.

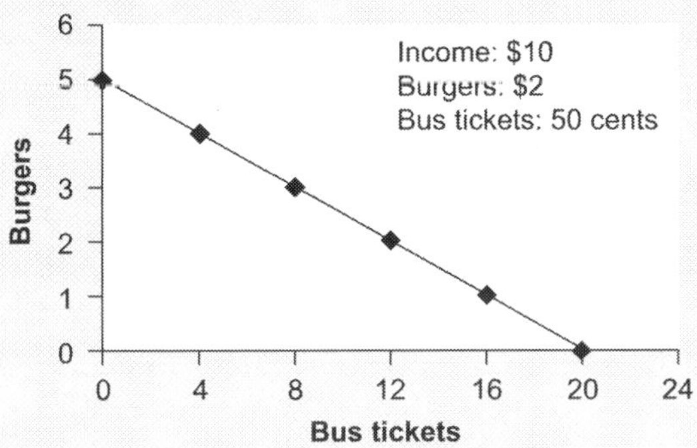

(a) First set of choices: Total income $10.

Quantity of Burgers (at $2)	Quantity of Bus Tickets (at 50 cents)
0	20
1	16
2	12
3	8
4	4
5	0

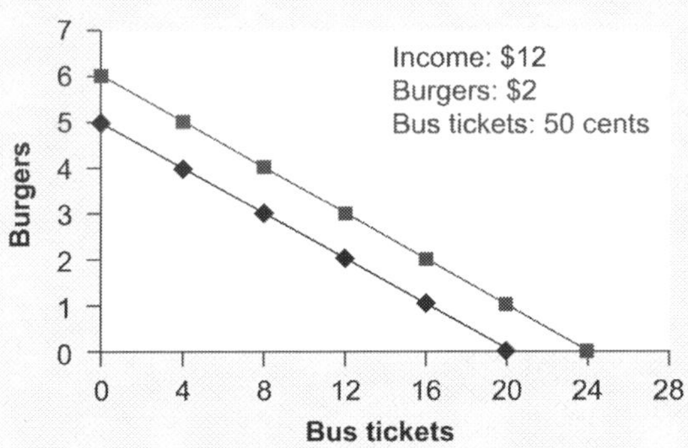

(b) Second set of choices: Total income $12.

Quantity of Burgers (at $2)	Quantity of Bus Tickets (at 50 cents)
0	24
1	20
2	16
3	12
4	8
5	4
6	0

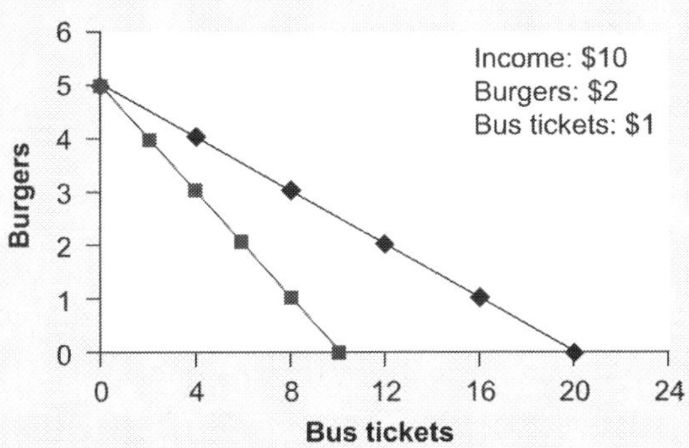

(c) Third set of choices: Total income $10.

Quantity of Burgers (at $2)	Quantity of Bus Tickets (at $1)
0	10
1	8
2	6
3	4
4	2
5	0

Clearing It Up: Sketching Budget Constraints:

As an economics student, you will need to know how to sketch budget constraints quickly and accurately. Here's a suggestion: Start by calculating, based on income and the prices of the two goods, how much of each good each person could buy if that person were not buying any of the other good. These calculations will determine the points on the two axes of the budget constraint. Then the other points form a straight line between these endpoints.

A change in income causes the budget constraint to shift so that the new budget constraint is parallel to the original. However, a change in prices causes the slope of the budget constraint to change so that the budget constraint is steeper or flatter. Why are the effects different? The slope of the budget constraint is determined by the relative price of the two goods, which is calculated by taking the price of one good and dividing it by the price of the other good. The *relative* price conveys the trade-off between the two goods, in this case burgers and bus rides. In Alphonso's first budget constraint in Exhibit 2-1a, if he gives up one burger, he can take four additional bus trips because the price of a burger is four times the price of a bus trip (that is, $2 versus 50 cents). The slope of this budget constraint shows that a loss of 1 burger equals a gain of 4 bus tickets. In Exhibit 2-1b, income changes but the relative prices of the two goods don't change, and so the slope of the budget constraint doesn't change either. In Exhibit 2-1c, however, giving up one burger means gaining only two bus trips (that is, $2 versus $1), and so the slope of the budget constraint changes to a loss of 1 burger means a gain of only 2 bus tickets.

PERSONAL PREFERENCES DETERMINE SPECIFIC CHOICES

What choice will Alphonso make along his budget constraint? The answer is simple: Alphonso will choose what he personally prefers. In economics, **utility** refers to the level of satisfaction or pleasure that people receive from their choices. Thus, when people make the choices that provide the highest level of satisfaction, economists say that they are "maximizing utility." In Alphonso's case, if he prefers to sit at home and eat, he buys a lot of burgers and chooses some point like A or B on the budget constraint in Exhibit 2-2. If he prefers to travel around town, he buys lots of bus tickets and chooses some point like D or E on the budget constraint. It's Alphonso's choice.

utility: The level of satisfaction or pleasure that people receive from their choices.

However, the logic of the budget constraint dictates that Alphonso's choice will be a point on the actual budget constraint itself: choice B with four burgers and four bus tickets—not a choice that is above the budget set or below it. Alphonso might desire a point like H in Exhibit 2-2 with five burgers and 16 bus tickets, offering more of both goods than choice B. However, choice H is outside the budget constraint, which means that Alphonso can't afford it. Conversely, Alphonso won't choose a point like J with two burger and four bus tickets, which is inside the boundary of the budget constraint, because he could instead select a choice on the budget set itself like B that would have at least as much of one good and more of the other—or a choice that would offer even more of both goods. In this simple model, Alphonso doesn't have any other goods on which to spend his money, and so if he doesn't spend his money, it is wasted.

The budget constraint diagram shows what choices are possible, but it does not specify which choice is made. If two people have the same income and face the same prices, then they have identical budget constraints; but if those two people have different personal preferences, they will make different choices.

The Origins of Economic Utility

In the late eighteenth century, a philosopher and occasional economist named Jeremy Bentham (1748–1832) constructed a philosophy called "utilitarianism," which was based on the "happiness principle" that all of society's decisions ought to be made according to the amount of pleasure and pain that they cause individuals. Bentham wrote: "The greatest happiness of the greatest number is the foundation of morals and legislation."

Utilitarianism may not sound very radical, but consider some of its implications for the world of the late eighteenth and early nineteenth century. The utilitarian philosophy did not say that the happiness of a king, queen, or member of the nobility was more important than the happiness of an average person. It did not place the happiness of men above the happiness of women. It did not say that the happiness of the unemployed, criminals, children, or the poor was any less important than the happiness of anyone else.

Bentham was the unofficial leader of a group called the Philosophical Radicals, who favored voting rights for all with a secret ballot, government programs to provide jobs for the unemployed, government-run banks to help the poor save money, better conditions in prisons, limits on child labor, and—important to economists—market competition and free trade among countries. The Philosophical Radicals weren't always right, but at least by modern standards, they were on the side of the angels more often than not.

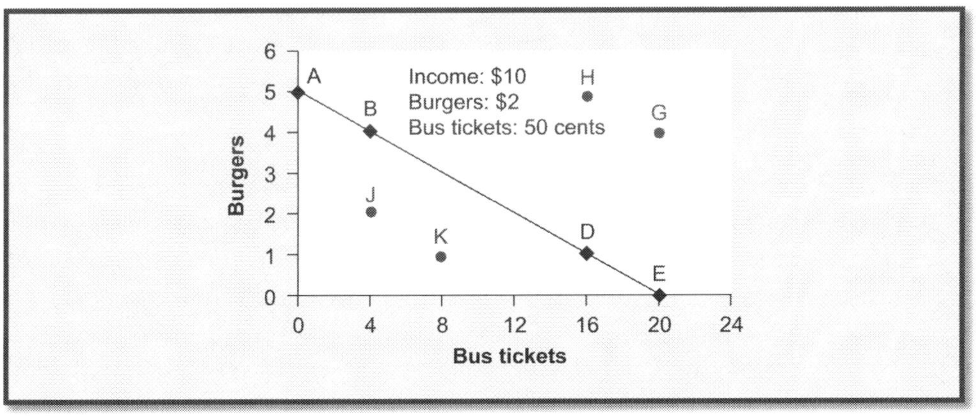

Exhibit 2-2 Personal Preferences Determine the Actual Choice:

If Alphonso likes burgers a lot, he will probably choose points A or B. If he likes bus tickets a lot, he will probably choose points D or E. Points H and G beyond the opportunity set are unattainable, given his level of income, no matter how much Alphonso might like them. Points J and K would be wasteful. For example, rather than choosing point J, he could have both more burgers and the same number of bus tickets at point B. Similarly, instead of choosing point K, he could have the same number of burgers but many more bus tickets at point D.

FROM A MODEL WITH TWO GOODS TO THE REAL WORLD OF MANY GOODS

The budget constraint diagram containing just two goods may seem so simple as to be simple-minded. In a modern economy, people choose from thousands of goods, not just two.

However, thinking about a model with many goods is straightforward. Instead of drawing just one budget constraint, showing the trade-off between two goods, you can draw multiple budget constraints, showing the possible trade-offs between many different pairs of goods. Or in more advanced classes in economics, you would use mathematical equations that include many possible goods and services that can be purchased, together with their quantities and prices, and show how the total spending adds up to the overall amount of money available. However, the graph with two goods clearly illustrates three basic concepts: (1) how the budget constraint is determined by income and prices; (2) how changes in income or relative prices cause a budget constraint to shift; and (3) how the personal preferences of an individual are represented by the point that is chosen on the budget constraint.

Choosing Between Labor and Leisure

The budget constraint applies to the labor-leisure choice just as it does to the decision of what quantity of goods to consume. But in the labor-leisure budget constraint, the decision isn't about what quantities of goods to buy, given their prices a limited amount of income; instead, it's about what number of hours to work, given the wage that can be earned and the limited number of hours in a day. Again, the first step is to use the budget constraint to show what is possible, while the second step is for each individual to make their personally preferred choice that maximizes utility.

AN EXAMPLE OF A LABOR-LEISURE BUDGET CONSTRAINT

Beulah has a job as an assistant manager of a fast-food restaurant. She can work as many as 60 hours per week if she chooses. Of course, most people don't have jobs that let them choose exactly how many hours to work each week; but most people have at least some flexibility about whether to look for a part-time or a full-time job or whether to work overtime or take on a second job. Thus, it isn't unreasonable to imagine people making choices about the number of hours they work. Exhibit 2-3 shows two of Beulah's labor-leisure budget constraints.

In Exhibit 2-3a, Beulah's wage is $9 per hour. The table and the budget constraint show the trade-off that she faces between income and leisure. Because Beulah receives an hourly wage, the more hours she works, the more her income rises and her leisure diminishes. The horizontal axis of the exhibit measures both labor hours and leisure hours at the same time, but in opposite directions. The quantity of hours of leisure is measured from left to right, while the quantity of hours of labor is measured from right to left. Since Beulah has a total of 60 hours available that she could work, the horizontal axis shows how she divides up this time between leisure and work.

HOW A CHANGE IN WAGES AFFECTS THE LABOR-LEISURE BUDGET CONSTRAINT

A change in the wage will shift Beulah's budget constraint. If her wage rises to $11 per hour, perhaps because she has gained more experience or training, then the trade-offs that she faces change as well. Both her original budget constraint and her new set of tradeoffs are shown in Exhibit 2-3b. A new wage changes the slope of the budget constraint because a new wage means a different trade-off between hours of leisure and income.

MAKING A CHOICE ALONG THE LABOR-LEISURE BUDGET CONSTRAINT

Living in a world of scarcity—no one has more than 24 hours in a day—requires that people must make choices about how to spend their time, but the fact of scarcity doesn't dictate what choices they make. In deciding how many hours to work, Beulah will make a choice that maximizes her utility; that is, she will choose according to her preferences for leisure time and income. If she chooses to work 60 hours per week, she will have more income to spend on food, rent, clothing, cars, vacations, or other material goods. However, if she prefers leisure time over material satisfactions, she may choose to work fewer hours so that she has more time for family, friends, and low-cost hobbies such as reading or yoga. Exhibit 2-4 illustrates both possibilities. If Beulah prefers a relatively high level of income, then she will choose a point close to A, with $540 of income, 60 hours of work and no leisure. If she prefers instead a relatively high level of leisure, she might choose a point like C with 50 hours of leisure, 10 hours of work, and $90 in income.

Clearing It Up: Measuring Labor and Leisure on the Same Axis

The labor-leisure budget constraint involves illustrating three factors—hours of labor, hours of leisure, and dollars of income—on only two axes. This illustration only works because the hours of both labor and leisure appear on the horizontal axis. After all, all leisure means no labor, and all labor means no leisure. On the horizontal axis, hours of leisure are measured from left to right, but hours of labor are measured from right to left. The trade-off here is between the two goods of leisure and income because labor is not a "good" in itself, but instead a mechanism for earning income.

Exhibit 2-3 Beulah's Labor-Leisure Opportunity Set

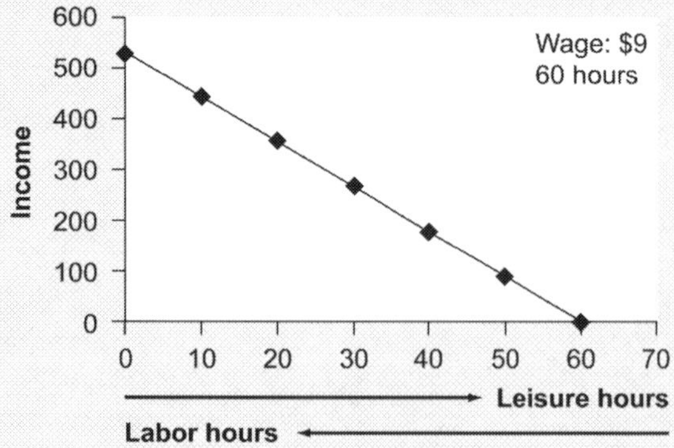

Hours worked	Leisure time	Income
0	60	$0
10	50	$90
20	40	$180
30	30	$270
40	20	$360
50	10	$450
60	0	$540

(a) First set of choices: Wage $9 per hour. The points on the opportunity set show what combinations of leisure and income that Beulah can have with her 60 hours of time, given that she can earn a wage of $9 per hour. The trade-off between leisure and income, which is the wage $9 per hour, determines the slope of the line.

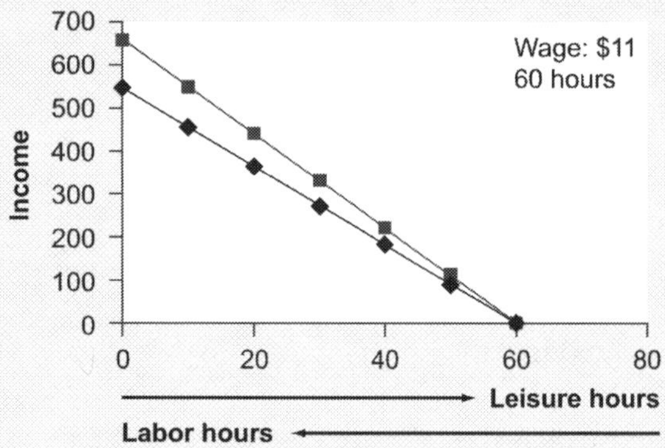

Hours worked	Leisure time	Income
0	60	$0
10	50	$110
20	40	$220
30	30	$330
40	20	$440
50	10	$550
60	*0*	*$660*

(b) Second set of choices: Wage $11 per hour. If Beulah's wage increases from $9 per hour to $11 per hour, her 60 hours of time has not changed, but the trade-off that she faces between leisure and income has changed. With the higher wage, giving up a certain number of hours of leisure brings a higher income, so the budget set rotates upward.

Beulah might desire a combination of income and leisure that is outside her budget constraint; for example, she would probably like to have both 60 hours of leisure and $540 of income, which is the choice shown at point S. However, the budget constraint shows the limits of what choices are possible, given the wage and hours available, and choices beyond the budget constraint are not possible. Moreover, Beulah will not choose a point inside the budget constraint like T, which is 50 hours of labor, 10 hours of leisure, and $200 of income. In effect, a choice like T would mean that Beulah was working for only $4 per hour (that is, $200 of income divided by 50 hours of work), when she can actually earn a wage of $9 per hour. Thus, the labor-leisure budget constraint illustrates: (1) how the budget set of possible choices for leisure and income are determined by the wage rate and the total quantity of hours that can be worked; (2) how changes in the wage rate cause the budget constraint to shift; and (3) how the personal preferences of an individual for choosing between leisure and income are represented by the point that is chosen on the budget constraint.

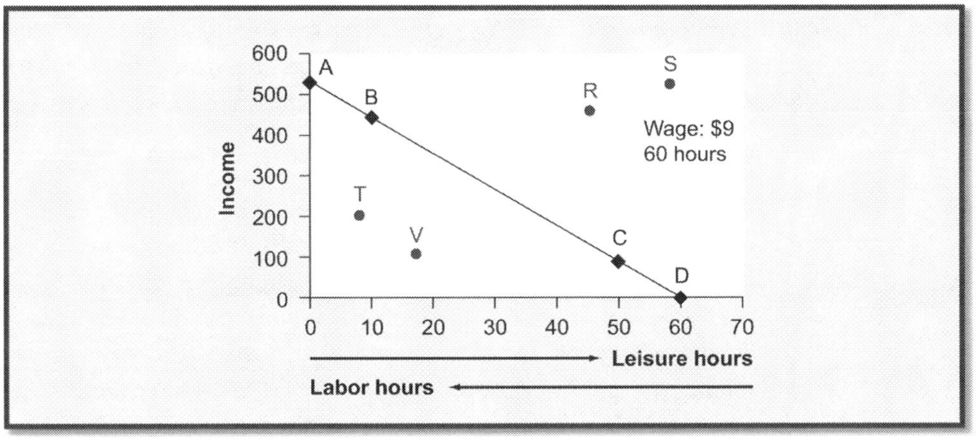

Exhibit 2-4 Beulah's Personal Choice on a Labor-Leisure Opportunity Set

If Beulah strongly prefers income, she will work a lot of hours and choose a point like A or B. If she strongly prefers leisure, she will work few hours and make a choice like C or D. Given that she has 60 hours of time and a wage of $9 per hour, she cannot choose points like R or S that are outside her budget set. Points like T or V inside her budget set would be wasteful; they would be like giving up hours of leisure but not being paid.

Choosing Between Present and Future Consumption

An intertemporal choice reaches across time. Borrowing money is an intertemporal choice, because it involves borrowing money to spend in the present but promising to repay in the future. Saving money is also an intertemporal choice, because it involves less consumption in the present, but the ability to consume more in the future. The intertemporal choice budget constraint shows the trade-off between present and future consumption.

INTEREST RATES: THE PRICE OF INTERTEMPORAL CHOICE

In the consumption choice budget constraint presented earlier, the trade-off between goods is determined by the relative prices of the two goods. In the labor-leisure budget constraint, the trade-off between leisure and income is based on the wage. In the intertemporal choice budget constraint, the trade-off between present consumption and future consumption is based on the interest rate or the rate of return. The price of borrowing money is the interest that you pay on the loan. The reward for saving money is the interest that you receive. Interest rates are worth more discussion, because they may seem less familiar than other prices.

The key to understanding the economic function of interest rates is to recognize that $100 you will receive in the future has less economic value than $100 you receive today. Imagine that a friend owes you $100, and when the time comes to pay, the friend says: "Hey, no problem, I'll have the money for you in five years." You protest, and your supposed friend says, "Hey, you are still getting repaid your full $100, so what are you complaining about?" You probably aren't going to persuade this loser, your former friend, to repay you sooner, but you can offer three arguments as to why $100 in the future doesn't have the same value as $100 today:

risk premium: A payment to make up for the risk of not being repaid in full.

inflation: Rise in the overall level of prices.

time value of money: The cost of having to wait for repayment.

1. *Risk of not being repaid.* The future is uncertain. Your friend could get hit by a bus. You could get hit by a bus. (The way this friendship is going, you could run over your former friend with a bus.) Having $100 in your pocket is a sure thing. Having a promise of $100 is uncertain. Anytime someone borrows money, whether the lender is a friend or a bank, the lender must be concerned about the risk of not being repaid. Part of the interest rate is a **risk premium**, that is, a payment to make up for the risk of not being repaid in full.
2. *Inflation.* In most years, there is a rise in the price level called **inflation**. In recent U.S. history, this increase has typically been 1-3% per year, but in some other countries the rate of inflation has been much higher. If the overall level of prices rises by 3% then on average a dollar will buy 3% less in terms of goods and services at the end of the year. If that 3% is being subtracted each year from the buying power of the currency, then being repaid $100 in the future will provide less buying power than receiving the money immediately. A lender demands an interest rate in part to compensate for any expected inflation, so that the money that is repaid in the future will have at least as much buying power as the money that was originally loaned. (The concept of inflation, along with its underlying causes and policy solutions, is discussed at length in the macroeconomics section of the book.)
3. *Time value of money.* Even if you knew with complete certainty that the $100 will be repaid in the future, and even if the rate of inflation is zero, it is still annoying to wait several years for repayment. If you have the money now, you can spend it on something now if you wish to do so and receive benefits from that spending. Being forced to wait is an intangible cost, but still a cost. This cost of having to wait is referred to as the **time value of money**.

Thus, when explaining to your friend why you should receive interest payments if you need to wait five years for your money, you can point out that an interest rate has three components:

Interest rate = Risk premium + Expected rate of inflation
+ Time value of money.

In effect, interest payments are a compensation for the risk of not being repaid, the fact that inflation tends to reduce the buying power of money over time, and the unpleasantness of having to wait to have money available.

Thinking about these three components of interest rates helps to explain why interest rates differ across times and places. At times and places when inflation is high, interest rates will also be high. Differences in interest rates at a point in time can usually be traced to the different risk premiums involved. For example, when the U.S. government borrows money the interest rate is quite low, perhaps an annual rate of 3–4%, because the chance that the federal government will not repay what it has borrowed is quite low. A large corporation might pay an annual interest rate of 6–7% because, although the firm is still unlikely not to pay back the loan, the risk is greater than with a federal government. A medium-size or small firm would pay a still higher interest rate because it has a greater risk of not repaying the loan. Individuals pay a relatively low interest rate when they borrow money from a bank to purchase a home because the bank (the lender) does a credit check before lending any money in the first place. The credit check is supposed to ensure that a home buyer has the financial means to cover the cost; if the buyer is unable to meet the payments, the bank can take the house and sell it. However, individuals pay a higher interest rate on credit card borrowing because there is a greater risk that such loans will not be repaid.

THE POWER OF COMPOUND INTEREST

Interest rates are usually expressed in annual terms. For example, an annual interest rate of 7% means that if you borrow $100 you will need to repay $107 a year from now, or if you save $100 you will receive $7 in interest payments a year from now. But what if you are planning to save money for a period of many years, allowing the interest to accumulate over time? The formula for starting with a certain amount of money in the present, and a certain interest rate or rate of return, and figuring how much it would be worth at a date in the future is:

$$(\text{Amount at present}) \times (1 + \text{interest rate})^{\text{number of years}} = \text{Amount at future time}$$

For example, Christopher is planning to make a financial investment of $500. He will put this money in a savings account that pays an interest rate of 6% annually and leave it in the account for some years as the interest accumulates.

Exhibit 2-5 applies this formula for Christopher and shows what his financial investment would be worth at various dates in the future. Notice that if he leaves the financial investment alone for 20 years, the original $500 will more than triple in value to $1,603; if he leaves the financial investment alone for 40 years, it will increase more than 10-fold to $5,143. How can a seemingly moderate interest rate like 6% per year produce such large increases? The answer lies in the power of **compound interest**, which refers to the situation when interest payments are allowed to accumulate, so that in later time periods, the interest rate is paid not only on the original amount, but also on the interest that has accumulated in previous years. In the equation for how a financial investment increases in value over time, the number of years is an exponent. When quantities are raised to high exponential powers, they will eventually expand very quickly. The exponent represents the power of compound interest—as time goes by, Christopher is not just earning interest on his original $500, but also on the earlier interest he earned. If

compound interest: When interest payments accumulate, so that in later time periods, the interest rate is paid on the interest that has been earned and reinvested in previous years.

interest rates are relatively low, compound interest doesn't make much of a practical difference over a short time period of a few years. But over several decades, even a relatively low interest rate will compound in a way that yields significant returns on the initial financial investment.

AN EXAMPLE OF INTERTEMPORAL CHOICE

Consider the case of Desdemona, who is lucky enough to receive a gift of $10,000 from a wealthy aunt. She faces a choice: how much money should she consume now, and how much should she save for future consumption? Again, the first step is to use the budget constraint to show the range of possible choices, while the second step is to illustrate the individually preferred choice that maximizes her utility.

Exhibit 2-5
Christopher's Potential Savings

Starting with $500, interest rate of 6%

After 1 year	$\$500\,(1 + .06)^1 = \$530$	After 10 years	$\$500\,(1 + .06)^{10} = \$895$
After 2 years	$\$500\,(1 + .06)^2 = \$562$	After 20 years	$\$500\,(1 + .06)^{20} = \$1,603$
After 5 years	$\$500\,(1 + .06)^5 = \$669$	After 40 years	$\$500\,(1 + .06)^{40} = \$5,143$

Exhibit 2-6 Desdemona's Intertemporal Budget Constraint
The points along the budget set represent the combinations of present and future consumption that are available to Desdemona, based on her inheritance of $10,000 and an interest rate of 9% per year. The trade-off between present consumption and future consumption—and thus the slope of the budget line—is determined by the interest rate. Choices like Q or P are unavailable to Desdemona, even if she would like them. She will not make choices like R or S because they give up present consumption without taking future consumption, which would be wasteful. Thus, she will choose among points like A through F, based on her personal preferences.

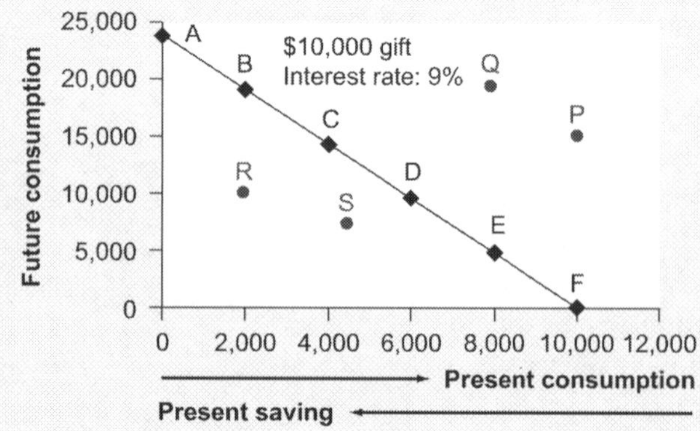

Consume in present	Save in present	Consume in future
0	$10,000	$23,673
$2,000	$8,000	$18,939
$4,000	$6,000	$14,204
$6,000	$4,000	$9,469
$8,000	$2,000	$4,734
$10,000	$0	$0

In the intertemporal choice budget constraint, the two axes represent consumption in the present and consumption in the future. Let's assume that if Desdemona saves some of the money, she can earn an annual interest rate of 9% for the next 10 years. Exhibit 2-6 shows Desdemona's choices in both a table and a budget constraint. The levels of future consumption that are available to her 10 years from now are calculated by using the formula for compound interest. At one extreme, she can consume all of the $10,000 in the present and have nothing left in the future. At the other extreme, she can save the entire $10,000, consume none of it in the present, and have $23,673 to spend 10 years from now. In Exhibit 2-6, both present consumption and present savings are shown on the horizontal axis. Consumption is measured from left to right; saving is measured from right to left. In effect, the horizontal axis shows how the income that is available in the present is divided into either consumption or savings. (This approach applies the same logic as the way in which hours of labor and leisure were both shown on the horizontal axis in the labor-leisure budget constraint.) If the interest rate rises, then the budget constraint has a steeper slope; a lower interest rate causes the budget constraint to shift downward to a flatter slope.

Desdemona will seek to maximize her utility and choose the option that brings her the greatest degree of satisfaction. Inevitably, this choice will be one of the points on the budget constraint such as A, B, C, D, E, or F. Even if Desdemona wants to choose a point like Q, with $8,000 of consumption in the present, $2,000 of savings, and $20,000 of future consumption, she can't have it because choice Q is outside her budget constraint. Moreover, Desdemona will not choose a point inside the budget constraint like R, with $2,000 in present consumption and $10,000 in future consumption because such a choice would be like throwing away money. Instead of choosing R, Desdemona would certainly prefer a choice like C with more consumption in both the present and the future.

In the real world, the trade-off between present and future consumption is considerably more complex than the basic intertemporal budget constraint shown here. Instead of making one decision in the present about whether to consume now or save for 10 years from now, people receive income in many different years and make decisions about how much to save over different periods of time. Moreover, financial investments usually don't pay a guaranteed rate of return, so people need take into account the risk and uncertainty of investments. Later chapters will take up the details of financial investing in greater detail. But the basic intertemporal budget constraint here illustrates three themes: (1) how the budget constraint of possible choices for present and future consumption are determined by the quantity of income in the present and the interest rate; (2) how changes in the interest rate will cause the intertemporal budget constraint to shift; and (3) how the personal preferences of an individual for present and future consumption are represented by the point that is chosen on the intertemporal budget constraint.

Three Implications of Budget Constraints: Opportunity Cost, Marginal Decision-Making, and Sunk Costs

The budget constraint framework has some possibly unexpected implications for how a sensible utility-maximizing individual will make decisions. Let's now draw out three of those implications, involving *opportunity cost, marginal decision making*, and *sunk costs.*

OPPORTUNITY COST

opportunity cost: Whatever must be given up to obtain something that is desired.

When most people want to know the cost of an item or a service, they look for a price tag. When economists want to determine cost, they go one step further. They use the idea of **opportunity cost**, which is whatever must be given up to obtain something that is desired. In the examples discussed earlier, if Alphonso wants more burgers, the opportunity cost is measured in bus tickets; if he wants more bus tickets, the opportunity cost is measured in burgers. In Beulah's labor-leisure choice, if she wants more income, the opportunity cost is hours of leisure; if she wants more leisure time, the opportunity cost is dollars of income. In Desdemona's intertemporal choice, the opportunity cost of greater consumption in the present is less consumption in the future and vice versa. The idea of opportunity cost, as its name implies, is that the cost of one item is the lost opportunity to do or consume something else.

Opportunity Costs

By David Moglen

Economic Actor	Nearly Always Trying to Maximize	Basic Action/ Choice	Opportunity Cost
Consumers	Utility	Buying a good yielding the most utility	Lost utility from second-best good
Businesses	Profit	Producing the good yielding the most profit	Lost profit from second most profitable good the business could make
Government	Unknown; no one agreed-upon target	Spending money in a certain way, change a certain tax, change or introduce a law or regulation	Unknown; no one agreed-upon second-best option
Country (as shown in a PPC graph)	Output/ efficiency	Produce more of one good	Lost output of second good
Labor	Wages + net nonmonetary advantages	Choose to work one hour	Lost utility from an hour of leisure time (the leisure trade-off)

Opportunity Cost in the Airport

After the terrorist plane hijackings on September 11, 2001, many steps were proposed to improve air travel safety. For example, the federal government could provide armed "sky marshals" who would travel inconspicuously with the rest of the passengers. The cost of having a sky marshal on every flight would be roughly $3 billion per year. Retrofitting all U.S. planes with reinforced cockpit doors to make it harder for terrorists to take over the plane would have a price tag of $450 million. Buying more sophisticated security equipment for airports, like three-dimensional baggage scanners and cameras linked to face recognition software, could cost another $2 billion.

But the single biggest cost of greater airline security doesn't involve spending money. It's the opportunity cost of additional waiting time at the airport. About 750 million passengers took plane trips in the United States in 2008. Since the 9/11 hijackings, security screening has become more intensive, and consequently, the procedure takes longer than in the past. Say that, on average, each air passenger spends one extra hour in the airport per trip. Economists commonly place a value on time to convert an opportunity cost in time into a monetary figure. Because many air travelers are relatively high-paid business people, conservative estimates set the average price of time for air travelers at $20 per hour. By these estimates, the opportunity cost of delay in airports is 750 million hours × 20 dollars/ hour, or $15 billion per year. Clearly, the opportunity costs of waiting time can be just as important as costs that involve direct spending.

In many cases, it is reasonable to refer to the opportunity cost as the price. If your cousin buys a new bicycle for $300, then $300 measures the amount of "other consumption" that he has given up. For practical purposes, there may be no special need to identify the specific alternative product or products that could have been bought with that $300, but sometimes the price as measured in dollars may not accurately capture the true opportunity cost. This problem can loom especially large when costs of time are involved. For example, consider a boss who decides that all employees will attend a two-day retreat to "build team spirit." The out-of-pocket monetary cost of the event may involve hiring an outside consulting firm to run the retreat. But an opportunity cost exists as well: during the two days of the retreat, none of the employees are doing any other work. Attending college is another case where the opportunity cost exceeds the monetary cost. The out-of-pocket costs of attending college include tuition, books, room and board, and other expenses. But in addition, during the hours that you are attending class and studying, it is impossible to work at a paying job. Thus, college imposes both an out-of-pocket cost and an opportunity cost of lost earnings—and both costs should be taken into account.

In some cases, making the opportunity cost explicit can alter behavior. Imagine, for example, that you are an employee who goes out to lunch every day and spends $8 at a local restaurant. You may know perfectly well that bringing a lunch from home would only cost $3 a day, but somehow referring to the opportunity cost of buying lunch at the restaurant as $5 each day (that is, the $8 it costs minus the $3 your lunch from home would cost) doesn't seem to matter much. However, if you work 250 days a year, that $5 per day adds up to $1,250 for a year—which is the cost of a decent vacation. If the opportunity cost is described as "a nice vacation" instead of "$5 a day," you might make different choices.

Can Economics Take Pride in Being the "Dismal Science"?

Economics is often called the dismal science. Yet few people would toss that phrase around so easily if they knew its origin. The "dismal science" phrase originated with British essayist Thomas Carlyle (1795-1881). In an 1849 article, Carlyle described the study of "political economy," as economics was then called, as a "dreary, desolate and indeed quite abject and distressing one; what we might call, by way of eminence, the *dismal science*."

This put-down has echoed through time. But not many people know why Carlyle disliked economics. The "dismal science" comment appeared in his essay "Occasional Discourse on the Negro Question." In that essay, Carlyle made the racist argument that white landowners should compel black people in the West Indies to give up their natural laziness and instead to work hard and have some purpose in their otherwise meaningless lives. Carlyle didn't just believe that black people should be ordered around by whites; he believed that all the "weak" people, black and white alike, should be compelled by the strong to do "the work they were appointed for," as he put it.

Carlyle thought economics was the "dismal science" because it rested on the assumption that people, regardless of race and social status, were best suited to make their own decisions about their own lives. Carlyle's insult is one that economists can wear with pride.

MARGINAL DECISION-MAKING AND DIMINISHING MARGINAL UTILITY

The budget constraint framework helps to emphasize that most choices in the real world aren't about getting all of one thing or all of another; that is, they aren't about choosing either the point at one end of the budget constraint or else the point all the way at the other end. Instead, most choices involve **marginal analysis**, which involves comparing the benefits and costs of choosing a little more or a little less of a good.

marginal analysis: Comparing the benefits and costs of choosing a little more or a little less of a good.

The utility that a person receives from consuming the first unit of a good is typically more than the utility received from consuming the fifth or the tenth unit of that same good. When Alphonso makes his choice between burgers and bus tickets, for example, the first few bus rides that he chooses might provide him with a great deal of utility— perhaps they help him get to a job interview or a doctor's appointment. But later bus rides might provide much less utility—they may only serve to kill time on a rainy day. Similarly, the first burger that Alphonso chooses to buy may be on a day when he missed breakfast and is ravenously hungry. However, if Alphonso has a burger every single day, the last few burgers may taste pretty boring. Similarly, if Beulah is working 60 hours per week and thinking about whether to take a few hours of leisure, that break may provide her with a great deal of utility. But if she is working only 10 hours a week, with 50 hours of leisure already, then taking a few more hours of leisure seems likely to provide much less utility.

The general pattern that consumption of the first few units of any good tends to bring a higher level of utility to a person than consumption of later units is a common pattern. Economists refer to this pattern the **law of diminishing marginal utility**, which means that as a person receives more of a good, the additional or marginal utility from each additional unit of the good declines.

law of diminishing marginal utility: As a person receives more of a good, the marginal utility from each additional unit of the good is smaller than from the previous unit.

The law of diminishing marginal utility explains why people and societies rarely make all-or-nothing choices. You wouldn't say, "My favorite food is (say) ice cream, so I will eat nothing but ice cream from now on." Instead, even if you get a very high level of utility from your favorite food, if you ate it exclusively, the additional or marginal utility from those last few servings would not be very high. Similarly, most workers don't say: "I enjoy leisure, so I'll never work." Instead, workers recognize that even though some leisure is very nice, a combination of all leisure and no income isn't so attractive. Thus, the budget constraint framework suggests that when people make choices in a world of scarcity, they will use marginal analysis and think about whether they would prefer a little more or a little less.

SUNK COSTS

sunk cost: Costs that were incurred in the past and cannot be recovered, and thus should not affect current decisions.

In the budget constraint framework, all decisions involve what will happen next: that is, what quantities of goods will be consumed, how many hours will be worked, or how much will be saved. These decisions do not look back to past choices. Thus, the budget constraint framework assumes that **sunk costs**, which are costs that were incurred in the past and cannot be recovered, should not affect the current decision.

Consider the case of Edgar who pays $8 to see a movie, but after watching the film for 30 minutes he knows that it's truly terrible. Should he stay and watch the rest of the movie because he paid $8, or should he leave? The money he spent is a sunk cost and unless the theater manager is feeling kindly, Edgar won't get a refund. But staying in the movie still means paying an opportunity cost in time. Thus, Edgar's choice is whether to spend the next 90 minutes suffering through a cinematic disaster or to do something—anything—else. The lesson of sunk costs is to forget about the money that's irretrievably gone and instead to focus on the marginal costs and benefits of future options.

production possibilities frontier: A diagram that shows the combinations of output that are possible for an economy to produce.

For people and firms alike, dealing with sunk costs can be frustrating. It often means admitting an earlier error in judgment. Many firms, for example, find it hard to give up on a new product that is doing poorly because they spent so much money in creating and launching the product. But the lesson of sunk costs is to ignore them and make decisions based on what will happen in the future.

The budget constraint or opportunity set framework provides a framework for thinking about how individuals make economic decisions like what to consume, how much to work, and how much to save. The purpose of this model is not to tell utility-maximizing individuals what they *should* do, but only to convey the range of available choices for what individuals *could* do, and to provide a way of showing what choices people actually make.

The Production Possibilities Frontier and Social Choices

In a world of scarcity, individuals cannot have everything they want and must instead make a choice along a budget constraint. Firms cannot have all the profits they want and must struggle to come up with new ways of pleasing customers. Society as a whole cannot have everything it might want, either. A production possibilities frontier is a graph that shows the combinations of output that are possible for an economy to produce. In effect, a **production possibilities frontier** is a budget constraint for the economy as a whole.

An example of a production possibilities frontier faced by every economy is the macroeconomic choice between consumption and real investment. Consumption refers to goods and services that are used up this year. Real investment (as opposed to financial investment) refers to expenditures on equipment (like machinery) that can be used to produce goods or services for some years into the future. Thus, expenditures on consumption often serve a more immediate need or desire, but expenditures on investment typically help to increase the economy's level of output in the future.

A production possibilities frontier for the choice between consumption and investment is shown in Exhibit 2-7 by the line labeled PPF_1. At point A, the economy is devoting all of its resources to producing goods for current consumption and nothing to investment. At points B, C, and D, the economy is gradually shifting toward lower levels of consumption and higher levels of investment. At point E, at the other end of the production possibilities frontier, the economy is devoting all of its resources to producing goods for real investment and no resources to current consumption. In a market-oriented economy, the choice between consumption and real investment is not made by the government or by any single organization, but rather is the result of many decisions made by households and firms. However, government policies can use taxes, regulations and other policies to influence the choices of individuals as to how much they should consume or save, and also to influence the eagerness with which firms will make real investments. Just as different people will make different choices along a budget constraint, according to their personal preferences, different societies will make choices about how much to consume and to invest.

Over time, societies that invest a greater share of GDP will tend to expand their ability to produce output. Therefore, a society that chooses

Exhibit 2-7 The Consumption and Investment Trade-Off

A production possibilities frontier shows the possible combinations of output that a society can produce. Points A, B, C, and D illustrate some possible choices along PPF_1, moving from all consumption at A to greater investment at B, C, and D. PPF_2 and PPF_3 show an outward shift of the frontier, which would happen as an economy grows and can afford more of both consumption and investment.

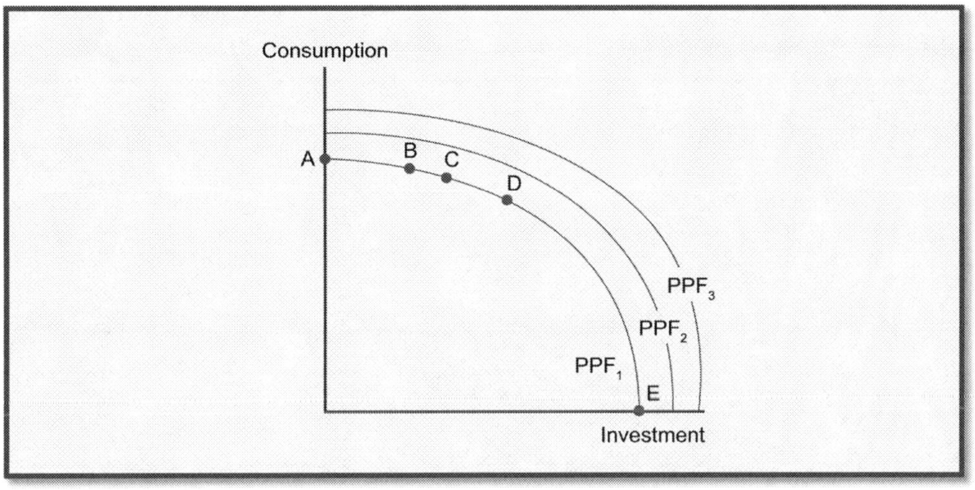

a high level of consumption and low level of investment, like point B, will find that in the future its production possibilities frontier shifts outward only a bit, perhaps from PPF_1 to PPF_2. However, a society that consumes relatively less in the present and invests more, like point D, will find that in the future its production possibilities frontier has shifted outward more dramatically, from PPF_1 to PPF_3. Thus, a consumption-investment production possibilities frontier shows the range of choices available to society, illustrates which choice will happen, and even has implications for how the PPF will shift in the future.

THE SHAPE OF THE PRODUCTION POSSIBILITIES FRONTIER AND DIMINISHING MARGINAL RETURNS

The budget constraints presented earlier in this chapter, showing individual choices about what quantities of goods to consume, how much to work and how much to save, were all straight lines. The reason for these straight lines was that the slope of the budget constraint was determined by relative prices of the two goods in the consumption budget constraint, by the wage in the labor-leisure budget constraint, and by the interest rate in the intertemporal budget constraint. However, the production possibilities frontier for consumption and investment was drawn as a curved line. Why does the PPF have a different shape?

Consider another example of a production possibilities frontier that arises when government decision makers must decide how much money to spend on competing government priorities, like education and improving health. Exhibit 2-8 shows a production possibilities frontier for this trade-off. In this diagram there are no specific numbers on the axes because there is no single way to measure levels of education

Exhibit 2-8 A Health vs. Education Production Possibilities Frontier

This production possibilities frontier shows a trade-off between devoting social resources to health and devoting them to education. At choices like A and B, most social resources go to health. At choices like D and E, most go to education. The curvature of the PPF shows that when a large share of resources is already devoted to health (as at point B), devoting still more resources to health and moving to point A produces only a small gain in health but a substantial loss in education. Thus, the curvature of the PPF demonstrates the law of diminishing marginal returns.

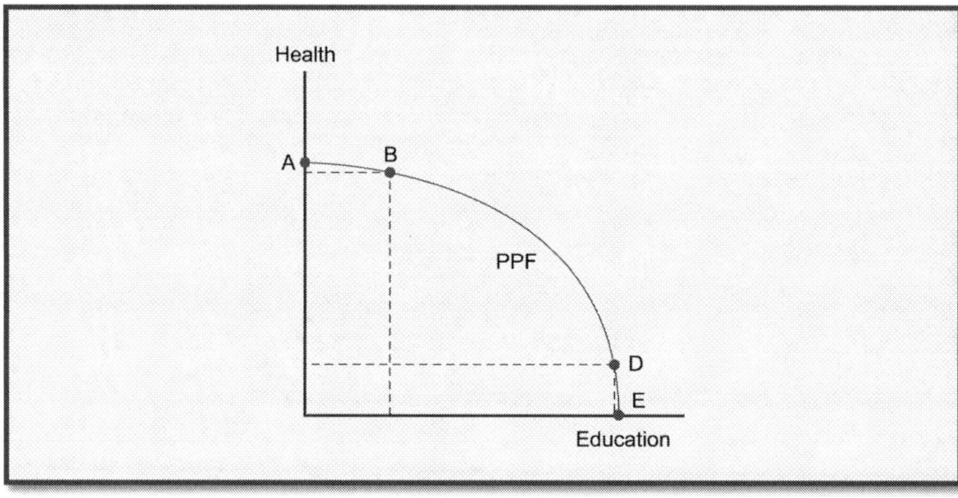

and health. However, when you think of improvements in education, you can think of accomplishments like more years of school completed, fewer high-school dropouts, and higher scores on standardized tests. When you think of improvements in health, you can think of longer life expectancies, lower levels of infant mortality, and fewer outbreaks of disease. At choice A, the government is committing all of its resources to producing health and none to education; at choice D, the government is committing all resources to education and none to health. As the economy grows over time this production possibilities frontier will shift to the right, making it possible for society to have more of both education and health. But in the immediate present, choosing more of one means choosing less of the other.

To understand why the PPF is curved, start by considering point A at the top left-hand side of the PPF. At point A, literally all of the available resources are being devoted to health and literally none to education. This situation would be extreme and even ridiculous. For example, children are seeing a doctor every day, whether they are sick or not, but not attending school. People are having cosmetic surgery on every part of their bodies, but no high school or college education exists. Now imagine that some of these resources are diverted from health to education, so that the economy is at point B instead of point A. Diverting some marginal resources away from A to B causes relatively little reduction in health because the last few marginal dollars going into health care services aren't producing much additional gain in health. However, putting those marginal dollars into education, which is

the law of diminishing returns: As additional increments of resources are added to producing a good or service, the marginal benefit from those additional increments will decline.

IN-CLASS PROJECT

The Production Possibilities Curve (PPC)

By David Moglen

Direction:

Graph—You will be assigned a group number from 1–5. Take the country associated with the same number as the question number you are assigned (below).

Once you have been assigned a group number, draw the graph with points A (before the shock) and B (after the shock) as described. Fully label the graph including estimated numeric values on x and y axes for points A and B. Label the axes according to the good and units of that good specified in the data.

Your points A or B could be a variety of different places and you must choose only one. Assume all examples start and end with output at potential—on the curve—unless otherwise indicated.

You should use k for thousand and m for million. Use a curved PPC since this is a single-country example.

***Explanation**—Say what is happening to the Land, Labor or Capital in your example to cause the change described. Be specific to the industry, e.g., if the factor you want to say is causing the shock you are given (below) is *Labor*, and the good is mechanical, maybe you say something (be specific) is happening to affect employment of *factory workers* (or whatever would correctly reflect the situation described).

Or as another example, if you wanted to use *capital* and the good is some kind of clothing, you would say what's happening with the *sewing machines.*

Use a curved PPC. In other words *name at least one input*—one thing you would need to produce this good—and say what is happening to it to cause the shock you are assigned (below).

1. Movement from inside to on the curve
2. Movement from on to inside the curve
3. Growth in the economy
4. Negative growth in the economy
5. Potential output for computers doubles

Data—Countries and their maximum output of two goods.

1. Japan (Daily)
   45,000 cars
   5 tons of gold

2. Saudi Arabia (Daily)
   8 million barrels of oil per day (MBPD oil)
   80 Airplanes

3. Denmark (Daily)
   48,000 tons of cheese
   12,000 customer service call center workers (cscw's)

4. Guatemala (Daily)
   60,000 tons of oak lumber
   30,000 tons of coal

5. France (Hourly)
   100 laptop computers
   400 tons of coffee

The Budget Constraint and the Production Possibilities Frontier

When you study economics, you may feel buried under an avalanche of diagrams: diagrams in the text, diagrams in the lectures, diagrams in the problems, diagrams on exams. Your goal should be to recognize the common underlying logic and pattern of the diagrams, not to memorize each of the individual diagrams.

This chapter uses only one basic diagram, although it is presented with different sets of labels. The consumption choice budget constraint, the labor-leisure budget constraint, and the intertemporal choice budget constraint for individuals, along with the production possibilities frontier for society as a whole, are all the same basic diagram. The exhibit shows an individual budget constraint and a production possibilities frontier for two goods, Good 1 and Good 2. The trade-off diagram always illustrates three basic themes: scarcity, trade-offs, and economic efficiency.

The first theme is scarcity. It is not feasible to have unlimited amounts of both goods. Budget constraints can shift, either as a result of movements of income or of prices. Production possibilities frontiers can shift, too, either as a national economy expands or as the trade-offs between the two goods shift. But even if the budget constraint or a PPF shifts, scarcity remains—just at a different level.

The second theme is trade-offs. As depicted in the budget constraint or the production possibilities frontier, it is necessary to give up some of one good to gain more of the other good. The details of this trade-off vary. In a budget constraint, the trade-off is determined by the relative prices of the goods: that is, the relative price of two goods in the consumption choice budget constraint; the relative price of labor and leisure (the wage) in the labor-leisure budget constraint; and the relative price of present and future consumption (the principal saved plus the interest rate or rate of return) in the intertemporal choice budget constraint. These trade-offs appear as a straight line. However, the trade-offs in many production possibilities frontiers are represented by a curved line because the law of diminishing returns holds that as resources are added to an area, the marginal gains tend to diminish. But regardless of the specific shape, trade-offs remain.

The third theme is economic efficiency or getting the most benefit from scarce resources. All choices on the production possibilities frontier show productive efficiency because in such cases, there is no way to increase the quantity of one good without decreasing the quantity of the other. Similarly, when an individual makes a choice along a budget constraint, there is no way to increase the quantity of one good without decreasing the quantity of the other. The choice on a production possibilities set that is socially preferred, or the choice on an individual's budget constraint that is personally preferred, will display allocative efficiency.

The basic budget constraint/production possibilities frontier diagram will recur throughout this book. Some examples include using these trade-off diagrams to analyze one source of the gains from international trade and to examine the trade-offs between environmental protection and economic output, between equality of incomes and economic output, and the macroeconomic trade-off between consumption and investment. Don't be confused by the different labels. The budget constraint/production possibilities frontier diagram is always just a tool for thinking carefully about scarcity, trade-offs, and efficiency in a particular situation.

The Trade-Off Diagram

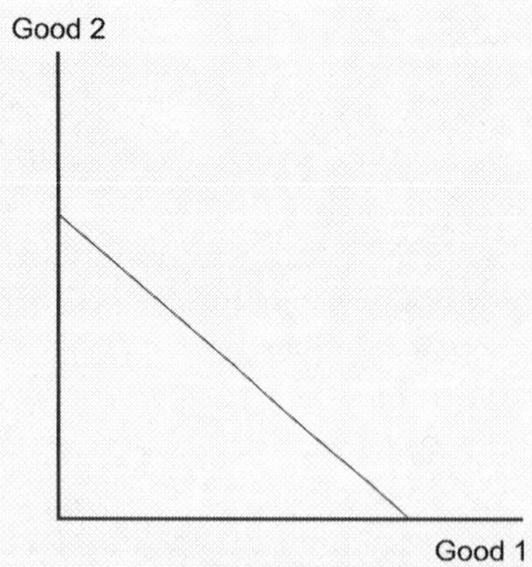

(a) An individual opportunity set.

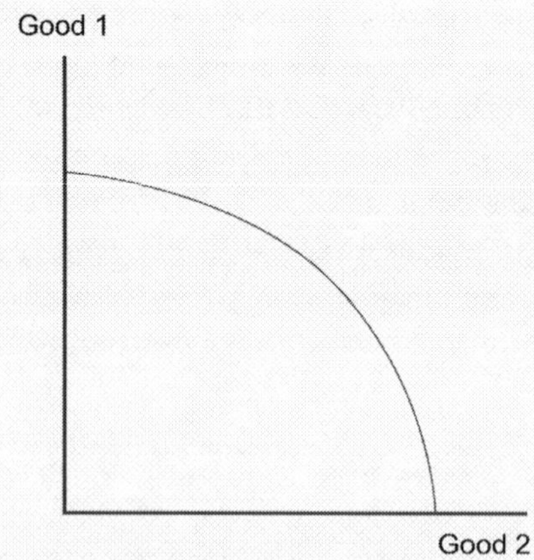

(b) A social production possibilities frontier.

completely without resources at point A, can produce relatively large gains. For this reason, the shape of the PPF from A to B is relatively flat, representing a relatively small drop-off in health and a relatively large gain in education.

Now consider the other end, at the lower right, of the production possibilities frontier. Imagine that society starts at choice D, which is devoting nearly all resources to education and very few on health, and moves to point E, which is devoting all spending to education and none to health. For the sake of concreteness, you can imagine in the movement from D to E, the last few doctors must become high school science teachers, the last few nurses must become school librarians rather than dispensers of vaccinations, and the last few emergency rooms are turned into kindergartens. The gains to education from adding these last few resources to education are very small. However, the opportunity cost loss to health will be fairly large, and thus the slope of the PPF between D and E is steep, showing a small gain in education and a large drop in health.

The lesson here is not that society is likely to make an extreme choice like devoting no resources to education at point A or no resources to health at point E. Instead, the lesson is that the gains from committing additional marginal resources to education depend on how much is already being spent. If very few resources are currently committed to education, then an increase of a certain amount can bring relatively large gains; on the other side, if a large number of resources are already being committed to education, then an increase of a certain amount will bring relatively smaller gains. This pattern is common enough that it has been given a name: **the law of diminishing returns**, which holds that as additional increments of resources are added to a certain purpose, the marginal benefit from those additional increments will decline. This pattern is common. When government spends a certain amount more on reducing crime, for example, the original gains in reducing crime could be relatively large. But additional increases typically cause relatively smaller reductions in crime, and paying for enough police and security to reduce crime to nothing at all would be tremendously expensive.

efficiency:
When it is impossible to get more of something without experiencing a trade-off of less of something else.

productive efficiency:
When it is impossible to produce more of one good without decreasing the quantity produced of another good.

The curvature of the production possibilities frontier shows that as additional resources are added to education, moving from left to right along the horizontal axis, the original gains are fairly large, but gradually diminish. Similarly, as additional resources are added to health, moving from bottom to top on the vertical axis, the original gains are fairly large, but again gradually diminish. In this way, the law of diminishing returns produces the outward-bending shape of the production possibilities frontier.

PRODUCTIVE EFFICIENCY AND ALLOCATIVE EFFICIENCY

The study of economics does not presume to tell a society what choice it should make along its production possibilities frontier. In a market-oriented economy with a democratic government, the choice will involve a mixture of decisions by individuals, firms, and government. However, economics can point out that some choices are unambiguously better

Exhibit 2-9 Productive and Allocative Efficiency

Productive efficiency means it is impossible to produce more of one good without decreasing the quantity that is produced of another good. Thus, all choices along a given PPF like B, C, and D display productive efficiency, but R does not. Allocative efficiency means that the particular mix of goods being produced—that is, the specific choice along the production possibilities frontier—represents the allocation that society most desires.

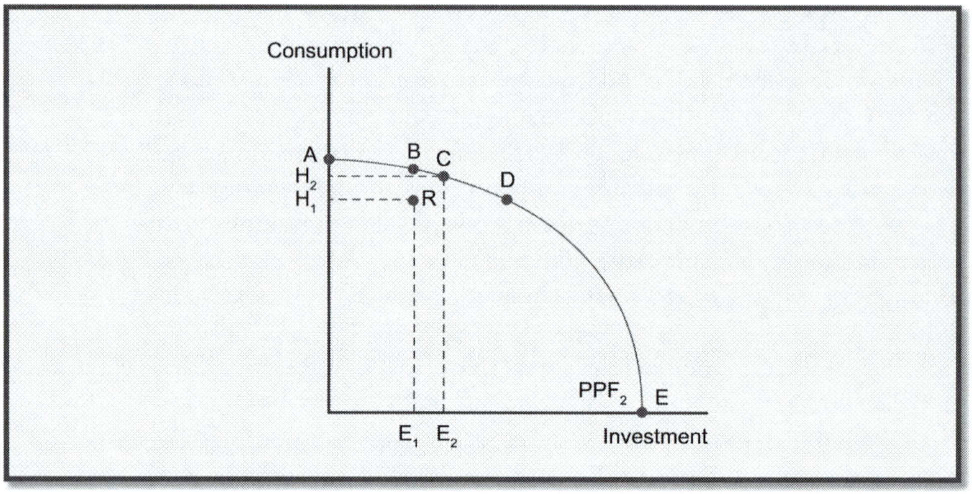

allocative efficiency:

When the mix of goods being produced represents the allocation that society most desires.

than others. In everyday usage, the concept of efficiency refers to lack of waste. An inefficient machine operates at high cost, while an efficient machine produces without wasting energy or materials. An inefficient organization operates with long delays and high costs, while an efficient organization meets schedules, is focused, and performs within budget.

To an economist, **efficiency** refers to the situation in which it is impossible to get more of one thing without experiencing a trade-off of less of something else. The production possibilities frontier can illustrate two kinds of efficiency: *productive efficiency* and *allocative efficiency*. Exhibit 2-9 illustrates these ideas using a production possibilities frontier between consumption and investment.

Productive efficiency means that, given the available inputs and technology, it is impossible to produce more of one good without decreasing the quantity that is produced of another good. Thus, all choices on the PPF in Exhibit 2-9, including A, B, C, D, and E, display productive efficiency. As a firm moves from any one of these choices to any other, either consumption increases and investment declines or vice versa. However, any choice inside the production possibilities frontier is productively inefficient and wasteful because it is possible to produce more of one good, the other good, or some combination of both goods. For example, point R is productively inefficient because it is possible at choice C to have more of both goods: investment on the horizontal axis is higher at point C than point R (E_2 is greater than E_1) and consumption on the vertical axis is also higher at point C than point R (H_2 is greater than H_1).

Allocative efficiency means that the particular mix of goods being produced—that is, the specific choice along the production possibilities frontier—represents the allocation that society most desires. How to determine what a society desires can be a controversial question, and it will be addressed in political science, sociology and philosophy classes as well as in economics. Only one of the productively efficient choices will be the allocatively efficient choice for society as a whole.

WHY SOCIETY MUST CHOOSE

Every economy faces two situations in which it may be able to expand consumption of all goods. In the first case, a society may discover that it has been using its resources inefficiently, in which case by improving efficiency and moving to the production possibilities frontier it can have more of some or all goods. In the second case, as an economy grows over a period of years, the production possibilities frontier for a society will tend to shift outward and society will be able to afford more of all goods. But improvements in productive efficiency take time to discover and implement, and economic growth happens only gradually. Thus, a society must face scarcity and choose between tradeoffs in the present. For government, this process often involves trying to identify where additional spending could do the most good and where reductions in spending would do the least harm. At the individual and firm level, the market economy coordinates a process in which firms seek to produce goods and services in the quantity, quality, and price that people want. But for both the government and the market economy in the short term, increases in production of one good typically mean offsetting decreases somewhere else in the economy.

Confronting Objections to the Economic Approach

It's one thing to understand the economic approach to decision-making and another thing to feel comfortable applying it. The sources of discomfort typically fall into two categories: that people don't act in the way that fits the economics model, and that even if people did act that way, they should try not to. Let's consider these arguments in turn.

A FIRST OBJECTION: PEOPLE, FIRMS, AND SOCIETY DON'T ACT LIKE THIS

The economic approach to decision-making seems to require more information than most individuals possess and more careful decision-making than most individuals actually display. After all, do you or any of your friends draw a budget constraint and mutter to yourself about maximizing utility before you head to the shopping mall? Do members of the U.S. Congress contemplate production possibilities frontiers before they vote on the annual budget? The messy ways in which people and societies operate somehow doesn't look much like neat budget constraints or smoothly curving production possibilities frontiers.

However, the economics approach can be a useful way to analyze and understand the trade-offs of economic decisions even if it doesn't describe how those decisions are actually made. To appreciate this point, imagine for a moment that you are playing basketball, dribbling to the right, and throwing a bounce-pass to the left to a teammate who is running toward the basket. A physicist or engineer could work out the correct speed and trajectory for the pass, given the different movements involved and the weight and bounciness of the ball. But when you're playing basketball, you don't perform any of these calculations. You just pass the ball, and if you're a good player, you will do so with high accuracy. Someone might argue: "The scientist's formula of the bounce-pass requires a far greater knowledge of physics and far more specific information about speeds of movement and weights than the basketball player actually has, so it must be an unrealistic description of how basketball passes are actually made." This reaction would be wrongheaded. The fact that a good player can throw the ball accurately because of practice and skill, without making a physics calculation, doesn't mean that the physics calculation is wrong.

Similarly, from an economic point of view, someone who goes shopping for groceries every week has a great deal of practice with how to purchase the combination of goods that will provide that person with utility, even if the shopper doesn't phrase decisions in terms of a budget constraint. Government institutions may work imperfectly and slowly, but in general, a democratic form of government feels pressure from voters and social institutions to make the choices that are most widely preferred by people in that society. Thus, when thinking about the economic actions of groups of people, firms, and society, it is reasonable as a first approximation to analyze them with the tools of economic analysis.

A SECOND OBJECTION: PEOPLE, FIRMS, AND SOCIETY SHOULDN'T DO THIS

The economics approach portrays people as self-interested. For some critics of this approach, even if self-interest is an accurate description of how people behave, these behaviors are not moral. Instead, the critics argue that people should be taught to care more deeply about others. Economists offer several answers to this concerns.

First, economics is not a form of moral instruction. Rather, it seeks to describe economic behavior as it actually exists. Philosophers draw a distinction between **positive statements**, which describe the world as it is, and **normative statements**, which describe how the world should be. In the study of economics, positive and normative arguments often blend into each other: for example, if an economist analyzes a proposal for building a subway system in a certain city and finds that the benefits are higher than the costs, then is this study a positive analysis that merely states what *will* happen or a normative analysis which describes what *should* happen? But even if the line between positive and normative statements isn't always crystal clear, economic analysis does try to remain rooted in the study of the actual people who inhabit the actual economy. Yes, if the world were populated by saints, the economy would look different. But it isn't.

Second, self-interested behavior and profit-seeking can be labeled with other names, such as personal choice and freedom. The ability to make personal choices about buying, working, and saving is an important personal freedom. Some people may choose high-pressure, high-paying jobs so that they can earn and spend a lot of money. Others may earn a lot of money and give it to charity or spend it on their friends and family. Others may devote themselves to a career that can require a great deal of time, energy and expertise but does not offer high financial rewards, like being an elementary school teacher or a social worker. Still others may choose a job that does not take lots of their time or provide a high level of income, but still leaves time for family, friends, and contemplation. Some people may prefer to work for a large company; others might want to start their own business. People's freedom to make their own economic choices has a moral value worth respecting.

Third, self-interested behavior can lead to positive social results. For example, when people work hard to make a living, they create economic output. Consumers who are looking for the best deals will encourage businesses to offer goods and services that meet their needs. Adam Smith, writing in the *Wealth of Nations*, christened this property the "invisible hand." In describing how consumers and producers interact in a market economy, Smith wrote:

> Every individual ... generally neither intends to promote the public interest, nor knows how much he is promoting it. He intends only his own security, only his own gain. And he is in this led by an invisible hand to promote an end which was no part of his intention. By pursuing his own interest he frequently promotes that of society more effectually than when he really intends to promote it.

The metaphor of the invisible hand suggests the remarkable possibility that broader social good can emerge from selfish individual actions.

Fourth, even people who focus on their own self-interest in the economic part of their life often set aside their own narrow self-interest in other parts of life. For example, you might focus on your own self-interest when asking your employer for a raise or negotiating to buy a car. But then you might turn around and focus on other people when you volunteer to read stories at the local library, help a friend move to a new apartment, or donate money to a charity. Thus, self-interest is a reasonable starting point for analyzing many economic decisions, without needing to imply that people never do anything that is not in their own immediate self-interest.

Facing Scarcity and Making Trade-offs

The study of economics is rooted in a fundamental insight about the human condition. The world we live in is a place of scarcity, whether measured in terms of time, money, natural resources, or material goods. As a result, people must face trade-offs and make choices. The main economic trade-offs for individuals are their decisions about what to consume, how much to work, and how much to save. For society as a whole and for government decision-makers, the task is to use scarce resources as efficiently as possible to meet people's needs. Economics delves into the questions of how individuals, firms and government will interact, and thus into the decisions that society will make about what to produce, how to produce, and for whom to produce.

Key Concepts and Summary

1. The real world is one of scarcity: that is, a world in which people's desires exceed what is possible. As a result, economic behavior involves trade-offs in which individuals, firms, government and society must give up one thing that they desire to obtain things that they desire more.
2. Individuals face three main categories of trade-offs: the consumption choice of what quantities of goods to consume, the labor-leisure choice of what quantity of hours to work, and the intertemporal choices that involve costs in the present and benefits in the future, or benefits in the present and costs in the future.
3. The **budget constraint**, sometimes called the **opportunity set**, illustrates the range of choices available. The slope of the budget constraint is determined by the relative price of the choices. Choices beyond the budget constraint are impossible. Choices inside the budget constraint are wasteful.
4. People will choose along their budget constraints in a way that maximizes their satisfaction or **utility**, which is based on their own distinctive personal preferences.
5. An interest rate has three components: the **risk premium** to cover the risk of not being repaid, the rate of expected **inflation**, and the **time value of money.** The formula for how **compound interest** accumulates over time is:

   $(\text{Amount at present}) * (1 + \text{Interest rate})^{\text{number of years}} = \text{Amount at future time}$

6. **Opportunity cost** measures cost by what is given up in exchange. Sometimes opportunity cost can be measured in money, but it is often useful to consider whether time should be included as well, or to measure it in terms of the actual resources that must be given up.
7. Most economic decisions and trade-offs are not all-or-nothing. Instead, they involve **marginal analysis**, which means they are about decisions on the margin, involving a little more or a little less.
8. The **law of diminishing marginal utility** points out that as a person receives more of something—whether it is a specific good or another resource—the additional marginal gains tend to become smaller.
9. Because **sunk costs** occurred in the past and cannot be recovered, they should be disregarded in making current decisions.
10. A **production possibilities frontier** defines a set of choices faced by society as a whole. The shape of the PPF is typically curved outward, rather than straight. Choices outside the PPF are unattainable and choices inside the PPF are wasteful. Over time, a growing economy will tend to shift the PPF outwards.

11. The **law of diminishing returns** holds that as increments of additional resources are devoted to producing something, the marginal increase in output will become smaller and smaller.
12. All choices along a production possibilities frontier display **productive efficiency**; that is, it is impossible to use society's resources to produce more of one good without decreasing production of the other good. The specific choice along a production possibilities frontier that reflects the mix of goods that society prefers is the choice with **allocative efficiency**.
13. **Positive statements** describe the world as it is, while **normative statements** describe how the world should be. Even when economics analyzes the gains and losses from various events or policies, and thus draws normative conclusions about how the world should be, the analysis of economics is rooted in a positive analysis of how people, firms and government actually behave, not how they should behave.

Review Questions

1. Explain why scarcity leads to trade-offs.
2. Name the three main categories of economic tradeoffs that individuals face.
3. What determines the slope of the consumption choice budget constraint? The labor-leisure budget constraint? The intertemporal budget constraint?
4. Explain why individuals make choices that are directly on the budget constraint, rather than inside the budget constraint or outside it.
5. Does the economic approach specify what choices people should make? Why or why not?
6. What does it mean to "maximize utility"?
7. What are the three components of the interest rate?
8. What is the formula for how compound interest accumulates over time?
9. What is opportunity cost?
10. What is the law of diminishing marginal utility?
11. What are sunk costs?
12. What does a production possibilities frontier illustrate?
13. Why is a production possibilities frontier typically drawn as a curve, rather than a straight line?
14. Explain why societies cannot make a choice above their production possibilities frontier and should not make a choice below it.
15. What are diminishing marginal returns?
16. What is productive efficiency? Allocative efficiency?
17. What's the difference between a positive and a normative statement?
18. Is the economic model of decision-making intended as a literal description of how individuals, firms, and the government actually make decisions?

IN-CLASS PROJECT

Steps for International Trade Using the PPC Graph

By David Moglen

Directions:

When an example has one country, the PPC is modeled as curved—which is more accurate? When two countries are trading, it is a useful simplification that improves the model to draw all lines straight.

1. Use the data to draw two straight-line PPCs in one, fully-labeled, X-Y space.

(Daily)	Trinidad = T	Sicily = S
Milk (in gallons) = M	5,000	100,000
Cell Phones = C	30,000	40,000

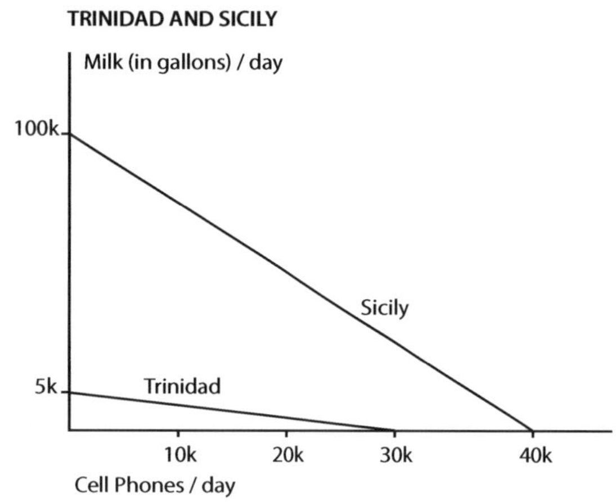

2. Set up tradeoff ratios. Change the numbers below Trinidad into a fraction.

	Trinidad	Now, do the same for Sicily:	Sicily
M (Milk)	5,000		100,000
C (Cell Phones)	30,000		40,000

Now, do the same for Sicily. Now, reduce the numerator to 1.

	Trinidad	Now, do the same for Sicily:	Sicily
M (Milk)	1		1
C (Cell Phones)	6		.4

3. Draw a "Combined PPC without Trade" line. This is just a straight line between the points where both countries have hypothetically put all their resources into producing one good. Go back to the original data. If both Trinidad and Sicily produce milk, up to 5,000 gallons can come from Trinidad and up to 100,000 Sicily. So, combined they can make up to 105,000. Mark the quantity of 105,000 on the Milk axis. Similarly for cell phones, 30,000 (from Trinidad) + 40,000 (from Sicily) = 70,000. Mark this quantity on the Cell Phones axis. Now draw a straight line between 70,000 phones and 105,000 gallons, and label it "Combined PPC without Trade."

4. Determine Specialization and draw a "Combined PPC with Trade" line. The tradeoff ratio fractions ask the question, how much does it cost to produce milk (the good in the numerator, the top of the fraction) in each country. In Trinidad the opportunity cost of a gallon of milk is 6 cell phones. In Sicily the cost to make the gallon of milk is 0.4 cell phones. Sicily has lower opportunity cost in the production of milk (their denominator is lower; 0.4 is less than 6) so they have comparative advantage in milk and should specialize in dairy. Trinidad should specialize in cell phones. Draw the point that would indicate both nations have gone 100% into their specialty. Trinidad produces 30,000 cell phones and Sicily produces 100,000 gallons of milk. That (30,000, 100,000) point is labeled "C." Draw lines to connect point C to the same axes intercepts (70,000 phones and 105,000 gallons) you found in Step 3. Label this line "Combined PPC with Trade."

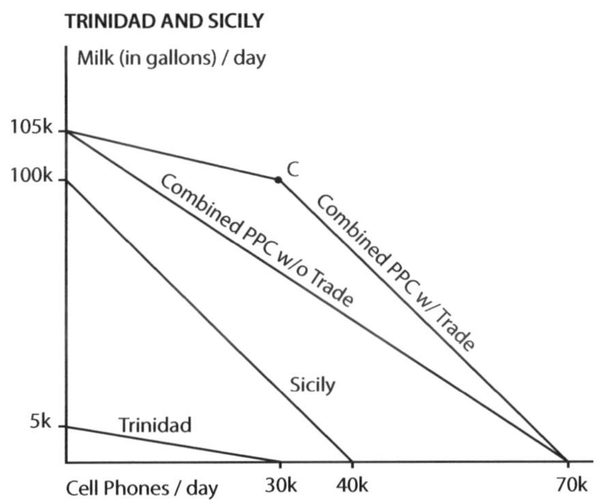

5. Write Terms of Trade Statements. Without more information (which is usually never given) we can't say exactly how many of Trinidad's cell phones will trade for a gallon of Sicilian milk, but we can state it as a range. Take the two denominators from the above fraction you had in Step 2 once you had already equalized the numerators to 1.

Terms of Trade Statement 1

One gallon of milk will trade for between _________ and _________ cell phones.

Insert the two denominators in the blanks. It is customary to put the smaller number first.

Terms of Trade Statement 1

One gallon of milk will trade for between 0.4 and 6 cell phones.

To do the same thing for one cell phone, you should go back to the original data. Flip the tradeoff ratios so that you are now looking at not Milk/Cell phones (M/C) but C/M for both countries. Now, do the same for Sicily, as in:

	Trinidad	Now, do the same for Sicily:	Sicily
C (Cell Phones)	30,000		40,000
M (Milk)	5,000		100,000

The fractions reduce to:

	Trinidad	Now, do the same for Sicily:	Sicily
C (Cell Phones)	1		1
M (Milk)	.167		2.5

Sicily = S (daily):	
Cell phones (C)	1
Milk (M)	2.5

And the Terms of Trade Statement is:

Terms of Trade Statement 2

One cell phone will trade for between 0.167 and 2.5 gallons of milk.

IN-CLASS PROJECT

Terms of Trade

By David Moglen

Directions

You will be assigned in class one of the pairs of nations (from 1-5) in the data section. In other words, since this is the trade example, now you are using the data from both countries in a given question.

Use the process explained in the "Steps for International Trade Using the PPC Graph" segment.

The answer has two parts: Draw four PPC "curves" (made up of all straight lines) on one graph. For example, the PPC for France, PPC for China, PPC for combined w/o trade, PPC for combined w/ trade. Clearly label all four lines and the axes, The heading above the graph should say France + China.

The second part is to give terms of trade statements for the two different goods. This means you will have two separate sentences, using the exact wording of correct terms of trade statements—one statement for each good. This completes your answer.

Assume straight-line PPCs.

Data

Countries and their maximum output of two goods.

1. **Japan (daily)**
   45,000 cars
   5 tons of gold

   Sweden (daily)
   20,000 cars
   10 tons of gold

2. **Saudi Arabia (daily)**
   8 mbpd oil (millions barrels per day)
   80 airplanes

   Mexico (daily)
   5 mbpd oil
   10 airplanes

3. **Denmark (daily)**
   48,000 tons of cheese
   12,000 customer service call center workers

   Germany (daily)
   25,000 tons of cheese
   50,000 csw's

4. **Guatemala (daily)**
   60,000 tons of oak lumber
   30,000 tons of coal

   Brazil (daily)
   80,000 tons of oak lumber
   1,000,000 tons of coal

5. **France (hourly)**
   100 laptop computers
   500 tons of coffee

   China (hourly)
   1,200 laptop computers
   400 tons of coffee

CHAPTER 3
Business Organization

3 Business Organization

By David Moglen

ORGANIZATION OF THE ECONOMY

The U.S. economy, like other nations, has three domestic sources of spending, and a fourth in its international trading partners. Together, the spending of these four economic actors adds up to GDP. The organization of these economic actors is the result of an evolving set of decisions by policymakers in government and the public at large.

Figure 1

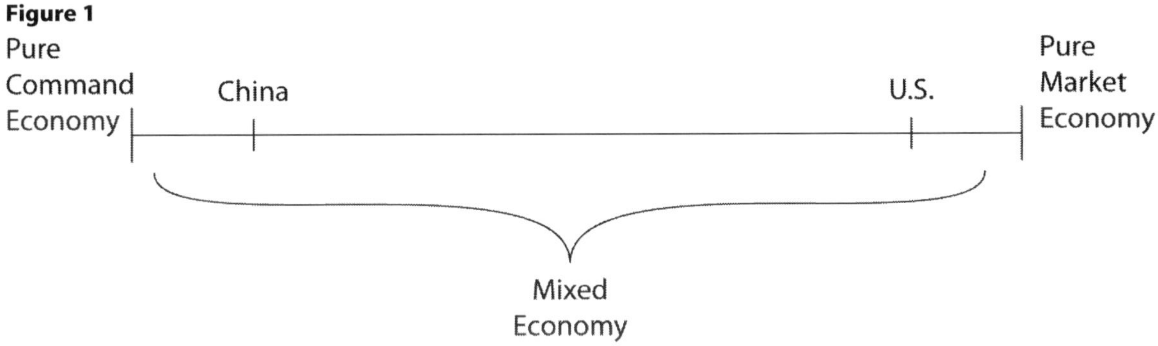

As you can see from the spectrum shown in Figure 1, the different possible types of economies range between two extremes – those of *pure market economies* and *pure command economies.* The latter are also known as *centrally planned economies.* The U.S. puts enough economic activity in the private sphere that it is routinely referred to as a market economy. However, strictly speaking, all modern national economies are *mixed economies* because they all contain at least some elements of *private sector* (consumers and business firms) ownership and control as well as some *public sector* (government) ownership and control. Additionally, historical economies and some regions in today's economies could be described as *traditional economies,* in that occupations, decisions about where to live, decisions about what to buy, and the bounds of social mobility are determined by heredity. In other words, if society says the son of a shoemaker will also be a shoemaker, and the daughter of a clothing designer will also be a clothing designer, that is called a *traditional economy.*

While the degree of public sector relative to private sector control determines where on the above spectrum we should place any specific country, the below relationship (shown in the *Simple Circular Flow Diagram*) applies to all types of economies.

Figure 2: Simple Circular Flow Diagram:

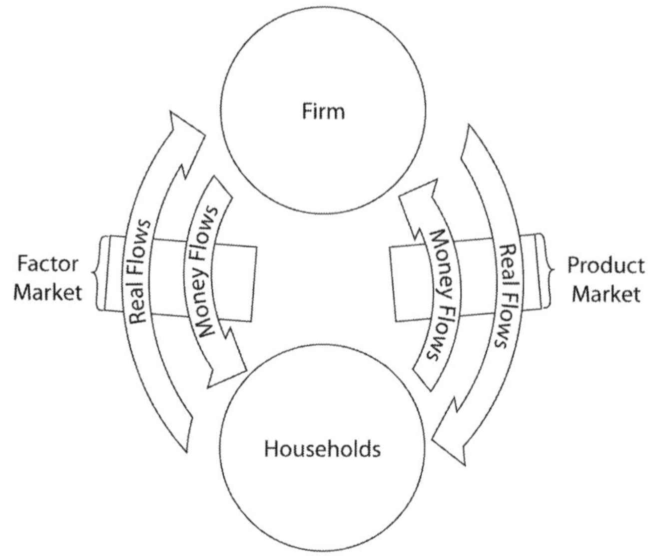

As you can see above in Figure 2, the firms buy inputs in the economy in the *factor market*. Households (as well as businesses, and government) buy output (produced by firms) in the *product market*. In other words, firms are the supply and households are the demand in the retail (product) market. Households are the supply and firms are the demand in the resource (factor) market. For example, you as an individual member of your household sell your labor to the company so you are a supplier in the labor market.

While this circular flow is universal, it is not the only universal aspect that applies to all economies worldwide. Another attribute common to all national economies is that they must answer the three *key economic questions*:

- What is produced
- How is it produced
- Who consumes it

Notice that even the extremes in the above spectrum, the pure market or the pure command economy, were they to exist in reality (recall it is better to call all real economies "mixed") would have to answer the above key economic questions in some way. So too would any (realistic) economies between those two poles. Other economic questions may go unanswered by some nations, such as how to maximize equity or how to maximize competition.

Another universal aspect common to all economies is that the private sector and public sector can both engage in *market activities* and *nonmarket activities.* Some examples are given in the chart below. The distinction is that market activities are exchanges in which both sides give something and both sides get something, such as in a purchase. In most cases, one side is giving up some money and the other side gives a good, service, or resource for that money. Nonmarket implies that one side gives and the other side does not provide anything in return, such as a subsidy, volunteering, or charity.

Sector	Market Activities	Nonmarket Activities
Private Sector	People buy goods Firms make and sell goods Firms pay workers	People give to charity People volunteer Firms establish charities
Public Sector	Federal government pays for roads and military County government sells permits and certificates	Federal government provides corporate and farm subsidies, welfare, food stamps, and foreign development assistance

As you can see from the chart above, while it may be tempting to draw a firewall between market and nonmarket activities, and to say that private sector is solely in the market and the public sector is strictly in the nonmarket activities, the reality is quite different. The guiding slogan for this structure should be "both can do both." Both the public and private sectors engage in both types of activities, the monetized market exchanges as well as nonmarket giving.

As we saw in Chapter Two, ("Opportunity Costs") consumers seek to nearly always maximize utility and their opportunity cost is the lost utility from the foregone (next best) purchase. Business firms seek to nearly always maximize profit and their opportunity cost is the lost profit from the foregone (next best) business venture. Opportunity cost and a goal as to what should be maximized are both undefined and ambiguous for government. Before we get to the main focus of Chapter Three, the attributes of three main business types, let's briefly cover the functions of government as understood by modern economists.

GOVERNMENT

The actions of the government can be broadly divided into two categories: *Actor* or *Referee.* The actor role for government is when it buys or sells anything. Any appropriation, or change in the budget (even a decrease in spending) is an example of the actor role. When the school district pays a fifth-grade teacher, or the state government builds a new university, the government is being an actor in the economy. The referee role means new laws or regulations are being passed or rolled back/repealed. The speed limit increasing from 55 to 65 miles per hour is an example of the referee role. So too is the decision made by European governments to ban pharmaceutical advertising on TV.

The following six roles of government are all up for debate, and often form the basis for the national debate raging in media, society and voting booths every election year. While some would like to see an expansion of government power in some or all of the following functions, others would like to see the function curtailed (reduced) or eliminated altogether, in favor of a privatized solution. That said, there is the most agreement about the first governmental function. Providing certain economic institutions is a role of government that is virtually universally accepted.

Roles of Government:

1. Promote Economic Institutions

Institutions are also referred to as social fabric, fabric of society, or social capital.

- Freedom of Contract
- Private Property

Enforcement of property laws also applies to intellectual property such as patented goods.

- A legal system that protects contracts, property rights, and other safeguards for business activity
- The corporate form or alternative mechanism to spread out risk and encourage risk-taking like starting a big business with a significant required investment
- Policies that promote the health and education (e.g. social capital) of the public

2. Promote Optimal Competition

Agencies like the Department of Justice, headed by the Attorney General, and the Federal Trade Commission (FTC) have the power to sanction monopolies and take them to court, where remedies up to and including the breaking up of the company can occur. These court cases against monopolies and cartels are part of Antitrust Law, and they are a major focus later in Chapter 15. Also theories like Joseph Schumpeter's "Creative Destruction" hold that a more laissez-faire approach is often better since monopoly power is an incentive to others to provide consumers the same utility in a way that circumvents (and partly or wholly) destroys the incumbent/ established monopoly's hold on the market. This logic says the government usually can let the market work out competition issues.

3. Correct for Externalities

Remember back to the assumptions of market theory. "Atomistic market participants" (e.g. many small producers) were assumed to be competing – not a monopoly. If there is a market failure in that bad effects from monopolies occur, as you see above, there are ways to correct for that. Similarly, inaccurate prices were an assumption of market theory – i.e. when there are negative externalities – third parties (not the buyer or seller) are negatively impacted. Air and water pollution are major examples, but others are harmful products like alcohol, cigarettes and weapons. The government has agencies empowered to compel firms to internalize these social costs into the offending producer's costs - then there is no more externality.

4. Promote Economic Growth and Stability

Many (but not all) economists hold that the government has a responsibility to enact policies to counter economic fluctuations. This is called countercyclical fiscal policy. Also many of these same economists believe the government should promote growth. In the U.S., ideal growth and stability is approximately 5% unemployment, 2-3% annual GDP growth, and 2-3% inflation.

5. Identify and Provide Public Goods

What is an inherently *public good* and what is an inherently (i.e. by definition) *private good* is a serious, continual debate in every country. Many countries have their energy sector like oil and gas companies in the public sector. In the U.S., it is beyond imagination that Exxon and Chevron and other oil companies would be owned by the government (but if they were they would probably be merged – i.e. the provider of the public good is often a government-owned monopoly). All developed countries (also known as the industrialized, or rich countries) provide health care as a public good except the U.S.

Transportation infrastructure (roads, highways, bridges, shipping ports and airports) is considered a public good. American public goods also include K-12 public education, community colleges, disaster relief, food, drug, and consumer product safety standards, libraries, shipping ports, airports, military, homeland security, courts, jails, prisons, Social Security, Medicare, Medicaid, the University of California and California State University systems, the majority of grants for basic research including the National Institutes of Health and their twenty-seven institutes and centers (see http://www.nih.gov/icd/) to name a few.

6. Correct Market Failures

One situation that has been evidently long-viewed as a market failure would be a completely free market in labor. So to avoid what are perceived as negative results from a free market in labor, tight immigration restrictions are in place. In particular, high-skilled labor enters on a very limited basis through the H1-B visa. A free market would put more American technology sector workers out of work in the short-run. Whether it's worth it due to other gains in the long-run is up for debate, although most economists agree that efficiency results from the free market rather than from barriers and "protectionism" like visa quotas.

Yet another situation that has been viewed as a market failure would be a free market in human organs, for example when someone needs a kidney. Such a market is illegal. It is the same with adoptions (no market exists legally).

Business Firms

The three main business types should be understood in terms of their advantages and disadvantages. While these are the only three you need to study, if you were to start a business you should learn about the hybrids – several additional business types that exist. A great starting point to survey this topic is provided by the article (link is provided) in the section entitled "Beyond the Three Basic Business Types: LLPs, LLCs, and S Corporations" which appears later in this chapter.

Sole proprietorships are the most simple business type to set up. One individual or a married couple ("mom and pop") sets this up to run their small business. There is no separation between business and personal income for tax purposes, nor is there separation of business and personal assets for liability purposes. This is called *unlimited liability*

Partnerships are set up by two or more partners. They also lack separation between business and personal income and assets.

Corporations, referring specifically to publicly traded corporations, do have a line between business assets and the personal assets of their owners (the stockholders), referred to *limited liability*. Taxes are assessed first on corporate profits and second on earnings when they are received by stockholders in the form of dividends and/or capital gains. This two-stage assessment of taxes is called *double taxation*.

Managers are separate from owners, which is called *absentee ownership*. This quality confers advantages (such as ability to hire the most specialized managers) as well as disadvantages to the corporation. For example, the principal-agent problem covers a variety of ways in which managers (executives) diverge from the goals of the owners (stockholders) who only want to maximize profits.

Figure 3: Breakdown of firms and sales by business type

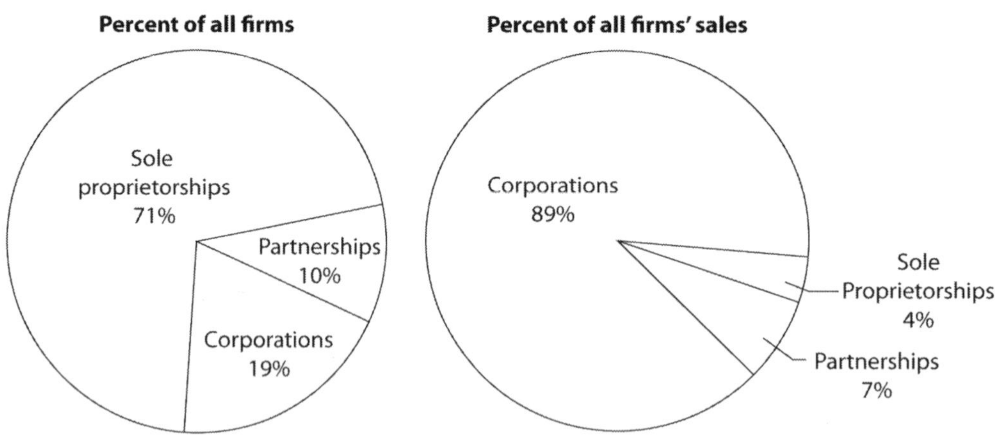

As you can see above in Figure 3 (from 2008, www.irs.ustreas.gov/taxstats) corporations only make up 19% of all registered business firms, but earn 89% of the sales revenue nationwide. While corporations are not in the majority if you add how many business firms of all types (mostly sole proprietorships) exist in the U.S., the majority of the profits made by all businesses are earned by corporations. This is because any larger firm is most likely to be a corporation. Furthermore, any publicly traded firm is most likely to be a corporation. The exception is a business organization called a Master Limited Partnership (MLP), which is a partnership that is allowed to sell stock shares to the public.

BUSINESS TYPE	ADVANTAGES	DISADVANTAGES
Sole Proprietorships (SP)	Inexpensive and simple to start	Limited life
	Best incentives for efficiency=best accountability	Unlimited liability
		Can't hire the most specialized managers (therefore lack potential ability to achieve maximum efficiency)
		Limited access to capital
Partnerships	Compared to SP, more specialized managers	Compared to corporations, less specialized managers
	Compared to SP, access to capital is better	Compared to corporations, less access to capital
	Accountability is better than in corporations	Limited life
		Unlimited liability
		Accountability is worse than in SP
Corporations	Limited liability	More expensive to start and more complicated paperwork
	Corporate personhood	Principal-Agent Problems
	Unlimited life	Double Taxation
	Best access to capital	More complicated and frequent financial reporting requirements

To clarify, access to capital refers to the amount of money and range of options to raise money available to the firm. In other words, it is financial capital – money the firm might need to spend on expansion, remodeling, or other non-recurring expenses. What are the firm's options to raise this money, beyond the fact they sell some product as part of their business?

The sole proprietor can only borrow from the bank, and the amount of their business loan is not very much. The partnership can do the same, although with greater borrowing power due to the partners' combined credit. But access to capital is most advantageous for the corporation; both the amount of funds they can access and the varieties available to them exceed that of the other two business types.

Besides the basic bank loan or credit line (short-term bank loan) that sole proprietors and partnerships can access (corporations can do that too), the corporate form enables a different type of *debt financing*. The corporation can issue *bonds*, which are loans from individual savers like yourself to the firm. For example, you could lend $1,000 today, with interest, to almost any firm you could name, from Coca Cola to Ford Motor Corporation, simply by buying one of their corporate bonds. Your stockbroker or online stock trading account would be the means to do this.

Even more significant than the varieties of debt financing which are available to it, the corporation can raise money by issuing *stock* shares, which is called *equity financing*. Each share is a very small percentage ownership of the actual firm. The first time a firm offers shares for sale to investors (i.e. the firm "goes public") it is called an IPO – initial public offering. They also can release more shares for sale later – even years later – in secondary offerings.

The *Principal-Agent Problem* is a huge area of study in economics and occurs anytime there is an agent (manager) in some control other than the real owner. For the firm the primary manager is the CEO (Chief Executive Officer). Others in the Agent category are the other executives, the board of directors, upper management/ supervisors, and even, to a much lesser extent, regular employees. The Principal is the owner – in this case, the stockholders. These shareholders have one primary goal: profit maximization. But the executives may want something else. Examples of the principal-agent problem, executives acting in their own interest more than the stockholders' interests, can be filed into one of four categories: "low and insufficient effort, inefficient or extravagant investments, entrenchment strategies or self dealing actions."*

Corporate Personhood

It sounds like a strange concept if you have never heard of this. What are the key court decisions that enable corporations to back political causes, officeholders, and ballot measures or initiatives?

YEAR	CASE NAME	BASIC MEANING
1886	Santa Clara County v. Southern Pacific Railroad	Corporations are legally people for most purposes
1976	Buckley v. Valeo	Money is a form of speech, and therefore entitled to First Amendment protections

* http://www.cer.ethz.ch/research/wp_07_63.pdf

2010	Citizens United v. FEC (Federal Elections Commission)	Strikes down laws limiting direct corporate contributions to Federal campaigns and requiring disclosure and transparency in political corporate spending. How complete this deregulation of campaign finance law will go remains to be seen as future cases work their way through the courts.

CONCLUSION

All economies on the spectrum from pure market to pure command must answer key economic questions such as what to produce and how to make it. In the predominantly market-based economies, these key questions are mainly answered by the price system. All modern economies can be described using a circular-flow diagram. Government has a variety of roles, although the extent of its engagement in each fuels political debates and power struggles, and the assertiveness of the state varies widely in different countries. Firms, or businesses, fall into three categories. Each can be described and compared to the others through their unique advantages and disadvantages.

Competition and cooperation between firms, the balance of power between the private and public sectors, and the role of corporate money in politics: these are the open questions over which policy wars are waged and corporate strategies are formed. These tensions and conflicts determine if you will get a good price or not for your car, your house, your education, whether there will be plenty of good jobs in the future, and the quality and availability of services from child care to medical care, from mail delivery to internet broadband (e.g. for watching videos on the web). The key actor besides business and government is the consumer: you. Collectively, you as consumers determine the fate of firms, the priorities of your policymakers, and the health of the economy.

EDITOR'S NOTES

Beyond the Three Basic Business Types: LLPs, LLCs, and S Corporations

The following article from *Medical Economics*, March 5, 2004, gives a very explanatory synopsis of business types beyond Sole Proprietorships, Partnerships and Corporations (called here C corps). Specifically, it analyzes the benefits and drawbacks of LLCs (Limited Liability Companies), LLPs (Limited Liability Partnerships), and S corporations. While it is written to advise doctors on how to set up their private practice, their analysis applies to most other professions as well. All you need to do is substitute the words "doctor" and "physician" for lawyer, accountant, architect, cabinet-maker, or any other good or service that a business might produce.

S CORP, C CORP, LLC, LLP—WHICH IS BEST?

By Dennis Murray

Publish date: March 5, 2004

Whether you're setting up a new practice or re-evaluating an existing one, here's help in sorting through your options.

Deciding which business structure is best for your medical practice can be one of the most difficult and financially significant things you'll do, besides treating patients. Set up your practice the right way and you'll enjoy tax benefits while adding an extra layer of protection against liability judgments. Set it up incorrectly and you might find yourself paying more taxes, and possibly being on the hook for a partner's negligence.

No business structure will protect you from liability for your own professional actions, but some may be able to protect you from suits arising from slip-and-fall injuries to your employees or patients. Nor will any structure give you total immunity for the actions of employees you supervise. But each type of business structure offers specific benefits and drawbacks. Understanding the differences will help you make the wisest choice, whether you're setting up a new practice or re-evaluating the structure of your current one.

All medical practices fall into two broad categories: unincorporated and incorporated. Most are incorporated, but some doctors still choose to set up shop in unincorporated practices. Let's look at those first, to understand why.

Unincorporated practices

Unincorporated practices are easier and less expensive to set up than incorporated businesses, which is why some doctors favor them. But the old saying, "you get what you pay for" may apply, because they don't offer the level of protection that incorporated practices do.

Here are the pros and cons of the key unincorporated setups:

Sole proprietorships. This is the simplest, cheapest way to get started in practice. Setting up a sole proprietorship involves minimal paperwork. When you die, so does the proprietorship. You and your business are treated as a single entity for tax purposes, so you simply report your practice's profits on Schedule C of your Form 1040. You also pay its debts from your own bank account. The downside—and it's a biggie—is that your personal assets can be claimed to settle any lawsuit against the business.

"I almost hate to see someone practice as a sole proprietorship or partnership nowadays," says Steven S. Goodman, of The Goodman CPA Group in Staten Island, NY. "Anyone who has become even the least bit successful should have a business structure that affords more liability protection."

A sole proprietorship can convert to an S corp or C corp—or, depending on the state you live in, to a limited liability partnership (LLP) or a limited liability company (LLC)—without triggering any taxes, says Goodman. The amount of paperwork needed varies widely, depending on where you live. So does the cost, which can typically run anywhere from $1,000 to $5,000. "Whatever the cost, though," he says, "it won't be substantial compared with the benefits gained."

General partnerships. This is much like a sole proprietorship in structure and simplicity, though having multiple partners does necessitate a bit more paperwork. More important, each doctor is personally liable for any claim against the partnership collectively, or against one of the partners individually, regardless of who's to blame. This is known as "joint and several liability." As with a sole proprietorship, if the judgment overshoots the coverage, you'll be responsible for paying the difference out of pocket.

General partnerships are starting to die out, largely because of the greater protections that corporations afford. In addition, most states are allowing physicians' practices to operate as LLPs or LLCs, both of which provide a better legal shield.

If you're currently in a general partnership, it's high time to switch to an LLP, an LLC, or a corporate structure. (More on these options later.) "That's a prudent move," Goodman says, "given the litigious society we live in."

Limited liability partnerships. This is the only type of unincorporated practice that will protect you from personal liability for your partners' or employees' malpractice. Your investment in the *business* still could be at stake if someone successfully sues the practice and the award exceeds your insurance limits. But at least you'll never have to worry about losing your house, savings, or personal investments because of the acts of another.

Don't confuse an LLP with a limited partnership that's established to invest in real estate, oil and gas, equipment leasing, and such. A limited partnership has general and limited partners. The general partner runs the organization, but limited partners don't; they simply fund it and receive income, capital gains, and tax benefits in return. An LLP, on the other hand, can be organized where every partner participates in decision making, regardless of seniority or income distribution. Moreover, the LLP has the option to create multiple classes of partners, each with different voting rights. Or, it can let a single physician run the show—whatever the doctors in the practice are most comfortable with.

Incorporated Practices

Incorporated practices are more formal, costly, and involve more paperwork than unincorporated ones. But they also provide more benefits. The main one is that like LLPs and LLCs, they protect you from personal liability for the professional acts of your colleagues. In the setups that follow, the doctors' personal assets are protected from judgments, which are considered business debts. The most any owner can lose is the total of his or her investment in the business—again, your personal assets are at risk for your own negligence.

C corporations. This structure has three levels of authority: shareholders (owners), a board of directors, and officers. C corporations can issue stock, which means physicians can buy into the practice or sell their shares without dissolving the corporate structure. There are generally no restrictions on how many shareholders the corporation can have, or on the number of shares it can issue. C corporations can issue two types of shares: preferred, which have priority when the practice is liquidated, and common shares. C corps can also issue voting and nonvoting shares, to allow for differences in seniority.

The major downside of C corporations is that profits are taxed twice, first at the corporate level and again when the physician shareholders receive their cut. C corporations usually get around the double-tax whammy by distributing the profits as year-end bonuses, so they're no longer taxable to the corporation. This is called "zeroing out" the profits. This should be done within reason, though, Goodman warns. An internist who draws a $40,000 salary and reports a $100,000 bonus may open himself up to increased scrutiny from the IRS. A real-life example of this potential pitfall, and its consequences, is described in detail in "The IRS cracks down on bonuses," Jan. 23, 2004.

S corporations. Like a C corporation, an S corporation can issue stock. However, it's limited to 75 shareholders and it can't issue both common and preferred shares of stock. In addition, profits in an S corporation have to be distributed in proportion to each owner's stake in the business.

The biggest advantage S corps have over C corps is that profits can flow directly to the owners' personal tax returns. Because of this, an S corporation's profits aren't double taxed. In that respect, an S corp is similar to an LLP (and another structure we'll discuss shortly, the LLC).

The major drawback of an S corporation is that, with the exception of health insurance premiums, you can't write off the entire cost of benefits. But that's a minor concern, says David J. Schiller, a tax attorney in Norristown, PA. Moreover, he says, it's offset by another important S corp benefit: "Losses that routinely occur at the startup of any practice are passed through to the shareholders and can offset their taxable income from other sources. Conversely, in a C corporation, such losses are trapped within the business and provide no immediate benefit to the doctors."

Having an established S corporation will also help you when you sell your share of the practice. But if you currently have a C corporation and you plan to reclassify it as an S corp to avoid double taxation on the sale of the assets, the IRS is one step ahead of you: It says you must have made the switch a full decade before the sale to avoid being taxed twice on the proceeds. If you're currently in a C corporation, meet with your tax adviser to go over your options. Depending on the timing and circumstances, it may be possible to get around this rule on a substantial amount of the proceeds, Schiller says.

Limited liability companies. Limited liability companies are a sort of hybrid; they offer the liability protection of a corporation, but are taxed like a sole proprietorship, if you practice alone, or a partnership, if you have associates. (Owners can choose to be classified as a corporation for tax purposes if they wish.) LLCs are generally structured like S corporations, but with a couple of twists. For one, an LLC can have an unlimited number of owners, which is great for a growing, multispecialty practice. There are also fewer restrictions on ownership of the practice. For instance, an LLC can be owned by another LLC, corporation, or a trust. Those aren't options for an S corporation.

"If you're in a group practice and you expect it to grow and take on more physicians, the LLC provides the easiest way in and out," Steven Goodman says. "With proper structuring, you can add physicians without an immediate tax effect. Moreover, the LLC has a major nontaxadvantage over the corporation: It isn't required to observe the same formalities that a corporation does in terms of meetings, minutes, etc."

Profits can also be distributed disproportionately in an LLC, which may offer some advantages. "For example, you may want to give the senior doctor or managing partner an extra percent or two in distributions," says CPA Sidney A. Blum, of Leonetti & Associates,

Business Structures at a Glance

	C Corp	S Corp	LLP or LLC	General Partnership	Sole Proprietorship
Shields owners from business liabilities	X	X	X		
Frees business from federal taxes		X	X	X	X
Allows deduction for full costs of all fringe benefits	X				
Frees business from complex restrictions on ownership	X		X	X	X

Dennis Murray. S corp, C corp, LLC, LLP—which is best? *Medical Economics*, Mar. 5, 2004; 81:44.

in Buffalo Grove, IL. "Likewise, if you merge your practice and the new doctors bring expensive equipment or new technologies with them, they may deserve a larger slice of the profits."

And then there's this piece of advice from Teaneck, NJ, attorney Martin M. Shenkman: "If you have a medical building, it should be owned in a separate LLC and leased back to the practice, to keep it safe from claims."

But if LLCs provide these advantages, why do S corps continue to be the recommended corporate structure for most medical practices? "Attorneys prefer S corporations because they've been around longer and more case law has been established on them, which means the liability protection is generally better tested," says David Schiller. "Furthermore, it's believed that the audit risk is less with an S corp than it is with an LLC. That's because LLCs are generally small businesses. Gross receipts of $1 million would be considered a lot for an LLC, and the audit prospects would be increased. Conversely, an S corp with $1 million in receipts wouldn't attract as much attention from the IRS, because corporations have historically been big businesses."

Finding the Right Fit

This completes our crash course in corporate structures. If you're still not sure which is the best one for your practice, don't be ashamed.

"There's no pat answer," Goodman says. "My advice is to meet with your accountant and a tax attorney and discuss your plans for the growth of the practice, and how long you plan to work. Are you the type of person who can follow formalities and take a salary, or are you used to running the show and being able to write a check whenever you want to? There are all sorts of variables that will affect your decision."

One such variable, as we've noted, is what the law will allow: Rules on corporate structures vary from state to state. So be sure you consult a local attorney who specializes in taxes. If your current attorney doesn't, ask him or your accountant to recommend someone who does.

For some doctors, having more than one type of corporate structure makes sense, to take advantage of the unique tax benefits that each of them provides. New York attorney David B. Mandell is a major proponent of this approach. "The biggest thing I see troubling physicians these days is that they want to do some kind of tax planning—qualified or nonqualified deferred compensation, or something else—and a lot of their partners don't," he says. "In a practice of, say, 15 doctors, five might really want to defer compensation, five are young and focused on paying off their loans and don't want to defer anything, and five don't care because they're too old to benefit.

"I often recommend one entity—usually an S corp—to manage the practice, including billing and collections," Mandell says. "Then, instead of all the doctors being paid as employees of the S corp, each creates his or her own corporation or LLC and is paid through that. It can even be another S corp. The type of structure used will depend on what state law allows. Using more than one structure can permit each physician to do some planning that's independent of the rest of the doctors in the practice. None of the other doctors has to know about it, vote on it, or get into the politics of it."

Mandell says it costs about $1,000 per physician to do the necessary paperwork to establish separate corporations. "There may be some hassles up front in terms of amending the original corporate agreement and tweaking the accounting procedures. But in most cases, the hurdles can be overcome."

IN-CLASS PROJECT

Economic Security and Government Involvement Issues

By David Moglen

This project examines two case studies of government involvement in private sector economic transactions. These recent historical events reveal not only the pitfalls and inefficiency of these particular actions, but also the genuine concerns about economic security that motivate such interventions. Keep in mind that the policy enacted is not always crystal clear, as in these cases. The government may have only signalled what their plan was, but it's enough to change the course of events. The end result is totally different from how these cases would have turned out in the absence of any government involvement.

Directions: After the class is divided in half, Group 1 and Group 2, you will then read the two articles (e.g., if you are in Group 2, read articles 2A and 2B). Whether you are Group 1 or Group 2, answer the same four questions below. The grid at the end of this project may help you organize your answers, but your teacher will advise as to whether the grid provides enough space for your complete answer; otherwise, plan on using an extra sheet of paper.

For Each:

1. How would you describe the central conflict your article reports? In other words, why is this news?

2. The result of this scenario can be either free market or government intervention.
Who are the stakeholders pursuing these results? Who wants what and why?
Groups to consider **(pick at least three)**

- A U.S. Company Called_______________, it's shareholders, employees, and customers (three groups who may or may not want the same result as each other)
- A Foreign Company Called ____________, it's shareholders, employees, and customers
- A foreign Gov't of the country: __________
- Foreign citizens of the country:___________
- U.S. Citizens
- U.S. Government
- Other firms who may be impacted
- Any other identifiable groups, individuals, agencies, or organizations

3. What goals are being pursued if the free market option occurs?
What goals are being pursued if the government-intervention option occurs?

4. Was the correct policy pursued? If yes, why was the current policy correct (in terms of economic and social impacts)?
If not, what would have been a better policy (in terms of economic and social impacts) to address the situation, and/or what are the flaws of the current policy?
In other words, what is and what should be the role of government in this situation?

Focus Questions specific to the article you are looking at; these questions convey info that is not made explicitly clear in the article. These are not additional to 1-4 above. If you fully answer 1-4 above, you will have already answered the focus question pertaining to your article below.

Article 1A & 1B:

CNOOC Unocal bid

Should U.S. have intervened, as was being discussed before Chevron completed the buy?

Article 2A & 2B:

"WASHINGTON (CNN)—United Arab Emirates-owned DP World said Thursday it would transfer its operations of American ports to a "U.S. entity" after congressional leaders reportedly told President Bush that the firm's takeover deal was essentially dead on Capitol Hill."

Should U.S. have intervened if DP World pursued its ownership rights rather than promising to transfer ownership to a U.S. entity?

Article 1A:

http://www.nytimes.com/2005/06/22/business/worldbusiness/22WIRE-CNOOC.html?hp&ex=1119499200&en=23bd8ddf523d1a8e&ei=5094&partner=homepage.

Article 1B:

http://www.forbes.com/2005/07/11/cnooc-unocal-review-cx_0712oxan_cnooc.html?partner=links&partner=links.

Article 2A:

http://articles.cnn.com/2006-03-09/politics/port.security_1_edward-h-bilkey-uae-firm-ports?_s=PM:POLITICS.

Article 2B:

http://www.nytimes.com/2006/03/10/politics/10ports.html?_r=1.

Chart to help work out questions 1-3 on page 1.

Situation/ Article	**Competing Goals**	**Competing Stakeholders and their roles**
1. CNOCC/Unocal		
2. Dubai Ports World buys ports management contract		

Filled in generically—you would have to say how any (really, all) of these things are implied by the situation you're analyzing:

Situation/ Article	**Competing Goals**	**Competing Stakeholders and their roles**

1. CNOCC/ Unocal	___________ (state and describe) vs. U.S. as a model globally for a Free Market, Free Trade, Laissez-Faire philosophy, which would tend to improve bargaining position in future Free Trade Agreement and International Relations.	The Countries involved, their governments and citizens The firms involved, their employees, shareholders (aka owners), and their customers Anyone else who will be affected one way or the other
2. Dubai Ports World buys ports management contract	_____________ (state and describe) vs. U.S. as a model globally for a Free Market, Free Trade, Laissez-Faire philosophy, which would tend to improve bargaining position in future Free Trade Agreement and International Relations.	The Countries involved, their governments and citizens The firms involved, their employees, shareholders (aka owners), and their customers Anyone else who will be affected one way or the othcr

Key Terms:

Actor
Bonds
Centrally planned economy
Circular flow model
Corporate personhood
Corporation
Debt financing
Double taxation
Economic Institutions
Equity financing
Externality
Factor market
Key economic questions
Limited liability/ unlimited liability
Limited life/ unlimited life
Market activity
Market failures
Mixed economy
Nonmarket activity
Partnership
Principal-agent problem
Private sector
Product market
Public good
Public sector
Pure command economy
Pure market economy
Referee
Sole proprietorship
Stocks
Traditional economy

Study Questions:

1. If you are setting up a dog-walking business, which of the three main business types would you select and why?
2. Firms sometimes engage in stock buybacks where they use cash to buy their own stock. Explain when this would be a good idea and when it would be a bad idea. How does this plan compare with returning money to shareholders as a dividend?
3. What are the economic incentives and goals of the competing parties in a hostile takeover? Make sure to mention management,

shareholders, and the corporate takeover specialist (individual or private equity company) in this process.

4. Firms sometimes “spinoff” part of their company (see ITT, Motorola, Marathon, and AT&T). What are the circumstances where this is a good idea for original company? How can an investor tell if the parent or the spinoff company is the better investment in the stock market?
5. Which type of economy is more likely to seek the following goals (answer for each one separately):
   a. Maximum competition
   b. Maximum income equality
   c. Maximum adherence to dominant culture
   d. Maximum entrepreneurship
6. How does a corporation reduce risk for those who invest their money in its activities? Are there some specific companies or sectors who help corporations or others in the economy to reduce negative impacts of certain risks?
7. What are some specific examples of actions by executives that would fit into each of the four categories stated in the principal-agent problem section? Describe a policy (either corporate or governmental) solution to the principal-agent problem.

CHAPTER 4
Demand and Supply

4 Demand and Supply

By William Baumol

DEMAND AND QUANTITY DEMAND

Noneconomists are apt to think of consumer demands as fixed amount. For example, when the production of a new model of computer is proposed, management asks "What is its market potential? How many will we be able to sell?" Similarly, government bureaus conduct studies to determine how many engineers will be "required" in succeeding years.

Economists respond that such questions are not well posed—that there is no *single* answer to such a question. Rather, they say, the "market potential" for computers or the number of engineers that will be "required" depends on a great number of things, *including the price that will be charged for each.*

> The **quantity demanded** of any product normally depends on its price. Quantity demanded also has a number of other determinants, including population size, consumer incomes, tastes, and the prices of other products.

The **quantity demanded** is the number of units consumers want to buy over a specified period of time.

Because of the central role of prices in a market, economy, we begin our study of demand by focusing on the dependence of quantity demanded on price. Shortly, we will bring the other determinants of quantity demanded back into the picture.

Consider, as an example, the quantity of milk demanded. Almost everyone purchases at least some milk. However, if the price of milk is very high, its "market potential" may be very small. People will find ways to get along with less milk, perhaps by switching to tea or coffee. If the price declines, people will be encouraged to drink more milk. They may give their children larger portions or switch away from juices and sodas. Thus:

> There is no *one* demand figure for milk, for computers, or for engineers. Rather, there is a different quantity demanded for each possible price.

Price (dollars per quart)	Quantity Demanded (billions of quarts per year)	Label in Fiqure 4-1
$1.00	45	A
0.90	50	B
0.80	55	C
0.70	60	E
0.60	65	F
0.50	70	G
0.40	75	H

Table 4-1
Demand Schedule for Milk

THE DEMAND SCHEDULE

Table 4-1 displays this information for milk in what we call a **demand schedule,** which indicates how much consumers are willing and able to buy at different possible prices during a specified period of time. The table shows the quantity of milk that will be demanded in a year at each possible price ranging from $1 to 40¢ per quart. We see, for example, that at a relatively low price, like 50¢ per quart, customers wish to purchase 70 billion quarts per year. But if the price were to rise to, say, 90¢ per quart, quantity demanded would fall to 50 billion quarts.

A **demand schedule** is a table showing how the quantity demanded of some product during a specified period of time changes as the price of that product changes, holding all other determinants of quantity demanded constant.

Common sense tells us why this should be so.[1] First, as prices rise, some customers will reduce their consumption of milk. Second, higher prices will induce some customers to drop out of the market entirely, for example, by switching to soda or juice. On both counts, quantity demanded will decline as the price rises.

As the price of an item rises, the quantity demanded normally falls. As the price falls, the quantity demanded normally rises.

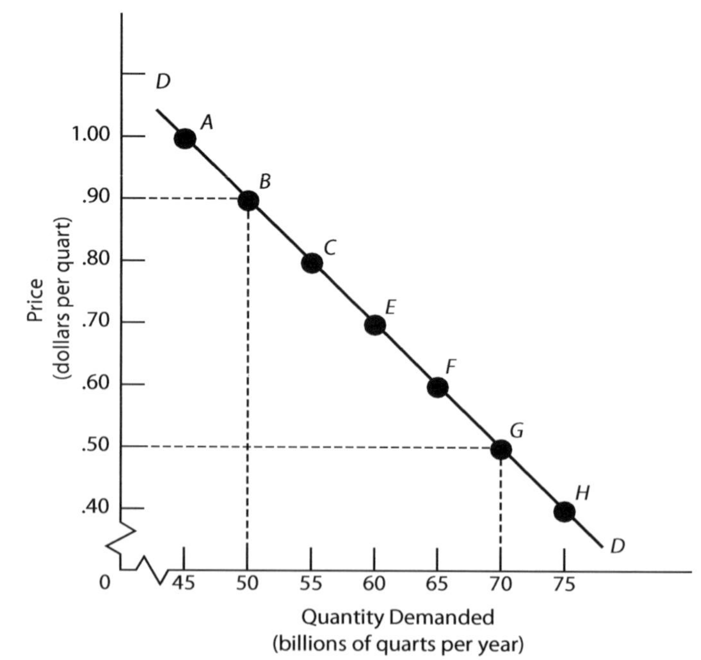

FIGURE 4-1
Demand Curve for Milk
This curve shows the relationship between price and quantity demanded. To sell 70 billion quarts per year, the price must be only 50¢ (point *G*). If, instead, price is 90¢, only 50 billion quarts will be demanded (point *B*). To sell more milk, the price must be reduced. That is what the negative slope of the demand curve means.

THE DEMAND CURVE

The information contained in Table 4-1 can be summarized in a graph like Figure 4-1, which we call a **demand curve**. Each point in the graph corresponds to a line in the table. For example, point *B* corresponds to the second line in the table, indicating that at a price of 90¢ per quart, 50 billion quarts per year will be demanded. Since the quantity demanded declines as the price increases, the demand curve has a negative slope.[2]

A **demand curve** is a graphical depiction of a demand schedule. It shows how the quantity demanded of some product during a specified period of time will change as the price of that product changes, holding all other determinants of quantity demanded constant.

Notice the last phrase in the definitions of the demand schedule and the demand curve: "holding all other determinants of quantity demanded constant." These "other things" include consumer incomes and preferences, the prices of soda and orange juice, and perhaps even advertising by the dairy association. We will examine the influences of these factors later in the chapter. First, however, let's look at the sellers' side of the market.

Supply and Quantity Supplied

The **quantity supplied** is the number of units sellers want to sell over a specified period of time.

Like quantity demanded, the quantity of milk that is supplied by dairy farmers is not a fixed number; it also depends on many things. Obviously, we expect more milk to be supplied if there are more dairy farms, or more cows per farm. Or cows may give less milk if bad weather deprives them of their feed. As before, however, let's turn our attention first to the relationship between **quantity supplied** and one of its major determinants—the price of milk.

Economists generally suppose that a higher price calls forth a greater quantity supplied. Why? According to that principle, as more of any farmer's (or the nation's) resources are devoted to milk production, the opportunity cost of obtaining another quart of milk increases. Farmers will therefore find it profitable to raise milk production only if they can sell the milk at a higher price—high enough to cover the additional costs incurred to expand production.

Looked at the other way around, we have just concluded that higher prices normally will be required to persuade farmers to raise milk production. This id ea is quite general and applies to the supply of most goods and services.[3] As long as suppliers want to make profits and the principle of increasing costs holds:

As the price of an item rises, the quantity supplied normally rises. As the price falls, the quantity supplied normally falls.

A **supply schedule** is a table showing how the quantity supplied of some product during a specified period of time changes as the price of that product changes, holding all other determinants of quantity supplied constant.

THE SUPPLY SCHEDULE AND THE SUPPLY CURVE

The relationship between the price of milk and its quantity recorded in Table 4-2. Tables like this are called **supply schedules**; they show

[1]This common-sense answer is examined more fully in Chapters 7 and 8.

[2]If you need to review the concept of *slope*, refer back to the appendix to Chapter 1, especially pages 20–23.

[3]This analysis is carried out in much greater detail in the next two chapters.

Price (dollars per quart)	Quantity Supplied (billions of quarts per year)	Label in Fiqure 4-2
$1.00	90	a
0.90	80	b
0.80	70	c
0.70	60	e
0.60	50	f
0.50	40	g
0.40	30	h

Table 4-2
Supply Schedule for Milk

A **supply curve** is a graphical depiction of a supply schedule. It shows how the quantity supplied of some product during a specified period of time will change as the price of that product changes, holding all other determinants of quantity supplied constant.

how much are willing to provide during a specified period at alternative possible prices. This particular supply schedule shows that a low price like 50¢ per quart will induce suppliers to provide only 40 billion quarts, while a higher price like 80¢ will induce them to provide much more—70 billion quarts.

As you might have guessed, when information like this is plotted on a graph, it is called a **supply curve**. Figures 4-2 is the supply curve corresponding to the supply schedule in Table 4-2 It slopes upward because quantity higher when price is higher.

Notice again the same phrase in the definition: "holding all other determinants of quantity supplied constant". We will return to these "other determinants" a bit later in the discussion. But first we are ready to put demand and supply together.

Equilibrium of Supply and Demand

To analyze how price is determined in a free market, we must compare the desires of consumers (demand) with the desires of producers (supply) and see whether the two plans are consistent. Table 4-3 and Figure 4-3 help us do this.

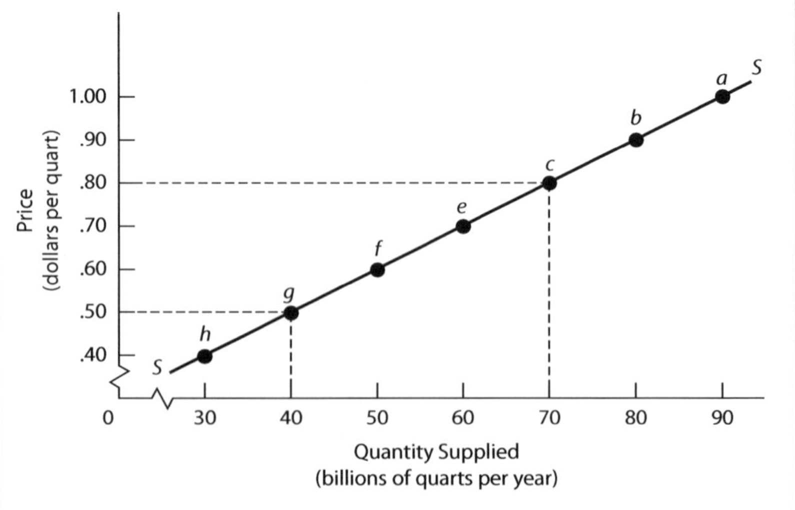

FIGURE 4-2
Supply Curve for Milk
This curve shows the relationship between the price of milk and the quantity supplied. To stimulate a greater quantity supplied, price must be increased. That is the meaning of the positive slope of the supply curve.

Price (dollars per quart)	Quantity Demanded	Quantity Supplied	Surplus or Shortage?	Price Will
	(billions of quarts per year)			
$1.00	45	90	Surplus	Fall
0.90	50	80	Surplus	Fall
0.80	55	70	Surplus	Fall
0.70	60	60	Neither	Remain the same
0.60	65	50	Shortage	Rise
0.50	70	40	Shortage	Rise
0.40	75	30	Shortage	Rise

Table 4-3
Determination of the Equilibrium Price and Quantity of Milk

Table 4-3 brings together the demand schedule from Table 4-1 and the supply schedule from Table 4-2. Similarly, Figure 4-3 puts the demand curve from Figure 4-1 and the supply curve from Figure 4-2 on a single graph. Such a graphic device is called a **supply-demand diagram,** and you will encounter many of them in this book. Notice that, for reasons already discussed, the demand curve has a negative slope and the supply curve has a positive slope. Most supply-demand diagrams are drawn with slopes like these.

There is only one point in Figure 4-3, point *E*, at which the supply curve and the demand curve intersect. At the price corresponding to point *E*, which is 70¢ per quart, the quantity supplied and the quantity demanded are both 60 billion quarts per year. This means that, at a price of 70¢ per quart, consumers are willing to buy just what producers are willing to sell.

At any lower price, such as 50¢, only 40 billion quarts of milk will be supplied (point *g*) whereas 70 billion quarts will be demanded (point G). Thus quantity demanded will exceed quantity supplied. There will be a **shortage** equal to 70-40 = 30 billion quarts. Alternatively, at a higher price like $1, quantity supplied will be 90 billion quarts (point *a*) while quantity demanded will be only 45 billion (point *A*). Quantity supplied will exceed quantity demanded, so there will be a surplus equal to 90-45 = 45 billion quarts.

A **shortage** is an excess of quantity demanded over quantity supplied. When there is a shortage, buyers cannot purchase the quantities they desire.

A **surplus** is an excess of quantity supplied over quantity demanded. When there is a surplus, sellers cannot sell the quantities they desire to supply.

Since 70¢ is the price at which quantity supplied and quantity demanded are equal, we say that 70¢ per quart is the **equilibrium price** in this market. Similarly, 60 billion quarts per year is the **equilibrium quantity** of milk. The term "equilibrium" merits a little explanation, since it arises so frequently in economic analysis.

An **equilibrium** is a situation in which there are no inherent forces that produce change; that is, a situation that does not contain the seeds of its own destruction. Think, for example, of a pendulum at rest at its center point. If no outside force (such as a person's hand) comes to push it, the pendulum will remain where it, is; it is in *equilibrium.* But if you give the pendulum a shove, its equilibrium will be disturbed and it will start to move upward. When it reaches the top of its arc, the pendulum will, for an instant, be at rest again. But this is not an equilibrium position, for a force known as gravity will pull the pendulum downward.

An **equilibrium** is a situation in which there are no inherent forces that produce change. Changes away from an equilibrium position will occur only as a result of "outside events" that disturb the status quo.

FIGURE 4-3

Supply Demand Equilibrium In a free market, price and quantity are determined by the intersection of the supply curve and the demand curve. In this example, the equilibrium price is 70¢ and the equilibrium quantity is 60 billion quarts of milk per year. Any other price is inconsistent with equilibrium. For example, at a price of 50¢, quantity demanded is 70 billion (point *G*), while quantity supplied is only 40 billion (point *g*), so that price will be driven up by the unsatisfied demand.

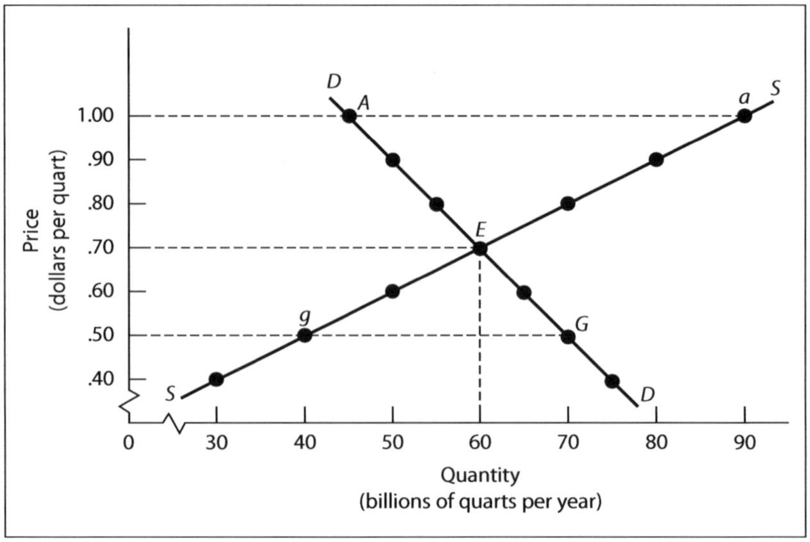

Thereafter, its motion from side to side will be governed by gravity and friction. Eventually, we know, the pendulum will return, to the point at which it started, which is its only equilibrium position. At any other point, inherent forces will cause the pendulum to move.

The concept of equilibrium in economics is similar and can be illustrated by our supply and demand example. Why is no price other than 70¢ an equilibrium price in Table 4-3 or Figure 4-3? What forces will change any other price?

Consider first a low price like 50¢, at which quantity demanded (70 billion) exceeds quantity supplied (40 billion). If the price were this low, many frustrated customers would be unable to purchase the quantities they desired. In their scramble for the available supply of milk, some would offer to pay more. As customers sought to outbid one another, the market price would be forced up. Thus a price below the equilibrium price cannot persist in a free market because a shortage sets in motion powerful economic forces that push price upward.

Similar forces operate if the market price is *above* the equilibrium price. If, for example, the price should somehow get to be $1, Table 4-3 tells us that quantity supplied (90 billion) would far exceed quantity demanded (45 billion). Producers would be unable to sell their desired quantities of milk at the prevailing price, and some would find it in their interest to undercut their competitors by reducing price. Such competitive price-cutting would continue as long as the surplus persisted, that is, as long as quantity supplied exceeded quantity demanded. Thus a price above the equilibrium price cannot persist indefinitely.

We are left with only one conclusion. The price 70¢ per quart and the quantity 60 billion quarts per year is the only price-quantity combination that does not sow the seeds of its own destruction. It is the only *equilibrium*. Any lower price must rise, and any higher price must fall. It is as if natural economic forces place a magnet at point *E* that attracts the market just like gravity attracts a pendulum.

At the Frontier

EXPERIMENTAL ECONOMICS

In theory, supply and demand curves determine prices. But does reality work the way the theory claims? Physicists use experiments to help answer such questions. However, for a long time it was believed that economists could not perform laboratory experiments. After all, people are not guinea pigs. Can economists recreate an entire economy, or even a single market, in a laboratory? And, even if this is done, how can the experimenter get the "guinea pigs" to act as they would in making real decisions-with real money at stake?

For a long time, economists felt that experimental methods were beyond their reach. So they relied almost exclusively on statistical inference to test their theories. But the statistical approach is an imperfect solution because it does not allow us to isolate just *one* influence at a time, as a scientifically controlled experiment does.

Lately, this view of experimental in economics has begun to change. While economists still rely mainly on statistical analysis, they have also begun to experiment. Market experiments are now conducted to test theories about the behavior of large firms, about government programs that provide financial assistance to poor people, and about a wide variety of other subjects.

Who are the subjects of these experiments? You guessed it. They are often college students who volunteer to participate. Some may volunteer because the experiments are interesting; but there is also money to be earned. In fact, that is what motivates participants to act as they would in a real market. One such experiment was conducted at UCLA and Los Angeles City College*. The objective was to see whether demand and supply curves do in fact determine price in the way the theory claims.

Students were divided into two groups: sellers and buyers. Each was given some money to start. Sellers purchased fictitious "goods" from the experimenter (who acted like a wholesaler), and then tried to sell them to buyers. If they could sell them at higher prices than they paid, sellers got to pocket the difference. Similarly, buyers could resell their purchases to the experimenter, who would pay according to a fixed schedule. They, too, got to keep any profits they made.

For example, seller A was able to buy from the wholesaler at the following prices:

Unit	1st	2nd	3rd	4th	5th	6th	7th	8th
Price	$2.30	2.30	2.30	2.31	2.31	2.36	2.50	2.70

That is, she could purchase up to three units of the commodity at a price of $2.30 per unit. However, if she bought a fourth unit, the price would go up to $2.31, and so on. It is clear that, if the market price was, say $2.35, seller A should want to supply five units, because she can obtain this many units from the wholesaler at lower prices. But seller A would be irrational to acquire the sixth unit from the wholesaler for $2.36 and then sell it for $2.35.

So the experimenters knew that, at a price of $2.35, seller A's theoretical quantity supplied was five units. And they could reach a similar conclusion for every other price and every other seller. Analogously, the experimenters were able to calculate the theoretical quantities demanded for each buyer. The theoretical price at which the supply and demand curves intersected was $2.44.

How did the actual prices turn out in the experiment? The experiment was repeated five times, each repetition involving about 20 transactions. The average actual price was slightly lower than the theoretical equilibrium price of $2.44, but the experimental price almost always fell in the $2.40-$2150 range. And the price came closer and closer to $2.44 as students acquired more experience. In the last two experiments, the average prices were $2.418 and $2.434—within 2.2 percent of the predicted equilibrium. Apparently, the experiments do work, and so does the theory-as a reasonable *approximation* to reality.

*See C.R. Plott, "Externalities and Corrective Policies in Experimental Markets," *The Economic journal*, vol. 93, March 1983, pages 106-127.

The analogy to a pendulum is worth pursuing further. Most pendulums are more frequently in motion than at rest. However, unless they are repeatedly buffeted by outside forces (which, of course, is exactly what happens to pendulums used in clocks), pendulums gradually return to their resting points. The same is true of price and quantity in a free market. Markets are not always in equilibrium, but, if they are not interfered with, experience shows that they normally *move toward equilibrium.*

The Law of Supply and Demand

In a free market, the forces of supply and demand generally push the price toward its equilibrium level, the price at which quantity supplied and quantity demanded are equal.

The **law of supply and demand** states that, in a free market, the forces of supply and demand generally push the price toward the level at which quantity supplied and quantity demanded are equal.

Like most economic "laws," the **law of supply and demand** is occasionally disobeyed. Markets sometimes display shortages or surpluses for long periods of time. Prices sometimes fail to move toward equilibrium. But the "law" is a fair generalization that is right far more often than it is wrong.

The last interesting aspect of the pendulum analogy concerns the "outside forces" of which we have spoken. A pendulum that is blown by the wind or pushed by a hand does not remain in equilibrium. Similarly, many outside forces can disturb equilibrium in a market. In 1990–1991, the world oil market was disturbed by a war in the Persian Gulf. In 1992, Hurricane Andrew struck Florida and disturbed equilibrium in the market for oranges.

Often these outside influences *change the equilibrium price and quantity* by shifting either the supply curve or the demand curve. If you look again at Figure 4-3, you can see clearly that any event that causes *either* the demand curve *or* the supply curve to shift will also change the equilibrium price and quantity. Such events constitute the "other things" that were held constant in our definitions of supply and demand curves. We are now ready to analyze how these outside forces affect the equilibrium of supply and demand, beginning on the demand side.

Shifts of the Demand Curve

Returning to our example of milk, we noted earlier that the quantity of milk demanded is influenced by a variety of things other than the price of milk. Changes in population, consumer income, and the prices of alternative beverages such as soda and orange juice presumably change the quantity of milk demanded even if the price of milk is unchanged.

Since the demand curve for milk depicts only the relationship between the quantity of milk demanded and the price of milk, holding all other factors constant, a change in any of these other factors produces *a shift of the entire demand curve.* More generally:

A change in the price of a good produces a **movement along a fixed demand curve.** By contrast, a change in any other variable that influences quantity demanded produces a **shift of the entire demand curve.** If consumers want to buy *more* at any given price than they wanted previously, the demand curve shifts to the right (or outward). If they desire *less* at any given price, the demand curve shifts to the left (or inward).

Figure 4-4 shows this distinction graphically. If the price of a quart of milk falls from 80¢ to 60¢ and quantity demanded rises accordingly, we move *along demand curve* D_0D_0 from point *C* to point *F*, as shown by the blue arrow. If, on the other hand, consumers suddenly decide that they like milk better than they did formerly, *the entire demand curve shifts outward from* D_0D_0 *to* D_1D_1, as indicated by the blue arrows. To make this general idea more concrete and to show some of its many applications, let us consider some specific examples.

1. ***Consumer incomes.*** If average incomes increase, consumers will purchase more of most foods, including milk, even if the price of milk remains the same. That is, *increases in income normally shift demand curves outward to the right,* as depicted in Figure 4-5(a). In this example, the quantity demanded at the old equilibrium price of 70¢ increases from 60 billion quarts per year (point *E* on demand curve D_0D_0) to 75 billion (point *R* on demand curve D_1D_1). We know that 70¢ is no longer the equilibrium price, since at this price quantity demanded (75 billion) exceeds quantity supplied (60

[4]This statement, like many others in the text, assumes that the demand curve is downward-sloping and the supply curve is upward-sloping.

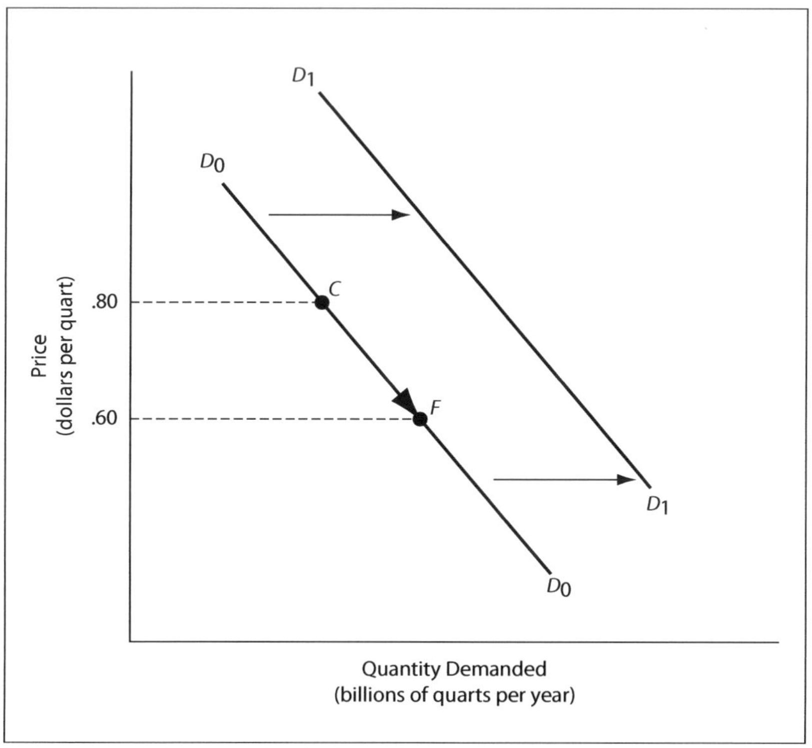

FIGURE 4-4

Movements Along Versus Shifts of a Demand Curve

If quantity demanded increases because the price of a commodity falls, the market moves along a fixed demand curve such as D_0D_0 (see the movement from *C* to *F*). If, on the other hand, quantity demanded increases due to a change in one of its other determinants (such as consumer tastes or incomes), the entire demand curve shifts outward, as shown here by the shift from D_0D_0 to D_1D_1.

billion). To restore equilibrium, price will have to rise. The diagram shows the new equilibrium at point *T*, where the price is 80¢ per quart and both quantities demanded and supplied are 70 billion quarts per year. This illustrates a general result.

Any factor that causes the demand curve to shift outward to the right, and does not affect the supply curve, will raise the equilibrium price and the equilibrium quantity.[4]

Everything works in reverse if consumer incomes fall. Figure 4-5(b) depicts a leftward (inward) shift of the demand curve that results from a decline in consumer incomes. For example, the quantity demanded at the previous equilibrium price (70¢) falls from 60 billion quarts (point *E*) to 45 billion (point *L* on demand curve D_2D_2). At the initial price, quantity supplied must begin to fall. The new equilibrium will eventually be established at point *M*, where the price is 60¢ and both quantity demanded and quantity supplied are 50 billion. In general:

> Any factor that shifts the demand curve inward to the left, and does not affect the supply curve, will lower both the equilibrium price and the equilibrium quantity.

2. ***Population.*** Population growth affects quantity demanded in more or less the same way as increases in average incomes. A larger population will presumably wish to consume more milk, even if the price of milk and average incomes are unchanged, thus shifting the entire demand curve to the right as in Figure 4-5(a). The equilibrium price and quantity both rise. Similarly, a decrease in population should shift the demand curve for milk to the left, as in Figure 4-5(b), causing equilibrium price and quantity to fall.
3. ***Consumer preferences.*** If the dairy industry mounts a successful advertising campaign extolling the benefits of drinking milk, families may decide to raise their quantities demanded. This would shift the entire demand curve for milk to the right, as in Figure 4-5(a). Alternatively, a medical report on the dangers of kidney stones may persuade consumers to drink less milk, thereby shifting the demand curve to the left, as in Figure 4-5(b). Again, these are general phenomena.

   If consumer preferences shift in favor of a particular item, that item's demand curve will shift outward to the right, causing both equilibrium price and quantity to rise (Figure 4-5[a]). Conversely, if consumer preferences shift against a particular item, that item's demand curve will shift inward to the left, causing equilibrium price and quantity to fall (Figure 4-5[b]).
4. ***Prices and availability of related goods.*** Because soda, orange juice, and coffee are popular drinks that compete with milk, a change in the price of any of these beverages can be expected to shift the demand curve for milk. If any of these alternative drinks become cheaper, some consumers will switch away from milk. Thus the demand curve for milk will shift to the left, as in Figure 4-5(b). Other price changes shift the demand curve for milk in the opposite direction. For example, suppose that cookies, a commodity that goes well with

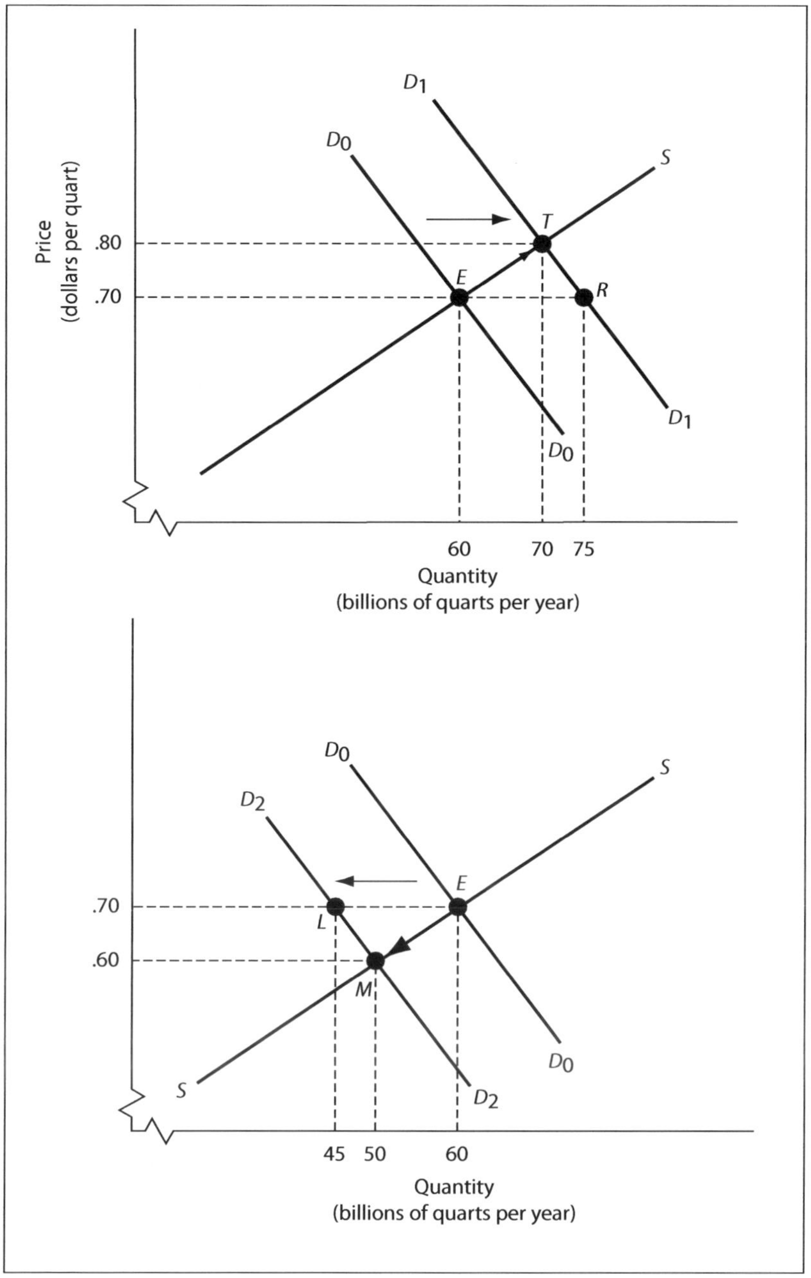

FIGURE 4-5
The Effects of Shifts of the Demand Curve
A shift of the demand curve will change the equilibrium price and quantity in a free market. In part (a), the demand curve shifts outward from D_0D_0 to D_1D_1. As a result, equilibrium moves from point *E* to point *T*; both price and quantity rise. In part (b), the demand curve shifts inward from D_0D_0 to D_2D_2, and equilibrium moves from point *E* to point *M*; both price and quantity fall.

milk, become less expensive. This may induce some consumers to drink more milk and thus shift the demand curve for milk to the right, as in Figure 4-5(a).

Increases in the prices of goods that are substitutes for the good in question (as soda is for milk) move the demand curve to the right, thus raising both the equilibrium price and quantity. Increases in the prices of goods that are normally used together with the good in question (such as cookies and milk) shift the demand curve to the left, thus lowering both the equilibrium price and quantity.

While the preceding list does not exhaust the possible influences on quantity demanded, enough has been said to indicate the principles involved. Let us therefore turn to a concrete example.

APPLICATION: Why Airlines Run Sales

Anyone who travels knows that airline companies reduce fares sharply to attract more customers at certain times of the year—particularly in winter (excluding the holiday period), when air traffic is light. There is no reason to think that air transportation gets cheaper in winter. Why, then, do airlines run such "sales"? A simple supply and demand diagram (see Figure 4-6) holds the answer.

Given the number of planes in airlines' fleets, the supply of seats is relatively fixed, as indicated by the steep supply curve *SS* in Figure 4-6, and is more or less the same in summer and winter. During seasons when people want to travel less, the demand curve for seats shifts leftward from its normal position, D_0D_0, to a position such as D_1D_1. Hence, equilibrium in the air-traffic market shifts from point *E* to point *A*. Thus both price and quantity decline at certain times of the year, not because flying gets cheaper or airlines get more generous, but because of the discipline of the market.

Shifts of the Supply Curve

Like quantity demanded, the quantity supplied on a market typically responds to a great number of influences other than price. The weather, the cost of feed, the number and size of dairy farms, and a variety of other factors all influence how much milk will be brought to market. Since the supply curve depicts only the relationship between the price of milk and the quantity of milk supplied, holding all other factors constant, a change in any of these other factors will cause the entire supply curve to shift. That is:

> A change in the price of the good causes a **movement along a fixed supply curve.** But price is not the only influence on quantity supplied. And, if any of these other influences changes, the **entire supply curve shifts**.

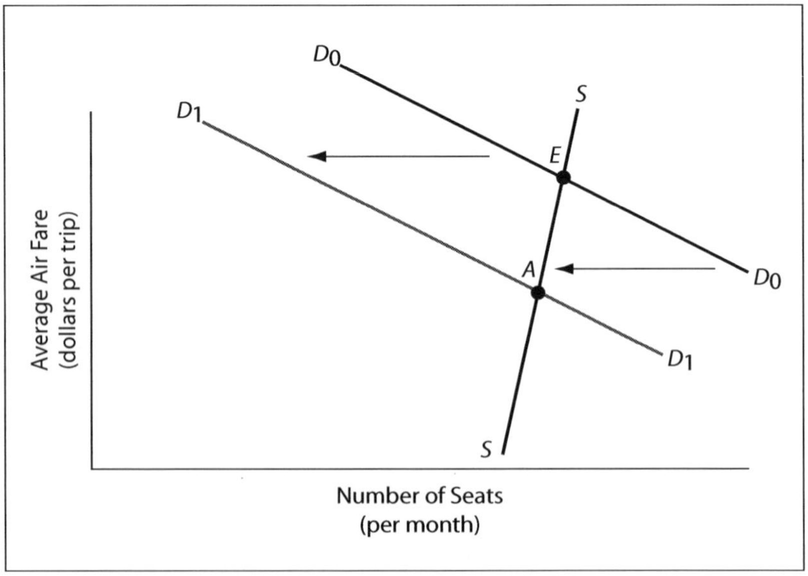

FIGURE 4-6
Seasonal Changes in Airline Fares
During seasons of slack demand for air travel, the demand curve shifts leftward from D_0D_0 to D_1D_1. In consequence, the market equilibrium point shifts from *E* to *A*, causing both price and quantity to decline.

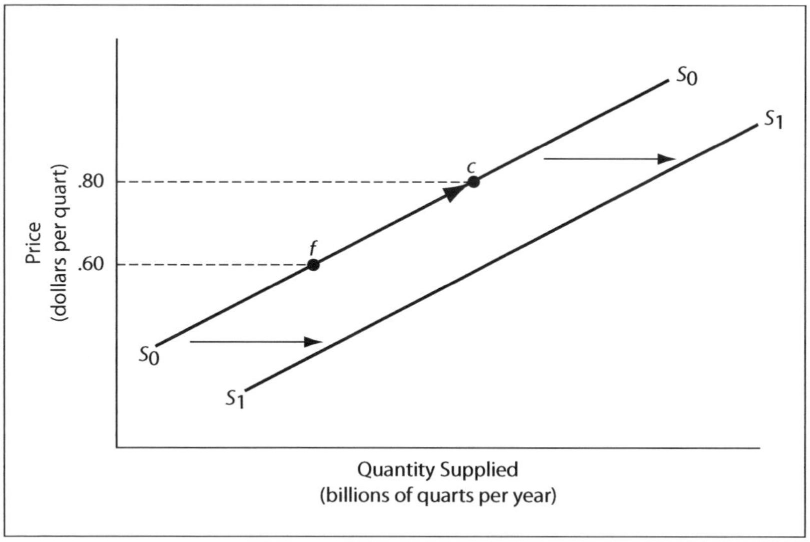

FIGURE 4-7

Movements Along Versus Shifts of a Supply Curve

If quantity supplied rises because the price increases, we move along a fixed supply curve such as S_0S_0 (see the red arrow from point *f* to point *c*). If, on the other hand, quantity supplied rises because some other factor influencing supply improves, the entire supply curve shifts outward to the right from S_0S_0 to S_1S_1 (see the blue arrows).

Figure 4-7 once again depicts the distinction graphically. A rise in price from 60¢ to 80¢ will raise quantity supplied by *moving along supply curve* S_0S_0 from point f to point c. But any rise in quantity supplied attributable to a factor other than price will *shift the entire supply curve outward to the right* from S_0S_0 to S_1S_1, as shown by the blue arrows. Let us consider what some of these other factors are, and how they shift the supply curve.

1. ***Size of the industry.*** We begin with the most obvious factor. If more farmers enter the milk industry, the quantity supplied at any given price will increase. For example, if each farm provides 600,000 quarts of milk per year when the price is 70¢ per quart, then 100,000 farmers provide 60 billion quarts, but 130,000 farmers provide 78 billion. Thus, when more farms are in the industry, the quantity of milk supplied will be greater at any given price and hence the supply curve will be farther to the right.

   Figure 4-8(a) illustrates the effect of an expansion of the industry from 100,000 farms to 130,000 farms—a rightward shift of the supply curve from S_0S_0 to S_1S_1. Notice that at the initial price of 70¢, the quantity supplied after the shift is 78 billion quarts (point *I* on supply curve S_1S_1), which exceeds the quantity demanded of 60 billion (point E on supply curve S_0S_0).

   We can see in the graph that the price of 70¢ is too high to be the equilibrium price; so the price must fall. Th e diagram shows the new equilibrium at point J, where the price is 60¢ per quart and the quantity is 65 billion quarts per year. The general point is that:

   > Any factor that shifts the supply curve outward to the right, and does not affect the demand curve; will lower the equilibrium price and raise the equilibrium quantity.

[5]Graphically, whenever a positively sloped curve shifts to the right, its intersection point with a negatively sloping curve must always move lower. Just try drawing it yourself.

This must *always* be true if the industry's demand curve has a negative slope, because the greater quantity supplied can be sold only if price is decreased to induce customers to buy more.[5]

Figure 4-8(b) illustrates the opposite case: a contraction of the industry from 100,000 farms to 62,500 farms. The supply curve shifts inward to the left and equilibrium moves from point *E* to point *V*, where price is 90¢ and quantity is 50 billion quarts per year. In general:

> Any factor that shifts the supply curve inward to the left, and does not affect the demand curve, will raise the equilibrium price and reduce the equilibrium quantity.

Even if no farmers enter or leave the industry, results like those depicted in Figure 4-8 can be produced by expansion or contraction of the existing farms.

2. ***Technological progress.*** Another influence that shifts supply curves is technological change. Suppose someone discovers that cows give more milk if Mozart is played during milking. Then, at any given price of milk, farmers will be able to provide a larger quantity of output; that is, the supply curve will shift outward to the right, as in Figure 4-8(a). This, again, illustrates a general influence that applies to most industries:

> Technological progress that reduces costs will shift the supply curve outward to the right.

Thus, as Figure 4-8(a) shows, the usual consequences of technological progress are lower prices and greater output.

3. ***Prices of inputs.*** Changes in input prices also shift supply curves. Suppose farm workers become unionized and win a raise. Farmers will have to pay higher wages and consequently will no longer be able to provide 60 billion quarts of milk profitably at a price of 70¢ per quart (point *E* in Figure 48[b]). Perhaps they will provide only 37.5 billion (point *U* on supply curve S_2S_2). This example illustrates that:

> Increases in the prices of inputs that suppliers must buy will shift the supply curve inward to the left.

4. ***Prices of related outputs.*** Dairy farms produce more than milk. If cheese prices rise sharply, farmers may decide to use some raw milk to make cheese, thereby reducing the quantity of milk supplied. On a supply-demand diagram, the supply curve would shift inward, as in Figure 4-8(b).

Similar phenomena occur in other industries, and sometimes the effect goes the other way. For example, suppose the price of beef goes up, which increases the quantity of meat supplied. That, in turn, will raise the number of cowhides supplied even without any change in price of leather. Thus, a rise in the price of beef will lead to a rightward shift in the supply curve of leather. In general:

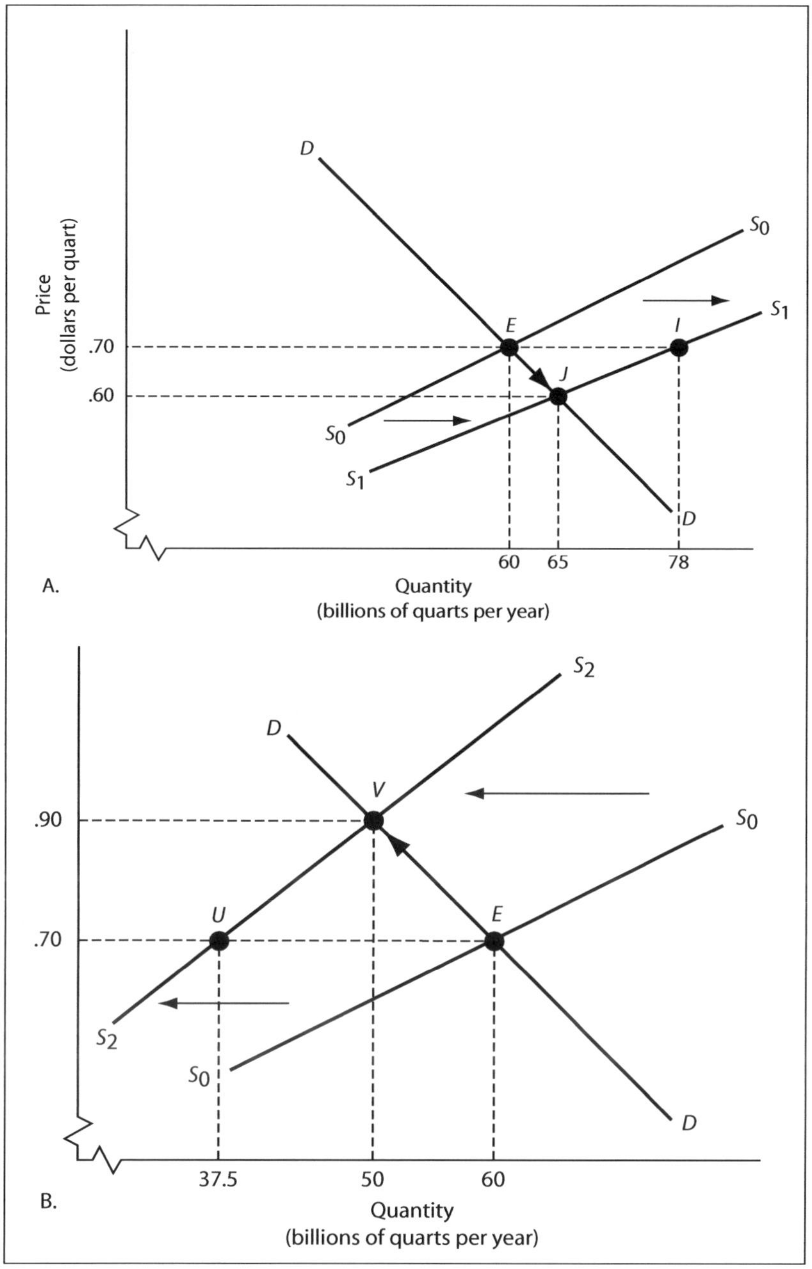

FIGURE 4-8
Effects of Shifts of the Supply Curve
A shift of the supply curve will change the equilibrium price and quantity in a market. In part (a), the supply curve shifts outward to the right, from S_0S_0 to S_1S_1. As a result, equilibrium moves from point *E* to point *J*; price falls as quantity increases. Part (b) illustrates the opposite case-an inward shift of the supply curve from S_0S_0 to S_2S_2. Equilibrium moves from point *E* to point *V*, which means that price rises as quantity falls.

A change in the price of one good produced by a multiproduct industry may be expected to shift the supply curves of all the other goods produced by that industry.

APPLICATION: A Computer in Every Home?

Twenty years ago, no one owned a home computer. Now there are tens of millions of them, and enthusiasts look forward to the day when computers will be as commonplace as television sets. What brought the computer from the laboratory into the home? Did Americans suddenly develop a craving for computers?

Hardly. What actually happened is that scientists in the 1970s invented the microchip—a stunning technological breakthrough that

FIGURE 4-9
The Effects of Rapid Technological Change on the Computer Market
The invention of the microchip and other technological breakthroughs caused the supply curve of computers to shift outward to the right-moving from S_0S_0 to S_1S_1. Consequently, equilibrium shifted from point *E* to point *A*. The price of microcomputers fell from \$10,000 to \$1500, and the quantity increased from 100,000 to 3 million per year.

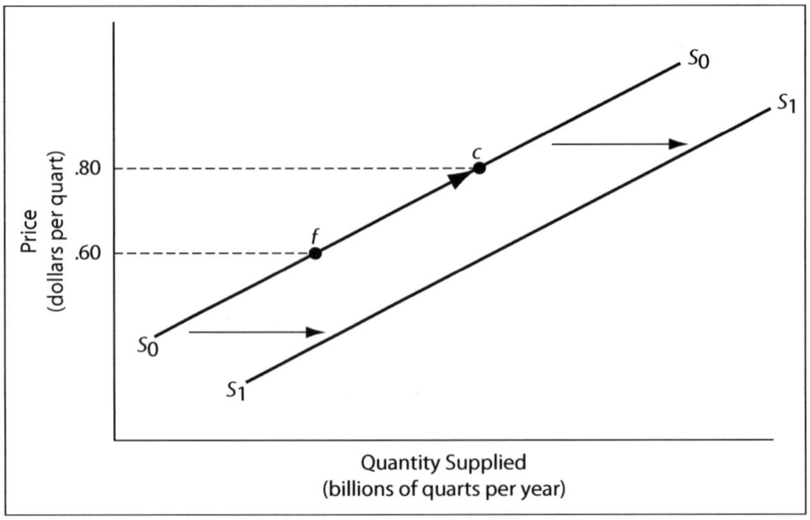

sharply reduced both the size and cost of computers. Within a few years, microcomputers were in commercial production. And, as the technology continued to improve, the cost of computers fell and fell and fell. Today, \$1500 will buy you more computing power than a multi-million, dollar computer could deliver two decades ago—and the machine will play games, too!

In terms of our supply and demand diagrams, the rapid technological improvement in computer manufacturing shifted the supply curve dramatically to the right. As Figure 4-9 shows, a large outward shift of the supply curve should lower the equilibrium price and raise the equilibrium quantity—which is just what happened to the computer industry. It was not the *demand curve* that shifted out, but the *supply curve.*

Demand and Supply Shifters

By David Moglen

Demand Shifters

Price is not a demand shifter. Like a shift in supply, price changes will not shift or change demand, they will cause movement along the demand curve, a change in quantity demanded (change in Qd).

1. Buyers' income
   - Level of GDP per capita aka PCI, or
   - A change in Distribution of income can shift Demand. While level of PCI would be assumed unchanged, if you were given: "Income becomes more unequal" as the shock, and the good in question is private helicopters, your response would be . . . demand increases.
   - But if you were given: "Income becomes more unequal" (same shock as above) but the good is: bargain retail (all shopping at Wal-Mart, Ross, K-Mart, the Dollar Store), your answer is . . . demand decreases.
2. Buyers' taste and preferences
   Any medical advice to eat or consume a certain product (or to avoide ay food or consumable item), advertising, fads/trends, religious or cultural changes that impact the consumption of a good all fall under "tastes". In the market for bread, pasta, and ceral (carbohydrates), what would the increasing popularity of the Atkins Diet do to demand?
3. Price of complements and substitutes
4. Buyers' expectations of future market conditions (especially the good's future price) but could more generally be their outlook on the economy, jobs, income, and sense of personal economic stability captured by a survey called consumer confidence (CC).
5. Number of buyers in the market (aka size of the market)

   For number of buyers, it could be described as a population (pop) increase (or decrease). If US population increases, then demand goes up for all goods, including, say, software.

   Also, it does not have to be the level of population—it could be the makeup of the population. If you are told that a demographic has changed (you then have to assume level of pop—as anything else in the economy—is unchanged and held constant).

   Example: If the shock is "population is aging" and the good is health care, the result is an increase in demand.

   If the shock is "population is aging" and the good is video games, the result is decrease in demand.

Supply Shifters

Price is not a supply shifter. Like a shift in demand, price changes will not shift or change Supply, they will cause movement along the supply curve, a change in quantity supplied (change in Qs).

1. Level of Productivity, Technology, or Human Capital used in production
2. Input prices (raw or intermediate materials that are needed to make output are called "inputs"). This also refers to the cost associated with any of the four "factors of production". Also called resource prices. Usually would be specific such as a change in the price of oil, employees' wages, the cost of buying or running a machine or factory, or rental costs.
3. Prices of other goods (specifically, the price of another goods the firm could produce instead).
4. Expectations about future prices for the good. Can also be firms generalized expectations about the economy, captured by a survey called business confidence (BC).
5. Number of firms in the industry; also might best be described as any of the following-Number of Suppliers/Producers/Resources
6. The firm's objective: e.g. profit maximizing or something else? This shifter is extremely rare, and generally means an industry has gone from public to private (privatized) or private to public (nationalized). A subtler shift would be industry becomes deregulated or more regulated.

SUMMARY —

1. The quantity of a product that is demanded is not a fixed number. Rather, **quantity demanded** depends on such factors as the price of the product, consumer incomes, and the prices of other products.
2. The relationship between quantity demanded and price, holding all other things constant, can be displayed graphically on a **demand curve**.
3. For most products, the higher the price, the lower the quantity demanded. So the demand curve usually has a negative slope.
4. The quantity of a product that is supplied also depends on its price and many other influences. A **supply curve** is a graphical representation of the relationship between **quantity supplied** and price, holding all other influences constant.
5. For most products, the supply curve has a positive slope, meaning that higher prices call forth greater quantities supplied.
6. A market is said to be in **equilibrium** when quantity supplied is equal to quantity demanded. The equilibrium price and quantity are shown by the point on a graph where the supply and demand curves intersect. The **law of supply and demand** states that price and quantity tend to gravitate to this point in a free market.
7. A change in quantity demanded that is caused by a change in the price of the good is represented by a **movement along a fixed demand curve**. A change in quantity demanded that is caused by a change in any other determinant of quantity demanded is represented by a **shift of the demand curve.**
8. This same distinction applies to the supply curve: Changes in price lead to **movements along a fixed supply curve**; changes in other determinants of quantity supplied lead to **shifts of the whole supply curve.**
9. Changes in consumer incomes, tastes, technology, prices of competing products, and many other influences cause shifts in either the demand curve or the supply curve and produce changes in price and quantity that can be determined from **supply-demand diagrams.**
10. An attempt by government regulations to force prices above or below their equilibrium levels is likely to lead to **shortages** or **surpluses**, black markets in which goods are sold at illegal prices, and to a variety of other problems. This is one of the **12 Ideas for Beyond the Final Exam.**

KEY CONCEPTS AND TERMS

Quantity demanded
Demand schedule
Demand curve
Quantity supplied
Supply schedule
Supply curve
Supply-demand diagram
Shortage
Surplus
Equilibrium price and quantity
Equilibrium
Law of supply and demand
Shifts in vs. movements along supply and demand curves
Price ceiling
Price floor

QUESTIONS FOR REVIEW

1. How often do you go to the movies? Would you go more often if a ticket cost half as much? Distinguish between your demand curve for movie tickets and your "quantity demanded" at the current price.
2. What would you expect to be the shape of a demand curve
   a. for a medicine that means life or death for a patient?
   b. for gasoline at an intersection with four gas stations?
3. The following are the assumed supply and demand schedules for footballs in Anytown, USA:

Demand Schedule		Supply Schedule	
Price	Quantity Demanded (per year)	Price	Quantity Supplied (per year)
$13	6,000	$13	71,000
11	13,000	11	63,000
9	29,000	9	29,000
7	50,000	7	11,000
5	61,000	5	0

   a. Plot the supply and demand curves and indicate the equilibrium price and quantity.
   b. What effect will an increase in the price of leather (a factor of production) have on the equilibrium price and quantity of footballs, assuming all other things remain constant? Explain your answer with the help of a diagram.
   c. What effect will a decrease in the price of soccer balls (a substitute commodity) have on the equilibrium price and quantity of

footballs, assuming again that all other things are held constant? Use a diagram in your answer.

4. Suppose the supply and demand schedules for Japanese cars in the United States are as follows:

Price (thousands)	Quantity Demanded (millions per year)	Quantity (millions per year)
$8	2.75	1.25
$10	2.50	1.50
$12	2.25	1.75
$14	2.00	2.00
$16	1.75	2.25
$18	1.50	2.50
$20	1.25	2.75

a. Graph these curves and show the equilibrium price and quantity.
b. Now suppose that a rise in anti-Japanese sentiment in the U.S. reduces the quantity demanded at each price by 500,000 (0.5 million) cars per year. What is the new equilibrium price and quantity? Show this solution graphically. Explain why the quantity falls by less than 500,000 cars per year.
c. Suppose *instead* that anti-American sentiment in Japan induces the Japanese to reduce their shipments to the U.S. by 500,000 cars per year (at each price). Find the new equilibrium price and quanity, and show it graphically. Explain again why quantity falls by less than 500,000.
d. What are the equilibrium price and quantity if the shifts described in parts (b) and (c) happen at the same time?

IN-CLASS PROJECT

Demand and Supply

By David Moglen

Directions

For the following exogenous shocks (you will be assigned one question, which is the same number as your group number, from 1–3):

Draw the Demand-Supply diagram with correctly labeled axes and the name of the market at the top.

Assume end-user, "product" market. I.e., what is the good that you as a normal consumer buy in the retail market relevant to the shock you have been assigned. That retail, final good should inform how you label the axes, especially the relevant quantity units on the horizontal axis, and what you will write above the graph for the name of the market/good.

Show Equilibrium points A (before the shock) and B (after the shock)and estimate numerical coordinates on X and Y axes.

Categorize the shifter—choose the entry from the list of Demand or Supply shifters that most closely describes the shock.

This is the only thing you need to write outside of the graph. If you are unsure of the shifter or are picking more than one shifter from the list, include an explanation of why the shifter you chose most closely categorizes the specific situation in your question.

1. "Moscow—Gazprom, the world's largest natural gas company, cut about a quarter of the gas supply to Ukraine's domestic market on Monday to force the country to settle a debt. . . . Europe draws about a fifth of its gas from Ukrainian pipelines so that any reduction of gas pressure there can deflate the whole, continent-wide natural network. Meanwhile, Russia and Ukraine feud often over prices and conditions. It is a weakness for the European Union that critics have compared with the United States' over-reliance on the unstable Persian Gulf for oil."[1]

   What is the impact in the end-user market for natural gas? Assume a starting price of $100/ 1,000 cubic meters of gas.

2. The chart below shows end of 2007–2008 survey results called Consumer Confidence.[2]

   What is the impact in the market for new Condominiums?

3. Chicago (MarketWatch)--Skybus Airlines announced it was shutting down Saturday, with the low-cost airline blaming the "insurmountable" pressures of rising jet fuel costs and a slowing economic environment.

Columbus, Ohio-based Skybus became the fourth airline this week to close or announce plans to do so. . . . Skybus made 74 daily flights to 15 U.S. cites, and offered some $10 flights.

The closely held company plans to file for bankruptcy protection next week, according to a Wall Street Journal report.

The shut-down came without warning Friday night. About 450 workers were affected, in addition to the travelers who held tickets for future flights, the report said.

Skybus marks the latest airline shut down in a string of carrier failures announced this week. Aloha Airlines halted operations Monday, and ATA Airlines shut down Thursday. Both have also applied for bankruptcy protection. Also, charter air-

line[3] Champion Air announced this week it would cease flight operations on May 31."
What is the impact of an increase in jet fuel prices in the market for air travel?

Don't forget to be specific on what to call the units that consumers like yourself buy in this market, and realistic prices people are paying.

[1]http://www.nytimes.com/2008/03/03/business/worldbusiness/03cnd-gazprom.html?ref=business

[2]http://www.conference-board.org/economics/ConsumerConfidence.cfm

[3]http://www.marketwatch.com/news/story/skybus-becomes-latest-airline-shut/story.aspx?guid=%7BA7CFE32B-59FC-40FC-B58E-54EE5979365F%7D

EXPERIMENT

Producers and Consumers

By David Moglen

Supplies

3X5 cards, any color, enough for every group of 4–5 students to get one. So a 40–student class should have about 10 cards.

Directions

Form your usual group. You will receive one 3X5 card per group. Write the name of a good your group will sell to the rest of the class. Imagine it's the month of December and the groups can be shopping for themselves, friends, or family. The time period is one month and people shop a lot in December. All groups have to spend $3,000 to $5,000.

But for now just take a minute or two to think of what good your group will produce and sell. It could be a good or a service, real or imagined, or a known major brand. There are no costs and winning is determined solely on revenue, not profits, so don't worry that the good you select will cost too much to produce. But do think about the $3,000 to $5,000 spending limit per group; you can't expect anyone to buy something from you for $5,000 per unit or more, or even anywhere close to that price because they will be over-budget.

Which brings us to the price. Determine your price, write it small on the card, and don't tell anyone outside of your group. Your teacher will come around within two-three minutes and write down on their own card the name of the good and your stated price for each group in the class.

During the shopping phase, groups will get to name their price for your good, in addition to the quantity of your good they will buy at that price. They will enter their shopping request in the space your teacher will have written on the board, like so:

T T T T

Where number of T's = number of groups in the class.

As soon as even one group is ready, they should walk up to the board and write above one of the T's the name of their good. If they want to include any details, features, brand, etc., they can write it there as well. Also, before shopping starts, the teacher should ask each group to verbally announce to the class any pitch they have for their good (briefly-takes 5–10 seconds per group). The left column of the T is labeled Q for the quantity the shopping group wants to buy. The right column of the T is labeled P for price per unit the group wants to pay for that good.

A sale has only gone through if the shoppers state a price equal or greater to your price.

Let's say you write down (on the card and on the board) that your good is glass kitchen tables, and you write on the card (and keep it secret) that your price is $400. Then a group comes up to the board during the shopping phase and writes under your good that they will buy 2 for $600, then you made a sale, two in fact, at your price of $400. So that is $800 of revenue.

If they offer even as low as $400, that would be a sale. But if they want to buy, say, 5 tables for $180 each, then you didn't make any sale. These offers did not "go through". You should, however write down on a sheet of paper every entry shoppers put on the board – even prices that are too low for you - under your good as you will need this data to draw your demand curve at the end of this experiment.

Winning

The group with the highest Total Revenue (=Sales) will win bonus points (or participation credits). To avoid collusion, there should not be second-place points on this project. There is one caveat: for the winning group to receive their bonus points, **they must have at least $1000 of their purchases actually go through**. So if they lowballed everyone and offered fifty cents for all their purchases, they cannot win. They have to have written on the board purchases totaling at least $1000 that have been accepted by the other groups.

Each group will turn in at the end of the exercise. (**Bold** indicates a specific item you are turning in:)

1. Producing Phase: The 3X5 card with the **name of the good** and your price written on it. This is also a good place to write your total revenue where **TR=your price quantity of units you sold**. This number is the sole basis on which the winning group is decided.

2. Shopping Phase: Send one or two members to the board and write under the goods on the board: quantities (in the Q column) and prices per unit (in the P column) that your group wants to buy. Your spending, using these prices you as a shopper are willing to pay, are used to show that you spent $3,000 to $5,000. **Show the math to indicate you are within these spending limits on a separate sheet of paper.** You do not need to buy every good, and you cannot buy your own good.

3. Demand-Supply Graph: **Write down on your paper all the shoppers' quantities and prices written on the board under your good.** Draw a demand curve for your good based on the data shoppers have given you for your good. For help on this, see the text on adding up individual's demand curves to get a market demand curve (you are only drawing the market demand curve). Draw your supply curve as a horizontal line, with a vertical value = your stated price. As always with any graph, fully label your axes, show point A as the intersection of D and S, and the time period should be per month.

Staple the sheet of paper to your 3X5 card and make sure all group members' names are written on either the paper or the card, or both if a stapler is unavailable.

CHAPTER 5
Price Controls

5 Price Controls

By William Baumol

A CASE STUDY: Rent Controls in New York City

New York is the only major city in the United States that has had rent controls continuously since World War II. The objective of rent control is, of course, to protect the consumer from high rents. But most economists believe that rent control does not help the cities or their inhabitants and that, in the long run, it makes almost everyone worse off. Elementary supply-demand analysis shows us what actually happens.

Figure 5-1 is a supply–demand diagram for rental units in New York. Curve *DD* is the demand curve and curve *SS* is the supply curve. Without controls, equilibrium would be at point *E*, where rents average $1200 per month and 3 million units are occupied. If rent controls are effective, they must set a ceiling price *below* the equilibrium price of $1200. But with a low rent ceiling, such as $800, the quantity of housing demanded will be 3.5 million (point *B*) while the quantity supplied will be only 2.5 million (point *C*).

The diagram shows a shortage of 1,000,000 apartments. This theoretical concept of a "shortage" manifests itself in New York City as an abnormally low vacancy rate—typically about half the national urban average.

As we expect, rent controls have spawned a lively black market in New York. The black market raises the effective price of rent-controlled apartments in many ways, including bribes, "key money" paid to move up on the waiting list, and requiring prospective tenants to purchase worthless furniture at inflated prices.

According to the diagram, rent controls reduce the quantity supplied from 3 million to 2.5 million apartments. How does this show up in New York? First, some property owners, discouraged by the low rents, have converted apartment buildings into office space or other uses. Second, some apartments have been inadequately maintained. After all, rent controls create a shortage which makes even dilapidated apartments easy to rent. Third, some landlords have actually abandoned their buildings rather than pay rising tax and fuel bills. These abandoned buildings rapidly become eyesores and eventually pose threats to public health and safety.

FIGURE 5-1

Supply–Demand Diagram for Rental Housing

When market forces are permitted to set rents, the quantity of dwellings supplied will equal the quantity demanded. But when a rent ceiling forces rent below the market level, the number of dwellings supplied (point *C*) will be less than the number demanded (point *B*). Thus, rent ceilings induce housing shortages.

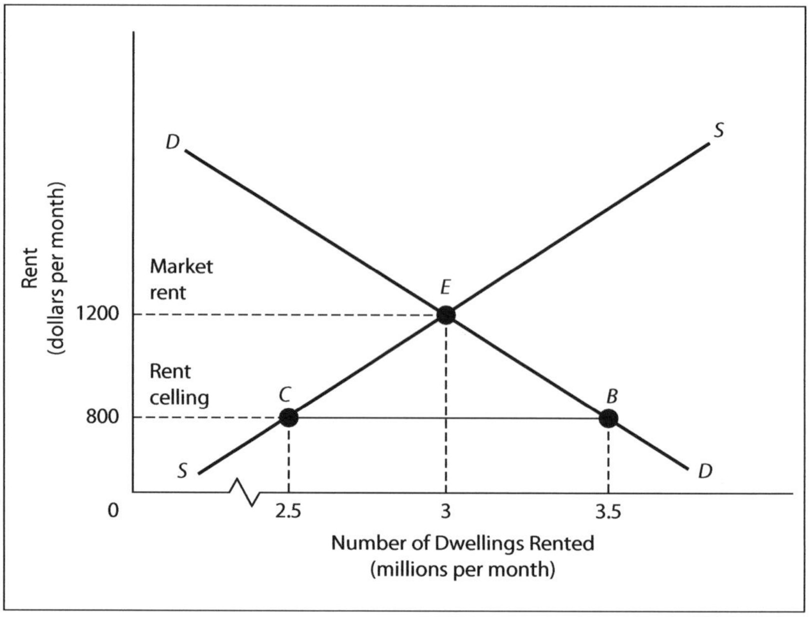

With all these problems, why do rent controls persist in New York City? And why are some other cities moving in the same direction? Part of the explanation is that most people simply do not understand the problems that rent controls create. Another part is that landlords are unpopular politically. But a third, and important, part of the explanation is that not everyone is hurt by rent controls. Those who benefit from controls fight hard to preserve them. In New York, for example, many tenants pay rents that are only a fraction of what their apartments would fetch on the open market. They are, naturally enough, quite happy with, this situation. This last point illustrates another very general phenomenon:

Virtually every price ceiling or floor creates a class of people with a vested interest in preserving the regulations because they benefit from them. These people naturally use their political influence to protect their gains, which is one reason why it is so hard to eliminate price ceilings or floors.

Restraining the Market Mechanism: Price Floors

A **Price Floor** is a legal minimum on the price that may be charged for a commodity.

Interferences with the market mechanism are not always designed to keep prices *low*. Agricultural price supports and minimum wages are two notable examples in which the law keeps prices *above* free-market levels. **Price floors** are typically accompanied by a standard set of symptoms:'

1. A surplus develops as sellers cannot find enough buyers. *Example:* Surpluses of various agricultural products have been a persistent, and costly, problem for the U.S. government. The problem is even more severe in the European Community, where the so-called common agricultural policy holds prices even higher.
2. Where goods, rather than services, are involved, the surplus creates a problem of disposal. Something must be done about the excess of quantity supplied over quantity demanded.

Example: The government has often been forced to purchase, store, and then dispose of large amounts of surplus agricultural commodities.

3. To get around the regulations, sellers may offer discounts in disguised and often unwanted-forms. *Example:* When airline fares were regulated by the government, airlines offered more and better food and stylish uniforms for flight attendants instead of lowering fares. Today, the food is worse but tickets cost much less.
4. Regulations that keep prices artificially high encourage overinvestment in the industry. Even inefficient businesses whose high operating costs would doom them in an unrestricted market can survive beneath the shelter of a generous price floor. *Example:* This is why the airline and trucking industries both went through painful "shake outs" of the weaker companies in the 1980s.

Once again, a specific example is useful.

A CASE STUDY: Milk Price Supports

America's extensive program of farm price supports began in 1933 as "a temporary method of dealing with an emergency"—farmers were going broke in droves. It is with us still today, even though the farm population of the United States is less than a sixth of what it was then.

One of the more absurd legacies of that "temporary emergency" is a maze of milk-marketing orders covering the pricing and distribution of milk in 44 milk producing regions of the country. By setting the prices of milk, butter, and cheese as high as three times those on world markets, the government ensures that America will suffer from chronic overproduction—as Figure 5-2 shows.

In the diagram, the equilibrium price for milk is 70¢ per quart, but we assume that the government sets *a price floor* at 90¢. At this high price, farmers produce 80 billion quarts per year—20 billion above the equilibrium quantity. But consumers want to purchase only 50 billion—10 billion below the equilibrium quantity. The result is a huge *surplus* of milk—30 billion quarts per year in the example.

In a market economy like ours, Congress cannot simply set prices by decree; it must do something to enforce the price floor. Normally, that "something" is buying up the surplus, that is, adding 30 billion quarts per year in *government demand* to the private demand shown in Figure 5-2.[1] That, of course, requires a lot of the taxpayers' money. In addition, all the surplus milk must be stored somewhere—usually as cheese—for milk does not keep well. That creates another bill for the taxpayer to pick up. But there is more. We pay again as consumers in the form of higher prices for milk—90¢ rather than 70¢ in the example. According

[1]Draw a new demand curve into Figure 5-2 which includes this government demand. It must be parallel to DD but 30 billion quarts farther to the right. If you draw it accurately, it will pass exactly through point *B*.

FIGURE 5-2
Analysis of Milk Price Supports
In this diagram, which repeats the supply and demand curves from Figure 5-3, the support price for milk (90¢ per quart) exceeds the equilibrium price (which is 70¢. Quantity supplied at the support price is 80 billion quarts per year (point *B*) while quantity demanded is only 50 billion (point *A*). To keep the price at 90¢, the government must buy up the 30-billion-quart surplus each year.

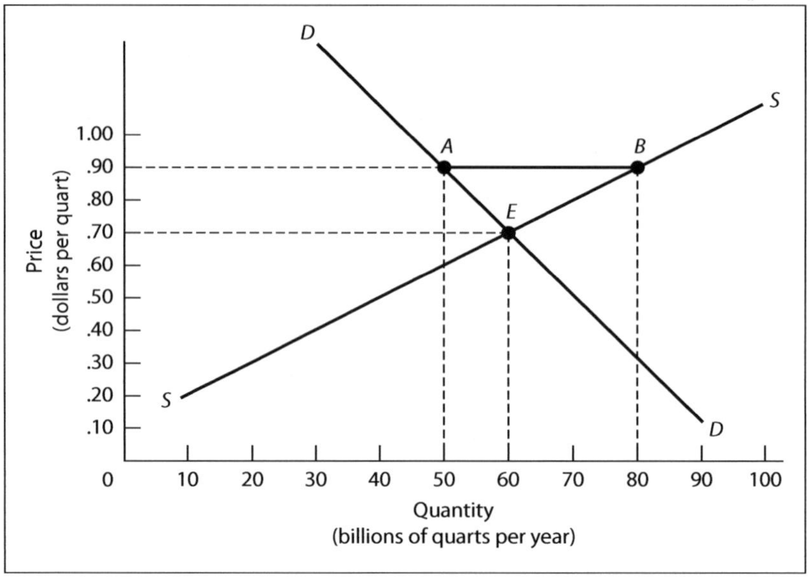

to current estimates, milk price supports cost American taxpayers and consumers together about \$10–\$12 billion a year.

Sometimes the government tires of all this and tries something else. For example, in 1986 it offered to pay dairy farmers to slaughter 1.6 million cows. The result? An uproar from beef raisers as meat prices collapsed.[2] As we said earlier, those who would flaunt the will of the market had better be prepared for unforeseen consequences.

A Can of Worms

Our two case studies—rent controls and milk price supports—illustrate some of the major side effects of price floors and ceilings, but barely hint at others. There are difficulties that we have not even mentioned, for the market mechanism is a tough bird that imposes suitable retribution on those who seek to circumvent it by legislative decree. Here is a partial list of other problems that may arise when prices are controlled.

FAVORITISM AND CORRUPTION

When price ceilings or floors create shortages or surpluses, someone must decide who gets to buy or sell the limited quantity that is available. This can lead to discrimination along racial or religious lines, political favoritism, or corruption in government. For example, it has been argued that the high U.S. support price for sugar has led to widespread corruption in Caribbean nations, as foreign producers vie for the valuable right to export sugar cane to the United States.

[2]See Review Question 8 at the end of the chapter.

UNENFORCEABILITY

Attempts to limit prices are almost certain to fail in industries with numerous suppliers, simply because the regulating agency must monitor the behavior of so many sellers. Ways will be found to evade or violate the law, and something akin to the free-market price will generally reemerge. But there is an important difference: since the evasion mechanism, whatever its form, will have some operating costs, those costs must be borne by someone. Normally, that someone is the consumer.

AUXILIARY RESTRICTIONS

Fears that a system of price controls will break down invariably lead to regulations designed to shore up the shaky edifice. Consumers may be told when and from whom they are permitted to buy. The powers of the police and the courts may be used to prevent the entry of new suppliers. Occasionally, an intricate system of market subdivision is imposed, giving each class of firms a protected sphere in which others are not permitted to operate. Laws banning conversion of rent controlled apartments to condominiums are one example. Milk-marketing orders are another. A few years ago, milk cost so much less in New Jersey than in New York that people were actually smuggling milk into New York State!

LIMITATION OF VOLUME OF TRANSACTIONS

To the extent that controls succeed in affecting prices, they can be expected to reduce the volume of transactions. Curiously, this is true regardless of whether the regulated price is *above* or *below* the free-market equilibrium price. If it is set above the equilibrium price, quantity demanded will be below the equilibrium quantity. On the other hand, if the imposed price is set below the free-market level, quantity supplied will be cut down. Since sales volume cannot exceed either the quantity supplied or the quantity demanded, a reduction in the volume of transactions is the result.[3]

MISALLOCATION OF RESOURCES

Departures from free-market prices are likely to produce misuse of the economy's resources because the connection between production costs and prices is broken. For example, Russian farmers used to feed their farm animals bread, instead of unprocessed grains, because price ceilings kept the price of bread ludicrously low. In addition, just as more complex locks lead to more sophisticated burglary tools, more complex regulations lead to the use of yet more resources for their avoidance. New jobs are created for executives, lawyers, and economists. It may well be conjectured that at least some of these expensive professionals could be put to better use elsewhere.

[3]See Review Question 9 at the end of the chapter.

Policy Debate

ECONOMIC ASPECTS OF THE WAR ON DRUGS

For years now, the U.S government has engaged in a highly publicized "war on drugs." At part of this effort, billions of dollars have been spent on trying to stop illegal drugs at the border. In some sense, interdiction has succeeded: literally tons of cocaine and other drugs have been seized by federal agents. Yet all these efforts have made barely to America's city streets. Simple economic reasoning explains why.

When drug interdiction works, it shifts the supply curve of drugs to the left, thereby driving up street prices. But that, in turn, raises the rewards for potential smugglers and attracts more criminals in to the "industry", which shifts the supply curve back to the right. The net result is that increased shipments of drugs to our shores replace much of what the authorities confiscate. This is why many economics believe that any successful anti-drug program must concentrate on reducing *demand* which would lower the street price of drugs, not on reducing *supply* which can only raise it.

Some economists-and some noneconomists as well-would go even further and advocate *legalization* of many drugs. While this remains a highly controversial position which few are ready to endorse, the reasoning behind it is straightforward. A stunningly high number of crimes committed in America—especially robberies and murders—are drug-related. One major reason is that street prices of drugs are so high that addicts must steal to get the money and drug traffickers are all too willing to kill to protect their highly profitable "businesses".

How would things differ if drugs were legal? Since Colombian farmers earn pennies for drugs that sell for hundreds of dollars on the streets of Los Angeles and New York, we may safely assume that drugs would be vastly cheaper under legalization. And that, proponents pointed out, would reduce drug-related crimes dramatically. When, for example, was the last time you heard of a gang killing connected with the distribution of cigarettes or alcoholic beverages?

The argument against legalization of drugs is largely moral: Should the state sanction potential lethal substances? But there is also an economic aspect. The vastly lower street prices of drugs that would increase drug use. Thus, while legalization would almost certainly reduce crime, it would also produce more addicts. The key question here-to which no one has a good answer-is: How many more addicts? If you think the increase in quantity demanded would be large, you are unlikely to find legalization an attractive option.

Economists put it this way. Free markets are capable of dealing with the three basic coordination tasks: deciding *what* to produce, *how* to produce it, and *to whom* the goods should be distributed. Price controls throw a monkey wrench into the market mechanism. Though the market is surely not flawless, and government interferences often have praiseworthy goals, good intentions are not enough. Any government that sets out to repair what it sees as a defect in the market mechanism must take care lest it cause even more serious damage elsewhere. As a prominent economist once quipped, societies that are too willing to interfere with the operation of free markets soon find that the invisible hand is nowhere to be seen-a point that the formerly communist nations grew to understand in a very painful way.

A Simple But Powerful Lesson

The lessons you have learned in this chapter may seem elementary, even obvious. In many respects, they are. But they are also very important, indeed, indispensable. Although the law of supply and demand is one of the simplest principles in economics, it is also one of the most powerful. Astonishing as it may seem, many people in authority, even highly intelligent people, fail to understand the law of supply and demand or cannot apply it to concrete situations.

For example, a few years ago the *New York Times* carried a dramatic front page picture of the president of Kenya setting fire to a large pile of elephant tusks that had been confiscated from poachers. The accompanying story explained that the burning was intended as a symbolic act to persuade the world to halt the ivory trade.[4] Economists claim no expertise on the likely psychological effect of burning elephant tusks, though one may doubt that it touched the hearts of criminal poachers. However, one economic effect was clear. By reducing the supply of ivory on the world market, the burning of tusks forced up the price of ivory, which raised the illicit rewards reaped by those who slaughter elephants. That could only encourage more poaching-precisely the opposite of what the Kenyan government sought to accomplish.

[4]The *New York Times*, July 19, 1989.

FIGURE 5-3

Dealing with the Surplus

This graph illustrates two of many approaches open to a government that has legislated an above-equilibrium minimum price (here of $3 per bushel) and has to deal with the ensuing surplus problem as well. First, as pane (a) demonstrates, regular consumers can buy whatever they are willing to take at the minimum price (point *a*). Subsequently, the government can use the taxpayers' money to buy up the surplus (*ab*). In this example, regular consumers end up spending $1,500 million per year (shaded area) and the government spends an additional $3,000 million per year (crosshatched area).

Second, as panel (b) demonstrates regular consumers can be given the *entire* crop (*de*), which farmers supply when promised the "target" price of $3 per bushel. As point *f* indicates, these consumers will buy that crop, but only for $1 per bushel. Subsequently, the government can use the taxpayers' money to pay farmers a subsidy equal to the difference between the promised "target" price of $3 and the realize market price of $1. In this example, regular consumers end up spending $1,500 million per year (shaded area), and the government spends another $3,000 million per year (crosshatched area).

Note: It is only a coincidence that the shaded areas in the two panels and the cross-hatched areas in the two panels and the crosshatched areas in the two panels are equal to each other.

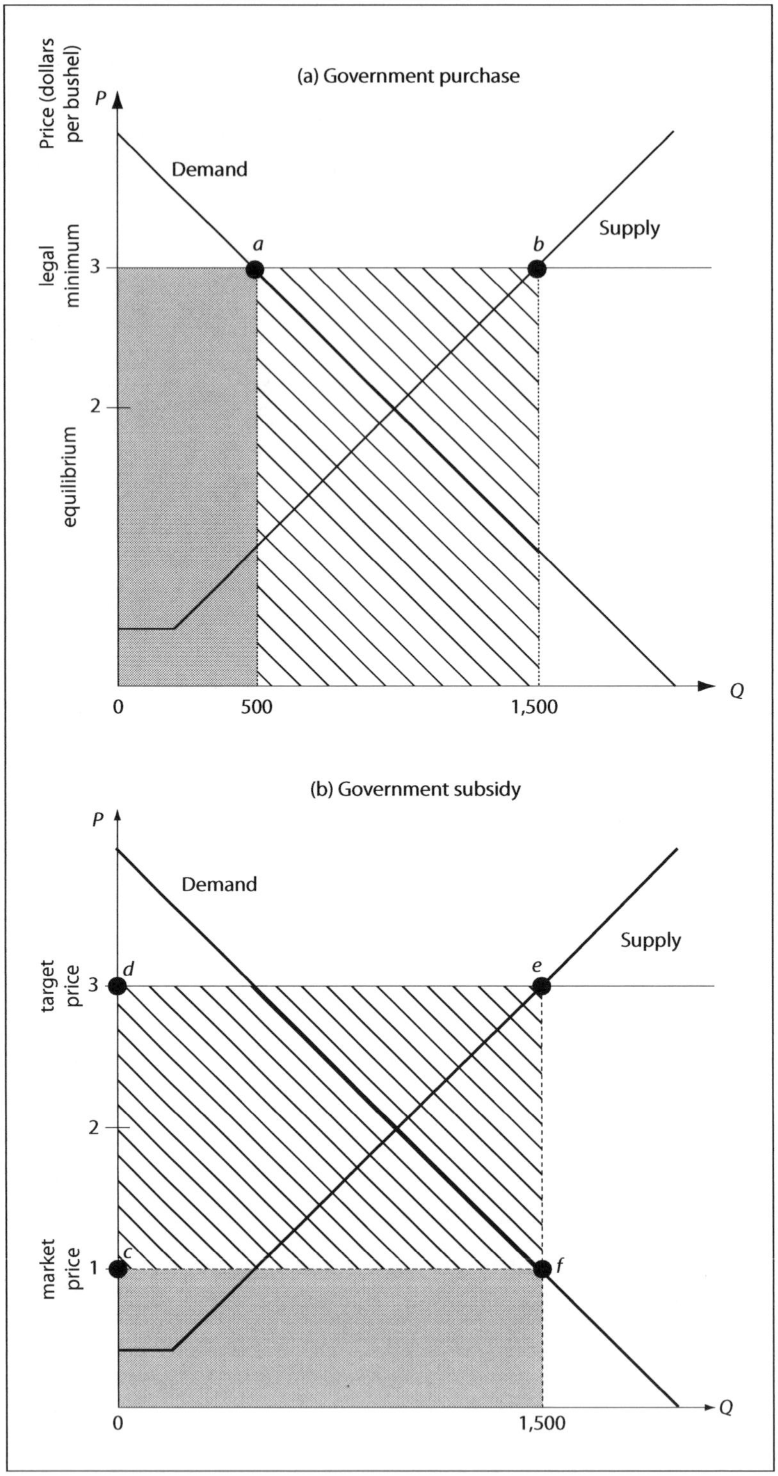

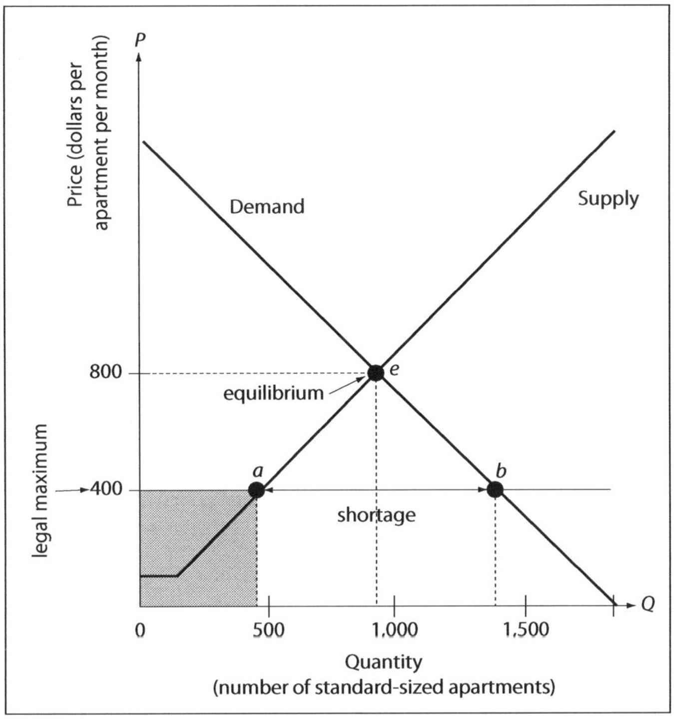

FIGURE 5-4

Setting a Maximum Price for Apartment Rental

In this apartment-rental market, free competition among sellers or buyers would establish an equilibrium at *e*, corresponding to a monthly rent of $800 per apartment and the renting of 1,000 apartments. If government, however, intervenes by setting a legal maximum rent of $400, a shortage of *ab* emerges. As price falls from the equilibrium level to the legal maximum, quantity demanded increases along *eb* while quantity supplied decreases along *ea*. A shortage of ab emerges. In this example, only 500 apartments are actually rented, for a total monthly payment of $400 per apartment times 500 apartments, or $200,000 (shaded). Yet would-be renters of another 1,000 apartments (distance ab) fail to find any that are available. To them the low rent is nothing but a cruel mockery.

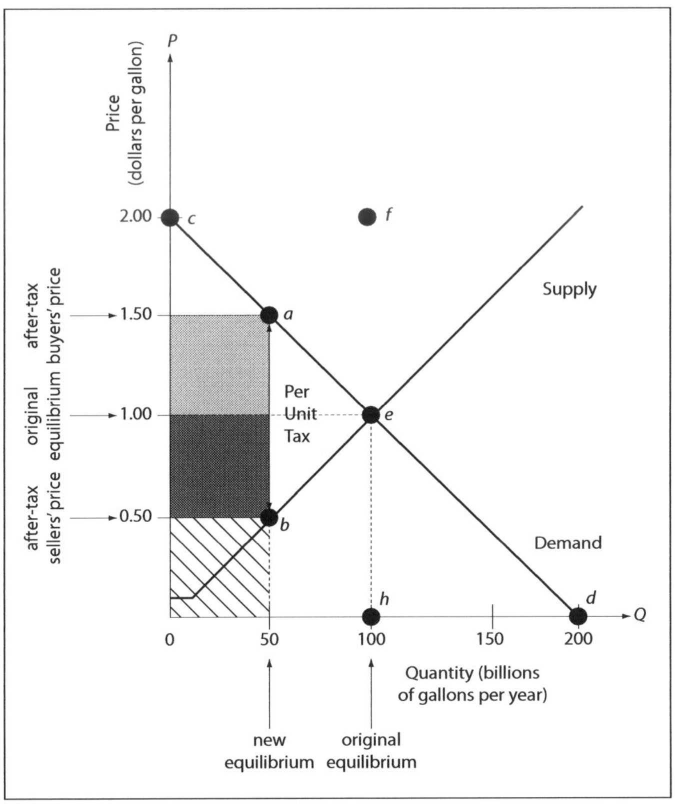

FIGURE 5-5

Imposing an Excise Tax on Gasoline

Equilibrium occurs at e, corresponding to a price of $1 per gallon per year. If government intervenes by imposing an excise tax of $1 per gallon, a $1 wedge appears between the price buyers pay (point a) and the price sellers ultimately receive (point b). A new and lower equilibrium quantity emerges (corresponding to the location of the wedge).

In this example, buyers ultimately pay $1.50 per gallon times 50 billion gallons, or $75 billion per year (the sum of the shaded plus dotted plus crosshatched areas). Sellers pass on to the government $1 per gallon times 50 billion gallons, or $50 billion per year (the sum of the shaded plus dotted areas). Thus the sellers' after-tax receipts only equal 50¢ per gallon times 50 billion gallons, or $25 billion per year (the crosshatched area). Compared to the original equilibrium price, buyers pay 50¢ more per gallon; sellers get 50¢ less. Thus, the tax burden, by coincidence, is equally shared.

Example 1

THE STORY OF RENT CONTROL

The story depicted by Figure 11 has been confirmed by the experience of renters in many cities throughout the world. In the United States, rent control was introduced in New York in 1943 and has since spread to many other cities, ranging from Boston and Washington, D.C., to Los Angeles and San Francisco, and to well over 200 smaller towns. At the time of their enactment, rent-control laws are typically justified as a long-overdue means of putting greedy, villainous landlords in their place and of helping their innocent, overcharged victims.

Inevitably, the kind of shortage depicted by distance *ab* in Figure 11 develops and tends to grow worse over time. The short-run decrease in quantity supplied (along *ea*) as landlords quickly convert rent-controlled apartments to uncontrolled office space, private condominiums, and similar alternative uses is followed by decreases in long-run supply (not shown in Figure 11). Such a leftward shift of the entire supply line occurs when new construction comes to a halt and existing rental units disappear. At first, landlords skimp on maintenance as their profits are squeezed between fixed revenues and rising costs. A vicious circle is set up. Poor maintenance of electrical wiring turns buildings into firetraps and causes accidents, so insurance rates go up. So do city taxes for fire protection. Lack of janitorial services forces people to share water facilities. Before long, tenants end up living in vermin-infested, badly ventilated quarters. Children get lead poisoning from eating peeling paint. Everyone gets sick from breathing garbage processed by inefficient incinerators. Everyone freezes in winter when old furnaces break down and go untended. In anger, residents turn to vandalism. Insurance rates go up some more, as do city taxes for police protection.

Eventually, the rental units become so dilapidated as to be unlivable. Finally, instead of paying taxes on useless buildings, landlords abandon them, as happened to 200,000 units in New York between 1965 and 1975. In due time, most abandoned buildings fall victim to vandals who strip them of heating, plumbing, electrical installations, windows, paneling, flooring, and stairways. Before long, they are littered with garbage, blackened by arsonists, and damaged beyond repair. The charred rubble becomes inhabited by homeless people. Thus entire slums are born, and what remains are eyesores and threats to public health and safety.

In the meantime, a black market develops in which people on waiting lists attempt to acquire scarce rental units at above-ceiling prices. A million different methods are in common use. They range from outright bribes to paying "key money" to requiring any new tenant to buy worthless furniture at incredibly inflated prices.

As with so many price-fixing programs, there is no certainty that this program truly helps the poor. In New York City, for example, many tenants in rent-controlled apartments (who recently paid a median rent of $330 a month) are middle and upper income families. Many landlords are small investors of moderate income.

DISCUSSION QUESTIONS

Farm Subsidies / Agricultural Price Supports

By David Moglen

Read the two article excerpts below and answer the questions that follow.

From page two of "Cornucopia Blues" by Brent Cunningham, online at http://www.thenation.com/article/cornucopia-blues:

"In *Enough*, Thurow and Kilman relay an anecdote about Ethiopia during the 2003 famine that shows the grim consequences of the Iron Triangle's stranglehold on food aid. As trucks laden with 1 million tons of US corn, wheat, peas, beans and lentils rolled into Nazareth, a city of around 230,000 people in central Ethiopia, they passed warehouses stuffed with 100,000 metric tons of Ethiopian grains, beans and peas—the surplus from a bumper crop two years earlier that had failed to sell when prices collapsed. (Here again was the legacy of structural adjustment: the dearth of storage facilities meant that farmers had no choice but to dump their grain on the market at the same time; and the stunted internal markets and an ancient transportation network that still relied heavily on donkeys meant that there was no way to move the glut of grain to the parts of the country that needed it.) The market was undermined further by the arrival of international food aid. "American farmers have a market in Ethiopia, but we don't have a market in Ethiopia," huffed Kadir Geleto, who managed a grain-trading operation in Nazareth."

Geleto understood that Ethiopian-grown grain alone couldn't feed the hungry when the rains failed, but he also knew that the deluge of American food aid had created a cycle of dependency that sapped the incentive of many of his countrymen to work to feed their families. Why, Geleto wondered, didn't America provide cash aid to buy up the local surplus and then send food aid to cover the rest of the shortage? During the 2003 famine, Andrew Natsios, the administrator of the US Agency for International Development, asked the same question. He knew that if he had the flexibility to buy surplus grain in Ethiopia, food aid would be cheaper and made available to the hungry faster than food shipped from the United States. As Thurow and Kilman write in Enough, Natsios also knew that the Iron Triangle had consistently quashed efforts to allow for such flexibility in American food policy. But by 2005, with the reverberations from the 2003 famine keeping world leaders nominally focused on ending hunger in Africa, Natsios convinced President Bush that "reforming the...food-aid program would complement his initiative to end famine in the Horn of Africa." Bush's budget that year included a proposal that one-quarter of the $1.2 billion in food-aid money be used to buy African crops. But when Natsios presented the idea in April of that year to the annual food-aid industry conference in Kansas City, he was nearly run out of town. Robert Zachritz of World Vision, a Christian aid group, described the reception Natsios received as "hostile." The law governing food aid didn't change. As Ó Gráda notes in Famine, "Public Law 480 has allowed U.S. food producers to match philanthropy with self-interest for over half a century."

1. What does the author mean when he links these problems to "structural adjustment"?
2. What happened when Mr. Nastios said that farm subsidies would be better spent buying from Ethiopian rather than American farmers?
3. Can you guess what might explain this reaction?

From "Another Year at the Federal Trough: Farm Subsidies for the Rich, Famous, and Elected

IN-CLASS PROJECT

Price Controls

By David Moglen

Directions

You will be given a group number from 1–3. Answer the corresponding questions.

1. Draw graph showing a quota of 10 million foreign-made cars per year when the equilibrium is 20 million auto imports per year. (Graph)

Categorize as winners or losers from the quota policy each of the following groups: consumers, domestic producers, foreign producers able to sell under the quota, the government (budgetary impact), and foreign producers unable to sell under the quota. Explain why each is in that category. (List)

*Why might this policy succeed; in other words, why might the "winners" beat the "losers" in getting this policy implemented and upheld? Mention the governing body who passes the law; what is that federal, state, or local government body called, where certain elected officials gathered in a room to pass this law? Now what exactly, in detail, is going on during the one-month period these lawmakers are considering a law that would require this price control. Describe as many activities as you can for what the winners will do to try to get the price control passed, so they can win, and what, if anything the losers do to counter-act this and fight for their goals. If you say the losers do nothing then explain why. (3–7 sentences)

2. Graph a subsidy to stabilize farmers' incomes by creating a binding price floor of $1 per pound of corn when equilibrium price is 50 cents per pound. (Graph)

Categorize as winners or losers from the price control policy each of the following groups: consumers, producers, foreign farmers whose countries receive the distributed excess output, and the governmen (budgetary impact). Explain why each is in that category. (List)

*Why might this policy succeed; in other words, why might the "winners" beat the "losers" in getting this policy implemented and upheld? Mention the governing body who passes the law; what is that federal, state, or local government body called, where certain elected officials gathered in a room to pass this law? Now what exactly, in detail, is going on during the one-month period these lawmakers are considering a law that would require this price control. Describe as many activities as you can for what the winners will do to try to get the price control passed, so they can win, and what, if anything the losers do to counter-act this and fight for their goals. If you say the losers do nothing then explain why. (3–7 sentences)

3. Graph the market for New York City rental units when equilibrium is $2000 per month and the rent control limit is $1000 per month. At the equilibrium rental price, 1 million units are rented. Assume one renter per unit. (Graph)

Categorize as winners or losers from the price control policy each of the following groups: current renters, potential renters (in the long run), landlords, and the government (budgetary impact). Explain why each is in that category. (List)

*Why might this policy succeed; in other words, why might the "winners" beat the "losers" in getting this policy implemented and upheld? Mention the governing body who passes the law; what is that federal, state, or local government body called, where certain elected officials gathered in a room to pass this law? Now what exactly, in detail, is going on during the one-month period these lawmakers are considering a law that would require this price control. Describe as many activities as you can for what the winners will do to try to get the price control passed, so they can win, and what, if anything the losers do to counter-act this and fight for their goals. If you say the losers do nothing then explain why. (3–7 sentences)

UNLOCKING THE MYSTERIES

Rent Control

By David Moglen

Mystery #1: How do landlords reduce the number of units rented out?

Take a look at this model below of a $700 rent control in Boston, Massachusetts, when the free market rental rate would have been $1,200.

Remember, renters are the demand and landlords are the supply. Notice this graph includes a line labeled SSR, or short run supply. Short run supply is vertical at the equilibrium quantity of two million units rented out at point A. Imagine that the city of Boston has just yesterday implemented rent-control, so you are still in the short run. While we know from where the $700 rent control price meets their SLR that landlords want to reduce the number of apartment units they provide to 1.3 million, in the short run they have to continue renting the same two million units to their current renters.

Why can't landlords immediately kick out 700,000 renters and get down to suppliers' ideal quantity of 1.3 million?

Think about it for a minute.

There are laws against evicting someone who has been on time with their rent. Even someone who missed their payment can't be kicked out the next day. Renters are on a lease, and while some leases will run out within the month, others may take about a full year for their lease to run out. Then, after a year, you are in the long run in this market and the landlords can reduce the number of units they rent out and force the 700,000 renters between Qs and Qe to go look for somewhere else to live.

While they can't reduce supply in the short run, how do the landlords reduce their units in the short run? In the graph, how do they go from point b' on their short run supply curve to point b on the long run supply curve?

A lot of these options for the landlords rely on whether the rent control law, and other city laws allow them. If there are no loopholes, and the landlord has no other options, they will most likely pursue the last choice on the list.

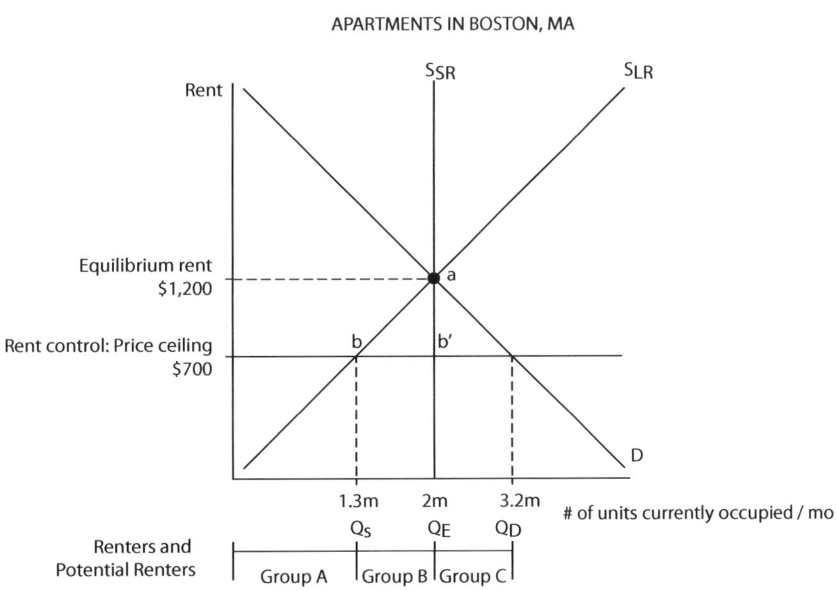

a. Convert to condominiums: a condo is simply their apartment unit sold off like a house or any other real estate. They have removed the 700,000 units from the market because they are not being rented out anymore because they have sold it to an owner-occupant.
b. Convert to luxury or furnished apartment.
c. Rezone property to business or mixed-use.
d. Abandon property, provide zero maintenance, and let it become a slum. Renters or squatters may remain there until city building inspectors condemn the property and remove any people inside.

Mystery #2: Alternative allocative mechanisms

Had Boston apartments been left to the free market, the price system would have determined who will get to buy this good. You would be at point A, with two million units rented at the price of $1,200. In other words, whoever had the money and was willing to rent would have gotten a unit.

Under rent control, not everyone willing to pay the $700 rent gets a unit. In fact, 3.2 million wish to rent and only 1.3 million actually get a place. So it is not the price system determining who gets what; price controls require an Alternative Allocative Mechanism:

a. Lottery
b. Waiting in line/first come, first served
c. Rationing
d. Seller's Preference

Mystery #3: Renter's who lose their apartment—are they for or against rent control?

If rent control leads to a shortage, and many renters eventually lose their homes, why do the renters support and even aggressively advocate for such a law?

If the renter is in the group who gets to keep their apartment and just pay the decreased rent, of course they are in favor of rent control. But what about the renters in the graph who lose their apartment due to the landlord converting it to a condo or leaving it without maintenance, abandoning the property for city building inspector to condemn and expel any squatters or remaining renters? Why would the person who loses their place to live advocate for the very rent control law that caused their effective eviction?

The answer primarily is that before the law is passed and leases have time to expire/abandoned buildings have time to become blighted, individual renters don't know if they are in the lucky group who gets to stay in their place with lower rent (Group A in the graph), or the unlucky group who loses their apartment (Group B). Everyone hears there is a possibility of a law mandating lower rent, and thinks they will benefit. Refer to Mystery 1, above; all renters continue to think they will be winners until a year passes.

Another reason most renters will support rent control proposals are the normative aspects. In Berkeley, rent control can be rationalized as essential for students and employees of UC Berkeley. In New York City and San Francisco, the argument can be made that maintaining an artistic population rather than being a white collar, Wall Street-only city requires some relief from the city's unaffordable rents. At many mobile-home parks, space rentals are rent-controlled in the interest of the mostly elderly and/or low-income residents.

Directions

Break into your small groups. Whichever group finishes all questions with 100% accuracy gets bonus points but must, when asked by the teacher, write out how you got your answer on the board for the class.

1. There is rent control. Demand decreases. Will the shortage increase or decrease?
2. There is rent control. The price ceiling decreases. Will the shortage increase or decrease?
3. There is an agricultural price support (Price Floor) for wheat. Supply decreases. Will the surplus increase or decrease?
4. There is an agricultural price support (Price Floor) for wheat. The price floor decreases. Will the surplus increase or decrease?

UNLOCKING THE MYSTERIES

Minimum Wage

By David Moglen

Minimum wage is a price control; specifically, as a wage floor, it should be modeled the same way as a price floor. As we know from the price floor example in the chapter, price floors cause a surplus. The market we are analyzing with a minimum wage is the Labor Market. So basic theory says a surplus will occur, which in the Labor Market is called unemployment. Supply of workers exceeds businesses' demand at the artificially high wage. While there is debate among economists as to whether there are any unemployment effects of miniumum wage,[1] part of the lack of an effect is readily apparent: how can changing the minimum wage from, say, $6.55 to $7.25 (the most recent increase) have any direct effect on a doctor making $200 per hour, or a mechanic making $50 per hour, or a factory worker making $15 per hour? In other words, it is a non-binding price control for most workers.

In the Labor market, the horizontal (quantity) axis is labeled L for number of workers, and the vertical (price) axis is labeled Wage. For a realistic equilibrium quantity (where number of workers the labor force supplies equals the number businesses demand-in other words, the intersection of supply and demand) we'll estimate L=150 million.

What should be our estimate for the equilibrium wage, in other words, the vertical measure of point A, equilibrium, where supply and demand cross? What is a wage that represents all 150 million workers in the economy, when some are paid very little, others get incredibly high salaries, and everyone else is somewhere in between? The wage that would represent all workers is the *average* hourly wage. It's been about $19 per hour in the most recent data.[2] So our estimate of equilibrium wage on the vertical axis reads $19. (*see* Panel A)

Now let's draw the minimum wage: a binding price floor at $7.25 per hour. Do you notice anything wrong with this picture? (*see* Panel B)

Right! The only way to draw a binding price floor—one that will have any impact of number of workers employed or their wage, is to draw it above equilibirum wage. But $7.25 is not above $19. For this market showing *all* U.S. workers, the horizontal price floor/ minimum wage line would have to be drawn well below equilibrium–a non-binding price floor.

Panel A

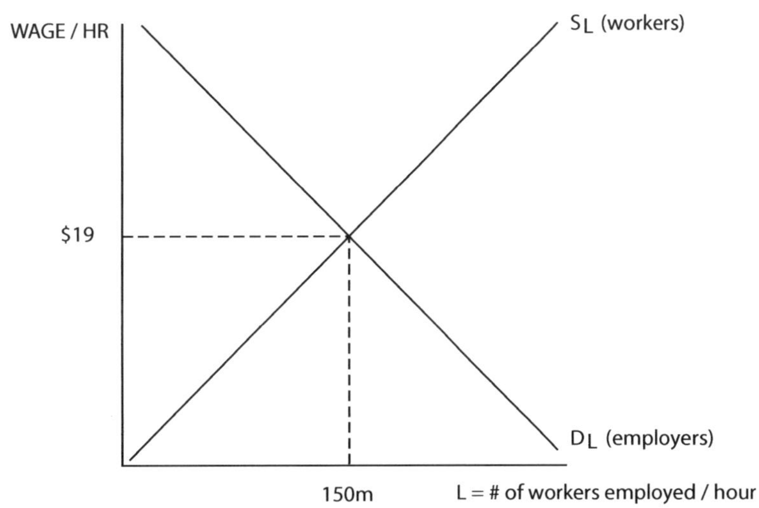

The only way to have a market where a minimum wage of $7.25 would have any impact is if we remove from the picture almost all workers, and leave in only the entry-level/ unskilled workforce. Now we have a model that at least makes sense when it says minimum wage causes unemployment, at least for this limited category of workers. We can leave it to economists to debate whether minimum wage induces unemployment for even the entry-level workers.[3] (*see* Panel C)

Panel B

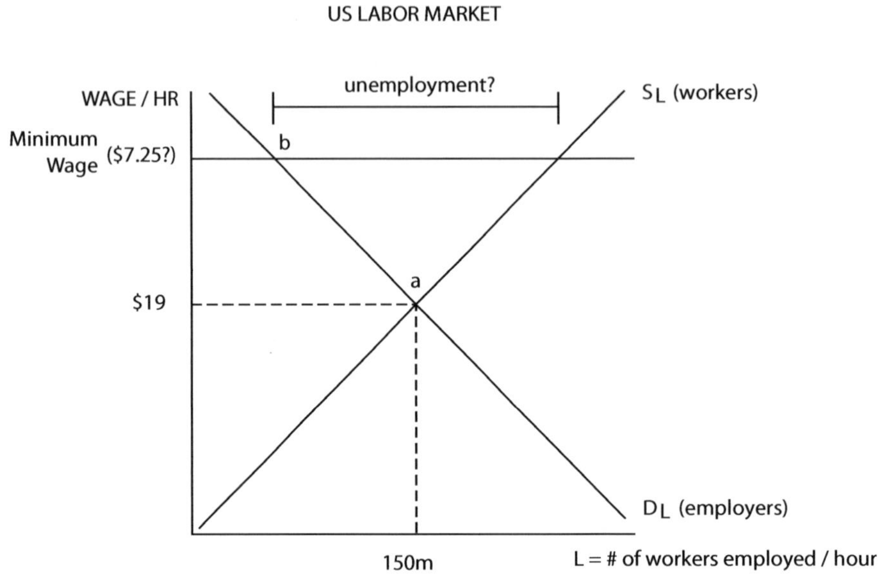

Panel C

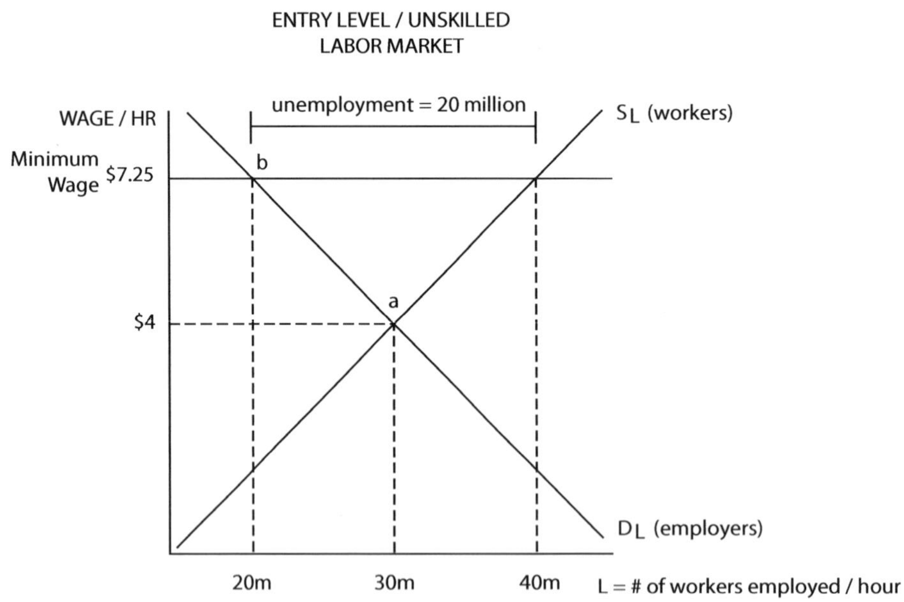

[1] http://en.wikipedia.org/wiki/minimum_wage.
[2] http://www.bls.gov/news.release/empsit.t24.htm
[3] http://en.wikipedia.org/wiki/minimum_wage.

The Minimum Wage

The Fair Labor Standards Act of 1938 set a minimum wage of 25 cents an hour, covering 43% of the nonagricultural labor force. By early 1989, the minimum wage had been increased 13 times, and its coverage more than doubled. Some workers do not receive the minimum wage because their industries are still not included; even in those that are, some firms do not comply with this law, because there are inadequate penalties for breaking it. By 1989, the minimum wage had become a heated issue because it had not been raised since 1981 and had therefore been eroded by inflation. It was still $3.35 an hour, even though the average U.S. wage had increased by more than 32%, from $7.25 to $9.60. Congress wanted the rate raised to $4.55 to compensate for inflation. President Bush opposed any increase above $4.25.

To analyze the minimum wage in the United States where some industries are covered by it and some are not, consider two cases. (1) Suppose the minimum wage is applied to only one industry; and (2) suppose it is applied to all industries. The U.S. economy is between these two polar cases.

CASE 1: Only One Industry is Covered by the Minimum Wage

This case can be described in panel *c* Unlocking the Mysteries: Minimum Wage. Suppose that there is initially a perfectly competitive, free-market wage of W_1, where supply equals demand for labor. Then the government imposes a minimum wage W_3, above W_1. Because of the higher wage, employers hire fewer workers. Equilibrium moves back up the demand curve from E_1 to E_3, with the number of workers employed falling from N_1 to N_3. As a result, there is the red efficiency loss because too few workers are hired in this industry.

Why then does the government introduce this policy? The answer is to provide a fairer, equitable wage and thus help to solve the poverty problem. In fact, this policy can indeed be expected to redistribute income, but not necessarily in the way intended, since some workers lose while others gain. The winners are the N_3 workers who still have a job in this industry and who enjoy a wage increase from W_1 to W_3. The losers are the N_3N_1 workers who lose their jobs in this industry or are not hired in the first place. They are left in lower productivity jobs paying lower wages elsewhere.

CASE 2: All Industries Are Covered by the Minimum Wage

The result in this case is the same in many respects. The winners are those who retain their jobs, where—as the losers are those who do not. There is now one important difference, however. Those who lose their jobs do not get jobs elsewhere. Because the whole economy is covered, there are no other jobs for them to get. Because they become unemployed, they lose far more than they do in case 1. Moreover, the overall efficiency loss to the economy is greater because their lost output is no longer partially offset by their output in other, lower productivity jobs. They don't get another job. The result is a large gap between the income of those who still have a job (whose wage has increased) and those who no longer have a job (whose wage has disappeared).

Since much, but not all, of U.S. employment is subject to the minimum wage, the world in which we live lies somewhere between case 1 and case 2. It is likely that some workers who lose their jobs because of a minimum wage will get lower productivity jobs elsewhere, but some will not. For those who obtain jobs elsewhere, there is an efficiency loss because they produce less. For those who remain unemployed, there is an even greater efficiency loss because they produce nothing.

THE MINIMUM WAGE AND TEENAGE UNEMPLOYMENT

Who are the workers who lose their jobs? The answer is often teenagers. Because they lack work experience and seniority, they tend to be the "last hired, first fired." Consequently, their unemployment rate is more than double the national average. *Minority* teenagers get the worst of both worlds; their unemployment rate is more than four times the national average. The University of Michigan's Charles Brown estimates that an increase in the minimum wage to $4.55 would result in 150,000 fewer jobs for teenagers over three years, with black teenagers suffering most.

One way to reduce the teenage unemployment problem is to institute a "two-tiered system," with a lower minimum wage for teenagers than for adults. Numerous such proposals have come before Congress. Indeed, since 1961 employers in higher education, retailing, and other services have been allowed to pay students 15% less than the minimum wage for part-time or summer work.[5] In 1989, President Bush proposed a lower minimum wage for new workers—many of whom are teenagers—during a six-month training period. Such proposals for a two-tiered minimum wage have been opposed by labor unions on the grounds that they are not fair. Employers might lay off adults with families to support in order to hire teenagers at a lower wage.

THE MINIMUM WAGE: Concluding Observation

The minimum wage can affect not only the wage of the unskilled, but it can also have a "ripple effect" in raising the wage of skilled workers who are above the minimum. The reason is that employers have sometimes regarded it as only fair to maintain a gap between the two wage levels, and workers have tried hard to maintain this gap by bargaining for increases in skilled wages whenever the minimum wage has been increased.

On the other hand, there are several reasons for believing that the minimum wage is less important than is often supposed.

1. *It has not been very effective in reducing inequality.* The reason is that it has raised the income, not just of the working poor, but of the non-poor as well. One estimate indicates that less than 20% of the benefits from an increased minimum wage would go to households living below the poverty line for a family of four. At the same time, over 60% of the benefits would go to households with incomes at least double the poverty level. (In many such cases, it would be teenage children still holding jobs who would benefit.)
2. *The minimum wage may* be less *damaging to efficiency than Figure* 21-6*c suggests.* It is true that, in perfect competition, the minimum wage does lead to the efficiency loss shown in that diagram. However, in the imperfectly competitive labor markets, it may lead to an efficiency gain.
3. *There are fewer clear winners and clear losers than the standard analysis implies.* It is frequently difficult to distinguish between the winners who get the minimum wage jobs and the losers who do, not. The reason is that, in minimum wage jobs, there is a high turnover rate (according to one estimate, over 12% *per month).* Therefore workers share these jobs to some extent. Accordingly, many individuals are both part-time winners (when they have one of the minimum wage jobs) *and* part-time losers (when they do not). This means that the concern about clear losers who end up without any jobs at all is sometimes exaggerated. It also means that there are fewer clear winners. Moreover, even for a "winner" who still has a job and has gotten a wage increase, part of this increase may be an illusion if employers who' have to pay the higher wage cover this additional cost by cutting back oh other benefits to labor such as on-the-job training.

Case in Point

MINIMUM WAGES

By Joseph Stiglitz and Carl Walsh

Legislating a minimum wage below which it is illegal to hire workers has been sharply criticized by economists as hurting exactly the people it is designed to help-those at the bottom of the wage scale.

Critics base their reasoning on the traditional demand and supply model of Part Two. There, an increase in wages above the market equilibrium results in lower employment. Those who manage to get jobs are better off; those who are forced into unemployment are worse off. If the objective is to reduce poverty, the minimum wage, from this perspective, seems counterproductive.

But as this chapter has pointed out, markets for labor are different from markets for many other commodities. Workers have to be motivated to work hard. High wages lead to increased productivity, less absenteeism, and lower labor turnover. Presumably, rational firms would take these consequences into account in setting wages. Even so, if the government forces firms to pay higher wages through minimum wage legislation, the increased productivity may largely offset the increased wages, making the employment effect very small.

In labor markets in which there is imperfect competition, minimum wages could actually lead to increased employment. Because of imperfect mobility, firms face an upward-sloping supply curve. Since all workers in a similar job have to be treated the same, the cost of hiring an additional worker may be much higher than the new employee's salary. Not only must the firm raise the wage offered to the *new* worker, it must also raise the wage paid to all existing workers. This cost discourages the firm from hiring additional employees. The imposition of a minimum wage limits the expense of hiring an additional worker to just that employee's wage. And because their marginal cost of adding to their workforce is lower, firms that are required to pay a minimum wage in fact will hire more workers.

These perspectives are consistent with several recent empirical studies that have shown there to be negligible, or even positive, employment effects from a minimum wage.

Some economists have also pointed to broader positive consequences of minimum wages: they induce firms to invest more in their workers in order to increase their workers' productivity. Gavin Wright, a distinguished economic historian at Stanford University, has argued that minimum wages played a vital role in the transformation of the South. It was a region that had been vastly poorer than the North from the end of the Civil War to the Great Depression, and its economy had been largely based on very low wages. The minimum wage catalyzed dramatic changes, shifting the South away from low wage industries to dynamic industries paying higher wages.

A further alleged advantage of raising the minimum wage is that it increases the incentive to work by increasing the income gap between someone on welfare and someone with a job.

IN-CLASS PROJECT

Immigrant Labor Market

By David Moglen

This project further applies your skills with price controls by taking the market for (legal and illegal) immigrant labor as an example of a market with both a quota (the limited number of immigration visas) and a minimum wage that is actually a binding price floor.

Notice the market is specified as entry-level immigrant labor. Highly-skilled or moderately skilled workers are not subject to a binding minimum wage, as explained the Unlocking the Mysteries: Minimum Wage feature.

Directions:

Everyone should answer all four questions.

1. If the visa quota and the minimum wage are both enforced, what is the wage and number of workers employed?
2. If only the visa quota is enforced, what is the wage and number of workers employed?
3. If only the minimum wage is enforced, what is the wage and number of workers employed?
4. If neither visa quota nor minimum wage are enforced, what is the wage and number of workers employed?

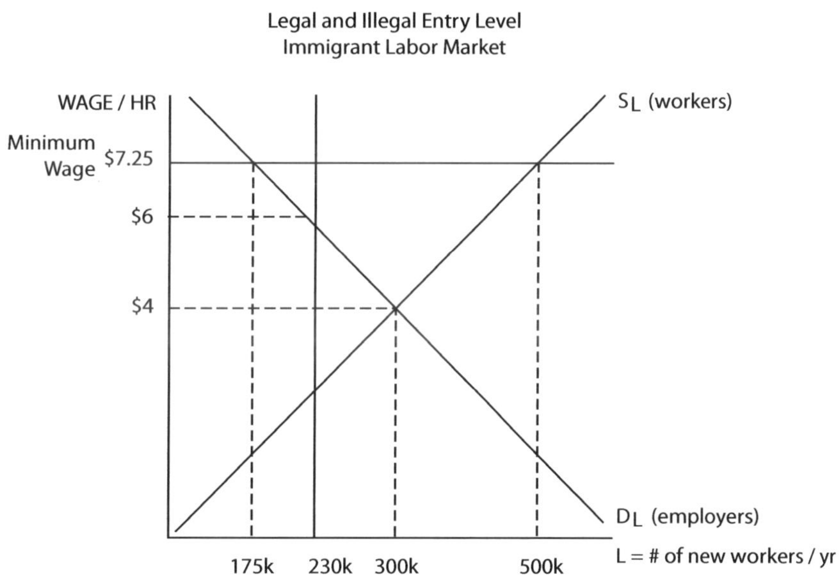

CHAPTER 6
Business Cycles

6 Business Cycles

Employment and Unemployment

By Neva Goodwin, Julie Nelson, and Johnathan Harris

Along with the growth rate of GDP, the rate of unemployment is one of the official measures of macroeconomic performance most discussed in the media, by policymakers, by business leaders, and by economists. Like the other indicators discussed in Chapters 5 and 6, the official unemployment rate is interesting because, in a crude way, it measures something about human well-being—or, in this case, ill-being.

Although some level of unemployment is unavoidable in a changing economy, a high rate of unemployment is a bad thing. Partly this is because high unemployment represents an inefficient utilization of national resources. The economy could be more productive if idle labor resources were put to work.

More dramatically, however, the experience of wanting and needing a job, but not being able to find one, can have a devastating effect on the job seekers themselves and on their families and communities. Besides the obvious strains and difficulties that accompany the loss of income, being unwanted by employers can be a profoundly unsettling experience in a society in which your identity is often tied up with "what you do." Higher rates of suicide, domestic violence, and depression often occur during periods of high and sustained unemployment. Social cohesion can also deteriorate when people feel marginalized from the mainstream of economic life.

How well is this social distress captured in official measures of employment and unemployment? What are some of the causes of unemployment How has unemployment varied over time? How has the nature of work changed in recent decades, and what will the future hold? These are the questions we will discuss in this chapter.

1. Measuring Employment and Unemployment

The U.S. Bureau of Labor Statistics (BLS), collects and publishes information on employment and unemployment. Every month, they interview

60,000 households, asking whether individual household members have jobs or are looking for work.[1]

Bureau of Labor Statistics (BLS): In the United States, the government agency that compiles and publishes employment and unemployment statistics

1.1 WHO IS "EMPLOYED"?

If you live in a U.S. household, you may someday get a telephone call from a BLS interviewer. After a few preliminaries he or she will ask you the questions shown in Box A of Figure 7.1. If you can answer "no" to *all* of these questions, you are part of the *civilian, noninstitutionalized, age sixteen and over population* about which this survey gathers data, and the interviewer will ask you questions about employment. If you answer any question in Box A "yes," the interviewer will not ask you about employment. Official employment and unemployment statistics do not include you. Trends in employment statistics over time, then, need to be analyzed in the light of considerations such as changes in age demographics, military policy, and rates of disability and incarceration.

If you are part of the surveyed population, you will then be asked the questions in Box B of Figure 7.1, starting with "Last week, did you do any work for pay or profit?"

Anyone who answers "yes" will be classified as **employed.** If you did *any* paid work last week—even if you worked for only an hour or two at a casual job—the interviewer will code you as "employed." If you answer "no," you will then be asked more questions. For example, if you have a paid job but just did not happen to put in any hours last week because you were sick, on vacation, or on certain kinds of leave, you will be coded as working and "employed." Also, if you did *un*paid work in a family-run business, such as a retail store or farm, you will be classified as "employed" as long as you worked in it more than fifteen hours a week.

employed person (BLS household survey definition): a person who did any work for pay or profit during the week before they are surveyed by the BLS or who worked fifteen hours or more in a family business

Note that the "family business" situation is the only case where unpaid work currently counts in the official statistics. If you work fewer

[1]Actually, the BLS publishes information from *two* surveys. In addition to the household survey, it collects data every month from nearly 400,000 employers. The information from the two surveys can sometimes point in different directions—for example, one survey may suggest a month-to-month gain in employment, while the other indicates a loss. Since employment growth is a politically sensitive topic, there is often debate about which set of numbers should be believed.

Table 7.1 Unemployment Rates for Different Groups

Group	Unemployment rate
All Workers	4.7
Race and ethnicity[a]	
White	4.2
Black or African American	8.5
Hispanic or Latino Ethnicity	5.6
Age	
Teenage (age 16–19)	15.6
Education	
Less than a high school diploma	7.3
Bachelor's degree and higher	2.1
Gender	
Adult Male	4.9
Adult Female	4.5

Source: BLS News: October 2007.
[a]People are allowed to indicate more than one racial group. However, data from people who indicated more than one race are not included in these statistics.

hours in your family business, or are, for example, occupied with caring for your children or other family members or doing community volunteer work, you will *not* be considered to be "employed." The BLS is currently seeking to improve its measures of people's productive activities, both paid and unpaid, by instituting a new "time use" survey. This survey gathers data on how much time people spend in activities including paid work, unpaid work taking care of home and family, unpaid volunteer work, and leisure. In the meantime, however, it is important to note that—based on a convention that originated with the first employment statistics collected in the 1940s—terms such as "labor," "work," and "employment" in official statistics generally refer to *paid* work only.

1.2 MEASURING UNEMPLOYMENT

If your answers to the household survey do *not* result in you being classified as "employed," you will be asked the questions about job search and availability shown in Box C of Figure 7.1. Activities such as contacting employers and sending out résumés count as "active" job search. Merely participating in a job training program or reading the want ads do not. The question about whether you could start a job probes to find out if, in fact, you are *available* for work. If, for example, you are a college student searching during April break for a summer job, but you aren't available to start the job until June, you would answer "no" to the availability question. If you can answer "yes" to *both* these questions you are classified as **unemployed.**

News in Context: New High in U.S. Prison Numbers

More than one in 100 adults in the United States is in jail or prison, an all-time high that is costing state governments nearly $50 billion a year and the federal government $5 billion more, according to a report released yesterday.

With more than 2.3 million people behind bars, the United States leads the world in both the number and percentage of residents it incarcerates, leaving far-more-populous China a distant second, according to a study by the nonpartisan Pew Center on the States.

The growth in prison population is largely because of tougher state and federal sentencing imposed since the mid-1980s. Minorities have been particularly affected …

Five states—Vermont, Michigan, Oregon, Connecticut and Delaware—now spend as much as or more on corrections as on higher education.

Source: N.C. Aizenman, *Washington Post*, February 29, 2008.

Do you think, in light of the very high incarceration rate in the United States, that official unemployment statistics are understated, overstated, or about right?

unemployed person (BLS definition): a person who is not employed, but who is actively seeking a job and who is immediately available for work

If you are either employed or unemployed, the BLS classifies you as part of the **labor force.** But what if you are neither "employed" nor "unemployed"? Then you are classified as **"not in the labor force."** Often people in this category are taking care of a home and family, in school, disabled, or retired.

labor force (BLS definition): made up of people who are employed or unemployed

"not in the labor force" (BLS definition): the classification given to people who are neither "employed" nor "unemployed"

Notice, in Figure 7.1, that the vast majority of U.S. residents who are not "employed" are either "not in the labor force" (about 79.5 million) or are not part of the surveyed population (about 70.8 million). In comparison, about 7.2 million people in this month, October 2007, were formally counted as "unemployed." (Figures are updated monthly at www.bls.gov.)

Every month, having made estimates of the number of employed and unemployed people in the country, the BLS calculates the official **unemployment rate.** This follows the formula:

$$\textit{unemployment rate} = \frac{\textit{number of people unemployed}}{\textit{number of people in the labour force}} \times 100$$

For example, in October 2007, looking at Figure 7.1 you can see that the BLS estimated that 146.0 million people were employed and

7.2 million people were unemployed. The unemployment rate was thus calculated as 4.7 percent:

$$unemployment\ rate = \frac{7.2\ million}{146.0\ million + 7.2\ million} \times 100 = 4.7\%$$

The unemployment rate represents the fraction of the officially defined labor force which is made up of people not currently working at paid jobs, but who are currently looking for and available for paid work.

unemployment rate: the percentage of the labor force made up of people who do not have paid jobs, but who are immediately available and actively looking for paid jobs

The unemployment rate reported in the media is often "seasonally adjusted." Over the course of a year, some swings in unemployment are pretty predictable. For example, agriculture and construction tend to employ fewer people in the cold winter months, and each year many students enter the labor force in June. The BLS releases "seasonally adjusted" figures that attempt to reflect only shifts in unemployment that are due to factors *other than* such seasonal patterns.

1.3 HOW PEOPLE ENTER AND EXIT UNEMPLOYMENT

Often, when we think of unemployed people, we think of someone who has lost their job—perhaps a friend or a relative who has been "downsized" from a position. Losing one's job, however, is not the only way of becoming unemployed.

The BLS classifies unemployed people according to four main reasons for unemployment:

- *Job losers* left their last job involuntarily;
- *Job leavers* have voluntarily quit their jobs;
- *Reentrants* are people who were in the labor force at some previous time, and have now joined it again after some period away;
- *Entrants* are people who have just joined the labor force for the first time.

On average, about half of the unemployed are job losers, although the proportions of the unemployed in each group varies over time. During recessions, people are more likely to have been laid off and less likely to want to voluntarily leave a job (since they are not sure they will find another) than in times of greater prosperity. Sometimes when one family member loses a job, other family members will enter (or reenter) the labor force in order to try to make up for the lost wages.

How do people *get out of* being unemployed? Obviously, one way is by getting a job. However, people can also leave unemployment by leaving the labor force. They may stop actively looking for work because they have decided to go to school or take care of children. Other people leave unemployment when they enlist in the military, go to jail (see News in Context), or die—thus moving out of the surveyed population. Some of these life changes may reflect deliberate, positive decisions. But some unemployed people may simply give up actively searching for work because they have had no success after months of looking.

1.4 DISCOURAGED WORKERS AND UNDEREMPLOYMENT

The fact that some "not in the labor force" people might want jobs but have given up looking for them has troubled employment analysts for some time. To the extent people give up on looking, the official unemployment rate *underestimates* people's need and desire for paid jobs.

In recent years, the BLS has added questions to the survey to try to determine how many people in the "not in the labor force" population may want employment, even if they are not currently searching for work. If someone says that they are available for work, want to work, and have looked for work recently even though they are not looking now, the BLS calls them "marginally attached workers." If they also say that the reason they are no longer looking is that they believe there are no jobs out there for them, they are called **discouraged workers.** They may have become discouraged because they believe their skills don't match available openings, because they have experienced discrimination, or because they have been turned away time after time.

discouraged workers: people who desire and are available for a job, but give discouragement as the reason for no longer looking for a job

But let's take a closer look at the people classified as "employed," too. In the BLS statistics a person is counted as "employed" if they do any paid work *at all* during the reference week, even if only for an hour or two. Some people prefer part-time work, of course, because of the time it leaves them for other activities such as schooling or family care. Some are limited to part-time work for health reasons. But others want and need full-time work, and are only settling for part-time work until they can find something better. The household survey asks people who work part-time about their reasons for doing so. In October 2007, 19.3 million people reported working fewer than thirty-five hours per week for reasons such as health or family responsibilities. In the same month, 4.3 million people reported working part-time for what the BLS calls "economic reasons"—that is, slack business conditions or because part-time work was all they could find.

What indicator, then, should we look at to see if the national employment situation is "bad" or "good"? The BLS now actually publishes various measures of labor underutilization that allow you to see the situation from a variety of different perspectives. For example, adding "marginally attached" workers and people who involuntarily work part-time to the number of unemployed, the rate of labor underutilization in October 2007 was 8.4 percent, as compared to the official unemployment rate of 4.7 percent.

The BLS also counts people as employed even if the kind of work they did does not begin to tap into their skills. Suppose you paint your aunt's living room for cash while you are waiting to hear back on job applications for management or computer positions. The BLS counts you as already employed. People who are working at jobs that underutilize their abilities, as well as those who work fewer hours than they like, can be said to be **underemployed.**

underemployment: working fewer hours than desired, and/or at a job that does not utilize one's skills

If we are concerned about human well-being, underemployment as well as unemployment should be of concern. While underemployment due to an underutilization of skills is certainly of considerable concern for both efficiency and quality-of-life reasons, official surveys do not currently attempt to measure this sort of underemployment.

DISCUSSION QUESTIONS

1. How would the BLS classify you, personally, on the basis of your activities last week? Can you think of an example where someone you would think of as *working* would not be considered by the BLS to be officially "employed"? Is it true that people who are *not working* are generally counted as "unemployed"?
2. Do you know anyone who is a "discouraged worker"? How about someone working part time "for economic reasons"?

2. TYPES OF UNEMPLOYMENT

While the BLS statisticians are mainly concerned with calculating the number of the unemployed, economists are more concerned with the cause of unemployment. Economists often apply a three-way categorization of types of unemployment, which—while abstract and not tightly related to BLS categories—can be helpful in thinking about some of the major causes of unemployment.

2.1 FRICTIONAL UNEMPLOYMENT

Frictional (or search) **unemployment** merely reflects people's transitions between jobs. The fact that some people are unemployed does not necessarily mean that there are no jobs available. In the fall of 2007, for example, while 7.2 million people were looking for jobs, there were also about 4.1 million job vacancies—that is, jobs looking for people! Even in a well-functioning economy, it may take many weeks for people and suitable jobs to find each other. An unemployment rate of zero percent could only happen if everyone who wants a job always takes one immediately—within a week. Not only is this unlikely, this is also in some ways undesirable. Taking the first job offered is often not the best thing for the person looking for the job, nor for the economy as a whole. Everybody benefits if people take the time to find good job matches—places where their skills and talents can be put to valuable use. Because information about job openings takes time to find, and employers may want to spend time interviewing and testing applicants, making a good job match is not an instantaneous process.

frictional unemployment: unemployment that arises as people are in transition between jobs

For the most part, economists don't worry too much about frictional unemployment, because some amount of frictional unemployment—say, 2 to 3 percent—is inevitable and much of it tends to be short-term. Things such as innovative Web technologies for matching job offers to job seekers may reduce frictional unemployment by reducing search time.

Many job seekers rely on state unemployment insurance programs to ease their income needs while they spend time searching for work. Unemployment compensation benefits are, in many states, set equal to half a worker's earnings or a state-set maximum (whichever is less). Workers who qualify can usually receive benefits for up to twenty-six weeks. Part of the justification for these programs is to allow people the time to make good matches.

2.2 STRUCTURAL UNEMPLOYMENT

Structural unemployment arises in an economy when a mismatch occurs between the kinds of jobs being offered by employers and the skills, experience, education, and/or geographical location of potential employees. One important cause of structural unemployment is sectoral shifts, such as will be described in Chapter 8, where employment in some sectors falls while employment in other sectors rises. The U.S. economy may have a lot of new jobs for financial analysts and nurses' aides in the Southwest, for example. But these won't do you much good if you live in the Northeast and have skills in engine assembly or Web design.

structural unemployment: unemployment that arises because people's skills, experience, education, and/or location do not match what employers need

On the positive side, structural unemployment arises from what economist Joseph Schumpeter (1883–1950) called "creative destruction." Schumpeter thought this was a good and necessary thing for capitalist economies. Technological and entrepreneurial innovations have often contributed to improved living standards, even though they cause some job opportunities to dry up. People skilled in outdated technologies—buggy-whip manufacturing is a classic example—necessarily become unemployed. Society could have tried to prevent unemployment in buggy-whip manufacturing by banning the introduction of the automobile, but the cost in economic growth would have been immense. If we, today, begin to move away from internal combustion engines due to their negative environmental impacts, the conventional auto industry will decline just as the buggy-whip industry declined at the end of the horse-and-buggy era. New technologies, new markets, and new concerns create new opportunities.

On the negative side, shifts in employment patterns by sector and industry are very disruptive, and often very painful, to the people who work in the declining sectors and to their families and communities. People in the declining sectors see the value of their specialized human capital depreciating rapidly. Whole towns and cities may become economically depressed when a major industry closes down, because the unemployed workers spend less at local businesses and property values plummet. Displaced workers *may* be able to train for a new career—especially if they are young and able to move to wherever the new jobs may be. But many displaced workers, particularly older ones, may never find the kind of pay and satisfaction that they had at their earlier occupations. Older displaced workers are more likely than younger ones to stay unemployed for long periods, or exit the labor force.

Governments at all levels have tried various policies to prevent or alleviate structural unemployment. The governments of some countries, notably Germany and Japan in the 1980s and 1990s, have followed industrial policies through which they directly encourage the development and retention of certain key industries through loans, subsidies, and tax credits. During negotiations on international trade (see Chapter 13), one sensitive issue is always the impact that increased trade might have on the employment levels in various industries in each country.

Government policies in the United States that target structural unemployment often focus on attempting to help displaced workers find new employment. For example, the Trade Adjustment Assistance Reform Act of 2002 provides benefits for certain workers displaced as a result of increased imports or the shifting of production to other countries. Workers who qualify for the program can receive retraining along with temporary income support payments and assistance with health insurance. The key feature of these programs is that they are targeted to particular workers, in particular sectors of the economy. There has been some question, however, as to whether they have actually been successful in getting displaced workers into new, good jobs. Business policies at the firm level are also relevant: Firms can help prevent structural unemployment if they make retaining and/or retraining their loyal employees a priority, even while responding to changes in technology and trade.

2.3 CYCLICAL UNEMPLOYMENT

Cyclical unemployment is unemployment due to macroeconomic fluctuations—specifically, unemployment that occurs due to a drop-off in aggregate demand. (As noted in Chapter 1, "aggregate demand" means the total demand for all goods and services in a national economy.) During recessions, unemployment rises as demand for the products of business falls off. During recoveries, this kind of unemployment should decrease.

cyclical unemployment: unemployment caused by a drop in aggregate demand

Traditionally, a **recession** has been defined as a case where GDP falls for two consecutive calendar quarters. Most economists look to the National Bureau of Economic Research (NBER), a nonprofit and nongovernmental economic research organization, to "officially" mark the beginning and end of recessions. The NBER determinations are strongly based on GDP data, though they also look at other indicators such as the levels of industrial production and wholesale-retail sales.

recession: traditionally defined as occurring when GDP falls for two consecutive calendar quarters, now "officially" marked by the National Bureau of Economic Research

Figure 7.2 shows the monthly unemployment rate in the United States from January 1969 to October 2007. Unemployment was at a low of 3.4 percent in 1969, and at a high of 10.8 percent in 1982. Notice in the figure that since 1982 the U.S. economy has apparently been characterized by less frequent and shorter recessions. However, while earlier recovery periods were characterized by immediate upswings in

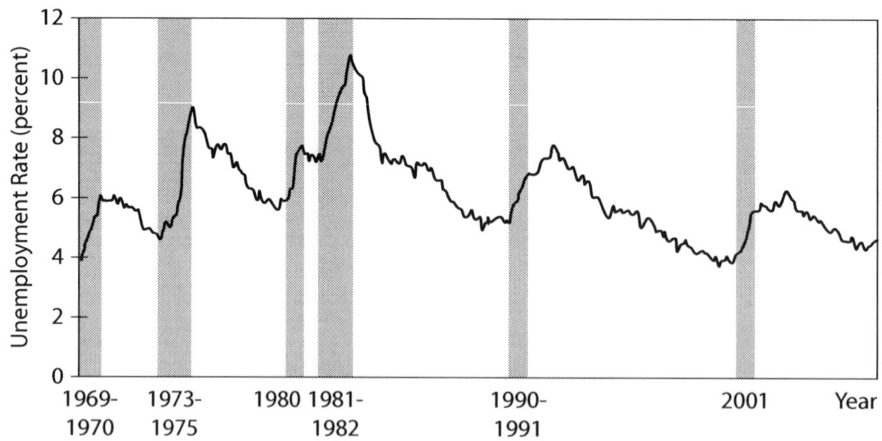

FIGURE 7.2

Unemployment Over the Business Cycle, U.S. 1969–2007

Unemployment rates rise during recessions (shown in grey). During the start of recent "recoveries," they have also continued to climb. (Source: U.S. BLS, Current Population Survey, and NBER.)

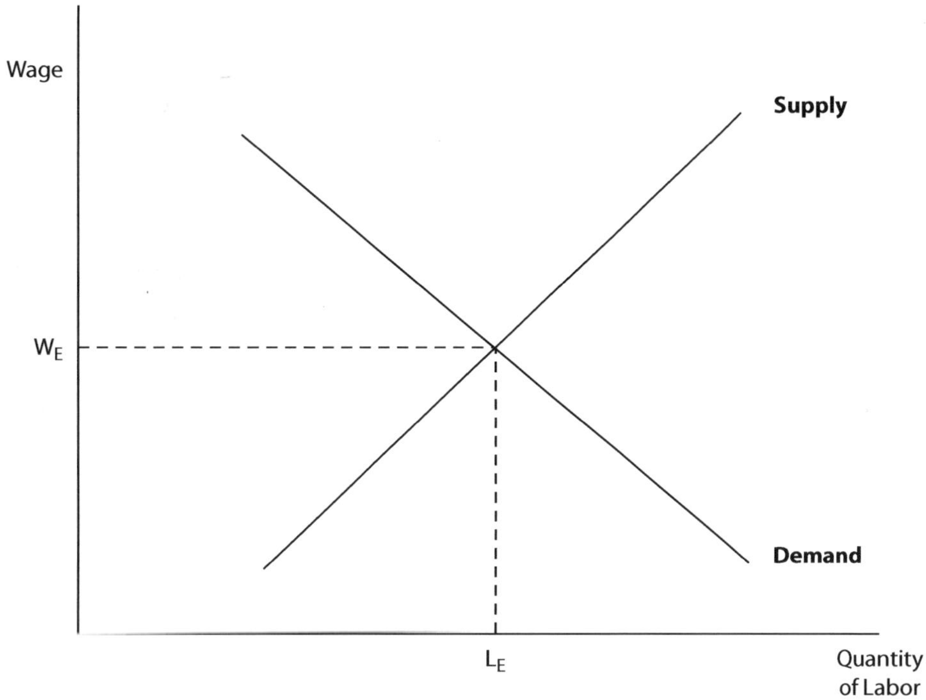

FIGURE 7.3

A Supply and Demand Model for Labor

In a smoothly functioning market, the equilibrium wage and quantity of labor would be set by market forces.

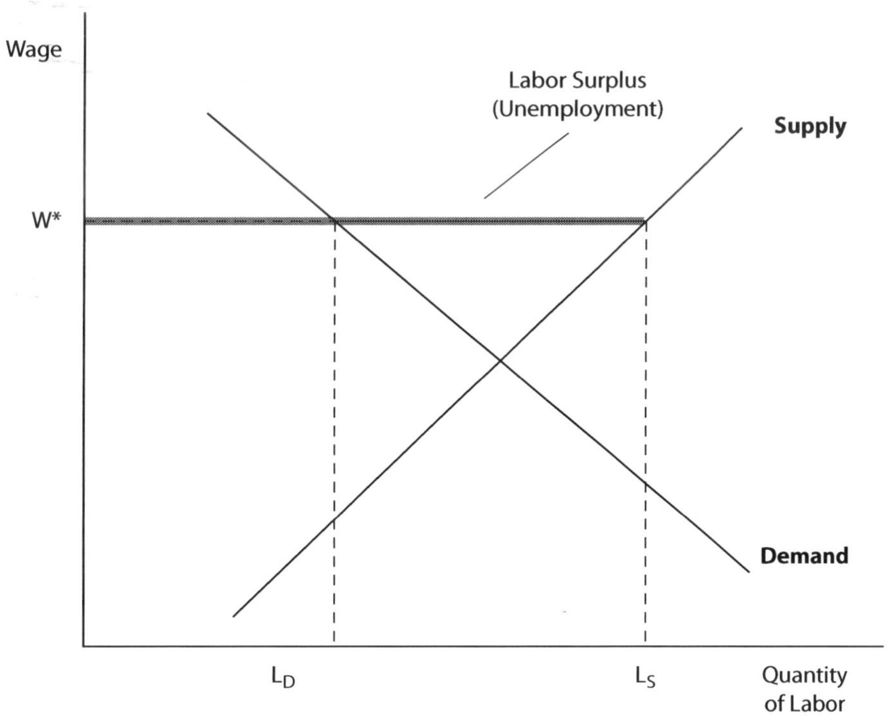

FIGURE 7.4

Classical Unemployment

In a classical (idealized) market for labor, the only thing that can cause true unemployment is something that interferes with the adjustments of free markets, such as a legal minimum wage.

employment, the recessions that NBER says ended in 1991 and 2001 were followed by continuing job slumps. The continued loss of jobs well into 2003, after the last recession, caused many commentators to call it the "jobless recovery." Apparently, while GDP grew, it grew too slowly to provide jobs for new entrants and keep up with increasing labor productivity. Is an economy really "recovering" if employment is still dropping or stagnating?

Not surprisingly, given that the field of macroeconomics was born out of the problems of the Great Depression, cyclical unemployment is of major concern to macroeconomists. While *structural* unemployment affects only some sectors of the economy and some amount of *frictional* unemployment seems inevitable, cyclical unemployment is spread broadly through the economy and can cause considerable economic hardship. For this reason, it seems that avoiding or minimizing cyclical unemployment should be an important goal of economic policy. Explanations of why macroeconomic fluctuations occur, and what kind of policies might be used to dampen them (and thus reduce cyclical unemployment) are discussed in Part Three of this book.

DISCUSSION QUESTIONS

1. Reflecting on the experience of you or someone you know, how long would you say it might normally take for someone to find a job in your area? Comparing your answers in a group, do you find different opinions? What might be some of the factors that make frictional unemployment last a longer or shorter period of time?
2. Do you know of places in your city or region (or nation) that have been particularly hard-hit by unemployment and underemployment, recently or in past decades? Do you know why this hardship occurred? Would you characterize this unemployment as frictional, structural, or cyclical?

3. THEORIES OF UNEMPLOYMENT

Why does unemployment arise, and what can be done about it? Economists favor different theories, depending on whether they take a more classical or a more Keynesian view.

3.1 THE CLASSICAL THEORY OF UNEMPLOYMENT

In classical economic theory, unemployment is seen as a sign that smooth labor market functioning is being obstructed in some way. The classical approach assumes that markets behave as described by the idealized supply-and-demand model presented in Chapter 4: The labor market is seen as though it were a single, static market, characterized by perfect competition, spot transactions, and institutions for double-auction bidding.

Such an abstract labor market is depicted in Figure 7.3. In Chapter 4 we examined markets for assets and produced goods, but in this case "quantity" is not measured as a number of *things* (such as apartments or swimsuits) but rather a quantity of labor *services.* We can think of this quantity as being measured, for example, by the number of workers working full days over a given time period. The "price" of labor is the (real) wage (in this case, per day). Workers supply labor, while employers demand it. We assume that every unit of labor services is the same, and every worker in this market will get exactly the same wage. The equilibrium wage in this example is W_E and the equilibrium quantity of labor supplied is at L_E.

Because the market pictured in Figure 7.3 is free to adjust, there is no involuntary unemployment. Everyone who wants a job at the going wage gets one. There may be many people who would offer their services on this market *if* the wage were higher—as the portion of the supply curve to the right of L_E demonstrates. But, given the currently offered wage rate, these people have made a rational choice not to participate in this labor market.

Within the classical model, the only way true, involuntary unemployment can exist is if something gets in the way of market forces. The presence of a legal minimum wage is commonly pointed to as one such factor. As illustrated in Figure 7.4, if employers are required to pay a minimum wage of W* ("W-star") that is above the equilibrium wage, this model predicts that they will hire fewer workers. At an artificially high wage W*, employers want to hire only L_D workers. But at that wage, L_S people want jobs. There is a situation of surplus, as we discussed in Chapter 4. The market is, in this case, prevented from adjusting to equilibrium by legal restrictions on employers. Now there are people who want a job at the going wage, but can't find one. That is, they are unemployed.

The minimum wage only affects a portion of the workforce, however—people who are relatively unskilled, including many teenagers. But unemployment tends to affect people at all wage levels. Classical economists suggest other "market interference" reasons for unemployment, as well. The economy might provide less than the optimal number of jobs, they believe, because:

- Regulations on, businesses reduce their growth, restricting growth in the demand for labor
- Labor-related regulations (such as safety regulations, mandated benefits, or restrictions on layoffs and firings) and labor union activities increase the cost of labor to businesses, causing them to turn toward labor-saving technologies and thus reducing job growth
- Public "safety net" policies such as disability insurance and unemployment insurance reduce employment by causing people to become less willing to seek work

Labor-market recommendations derived from a classical point of view tend to focus on getting rid of regulations and social programs that are seen as obstructing proper market behavior.

Like other classical proposals, such labor market proposals assume that the economy works best under the principle of laissez-faire—"leave it alone."

3.2 IMPERFECT LABOR MARKETS

The classical theory of labor markets depends on rapid market adjustment—in particular, the elimination of any labor surplus through falling wages and a resulting full-employment equilibrium at a lower wage rate. But is this realistic? John Maynard Keynes, reflecting on the experiences of the Great Depression, pointed out that certain aspects of real-world human psychology and institutions make it unlikely that wages will fall quickly in response to a labor surplus. No one likes to feel that they are losing something. (How would you feel if your boss told you she was *cutting* your wage?) Employers may be slow to reduce wages because they fear that workers will strongly resist such a move—perhaps with strikes, mass demonstrations, or even violence.

As the classical-Keynesian synthesis (introduced in Chapter 1) took form, many economists came to favor a more Keynesian explanation for cyclical unemployment. Given enough time, they argued, markets might be able to adjust as described in the classical model. But Keynesian-oriented economists also developed **"sticky wage" theories,** which hypothesize that wages may stay at a level above equilibrium for some time. Wages may eventually adjust in the way shown in the classical model, but too slowly to keep the labor market always in equilibrium.

"sticky wage" theories: theories about why wages may stay at above-equilibrium levels, despite the existence of a labor surplus

In addition to psychological resistance to wage cuts, as mentioned above, a minimum wage might also make wages "sticky." Wages may also become set at particular levels by long-term contracts, such as many large employers negotiate with labor unions.

More recently, economists have also come up with other theories. One is that the efforts of "insiders" may contribute to keeping wages high. "Insiders" are people who already have jobs within an organization. Insiders may be able to keep their wages high by setting up various barriers that prevent their employer from dismissing them and hiring lower-priced "outsiders." Insiders may have contracts that specify a high wage and that make them difficult to fire. Or they may refuse to cooperate with new workers or harass them, reducing new workers' productivity. In the **insider-outsider theory,** employed workers use the power they derive from such labor turnover costs to keep their wages artificially high.

insider-outsider theory: the theory that "insider" workers who are already employed may have the power to prevent "outsider" workers from competing with them and lowering their wages

Yet another recently developed explanation is that employers may find it to their advantage to pay employees wages that are somewhat higher than would be strictly necessary to get them to work. Managers don't just offer "the going wage" and then sit back. They must attract, train, and motivate workers if their enterprise is to be productive. **Efficiency wage theory** suggests that paying higher-than-necessary wages may improve employee productivity. Workers may be healthier and better nourished, and therefore more able to do quality work, when they are better paid. (This is especially true when talking about wage rates at the low end of the scale.) Also, workers may quit less often if they know they are getting "a really good deal" from their employer than if they are getting barely enough to motivate them to take the job, or just the same as they could get anywhere else. A lower likelihood of quitting makes employees more valuable to an employer because the employer saves on the costs of training new workers. Workers may also work more efficiently if being caught shirking means potentially losing their "really good deal." If the higher-than-necessary efficiency wages creates a pool of unemployed people, this only further reinforces employees' incentives to work hard because then they will be even more afraid of losing their good jobs.

efficiency wage theory: the theory that an employer can motivate workers to put forth more effort by paying them somewhat more than what they could get elsewhere

In sum, in the classical-Keynesian synthesis, legally or contractually set wages, fear of worker unrest, the power of insiders, and efficiency wages are thought sometimes to cause wages to be "sticky." By making real-world labor markets work differently from the market pictured in the classical model, these phenomena mean that it is unrealistic to expect that labor markets can adjust rapidly to maintain full employment.

What sort of policies do "sticky wage" theories lead to? To the extent that unemployment is seen as a real problem in these theories, more government activity to relieve unemployment-related hardship may be proposed, such as the aggregate demand policies we will discuss in Part Three of this book, or programs of unemployment benefits or job creation. Some economists also argue that a moderate level of economy-wide price inflation tends to relieve some "sticky wage" unemployment. How could this be so? Suppose you are working for $12 per hour now, and your employer says he wants to cut your wage to $10 per hour. You would probably resist—especially if you see that other people are *not* suffering such wage cuts. But suppose, instead, that your wage stays at $12 per hour, and, over time, inflation reduces the purchasing power of your wage to $10 per hour (in terms of prices of the base year). Your *nominal* wage has stayed the same, but your *real* wage (and thus your real cost to your employer) has fallen. Since this has happened more subtlety—and is felt more economy-wide—than a cut in your personal nominal wage, you may not feel as compelled to resist. According to some theories, such a drop in the wage (in real terms) should cause employment to increase.

3.3 UNEMPLOYMENT AND AGGREGATE DEMAND

While Keynesian economics is often closely associated with "sticky wage" theories, Keynes' own critique of classical views (as explained in Chapter 19 of his 1936 book, *The General Theory*) actually went much farther. He questioned whether the theory of a smoothly functioning labor market, as portrayed in Figure 7.3, is really a good starting place for thinking about macroeconomics and unemployment. This view is carried forward today by a number of economists (who sometimes call themselves Keynesian, or also post-Keynesian or institutionalist).

Recall that the supply-and demand diagram, as we introduced it in Chapter 4, was meant to be a way of thinking about a single spot market in which a single, completely standardized good is being traded. But "the economy" as a whole is not just one smoothly functioning market in which prices move to equate quantity supplied and quantity demanded. It is made up of markets for potatoes and markets for health care, markets for steelworkers and markets for schoolteachers, markets for real estate and markets for credit, markets for goods and services to be delivered now and for goods and services to be delivered months (or longer) in the future—as well as nonmarket institutions and transfers of all sorts. All these arenas of economic action have their own institutional peculiarities, and all are interwoven by a network of flows of incomes and payments. Hence, economists who are critical of classical theory see diagrams such as Figure 7.3 and 7.4, which portray only an idealized, abstract, detached, and institutionless labor market, as fundamentally misleading and beside the point.

In the real world, where issues of motivation, labor relations, and power are important, even the classical idea that minimum wages cause substantial unemployment may be called into question. In a well-known study, economists David Card and Alan Krueger found that a moderate increase in the minimum wage in New Jersey did not cause low-wage employment to decline, and may even have increased it. The study came under fire from economists who believed (given graphs such as Figure 7.4) that such a result simply could not be true. But the classical world assumes perfect competition, whereas real-world employers may have enough power in the labor complicated than a simple supply-and-demand model suggests.

Keynes' own focus was on the level of aggregate demand in the economy, and on businesses expectations about future profitability (to be discussed more in Chapter 9). Keynes believed that even if wages *did* fall quickly in a number of labor markets, this might do more harm than good. To see why, examine Figure 7.5. Workers' incomes give them the

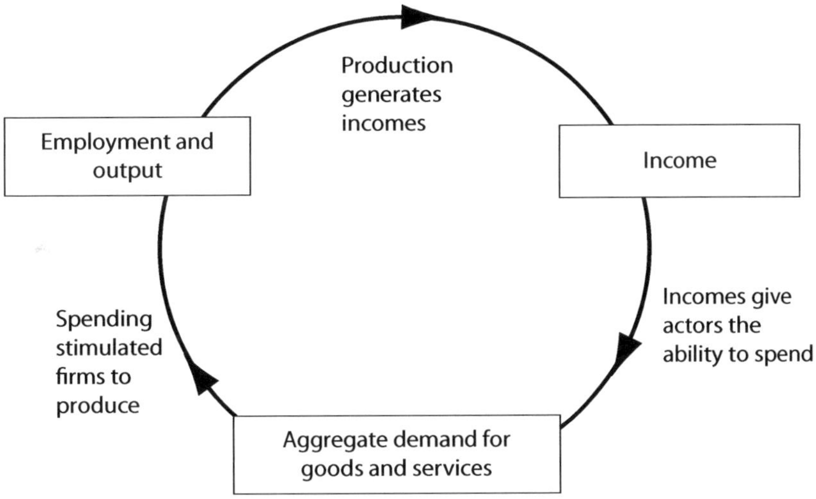

FIGURE 7.5

The Keynesian model of Employment Determination

In the Keynesian model, aggregate employment depends on the level of aggregate demand in the economy as a whole. If total spending is low, then employers will not want to produce a great deal because they do not want to end up with unsold goods. If production is low, they will not need many workers. If few workers are hired, then aggregate income will be low—in what can become a vicious cycle.

ability to spend on goods and services, and this spending stimulates firms to produce. The cycle is completed when this production in turn generation incomes. But what happens when wages fall? Workers who have lower wages will have less to spend, reducing demand for goods being produced by businesses all over the economy. If businesses cannot sell their goods, they will tend to cut back on their investments and on their number of workers. Prices as well as wages may fall (as was observed during the Great Depression), keeping real wages constant and thus giving employers no incentive to hire more workers. Low aggregate demand for goods and services could lead to a vicious cycle of unemployment, low incomes, and low spending in the economy as a whole.

Rather than blaming unemployment on "the wage being too high," as illustrated in a graph of a hypothetical unified national labor market, Keynes identified the cause of cyclical unemployment as *insufficient labor demand* in many individual labor markets, economy-wide, leading to a glut of workers overall. Fixing the problem of unemployment in a recession or depression, then, to Keynes and his followers, is not just a matter of making labor markets work more smoothly. Rather, aggregate demand in the economy has to be increased in order to stimulate hiring. Questions of aggregate demand and Keynesian policy will be taken up in Part Three of this book.

3.4 IS THERE A "NATURAL" RATE OF UNEMPLOYMENT?

Because of macroeconomists' special interest in cyclical unemployment, many have adopted a somewhat unfortunate term—the **"natural" rate**

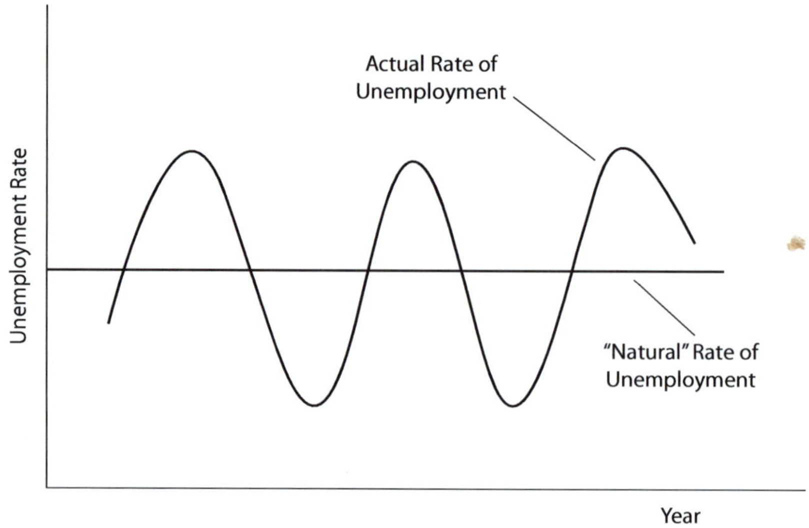

FIGURE 7.6

The "Natural" Rate of Unemployment

In this highly stylized graph, recessions cause unemployment to rise above its "natural" rate and booms cause unemployment to fall below it.

of unemployment—to describe the rate of unemployment *that they hypothesize would occur in the absence of cyclical fluctuations.* Figure 7.6 shows what might happen in a highly stylized business cycle in which actual unemployment fluctuates around a "natural rate." Booms are said to reduce unemployment below a stable "natural rate," and recessions to make unemployment rise above it.

"natural" rate of unemployment: the rate of unemployment that would prevail in the absence of business cycles, according to some theories

A related concept is that of the **non-accelerating inflation rate of unemployment (NAIRU).** This is conceptualized as the lowest rate of unemployment that can be maintained without causing the economy to "overheat." The concept of the NAIRU can best be understood by looking back at the Phillips curve graph we created in Chapter 2, reproduced as Figure 7.7. In this graph, you can see that inflation rises steadily but not dramatically as unemployment is reduced toward 4 percent. But as the unemployment rate passes below about 4 percent, the Phillips curve distinctly bends upward, with inflation rising more sharply from year to year. Since unemployment below about 4 percent seems to be associated with rapidly rising inflation, we could say that the NAIRU during 1963–69 appears to be about 4 percent, as represented in the graph by the vertical line.

non-accelerating inflation rate of unemployment (NAIRU): the lowest rate of unemployment that can be sustained without causing rapidly rising inflation

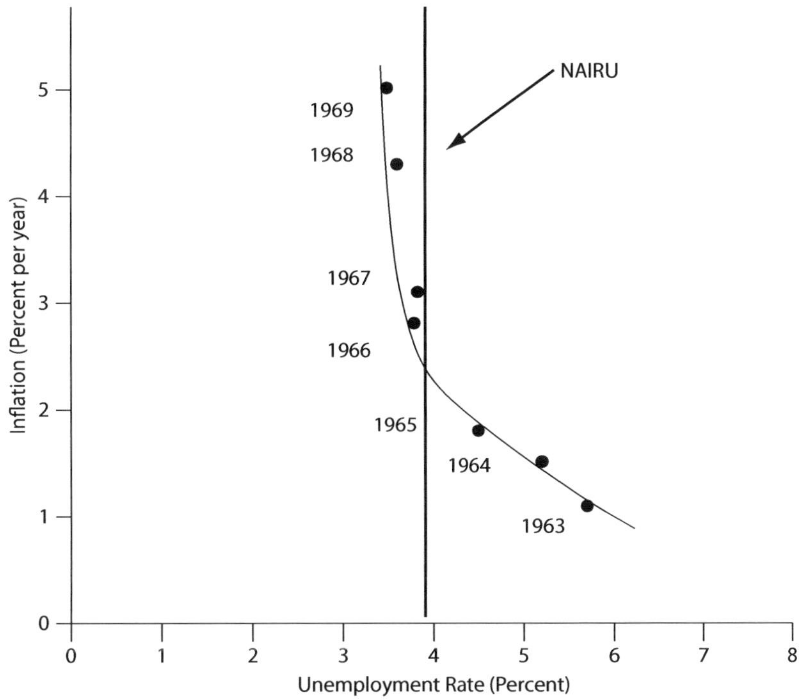

FIGURE 7.7

The Non-Accelerating Inflation Rate of Unemployment (NAIRU)

Very low rates of unemployment can be a sign of an "overheated" economy. During the 1963–69 period, it seems that an unemployment rate below about 4 percent was associated with accelerating inflation rates.

If the world were as simple these two figures suggest, the "natural" rate and the NAIRU would mean essentially the same thing. Unemployment higher than the NAIRU, like unemployment higher than the "natural" rate, would be associated with low production and a sluggish economy. Unemployment lower than NAIRU or "natural" rate would be associated with higher production and inflation.

But the world is not so simple. If you refer back to Figure 2.4 in Chapter 2, you will see that after 1969 the relation between inflation and unemployment doesn't look a bit like the Phillips curve in Figure 7.7. Over longer periods of time, it is clear that if a NAIRU exists at all, it certainly moves around. Some economists argue that NAIRU is a useful concept, even if it can be difficult to say just what number should be associated with it. Other economists believe the concept is no longer useful.

The concept of a "natural" rate has even more significant problems. First, the word "natural" sometimes leads people to think that there is something *right* or *inevitable* about unemployment at the "natural" rate—no matter how much *non*cyclical unemployment (such as structural unemployment from shifts in international trade) people may be suffering. Second, the concept reflects one particular theory, that of the classical school of macroeconomics. The inventor of the "natural rate of unemployment" concept was economist Milton Friedman, who was a great believer in the efficiency of market forces.

Second, as with the NAIRU, the study of history shows that it is very difficult to match a particular number with the "natural" rate idea. Figure 7.8 reproduces data from the previous section. You can see that the actual pattern is not the flat line suggested in theory in Figure 7.6. If we were to suppose that unemployment was fluctuating around *some* specific rate, it might appear that this rate climbs during the 1970s and then gently falls after the early 1980s, as illustrated in Figure 7.8. (This is one of many possibilities. Others might picture the "natural" rate rising in steps like a staircase, or in other patterns.)

A "natural" rate that changes over time is a slippery concept, however. A current unemployment rate of 5 percent would be considered excessive due to cyclical considerations if you believe that the "natural" rate is 4 percent. But the same rate would be considered to be a sign of a vibrant macroeconomy if you believe that the "natural" rate is 6 percent. Because of this problem, a number of economists do not believe that the "natural" rate concept is very useful.

While economists from the classical school believe that the economy will tend to return to an equilibrium position whenever it is pushed away, and thus favor the concept of a "natural" rate, other economists question whether an economy is really a stable system at all. Some economists, including John Maynard Keynes and Joseph Schumpeter, envisioned economies as more dynamic and evolving. While Keynes is often associated with a rather pro-government political stance, and Schumpeter with the more libertarian, small-government views held by adherents of the Austrian school of economics, both Keynes and Schumpeter stressed the inherent *instability* of economic systems. To them, factors such as uncertainty, innovation, institutions, and technological advance made economies quite unpredictable.

To use a hiking analogy, classically minded economists believe that the path of an economy is like a walking trail already laid out through the woods. While a hiker (economy) sometimes steps off the trail (diverges from the "natural" path), he always returns to it. The path of an economy as envisioned by Keynes and Schumpeter and others, on the other hand, is more akin to the path taken by a hiker who ventures into the unknown wilderness, creating the trail as she goes. As society and institutions evolve, these economists and their followers believe the economy can move in any direction, often quite unpredictably.

DISCUSSION QUESTIONS

1. Which arguments seem most convincing to you, those of classical labor market theorists, "sticky wage" theorists, or economists concerned with aggregate demand? What are some strengths and weaknesses of each argument? (Is one argument more elegant—that

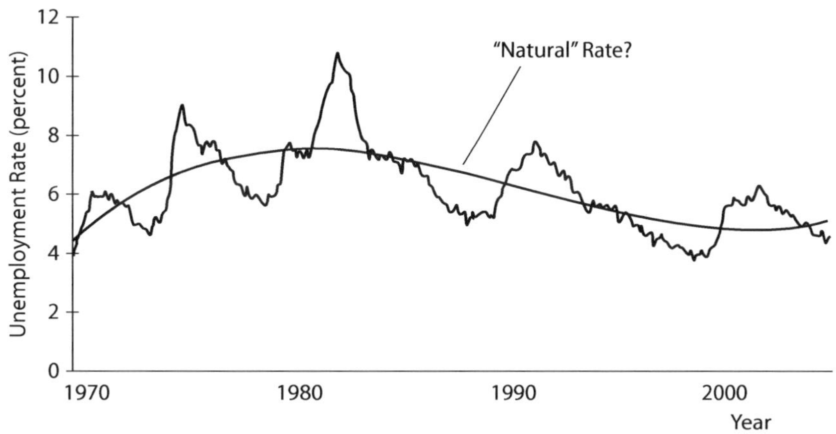

FIGURE 7.8

Empirical Data and the "Natural" Rate

Looking at real-world data, there does not seem to be any one constant rate around which unemployment fluctuates. In recent decades the "natural" rate might be considered to be anywhere from about 4 percent to over 7 percent. (Source: U.S. BLS, Current Population Survey.)

is, does it seem to explain a great deal with a minimum of fuss? Is one argument more realistic?)

2. Can you, looking at Figure 7.2 or 7.7, predict where the unemployment rate is headed next?

4. EMPLOYMENT, UNEMPLOYMENT, AND WELL-BEING

Because the world we live in is constantly changing, macroeconomics also has to adapt to take into account changes in the labor force, the changing the nature of work, and the evolution of people's goals regarding employment. This section looks at some of the current challenges to how we think about employment and unemployment issues on a national scale.

4.1 THE CHANGING LABOR FORCE

The labor laws and labor-related social policies that were enacted during and after the Great Depression made certain assumptions about what a "good job" was. Most workers were men, and the assumption was that men who were employed full time—perhaps with options for overtime hours as well—could provide for their families, and form the base of a solid, reliable workforce and a stable society. These assumptions influenced macroeconomic thinking, as well. Full-time employment of the male "breadwinner" was the explicit or implicit goal of employment policies.

Over the second half of the twentieth century, however, the composition of the labor force changed considerably. Women's labor force participation (LFP) rate rose dramatically, while men's LFP dipped. The labor force participation rate is calculated as

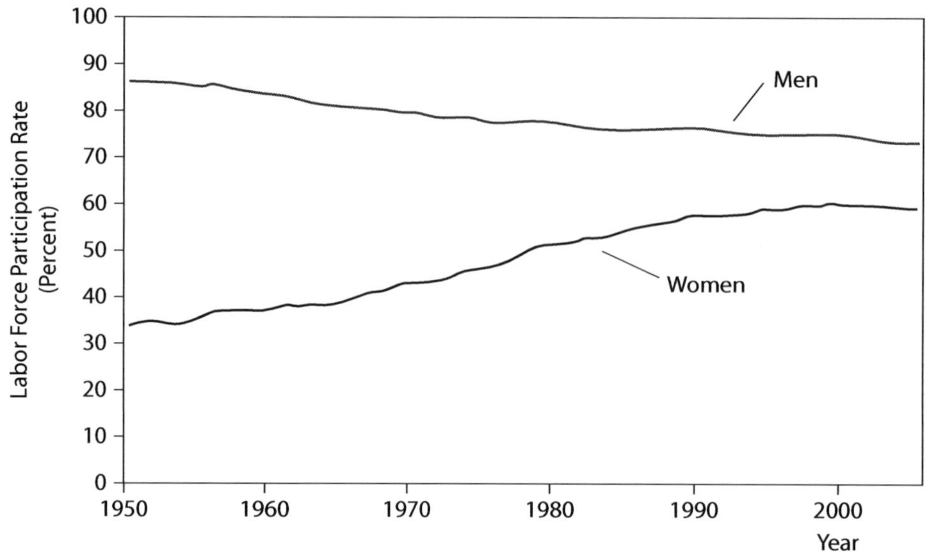

FIGURE 7.9

Labor Force Participation Rates by Sex, 195–2007

During the latter half of the twentieth century, women's rate of participation in paid labor market activities increased dramatically, while men's tapered off. (Source: U.S. BLS, Labor Force Statistics from the Current Population Survey, Historical Data)

$$\textit{labour force participation} = \frac{\textit{number of people in the labour force}}{\textit{number of people in the civilian noninstitutionalized age 16 and over population}} \# 100$$

The LFP rate indicates the fraction of potential paid workers who are either in paid jobs, or who are seeking and available for paid work. Figure 7.9 shows the labor force participation (LFP) rates of men and women (age sixteen and older). In 1950, many women worked only until they were married, or after their children were grown, so that women's LFP was only 34 percent. During the next four decades, women increasingly entered the labor market, until women's LFP rate flattened out at about 59–60 percent from the mid-1990s onward. The rise of the civil rights and women's movements during the 1960s and 1970s certainly contributed to this expansion in women's labor market activities. Some economists also point to expansion of the service sector (discussed in Chapter 8), reductions in the average number of children per family, and other factors to help explain this increase.

Men's LFP, meanwhile, dropped from 86 percent in 1950 to 73 percent in recent years. Tendencies such as increased time spent in schooling before beginning work, and earlier retirement from work, explain some of this change. In 1950, 70 percent of the people in the labor force were male; now, the figure is only 54 percent.

The labor force has changed in other ways as well. In 1975, Hispanics or Latinos made up only about 4 percent of the U.S. labor force. Currently, this statistic is 13 percent.

4.2 THE CHANGING NATURE OF WORK

For most of the twentieth century, people often thought of "a job" (or at least *a good* job) as something you typically did Monday through Friday, forty hours a week, for a wage or salary and benefits (such as health insurance and pension plans). People often expected to stay in the same job for years, or even decades. In recent years, it has become popular to talk about how employment is becoming more "flexible." The term "flexibility" has two very different meanings in the context of macroeconomics and labor economics, however.

One meaning of "flexible" work is work that is more suited to people's varying needs, especially given family constraints, desires to get an education, and so on. Some workers—especially professional and managerial workers—now enjoy "flextime" or the ability to set their starting and ending times. Job-sharing and part-time work allow employment to be more easily combined with family care, studying, or leisure pursuits. It is still the case, however, that many jobs are inflexible and not "family friendly." The United States is practically alone among industrial nations in not offering paid job-guaranteed leaves for new parents. A lack of flexibility creates problems for people who want "good jobs" with good pay and promotion opportunities, but who want to be able to pursue other life goals and make other important contributions as well. The term "flexibility" can also refer to people's ability to change jobs when they want to, or retrain for new careers.

But the term "flexibility" has also been used to refer to policies that make things easier for employers—and often make life more difficult from a worker's perspective. Many employers would like to be able to have complete discretion over setting their workers' hours and pay, to be able to terminate employees quickly and without fuss, and to offer little in the way of benefits. Increasingly, some firms have hired "independent contractors" or "consultants," or part-time workers, to avoid having to pay the benefits that they pay their regular full-time employees. More people now work non-standard workweeks, whether they want to or not, in an economy that is increasingly "24/7" (twenty-four hours a day, seven days a week). Given short hours and low pay, some workers find themselves working two or more part-time jobs to get by.

Since labor unions often try to block such "flexibilization" of work by bargaining for guaranteed hours, increased benefits, and assurances of job security, the reduction in union power is one component of this phenomenon. Union membership topped out at about one-third of the workforce in the mid-1950s, with significant membership from private industry. Currently, only about 13 percent of workers are union members, and many of these are public sector employees such as teachers, police, and firefighters.

To some extent, "flexibility" from the employee's perspective is also in the interest of employers. Workers who are better rested and less stressed about their families, because of accommodating schedules and expectations, can be more productive. And to some extent, "flexibility" from the employer's perspective is also in the workers' interest.

An overly rigid labor market, in which workers are too expensive and difficult to fire, could cause employers to try to minimize the number of workers they must hire, thus reducing the number of jobs. From a well-being perspective, the question is how a good balance can be achieved.

Another aspect of work patterns that has changed substantially in the last few decades is the pattern of *hours* of work. While some observers claim that people in the United States are now working increased hours, and others claim that we are now benefiting from increased leisure, the *average* workweek has, in fact, changed little in the last thirty or so years. What has happened, however, is that some *groups* of people are increasingly working very long hours, and others very short hours, so that there are now more people at both extreme ends of the spectrum.

In 2000, 26.5 percent of employed men and 11.3 percent of employed women worked fifty or more hours per week, up from 21 percent and 5.2 percent, respectively, in 1970. Often people in this group are professionals or managers with heavy job responsibilities. People in such job categories usually receive fringe benefits from their employers—but do not, by law, have to be paid extra when they work overtime. On the other hand, the number of people working *short* hours has also been increasing. In 2000, 8.6 percent of employed men and 19.6 percent of employed women worked thirty hours a week or less, up from 4.5 percent and 15.5 percent in 1970. Often these employees are in hourly wage jobs where overtime pay would be required by law (if the employers would offer the extra hours). Part time workers are less likely than full time workers to be offered fringe benefits.

Is the increasing divergence in the hours that people work evidence that they are now able to tailor their workweeks to their own convenience? Or that their employers are making them work too much, on the one hand, or offering so little work that they find it hard to get by financially, on the other? Survey evidence suggests that, in many cases, it is the latter. Jerry A. Jacobs and Kathleen Gerson, in their book *The Time Divide,* report that "Those who work few hours on average prefer to work more, while those who work many hours on average prefer to work less."[2] In one survey, 80 percent of men and 90 percent of women working over fifty hours per week stated that they would prefer to work less. Those who worked between fifty and sixty hours stated that, on an average, they would prefer thirteen fewer hours. On the other hand, many people working short hours wanted to work more. Most people tend to prefer workweeks between twenty-five and forty hours.

This is important when thinking about the macroeconomics of labor markets, since any given number of total employment hours can have very different well-being consequences depending on how the hours are spread across the population of workers. One case would be an economy in which some groups of people work very long hours, while other people are unemployed or underemployed. Another case would be where working hours are distributed more evenly, allowing workers to have time for family care while reducing the number of unemployed.

Several countries in Europe have moved toward shorter standard working hours, often for macroeconomic reasons of reducing unemployment, but also to encourage strong families and to reduce consumption for ecological reasons. Most European countries have legal limits on the number of hours per week an employee is allowed to work, and vacation time of at least one month per year is standard—even for workers who are just starting out. Because of these different patterns of employment, a typical full-time worker in Europe now works an average of about two hundred hours (the equivalent of five forty-hour weeks) less per year than a full-time worker in the United States.

4.3 CONCLUDING THOUGHTS

Whether an economy is able to generate and sustain "good jobs" (and good families and communities) depends on the whole institutional structure and dynamics of the national economy. The actions of business, governmental units, nonprofits (including unions, industry associations, and universities) and households all work together to determine the numbers and types of jobs that are generated, the number of workers in the labor force, and the skills with which workers are equipped. The responses of a country's business leaders, policymakers, workers and consumers to natural resource constraints and to the challenges and opportunities offered by participation in global markets for goods, services, and finance further significantly impact the employment situation. Studying macroeconomics only begins to equip one for addressing these challenges.

REVIEW QUESTIONS

1. What population is included in the official household survey that measures employment and unemployment?
2. What questions are asked to determine if someone is "employed"?
3. What makes a person count as "unemployed"?
4. How is the unemployment rate calculated?
5. What groups tend to have particularly high unemployment rates? Particularly low rates?
6. List four ways a person may enter unemployment.
7. What are "discouraged workers," and why are they of concern?
8. List the three types of unemployment, and describe them.
9. What policies may be used to combat frictional and structural unemployment?
10. Describe the classical theory of unemployment.
11. What are some of the reasons an economy might offer less than the optimal number of jobs, according to classical theory?
12. Describe how "sticky wages" could lead to unemployment.
13. What are some reasons that wages might be "sticky"?
14. Explain the "insider-outsider" theory of sticky wages.
15. What are "efficiency wages," and why might payment of them lead to unemployment?
16. On what grounds do some economists criticize classical and "sticky wage" theories?

17. In the Keynesian model of employment determination, what is the key factor explaining the level of employment in an economy?
18. Compare and contrast the concepts of the "natural rate of unemployment" and the "non-accelerating inflation rate of unemployment."
19. What are some problems with the "natural" rate and NAIRU concepts?
20. How is the labor force participation rate calculated?
21. What have been some of the major changes in the characteristics of the labor force over the last several decades?
22. What sorts of "flexibility" are good for workers? For employers?
23. How has the number of hours worked by different groups changed over the last few decades?

EXERCISES

1. The small nation of Neverland counts its unemployed using the same methods as the United States. Of the population of 350 people, seventy are under age sixteen, 190 are employed in paid work, and eighty are adults who are not doing paid work or looking for work because they are doing full-time family care, are retired or disabled, or are in school. The rest are unemployed. (No one is institutionalized, and the country has no military.) Calculate the following:
   a. The number of unemployed.
   b. The size of the labor force
   c. The unemployment rate
   d. The labor force participation rate (overall, for both sexes)
2. The population of Tattoonia is very small. Luis works for pay, full-time. Robin works one shift a week as counter help at a fast-food restaurant. Sheila is retired. Shawna does not work for pay, but is thinking about getting a job and has been flipping through the want ads to see what is available. Bob has given up looking for work, after months of not finding anything. Ana, the only child in the country, is twelve years old.

   a. How would a household survey, following U.S. methods, classify each person?

   b. What is the labor force participation rate in Tatoonia?

   c. What is the unemployment rate in Tatoonia?
3. Suppose an economy is suffering unemployment due to "too high" wages, as theorized by classical economists.

   a. Draw and numerically label a graph illustrating this case, in which the going wage is $20, the equilibrium wage is $15, fifty million people want to work, but only thirty million are employed.

   b. Describe some of the assumptions about labor markets that underlie this graph.
4. A computer software company advertises for employees, saying "We offer the best-paid jobs in the industry!" But why would any company want to pay more than it absolutely *has to, to* get workers? Can this phenomenon help to explain the existence of unemployment? Explain in a paragraph.

5. Match each concept in Column A with a definition or example in Column B.

Column A	Column B
a. "Not in the labor force"	1. The theory that unemployment is caused by insufficient aggregate demand
b. "Sticky wage" theory	2. The lowest unemployment rate, in theory, consistent with inflation that does not rapidly rise
c. Jobless recovery	3. A theory proposed by Milton Friedman
d. Frictional unemployment	4. Occurs when the skills, experience, and education of workers do not match job openings
c. Employed	5. The theory that people who already hold jobs may set up barriers that keep employment from expanding
f. Trade Adjustment Assistance Reform Act	6. Immediately available for and currently looking for paid work
g. Unemployed	7. Military personnel
h. Keynes' alternative to theories that say that unemployment is caused by high wages	8. A policy response to structural unemployment
i Structural unemployment	9. Worked 15 hours or more in a family business
j. Insider-outsider theory	10. Occurs as people move between jobs
k. Natural rate of unemployment	11. When GDP rises but employment does not
l. Not included in the household survey covering employment	12. The theory that unemployment may occur because wages are slow to fall
m. Reentrant	13. Someone who joins the labor force after some period away from it
n. NAIRU	14. A retired person

6. Locate the most recent news release on employment and unemployment statistics at the Bureau of Labor Statistics website (*www.bls.gov*). In a paragraph, describe how the labor force, overall unemployment rate, and unemployment rates by race and ethnicity, age, and education differ from the numbers (for October 2007) given in the text.

NOTES

1. The data in this section are from Jerry A. Jacobs and Kathleen Gerson, *The Time Divide: Work, Family, and Gender Inequality* (Cambridge: Harvard University Press, 2004).
2. Jacobs and Gerson, *The Time Divide*, pp. 65–66.

Unemployment

By Joseph Stiglitz and Carl Walsh

While increasing living standards is the central economic goal over the long run, when the economy goes into a downturn, unemployment becomes a source of immediate concern. To an economist, unemployment represents an underutilization of resources. People who are willing and able to work are not being productively employed. To the unemployed individuals and their families, unemployment represents economic hardship and changes in their way of life. If a person is unemployed for a long time, he will be unable to meet his current expenses—like utilities and rent—and will have to move to cheaper housing and reduce other aspects of his standard of living.

Unemployment not only costs individuals their paychecks, it can deal a powerful blow to their self-respect. Unemployed workers in today's urban America cannot fall back on farming or living off the land as they might have done in colonial times. Instead, they and their families may be forced to choose between poverty and the bitter taste of government or private charity. Many of these families break up under the strain.

Unemployment presents different problems for each age group of workers. For the young, having a job is necessary for developing job skills, whether they are technical skills or such basic work prerequisites as punctuality and responsibility. Persistent unemployment for them not only wastes valuable human resources today but also reduces the future productivity of the labor force. Individuals fail to obtain critical on-the-job training that improves their skills, and to develop work habits that improve their on-the-job productivity. Furthermore, young people who remain unemployed for an extended period are especially prone to becoming alienated from society and turning to anti-social activities such as crime and drug abuse.

For the middle-aged or elderly worker, losing a job poses different problems. Despite federal and state prohibitions against age discrimination, employers are often hesitant to hire an older worker. They may fear she is more likely than a younger person to become sick or disabled. They may worry about being able to "teach old dogs new tricks." If older workers are unemployed for long periods of time, they may have lost some of their skills. Even if the unemployed older worker succeeds in getting a job, it often entails reduced wages and lower status than in her previous job and may make less than full use of her skills. The toll of such changes is a heavy burden of stress on the dislocated worker and her family.

In addition to these personal losses, unemployment poses heavy costs for communities. If people in a town are thrown out of work—say, because a big employer closes down or decides to move—everyone else in town is likely to suffer as well, since there will be fewer dollars circulating to buy everything from cars and houses to gasoline and groceries. As more unemployment results in fewer people paying local taxes, the quality of schools, libraries, parks, and police can be threatened.

Unemployment may also reinforce racial divisions in society as a whole. The rate of unemployment for blacks is generally more than twice that for whites. During the 1980s and early 1990s, among blacks between the ages of sixteen and nineteen who were just beginning to look for work, unemployment averaged 37 percent, nearly reaching 50 percent in the recession years of 1982 to 1983.

Unemployment represents a tragedy for the individual and the family a source of dislocation and stress for a community, and a waste of productive resources for society as a whole.

THE MAGNITUDE OF THE PROBLEM

Living in the midst of the approximately 125 million people who get up and go to work every morning is a fluctuating group of several million healthy people who do not. During the recession year of 1991, 8.5 million people were out of work, and one-fourth of those people were jobless for fifteen weeks or more. From the standpoint of the economy as a whole, the potential production of workers who cannot find jobs is a major loss. One calculation puts the loss in output from the high unemployment of the early 1980s at between $122 billion and $320 billion a year, for a per capita loss of between $500 and somewhat more than $1,300. In other words, using the latter number, every man, woman, and child in the United States would have had (on average) an additional $1,300 to spend if the unemployed workers had been gainfully employed.

UNEMPLOYMENT STATISTICS

In the United States, unemployment data are collected by the Department of Labor, which surveys a representative mix of households and asks each whether a member of the household is currently seeking employment. The unemployment rate is the ratio of the number seeking employment to the total labor force. If there are 120 million Americans employed and 10 million say they are looking for a job but cannot find one, then the total labor force is 130 million, and the

$$\text{unemployment rate} = \frac{\text{number unemployed}}{\text{labor force}}$$

$$= \frac{\text{number unemployed}}{\text{number employed} + \text{number unemployed}}$$

$$= \frac{\text{10 million}}{\text{120 million} + \text{10 million}} = 7.7 \text{ percent.}$$

Figure 4.4 plots the unemployment rate for the United States since 1960. The figure illustrates two facts. First, unemployment is persistent. Second, the level of unemployment can fluctuate dramatically. In the worst days of the Great Depression, over one quarter of the U.S. labor force was unemployed. The unemployment rate among those who worked in manufacturing was even worse—at one point, one out of three workers in manufacturing had lost their jobs. As recently as 1983, the unemployment rate in the United States was nearly 10 percent. The level of unemployment in the early 1990s, at 5.4 to 7.4 percent, while much lower than that of the early 1980s, is still higher than the rate that prevailed in the mid-1960s, around 4 percent.

Unemployment in other countries has often been worse than in the United States (Figure 4.5). In European countries, it reached over 10 percent during much of the 1980s, and in many developing countries over 20 percent.

FIGURE 4.4 OVERALL U.S. UNEMPLOYMENT RATE

Unemployment is persistent in the U.S. economy, rising during recessions and falling during booms, but never touching zero. Source: ERP (1996), Table B-37.

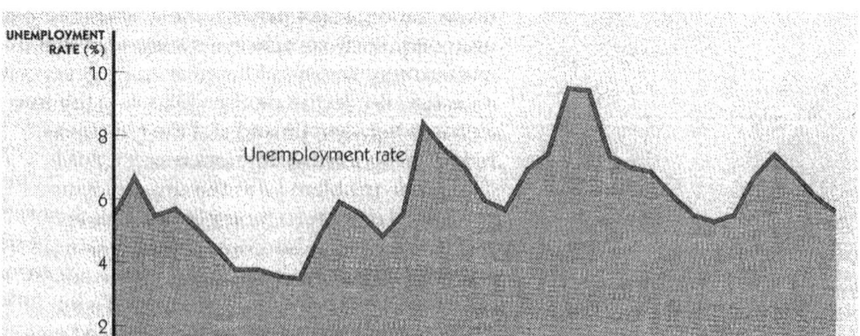

FIGURE 4.5 INTERNATIONAL UNEMPLOYMENT COMPARISONS

In other developed countries, the unemployment rate is often much higher than has been observed in the United States in recent years. Source: ERP(1996), Table B-105.

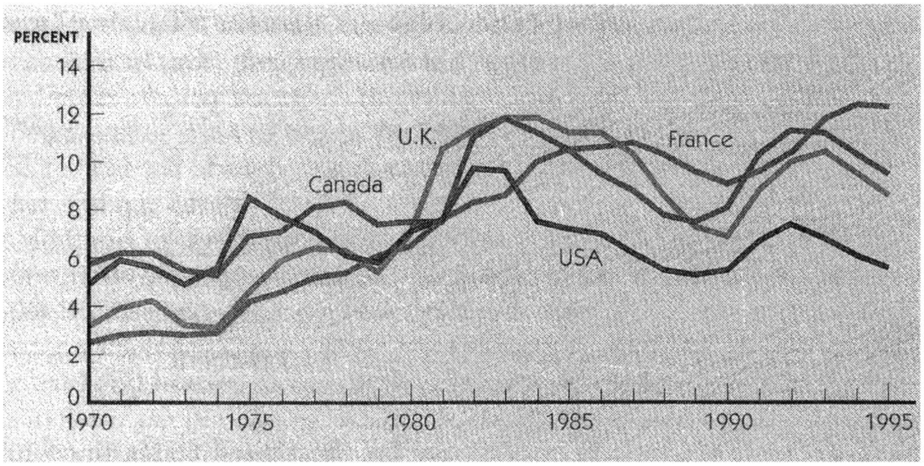

PROBLEMS WITH THE UNEMPLOYMENT STATISTICS

Unemployment statistics are supposed to measure the number of workers who are actively seeking employment but cannot find a job. Information is obtained from a survey of households, and the results of such survey often depend on how the survey is conducted. For instance, in January 1994, the Bureau of Labor Statistics changed the manner in which it conducted its monthly survey. The timing could not have been worse: the economy was pulling out of a recession and a major policy initiative, the 1993 deficit reduction, was just going into effect. Policymakers wanted to know how the economy was doing. It was as if at the very moment a physician tried a new medicine on a sick patient, she also used a new, imperfectly calibrated thermometer. Early comparisons suggested that under the new measure, the unemployment rate would appear to be .6 percent higher than under the older measure. But in the months following the introduction of the survey, the differences between the old and the new measures narrowed considerably; currently the gap between them is negligible.

Another problem with the unemployment measure is that, especially in a prolonged downturn, many individuals are *discouraged* from even looking for a job. Because they are not actively seeking employment, the statistics will not count them as unemployed, and thus will provide an underestimate of the number who would choose to work if a job were available. The fraction of the working age population that is employed or seeking employment is called the **labor force participation rate**. Because of discouraged workers, the labor force participation rate tends to decline in recessions.

Despite these ambiguities, when the unemployment rate increases by more than a trivial amount, it is safe to conclude that the economy has slowed down. Some individuals have been laid off and have not found new jobs, and firms may have slowed down the pace at which they hire new workers.

FORMS OF UNEMPLOYMENT

Economists distinguish between different kinds of unemployment. Right before Christmas, there is a huge demand for retail salespeople to work in department stores and shopping malls across the country. In many parts of the country construction slows down in the winter because of the climate. For the same reason, tourism often increases in the summer, and so does the number of jobs that cater to tourists. The supply of labor also increases in the summer, as high school and college students enter the labor force on a temporary basis. Unemployment that varies with the seasons is called **seasonal unemployment**. Since these movements in employment and unemployment reflect normal seasonal patterns, the unemployment rate you see reported on the news is adjusted according to the average amount of seasonal unemployment. These adjustments are called seasonal adjustments. Thus, if, on average, the unadjusted unemployment rate is normally .4 percent higher in the summer than at other times, the seasonally adjusted unemployment rate for July will be the measured unemployment rate minus .4 percent.

While workers in construction, agriculture, and tourism regularly face seasonal unemployment, other workers become unemployed only as part of a normal transition from one job to another. This kind of unemployment is referred to as **frictional unemployment**. If people could move from job to job instantaneously, there would be no frictional unemployment. In a dynamic economy such as America's, with some industries growing and other declining, there will always be movements from one job to another, and hence there will always be frictional unemployment.

Most bouts of unemployment are short-lived; the average person who loses a job is out of work for only three months. However, about 10 percent of the jobless have been unemployed for more than six months. This kind of long- term unemployment often results from structural factors in the economy, and is called **structural unemployment**. Substantial structural unemployment is found quite often side by side with job vacancies, because the unemployed lack the skills required for the newly created jobs. For example, there may be vacancies for computer programmers, while construction workers are unemployed. By the same token, there may be job shortages in those parts of the economy that are expanding (as in the Sunbelt) and unemployment in areas that are suffering decline (as in Michigan during the period of decline in demand for U.S. cars).

Unemployment that increases when the economy goes into a slowdown and decreases when the economy goes into a boom is called **cyclical unemployment** and is the fundamental concern of this part of the book. Government policy is particularly interested in reducing both the frequency and magnitude of this kind of unemployment, by reducing the frequency and magnitude of the recessions that give rise to it. Government also seeks to reduce its impact, by providing unemployment compensation for those temporarily thrown out of work.

As the economy goes into a recession, the demand for labor—the number of hours to be worked—decreases; if the decreased demand were spread uniformly among all workers, the social disruption would be limited; but in fact, most workers have a slight reduction in work, while a few workers simply lose their jobs. And unskilled workers and minorities are especially likely to become unemployed. Unemployment rates among these groups often soar in a downturn.

FORMS OF UNEMPLOYMENT
Seasonal
Frictional
Structural
Cyclical

INFLATION

In the 1920s, the,years of silent pictures, a movie ticket cost a nickel. By the late 1940s, in the heyday of Hollywood, the price was up to $.50. By the 1960s, the price of a movie was $2.00, and now it is over $7.00. This steady price rise is no anomaly. Most other goods have undergone similar increases over time. This increase in the general level of prices is called inflation. While unemployment tends to be concentrated in certain groups within the population, everyone is affected by inflation. Thus, it is not surprising that when inflation becomes high, it almost always rises to the top of the political agenda.

It is not inflation if the price of only one good goes up. It is inflation if the prices of *most* goods go up. The **inflation rate** is the rate at which the *general* level of prices increases.

MEASURING INFLATION

If the prices of all goods rose by the same proportion, say by 5 percent, over a period of a year, measuring inflation would be easy: the rate of inflation for that year would be 5 percent. The difficulties arise from the fact that the prices of different goods rise at different rates, and some goods even decline in price. Over the past twenty years, while the price of fruits and vegetables has increased by 220 percent, the price of gasoline by 138 percent, and the price of medical care by 383 percent, the price of computers has declined by over 90 percent. To determine the change in the overall price level, economists calculate the *average* percentage increase in prices. But since some goods loom much larger in the typical consumer's budget than others, this calculation must reflect the relative purchases of different goods. A change in the price of housing, for example, is much more important than a change in the price of pencils. If the price of pencils goes down by 5 percent but the price of housing goes up by 5 percent, the overall measure of the price level should go up.

Economists have a straightforward way of reflecting the differing importance of different goods. They ask, what would it cost consumers to purchase the same bundle of goods this year that they bought last year? If, for example, it cost $22,000 in 1996 to buy what it cost consumers only $20,000 to purchase in 1995, we say that prices, *on average*, have risen by 10 percent. Such results are frequently expressed in the form of a **price index**; which, for ease of comparison, measures the price level in any given year relative to a common base year.

The price index for the base year is, by definition, 100. The price index for any other year is calculated by taking the ratio of the price level in that year to the price level in the base year and multiplying it by 100. For example, if 1995 is our base year and we want to know the price index for 1996, we first calculate the ratio of the cost of a certain bundle of goods in 1996 ($22,000) to the cost of the same bundle of goods in 1995 ($20,000), which is 1.1. The price index in 1996 is therefore 1.1 x 100 = 110. The index of 110, using 1995 as a base, means that prices are 10 percent higher, on average, in 1996 than in 1995.

There are several different price indices, each using a different bundle of goods. To track the movement of prices that are important to American households, the government collects price data on the bundle of goods that represents how the average household spends its income. This index is called the **consumer price index**, or CPI. To determine this bundle, the government, through the Bureau of Labor Statistics of the Department of Labor, conducts a Consumer Expenditure Survey, which is updated once a decade or so.

THE AMERICAN EXPERIENCE WITH INFLATION

As we have learned, the inflation rate is the percentage increase in the price level from one year to the next. Figure 4.6 shows the inflation rate for the United States during this century. Three interesting features stand out.

First, prices were relatively stable for much of the century, with the inflation rate under 5 percent except in three periods: around World War I, around World War II, and during the period 1973–1981. Indeed, from the start of the twentieth century until the early 1960s, average inflation ran at only about 1 percent per year.

Second, prices can actually come down. During the recession that followed World War I, prices fell by more than 15 percent, and in the Great Depression of the 1930s by more than 30 percent. It may seem hard to believe in an era when inflation seems the ever-present threat, but at the end of the nineteenth century, the concern was **deflation**, which is a steady decline of the price level. Borrowers at that time who were in debt and had not anticipated the fall in prices found that the dollars they had to pay back were worth far more than the dollars that they had borrowed. They were as upset about this as investors (lenders) are today when inflation makes the value of the dollars they get back from an investment or loan worth less than the value of the dollars they originally put in.

Finally while prices on average have been stable and there have even been periods of price decline, there have also been a few periods of high inflation, when prices increased rapidly. The most notable recent episode was in the late 1970s and early 1980s. In 1980 alone, prices rose by more than 13 percent.

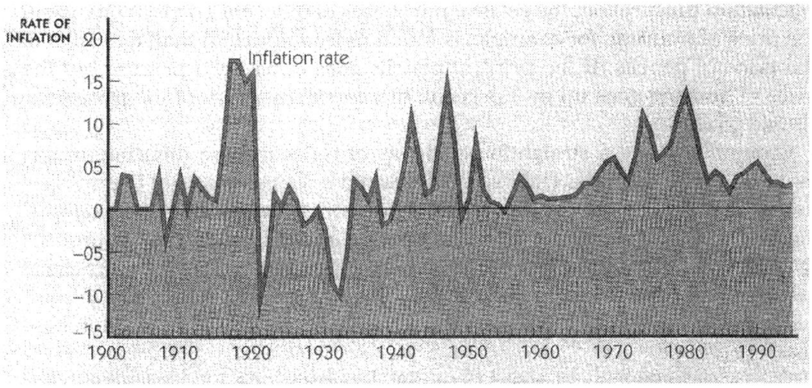

Figure 4.6 The Inflation Rate
The inflation rate is the percentage increase in the price level in a given year. Notice that inflation was low through most of the early part of this century (although high during World Wars I and II), rose sharply in the 1970s, and then fell somewhat in the 1980s. Sources: ERP (1996), Table B-60; Historical Statistics of the United States.

THE IMPORTANCE OF INFLATION

In modern economies, much has been done to ease the pain of inflation. For workers, rising levels of prices are usually accompanied by higher wages, and if a worker faces higher prices but has commensurately more money in her pocket, she is just as well off. The U.S. government has taken steps to adjust the income of retirees to changes in the price level. Most significant, Social Security payments are now "indexed," that is, adjusted, to keep up with changes in the cost of living.

Why, then, does fighting inflation rank so high as a priority in economic policy? There seem to be three answers.

The first is that some groups still suffer. Anyone whose income does not adjust fully is made worse off by increases in the price level. Second, when the rate of inflation suddenly increases, those who have lent money find that the dollars they are being paid back with are worth less. Thus, creditors (those who lend money) are worse off, while debtors are better off. When the inflation rate varies, both borrowing and lending become riskier.

Third, many feel that something is fundamentally wrong with the economy when what cost $1 five years ago costs $2 today. Sometimes these observers are right. Inflation can reflect gross errors in government economic policy, such as spending that is far in excess of revenues, or excessive provision of credit. But frequently inflation gets the blame when something else is the underlying problem. The steep increase in oil prices in 1973 set off a worldwide inflationary spiral. With Americans paying more to the oil-exporting countries, the United States was, in a sense, poorer. Someone had to take a cut. Furthermore, the worldwide economic downturn set off by the 1973 oil price rise made the cut that had to be taken that much larger. Thus, workers' real wages fell. They blamed inflation for their declining standard of living. But inflation was not really the culprit—higher oil prices were.

As the economy has adapted to inflation, economists have increasingly debated about how concerned we should be about moderate rates of inflation—the 3 to 6 percent inflation that has occurred regularly during the past few decades. They worry that the cures for moderate inflation may be worse than the disease. Still, most economists think

Using Economics: Calculating the Consumer Price Index

Encapsulating the movements of masses of prices into an index provides an easy way to look at price trends over time. Suppose that in 1990 the average American family spent $1,000 per month to buy a basket of goods. Assume that in 1996 it cost $1,200 to buy the same basket. Then the price index for 1996 is just the ratio of the cost in 1996 to the cost in 1990, times 100. That is,

CPI for 1996 = i,2oyi#ooo x 100 = 120.

The advantage of an index is that once there is an index number for any given year, we can compare it with any other year. The CPI for 1973 was 44, and for 1994 it was 148. Between those years, the index rose by 104, so the increase was

100 X 104/44 = 236 percent.

On average, prices rose by 236 percent from 1973 to 1994.

The figure below shows the level of the consumer price index from 1900 to the present, using 1983 as the base year. For example, prices in 1920 were 20 percent of what they were in 1983.

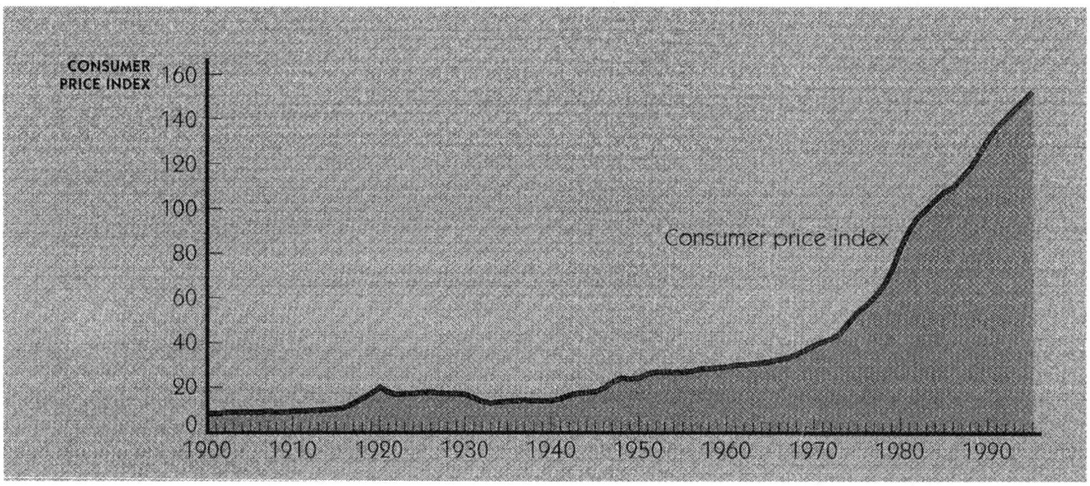

Policy Perspective: the Price Index Makes a Difference

Price indices have increasingly come to play an important role in economic life, in spite of the dry, technical flavor that seems to pervade most discussion of them. The Social Security benefits of the elderly increase with the cost of living index, and tax brackets and tax exemptions also change with the index. If the index overstates the cost of living (rate of inflation) increases, the real benefits (purchasing power) of the elderly increase, and real inflation-adjusted tax revenues decrease. Both distortions increase the budget deficit of the government—the first by increasing the outlays, the second by reducing the receipts of government.

By early 1994, it had become apparent that the price index used by the federal government for adjusting both benefits and tax brackets was seriously flawed—overstating the rate of inflation by between .5 and 1.5 percent a year. Several scheduled changes will go part of the way in correcting those errors. But in the interim, until those revisions are instituted, the Treasury will lose an estimated $100 billion or more as a result of the biased index.

The upward bias stems from three problems. The first is the "fixed basket problem." Price indices are generally calculated by comparing how much it costs to purchase a particular market basket of goods that represents an average consumer's expenditure pattern. But expenditure patterns change steadily over time, while the market basket is revised only infrequently (for instance, 1997 will be the first revision since 1982 through 1984). As people buy more of the goods which have become relatively less expensive, and less of the goods which have become relatively more expensive, the index increasingly overweights goods whose prices are rising.

The second major problem is "quality adjustments." New products, which can do new and better things than older products, constantly enter the market. To compare the prices of the new products with the old, some quality adjustment must be made. If the price goes up by 10 percent, but the product lives longer and does better than the old one, in a real sense the price increase is less than 10 percent and may even be a price reduction. The quality adjustments may sometimes be easy: one machine can do what two machines did before. But usually the comparisons are difficult. If we measure the quality of computers by calculations per minute, memory, and disk storage, the rate of decrease in computer prices is phenomenal. But even this does not fully reflect the quality improvement. We can do things with the computer now that were unimaginable twenty-five years ago at any price. And how do we treat a new drug that cures a previously incurable disease? The Bureau of Labor Statistics tries to make adjustments for quality. But the consensus is that these adjustments are imperfect and result in an overestimate in the inflation rate of between a few tenths of a percent to more than 1 percent.

A third set of problems is technical, having to do with the way the data are collected and the details of the calculation.

But many economists believe that the scheduled revisions will not fully eliminate the CPI bias. They argue that, as a result, Social Security and taxes should be indexed to the CPI rate of inflation minus 1 or .5.

that double-digit inflation levels, at the very least, are symptomatic of some kind of malfunction in the economy. Certainly there is a consensus that the kinds of rapid inflation experienced in Israel and some Latin American countries are extremely disruptive to the economy.

ALTERNATIVE MEASURES OF INFLATION

The consumer price index is one measure of inflation, based on what the average consumer pays. Other price indices can be calculated using different market baskets. A different measure of prices is the **producer price index**, which measures the average level of prices of goods sold by producers. This index is useful because it gives us an idea of what will happen to consumer prices in the near future. Usually, if producers are receiving higher prices from their sales to wholesalers, eventually retailers will have to charge higher prices. This will be reflected in a higher consumer price index.

Earlier in the chapter we observed that real GDP is nominal GDP adjusted for the price level. The price index we use for calculating real GDP is called the **GDP deflator**. It represents a comparison between what it would cost to buy the total mix of goods and services within the economy today and in a base year. In other words, the GDP deflator is a weighted average of the prices of different goods and services, where the weights represent the importance of each of the goods and services in GDP.

CONNECTING THE THREE MAJOR VARIABLES

Often the major macroeconomic variables move together in systematic ways. For example, when the economy is in a recession, as it was in 1982, unemployment tends to be higher, inflation tends to be lower, and growth comes to a standstill. These connections make sense. After all, when the economy is suffering tough times, businesses reduce their output, lay off workers, and do not hire new workers. In addition, businesses that are having a hard time selling products in a competitive market are less likely to raise prices.

FLOWS AND STOCKS

GDP, GNP, and NDP are all measures of output *per year*. Rate measurements such as these are called **flows**. When a news report says, "The quarterly GDP statistic, just released, shows that GDP was $4 trillion per year," it does not mean that $4 trillion of goods and services was produced during the quarter. Rather, it means that $1 trillion was produced during the quarter, so that if that rate of production were maintained for a whole year, the total value of goods and services would be $4 trillion.

Flow statistics need to be contrasted with **stock** statistics, which measure an item at a single point in time. Among the most important stocks is the capital stock—the total value of all the buildings and machines that underlie the productive potential of the economy.

The relationships between stocks and flows are simple. The stock of capital at the end of 1996, for example, consists of the stock of capital at the end of 1995 plus or minus the flows into or out of this stock during 1996. Investment is the flow into the capital stock. Depreciation is the flow out of the capital stock.

Similarly, we can look at the *number* of unemployed individuals as a stock. This number at the end of 1996 consists of the number at the end of 1995 plus or minus the flows into or out of the unemployment pool during 1996. Layoffs, firings, resignations, and new entry into the labor force can be thought of as flows into the unemployment pool; new hires represent flows out of the unemployment pool.

The Recession Has (Officially) Ended

By Catherine Rampell

September 20, 2010, 10:45 am
1:50 p.m. | Updated

The recession officially ended in June 2009, according to the Business Cycle Dating Committee of the National Bureau of Economic Research, the official arbiter of such dates.

As many economists had expected, this official end date makes the most recent downturn the longest since World War II. This recent recession, having begun in December 2007, lasted 18 months. Until now the longest postwar recessions were those of 1973-5 and 1981-2, which each lasted 16 months.

The newly-declared end-date to the recession also confirms what many had suspected: The 2007-9 recession was the deepest on record since the Great Depression, at least in terms of job losses.

Recession and expansion dates are based on various economic indicators, including gross domestic product, income, employment, industrial production and wholesale-retail sales. The Business Cycle Dating Committee typically waits to declare that the economy has turned until well after the fact, when it has a longer track record of economic data to confirm a new trend.

The bureau took care to note that the recession, by definition, meant only the period until the economy reached its low point — not a return to its previous vigor.

"In determining that a trough occurred in June 2009, the committee did not conclude that economic conditions since that month have been favorable or that the economy has returned to operating at normal capacity," the bureau said. "Rather, the committee determined only that the recession ended and a recovery began in that month."

The committee had previously met in April to consider whether an end to the recession could be declared, but members decided that the data were still inconclusive. Since then, however, the Bureau of Economic Analysis has released revised numbers for output and income growth over the last year, and the addition of this new information helped push the committee toward declaring an official turning point.

"That gave us the definitive picture of what happened in 2009," said Robert J. Gordon, a member of the committee for over 30 years and an economics professor at Northwestern. "At this point we're not going to get any new information to consider until July 2011. So we knew that if we're going to do anything, we should probably do something now."

Professor Gordon also said that nearly every indicator that the committee looked at simultaneously reached its low point in June

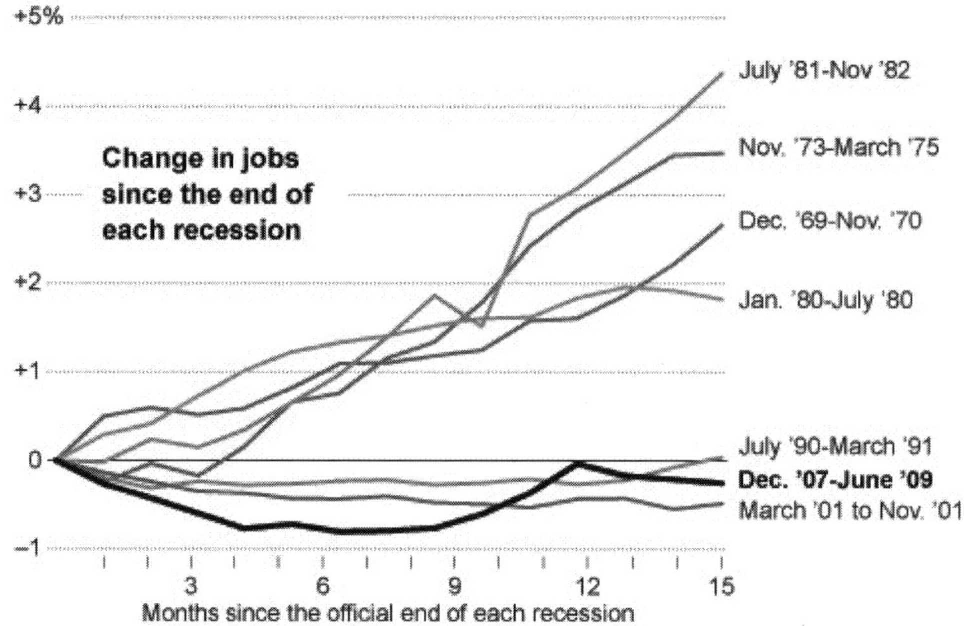

Source: Bureau of Labor Statistics

2009, which made that month a relatively easy selection as the official turning point. The main exception to this trend was employment, which hit its trough six months later, in December 2009.

This lag has led many to refer to the current situation as a "jobless recovery," and had even prompted suggestions that the weak job market should play a bigger role in determining recession start and end dates.

Professor Gordon notes, however, that the lag between a turnaround in gross domestic product and a turnaround in the job market was even worse after the 2001 recession.

"In that episode employment continued falling for 19 months after output troughed," he said. "If anything the case for putting employment more prominently in the committee dating was weaker this time."

Still, the magnitude of job losses was certainly worse in the 2007-9 recession, he said. From December 2007 to June 2009, the American economy shed more than 5 percent of its nonfarm payroll jobs; through December 2009, the month that employment bottomed, the economy had shed more than 6 percent of these jobs.

In terms of unemployment, which is measured by a different government survey and considers only people who are actively looking for work, the rate most recently peaked last October at 10.1 percent. It had gotten higher in 1982, when it reached 10.8 percent. But the composition of the work force looked very different in the 1980s — it was younger, and younger people tend to have higher unemployment rates — and so if you adjust for age, unemployment this time around looks much worse.

Additionally, a broader measure of unemployment, which also includes people who are reluctantly working part-time when they wish to be working full-time and those who have given up on looking for work altogether, also shows that unemployment this time around was far worse than in any previous postwar recession.

Whether the decline in output represented a record loss, however, depends on what metric you use.

In terms of how much inflation-adjust output declined, this most recent recession had the most severe contraction since World War II, according to Robert E. Hall, a Stanford economics professor and committee chair. But some economists say that a better measure would be how far output falls relative to where the economy would have been if growing "normally."

"It's definitely not as deep as 1981-82 when measured relative to economy's potential growth rate," Professor Gordon said.

He said that he does not believe the economy is headed for a "double dip" recession — the committee itself does not engage in forecasting — because trends in income and jobs indicate that the economy is still slowly but surely trending upward.

But the anemic growth since the cycle trough in June 2009 is still extraordinarily worrying. The deeper recession of the 1980s was followed by a strong, robust bounce-back in growth; this current recovery is barely trudging along.

"What's really unique about this recession is the amount of unemployment in combination with the slowness of the recovery," he said. "That's just not happened before. We had a sharp recession followed by a sharp recovery in the 1980s. And in '91 and '01 we had slow recoveries, but those recessions were shallow recessions so the slowness didn't matter much."

Professor Gordon estimates that economy needs a long-run output growth rate of 2.5 percent to keep the unemployment rate, now at 9.6 percent, even constant.

But with an annual growth rate of a measly 1.6 percent in the second quarter of this year, and private forecasts that the third quarter won't be much better, unemployment may actually "inch up" in the months ahead, Professor Gordon says.

"That's why the political news is so entirely dominated by the word 'jobs,' " he said. "The amount of unemployment we've already got and the slowness of recovery lead to predictions that we could have 9-plus percent unemployment even through the next presidential election."

IN-CLASS PROJECT

Accuracy of the Unemployment Rate

By David Moglen

Directions: Read these two articles and answer the questions at the end. If assigned as a group project, all groups should answer at least the main question, #1, and even #2 as well at the teacher's discretion.

Important note—a written answer of one or two sentences is required by the first sentence in question 1 and question 2, but the rest of those questions are answered using numbers and symbols only and very few words. Questions 3 and 4 ask for regular, short-answer responses.

The reserve Army

Feb. 12th 2004 From The Economist print edition http://www.economist.com/node/2424216

The Truth About the Job Numbers

The "self-employed" are not this bad economy's saviors.
By Robert B. Reich Web Exclusive: 09.09.04 Print Friendly | Email Article
http://www.prospect.org/cs/articles?article= the_truth_about_the_job_numbers.

The following Questions all make reference to the first article:

The reserve army From The Economist Feb. 12th 2004.

1. What is the importance of an unemployment rate that does or does not determine who is "enjoying a spot of leisure" in paragraph three? Are there any other reasons the unemployment rate tends to over- or under-state actual unemployment? Consider other skew factors in the rate such as discouraged workers, the role of underemployed workers.

Note—Your answer should separately analyze how the inclusion or exclusion of at least three groups in the official unemployment rate results in an official rate that over- or under-states actual unemployment. State clearly for each of the three groups you choose to analyze whether the fact our official rate includes or excludes them results in EITHER an overstated or understated rate. For some groups you will explain why the fact our official rate excludes (or includes) them results in understatement. For others you will explain why their inclusion or exclusion in the official data results in overstatement. However, for any one skew factor, you will not say it results in **understatement** and/or **overstatement** (specify one or the other for each skew factor).

Skew factor you must analyze: Those "enjoying a spot of leisure" (included)

Skew factors you could analyze (pick any two):

Students	(excluded)
Military	(excluded)
Those in the informal economy	(excluded)
Underemployed e.g. part-time workers	(included)
Those who have given up looking for a job	(excluded)

Use example numbers—either use the link at the end to access the real data in the U.S., or use an estimate. For example, your starting point (before incorporating, separately, each of the three skew factors) is that the official unemployment rate as currently reported is:

$$\frac{\#\ looking}{Labour\ Force\ (LF)} * 100 = Unemp\ rate$$

$$\frac{15\ million}{150\ million} * 100 = 10\%$$

2. What is meant by "The Reserve Army" (the article's title)? Explain the argument in paragraph ten that more gains for many economies could come from (Policy 1) bringing working-age people who are not looking for a job back into the workforce than (Policy 2) lowering unemployment to the natural rate of unemployment. Gains should be explained in terms of number of new workers or dollar value of additional output (use example #'s).

3. How could the natural rate of unemployment itself be reduced? Specifically how could (a) structural unemployment and (b) frictional unemployment be reduced? You may want to review: "Defining the Natural Rate of Unemployment and Analyzing its Determinants" to answer this question.

Note: the answer is not to simply declare a new estimate of the natural rate; suggest policies for (a) and (b) that would alter the real economic situation in a way that would compel economists to change their estimate of the natural rate to reflect the new reality.

4. Paragraph five states: "According to the household measure, nearly 139m Americans were in work in January, even more than had jobs at the height of the boom in March 2000. By the payroll measure, some 130m were in work—a fall of nearly 2% since employment peaked." In what ways does the fact that the difference between the two numbers (9m) is due to people reporting self-employment in the household survey improve that survey's accuracy in measuring jobs and output, and in what ways does the inclusion of such workers worsen its accuracy?

Additional Source: http://www.bls.gov/cps/.

DISCUSSION QUESTIONS

1. What was the labor force experience of your grandparents (or others you know that are in that generation? Of your parents (or their generation)? What do you expect your own labor force participation to be like? Do the patterns in your family reflect the national pattern of changes discussed in the text, or not?
2. What evidence have you seen—in your own family, or through the media—of increasing "flexibility" in labor markets? Do you think these changes have been beneficial, harmful, or both?

CHAPTER 7
National Economic Accounting

7 National Economic Accounting

By Timothy Taylor

Macroeconomics and microeconomics are two different perspectives on the subject of economics. What seems sensible from a microeconomic point of view can have unexpected or counterproductive results at the macroeconomic level. For example, imagine that you are sitting at an event with a large audience, like a live concert or a basketball game. A few people decide that they want a better view, and so they stand up. However, when these people stand up, they block the view for some other people, and the others need to stand up as well if they wish to see. Eventually, nearly everyone is standing up, and as a result, no one can see much better than before. The individually rational decision of some individuals at the micro level—stand up to see better—ended up being self-defeating at the macro level. Or consider the case of a farmer who finds out that the long-range weather forecast is for an especially fine growing season. The farmer decides to plant extra acreage to take advantage of the fine weather. However, if all farmers see the same forecast, and all decide to plant extra, then the result will be a shift out to the right of the supply curve that depresses the equilibrium market price for all farmers. In this case, the microeconomic rational behavior of individual farmers who are seeking higher profits ends up with an outcome—low prices—that none of them desired. Finally, consider the case of a country in which many foreign individuals and firms are making financial investments. A rumor circulates that the economy of this country may be weakening, and that some of its leading companies may go bankrupt. The foreign investors become worried. They start selling their assets in the country and declining to make any new investments. But when many foreign investors react in this way, the country's economy actually does become much weaker from a lack of loans and financial investment capital, and many leading companies go bankrupt as a result. Again, individually rational, cautious decisions by investors—in this case, reducing the amount invested in the country—leads to a self-fulfilling prophecy that their investments turn out poorly.

These stories have a common theme: Individually rational motivations help economic agents coordinate their behavior in some ways, but in some cases they can also lead to undesired outcomes. In such cases, society may wish to create other coordinating mechanisms. In the case of people in a crowd trying to see better, for example, the coordinating mechanism is often social pressure: that is, the group accepts that people will stand up in moments of excitement, but if someone stands at other times, then others in the audience yell at them to sit down. In macroeconomic settings, government may in certain situations be able to play a coordinating role to avoid unwanted outcomes.

This chapter begins the discussion of macroeconomics by focusing on the single most common measure of the size of the macro economy: gross domestic product or GDP. Since the macro economy involves all the buying and selling transactions that occur, GDP can be measured in two ways: by looking at the overall demand for goods and services, or by looking at what is produced. The chapter will discuss comparing GDP across countries, patterns of GDP in the long run and the short run, and the extent to which GDP captures or does not capture the broader concept of a society's standard of living.

The chapters that follow will first discuss macroeconomic goals, then frameworks for analysis, and finally policy tools. Exhibit 21-1 illustrates the structure. In thinking about the overall health of a macro economy, it is useful to consider four goals. *Economic growth*, which can be approximated by the growth of gross domestic product, ultimately determines the prevailing standard of living in a country. *Unemployment*, the situation in which people want to work but can't find a job, is not only potentially devastating for individuals and families—but society as a whole loses the value of the output that could have been produced. *Inflation* refers to a rise in the overall level of prices. The difficulty arises because not all prices rise at the same time. For example, if many people face a situation where the prices that they pay for food, shelter, and health care are rising much faster than the wages they receive for their labor, there will be widespread unhappiness. Finally, a sustainable *balance of trade* refers to the flows of goods and financial capital back and forth between countries. Although the gains from trade in the global economy can produce economic gains for all nations, trade imbalances can also be a source of macroeconomic disruption and instability. One or more of these statistics are in the news almost every day. The next four chapters—from Chapters 22–25—will explore and explain these four goals.

None of these macroeconomic goals is straightforward to analyze from a microeconomic perspective. For example, microeconomic analysis of supply and demand can explain why equilibrium quantity might increase in a single market for a good or a service, but it does not offer a simple method for explaining overall growth in the entire macroeconomy. Microeconomic analysis can explain why a firm or an industry might hire more or fewer workers, but it does not offer a simple method for explaining why many or most firms might become unwilling to hire at the same time, thus creating the macroeconomic problem of unemployment. Microeconomic analysis can explain why the price might rise or fall for a particular product, but it doesn't offer any simple way of discussing why most prices might all rise by about the same amount at

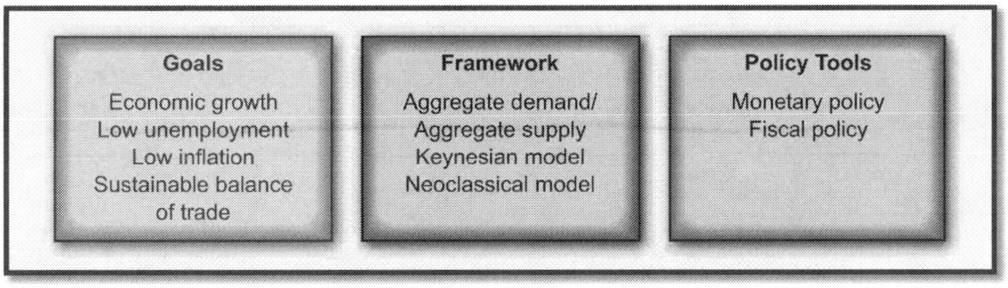

Exhibit 8-1 U.S. Consumption Choices in 2006–2007

the same time in a process of inflation. Finally, microeconomic analysis can explain why a firm might have success selling its goods abroad and why consumers might want to buy goods from abroad, but it offers no easy framework for discussing the implications of the overall balance of exports and imports—that is, the balance of trade.

Several different analytical frameworks exist for thinking about how these four macroeconomic goals relate to each other, and how pursuing one goal may in some cases or over the short run or the long run involve trade-offs with other goals. These frameworks have names like "aggregate supply and aggregate demand models," "sticky price Keynesian models," and "flexible price neoclassical models." At this point, these names are just empty words, but they will be explained from Chapters 26–28.

With the goals and frameworks in mind, the stage is set to discuss how the macroeconomic policy tools available to government, working through the analytical frameworks, will affect the ultimate policy goals. *Monetary policy* includes policies that affect money, banking, interest rates, and exchange rates, and these policies are discussed in Chapters 29–31.

Fiscal policy means policies that involve government taxes or spending, and applications of fiscal policy are discussed in Chapters 32–33. Chapter 34, the final chapter of the macroeconomic section, offers overall lessons of macroeconomics in a global context.

Measuring the Size of the Economy: Gross Domestic Product

The size of a nation's overall economy is typically measured by its **gross domestic product** or **GDP**, which is the value of the output of all goods and services produced within a country. The measurement of GDP thus involves counting up millions of different goods and services—cars, haircuts, computers, steel, bananas, college educations, and everything else—and summing them into a total value. As a conceptual matter, this task is straightforward: take the quantity of everything produced, multiply it by the price that everything for which everything sold, and add up the total. In 2009, the U.S. GDP totaled $14.2 trillion.

gross domestic product (GDP): The value of the output of all goods and services produced within a country.

Each of the market transactions that enter into GDP must involve both a buyer and a seller. Thus, the GDP of an economy can be measured either by the total of what is demanded in the economy, or by the total of what is produced in the economy.

GDP Measured by Components of Demand

GDP as measured by demand is commonly divided into five parts: consumption, investment, government, exports, and imports. Exhibit 21-2 shows how these five factors add up to the GDP in 2009. Exhibit 21-3a shows the levels of consumption, investment and government consumption over time, expressed as a percentage of GDP, while Exhibit 21-3b shows the levels of exports and imports as a percentage of GDP over time. A few patterns about each of these components are worth noticing.

Exhibit 21-2
Components of GDP in 2009: From the Demand Side

	Components of GDP on the Demand Side (in trillions of dollars)	Percentage of Total
Consumption	$9.9	70.2%
Investment	$1.6	11.3%
Government	$2.9	20.6%
Exports	$1.6	11.4%
Imports	–$1.9	–13.5%
Total	*$14.2*	*100%*

Exhibit 21-3 Components of GDP on the Demand Side

(a) Consumption is about two-thirds of GDP, but it moves relatively little over time. Investment hovers around 15% of GDP, but it increases and declines more than consumption. Government spending on goods and services is around 20% of GDP.

(b) Exports are added to total demand for goods and services, while imports are subtracted from total demand. Thus, if exports are equal to imports, international trade as a whole has no impact on the size of GDP. If exports exceed imports, as in most of the 1960s and 1970s in the U.S. economy, a trade surplus exists. If imports exceed exports, as in recent years, than a trade deficit exists.

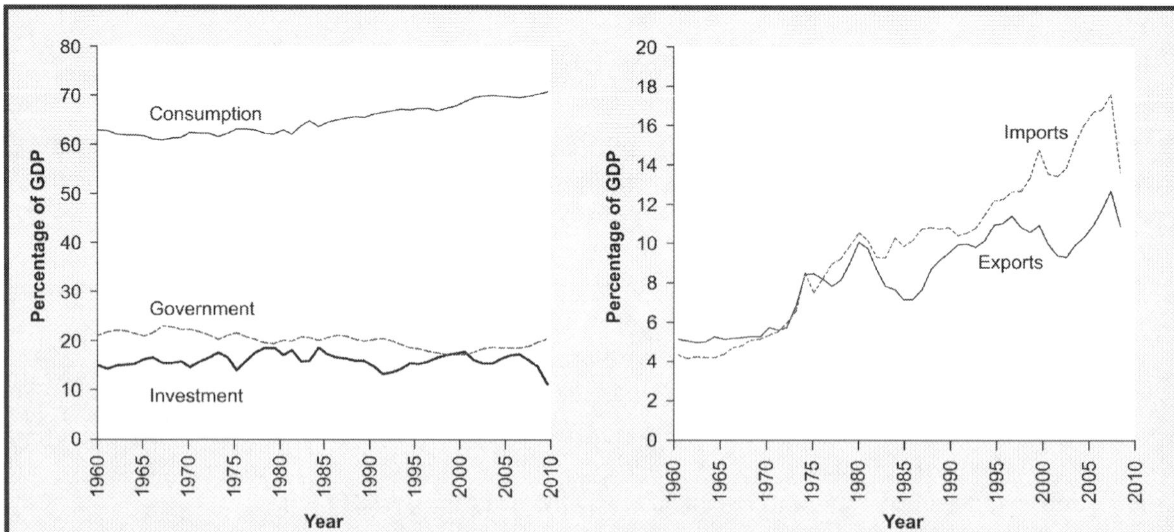

(a) Demand from consumption, investment, and government
(b) Imports and exports

How Statisticians Measure GDP

Economists have an old, sad joke that there are two things you never want to watch being made: sausages and economic statistics. The joke comes to mind in considering the task of the government economists at the Bureau of Economic Analysis, within the U.S. Department of Commerce, who piece together estimates of GDP from a variety of sources.

Once every five years, in the second and seventh year of each decade, the Bureau of the Census carries out a detailed census of businesses throughout the United States. In between, the Census bureau carries out a monthly survey of retail sales. These figures are adjusted with foreign trade data, to account for exports that are produced in the United States and sold abroad and for imports that are produced abroad and sold here. Once every 10 years, the Census Bureau does a comprehensive survey of housing and residential finance. Together, these sources provide the main basis for figuring what is produced for consumers.

For investment, the Census Bureau does a monthly survey of construction and an annual survey of expenditures on physical capital equipment.

For what is purchased by the federal government, the statisticians rely on the U.S. Department of the Treasury. An annual Census of Governments gathers information on state and local governments. Because a lot of government spending at all levels is involves hiring people to provide services, a large portion of government spending can also be tracked through payroll records collected by state governments and by the Social Security Administration.

With regard to foreign trade, the Census Bureau compiles a monthly record of all import and export documents. Additional surveys cover transportation and travel, and adjustment needs to be made for financial services that are produced in the United States for foreign customers.

Many other sources contribute to the estimates of GDP. Information on energy comes from the U.S. Department of Transportation and Department of Energy. Information on health care is collected by the Health Care Financing Administration. Surveys of landlords find out about rent. The Department of Agriculture collects statistics on farming.

All of these bits and pieces of information arrive in different forms, at different time intervals. The Bureau of Economic Analysis melds them together to produce estimates of GDP on a quarterly basis (that is, every three months). These estimates are then updated and revised. The "advance" estimate of GDP for a certain quarter is released one month after a quarter. The "preliminary" estimate comes out one month after that. The "final" estimate is published one month later, but it isn't actually final. In July, roughly, updated estimates for the previous calendar year are released. Then, once every five years, after the results of the latest detailed five-year business census have been processed, the BEA revises all of the past estimates of GDP according to the newest methods and data, going all the way back to 1929.

When you read newspaper reports of recent GDP announcements, be aware that the "advance," "preliminary" and "final" announcements of quarterly GDP during a year usually don't change much. However, the annual revisions released each summer can be substantial; enough to make GDP growth appear quite different than the quarterly reports released earlier that year.

Consumption (C) by households is the largest component of GDP, accounting for about two-thirds of the GDP in any year. However, consumption is a gentle elephant: when viewed over time, it doesn't jump around too much.

Investment (I) by businesses refers to real purchases of physical plant and equipment by businesses. Investment demand is far smaller than consumption demand, typically accounting for only about 15–20% of GDP. However, it moves up and down more noticeably than consumption. Investment is a cat in a bag: it jumps around unexpectedly.

Government (G) demand in the United States appears relatively small, at about 20% of GDP. This proportion may seem too low. Indeed, government in the United States (including the federal, state and local levels) collects about one-third of GDP in taxes. However, much of that money is passed directly to citizens, through programs like Social Security, welfare payments to the poor, or interest payments on past government borrowing. In these cases, the money that passes through government hands is counted as part of consumption. The only part of government spending counted in demand is—returning to the basic definition of GDP—government purchases of goods or services produced in the economy. Examples would include when the government buys a new fighter jet for the Air Force or when it pays workers who deliver government services.

When thinking about the demand for domestically produced goods in a global economy, it is important to count demand for exports (X)—that is, domestically made goods that are sold abroad. However, if one is going to add in the extra demand generated by foreign buyers, one must also subtract out imports (M)—that is, goods produced in other countries that are purchased in this country. The gap between exports and imports is called the **trade balance**. If a country's exports are larger than its imports, then a country is said to have a **trade surplus**. In the United States, exports typically exceeded imports in the 1960s and 1970s, as shown in Exhibit 21-3b. But since the early 1980s, imports have typically exceeded exports, and so the United States has experienced a **trade deficit** in most years. Indeed, the trade deficit grew quite large in the late 1990s and in the mid-2000s. Exhibit 21-3 also shows that imports and exports have both risen substantially in recent decades, even after the declines during the recessionary period in 2008 and 2009, illustrating the process of globalization. If exports and imports are equal, then foreign trade has no effect on the total GDP of the economy. However, even if exports and imports are balanced overall, foreign trade might still have powerful effects on particular industries and workers by causing nations to shift workers and physical capital investment toward specializing in one industry rather than another.

trade balance:
Gap between exports and imports.

trade surplus:
When exports exceed imports.

trade deficit:
When imports exceed exports.

Based on these five components of demand, GDP can be measured as:

$$\text{GDP} = \text{Consumption} + \text{Investment} + \text{Government} + \text{Trade balance}$$
$$\text{GDP} = C + I + G + (X - M).$$

Remember this definition. It will prove important for analyzing connections in the macro economy and for thinking about macroeconomic policy tools.

durable goods:
Longlasting goods like cars and refrigerators.

nondurable goods:
Shortlived goods like food and clothing.

GDP MEASURED BY WHAT IS PRODUCED

Everything that is purchased with components of demand must also be produced. Exhibit 21-4 breaks down what is produced into five categories: **durable goods**, **nondurable goods**, services, structures, and the change in **inventories**. Before going into detail about these categories, notice that total GDP measured according to what is produced is exactly the same as the GDP measured by looking at the five components of demand. Since every market transaction must have both a buyer and a seller, GDP must be the same whether measured by what is demanded or what is produced. Exhibit 21-5 shows these components of what is produced, expressed as a percentage of GDP, since 1960. Again, a few patterns stand out.

inventories: Goods that have been produced, but not yet been sold.

In thinking about what is produced in the economy, many non-economists immediately focus on solid, long-lasting goods, like cars and computers. But by far the largest part of GDP is services, rather than goods. Moreover, services have been a growing share of GDP over time. A detailed breakdown of the leading service industries would include health care, education, law, and financial services. It has been decades since most of the U.S. economy involved making solid objects. Instead, the most common jobs in a modern economy involves a worker looking at pieces of paper; meeting with co-workers, customers or suppliers; making phone calls; or looking at a computer screen.

Even within the overall category of goods, long-lasting durable goods like cars and refrigerators are about the same share of the economy as short-lived nondurable goods like food and clothing. The category of structures includes everything from homes, to office buildings, shopping malls, and factories. Inventories is a small category that refers to the goods that have been produced by one business but have not yet been sold to consumers, and are still sitting in warehouses and on shelves. The amount of inventories sitting on shelves will tend to decline if business is better than expected, or to rise if business is worse than expected.

Exhibit 21-4

Components of GDP on the Supply Side in 2009

	Components of GDP on the Supply Side (in trillions of dollars)	Percentage of Total
Goods		
Durable goods	$1.9	13.4%
Nondurable goods	$1.9	13.4%
Services	$9.4	66.2%
Structures	$1.1	7.7%
Change in inventories	–$0.2	–1.1%
Total	*$14.2*	*100%*

Exhibit 21-5 Components of Supply

Services are the largest single component of aggregate supply, representing over half of GDP. Nondurable goods used to be larger than durable goods, but in recent years, both categories are about 20% of GDP. Structures hover around 10% of GDP. The change in inventories, the final component of aggregate supply, is not shown here; it is typically less than 1% of GDP

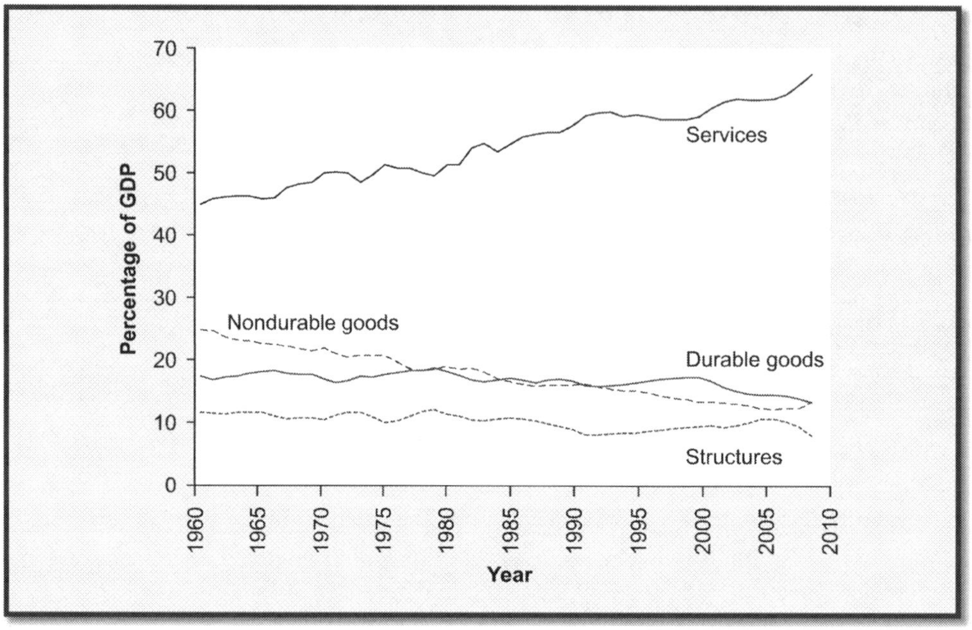

double counting:
A potential mistake to be avoided in measuring GDP, in which output is counted two or more times as it travels through the stages of production.

final goods and services:
Output used directly for consumption, investment, government, and trade purposes; contrast with "intermediate goods."

intermediate goods and services:
Output provided to other businesses at an intermediate stage of production, not for final users; contrast with "final goods and services."

THE PROBLEM OF DOUBLE COUNTING

One danger for the statisticians who calculate GDP is to avoid the mistake of **double counting**, in which output is counted two or more times as it travels through the stages of production. This problem arises because in an economy with a division of labor, most products must work through an interconnected network of producers. For example, imagine what would happen if the government statisticians who calculate GDP first counted the value of mining iron ore, and then counted the value of the steel that used that iron ore, and then counted the value of the car that used that steel. In this example, the value of the original iron ore would have been counted three times—once at each stage of production.

To avoid this problem, which could overstate the size of the economy considerably, government statisticians count just the **final goods and services** in the chain of production that are sold for consumption, investment, government, and trade purposes. This need to avoid double counting (or triple counting, or worse) explains why neither the method of measuring GDP—what is demanded or what is produced—includes the many **intermediate goods and services** that businesses provide to other businesses. The value of what businesses provide to other businesses is captured in the final products at the end of the production chain. Similarly, the value of people's work is included in the price of the goods and services that are eventually produced.

Cousins of GDP

In the world of economic statistics, too much is never enough. There are several different but closely related ways of measuring the size of the economy other than GDP.

One of the closest cousins of GDP is GNP, or gross national product. GDP includes only what is produced by labor and capital located within a country's borders. However, GNP adds what is produced by a nation's labor and capital that are located in the rest of the world, and subtracts out any payments sent home to other countries by foreign labor and capital located in the United States. In other words, GNP is based more on production of citizens and firms from a country, wherever they are located, and GDP is based on what happens within the geographic boundaries of a certain country. For the United States, the gap between GDP and GNP is relatively small; in recent years, only about 0.2%. But for small nations, which may have a substantial share of their population working abroad and sending money back home, the difference can be substantial.

Net national product, or NNP, is calculated by taking GNP and then subtracting the value of how much physical capital is worn out, or reduced in value because of aging, over the course of a year. The process by which capital ages and loses value is called "depreciation." The NNP can be further subdivided into national income, which includes all income to businesses and individuals, and personal income, which includes only income to people.

For practical purposes, it isn't vital to memorize these definitions. However, it is important be aware that these differences exist and to know what statistic you are looking at, so that you don't accidentally compare, say, GDP in one year or for one country with GNP or NNP in another year or another country.

The concept of GDP is fairly straightforward: it's just the value of all final goods and services bought and sold in the economy everything. But in a decentralized, market-oriented economy, actually calculating the more-than $14 trillion dollar U.S. GDP—along with how it is changing every few months—is a full-time job for a brigade of government statisticians.

Comparing GDP among Countries

When comparing the GDP of different countries, two issues immediately arise. First, the GDP of a country is measured in its own currency: the United States uses the U.S. dollar; Canada, the Canadian dollar; most countries of western Europe, the euro; Japan, the yen; Mexico, the peso; and so on. Thus, comparing GDP between two countries requires converting from one currency to another. A second problem is that countries have very different numbers of people. For instance, the United States has a much larger economy than Mexico or Canada, but it also has roughly three times as many people as Mexico and nine times as many people as Canada. Thus, comparing GDP across countries requires a way of adjusting for different currencies and for different population levels.

exchange rate: The rate at which one currency exchanges for another.

CONVERTING CURRENCIES WITH EXCHANGE RATES

To compare the GDP of two different countries with different currencies, it is necessary to use an **exchange rate**, which is the rate at which one currency exchanges for another. Exchange rates can always be expressed either as the units of country A currency that need to be traded for a single unit of country B currency, or units of country B currency that need to traded for a single unit of country A currency. For example, the exchange rate between the Mexican peso and the U.S. dollar can be expressed either as approximately 11 Mexican pesos per 1 U.S. dollar; or to put it the other way, it takes 1/13 of a U.S. dollar (about 8 cents) to buy a peso. It is equally accurate to express the exchange rate in either way, so you can choose whichever measure is more convenient. Exchange rates are published each day in the "Business" section of major newspapers and are available at banks and many websites. An illustrative list of exchange rates from early 2010 appears in Exhibit 21-6. Each exchange rate is expressed in two ways: the foreign currency per one U.S. dollar, and the amount in U.S. dollars to buy a unit of foreign currency. These two measures are the reciprocals of each other; in mathematical terms, multiplying the currency per U.S. dollar exchange rate times the U.S. dollars per foreign currency exchange rate will always equal 1.

Using the exchange rate to convert GDP from one currency to another is straightforward. Say that the task is to compare Japan's GDP of 500 trillion yen with the U.S. GDP of $14 trillion. The exchange rate is 90 yen = $1. (These numbers are realistic for early 2010, but rounded off to simplify the calculations.) To convert Japan's GDP into U.S. dollars, multiply:

$$\text{Japan's GDP in yen} \times \frac{\$}{\text{yen}} = \text{exchange rate}$$

$$500 \text{ trillion yen} \times \frac{\$1}{90 \text{ yen}} = \$5.55 \text{ billion dollars}$$

Of course, it is equally possible to convert the U.S. GDP into yen:

$$\text{U.S. GDP in } \$ \times \frac{\text{yen}}{\$} = \text{U.S. GDP in yen}$$

$$\$14 \text{ trillion} \times \frac{90 \text{ yen}}{\$1} = 1{,}260 \text{ trillion yen}$$

In either case, GDP in the United States is more than double that of GDP in Japan.

To compare the size of several economies, you must convert all of the different measures of GDP into a common currency. The second column of Exhibit 21-7 shows the size of each country's GDP, measured in billions of units of its own currency. The third column shows the exchange rate, measured in U.S. dollars per unit of foreign currency. The fourth column takes the GDP in each country's own currency,

Clearing It Up

Write Out the Exchange Rate Units

The most common mistake that students make when using exchange rates to convert between currencies is to put the exchange rate upside down: for example, they might use the U.S. dollars per euro exchange rate when they meant to use the euros per U.S. dollar exchange rate. To avoid this error, write out the currency units when doing these calculations. Then, you will notice that that the currency units that you are converting away from cancel out in the numerator and denominator of the multiplication calculation, as shown in the conversion of U.S. and Japanese GDP in the text, leaving behind the currency units into which you are converting.

Country (currency)	Currency per U.S. Dollar	U.S. Dollar Equivalent
Brazil (real)	1.792	0.558
Britain (pound)	0.668	1.497
Canada (dollar)	1.027	0.974
China (yuan)	6.826	0.146
Egypt (pound)	5.477	0.183
Euro	0.736	1.359
India (rupee)	45.520	0.022
Indonesia (rupiah)	9195.000	0.000
Japan (yen)	90.025	0.011
Mexico (peso)	12.632	0.079
Nigeria (naira)	150.600	0.007
Russia (ruble)	29.766	0.034
South Africa (rand)	7.403	0.135
United States (dollar)	1.000	1.000

Exhibit 21-6 Examples of Exchange Rates in Early 2010

multiplies by 1/exchange rate in the third column, and thus expresses the GDP for each country in U.S. dollars.

CONVERTING TO PER CAPITA GDP

The U.S. economy has the largest GDP in the world, by a considerable amount. But the United States is also a populous country; in fact, it is the third-largest country by population in the world, although well behind China and India. So is the U.S. economy larger than other countries just because the United States has more people than most other countries, or because the U.S. economy is actually larger on a per-person basis? This question can be answered by calculating a country's **per capita GDP**; that is, the GDP divided by the population.

per capita GDP: GDP divided by the population.

The second column of Exhibit 21-8 lists the GDP of the same selection of countries that appeared in the previous two exhibits, showing their GDP as converted into U.S. dollars. The third column gives the population for each country. The fourth column lists the per capita GDP, which is calculated by dividing the second column by the third.

Exhibit 21-8 illustrates that a country with a small population can have a smaller GDP, but a larger per capita GDP, than a country with a

Exhibit 21-7 Exchange Rates and Gross Domestic Product (GDP), 2008

The second column shows the size of each country's GDP, measured in billions of units of its own currency in 2008. The third column shows the exchange rate, measured in terms of how many units of domestic currency to each U.S. dollar. The fourth column takes the GDP in the nation's own currency, multiplies by 1/exchange rate in the third column, and thus calculates the country's GDP in U.S. dollars.

Country	GDP in Domestic Currency	Domestic Currency/ U.S. Dollars	GDP (in billions of U.S. dollars)
Brazil	2,080 billion reals	1.792	$1,161
Canada	1,437 billion dollars	1.027	1,400
China	29,556 billion yuan	6.826	4,330
Egypt	892 billion pounds	5.477	163
Germany	2,686 billion euros	0.736	3,650
India	55,534 billion rupees	45.520	1,220
Indonesia	4,726,230 billion rupiah	9195.000	514
Japan	442,022 billion yen	90.025	4,910
Mexico	13,768 billion pesos	12.632	1,090
Nigeria	31,927 billion nairas	150.600	212
Russia	47,922 billion rubles	29.766	1,610
South Africa	2,050 billion rand	7.403	277
United Kingdom	1,770 billion pounds	0.668	2,650
United States	14,258 billion dollars	1.000	14,258

Exhibit 21-8
Per Capita GDP in 2008

Country	GDP (in billions of U.S. dollars)	Population (in millions)	Per Capita GDP (U.S. dollars)
Brazil	1,161	192	6,048
Canada	1,400	33	42,028
China	4,330	1,326	3,266
Egypt	163	82	1,999
Germany	3,650	82	44,436
India	1,220	1,140	1,070
Indonesia	514	228	2,252
Japan	4,910	128	38,448
Mexico	1,090	106	10,249
Nigeria	212	151	1,401
Russia	1,610	142	11,354
South Africa	277	49	5,689
United Kingdom	2,650	61	43,160
United States	14,258	307	46,442

larger population. For example, the GDP of China is much larger than that of Mexico, but the per capita GDP of Mexico is much larger than China. Looking ahead several decades, it is quite possible that economic growth in China will cause China to have the largest overall economy in the world—while still having a much lower per capita GDP than the United States. After all, because China has more than four times as many people as the United States, its per capita GDP needs only to be more than one-fourth as large as the U.S. per capita GDP for China's total GDP to exceed that of the United States. The high-income nations of the

Exhibit 21-9 U.S. GDP, 1900–2009

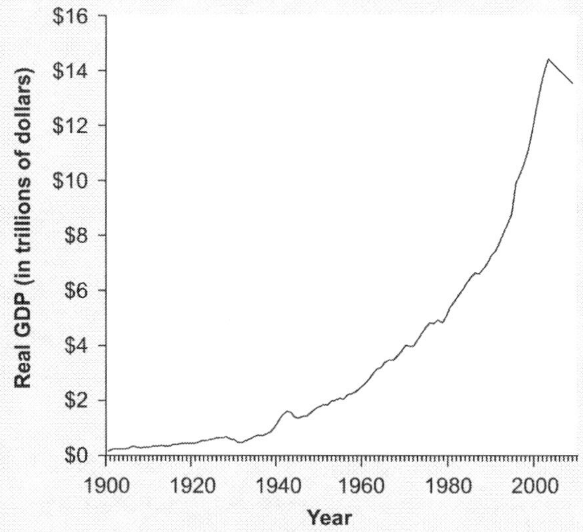

(a) GDP in the United States in 2009 was about $14 trillion. After adjusting to remove the effects of inflation, this represents a roughly 20-fold increase in the economy's production of goods and services since the start of the twentieth century.

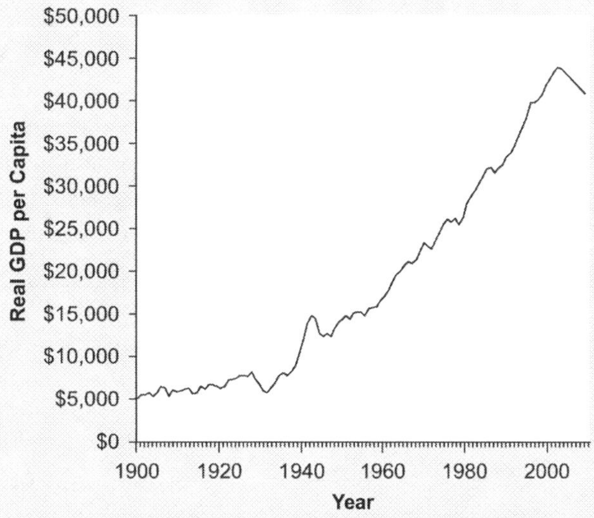

(b) Per capita GDP in the United States in 2005 exceeded $45,000. This represents roughly an eight-fold increase, even after adjusting for the effects of inflation, since the start of the twentieth century.

world—including the United States and Canada, the western European countries and Japan—typically have per capita GDP in the range of $20,000 to $50,000. Middle-income countries, which include much of Latin America, Eastern Europe, and some countries in East Asia, have per capita GDP in the range of $6,000 to $12,000. The low-income countries in the world, many of them located in Africa and Asia, often have per capita GDP of less than $2,000 per year, and in some cases even less than $1,000 per year.

The Pattern of GDP over Time

For most high-income countries of the world, the long-term pattern of GDP looks generally similar. GDP rises gradually over time, but the road can be bumpy.

Exhibit 21-9 illustrates this general pattern with data on U.S. GDP and per capita GDP. These GDP data are presented after adjusting for inflation. As the discussion of inflation in Chapter 24 will explore in detail, GDP can rise either because a greater quantity of goods and services are being produced, or because the prices of goods and services are higher as a result of inflation. By stripping out the effects of inflation, the remaining rise in GDP shown in the exhibits represents only an increase in the quantity of goods and services produced. Chapter 24 will also discuss just how this adjustment for inflation is performed.

Exhibit 21-9a shows the pattern of total U.S. GDP since 1900. The generally upward long-term path of GDP has been regularly interrupted by short-term declines in GDP. A significant decline in national output is called a **recession**. An especially lengthy and deep recession is called a **depression**. The severe drop in GDP that occurred during the Great Depression of the 1930s is clearly visible, as is the Great Recession of 2007–2009. The most significant human problem associated with recessions (and their larger, uglier cousins, depressions) is that a slowdown in production means that many firms will need to hire fewer people, or even to lay off or fire some of the workers that they have. Losing a job imposes painful financial and personal costs on the worker, and often on their extended family as well. In addition, even those who keep their jobs are likely to find that wage raises are scanty at best—or they may even be asked to take pay cuts. Exhibit 21-9b shows the corresponding rise in per capita GDP (again adjusted for inflation). Even though the U.S. population nearly quadrupled over the twentieth century, GDP on a per capita basis has multiplied eight-fold since 1900. The per capita growth rate of GDP over the twentieth century averaged about 2% per year.

recession:
A significant decline in national output.

depression:
An especially lengthy and deep decline in output.

Exhibit 21-10 lists the pattern of recessions and expansions in the U.S. economy since 1900. The highest point of the economy, before the recession begins, is called the **peak**; conversely, the lowest point of a recession, before a recovery begins, is called the **trough**. Thus, a recession lasts from peak to trough, and an economic upswing runs from trough to peak. The movement of the economy from peak to trough and trough to peak is called the **business cycle.** It is intriguing to notice that the three longest trough-to-peak expansions of the twentieth century have happened since 1960. The most recent recession started in December 2007 and seems to have ended in summer 2009.

peak:
During the business cycle, the highest point of output before a recession begins.

trough:
During the business cycle, the lowest point of output in a recession, before a recovery begins.

business cycle:
The relatively short-term movement of the economy in and out of recession.

These patterns of GDP growth suggest that the health of the macroeconomy, as measured by GDP, poses two main issues: economic growth and recessions. The time frame for worrying about economic growth is over the long term; the time frame for worrying about recessions is the short term. This long-term/short-term approach to thinking about GDP will play a central role in macroeconomic analysis.

How Well Does GDP Measure the Well-Being of Society?

The level of per capita GDP clearly captures some element of what is meant by the phrase "standard of living." Most of the migration in the world, for example, involves people who are moving from countries with relatively low per capita GDP to countries with relatively high per capita GDP. Similarly, it is not common to find many people in a high-income country who choose to deny themselves the benefits of electricity, plumbing, modern medicine, automobile and plane travel, and choose instead to live only with the income levels and technologies that were available 50 or 100 years ago in high-income countries—or with the technologies that are still in common use in low-income countries.

However, "standard of living" is a broader term than GDP. GDP focuses on production that is bought and sold in markets. Standard of

Trough	Peak	Months of Contraction	Months of Expansion
December 1900	September 1902	18	21
August 1904	May 1907	23	33
June 1908	January 1910	13	19
January 1912	January 1913	24	12
December 1914	August 1918	23	44
March 1919	January 1920	7	10
July 1921	May 1923	18	22
July 1924	October 1926	14	27
November 1927	August 1929	23	21
March 1933	May 1937	43	50
June 1938	February 1945	13	80
October 1945	November 1948	8	37
October 1949	July 1953	11	45
May 1954	August 1957	10	39
April 1958	April 1960	8	24
February 1961	December 1969	10	106
November 1970	November 1973	11	36
March 1975	January 1980	16	58
July 1980	July 1981	6	12
November 1982	July 1990	16	92
March 1991	March 2001	8	120
November 2001	December 2007	8	73
June 2009	—	18	—

Exhibit 21-10 Dates of U.S. Business Cycles since 1900

living includes all elements that affect people's happiness, whether they are bought and sold in the market or not. To illuminate the gap between GDP and standard of living, it's useful to spell out some things that GDP does not cover that are clearly relevant to standard of living.

SOME DIFFERENCES BETWEEN GDP AND STANDARD OF LIVING

GDP includes spending on recreation and travel, but it does not cover leisure time. Clearly, however, there is a substantial difference between an economy that is large because people work long hours, and an economy that grows because people work the same number of hours but are more productive with their time. For example, the per capita GDP of the U.S. economy is larger than the per capita GDP of Germany, as was shown in Exhibit 21-8, but it's also true that the average U.S. worker works several hundred hours more per year more than the average German worker. The calculation of GDP doesn't take the German worker's extra weeks of vacation into account.

GDP includes what is spent on environmental protection, health care, and education, but it does not include actual levels of environmental cleanliness, health, and learning. Thus, GDP includes the cost of buying pollution-control equipment, but it does not address whether the air and water are actually cleaner or dirtier. GDP includes spending on medical care, but does not address whether life expectancy or infant mortality have risen or fallen. Similarly, it counts spending on

The Human Development Index

Economists have long recognized that GDP is not a complete measure of social well-being. In 1990, an economist named Mahbud ul Haq at the United Nations Development Programme decided to do something about it. The UNDP began publishing an annual Human Development Report. Each year, along with a discussion of economic and social issues affecting low-income countries, the Report includes a Human Development Index, which ranks countries in three broad areas: health, as measured by life expectancy; education, as measured by school enrollment and adult literacy; and material standard of living, as measured by per capita GDP.

By blending per capita GDP with measures of health and education, countries with good levels of health and education may rank higher in the Human Development Index than other countries that have greater per capita GDP. For example, in the rankings published in 2009, the U.S. per capita GDP was 30% higher than that of Australia. However, life expectancy in Australia was three years greater than in the United States and a higher proportion of Australians are enrolled in school (including college) than in the United States. Thus, in the HDI rankings, Australia ranked above the United States.

To choose another example, the per capita GDP of Russia is about one-third above that of Costa Rica. In addition, the average education level is higher in Russia. However, live expectancy in Costa Rica is 79 years while in Russia it is only 66 years, and given the formula used for computing the HDI rankings, Costa Rica ends up well ahead of Russia.

The HDI rankings are controversial. Are these factors, measured in these specific ways, the right ones to include? What about making additional adjustments for gender or racial equality, the level of poverty, or environmental quality? Are the three factors weighted properly, or is, say, adult literacy getting too much weight and per capita GDP too little weight? The UNDP readily acknowledges: "The concept of human development is much deeper and richer than what can be captured in any composite index or even by a detailed set of statistical indicators."

education, but doesn't address directly how much of the population can read, write, or do basic mathematics.

GDP includes production that is exchanged in the market, but it does not cover production that is not exchanged in the market. For example, hiring someone to mow your lawn or clean your house is part of GDP, but doing these tasks yourself is not part of GDP. One remarkable change in the U.S. economy in recent decades is that as of 1970, only about 42% of women participated in the paid labor force. By the first decade of the 2000s, about 60% of women participated in the paid labor force. As women have entered the labor force, many of the services that they used to produce in the nonmarket economy like food preparation and child care have shifted to some extent into the market economy, which makes the GDP appear larger even if more services are not actually being consumed.

GDP includes newly produced goods and services, but does not count the buying and selling of previously existing assets. For example, a house built this year is counted in GDP, but a house built in the past that is sold this year is not part of GDP—because nothing new was produced this year. Although the price of the old house is not part of GDP, the amount paid to a realtor for the service of assisting with the transaction is counted in this year's GDP. GDP has nothing to say about the level of inequality in society. Per capita GDP is only an average. When per capita GDP rises by 5%, it could mean that everyone in the society has risen by 5%, or that some groups have risen by more while others have risen by less—or even declined.

GDP has nothing in particular to say about the amount of variety available. If a family buys 100 loaves of bread in a year, GDP doesn't care whether they are all white bread, or whether the family can choose from wheat, rye, pumpernickel and many others—it just looks at whether the total amount spent on bread is the same.

GDP has nothing much to say about what technology and products are available. The standard of living in, say 1950 or 1900 wasn't affected only by how much money people had—it was also affected by what they could buy. No matter how much money you had in 1950, you could not buy a CD player or a portable phone.

In certain cases, it isn't clear that a rise in GDP is even a good thing. If a city is wrecked by a hurricane, and then experiences a surge of rebuilding construction activity, it would be peculiar to claim that the destruction of the hurricane was therefore economically beneficial. If people are led by a rising fear of crime to pay for installation of bars and burglar alarms on all their windows, it is hard to believe that this increase in GDP has made them better off. Some people would argue that sales of certain goods, like pornography or extremely violent movies, do not represent a gain to society's standard of living.

DOES A RISE IN GDP OVERSTATE OR UNDERSTATE THE RISE IN THE STANDARD OF LIVING?

The fact that per capita GDP does not fully capture the broader idea of standard of living has led to a concern that the increases in GDP over time are illusory. It is at least theoretically possible that while the measured GDP is rising, the standard of living could be falling if human health, environmental cleanliness, and other factors that aren't included in GDP are worsening. Fortunately, this fear appears to be overstated.

In some ways, the rise in GDP understates the actual rise in the standard of living. For example, the typical workweek for a U.S. worker has fallen over the last century from about 60 hours per week to less than 40 hours per week. Life expectancy and health have risen dramatically, and so has the average level of education. Since 1970, the air and water in the United States have generally (with some exceptions) been getting cleaner. New technologies have been developed for many functions, including entertainment, travel, information, and health. A much wider variety of basic products like food and clothing is available today than several decades ago. Because GDP does not capture leisure, health, a cleaner environment, the possibilities created by new technology, or an increase in variety, the actual rise in the standard of living for Americans in recent decades has exceeded the rise in GDP.

On the other side, rates of crime, levels of traffic congestion, and inequality of incomes are higher in the United States now than they were in the 1960s. Moreover, a substantial number of services that used to be provided, primarily by women, in the non-market economy are now part of the market economy that is counted by GDP. By ignoring these factors, GDP would tend to overstate the true rise in the standard of living.

The positive factors ignored by GDP are probably larger than the negative factors ignored by GDP, in which case GDP over time would understate the true rise in the standard of living. But that judgment is a controversial one.

GDP IS ROUGH, BUT USEFUL

It would be foolish and blinkered to believe that a high level of GDP should be the only goal of macroeconomic policy or government policy more broadly. But even though GDP does not measure broader standard of living with any precision, it still reveals something important about the standard of living. In most countries, a significantly higher per capita GDP occurs hand in hand with other improvements in everyday life along many dimensions like education, health, environmental protection.

No single number can capture all the elements of a term as broad as "standard of living." Per capita GDP has real limitations, which must always be kept in mind. Nonetheless, per capita GDP is a reasonable, rough-and-ready measure of the standard of living.

Conclusion

There is sometimes a tendency to speak as if certain parts of the economy deserve more emphasis than others: for example, that high-technology industries are more important to the economy than established industries, like making paper, or service jobs in areas, like tourism. Even within the high-tech industries, certain hot new firms—perhaps those involved in the Internet or in biotechnology—are sometimes claimed to be more important than older established firms.

This desire to treat certain industries like favorite children is often misguided, because an economy is not like a country's Olympic team. In the Olympics, a country can celebrate if a few of its top athletes perform well. In the Olympics, it doesn't matter if the rest of the people in the country, watching on television, are fat and lazy and out of shape. But in an economy, every business counts. For an economy as a whole, it doesn't work especially well to have a few wonderful, world-class companies, while the rest of the economy is flabby and inefficient. After all, people work everywhere in the economy and buy goods from everywhere in the economy. Everyone throughout the economy needs good products, good jobs, good pay, and a generally rising standard of living.

Key Concepts and Summary

1. In a number of cases, behavior that seems rational at the microeconomic level for individuals and firms can end up leading to unexpected or even counterproductive outcomes at the macroeconomic level.
2. The size of a nation's economy is commonly measured by its **gross domestic product** or **GDP**, which measures the value of the output of all goods and services produced within the country. GDP is measured by taking the quantities of all goods and services produced, multiplying them by their prices, and summing the total.
3. Since GDP measures what is bought and sold in the economy, it can be measured either by the sum of what is demanded in the economy or what is produced. Demand can be divided into consumption, investment, government, exports, and imports. What is produced in the economy can be divided into **durable goods**, **nondurable goods**, services, structures, and **inventories**.
4. To avoid **double**-counting, GDP counts only final output of goods and services, not the production of intermediate goods or the value of labor in the chain of production.
5. In comparing GDP figures between countries, it is necessary to useful to convert to a common currency using **exchange rates** and to divide by population to calculate **per capita GDP**.
6. In the long term, the key issue concerning GDP is real per capita growth. In the short run, the key issue concerning GDP is shortening or reducing the size of **recessions** and **depressions**—or avoiding them completely.
7. GDP is an indicator of a society's standard of living, but it is only a rough indicator. GDP does not directly take account of leisure, environmental quality, levels of health and education, activities conducted outside the market, changes in inequality of income, increases in variety, increases in technology, or the (positive or negative) value that society may place on certain types of output.

Review Questions

1. What are the main components of measuring GDP with what is demanded?
2. What are the main components of measuring GDP with what is produced?
3. Would you usually expect GDP as measured by what is demanded to be greater than GDP measured by what is supplied, or the reverse?
4. Why is double counting a danger when measuring GDP?
5. What are the two main difficulties that arise in comparing the GDP of different countries?
6. What are the typical patterns of GDP for a highincome economy like the United State's in the longrun and the short-run?
7. List some of the reasons why GDP should not be considered a precise measure of the standard of living in a country.

DISCUSSION QUESTIONS

Calculating and Modifying GDP

By David Moglen

You are given the following information; show the traditional GDP calculation and the show the GDP with the given suggested improvement, for both countries:

	U.S. (in \$, U.S.)	Germany (in \$, U.S.)
Equality adjustment (OECD)	-500 Billion	+600 Billion
Government Spending	2,500 Billion	1,500 Billion
Consumption	7,000 Billion	4,000 Billion
Leisure adjustment (OECD)	0	400 Billion
Gross Private Investment	2,500 Billion	1,200 Billion
Exports	400 Billion	300 Billion
Imports	900 Billion	600 Billion
Informal Economy	800 Billion	500 Billion
In-home labor	400 Billion	200 Billion
Volunteer Work (outside of home)	400 Billion	200 Billion
Harmful Production: Cost to society of Pollution, False Advertising, & Defective Products	200 Billion	100 Billion

1. What are both countries' GDPs with both OECD adjustments?
2. What are both countries' GDPs with the equality adjustment only as well as including the value of in-home labor by homemakers and others doing chores and the value of the informal economy?
3. What are both countries' GDPs including both in-home and outside-of-the-home unpaid labor, and adjusting for the cost to society of harmful production?
4. Take the same data in #3, and leave out the adjustment for harmful production and add in the informal economy.

CHAPTER 8

Long-Run Economic Growth

C I g + (X - m)

8 Long-Run Economic Growth

By Timothy Taylor

Every country worries about economic growth. In the United States and other high-income countries, will economic growth continue to provide the same remarkable gains in standard of living that it has in the last century? Can middle-income countries like South Korea, Brazil, Egypt, or Poland catch up to the higher-income countries, or must they remain in the second tier of percapita incomc? Of thc world's population of 6.7 billion people, 2.6 billion are scraping by on incomes that average less than $2 per day. Can the world's poor be lifted from their fearful poverty? As economist Robert E. Lucas Jr., the 1995 Nobel laureate in economics, once noted: "The consequences for human welfare involved in questions like these are simply staggering: Once one starts to think about them, it is hard to think about anything else."

Dramatic movements in a nation's standard of living are possible. After the Korean War in the late 1950s, the Republic of Korea, often referred to as South Korea, was one of the poorest economies in the world, along with low-income countries of Africa and south Asia. Most South Koreans worked in peasant agriculture. Per capita GDP was perhaps $200 per year. But from the 1960s to the early twenty-first century, a time period well within the lifetime and memory of a single adult, the economy of South Korea has blossomed. Over these four decades, per capita GDP increased by more than 6% per year. Per capita GDP for the Republic of Korea now exceeds $27,000, which places South Korea firmly among the middle-income countries of the world, near nations like Italy, New Zealand and Israel. Measured by total GDP, South Korea ranked as the world's 13th-largest economy overall in 2008—just slightly larger than the economy of Canada. This transformation for a nation of 48 million people is extraordinary.

South Korea is a standout example, but it is not the only case of rapid and sustained economic growth. Other nations of East Asia, like Thailand and Indonesia, have seen very rapid growth as well. The economy of China has grown enormously since market-oriented economic reforms were enacted around 1980. In a longer historical perspective, per capita GDP in high-income economies like the United States has grown dramatically as well, as the U.S. economy has been transformed from primarily rural and agricultural economies to a modern economy based on services, manufacturing and technology.

This chapter begins with a brief overview of patterns of economic growth around the world in the last two centuries. It then discusses the power of even seemingly low levels of economic growth to transform living standards over time; the key macroeconomic ingredients for growth; and the link from worker productivity to economic growth. The discussion concludes by examining the prospects for countries with lower levels of per capita GDP to catch up to the high-income countries.

The Relatively Recent Arrival of Economic Growth

Economic growth is a relatively recent experience for the human race: it didn't really start until about 1800. Before then, while kings and conquerors could afford some extravagances, the standard of living of average people hadn't changed much for centuries. The famous economist John Maynard Keynes wrote in 1930:

> From the earliest times of which we have record—back, say, to two thousand years before Christ—down to the beginning of the eighteenth century, there was no very great change in the life of the average man living in the civilized centers of the earth. Ups and downs certainly. Visitations of plague, famine, and war. Golden intervals. But no progressive, violent change.

But progressive, powerful economic change started in the late eighteenth and early nineteenth centuries, first in Great Britain, and soon spreading to the United States, Germany, and other countries. The **Industrial Revolution** arrived—a term which refers to the widespread use of power-driven machinery and the economic and social changes that resulted in the first half of the 1800s. Ingenious machines—the steam engine, the power loom, and the locomotive—performed tasks that would have taken vast numbers of workers. The jobs for ordinary people working with these machines were often dirty and dangerous by modern standards, but their alternative jobs for that time in peasant agriculture and small-village industry were often dirty and dangerous, too. The new jobs of the Industrial Revolution typically offered higher pay and chance for social mobility. A self-reinforcing cycle began: new inventions and investments created profits, profits provided funds for new investment and invention, and the investments and inventions provided opportunities for further profits. Slowly, a group of national economies in Europe and North America emerged from centuries of economic stagnation and lifted off. During the last two centuries, the average rate of growth of per capita GDP in the leading industrialized countries has averaged about 2% per year.

Industrial Revolution: The widespread use of powerdriven machinery and the economic and social changes that occurred in the first half of the 1800s.

A growth rate of just 2% per year might seem too slow to explain the phenomenal changes in the standard of living over the last two centuries. But never forget that seemingly low rates of growth, compounded over time, can have mighty results. Thus, if a country's per capita GDP starts at a level of 100, and then grows for 200 years at 2%, its per capita GDP at the end of that period will be:

$$100 (1 + .02) 200 = 5{,}248$$

In other words, a 2% annual growth rate continued over 200 years means that per capita GDP will rise by a multiple of more than 52!

The Industrial Revolution led to a widening of the inequality between nations as some economies took flight, while others, like many of those in Africa or Asia, remained close to a subsistence standard of living. By one calculation, the 17 countries of the world with most developed economies had, on average, 2.4 times the per capita GDP of the world poorest economies in 1870; by 1960, the most developed economies had 4.2 times the per capita GDP of the poorest economies.

However, by the middle of the twentieth century, some countries had shown that catching up was possible. Japan's economic growth took off in the 1960s and 1970s, with a growth rate of real per capita GDP averaging 11% per year during those decades. Certain countries in Latin America experienced a boom in economic growth in the 1960s as well: in Brazil, for example, per capita GDP expanded by an average annual rate of 9% from 1968 to 1973. In the 1970s, some economies in east Asia zoomed as well, including South Korea, Thailand, and Taiwan. In these countries, growth rates of 11–12% per year in per capita GDP were not uncommon. More recently, the economy of China, with its population of 1.3 billion people, grew at a per capita rate 9% per year from 1984 into the 2000s. India, with a population of 1.1 billion, has shown promising signs of economic growth in the 1990s, with growth in per capita GDP of about 4% per year during the 1990s and climbing toward more like 7–8% per year in the 2000s.

These waves of catch-up economic growth have not touched all shores. In certain African countries like Niger, Tanzania, Nigeria, and Sudan, for example, per capita GDP at the start of the 2000s was still less than $300, not much higher than it was in the nineteenth century and for centuries before that. But in thinking about the overall situation of low-income people around the world, the good economic news from China (population: 1.3 billion) and India (population: 1.1 billion) is nonetheless astounding and heartening.

Economic growth in the last two centuries has made a striking change in the human condition. Richard Easterlin, an economist at the University of Southern California, wrote in 2000:

> By many measures, a revolution in the human condition is sweeping the world. Most people today are better fed, clothed, and housed than their predecessors two centuries ago. They are healthier, live longer, and are better educated. Women's lives are less centered on reproduction and political democracy has gained a foothold. Although western Europe and its offshoots

have been the leaders of this advance, most of the less developed nations have joined in during the 20th century, with the newly emerging nations of sub-Saharan Africa the latest to participate. Although the picture is not one of universal progress, it is the greatest advance in the human condition of the world's population ever achieved in such a brief span of time.

Worker Productivity and Economic Growth

productivity: What is produced per worker, or per hour worked.

Per capita GDP offers one measure of economic prosperity; that is, taking the total output of goods and services in an economy—the GDP—and dividing by the population. A useful alternative measure is to start with GDP and divide by the number of workers in an economy, or the number of hours that are worked. The value of what is produced per worker, or per hour worked, is called **productivity**.

An economy's rate of productivity growth is closely linked to the growth rate of its per capita GDP, although the two aren't identical. For example, if the percentage of the population who hold jobs in an economy increases, per capita GDP will increase but the productivity of individual workers need not be affected. But over the long term, the only way that per capita GDP can grow continually is if the productivity of the average worker rises.

A common measure of U.S. productivity is output per hour in the business sector. This measure excludes government workers, because their output is not sold in the market and so their productivity is hard to measure, and farming, which accounts for only a relatively small share of the U.S. economy. Exhibit 22-1 shows that the average amount produced by a U.S. worker in an hour averaged about $53 in 2009, about twice as much as an average worker produced per hour in 1966. Exhibit 22-2 shows average annual rates of productivity growth averaged over five-year periods since 1960. U.S. productivity growth was fairly strong in the 1960s but then dropped lower in the 1970s and 1980s, before rising again in the second half of the 1990s and especially the first half of the 2000s. In fact, the rate of productivity increase measured by the change in output per hour worked averaged 3% per year from 1960–1973; 1% per year from 1973 to 1982; 1.7% per year from 1982 to 1995; 2.1% from 1995 to 1999; 3.5% from 2000 to 2004; and then back to 2.1% from 2005–2009.

A hot controversy has been boiling among economists in recent years about the resurgence of U.S. productivity in the second half of the 1990s. One school of thought argued that the United States had developed a "new economy," based on the extraordinary advances in communications and information technology of the 1990s. The most optimistic proponents of the new economy argued that it would generate higher average productivity growth for decades to come. The pessimists, on the other hand, argued that even five or ten years of stronger

Exhibit 22-1 Output per Hour Worked in the U.S. Economy, 1960–2009

Output per hour worked is a measure of worker productivity. In the U.S. economy, worker productivity rose more quickly in the 1960s and since the mid-1990s than during the 1970s and 1980s. However, these growth rate differences are only a few percentage points per year, so you have to look carefully to see them in the upward slope of the figure. The average U.S. worker produced nearly $53 per hour in 2009. The output-per-hour numbers have been adjusted to remove the effects of price inflation. 1960 1965 1975 1985 1995 2005 2010

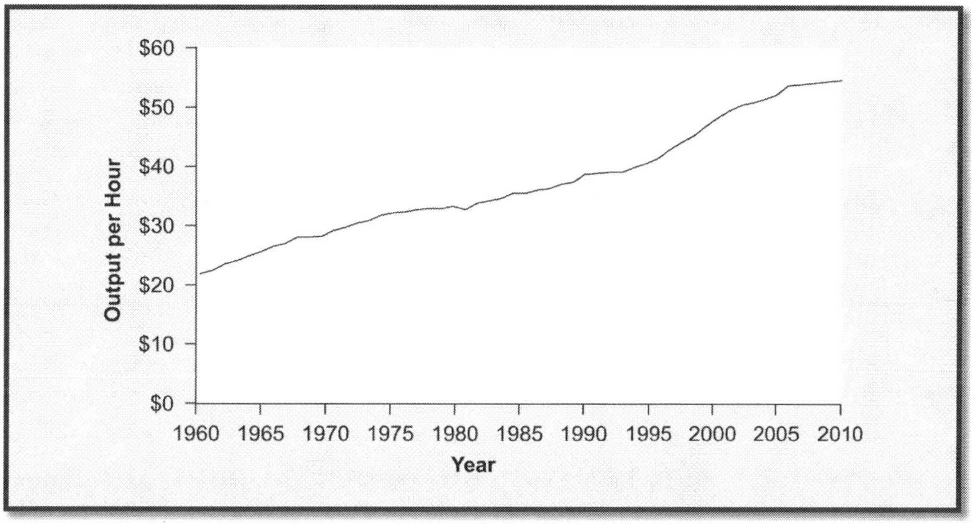

Exhibit 22-2 Annual Rate of Productivity Growth in Output per Hour Worked: Five-Year Averages U.S. growth in worker productivity was very high in the early 1960s, then declined to lower levels in the 1970s and the 1980s. The late 1990s and early 2000s saw a productivity rebound, but then productivity sagged in the late 2000s. Some think the productivity rebound of the late 1990s and early 2000s marks the start of a "new economy" built on higher productivity growth, but this cannot be determined until more time has passed.

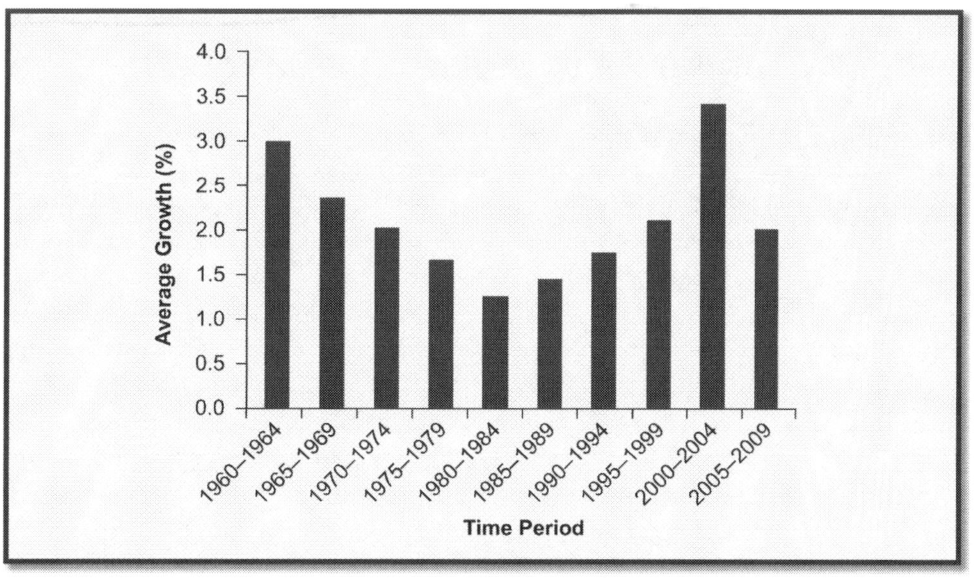

productivity growth doesn't prove that higher productivity will last for the long term. It's hard to infer anything about longterm productivity trends during the later part of the 2000s, because the steep recession of 2007–2009, with its sharp but not completely synchronized declines in output and employment, complicates any interpretation. Of course, the controversy over the path of productivity rates will gradually be resolved by the passage of time and additional data.

Productivity growth is also closely linked to the average level of wages received by workers. Over time, the amount that firms are willing to pay workers will depend on the value of the output that those workers produce. If a few employers tried to pay their workers less than what those workers produced, then those workers will receive job offers with higher wages from other profit-seeking employers. If a few employers mistakenly paid their workers more than what those workers produced, the employers would soon end up making losses, and would either have to reduce wages or go out of business. Over the long run, productivity per hour is the most important determinant of the average wage level in any economy.

The Power of Sustained Economic Growth

Nothing is more important for people's standard of living than sustained economic growth. Even small changes in the rate of growth, when compounded over long periods of time, make an enormous difference in the standard of living. Consider Exhibit 22-3, in which the rows of the table show several different rates of growth in per capita GDP and the columns show different periods of time. Assume for simplicity that an economy starts with a per capita GDP of 100. The table then applies the formula

$$\text{GDP at starting date} \times (1 + \text{growth rate of GDP})^{\text{years}} = \text{GDP at end date}$$

to calculate what GDP will be at the given growth rate at the future time. For example, an economy that starts with a GDP of 100 and grows at 3% per year will reach a GDP of 209 after 25 years; that is, $100\,(1.03)^{25} = 209$.

The slowest rate of per capita GDP growth in the table, just 1% per year, is similar to what the United States experienced during its weakest years of productivity growth. The second highest rate, 3% per year, is close to what the U.S. economy experienced during the strong economy of the late 1990s and into the 2000s. The higher rates of per capita growth, 5% or 8% per year, represent the experience of rapid growth in economies like Japan, Korea, and China. Exhibit 22-3 teaches that even a few percentage points of difference in economic growth rates will have a profound effect if sustained and compounded over time. For example, an economy growing at a 1% annual rate over 50 years will see its per capita GDP rise by a total of 64%, from 100 to 164 in this example. However, a country growing at a 5% annual rate will see (almost) this same amount of growth—from 100 to 163—over just 10 years. Rapid rates of economic growth can be transforming. At an 8% rate of growth, young adults starting at age 20 would see the average standard of living

Clearing It Up
Compound Growth Rates and Compound Interest Rates

The formula for growth rates of GDP over different periods of time, as used in Exhibit 22-1, is exactly the same as the formula for how a given amount of financial savings grows at a certain interest rate over time, as presented back in Chapter 2. Both formulas have the same ingredients: an original starting amount, in one case GDP and in the other case an amount of financial saving; a percentage increase over time, in one case the growth rate of GDP and in the other case an interest rate; and an amount of time over which this effect happens. Just as compound interest means earning interest on past interest, which causes the total amount of financial savings to grow dramatically over time, compound rates of economic growth means that the rate of growth is being multiplied by a base that includes past GDP growth, which can cause an economy to grow dramatically over time.

Exhibit 22-3 Growth of GDP over Different Time Horizons

At time zero, GDP =100. Apply the formula:
GDP at starting date × (1 + growth rate of GDP)^{years} = GDP at end date

	10 Years	25 Years	50 Years
1%	110	128	164
3%	134	209	438
5%	163	338	1,147
8%	216	685	4,690

in their country more than double by the time they had reached age 30, and grow nearly seven-fold by the time they had reached age 45.

The Aggregate Production Function

To analyze the sources of economic growth, whether measured by per capita GDP or by worker productivity, it is useful to think about a **production function**, which is a process of turning economic inputs like labor, machinery, and raw materials into outputs like goods and services used by consumers. A microeconomic production function would describe the inputs and outputs of a firm, or perhaps an industry. In macroeconomics, the connection from inputs to outputs for the entire economy is called an **aggregate production function**.

production function:
The process of a firm turning economic inputs like labor, machinery, and raw materials into outputs like goods and services used by consumers.

aggregate production function:
The process of an economy as a whole turning economic inputs like labor, machinery, and raw materials into outputs like goods and services used by consumers.

Components of the Aggregate Production Function

Exhibit 22-4 presents two aggregate production functions. In the first production function (Exhibit 22-4a), the output is GDP. The inputs are population, human capital, physical capital, and technology.

The category of population is reasonably self-explanatory: more population usually means more workers, who can then produce additional output. The category of **physical capital** includes the plant and equipment used by firms. **Human capital** is the name that economists give the skills and education of workers. As the phrase "human capital" implies, economists make a useful analogy between the intangible skills of workers and the physical capital of the economy. In both cases, investments are made that pay off in longer-term productivity in the future.

physical capital:
The plant and equipment used by firms in production.

human capital:
The skills and education of workers.

Exhibit 22-4 Aggregate Production Functions

An aggregate production function shows what goes into producing the output for an overall economy.

(a) This aggregate production function has GDP as its output.

(b) This aggregate production function uses GDP per capita, which because it is calculated on a per-person basis means that the "population" input is already figured into the other factors and doesn't need to be listed separately.

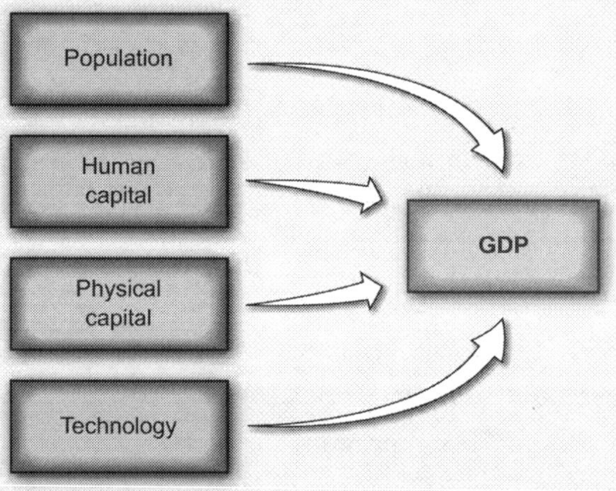

(a) Aggregate Production Function with GDP as its Output

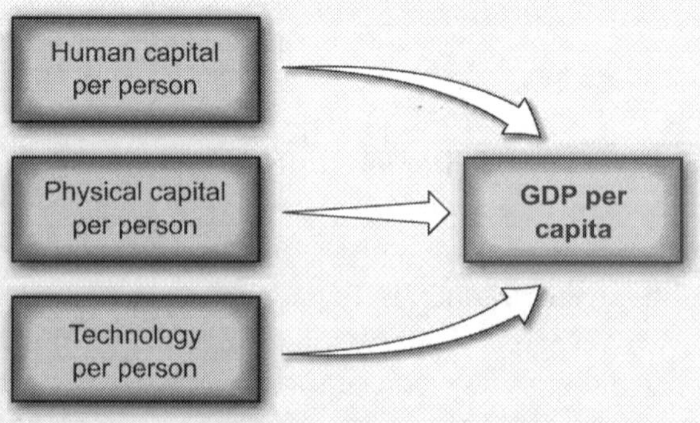

(b) Aggregate Production Function with GDP per Capita as its Output

The category of **technology** is the joker in the deck. When most people think of new technology, inventions like the laser, the transistor, or some new wonder drug come to mind. Such prominent inventions are included in the category of technology, but much more is included as well. The economy is full of small new technologies: the bleach that cleans clothes a little whiter, the portable phone that shrinks a little smaller; the improved design of a car tire that grabs the road better; the computer monitor that tilts at a slightly more comfortable angle. Added together, the vast number of ongoing small changes like But technology, as economists use the term, includes still more. It includes new ways of organizing work, like the invention of the assembly line, as well as new methods for assuring better quality of output in factories. In short, technology comprises all the advances by which people figure out how to make the existing machines produce more or higher quality, as well as including different and altogether new products.

technology:
All the ways in which existing machines produce more or higher quality, as well as producing different and altogether new products.

When discussing economic growth, it is often useful to focus on per capita GDP, to avoid studying changes in the size of GDP that represent only having more people in the economy, and focus on those increases in GDP which represent an actual rise in the standard of living on a per person basis. Using per capita GDP also makes it easier to compare countries with smaller numbers of people, like Belgium or Uruguay or Zimbabwe with countries that have larger populations like the United States or the Russian Federation or Nigeria.

For this purpose, divide everything in the first aggregate production function in Exhibit 22-4a by the population. This creates a revised aggregate production function where the output is per capita GDP (that is, GDP divided by population) and the inputs are the average level of human capital per person, the average level of physical capital per person, and the level of technology per person—see Exhibit 22-4b. In effect, any growth that occurs because of a rise in population is divided out.

When society has a higher level of capital per person, it is called **capital deepening**. The idea of capital deepening can apply both to additional human capital per worker and to additional physical capital per worker.

capital deepening:
When an economy has a higher average level of physical and/ or human capital per person.

Exhibit 22-5 illustrates the human capital deepening for U.S. workers by showing that the proportion of the U.S. population with a high school and a college degree is rising. As recently as 1970, for example, only about half of U.S. adults had at least a high school degree; by the start of the twenty-first century, more than 80% of adults had a high school degree. The idea of human capital deepening also applies to the years of experience that workers have, but the average experience level of U.S. workers hasn't changed much in recent decades. Thus, the key dimension for deepening human capital in the U.S. economy focuses more on additional education and training than on a higher average level of work experience.

Physical capital deepening in the U.S. economy is shown in Exhibit 22-6, which shows that the rise in the average amount of physical capital per worker has risen substantially over time. The average U.S. worker in the late 2000s was working with physical capital worth three times as much as the average worker of the early 1950s.

Not only does the current U.S. economy have better-educated workers with more physical capital than it did several decades ago, but these workers can use more advanced technologies. Growth in technology is impossible to measure with a simple line on a graph, but evidence that we live in an age of technological marvels is all around us: discoveries in genetics; in the structure of particles; the wireless Internet; and other inventions almost too numerous to count. The U.S. Patent and Trademark Office has typically been issuing more than 150,000 patents annually in recent years.

This recipe for economic growth and worker productivity—a mix of human capital, physical capital, and technology—applies beyond the border of the U.S. economy. In South Korea's economy, for example, universal enrollment in primary school (the equivalent of kindergarten through sixth grade in the United States) had already been achieved back in 1965, when Korea's per capita GDP was still near its rock bottom low. By the late 1980s, Korea had achieved almost universal secondary school education (the equivalent of a high school education in the United States). With regard to physical capital, Korea's rates of investment had been about 15% of GDP at the start of the 1960s, but doubled to 30–35%

Exhibit 22-5 A Human Capital Deepening in the U.S. Economy: Education Level of Those Age 25 and Older

Rising levels of education show the deepening of human capital in the U.S. economy. Notice that even today, relatively few American adults have completed a four-year college degree. There is clearly room for additional deepening of human capital to occur.

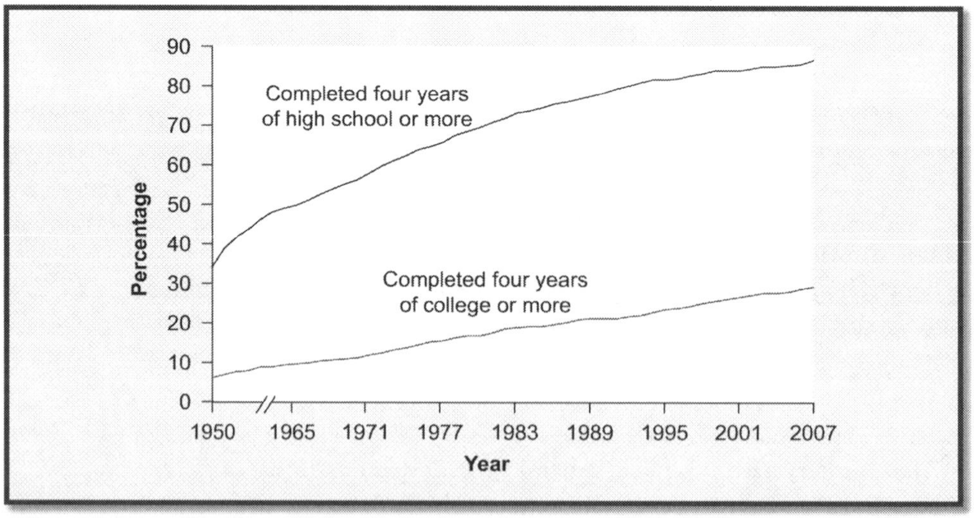

Exhibit 22-6 Physical Capital per Worker in the United States, 1950–2008

The value of the physical capital, measured by plant and equipment, used by the average worker in the U.S. economy has risen over the decades. The increase may have leveled off a bit in the 1970s and 1980s, which were not, coincidentally, times of slower-than-usual growth in worker productivity. There is a renewed increase in physical capital per worker in the late 1990s, followed by a flattening in the early 2000s. (The numbers in the graph are adjusted to remove the effect of price inflation.)

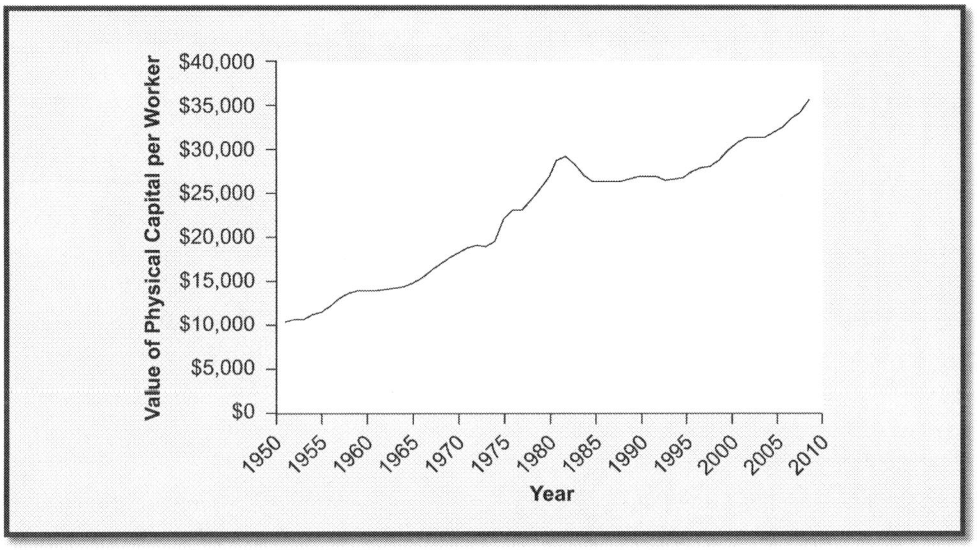

of GDP by the late 1960s and early 1970s. With regard to technology, South Korean students went to universities and colleges around the world to get scientific and technical training, and South Korean firms reached out to study and form partnerships with firms that could offer them technological insights. These factors combined to foster South Korea's high rate of economic growth.

GROWTH ACCOUNTING STUDIES

Since the late 1950s, economists have performed "growth accounting" studies to calculate what specific portion of economic growth is accounted for by deepening of physical capital, deepening of human capital, and technology. The usual approach of these studies is to estimate how much of per capita economic growth can be attributed to growth in physical capital and human capital, which can be measured at least roughly, and then to attribute whatever residual increase in output that can't be explained by these factors to growth in technology. The exact numerical estimates differ from study to study and from country to country, depending on how researcher measured these three main factors being considered over what time horizons. But for studies of the U.S. economy, three lessons commonly emerge from these growth accounting studies.

First, technology is typically the most important contributor to U.S. economic growth. Growth in human capital and physical capital often explain only half or less than half of the economic growth that occurs.

Girl's Education and Economic Growth in Low-Income Countries

In the low-income countries of the world, in the early 2000s, about 110 million children between the ages of 6–11 are not in school—and about two-thirds of them are girls. In Bangladesh, for example, the illiteracy rate for those aged 15–24 was 61% for females, compared to 40% for males. In Egypt, for this age group, illiteracy was 38% for females and 24% for males. Cambodia had 59% illiteracy for females and 25% for males. Nigeria had 18% illiteracy for females in the 15–24 age bracket and 11% for males.

Whenever any child does not receive a basic education, it is both a human and an economic loss. In low-income countries, wages typically increase by an average of 10 to 20 percent with each additional year of education. But there is some intriguing evidence that helping girls in low-income countries to close the education gap with boys may be especially important, because of the social role that many of the girls will play as mothers and homemakers.

Girls in low-income countries who receive more education tend to grow up to have fewer, healthier, better educated children. Their children are more likely to be better-nourished and to receive basic health care like immunizations.

Economic research on women in low-income economies backs up these findings. When 20 women get one additional year of schooling, as a group they will on average have one less child. When 1,000 women get one additional year of schooling, on average 1–2 fewer women from that group will die in childbirth. When a woman stays in school an additional year, that factor alone means that on average, each of her children will spend an additional half-year in school.

Of course, these benefits should be combined with the benefits of education that apply to both genders, like more productive workers, broader personal horizons, and greater control over one's life.

New ways of doing things are tremendously important to economic growth.

Second, while investment in physical capital is essential to growth in worker productivity and per capita GDP, building human capital is at least as important as physical capital. Economic growth is not just a matter of more machines and buildings. One vivid example of the power of human capital and technological knowledge occurred in Europe in the years after World War II. During the war, a large share of Europe's physical capital—factories, roads, vehicles—was destroyed. However, the powerful combination of skilled workers and technological knowledge, working within a marketoriented economic framework, rebuilt Europe's productive capacity to an even higher level within less than two decades.

A third lesson is that these three factors of human capital, physical capital, and technology work together. Workers with a higher level of education and skills are often better at coming up with new technological innovations. These technological innovations are often ideas that cannot increase production until they become a part of new investment in physical capital. New machines that embody technological innovations often require additional training, which builds skills of workers further. If the recipe for economic growth is to succeed, an economy needs all the ingredients of the aggregate production function.

A Healthy Climate for Economic Growth

The sources of economic growth—technology, human capital, and physical capital—need to combine within a healthy overall economic climate. At the microeconomic level, a healthy economic climate will have a market orientation, because the rewards that are available in a market provide incentives to encourage economic growth. Workers have an incentive to acquire additional human capital because in a market-oriented economy, the additional education and skills will pay off in higher wages. Firms have an incentive to make investment in physical capital and in training their workers, because they expect to earn higher profits as a result. Both individuals and firms look for new technologies, because small inventions can make your work easier or improve your products, and major inventions can be worth a fortune. This market orientation of healthy economies typically reaches beyond national borders and includes openness to international trade.

A general orientation toward markets doesn't rule out some important roles for government. Government often plays a role in setting up and funding the education system, especially at the primary and secondary level. Government regulations and taxes can favor savings and investment, or discourage it. Governments can administer laws in a fair and impartial way, or they can offer favoritism and patronage that encourages business to try to make money by lobbying government ministers, rather than by providing goods and services that consumers desire. Governments can encourage international trade, or surrender to protectionism. Governments can play a key role in overseeing the safety of banks and the financial system, in enforcing contracts, and in supporting infrastructure projects like roads and electricity generators. Governments can support scientific research and technical training that helps to create and spread new technologies, or not. Governments can protect the ability of inventors to profit from their inventions, or not. Governments also have a role to play in preventing the economy from sinking deep into recession or inflation, either of which can create a situation where individuals and firms are under such great stress from dismal macroeconomic conditions that they have little chance to plan the investments and discoveries that lead to economic growth.

Thus, the full recipe for growth in per capita GDP and worker productivity would include human capital deepening, physical capital deepening, and technological gains, operating in a market-oriented economy with supportive government policies.

Future Economic Convergence?

Some low-income and middle-income economies around the world have shown a pattern of **convergence**, in which their economies grows faster than those of high-income countries. GDP increased by an average rate of 2.7% per year in the 1990s and 2.3% per year from 2000–2008 in the high-income countries of the world, which includes the United States, Canada, the countries of the European Union, Japan, Australia and New

convergence:
When economies with low per capita incomes are growing faster than economies with high per capita incomes.

Exhibit 22-7

Economic Growth Around the World

Country	Average Growth Rate of GDP 1990–2000	2000–2008
Fast-Growth Club (5% or more per year in both time periods)		
Cambodia	7.1%	9.1%
China	10.6%	9.9%
India	6.0%	7.1%
Ireland	7.5%	5.1%
Jordan	5.0%	6.3%
Lao	6.5%	6.8%
Mozambique	6.4%	7.3%
Sudan	5.4%	7.3%
Uganda	7.1%	7.3%
Vietnam	7.9%	7.3%
Slow-Growth Club (2% or less per year in both time periods)		
Central African Republic	2.0%	0.8%
France	2.0%	1.8%
Germany	1.8%	1.3%
Guinea-Bissau	1.2%	0.2%
Haiti	−1.5%	0.3%
Italy	1.6%	1.2%
Jamaica	0.9%	1.4%
Japan	1.3%	1.3%
Switzerland	1.0%	2.0%
World Overview		
High income	2.7%	2.3%
Low income	3.8%	5.6%
Middle income	4.7%	6.1%

Zealand. Exhibit 22-7 lists 10 countries of the world which belong to an informal "fast growth club:" specifically, these countries averaged GDP growth (after adjusting for inflation) of at least 5% per year in both the time periods from 1990–2000 and from 2000–2008. Since economic growth in these countries has been exceeding the average of the world's high-income economies, the economies of these countries have been converging with the high-income countries. The second part of Exhibit 22-7 lists the "slow growth club," which consists of countries that averaged GDP growth of 2% per year or less (after adjusting for inflation) during both time periods. The final portion of the exhibit shows GDP growth rates for the countries of the world divided by income.

Each of the countries in Exhibit 22-7 has its own unique story of investments in human and physical capital, technological gains, market forces, government policies, and even lucky events. But an overall pattern of convergence over the last two decades is clear. The low-income countries have GDP growth faster than the middle-income countries,

The Challenges of Africa's Geography and Climate for Economic Growth

Many of the poorest countries of the world are in Africa, where the per capita GDP early in the twenty-first century was still only about $500. There are many reasons for poor economic performance, but some recent economic research has suggested that Africa's economic growth may have been limited by its geography and climate.

In many parts of the world, water transportation by river and ocean has helped to link together economies, but this doesn't work well for Africa. Other continents have major river systems that can be navigated by ocean-going vessels: like the Mississippi in North America, the Amazon in South America, the Rhine in Europe, or the Yangtze in Asia. But major rivers in Africa like the Nile, the Niger, the Congo, and the Zambezi have a number of steep waterfalls. Small boats might be transported around such waterfalls, but not large vessels. Moreover, Africa has a relatively straight coastline and thus relatively few natural ports with access to the ocean. Western Europe has one-eighth the land area of Africa, but its winding coastline is actually 50 percent longer.

As a result, in low-income countries in the world outside of Africa, more than half of the population lives within 60 miles of a sea or river. But in Africa, only one-fifth of the population lives within 60 miles of a sea or river.

Much of Africa has poor soil quality and little rain, which makes the challenges of agriculture different and more difficult than in other regions.

Africa is more tropical than any other region of the world; specifically, 93% of the land area of Africa is between the tropic of Cancer (an imaginary line drawn around the world at a latitude of 23.5 degrees north of the equator) and the tropic of Capricorn (an imaginary line drawn around the world at a latitude of 23.5 degrees south of the equator).

A tropical climate poses many challenges for economic growth. Many technologies that are developed for climates like the United States or Europe, like those for agriculture and construction, don't transfer well to tropical climates. Certain plant, animal, and human diseases that would be killed off or weakened by winter, like the malaria carried by mosquitoes, seem to thrive in a tropical climate. Moreover, Africa's tropical location means that it is a long way from the world's major markets in North America and Europe.

None of these arguments prove that Africa's economies cannot grow; indeed, a number of African countries have shown encouraging progress toward faster growth in the 2000s. Nor do these arguments disprove the general recipe for economic growth of investments in human capital, physical capital, and technology, operating in a market-oriented environment. But they do suggest that the nations of Africa face some distinctive economic challenges and will have to discover their own unique path to economic growth.

which in turn have GDP growth faster than the high-income countries. More specifically, two prominent members of the fast-growth club are China and India, which between them have nearly 40% of the world's population. Some prominent members of the slow-growth club are high-income countries like France, Germany, Italy and Japan. Will this pattern on economic convergence persist into future decades? This question is controversial among economists. Here are some of the main arguments on both sides.

ARGUMENTS FAVORING CONVERGENCE

Several arguments suggest that low-income countries might have an advantage achieving greater worker productivity and economic growth in the future. A first argument is based on diminishing marginal returns. Even though deepening human and physical capital will tend to increase per capita GDP, the law of diminishing returns suggests that as an economy continues to increase its human and physical capital, the marginal gains to economic growth will diminish. For example, raising the average education level of the population by two years from a tenth grade level to a high school degree (while holding all other inputs constant) would produce a certain increase in output. An additional two-year increase, so that the average person had a two-year college degree, would increase output further, but the marginal gain would be smaller. Yet another additional two-year increase in the level of education, so that the average person would have a four-year college bachelor's degree, would increase output still further, but the marginal increase would again be smaller. A similar lesson holds for physical capital. If the quantity of physical capital available to the average worker increases, by, say, $5,000 to $10,000 (again, while holding all other inputs constant), it will increase the level of output. An additional increase from $10,000 to $15,000 will increase output further, but the marginal increase will be smaller.

Low-income countries like China and India tend to have lower levels of human capital and physical capital; as a result, an investment in capital deepening should have a larger marginal effect in low-income countries than in high-income countries, where levels of human and physical capital are already relatively high. This factor should give low-income economies a chance for converging economic growth.

A second argument is that low-income countries may find it easier to improve their technologies than high-income countries. The reason is high-income countries must continually invent new technologies, whereas low-income countries can often find ways of applying technology that had already been invented and is well-understood. An economist named Alexander Gerschenkron (1904–1978) gave this phenomenon a memorable name—"the advantages of backwardness." Of course, he didn't literally mean that it was an advantage to have a lower standard of living. But he was pointing out that a country that is behind has some extra potential for catching up.

Finally, optimists argue that many countries have observed the experience of those countries that have grown more quickly and have learned from it. Moreover, once the people of a country begin to enjoy the benefits of an increased standard of living, they may be more likely to build and support the market-friendly institutions that will help provide this standard of living.

ARGUMENTS THAT CONVERGENCE IS NEITHER INEVITABLE NOR LIKELY

If the growth of an economy depended only on the deepening of human capital and physical capital, then the growth rate of that economy would be expected to slow down over the long run as these inputs run into diminishing marginal returns. However, there is another crucial factor in the aggregate production function: technology.

The development of new technology can provide a way for an economy to sidestep the diminishing marginal returns of capital deepening. Exhibit 22-8 shows how. The horizontal axis of the figure measures the amount of capital deepening, which on this figure is an overall measure that includes deepening of both physical and human capital. The amount of human and physical capital per worker increases as you move from left to right from C_1 to C_2 to C_3. The vertical axis of the diagram measures per capita output. Start by considering the lowest line in this diagram, labeled Technology 1. Along this aggregate production function, the level of technology is being held constant, so the line shows only the relationship between capital deepening and output. As capital deepens from C_1 to C_2 to C_3 and the economy moves from R to U to W, per capita output does increase—but the way in which the line starts out steeper on the left but then flattens as it moves to the right shows the diminishing marginal returns, as additional marginal amounts of capital deepening increase output by ever-smaller amounts. The shape of the aggregate production line Technology 1 shows how the ability of capital deepening by itself to generate sustained economic growth is limited, since diminishing returns will eventually set in.

Now bring improvements in technology into the picture. Improved technology means that with a given set of inputs, more output is possible. The production function labeled Technology 1 is based on one level of technology, but Technology 2 is based on an improved level of technology, so for every level of capital deepening on the horizontal axis, it produces a higher level of output on the vertical axis. In turn, production function Technology 3 represents a still higher level of technology, so that for every level of inputs on the horizontal axis, it produces a higher level of output on the vertical axis than either of the other two aggregate production functions.

Most healthy, growing economies are both deepening their human and physical capital and increasing technology at the same time. As a result, the economy can move from a choice like point R on the Technology 1 aggregate production function to a point like S on Technology 2 and on a point like T on the still higher aggregate production function Technology 3. With the combination of technology and capital deepening, the rise in per capita GDP in high-income countries does not need to fade away because of diminishing returns. The gains from technology can offset the diminishing returns involved with capital-deepening.

Will technological improvements themselves run into diminishing returns over time; that is, will it become continually harder and more costly to discover new technological improvements? Perhaps someday.

Exhibit 22-8 Capital Deepening and New Technology I

magine the economy starts at point R, with the level of physical and human capital C_1 and the GDP per capita at G1. If the economy relies only on capital deepening, while remaining at the technology level shown by the Technology 1 line, then it would face diminishing marginal returns as it moved from point R to point U to point W. However, now imagine that capital deepening is combined with improvements in technology. Then, as capital deepens from C_1 to C_2, technology improves from Technology 1 to Technology 2, and the economy moves from R to S. Similarly, as capital deepens from C_2 to C_3, technology increases from Technology 2 to Technology 3, and the economy moves from S to T. With improvements in technology, there is no longer any reason that economic growth must necessarily slow down.

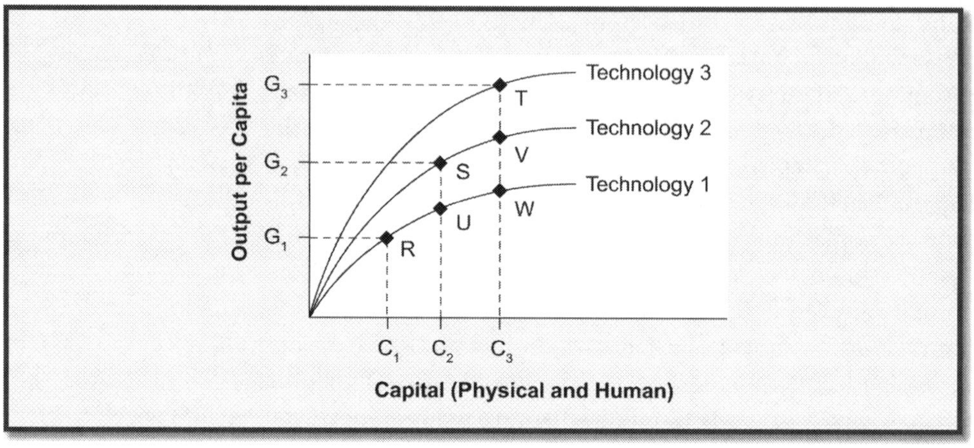

But at least over the last two centuries since the Industrial Revolution, improvements in technology haven't run into diminishing marginal returns. Modern inventions, like the Internet or discoveries in genetics or materials science, don't seem to provide smaller gains to output than earlier inventions like the steam engine or the railroad. One reason that technological ideas don't seem to run into diminishing returns is that the ideas of new technology can often be widely applied at a marginal cost that is very low or even zero. A specific additional machine, or an additional year of education, must be used by a specific worker or group of workers. But a new technology or invention can be used by many workers across the economy at very little marginal cost.

The argument that it is easier for a low-income country to copy and to adapt existing technology than it is for a high-income country to invent new technology isn't necessarily true, either. A society's performance when it comes to adapting and using new technology isn't automatic, but is the result of whether the economic, educational, and public policy institutions of the country are supportive. In theory, perhaps, low-income countries have many opportunities to copy and adapt technology, but if they lack the appropriate supportive economic institutions, the theoretical possibility that backwardness might have certain advantages is of little practical relevance.

THE SLOWNESS OF CONVERGENCE

Although economic convergence between the high-income countries and the rest of the world seems possible and even likely, it will proceed only slowly. Consider, for example, one country that starts off with a per capita GDP of $40,000, which would roughly represent a typical high-income country today, and another country that starts out at $4,000, which is roughly the level in low-income but not impoverished countries like Indonesia, Guatemala, or Egypt. Say that the rich country chugs along at a 2% annual growth rate of per capita GDP, while the poorer country grows at the aggressive rate of 7% per year. After 30 years, per capita GDP in the rich country will be $72,450 (that is, $40,000 (1 + .02)30), while in the poor country it will be $30,450 (that is, $3,000 (1 + .07)30). Convergence has occurred; the rich country used to be 10 times as wealthy as the poor one, and now it is only about 2.4 times as wealthy. But even after 30 consecutive years of very rapid growth, people in the low-income country are still likely to feel quite poor compared to people in the rich country. Moreover, as the poor country catches up, its opportunities for catch up growth are reduced, and its growth rate may slow down somewhat.

The slowness of convergence illustrates again that small differences in annual rates of economic growth accumulate to huge differences over time. The high-income countries have been building up their advantage in standard of living over decades—more than a century in some cases. Even in an optimistic scenario, it will take decades for the low-income countries of the world to catch up significantly.

Key Concepts and Summary

1. Since the **Industrial Revolution** of the nineteenth century, a process of economic growth began in which the world's leading economies—mostly those in Western Europe and North America—expanded per capita GDP at an average rate of about 2% per year. In the last half century, countries like Japan, Korea, and China, have shown potential for catch-up growth at higher rates, which has helped them to converge with the leading economies.
2. **Productivity** can be measured as the level of GDP per worker or GDP per hour. The rate of productivity growth is the primary determinant of its rate of long-term economic growth.
3. Over decades and generations, seemingly small differences of a few percentage points in the annual rate of economic growth make an enormous difference in per capita GDP.
4. An **aggregate production function** specifies how certain inputs in the economy, like human capital, physical capital, and technology, lead to the output measured as per capita GDP.
5. **Capital deepening** refers to a greater amount of capital per worker. It can apply to a greater amount of **human capital** per worker, in the form of higher education or skills, or to a greater amount of **physical capital** per worker.

6. **Technology**, in its economic meaning, refers broadly to all new methods of production, which include major scientific inventions but also small inventions and even better forms of management or company organization.
7. The recipe for growth in per capita GDP is to improve human capital, physical capital, and technology, in a market-oriented environment with supportive public policies and institutions.
8. **Convergence** refers to the issue of when, or if, countries with lower levels of per capita GDP will catch up to countries with higher levels of per capita GDP.
9. Because high-income economies will run into diminishing marginal returns to their investments in human capital and physical capital, and because high-income economies must continually invent new technologies, lower-income economies have a chance for convergent growth. However, many high-income economies have developed economic and political institutions that provide a healthy economic climate for an ongoing stream of technological innovations. The ongoing stream of technological innovations can counterbalance diminishing returns to investments in human and physical capital.

Review Questions

1. What was the Industrial Revolution?
2. How is per capita GDP calculated differently from worker productivity?
3. How do gains in worker productivity lead to gains in per capita GDP?
4. How much should a nation be concerned if its rate of economic growth is just 2% slower than other nations?
5. What is an aggregate production function? Describe one.
6. What is capital deepening?
7. What do economists mean when they refer to improvements in technology?
8. What is the overall recipe for growth in per capita GDP or worker productivity?
9. For a high-income economy like the United States, what elements of the aggregate production function are most important in bringing about growth in per capita GDP?
10. What do economists mean by convergence?
11. List some arguments for and against the likelihood of convergence.

Figure 8.7 **Productivity and Wages in U.S. Manufacturing: 1978 to 2006**

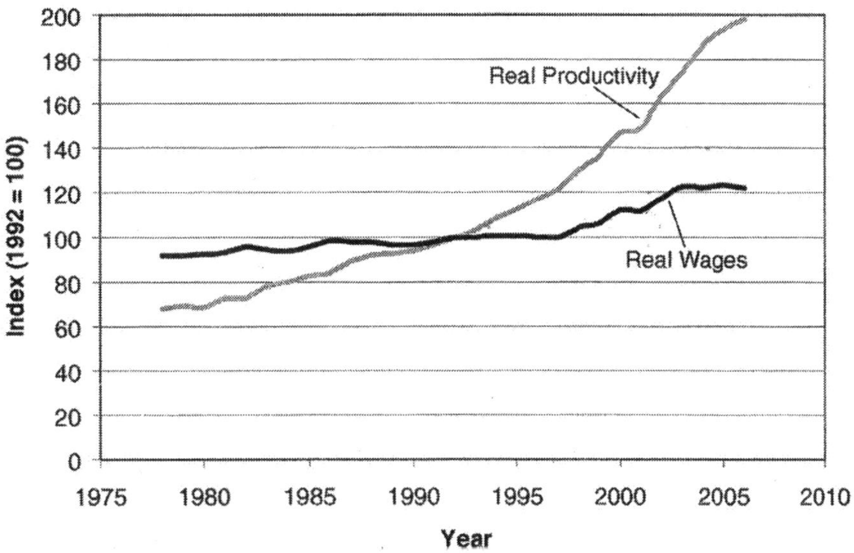

In recent decades, the average real hourly wage in manufacturing has not increased as quickly as real output per hour. (Source: U.S. Bureau of Labor Statistics, http://www.bls.gov/fls/prodsupptabletoc.htm)

CHAPTER 9
Classical and Keynesian Economics

9 Classical and Keynesian Economics

By Neva Goodwin, Julie Nelson, and Jonathan Harris

3. Macroeconomics in Context

Macroeconomics, as a field of study, is not a set of principles that is set in stone. Rather, the field has developed and changed over time as new empirical and theoretical techniques have been invented and as historical events have raised new questions for which people have urgently desired answers. To give you an idea about how the various principles in this book fit into social and historical context, we end this chapter with a short overview of the major historical developments in macroeconomics. This is not just dusty history; you will see as you progress through this textbook that many themes keep arising in just slightly new forms, while other challenges are unique to our twenty-first-century world.

3.1 THE CLASSICAL PERIOD

Centuries ago, most people in Europe were involved in agriculture or in home production, such as when a family would work together to card, spin, and weave raw wool into cloth. Merchants were a minority, and industrial production and large-scale trade were unknown. All this changed with the coming of the Industrial Revolution, which began in England in the mid-eighteenth century. In many countries technological progress led to new methods of production, and more productive economies both increased and diversified their output. Necessities like food and clothing used up a decreasing proportion of the average family income, while a growing fraction of the population was able to acquire more comforts and luxuries—better bedding, plumbing, housing, and transportation, to name just a few of the improvements to living standards. Academic thinkers started to try to understand and explain how these changes came about—and **classical economics** was born.

classical economics: the school of economics, originating in the eighteenth century, that stressed issues of growth and distribution, based on an image of smoothly-functioning markets

During this period macroeconomic study focused on economic growth and distribution. The most famous classical economist was Scottish philosopher Adam Smith (1723–90) whose 1776 book *An Inquiry into the Nature and Causes of the Wealth of Nations* set the

Neva Goodwin, Julie Nelson, and Johnathan Harris, *Macroeconomics in Context*, pp. 14–19.

terms of discussion for centuries to come. Smith attributed the growing "wealth of nations" to various factors. One was changes in the organization of work, particularly the **division of labor** that assigned workers to **specialized,** narrowly defined tasks. Whereas in family-based production each individual had usually performed a variety of tasks, in industrial production a person would repeat one very specific task over and over, presumably becoming more proficient with increased practice. Another factor was technological progress, such as the invention of new machines powered by burning coal. The third was the accumulation of funds to invest in plants and machinery ("capital accumulation"). Classical economists were also particularly concerned with theorizing about how the funds generated by selling output would come to be distributed between the people who worked in factories and the capitalists who owned the factories.

division of labor: an approach to production in which a process is broken down into smaller tasks, with each worker assigned only one or a few tasks

specialization: in production, a system of organization in which each worker performs only one type of task

Classical economists, from Adam Smith through Karl Marx, were interested in several questions that are still among the most important issues for macroeconomics: How is the total wealth generated by a society divided between those who own the means of production and those who work for them? Is the existing division optimal? What are the forces that determine how society's wealth will be divided?

Smith is particularly known for promulgating the idea that market systems could coordinate the self-interested actions of individuals so that they would ultimately serve, the social good. While Smith himself supported a number of government interventions and discussed the moral basis for social and economic behavior at length in others of his works, the school of classical economics has been popularly identified with the idea that individual self-interest is a positive force and that governments should let markets function without interference—that economies should be **laissez-faire.**

laissez-faire economy: an economy with little government regulation

The classical economists did not much address the problem of economic fluctuations. A smoothly functioning market system, a number of them thought, should be entirely self-regulating. At the macroeconomic level, full employment should generally prevail. This view was summarized in **Say's Law,** named after French classical economist Jean-Baptiste Say (1767–1832), which was said to prove that "supply creates its own demand." The example Say gave was of a tradesman, for example a shoemaker, who sold $100 worth of shoes. Say argued that the shoemaker would naturally want to spend the $100 on other goods, thereby creating a level of demand that was exactly equal in monetary value to the supply of shoes he had provided. If this example is extended to the whole economy, it suggests that the quantities demanded and quantities supplied of goods will exactly balance, meaning that employment—producing shoes or something else—will be available for anyone willing to work. Classical economists discussed issues related to a country's monetary system, but tended to assume that monetary issues affected only the price levels, and not the level of production, in a country.

Say's Law: the classical belief that "supply creates its own demand

3.2 THE GREAT DEPRESSION, KEYNES, AND MONETARISM

Yet economies did not seem to be working so smoothly, in practice. Some periods, like 1904–06 and the 1920s in the United States, were boom years where everyone seemed eager to invest and spend. People with extra funds would buy stocks (ownership shares in companies) or deposit their funds in banks (to be lent to others) with great confidence and optimism. On the other hand, these booms seemed to frequently end in painful recessions. Suddenly the tide would turn and everyone would want to sell—not buy—and stock prices would plummet. A lack of confidence in banks would lead to "bank runs" or "banking panics," such as occurred in 1907 and 1930–33 in the United States, when many people tried to pull out their deposits all at once. With financial markets in tatters, businesses and individuals would be unable or unwilling to maintain or expand their activities. With people cutting back on spending, produced goods would go unsold. Industries would cut back on production. People would become unemployed.

A great many people in the United States (and much of the rest of the industrialized world) suffered considerable hardship during the Great Depression that followed the 1929 stock market crash. Production dropped by about 30 percent between 1929 and 1933. At its worst, the unemployment rate during the Great Depression topped 25 percent—one in four workers could not find a job. High unemployment persisted throughout the 1930s, and classical economic theory did not seem to be of much help in either explaining or correcting the situation.

The publication of British economist John Maynard Keynes' *The General Theory of Employment, Interest, and Money* in 1936 was a watershed event. In this book, Keynes (pronounced "canes") argued that Say's Law was wrong. It *is* possible for an economy to have a level of demand for goods that is insufficient to meet the supply from production, he said. In such a case, producers, unable to sell their goods, will cut back on production, laying off workers, and thus creating economic slumps. The key to getting out of such a slump, Keynes argued, is to increase **aggregate demand**—the total demand for goods and services in the national economy as a whole.

aggregate demand: the total demand for all goods and services in a national economy

Keynes suggested a number of ways to achieve this. People could be encouraged to consume more, the government could buy more goods and services, or businesses could be encouraged to spend more. Some economists thought that the best way to encourage business spending was to keep interest rates low, so that businesses could borrow easily to invest in their enterprises. But, while Keynes believed that increasing investment spending would be the key to getting out of a depression, he thought that low interest rates alone would be insufficient to tempt discouraged and uncertain business leaders to start investing again. He wrote in *The General Theory* that the solution to business cycles lay in the government taking more direct control of the level of national investment. In his view capitalist economies were inherently unstable, and only a more socially oriented direction of investment could cure this instability.* This policy, however, was not generally adopted and the Great Depression continued for the remainder of the 1930s.

In actuality, it was the high government spending associated with national mobilization for World War II that finally brought the Great Depression to an end. Perhaps this is one reason why the followers of what came to be known as **Keynesian economics** did not follow Keynes on all points. While they retained his emphasis on deficiencies in aggregate demand, they tended to emphasize the use of fiscal policy to keep employment rates up. **Fiscal policy** is the manipulation of levels of government spending and taxation to raise or lower the level of aggregate demand.

Keynesian economics: the school of thought, named after John Maynard Keynes, that argued for the active use of fiscal policy to keep aggregate demand high and employment rates up

fiscal policy: the manipulation of levels of government spending and taxation to raise or lower the level of aggregate demand

Other economists in these post-WWII years—most notably University of Chicago economist Milton Friedman—took a different tack. While the Keynesians argued that active government fiscal policies were the way to get *out* of a recession, the **monetarists** argued that bad government **monetary policies** were how economies tend to get *into* bad situations in the first place. It was primarily the United States government's poor use of its monetary policy tools, such as banking regulations and the issuance of currency (most often understood as "printing money"), that led to the Great Depression, they said. They blamed government policies encouraging overly "loose" money (that is, easy credit, low interest rates, and high levels of money supply) for the overspending of the late 1920s. Then, they claimed, "tight" money policies (tight credit, higher-than-optimal interest rates, and low money supply) during the early 1930s turned what could have been a more minor slump into a major depression. They argued that governments should focus on keeping the money supply steady, and not try to take an active role in directing the economy, even when unemployment is high. Like the classical economists, they believed that the economy should best be left to adjust on its own.

monetarist economics: the school that focused on the effects of monetary policy, and argued that governments should aim for steadiness in the money supply rather than play an active role

monetary policy: the use of tools controlled by the government, such as banking regulations and the issuance of currency, to try to affect the levels of money supply, interest rates, and credit

As time went on, the Keynesian approach was expanded to include a role for monetary policy. This approach had a strong influence on macroeconomic policymaking in the United States and many other countries up through the 1960s. The idea became popular that the government might even be able to "fine tune" the economy, counteracting any tendencies to slump with expansionary (high spending and/or loose money) policies, and any excessive expansion with contractionary (low spending and/or tight money) policies, thereby largely eliminating business cycles. A related idea was that the government could choose to "trade off" unemployment and inflation—letting the economy suffer a little more inflation to get the unemployment rate down, or vice versa.

* It is the return of confidence, so to speak in ordinary language, which is so insusceptible to control in an economy of individualistic capitalism … I conclude that the duty of ordering the volume of investment cannot safely be left in private hands" *The General Theory* (NY: Harcourt Brace Jovanovich, [1936] 1964), p. 317, 320.

3.3 SYNTHESIZING CLASSICAL AND KEYNESIAN ECONOMICS

In the early 1970s this rosy picture was shattered, however, as many industrialized countries began to experience rising unemployment *without* a decrease in inflation. To explain this, many macroeconomists began combining elements of both classical and Keynesian economics, making a distinction between the long-run and the short-run as follows:

- Classical theories assert, first, that economies should naturally settle at full-employment levels of output and, second, that the primary outcome of changes in money supply are changes in the price level or rate of inflation. In an idealized smoothly functioning market system—as we will see in detail in a later chapter—any unemployment (that is, surplus of labor) should be corrected by a drop in the (equilibrium) wage. In the emerging synthesis, full employment and purely inflationary effects came to be thought of as *long-run* outcomes, which occur only after all markets have had sufficient time to adjust.
- Keynesian economists after World War II had come to accept the idea that their theories should be explainable in terms of market models, but explained unemployment as being due to the fact that markets for labor do not adjust quite as quickly as classical theory implies. Keynesian economists argued that wages are "sticky" in real-world markets and will not fall fast enough during a slump for full employment to be quickly restored. Fiscal and monetary policies were thought, in this emerging synthesis, to be effective mechanisms for coping with this *short-run* phenomenon.

Thus the dominant macroeconomic theory that emerged argued that in the short run—a period of some months or years—we are in a primarily Keynesian world where fiscal and monetary policies can be effective. In the long run, however—after such a period of time that even "sticky" markets are able to adjust—we are in a classical world, where markets adjustments assure full employment and money only affects prices.

Economists thus explained the inflation that occurred in the first few years of the 1970s (in spite of the simultaneous presence of unemployment) as the long-run outcome of expansionary monetary policies of the previous years. It appeared that short run active (Keynesian) government policies could have unintended negative long-term (classical) consequences.

While many economists have come to agree on this general theoretical picture, debates have continued, now centered around the question of whether the short-run benefits of active government policies are worth their long-run, presumably mostly negative, consequences.

Macroeconomists at the more classical end of the spectrum tend to emphasize market efficiency and a small role for government. They are suspicious about the use of monetary policy because of the possible negative effects we just discussed. They are suspicious about the use of fiscal policy, as well, arguing that increases in government spending or taxation primarily lead to a larger government. Large governments, they believe, discourage private sector activities and economic growth.

Economists on the more Keynesian end of the spectrum, meanwhile, tend to emphasize the way in which unemployment can cause severe human suffering and be very persistent. They argue for a more active role for government. Waiting for markets to adjust on their own, they believe, may mean waiting too long. And, as Keynes himself put in, "In the long run, we are all dead."

While it might seem that many economists have finally come to at least a general agreement about how the macroeconomy works, real-world developments have brought still new issues to public attention.

3.4 SUBSEQUENT CHALLENGES

In 1973–74 the macroeconomic environment of the United States and most other industrialized economies took a sharp hit when countries belonging to the Organization of Petroleum Exporting Countries (OPEC) cut production, drastically increased the price at which they would sell crude oil, and even for several months completely stopped shipping oil to certain nations. The price of oil, a key input to many production and consumption activities, suddenly quadrupled. Stock markets fell, inflation rose, and unemployment shot up as people struggled to adjust. People waited in long lines at gas stations, or were even limited to buying gas only on certain days. The price of crude oil continued to rise until at its peak in 1979 a barrel of crude oil in the United States cost over ten times as much as it had in 1973.

This crisis brought increased attention to two areas. First, the oil price shock made it clear how closely national economies are tied to each other. While many previous theories had neglected to take into account international linkages, the implications of globalization now became more prominent in macroeconomic thinking. Second, while Keynes had led the field into paying attention to aggregate *demand,* this "supply shock" encouraged economists to think more about the *supply* side of the economy—the resources and technology that allow production to occur. In later chapters of this book, you will study some of the theories economists have created to try to explain these phenomena.

3.5 MACROECONOMICS FOR THE TWENTY-FIRST CENTURY

While issues of economic growth and the business cycle preoccupied macroeconomic thinking for generations, once again, in the twenty-first century, new developments are demanding new ways of looking at the economic world.

First, the environmental impact of long-term, fossil-fuel-based economic growth is becoming increasingly a topic of economic, social, and

Figure 1.4 **Growth in Atmospheric Carbon Dioxide, 1800–2004**

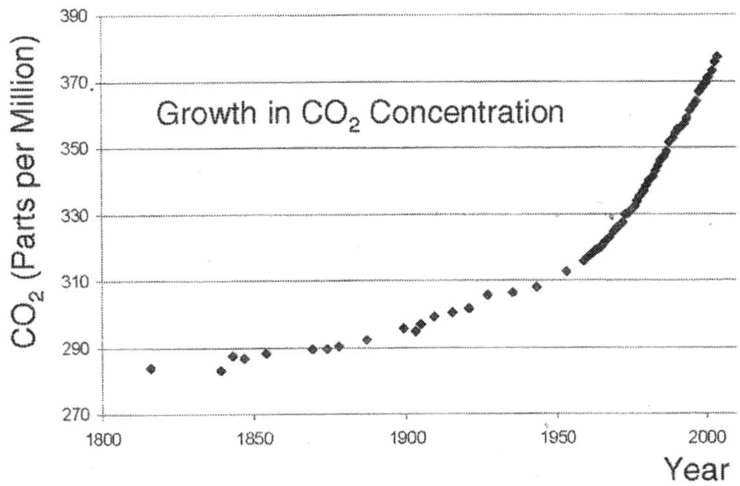

As fossil-fuel based industrialization and deforestation have increased, so has the atmospheric concentration of the gases involved in global warming. (Source: Carbon Dioxide Information Analysis Center, http://cdiac.ornl.gov/ftp/trends/co2/siple2.013 and http://cdiac.ornl.gov/trends/co2/sio-mlo.htm)

political concern. Most previous theories assumed that resources and the capacity of the environment to absorb the by-products of economic growth were essentially unlimited—or at least that continued developments in technology would keep problems of depletion and pollution at bay. This is increasingly questioned as the scale of human economic activity grows larger.

The graphs of economic growth, seen earlier in this chapter, illustrate an impressive human ability to increase production. The growth in global atmospheric carbon dioxide illustrated in Figure 1.4 is equally impressive, but more sobering, as it shows the human ability to affect our environment significantly—sometimes in dangerous ways. Carbon dioxide is released in fossil-fuel-burning industrial production, transportation, and heating, and more is released the more such production takes place. Deforestation also contributes to increases in atmospheric CO_2 Carbon dioxide is the main gas involved in global climate change, a problem that scientists say is already starting to cause floods, droughts, and irreversible disturbances to ecosystems.

Unless slowed or reversed, within the next twenty years we can expect to see increasingly dramatic disturbances to agriculture, disruptions in water supply, and an expansion of the reach of tropical diseases. How national and international economic environments can be made ecologically sustainable, while keeping employment and standards of living high, is rising in prominence as a macroeconomic issue. New thinking about the relation between production and living standards, and about the quality of our working lives, will likely be central to these discussions.

Second, the persistence of substantial global poverty, as mentioned in the earlier discussion of social sustainability, has called into question the appropriateness of traditional ideas about economic development. Questions of *what, how* and *for whom*—rather than just "how much"—are becoming increasingly important in evaluating the effect of economic activity on human well-being. The lopsided global distribution of resources, disparities in power, war and peace, and global institutions of trade and finance will become increasingly important issues as economists continue to participate in the humanitarian attempt to increase human well-being on a global scale.

The Keynesian Perspective

by Timothy Taylor

An argument is sometimes made that an occasional recession should not cause too much concern, because it will soon be over, and in the meantime, tough economic times create a powerful incentive for firms to become more productive lest they be driven into bankruptcy. Perhaps the most compelling criticism of this argument that recessions should be viewed without overmuch concern came from the great economist John Maynard Keynes. Soon after the steep recession of 1920–1921, Keynes wrote:

> Now "in the long run" this [idea that recessions are part of a process of long-term economic growth] is probably true. . . . But this long run is a misleading guide to current affairs. *In the long run* we are all dead. Economists set themselves too easy, too useless a task if in tempestuous seasons they can only tell us that when the storm is long past the ocean is flat again.

The worst economic storm of the twentieth century was the Great Depression of the 1930s. Over several years, the U.S. GDP plummeted by 30%. Unemployment rocketed from 3.2% in 1929 to 24.9% in 1933, and even as late as 1939, unemployment still hovered above 17%. So few dollars were chasing so many goods that deflation resulted, with the price level falling by 24% from 1929 to 1933. (In a situation of deflation, if you have money to spend, every dollar *increases* substantially in purchasing power.) The human misery of the Depression was even worse than these grim statistics imply. Up to a million Americans were homeless. Hunger and malnutrition were widespread. In the early 1930s, comparatively few government social programs existed. Millions of people had literally no way to make a living—no way to feed or shelter themselves or their families.

Yet in the early years of the Great Depression, many well-known economists did not perceive anything fundamentally wrong with the economy. After all, the

Timothy Taylor, "The Keynesian Perspective," *Principles of Macroeconomics*, pp. 501–512.

1920s had seen several recessions: from January 1920 to July 1921, from May 1923 to July 1924, and from October 1926 to November 1927. But even including these recessions, real GDP had risen at a healthy annual average rate of 2.6% per year from 1919 to 1928. Thus, some economists argued that recessions every few years were part of the process of a growing economy. However, other economists, like Keynes, focused on the human costs of suffering through a recession every few years. More recently, the U.S. economy suffered a recession starting in December 2007, and the number of unemployed Americans rose from 6.8 million in May 2007 to 15.6 million in October 2009. It would not have been helpful to tell those additional 8.8 million unemployed workers that their joblessness is part of a process of long-term growth.

This chapter begins with a Keynesian diagnosis of causes of recession. The chapter then discusses the components of aggregate demand—consumption, investment, government spending, exports, and imports. The discussion will use the model of aggregate supply and aggregate demand to show how recessions occur and can be counteracted. This Keynesian model implies trade-offs between unemployment and inflation. The discussion then presents a macroeconomic model called the expenditure-output model. Finally, the chapter addresses the question of whether Keynesian economics should be viewed as opposing or complementary to a market-oriented economy.

The Building Blocks of Keynesian Analysis

Keynesian economics focuses on explaining why recessions and depressions occur and offering a policy prescription for minimizing their effects. Not all of what is now called "Keynesian economics" can be found in an exact form in the writings of John Maynard Keynes, because these ideas have evolved over time. However, the Keynesian view of recession is based on two key building blocks. First, aggregate demand is not always automatically high enough to provide firms with an incentive to hire enough workers to reach full employment. Second, the macroeconomy may adjust only slowly to shifts in aggregate demand because of stickiness of wages and prices. Let's consider these two claims in turn, and then see how they are represented in the model of aggregate supply and aggregate demand.

The Importance of Aggregate Demand in Recessions

A first element of the Keynesian diagnosis of recession is that a shift in aggregate demand is a more likely explanation of recession than a shift in aggregate supply. After all, even during the Great Depression, the physical capacity of the economy to supply goods did not alter much. No flood or earthquake or other natural disaster ruined factories in 1929 or 1930. No outbreak of disease decimated the ranks of workers. No key input price, like the price of oil, soared on world markets. The U.S. economy in 1933 had just about the same factories, workers, and state of technology as it had had four years earlier in 1929—and yet the economy shrunk dramatically. Indeed, most recessions are not accompanied by destruction of machinery and equipment on the supply side of the economy. It seems more plausible that they are caused by shifts of aggregate demand.

As Keynes recognized, the events of the Depression contradicted Say's law that "supply creates its own demand." Instead, Keynes argued, an economy has periods when its potential GDP changes little, but aggregate demand falls by a lot. One likely cause is that the demand for physical investment spending by firms can shift quickly. When firms are pessimistic or uncertain about the economic future, they postpone investment projects. When businesses become more optimistic, they may have a backlog of projects in mind that they can start up all at once. Thus, the investment component of aggregate demand is likely to surge and decline rapidly.

More recent analysis in a Keynesian spirit has also emphasized how a country's ailing financial system—especially if its banks are performing poorly—can drag down the economy. As the U.S. economy staggered into Depression during the early 1930s, many businesses and households were unable to repay their loans, and banks went bankrupt as a result. Of the 24,000 U.S. banks in operation in 1929, only 14,400 remained in 1933. When so many banks went out of business, the availability of loans diminished for firms seeking to invest and for households seeking to buy a home or car. Thus, the reduction in aggregate demand injured the banking system, making the reduction in aggregate demand even worse, creating a vicious cycle of worsening depression. The U.S. recession from 2007–2009 was also worsened by a weakened banking system.

Wage and Price Stickiness

A second major element of the Keynesian diagnosis of recession involves the stickiness of wages. If markets throughout the economy all had flexible and continually adjusting prices, then a shift in aggregate demand would result in changes in prices and wages, but not in any additional unemployment. To put it another way, if all prices and wages were flexible and continually adjusting, the economy would always head for its natural rate of unemployment, as discussed in Chapter 23.

Keynes emphasized one particular reason why wages were sticky: the *coordination argument*. The coordination argument points out that even if most people would be willing—at least hypothetically—to see a decline in their own wages in bad economic times *as long as everyone else also experienced such a decline,* a market-oriented economy has no obvious way to implement a plan of coordinated wage reductions. The discussion of unemployment in Chapter 23 proposed a number of reasons why wages might be sticky downwards, most of which come down to the argument that businesses avoid wage cuts, because they may in one way or another depress morale and hurt the productivity of the existing workers.

Some modern economists have argued in a Keynesian spirit that along with wages, other prices may be sticky, too. Many firms don't change their prices every day or even every month. For example, many companies publish sales catalogs every six months or every year, instead of announcing that the prices may change on any given day. When a firm considers changing prices, it must consider two sets of costs. First, changing prices uses company resources: managers must analyze the competition and market demand and decide what the new prices will be, sales materials must be updated, billing records will change, and product labels and price labels must be redone. Second, frequent price changes may leave customers confused or angry—especially if they find out that a product now costs more than expected. These costs of changing prices are called **menu costs**—like the costs of printing up a new set of menus with different prices in a restaurant. Prices do respond to forces of supply and demand, but from a macroeconomic perspective, the process of changing all prices throughout the economy takes time.

menu costs: The costs that firms face in changing prices.

To understand the effect of sticky wages and prices in the economy, consider Exhibit 27-1. Exhibit 27-1*a* illustrates the overall labor market, while Exhibit 27-1*b* illustrates a market for goods and services. The original equilibrium E_0 in each market occurs at the intersection of demand curve D_0 and supply curve S_0. When aggregate demand declines, the demand for labor shifts to the left to D_1 in Exhibit 27-1*a* and the

The Slow Speed of Price Adjustments

Probably few companies anywhere in the world know more about inflation and pricing strategies than the business magazine *Fortune*. But consider how the cover price of *Fortune* has changed over time. In May 1970, the cover price was raised $1.50 to $2.00. The price increases from 1970 to 2000 are shown in the first column of the table. The second column shows the Consumer Price Index for those years (using a base period where the average price level from 1982–84 was set equal to 100), and the third column converts the nominal cover price into real 2009 dollars.

Apparently, *Fortune* used to be a lot more expensive in 1970, measured in real dollars. During the high inflation of the 1970s, the magazine allowed its real price to fall. Since then, *Fortune*'s pricing strategy is apparently to wait until the price level has increased about 10–15%—and the real price of the magazine has been eroded by that amount—before it bumps up the nominal price to about the same real level. However, by 2009 the real price had been allowed to fall even further.

	Cover Price	CPI	Real Price
May 1970	$2.00	38.8	$11.13
January 1980	$2.50	82.4	$6.55
May 1982	$3.00	96.5	$6.71
May 1985	$3.50	107.6	$7.02
April 1990	$3.95	130.7	$6.52
May 1994	$4.50	148.2	$6.56
October 1997	$4.95	160.5	$6.66
May 2001	$4.99	177.1	$6.08
December 2009	$4.99	215.9	$4.99

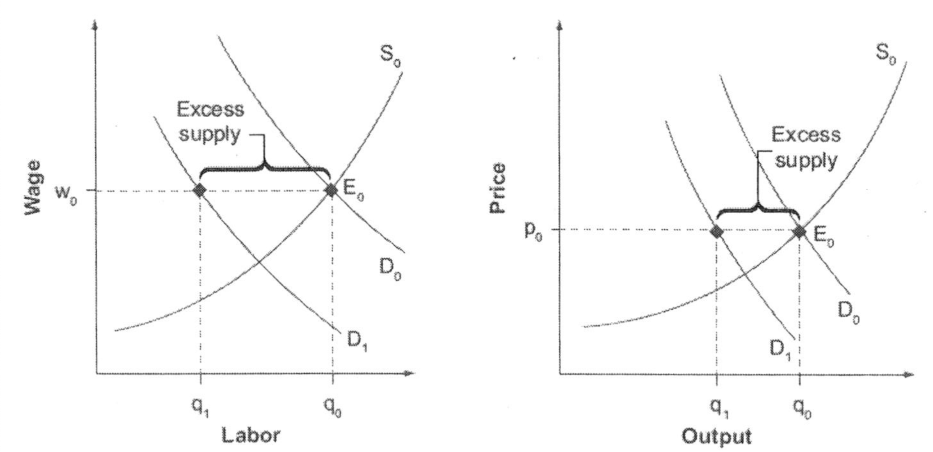

(a) Sticky wages in the labor market

(b) Sticky prices in the goods market

Exhibit 27-1 Sticky Prices and Falling Demand in the Labor and Goods Market

In both *a* and *b*, demand shifts left from D_0 to D_1. However, the wage in *a* and the price in *b* do not decline. In *a*, the quantity demanded of labor at the original wage w_0, but the new demand curve for labor D_1, will be q_1. In *b*, the quantity demanded of goods at the original price p_0 but the new demand curve D_1 will be q_1. An excess supply of labor will exist, called unemployment. An excess supply of goods will also exist, where the quantity demanded is substantially less than the quantity supplied. Thus, sticky wages and sticky prices combine with a drop in demand bring about unemployment and recession.

demand for goods shifts to the left to D_1 in Exhibit 27-1*b*. However, because of sticky wages and prices, the wage for a time remains at its original wage level w_0 and the price remains at its original level p_0. As a result, a situation of excess supply—where the quantity supplied exceeds the quantity demanded at the existing wage or price—exists in markets for both labor and goods, and q_1 is less than q_0 in both Exhibit 27-1*a* and Exhibit 27-1*b*. When many labor markets and many goods markets all across the economy find themselves in this position, the economy is in a recession: that is, firms cannot sell what they wish to produce at the existing market price and don't wish to hire all workers who are willing to work at the existing market wage.

The Two Keynesian Assumptions in the AS-AD Model

These two Keynesian assumptions—the importance of aggregate demand in causing recession and the stickiness of wages and prices—are illustrated by the AS-AD diagram in Exhibit 27-2. The original equilibrium of this economy occurs where the aggregate

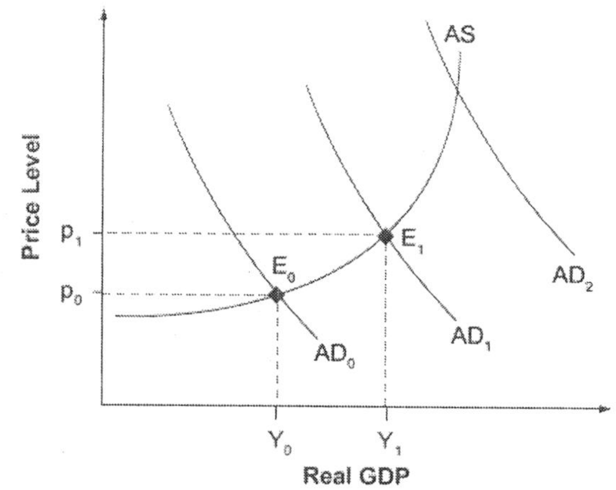

Exhibit 27-2
A Keynesian Perspective on Recession

The equilibrium E_0 illustrates the two key assumptions behind Keynesian economics. The importance of aggregate demand is shown because this equilibrium is a recession which has occurred because aggregate demand is at AD_0 instead of AD_1. The importance of sticky wages and prices is shown because the economic logic of the AS curve is built on the assumption of fixed prices for inputs, like wages, and because the intersection E_0 occurs in the relatively flat portion of the AS curve where the price level for outputs doesn't change by much.

demand function AD_0 intersects with AS. Since this intersection occurs well below the full employment level, this economy is suffering a recession and high cyclical unemployment.

This description of the recession encompasses the two key building blocks of Keynesian economics. The importance of aggregate demand is illustrated because the output of the economy is being determined by the fact that AD_0 is far to the left of AD_1 and potential GDP. The importance of sticky wages and prices is illustrated because the aggregate supply curve is built on an assumption that the prices of inputs like wages are being held constant—so the AS curve assumes sticky wages. Because shifts of aggregate demand happens primarily in the flatter portion of the AS curve, to the left of the potential GDP level of output, they will have little impact on the price level—which fits well with the notion that prices are sticky and don't alter by much. Thus, the AS-AD model is well-designed to explain how the combination of a fall in demand and sticky wages and prices bring about a recession.

The Components of Aggregate Demand

What economic events or policies might cause aggregate demand to shift to the left, away from the potential GDP level of output? Conversely, what economic events or policies could cause AD to shift to the right? This section investigates the Keynesian approach by considering in turn each of the components of aggregate demand—consumption, investment, government, exports and imports.

What Causes Consumption to Shift?

Consumption is the largest component of aggregate demand. If consumption increases at every given price level, then the aggregate demand curve will shift to the right. If consumption declines, then the AD curve will shift to the left.

For most people, the single most powerful determinant of how much they consume is how much income they have in their take-home pay, after the government subtracts taxes. This insight suggests two factors that affect consumption: income and taxes. Higher incomes or tax cuts will tend to lead to more consumption and cause AD to shift out to the right. Lower incomes or tax increases will cause AD to shift to the left.

But in thinking about how much to consume in the present, people will also think about their *expectations about future incomes*. An economic theory known as the **permanent income hypothesis** points out that when individuals think about how much to consume, they won't look just at the current paycheck, but will look into the future, too, and calculate their expected "permanent income" over their lifetime. An implication of the permanent income hypothesis is that if people believe that their income is especially high this year, and is likely to be lower in the future, then they are likely to save more in the present. Conversely, if people think that their income is especially low this year, but will rise in the future, then they may not worry about saving much at all in the present. The permanent income hypothesis also implies that a temporary tax cut, which increases take-home income for only one year, will have a much smaller impact on current consumption than a permanent tax cut, which is expected to increase take-home income for many years.

permanent income hypothesis: When individuals think about how much to consume, they look into the future and consider how much income they expect to earn in their lifetime

Choices about whether to save or borrow in the present will also be influenced by the interest rate. For a borrower, the interest rate is the price that is paid for borrowing; for a saver, the interest rate is the price that is received for saving. Lower real interest rates will tend to encourage consumer borrowing for purchases of big-ticket items like cars or refrigerators and cause AD to shift to the right. Conversely, higher real interest rates will tend to discourage purchases on credit and thus shift AD to the left.

Finally, a variety of other factors combine to determine how much people save, including personal preferences and wealth. If household preferences about saving shift in a way that encourages consumption rather than saving, then AD would shift out to the right. When households experience a rise in wealth, then they may be willing to consume a higher share of their income and to save less. When the U.S. stock market rose dramatically in the late 1990s, for example, U.S. rates of saving declined, probably in part because people felt that their wealth had increased and there was less need to save. On the other side, when the U.S. stock market declined about 40% from March 2008 to March 2009, as the recession took hold and many people felt far greater uncertainty about their economic future, rates of saving increased while consumption declined.

What Causes Investment to Shift?

When a firm makes an investment in physical assets, like plants or equipment, or in intangible assets, like skills or a research and development project, it is spending in the present in the expectation (or perhaps the hope) that the future will bring a worthwhile rate of return. When a firm plans its investment demand, it calculates an expected rate of return—that is, the percentage return that the firm expects to receive over time, after all the costs of the investment are taken into account. If firms believe that they can make a high expected return, they will be more eager to invest.

The expected rate of return depends on several factors. One consideration is the range of investment opportunities open to the firm. The creation of new technologies, for example, may offer investment opportunities with a high expected rate of return. Another key factor is that if the economy appears likely to grow in the next few years, then businesses will perceive a growing market for their products, and their higher degree of business confidence will encourage investment. In the second half of the 1990s, the U.S. economy experienced both a wave of new information and communications technologies, like the Internet and vastly improved mobile phones, while also having a long period of sustained economic growth sometimes called the "dot-com boom." For both reasons, U.S. investment levels surged at this time from 18% of GDP in 1994 to 21% of GDP in 2000. However, a recession started in the U.S. economy in 2001, and many firms came to believe that the returns from investing in new computers was not as high as they had thought, so U.S. investment levels quickly sank back to 18% of GDP by 2002.

When considering the expected rate of gains from investment opportunities, firms need to take into account not only the direct costs of investments—like buying a new piece of machinery—but also an opportunity cost that involves the interest rate. When a firm borrows funds to make an investment in physical plant or equipment, this opportunity cost is readily apparent in the interest payments that the firm has to make. But even if a firm doesn't need to borrow money for a certain investment—perhaps because it is earning enough profits to finance its investment using its own internal funds—the firm could have chosen to invest those profits and receive interest payments. The interest payments that could have been received, but are not, because of the decision to invest profits in new plant and equipment, are also an opportunity cost of the investment decision. In either case, a higher real interest rate discourages a firm from investing in tangible or intangible capital by raising its cost.

Developments in the rest of the economy or in public policy can also affect the expected rate of return on investment. For example, if the price of energy declines, then investments that use energy as an input will have a higher expected rate of return. If government offers special incentives through the tax code for investment, then investment will look more attractive; conversely, if government removes special investment incentives from the tax code, or increases other business taxes, then investment will look less attractive.

Firms often have some flexibility about when to invest. It's easy to postpone or scale back physical investment decisions for a time if economic conditions are unfavorable, and it's often possible to accelerate or increase investments if economic conditions appear more favorable. Thus, investment often happens in waves, surging and then ebbing. A decline in investment would shift AD back and to the left, and unless it was offset by other portions of aggregate demand, it could bring on a recession.

What Causes Government Demand to Shift?

Governments make decisions for political reasons, which in turn can depend on the philosophy of those who are in power. Government presiding over an economy with a low level of GDP may decide that there is too little tax revenue to justify much government spending, or alternatively, it may decide that the economy is in desperate need of government programs and higher spending. Conversely, a government with a high level of GDP may decide that in a high-income country, people can afford a high level of government services, or it may decide that in a high-income country, most people should be responsible for purchasing their own goods and service and so the government services and government spending should be low. In any given year, a government can decide to run a budget surplus—that is, to collect more in taxes than it spends—or to run a budget deficit—that is, to spend more than it collects in taxes. Whatever its political justification, an increase in the government spending component of demand will cause AD to shift to the right, while a decline in government spending demand will cause AD to shift to the left.

What Causes Exports and Imports to Shift?

Two sets of factors can cause shifts in export and import demand: changes in relative growth rates between countries and changes in relative prices between countries. The level of demand for a nation's exports tends to be most heavily affected by what is happening in the economies of the other countries that would be purchasing those exports. For example, if major importers of American-made products like Canada, Japan, and Germany have recessions, exports of U.S. producers to those countries are likely to decline. Conversely, the quantity of a nation's imports is directly affected by the amount of income in the domestic economy: more income will cause a higher level of imports.

One implication of thinking about exports and imports in this way is that the trade deficit in an economy will tend to arise (or an existing trade surplus will shrink) when an economy is growing strongly, while a trade surplus will tend to arise (or an existing trade deficit will shrink) when an economy is stagnant or shrinking. A more rapidly growing domestic economy draws in more imports, but doesn't affect exports (which are determined by what happens in other countries), thus reducing the balance of trade. Conversely, a domestic recession will reduce imports, along with all other consumption, but will not much affect exports, thus increasing the balance of trade. For example, the U.S. economy ran very large trade deficits in the mid-2000s during a period of sustained growth, but the trade deficit fell by about half when the recession took full hold in 2009.

Exports and imports can also be affected by relative prices of goods in domestic and international markets. If U.S. goods are relatively cheaper compared with goods made in other places, perhaps because a group of U.S. producers has mastered certain productivity breakthroughs, then U.S. exports are likely to rise. But if U.S. goods become relatively more expensive, perhaps because a change in exchange rate between the U.S. dollar and other currencies has pushed up the price of inputs to production in the United States, then exports from U.S. producers are likely to decline. Chapter 31 will discuss exchange rates in more detail.

Exhibit 27-3 summarizes the reasons given in this section for why the aggregate demand curve might shift to the left, from AD_1 to AD_2, or alternatively to the right, from

Exhibit 27-3 Reasons for Shifts in the Components of Aggregate Demand

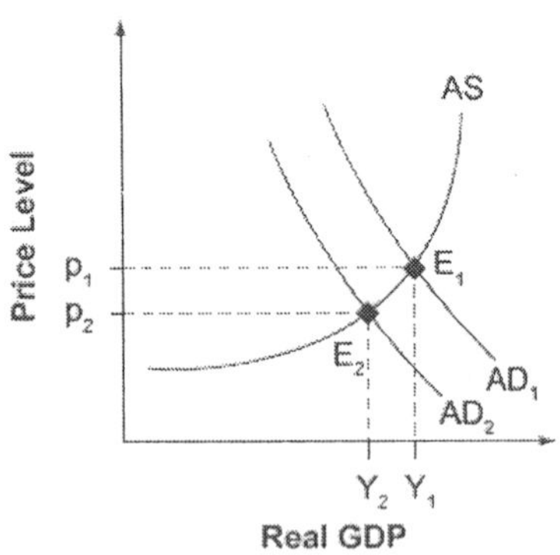

Reasons for a Shift of Aggregate Demand to the Left from AD_1 to AD_2	Reasons for a Shift of Aggregate Demand to the Right from AD_2 to AD_1
Consumption	*Consumption*
• Rise in taxes	• Decrease in taxes
• Fall in income	• Increase in income
• Rise in interest rates	• Fall in interest rates
• Desire to save more	• Desire to save less
• Decrease in wealth	• Rise in wealth
• Fall in future expected income	• Rise in future expected income
Investment	*Investment*
• Fall in expected rate of return	• Rise in expected rate of return
• Rise in interest rates	• Drop in interest rates
• Drop in business confidence	• Rise in business confidence
Government	*Government*
• Reduction in government spending	• Increase in government spending
Export and Import	*Export and Import*
• Decrease in foreign demand	• Increase in foreign demand
• Relative price increase of U.S. goods	• Relative price drop in U.S. goods

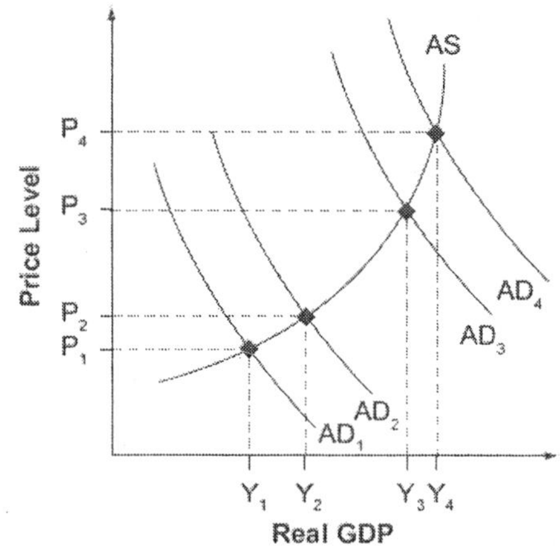

Exhibit 27-4 When Shifts in Aggregate Demand Increase the Price Level

A shift of aggregate demand to the right from AD_1 to AD_2 leads to a relatively small increase in the price level from P_1 to P_2, but a relatively large increase in real GDP from Y_1 to Y_2. When unemployment is relatively high, the inflationary increase in the price level is small. However, a similar shift of aggregate demand to the right from AD_3 to AD_4 leads to a relatively large increase in the price level from P_3 to P_4, and only a relatively small increase in real GDP from Y_3 to Y_4. When unemployment is relatively low, because the equilibrium is occurring in the near-vertical portion of the AS curve, close to potential GDP, then the pressure for inflationary price increases can be larger. This pattern suggests the trade-off that when unemployment is high, inflation may be low, and when unemployment is low, inflation may be high.

AD_2 to AD_1. Many of the reasons involve economic events, like changes in preference for saving, or the rate of growth in other economies that purchase exports. But some of the factors that shift aggregate demand can be affected by government policy.

The Phillips Curve

The Keynesian economic framework is based on an assumption that prices and wages are sticky and do not adjust rapidly. This assumption made some sense during the Great Depression, when Keynes was writing, and more generally during any recession when the intersection of AD and AS is below the potential GDP level of output. However, do prices still remain sticky when an economy is not in recession, but instead is near or even above its potential GDP?

The Discovery of the Phillips Curve

In the 1950s, a British economist named A.W. Phillips was studying the Keynesian analytical framework. He noticed that when the economy is in a recession, with real GDP well below potential GDP and high unemployment, the Keynesian theory implied that pressures for inflationary increases in the price level also tend to be low. However, when the level of output is at or even pushing beyond potential GDP, so that unemployment is low, Keynesian theory implied that the economy is at greater risk of inflationary pressures.

Exhibit 27-4 illustrates how during a recession, a move of aggregate demand from AD_1 to AD_2 barely shifts the equilibrium price level at all. However, if the economy is already near potential GDP at AD_3, then a move to AD_4 will increase the price level. When the level of output lies in the flatter part of the AS curve, far below potential GDP, then an increase in aggregate demand can easily encourage more firms to produce more. However, when an economy is already near potential GDP, it becomes increasingly difficult for an additional rise of aggregate demand to bring forth more supply—because the factories and workers in the economy are near full employment already. In this situation, the rise in aggregate demand begins to translate into a higher price level, rather than more output.

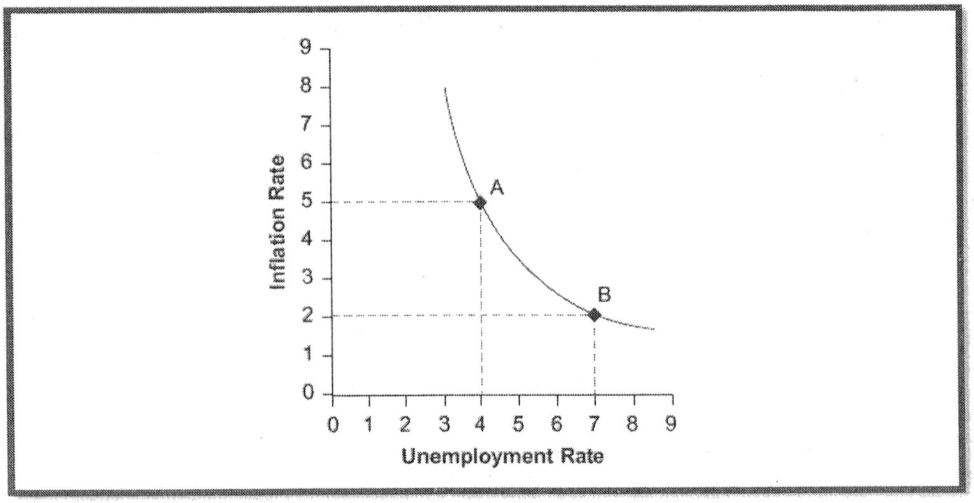

Exhibit 27-5
A Keynesian Phillips Curve Trade-off between Unemployment and Inflation

A Phillips curve illustrates a trade-off between the unemployment rate and the inflation rate; if one is higher, the other must be lower. For example, point A illustrates an inflation rate of 5% and an unemployment rate of 4%. If the government attempts to reduce inflation to 2%, then it will experience a rise in unemployment to 7%, as shown at point B.

Phillips went searching in the historical data to see if these theoretical predictions held true: Is inflation high when unemployment is low, and vice versa? Phillips graphed annual British data over 60 years, with unemployment rates on the horizontal axis and the rise in wages (as a measure of inflation) on the vertical axis. He found that the British data over this period of time did indeed trace out a downward-sloping curve, which became known as a **Phillips curve.** Exhibit 27-5 shows a theoretical Phillips curve. In this example, society must choose between a point like A, with 4% unemployment and 5% inflation, and a point like B, with 7% unemployment and 2% inflation.

Phillips curve: The trade-off between unemployment and inflation.

The Instability of the Phillips Curve

American economists began graphing unemployment and inflation data to see if the Phillips curve relationship held in the U.S. economy as well. Exhibit 27-6*a* is based on U.S. unemployment and inflation data for the years 1960–69. Over this time, the U.S. economy seemed first to move down a Phillips curve, then back up toward the middle. With the image of the Phillips curve in mind, macroeconomists in the 1960s sought to identify the optimal point on the Phillips curve. The extremes of the Phillips curve—high unemployment or high inflation—were both undesirable. But in the middle ground, which point should be favored?

But by the 1970s, this debate became obsolete. Instead of a trade-off between unemployment and inflation, several deep recessions occurred in which unemployment and inflation rose *at the same time.* The U.S. economy experienced this pattern in the deep recession from 1973–75, and again in the back-to-back recessions from 1980–82. For example, the U.S. unemployment rate rose from 4.9% in 1973 to 8.5% by 1975, while inflation was rising from 3.2% in 1972 to 11% in 1974. The unemployment rate rose from 5.8% in 1979 to 9.7% in 1982, while inflation had risen from 7.6% in 1978 to 13.5% in 1980. Exhibit 27-6*b* graphs the data on U.S. unemployment and inflation from 1960–2009. It is clearly impossible to draw a single smooth curve through this forest of data points. Many nations around the world saw similar increases in unemployment and inflation. This pattern was known as **stagflation**—an unhealthy combination of a stagnating economy with high inflation.

stagflation: When an economy experiences stagnant growth and high inflation at the same time.

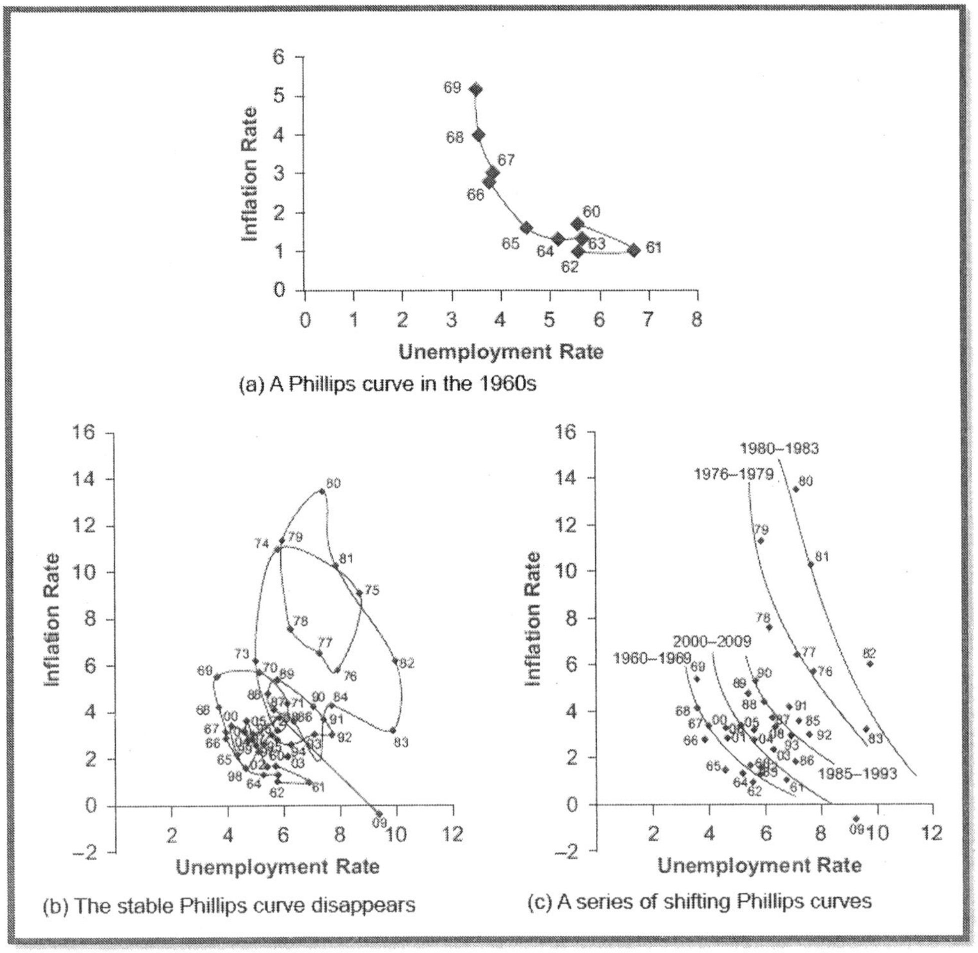

Exhibit 27-6 The Evolution of the Keynesian Phillips Curve

(a) The points on this figure show the unemployment rate and the inflation rate for each year from 1960–69, with the last two digits of the year beside each point. The data for the 1960s traces out a relatively clear Phillips curve.

(b) The Phillips curve trade-off between unemployment and inflation looked fairly clear in the 1960s. But since the 1970s, that pattern has broken down. It seems crystal clear that it would be impossible to draw a single Phillips curve holds true over the recent decades of U.S. experience.

(c) Over the long term of several decades, it's difficult to see one single Phillips curve in the macroeconomic data. But when the data is separated into short-run periods, and a few years are removed from the diagram to simplify the figure, then several different Phillips curves can be traced out. For example, a Phillips curve for 1960–69 is at the lower left of the figure. A Phillips curve for 1980–83 is in the upper right. In between are Phillips curves for the 1986–93 period, for the 1976–79 period, and for the 2000–2009 period. A downward-sloping Phillips curve often does exist in the short run, but be aware that the relationship can and does shift in the long run.

Critics of a Phillips curve will sometimes point to a diagram like Exhibit 27-6*b* and argue that the Phillips curve doesn't exist, but that argument goes too far. Consider again the patterns of U.S. unemployment and inflation as portrayed in Exhibit 27-6*c*. The diagram shows five Phillips curves for the U.S. economy: one based on the years from 1960–1969; one based on the years from 1980–83; and three middle ones based on the years from 1976–79, 1986–93, 2000–2009. The diagram shows that a Phillips curve trade-off between unemployment and inflation does hold for periods of several years, but then the Phillips curve itself can shift.

This idea that a Phillips curve can shift over time is quite reasonable. After all, the original Phillips curve was based on a short-term Keynesian model, which looked at movements in aggregate demand in an economy where aggregate supply was not moving and prices did not adjust rapidly. Aggregate supply had been relatively stable in the 1960s, so the Phillips curve looked relatively stable. But then aggregate supply shifts to the left in 1974–75 and again in 1979–80, driven in part by higher prices for the key economic input of imported oil. These shifts in the AS curve led to shifts in the Phillips curve as shown in Exhibit 27-6*c*. Thus, a downward-sloping Phillips curve should be interpreted as valid for short-run periods of several years, but over longer periods when aggregate supply shifts, the downward-sloping Phillips curve can shift so that unemployment and inflation are both higher (as in the 1970s and early 1980s) or both lower (as in the early 1990s or first decade of the 2000s).

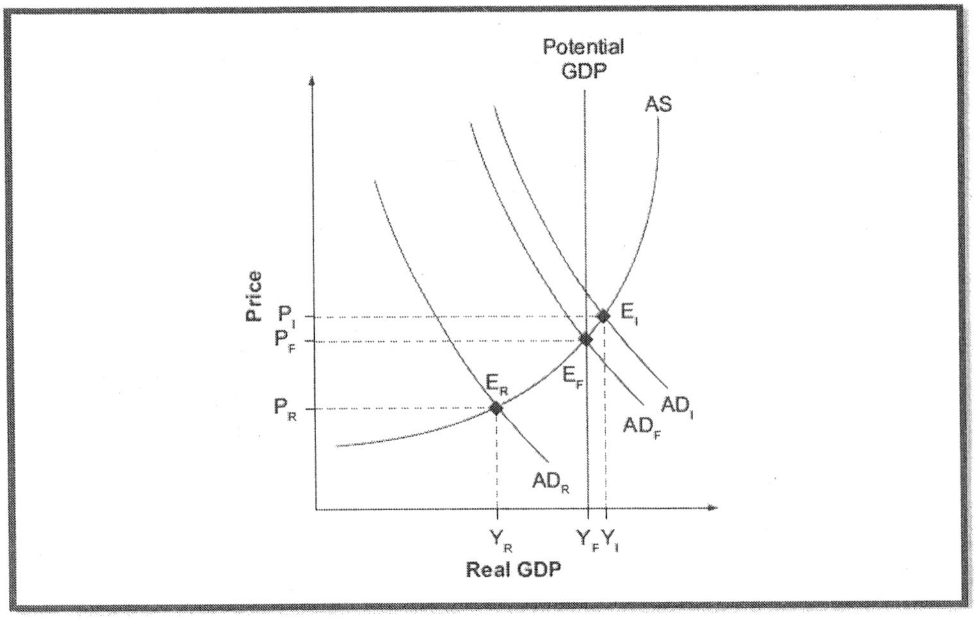

Exhibit 27-7 Fighting Recession and Inflation with Keynesian Policy

If an economy is in recession, with an equilibrium at E_R, then the Keynesian response would be to enact a policy to shift aggregate demand to the right from AD_R toward AD_F. If an economy is experiencing inflationary pressures with an equilibrium at E_I, then the Keynesian response would be to enact a policy response to shift aggregate demand to the left from AD_I toward AD_F.

Keynesian Policy for Fighting Unemployment and Inflation

Keynesian macroeconomics was born in the Great Depression, when the main concern was how to fight recession. Keynes argues that the solution to a recession would include policies to shift the aggregate demand curve to the right, like tax cuts for consumers and businesses to stimulate consumption and investment, or direct increases in government spending. For example, if aggregate demand was originally at AD_R in Exhibit 27-7, so that the economy was in recession, the appropriate policy would be for government to shift aggregate demand to the right from AD_R to AD_F, where the economy would be at potential GDP and full employment. Keynes noted that while it would be nice if government could spend additional money on housing, roads, and other amenities, he also argued that if the government couldn't agree on how to spend money in practical ways, then it could spend in impractical ways. For example, Keynes suggested building monuments, like a modern equivalent of the Egyptian pyramids. He proposed that the government could bury money underground, and let mining companies get started to dig the money up again. These suggestions were slightly tongue-in-cheek, but their purpose was to emphasize that a Great Depression is no time to quibble over the specifics of government spending programs and tax cuts when the goal should be to pump up aggregate demand by enough to lift the economy to potential GDP.

The other side of Keynesian policy occurs when the economy is operating at or even above potential GDP. In this situation, unemployment is low, but inflationary rises in the price level are a concern. The Keynesian response would be to use tax increases or government spending cuts to shift AD to the left. The result would be downward pressure on the price level, but very little reduction in output or very little rise in unemployment. If aggregate demand was originally at AD_I in Exhibit 27-7, so that the economy was experiencing inflationary rises in the price level, the appropriate policy would be for government to shift aggregate demand to the left from AD_I toward AD_F, which reduces the pressure for a higher price level while the economy remains at full employment.

The Neoclassical Perspective

by Timothy Taylor

In Chicago, Illinois, the highest recorded temperature was 105° in July 1995, while the lowest recorded temperature was 27° below zero in January 1958. Understanding why these extreme weather patterns occurred would be interesting. But if you wanted to understand the typical weather pattern in Chicago, instead of focusing on one-time extremes, you need to look at the entire pattern of data over time.

A similar lesson applies to the study of macroeconomics. It's interesting to study extreme situations, like the Great Depression of the 1930s or what many have called the Great Recession of 2007–2009. But if you want to understand the typical patterns, you need to look at the long-term. Consider the unemployment rate. Since 1955, the highest annual unemployment rate was 9.7% in 1982 and the lowest was 3.5% in 1969. (The annual unemployment rate in 2009 was 9.3%.) But even as the U.S. unemployment rate rose during recessions and declined during periods of sustained growth, it kept returning to the general neighborhood of 5.0–5.5%. For example, in 1960, the unemployment rate was 5.5%. In 1972, the unemployment rate was 5.6%. In 1979, the unemployment rate was 5.8%. In 1988, the unemployment rate was 5.5%. In 1996, the unemployment rate was 5.6%. In 2004, the unemployment rate was 5.5%. When the nonpartisan Congressional Budget Office carried out its long-range economic forecasts in 2010, it assumed that from 2015–2020, after this recession is safely in the past, the unemployment rate would be 5.0%. From a long-run perspective, the economy seems to keep adjusting back to a roughly similar level of unemployment.

The neoclassical perspective on macroeconomics emphasizes that in the long run, the economy seems to rebound back to its potential GDP and its natural rate of unemployment. This chapter begins with two building blocks of neoclassical economics: in the long run, the size of the economy is determined by potential GDP, and wages and prices will adjust in a flexible manner. A neoclassical version of the aggregate supply and aggregate demand model can illustrate these building blocks. If the neoclassical assumptions hold true—and some controversy exists over the extent to which they hold true—several policy implications follow. For example, the government should focus more on long-term growth and on controlling inflation than on worrying about recession or cyclical unemployment. The overall theme is not that Keynesian economics is "wrong" while neoclassical economics is "right," nor vice versa, but rather that the two approaches complement each other, with Keynesian economics more useful for analyzing the macroeconomic short run and neoclassical economics more useful for the long run.

Timothy Taylor, "The Neoclassical Perspective," *Principles of Macroeconomics*, pp. 533–546.

The Building Blocks of Neoclassical Analysis

Neoclassical economics argues that over time, the economy adjusts back to its potential GDP level of output. The neoclassical approach is based on two key building blocks. First, over the long term the expansion of potential GDP due to economic growth will determine the size of the economy. Second, even if the Keynesian assumption of price and wage stickiness is reasonable in the short run, over the longer run levels of prices and wages will adjust in a flexible manner. Let's consider these two claims in turn, and how they can be embodied in the aggregate supply-aggregate demand model.

THE IMPORTANCE OF POTENTIAL GDP IN THE LONG RUN

Over the long run, the level of potential GDP determines the size of real GDP. For example, the U.S. GDP was approximately 25 times larger in 2000 than it was in 1900.

The reasons for this phenomenal change are based in how the productive power of labor, physical capital, and technological capabilities have expanded. The U.S. population rose by a factor of 3.6 in the twentieth century, from 76 million in 1900 to 275 million by 2000. The human capital of modern workers was far higher, too, because the education and skills of workers have risen dramatically. In 1900 only about one-eighth of the U.S. population had completed high school and just one person in 40 had completed a four-year college degree. By 2000, more than four-fifths of Americans had a high school degree and one out of four had a four-year college degree as well. The average amount of physical capital per worker has grown dramatically, but even more important, the technology available to modern workers is extraordinarily better than a century ago: cars, airplanes, electrical machinery, telephones, computers, chemical and biological advances, materials science, health care—the list of technological advances could run on and on. Horse-drawn plows were effective tools for farmers back in 1900, but a plow made of high-strength, low-weight materials mounted on the front of a powerful tractor, and combined with modern seeds, fertilizer, irrigation, and computerized knowledge of soils types, crop possibilities, and weather, is a truly remarkable combination of technologies. The number of bushels of corn that a U.S. farmer could grow on an acre of land was roughly six times higher in 2000 than it was in 1900. Put these factors together—more workers, higher skill levels, larger amounts of physical capital per worker, and amazingly better technology—and potential GDP for the U.S. economy has clearly increased a great deal since 1900. Sure, in certain years the economy may fall below its potential GDP, perhaps because of a Keynesian lack of aggregate demand. From 2007 to 2009, the U.S. economy tumbled into recession. At other times, like in the late 1990s, the economy runs at potential GDP—or even slightly ahead—for a time. One line in Exhibit 28-1 shows the actual data for the increase in nominal GDP since 1960. The slightly smoother line shows the potential GDP since 1960 as estimated by the nonpartisan Congressional

Exhibit 28-1 Potential and Actual GDP (in nominal dollars)

Actual GDP falls below potential GDP during and after recessions, like the recessions of 1980 and 1981–82, 1990–91, 2001, and 2007–2009. In other cases, actual GDP can be above potential GDP for a time, as in the late 1990s.

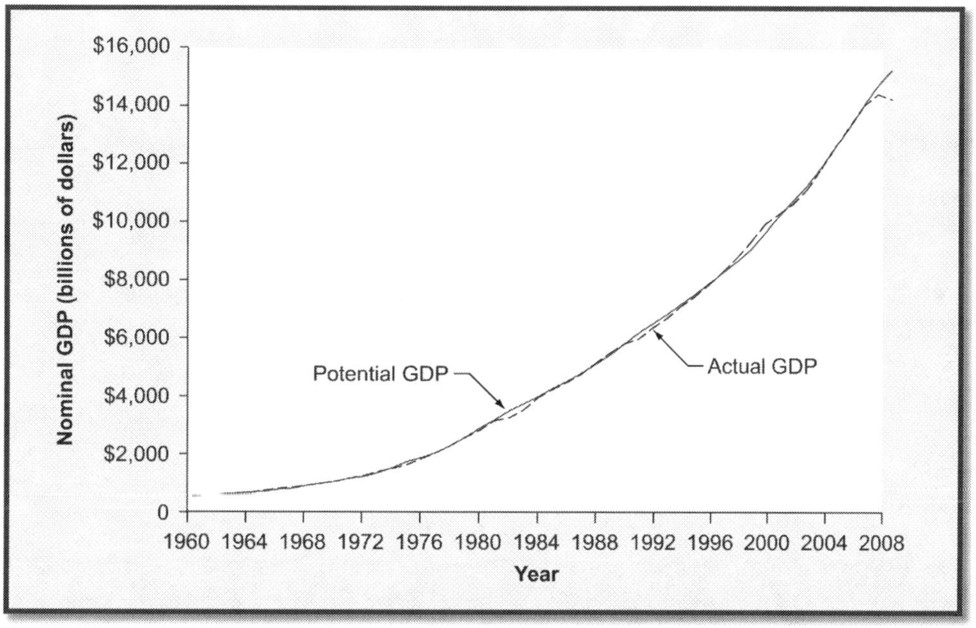

Budget Office. During periods of recession, like 1980–82, 1990–91, and 2007–2009, actual GDP is below its potential. In the red-hot economy of the late 1990s, however, actual GDP was above its potential for a time. Most economic recessions and upswings are times when the economy is 1–3% below or above potential GDP. Clearly, short-run fluctuations around potential GDP do exist, but over the long run, the upward trend of potential GDP determines the size of the economy.

In the neoclassical version of the model of aggregate supply and aggregate demand, potential GDP is shown as a vertical line. Neoclassical economists who focus on potential GDP as the primary determinant of real GDP argue that the aggregate supply curve should look the same as potential GDP—that is, the aggregate supply curve is a vertical line drawn at the level of potential GDP, as shown in Exhibit 28-2. A vertical AS curve means that the level of aggregate supply (or potential GDP) will determine the real GDP of the economy, regardless of the level of aggregate demand. Over time, economic growth shifts potential GDP and the vertical AS curve gradually to the right.

THE ROLE OF FLEXIBLE PRICES

How does the macroeconomy adjust back to its level of potential GDP in the long run? What if aggregate demand increases or decreases? The neoclassical view of how the macroeconomy adjusts is based on the insight that even if wages and prices are sticky in the short run, they can be flexible over time. To understand the neoclassical view of how the

Exhibit 28-2 A Vertical AS Curve

In the neoclassical model, the aggregate supply curve is drawn as a vertical line at the level of potential GDP. If AS is vertical, then it determines the level of real output, no matter where the aggregate demand curve is drawn. Over time, the AS curve shifts to the right as productivity increases and potential GDP expands.

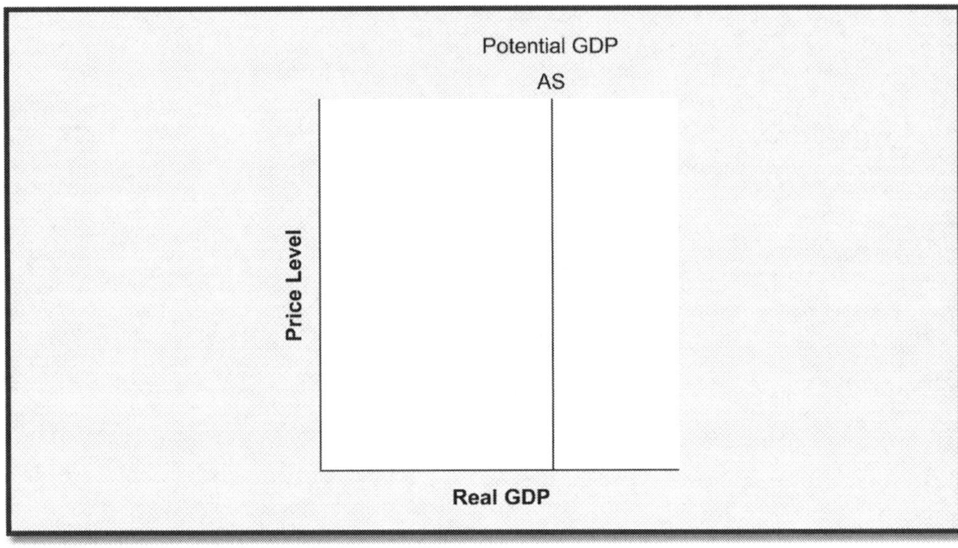

Exhibit 28-3 The Rebound to Potential GDP after AD Increases

The original equilibrium E_0, at an output level of 50 and a price level of 120, happens at the intersection of the aggregate demand curve AD_0 and the short-run aggregate supply curve AS_0. The output at E_0 is equal to potential GDP. Aggregate demand shifts right from AD_0 to AD_1. The new equilibrium is E_1, with a higher output level of 55 and an inflationary increase in the price level to 125. With unemployment rates unsustainably low, wages are bid up by eager employers. Higher wages are an economy-wide increase in the price of a key input, which shifts short-run aggregate supply to the left from AS_0 to AS_1. The new equilibrium E_2 is at the same original level of output, 50, but at a higher price level of 130. Thus, the long-run aggregate supply curve ASN, which is vertical at the level of potential GDP, determines the level of real GDP in this economy in the long run.

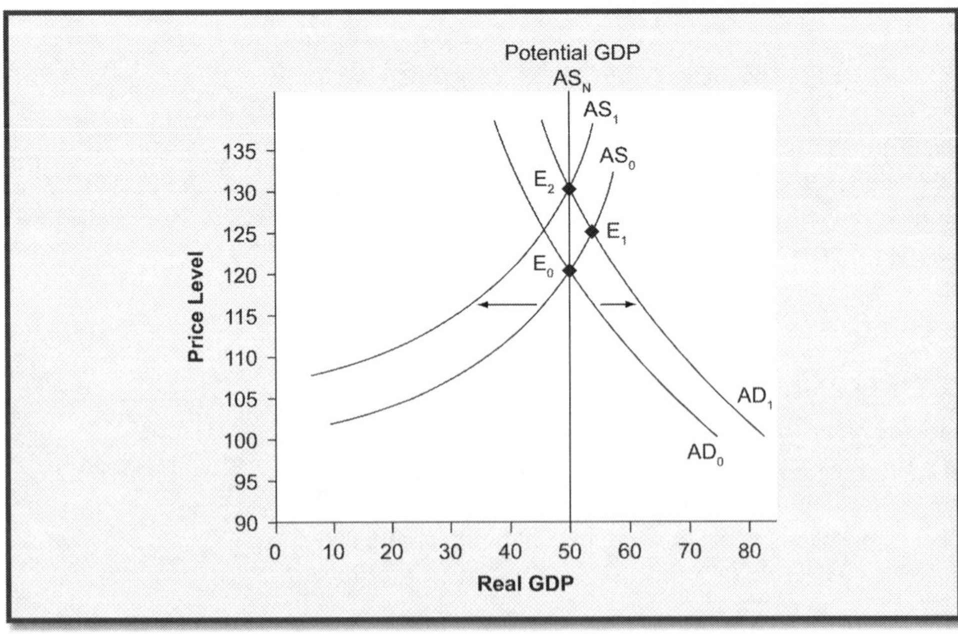

Exhibit 28-4 A Rebound Back to Potential GDP from a Shift to the Left in Aggregate Demand

The original equilibrium E_0, at an output level of 50 and a price level of 120, happens at the intersection of the aggregate demand curve AD_0 and the short-run aggregate supply curve AS_0. The output at E_0 is equal to potential GDP. Aggregate demand shifts left from AD0 to AD1. The new equilibrium is E_1, with a higher output level of 45 and downward pressure on the price level of 115. But with high unemployment rates, wages are held down. Lower wages are an economy-wide decrease in the price of a key input, which shifts short-run aggregate supply to the right from AS_0 to AS_1. The new equilibrium E_2 is at the same original level of output, 50, but at a lower price level of 110. Thus, the long-run aggregate supply curve ASN, which is vertical at the level of potential GDP, ultimately determines the real GDP of this economy.

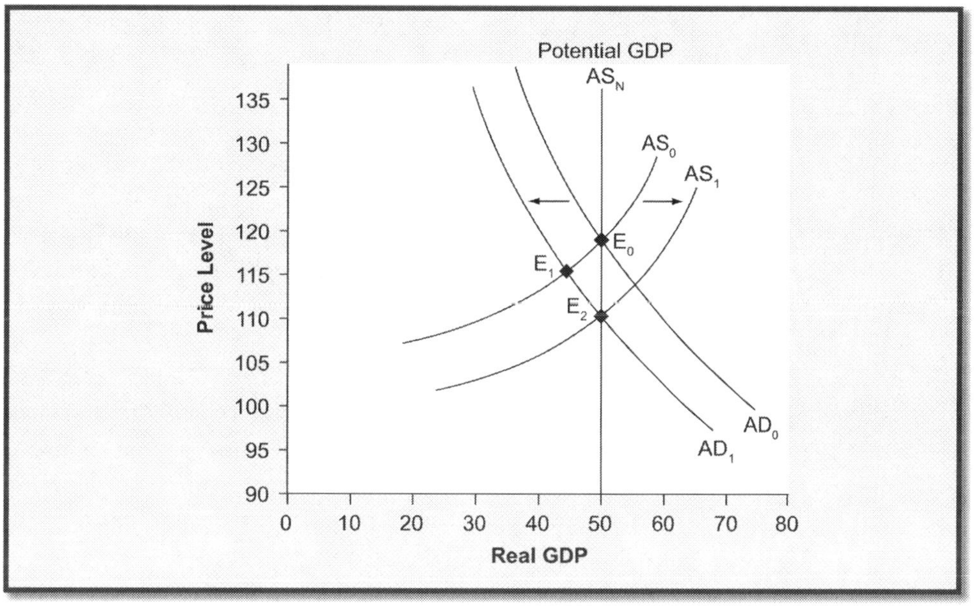

macroeconomy works, let's follow the connections from the short-run to the long-run situation.

The aggregate demand and aggregate supply diagram shown in Exhibit 28-3 shows two aggregate supply curves. The original aggregate supply curve AS_0 is a short-run or Keynesian AS curve. The vertical aggregate supply curve ASN is the long-run or neoclassical AS curve, which is located at potential GDP. The original aggregate demand curve, labeled AD_0, is drawn so that the original equilibrium occurs at point E_0, at which point the economy is producing at its potential GDP.

Now imagine that some economic event boosts aggregate demand: perhaps a surge of export sales or a rise in business confidence that leads to more investment, or perhaps a policy decision like higher government spending or a tax cut that leads to additional aggregate demand. The short-run Keynesian analysis is that the rise in aggregate demand will shift the aggregate demand curve out to the right from AD_0 to AD_1, leading to a new equilibrium at point E_1 with higher output, lower unemployment, and pressure for an inflationary rise in the price level.

But in the long-run neoclassical analysis, the chain of economic consequences is just beginning. As economic output rises above potential GDP, the level of unemployment falls. Eager employers are trying to bid workers away from other companies and to encourage their current workers to exert more effort and to put in longer hours. This high demand for labor will drive up wages. Most workers have their salaries reviewed only once or twice a year, and so it will take time before the higher wages filter through the economy. But as wages do rise, it will mean a leftward shift in the short-run Keynesian aggregate supply curve back to AS_1, because the price of a major input to production has increased. The economy moves to a new equilibrium E_2. The new equilibrium has the same level of real GDP as did the original equilibrium E_0. However, an inflationary increase in the price level has occurred.

This description of the short-run shift from E_0 to E_1 and the long-run shift from E_1 to E_2 is a step-by-step way of making a simple point: the economy can't sustain production above its potential GDP in the long run. An economy may produce above its level of potential GDP in the short run, under pressure from a surge in aggregate demand. But over the long run, that surge in aggregate demand ends up as an increase in the price level, not as a rise in output.

The rebound of the economy back to potential GDP also works in response to a shift to the left in aggregate demand. Exhibit 28-4 again starts with two aggregate supply curves, with AS_0 showing the original short-run Keynesian AS curve and ASN showing the vertical long-run neoclassical aggregate supply curve. A decrease in aggregate demand—say, because of a decline in consumer confidence that leads to less consumption and more saving—causes the original aggregate demand curve AD_0 to shift back to AD_1. The shift from the original equilibrium E_0 to the new equilibrium E_1 results in a decline in output. As output falls below potential GDP, unemployment rises.

Again, from the neoclassical perspective, this short-run scenario is only the beginning of the chain of events. The higher level of unemployment means more workers looking for jobs. As a result, employers can hold down on pay increases—or perhaps even replace some of their higher-paid workers with unemployed people willing to accept a lower wage. As wages stagnate or fall, this decline in the price of a key input means that the short-run Keynesian aggregate supply curve shifts to the right from its original AS_0 to AS_1. The overall impact in the long run, as the macroeconomic equilibrium shifts from E_0 to E_1 to E_2, is that the level of output returns to potential GDP, where it started. But there is downward pressure on the price level—or at least pressure for a lower level of inflation.

Thus, in the neoclassical view, changes in aggregate demand can have a short-run impact on output and on unemployment, but only a short-run impact. In the long run, when wages and prices are flexible, potential GDP and aggregate supply determine the size of real GDP.

HOW FAST IS THE SPEED OF MACROECONOMIC ADJUSTMENT?

How long does it take for wage and prices to adjust, and for the economy to rebound back to its potential GDP? This subject has been highly contentious. Keynesian economists argue that if the adjustment from recession to potential GDP takes a very long time, then neoclassical theory may be more hypothetical than practical. In the immortal words of John Maynard Keynes quoted in the previous chapter, "In the long run we are all dead." Neoclassical economists respond that even if the adjustment takes as long as, say, ten years—and it may happen in five years or less—then it becomes of central importance in understanding the economy.

One subset of neoclassical economists holds that the adjustment of wages and prices in the macroeconomy might be quite rapid indeed. The theory of rational expectations holds that people form the most accurate possible expectations about the future that they can using all information available to them. In an economy where most people have **rational expectations**, economic adjustments may happen very quickly.

rational expectations: The theory that people form the most accurate possible expectations about the future that they can using all information available to them.

To understand how rational expectations may affect the speed of price adjustments, think about a situation in the real estate market. Imagine that several events are announced that seem likely to push up the value of homes in the neighborhood. For example, perhaps a local employer announces that it is going to hire many more people or the city announces that it is going to build a local park or a library in that neighborhood. The theory of rational expectations points out that even though none of the changes will happen immediately, home prices in the neighborhood will rise immediately, because the expectation that homes will be worth more in the future will lead buyers to be willing to pay more for homes in the present. The amount of the immediate increase in home prices will depend on how likely it seems that the announcements about the future will actually happen and on how distant the local jobs and neighborhood improvements are in the future. The key point is that because of rational expectations, prices do not wait on events, but adjust immediately.

At a macroeconomic level, the theory of rational expectations points out that if the aggregate supply curve is vertical over time, then people should rationally expect this pattern. When a shift in aggregate demand occurs, people and businesses with rational expectations will know that its impact on output and employment will only be temporary, while its impact on the price level will be permanent. If firms and workers perceive the outcome of the process in advance, and if all firms and workers know that everyone else is perceiving the process in the same way, then they have no incentive to go through an extended series of short-run scenarios, like a firm first hiring more people when aggregate demand shifts out and then firing those same people when aggregate supply shifts back. Instead, everyone will recognize where this process is heading—toward a change in the price level—and then will act on that expectation. In this scenario, the expected longrun change in the price level may happen very quickly, without a drawn-out zigzag of output and employment first moving one way and then the other.

The theory that people and firms have rational expectations can be a useful simplification, but as a statement about how people and businesses actually behave, the assumption seems too strong. After all, many people and firms are not especially well informed either about what is happening in the economy or about how the economy works.

Do You, and Everyone around You, Have Rational Expectations?

Here's a social experiment to reveal both your rationality and your expectations about the rationality of others. You and everyone else in a group of people are asked to choose a number between 0 and 100. The winner is whoever makes a guess that is closest to one-half of the average of all the numbers chosen. What number should you pick? Think about it for a moment.

You might begin by reasoning that if the guesses of the other parties are distributed randomly over the interval from 0 to 100, then the average of the other guesses will be 50, and therefore you should guess 25. But if everyone reasons in this way, then everyone will guess 25, and so you should guess 12 or 13. But if everyone follows the logic of this choice, then every else will guess 12 or 13 as well, so you should guess 6. But if everyone else follows the logic of this choice, then everyone will guess 6 and you should guess 3. You can see where this train of logic is headed. If everyone is fully rational, and everyone expects everyone else to be fully rational, then everyone should guess zero. A group of economists who call themselves "experimental economists" organize games like this and see how people respond. When the game is first played, guesses of about 25 are common. As the game is then repeated, the guesses sink lower and lower. But very few people ever guess zero.

These results suggest several conclusions. People are not fully rational in their expectations, and they do not expect others to be fully rational, either. However, when people repeat a situation several times, they do learn and adapt their behavior in the direction of greater rationality.

adaptive expectations: The theory that people look at past experience and gradually adapt their beliefs and behavior as circumstances change.

It is probably more realistic to believe that people and firms act with **adaptive expectations**: they look at past experience and gradually adapt their beliefs and behavior as circumstances change, but are not perfect synthesizers of information and accurate predictors of the future in the sense of rational expectations theory. If most people and businesses have some form of adaptive expectations, then the adjustment from the short-run and long-run will be traced out in incremental steps that occur over time.

The empirical evidence on the speed of macroeconomic adjustment of prices and wages is not clear-cut. Indeed, the speed of macroeconomic adjustment probably varies among different countries and time periods. But a reasonable guess is that the initial short-run effect of a shift in aggregate demand might last two to five years, before the adjustments in wages and prices cause the economy to adjust back to potential GDP. Thus, one might think of the short run for applying Keynesian analysis as time periods less than 2–5 years, and the long run for applying neoclassical analysis as longer than five years. For practical purposes, this guideline is frustratingly imprecise, but when analyzing a complex social mechanism like an economy as it evolves over time, some imprecision seems unavoidable.

Policy Implications of the Neoclassical Perspective

The neoclassical school of macroeconomics argues that the economy has a self-correcting tendency to move back to potential GDP. If one accepts this theory, then it has implications for how to view the main problems of the macroeconomy. For example, fighting recession seems relatively less important, while encouraging long-term growth seems

Data on Inflation Expectations

Expectations about inflation may seem like a highly theoretical concept, but in fact, data do exist on this subject.

Joseph Livingston, a financial journalist for the Philadelphia Inquirer, started a twice-a-year survey of economists about their expectations of inflation in 1946. After Livingston's death in 1969, the survey was continued by the Federal Reserve Bank of Philadelphia. The Institute of Survey Research at the University of Michigan started carrying out a survey of inflation expectations of 500 random households in 1948. Finally, the American Statistical Association together with a private organization called the National Bureau of Economic Research started carrying out a survey of professional economic forecasters that included expectations about inflation in 1968.

Economic research can then compare these expectations to the actual inflation that occurred, but the results are mixed. Expectations do not seem to be purely adaptive and based on past experience of inflation; instead, people are clearly looking ahead. In fact, the average forecast of households is roughly as accurate as the average forecasts of the professionals. However, expectations do not seem to be perfectly rational forecasts of the future, either, because people often repeat past errors. For example, all parties have a tendency to overestimate future inflation when inflation is currently low and to underestimate future inflation when inflation is currently high. However, the forecasts of economists have become notably more accurate in the last few decades. Economists are actively researching how expectations of inflation and other economic variables are formed and changed.

more important. For similar reasons, fighting unemployment seems relatively less important, while fighting inflation seems more important. Let's consider these choices in turn, along with their implications for the shape of the Phillips curve trade-off between unemployment and inflation.

FIGHTING RECESSION OR ENCOURAGING LONG-TERM GROWTH?

Late in 2007, the U.S. economy entered a severe recession. Real GDP declined through the middle of 2009. Most Keynesian economists would probably focus on the immediate recession. But neoclassical economists might well argue that the economy will rebound out of the recession in a year or two. From the neoclassical point of view, perhaps a more important question is the growth rate of long-term productivity, which determined the rate at which potential GDP expands. As measured by growth in output per hour in the business sector, productivity growth was very strong from 1998 to 2003, growing at an annual rate of 3.4%. However, productivity growth then sagged to less than 2% per year in 2006 and 2007. The year 2009 actually saw high productivity growth at a rate of 3.8%. However, it was a peculiar year for the economy, with a deep recession seeming to come to an end in mid-year, but no one being quite certain that the worst was over. As a result, firms expanded output in the second half of 2009 without doing much hiring. More output with about the same labor input looks good for productivity, but it is unlikely to continue for the long-run. From a neoclassical perspective, the key question of the next few years is whether productivity growth returns to the high levels of the late 1990s and early 2000s, or whether it ends up at the slower rates of 2006 and 2007.

Neoclassical economists are often skeptical of the government's ability to manipulate aggregate demand skillfully and in a timely manner, as Keynesian economics recommends. Instead, neoclassical economists are likely to focus their attention on the underpinnings of long-run productivity growth: namely, an economy's investments in human capital, physical capital, and technology, operating together in a market-oriented environment that rewards innovation.

FIGHTING UNEMPLOYMENT OR INFLATION?

In the neoclassical model, the level of real GDP is determined by potential GDP, which is illustrated with a vertical aggregate supply curve. Unemployment can be divided into two categories, as explained in Chapter 23: cyclical unemployment and the natural rate of unemployment. Cyclical unemployment is created when the economy is producing below potential GDP, giving potential employers less incentive to hire. When the economy is producing at potential GDP, cyclical unemployment will be zero. Historical evidence shows that the unemployment rate never falls to 0%, not even when the economy is producing at or even slightly above potential GDP. The unemployment rate that is created by the forces of supply and demand in the labor market, even when the economy is at potential GDP, is called the natural rate of unemployment.

The neoclassical view of unemployment tends to focus attention away from the problem of cyclical unemployment—that is, unemployment caused by recession—while putting more attention on the issue of the rates of unemployment that prevail even when the economy is operating at potential GDP. To put it another way, the neoclassical view of unemployment tends to focus on how public policy might be adjusted to reduce the natural rate of unemployment. Such policy changes might involve redesigning unemployment and welfare programs so that they still support those in need, but also offer greater encouragement for job-hunting. It might involve redesigning business rules with an eye to whether they are unintentionally discouraging businesses from taking on new employees. It might involve building institutions to improve the flow of information about jobs and the mobility of workers, to help bring together workers and employers more quickly.

Neoclassical economists will not tend to see aggregate demand as a useful tool for reducing unemployment; after all, if economic output is determined by a vertical aggregate supply curve, then aggregate demand has no effect on unemployment. Instead, neoclassical economists believe that aggregate demand should be allowed to expand only to match the gradual shifts of aggregate supply to the right—keeping the price level much the same and inflationary pressures low.

If aggregate demand rises rapidly in the neoclassical model, it leads only to inflationary pressures. Exhibit 28-5 shows a vertical long-run AS curve and three different levels of aggregate demand, rising from AD_0 to

Exhibit 28-5 How Aggregate Demand Determines the Price Level in the Long Run

As aggregate demand shifts to the right from AD_0 to AD_1 to AD_2, real GDP in this economy and the level of unemployment do not change. However, there is inflationary pressure for a higher price level as the equilibrium changes from E_0 to E_1 to E_2.

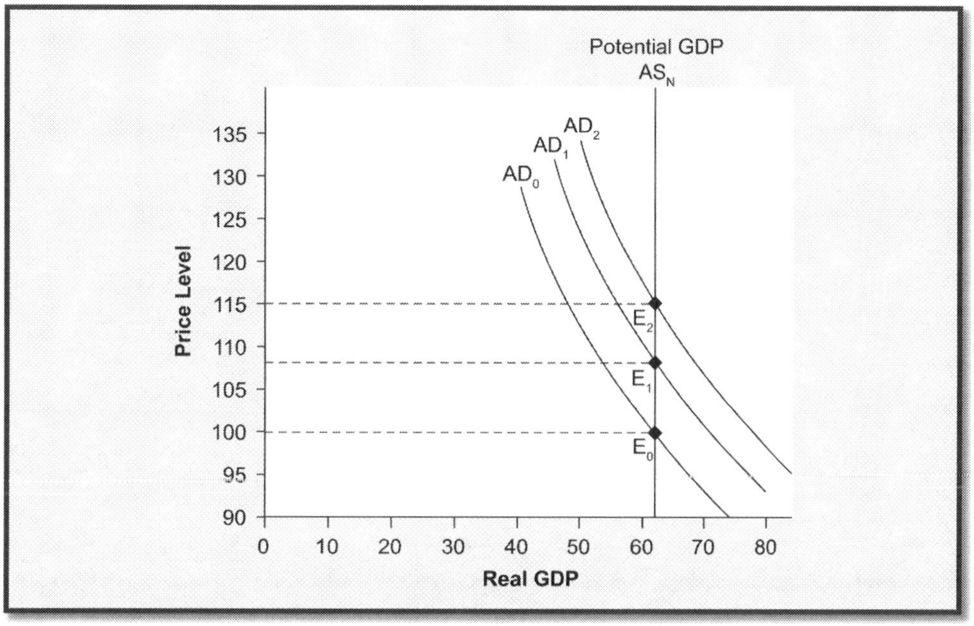

AD_1 to AD_2. As the macroeconomic equilibrium rises from E_0 to E_1 and E_2, the price level rises. But real GDP does not budge. Nor does the rate of unemployment, which adjusts to its natural rate. Conversely, reducing inflation has no long-term costs, either. Think about Exhibit 28-5 in reverse, as the aggregate demand curve shifts from AD_2 to AD_1 to AD_0, and the equilibrium moves from E_2 to E_1 to E_0. During this process, the price level falls, but neither real GDP nor the natural rate of unemployment is changed.

A shift to the left in aggregate supply can also push up the price level. Exhibit 28-6 shows a shift to the left of a vertical aggregate supply, which might result from an increase in prices of key inputs, like oil or wages. It can also result from a breakdown of key market institutions, like banks, which could prevent the economy from operating as smoothly as it had before. A shift back to the left of AS means that potential GDP has fallen, and perhaps conditions of the labor market have shifted in such a way such that the natural rate of unemployment is higher as well. But at the new AS curve, it remains true that aggregate supply determines the level of output, while changes in aggregate demand will determine the price level.

THE NEOCLASSICAL PHILLIPS CURVE TRADE-OFF

A neoclassical long-run aggregate supply curve will imply a vertical shape for the Phillips curve trade-off between inflation and unemployment. Exhibit 28-7a shows the vertical AS curve, with three different

Exhibit 28-6 How a Shift to the Left in AS Can Push Up the Price Level

A shift in aggregate supply to the left from AS_0 to AS_1 causes inflationary pressure for a higher price level as the equilibrium shifts from E_0 to E_1.

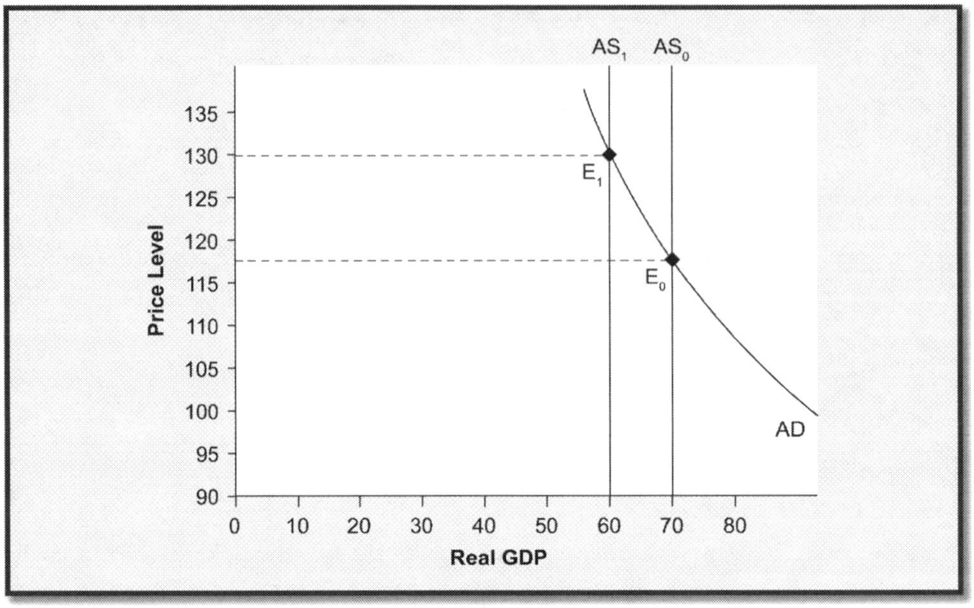

Exhibit 28-7 From a Long-Run AS Curve to a Long-Run Phillips Curve

(a) With a vertical AS curve, shifts in aggregate demand do not alter the level of output but do lead to inflationary changes in the price level. Because output is unchanged between the equilibria E_0, E_1 and E_2, all unemployment in this economy will be due to the natural rate of unemployment.

(b) If the natural rate of unemployment is 5%, then the Phillips curve will be vertical. That is, regardless of inflationary changes in the price level, the unemployment rate remains at 5%.

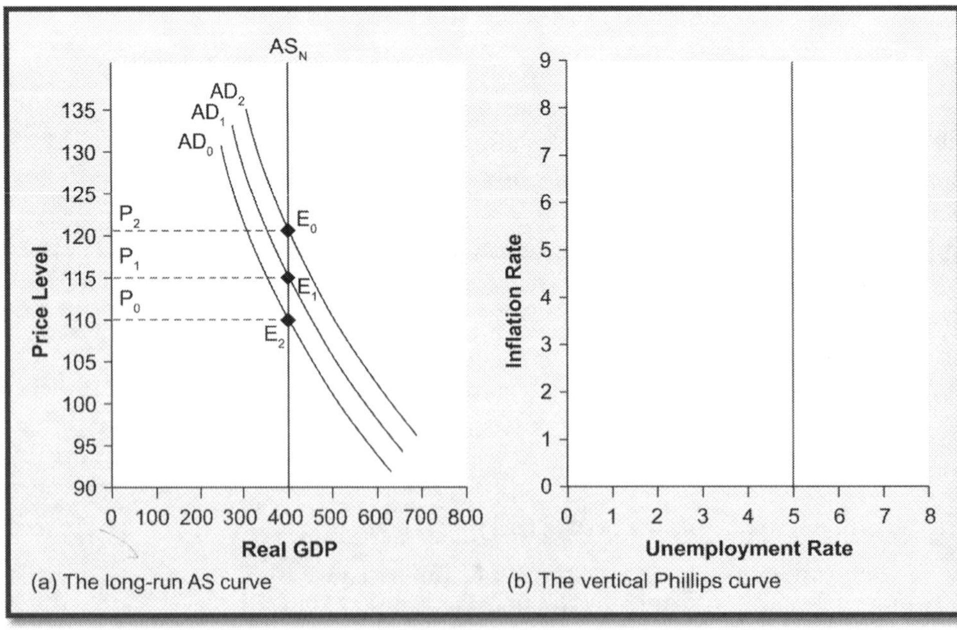

levels of aggregate demand resulting in three different equilibria at three different price levels. At every point along that vertical AS curve, potential GDP and the rate of unemployment remains the same. Assume that in this economy, the natural rate of unemployment when the economy is producing at potential GDP is 5%. As a result, the long-run Phillips curve relationship shown in Exhibit 28-7b is a vertical line, rising up from 5% unemployment, at any level of inflation.

The unemployment rate on the long-run Phillips curve will be the natural rate of unemployment. A small inflationary increase in the price level from AD_0 to AD_1 will have the same natural rate of unemployment as a larger inflationary increase in the price level from AD_0 to AD_2. The macroeconomic equilibrium along the vertical aggregate supply curve can occur at a variety of different price levels, and the natural rate of unemployment can be consistent with all different rates of inflation. The great economist Milton Friedman (1912–2006) summed up the neoclassical view of the longterm Phillips curve trade-off in a 1967 speech: "[T] here is always a temporary trade-off between inflation and unemployment; there is no permanent trade-off."

In the Keynesian perspective, the primary focus is on getting the level of aggregate demand right in relationship to an upward-sloping aggregate supply curve; that is, AD should be adjusted so that the economy produces at its potential GDP, not so low that cyclical unemployment results and not so high that inflation results. In the neoclassical perspective, aggregate supply will determine output at potential GDP, unemployment is determined by the natural rate of unemployment churned out by the forces of supply and demand in the labor market, and shifts in aggregate demand are the primary determinant of changes in the price level.

MACROECONOMISTS RIDING TWO HORSES

When a circus performer stands up on two horses, with a foot on each one, much of the excitement for the viewer resides in contemplating the gap between the two. As modern macroeconomists ride into the future with one foot on the short-term Keynesian perspective and another foot on the long-term neoclassical perspective, the balancing act may appear to be an uncomfortable one, but there doesn't seem to be any way to avoid it. Each approach, Keynesian and neoclassical, has its strengths and weaknesses.

The short-term Keynesian model, built on the importance of aggregate demand as a cause of business cycles and a degree of wage and price rigidity, does a sound job of explaining many recessions and why cyclical unemployment rises and falls. However, Keynesian economics does a less good job of capturing the reality that the economy does usually seem to revert to a natural rate of unemployment over time. By focusing on the short run adjustments of aggregate demand, Keynesian economics creates some danger of overlooking the long-term causes of economic growth or the natural rate of unemployment that exists even when the economy is producing at potential GDP.

The neoclassical model, with its emphasis on aggregate supply, focuses on the underlying determinants of output and employment in markets, and thus tends to put more emphasis on economic growth and how labor markets work. However, the neoclassical view is not especially helpful in explaining why unemployment moves up and down over short time horizons of a few years. Nor is the neoclassical model especially helpful when the economy is mired in an especially deep and long-lasting recession, like the Depression. Keynesian economics tends to view inflation as a price that might sometimes be paid for lower unemployment; neoclassical economics tends to view inflation as a cost that offers no offsetting gains in terms of lower unemployment.

The Keynesian and neoclassical approaches differ in their views of government macroeconomic policy, too. Keynesian macroeconomic policy requires some optimism about the ability of the government to recognize a situation of too little or too much aggregate demand, and to adjust aggregate demand accordingly with the right level of changes in taxes or spending, all enacted in a timely fashion. Conversely, even when neoclassical economists admit that a Keynesian increase in aggregate demand might in theory help to avoid a recession, they often argue it is unlikely to work well in practice. After all, neoclassical economists argue, it takes government statisticians months to produce even preliminary estimates of GDP so that politicians know whether a recession is occurring—and those preliminary estimates may be revised substantially later. Moreover, the political process can take more months to enact a tax cut or a spending increase; the amount of those tax or spending changes will be determined as much by political considerations as economic ones; and then the economy will take still more months to put changes in aggregate demand into effect through spending and production.

But macroeconomics cannot be summed up as an argument between one group of economists who are pure Keynesians and another group who are pure neoclassicals. Instead, many economists believe that all of these statements are true—it's just that the Keynesian statements are more relevant in the short run and the neoclassical statements in the long run. Robert Solow, the Nobel laureate in economics in 1987, described the dual approach in this way: "At short time scales, I think, something sort of 'Keynesian' is a good approximation, and surely better than anything straight 'neoclassical.' At very long time scales, the interesting questions are best studied in a neoclassical framework, and attention to the Keynesian side of things would be a minor distraction. At the fiveto- ten-year time scale, we have to piece things together as best we can, and look for a hybrid model that will do the job."

Many modern macroeconomists spend considerable time and energy trying to construct models that blend the most attractive aspects of the Keynesian and neoclassical approaches. It's possible to construct a somewhat complex mathematical model where aggregate demand and sticky wages and prices matter in the short run, but wages, prices and aggregate supply adjust in the long run. However, creating an overall model that encompasses both short-term Keynesian and long-term neoclassical models is not easy. Even if one of these hybrid models eventually becomes well accepted in the economics profession, it will probably still feel like riding two separate horses, but now with a double-saddle arrangement linking them together more closely, so that the rider is not quite so precarious.

Key Comments and Summary

1. Neoclassical economics argues that in the long run, the economy will adjust back to its potential GDP level of output through flexible price levels.
2. In the neoclassical view, potential GDP and the natural rate of unemployment are determined in the long run by market forces. Thus, the neoclassical perspective views the long-run AS curve as vertical.
3. A **rational expectations** perspective argues that people have excellent information about economic events and how the economy works, and that as a result, price and other economic adjustments will happen very quickly. **Adaptive expectations** is a milder theory in which people have limited information about economic information and how the economy works, and so price and other economic adjustments can be slow.
4. Neoclassical economists tend to put relatively more emphasis on long-term growth than on fighting recession, because they believe that recessions will fade in a few years and long-term growth will ultimately determine the standard of living.
5. Neoclassical economists tend to focus more on reducing the natural rate of unemployment caused by economic institutions and government policies than the cyclical rate of unemployment caused by recession.
6. Neoclassical economists see no social benefit to inflation. With an upward sloping Keynesian AS curve, inflation can arise because an economy is approaching full employment. But with a vertical long-run neoclassical AS curve, inflation does not accompany any rise in output.
7. If aggregate supply is vertical, then aggregate demand does not affect the quantity of output. Instead, aggregate demand can only cause inflationary changes in the price level.
8. A vertical aggregate supply curve, where the quantity of output is consistent with many different price levels, also implies a vertical Phillips curve.
9. Many mainstream economists take a Keynesian perspective, assuming sticky wages and prices and emphasizing the power of aggregate demand, for purposes of short-run analysis and a neoclassical perspective, assuming adjustment of wages and prices and emphasizing the power of long-run supply, for purposes of long-run analysis.

Review Questions

1. Does neoclassical economics focus on the long term or the short term?
2. Does neoclassical economics view prices and wages as sticky or flexible?
3. What shape is the long-run aggregate supply curve?
4. What is the difference between rational expectations and adaptive expectations?
5. Do neoclassical economists tend to focus more on economic growth or on recessions? Explain briefly.
6. Do neoclassical economists tend to focus more on cyclical unemployment or on inflation? Explain briefly.
7. Do neoclassical economists see a value in tolerating a little more inflation if it brings additional economic output?
8. If aggregate supply is vertical, what role does aggregate demand play in determining output? In determining the price level?
9. What is the shape of the neoclassical long-run Phillips curve?

Keynesian vs. Classical Theory

By David Moglen

Is the priority cutting the deficit or growing the economy? Consider this passage from British historian Peter Clarke, author of the biography "Keynes". When Britain went from prioritizing deficit reduction to favoring policies dedicated to improving the economy, they had better results. This poses the salient distinction: Classical theory says focus on the deficit and the economy will take care of itself. Keynesian theory says focus on the economy, and the deficit will take care of itself.

KEYNES

By Peter Clarke

There is another way of looking at the whole issue of public spending and public debt. This too can be illustrated from official British government statistics.[34] In 1914 the British national debt amounted to 29 per cent of GDP; by 1920 it was 148 per cent. The World War was responsible for a burden that made inter-war chancellors 'slaves to the debt' and led them into frantic efforts, especially in 1931, to balance the budget at all costs. Yet twenty years of Treasury frugality only succeeded in reducing the national debt by 1940 to 136 per cent of GDP. Where upon the Second World War—financed this time on basically Keynesian lines—pushed up the debt, not this time by 520 per cent in real terms as in the First World War, but by 80 per cent.

The burden of internal debt that the British government carried in 1945 was thus 240 per cent of GDP. But postwar chancellors, no longer slaves to the debt in an era of alleged Keynesian profligacy, had different priorities, notably economic growth. The results are sobering, one way or another. By 1965 the national debt was only 96 per cent of GDP; by 1980 it had been halved again, down to 48 per cent, and was at much the same level at the end of the century. The reason, of course, is not that the debt itself had declined; indeed at current prices the outstanding debt nominally on the books in 1945 (£21,366 million) was twenty times greater by 2000. The real reason was, of course, the growth of GDP meanwhile more than a hundred times greater at current prices over the same period. Some of this was inflation, but the real burden of the debt had none the less been reduced by 80 per cent. The actual moral seems to be twofold. First, be wary of expensive wars, especially if financed through debt rather than taxation. Secondly, that by looking after output and employment, it was indeed true, as Keynes had put it in 1934, that the budget could look after itself.

CHAPTER 10
The Multiplier Model

10 The Multiplier Model

By Timothy Taylor

In the Keynesian economic model, too little aggregate demand brings unemployment and too much brings inflation. Thus, you can think of Keynesian economics as pursuing a "Goldilocks" level of aggregate demand: not too much, not too little, but looking for what is just right.

The Expenditure-Output Model

The fundamental ideas of Keynesian economics were developed before the AS-AD model was popularized. From the 1930s up to the 1970s, Keynesian economics was often explained with a different model, known as the expenditure-output approach. (Some classes will choose to skip this discussion of the Keynesian cross model and move straight to the closing section of this chapter, which can be done without loss of continuity.) This approach is strongly rooted in the fundamental assumptions of Keynesian economics: it focuses on the total amount of expenditure or demand in the economy, with no explicit mention of aggregate supply or of the price level (although as you will see, it is possible to draw some inferences about aggregate supply and price levels based on the diagram). This laser-like focus on expenditures in the economy has a payoff. It allows a closer analysis of how shifts in demand or spending affect the rest of the economy; for example, it shows how a tax cut or spending increase of a certain amount, like $10 billion, can have more than $10 billion worth of impact on equilibrium GDP.

The Axes of the Expenditure-Output Diagram

The **expenditure-output model,** sometimes also called the "Keynesian cross diagram," determines the equilibrium level of real GDP by the point where the total or aggregate expenditures in the economy are equal to the amount produced in the economy. Thus, the axes of the Keynesian cross diagram as presented in Exhibit 27-8 show real GDP on the horizontal axis as a measure of output and aggregate expenditures on the vertical axis as a measure of spending.

expenditure-output model: A macroeconomic model in which equilibrium output occurs where the total or aggregate expenditures in the economy are equal to the amount produced; also called the "Keynesian cross model."

Remember that GDP can be thought of in several equivalent ways: it measures both the value of spending on final goods and also the value of the production of final goods. All sales of the final goods and services that make up GDP will eventually end up as income for workers, for managers, and for investors and owners of firms. The sum of all the income received for contributing resources to GDP is called **national income (Y).** At some points in the discussion that follows, it will be useful to refer to real GDP as "national income." Both of these axes are measured in real (inflation-adjusted) terms.

national income (Y): The sum of all income received foı producing GDP.

The Potential GDP Line and the 45-degree Line

The Keynesian cross diagram contains two lines that serve as conceptual guideposts to orient the discussion. The first conceptual line is a vertical line shows the level of potential GDP. Potential GDP means the same thing here that it means in the AS-AD diagrams: it refers to the quantity of output that the economy can produce with full employment of its labor and physical capital.

The second conceptual line on the Keynesian cross diagram is the 45-degree line, which starts at the origin and reaches up and to the right. A line that stretches up at a 45-degree angle represents the set of points (1, 1), (2, 2), (3, 3) and so on, where the measurement on the vertical axis is equal to the measurement on the horizontal

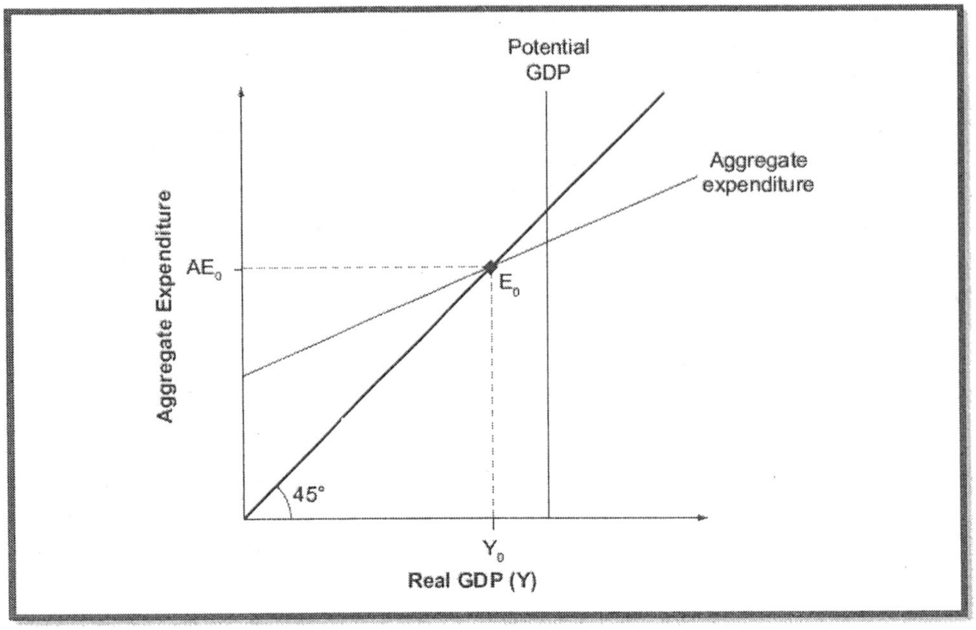

Exhibit 27-8 The Expenditure-Output Diagram

The aggregate expenditure-output model, sometimes called the Keynesian cross diagram, has aggregate expenditures on the vertical axis and real GDP as a measure of output on the horizontal axis. A vertical line shows potential GDP or full employment GDP. The 45° line shows all points where aggregate expenditures and output are equal. The aggregate expenditure schedule shows how total spending or aggregate expenditure increases as output or real GDP rises. The intersection of the aggregate expenditure schedule and the 45° line will be the equilibrium. Equilibrium occurs at E_0, where aggregate expenditure AE_0 is equal to the output level Y_0.

axis. In this diagram, the 45-degree line shows the set of points where the level of aggregate expenditure in the economy, measured on the vertical axis, is equal to the level of output or national income in the economy, measured by GDP on the horizontal axis. When the macroeconomy is in equilibrium, it must be true that the aggregate expenditures in the economy are equal to the real GDP—because by definition, GDP is the measure of what is spent on final sales of goods and services in the economy. Thus, the equilibrium calculated with a Keynesian cross diagram will always end up where aggregate expenditure and output are equal—which will only occur along the 45-degree line.

The Aggregate Expenditure Schedule

The final ingredient of the Keynesian cross or expenditure-output diagram is the aggregate expenditure schedule, which will show the total expenditures in the economy for each level of real GDP. The next section will explain the aggregate expenditure schedule in detail. But first, notice that the intersection of the aggregate expenditure line with the 45-degree line—at point E_0 in Exhibit 27-8—will show the equilibrium for the economy, because it is the point where aggregate expenditure is equal to output. After developing an understanding of what the aggregate expenditures schedule means in the next section, we'll return to this equilibrium and how to interpret it.

Building the Aggregate Expenditure Schedule

The aggregate expenditure schedule shows, either in the form of a table or on a graph, how aggregate expenditures in the economy rise as real GDP or national income rises. Thus, in thinking about the components of the aggregate expenditure line—consumption, investment, government spending, exports and imports—the key question is how expenditures in each category will adjust as national income rises.

Students sometimes question whether a fixed marginal propensity to consume makes sense. "After all," they say, "a low-income household can't afford to save much and a high-income household can afford to save a lot, so surely the MPC is higher for a low-income household than a high-income one?" It is true that high-income households typically save a higher proportion of their income than low-income households. But the macroeconomic perspective on consumption and saving considers the overall economy, taking all different kinds of households together. From a macroeconomic perspective, using one MPC to represent an overall average for the economy is a reasonable, if rough, approximation.

Clearing It Up

Does a Fixed MPC Make Sense?

Consumption as a Function of National Income

How do consumption expenditures increase as national income rises? People can do two things with their income: consume it or save it. (For the moment, let's ignore the need to pay taxes with some of it.) Each person who receives an additional dollar faces this choice. The **marginal propensity to consume**, or MPC, is the share of the additional dollar a person decides to consume. The **marginal propensity to save**, or MPS, is the share of the additional dollar a person decides to save. It must always hold true that

$$\text{MPC} + \text{MPS} = 1$$

marginal propensity to consume (MPC): The share of an additional dollar of income that goes to consumption.

marginal propensity to save (MPS): The share of an additional dollar that goes to saving.

For example, if the marginal propensity to consume out of the marginal amount of income earned is .9, then the marginal propensity to save is .1.

With this relationship in mind, consider the relationship among income, consumption and savings shown in Exhibit 27-9. An assumption commonly made in this model is that even if income were zero, people would have to consume *something*. In this example,

Exhibit 27-9 The Consumption Function

In the expenditure-output model, how does consumption increase with the level of national income? Output on the horizontal axis is conceptually the same as national income, since the value of all final output that is produced and sold must be income to someone, somewhere in the economy. At a national income level of zero, 600 is consumed. Then, each time income rises by 1,000, consumption rises by 800, because in this example, the marginal propensity to consume is .8. The pattern of consumption shown in the table is plotted on the diagram. To calculate consumption, multiply the income level by .8, for the marginal propensity to consume, and add 600, for the amount that would be consumed even if income was zero. Consumption plus savings must be equal to income.

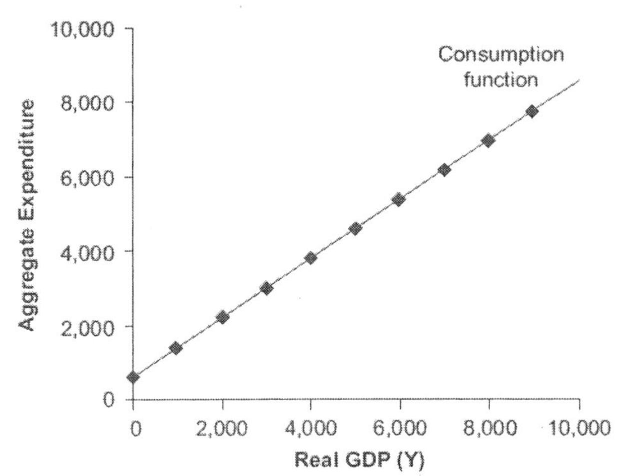

Income	Consumption	Savings
0	600	–600
1,000	1,400	–400
2,000	2,200	–200
3,000	3,000	0
4,000	3,800	200
5,000	4,600	400
6,000	5,400	600
7,000	6,200	800
8,000	7,000	1,000
9,000	7,800	1,200

consumption would be 600 even if income were zero. Then, the MPC is .8 and the MPS is .2 in this example. Thus, when income increases by 1,000, consumption rises by 800 and savings rises by 200. At an income of 4,000, for example, total consumption will be the 600 that would be consumed even without any income, plus 4,000 multiplied by the marginal propensity to consume of .8, or 3,200, for a total of 3,800. The total amount of consumption and saving must always add up to the total amount of income. (Exactly how a situation of zero income and negative savings would work in practice is not important, because even low-income societies are not literally at zero income, so the point is hypothetical.) This relationship between income and consumption, illustrated in the figure beside the table, is called the **consumption function.**

consumption function: The relationship between income and expenditures on consumption.

However, a number of factors other than income can also cause the entire consumption function to shift. These factors were summarized in the earlier discussion of consumption, and listed in Exhibit 27-3. When the consumption function moves, it can shift in two ways: either the entire consumption function can move up or down in a parallel manner, or the slope of the consumption function can shift so that it becomes steeper or flatter. For example, if a tax cut leads consumers to spend more, but doesn't affect their marginal propensity to consume, it would cause an upward shift to a new consumption function that is parallel to the original one. However, a change in household preferences for saving that reduced the marginal propensity to save would cause the slope of the consumption function to become steeper: that is, if the savings rate is lower, then every increase in income leads to a larger rise in consumption.

Investment as a Function of National Income

Investment decisions are forward-looking, based on expected rates of return. Precisely because investment decisions depend primarily on perceptions about future economic conditions, they do *not* depend primarily on the level of GDP in the current year. Thus, on a Keynesian cross diagram, the investment function can be drawn as a horizontal line, at a fixed level of expenditure. Exhibit 27-10 shows an investment function where the level of investment is, for the sake of concreteness, set at the specific level of 500. Just as a consumption function shows the relationship between consumption levels and real GDP (or national income), the investment function shows the relationship between investment levels and real GDP.

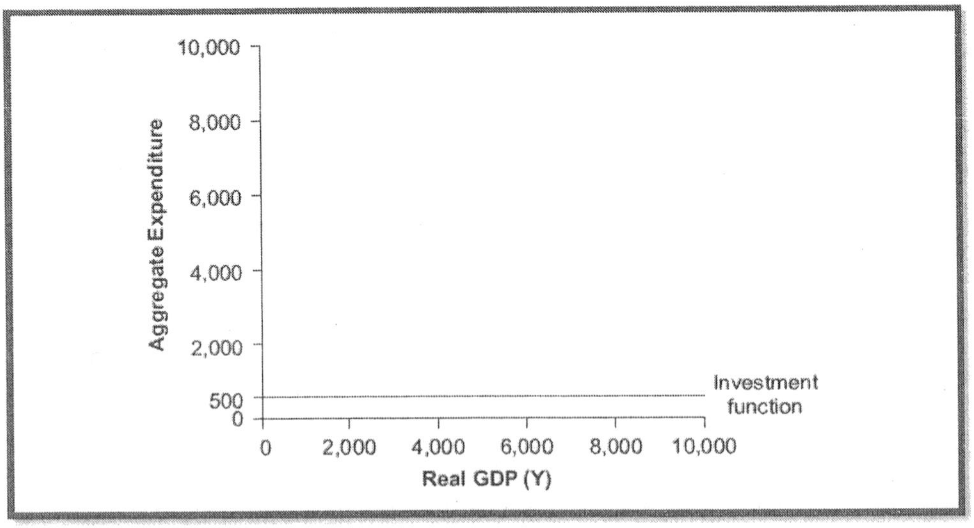

Exhibit 27-10 The Investment Function

The investment function is drawn as a flat line because investment is based on expectations about the future and so it doesn't change with the level of current national income. In this example, investment expenditures are at a level of 500. However, changes in factors like technological opportunities, expectations about near-term economic growth, and real interest rates would all cause the investment function to shift up or down.

The appearance of the investment function as a horizontal line does *not* mean that the level of investment never moves. The horizontal line for investment means only that in the context of this two-dimensional diagram, the level of investment on the vertical aggregate expenditure axis does not vary according to the current level of real GDP on the horizontal axis. However, all the other factors that vary investment—new technological opportunities, expectations about near-term economic growth, real interest rates, the price of key inputs, and tax incentives for investment—can cause the horizontal investment function to shift up or down.

Government Spending and Taxes as a Function of National Income

In the Keynesian cross model, government spending appears as a horizontal line, as in Exhibit 27-11 where government spending is set at a level of 1,300. As in the case of investment spending, this horizontal line does not mean that government spending is unchanging. It means only that government spending changes for political reasons, rather than shifting in a predictable way with the current size of the real GDP shown on the horizontal axis.

The situation of taxes is different, because taxes often rise or fall with the size of the economy. For example, income taxes are based on the level of income earned and sales taxes are based on the amount of sales made, and both income and sales tend to be higher when the economy is growing and lower when the economy is in a recession. For the purposes of constructing the basic Keynesian cross model, it is helpful to view taxes as a proportionate share of GDP. (Specific taxes will be discussed in more detail in Chapter 32.) In the United States, for example, taking federal, state, and local taxes together, government typically collects about 30-35% of income as taxes.

Exhibit 27-12 revises the earlier table on the consumption function so that it takes taxes into account. The first column shows national income. The second column calculates taxes, which in this example are set at a rate of 30%, or .3. The third column shows after-tax income; that is, total income minus taxes. The fourth column then calculates consumption in the same manner as before; multiply after-tax income by .8, representing the marginal propensity to consume, and then add 600, for the amount that

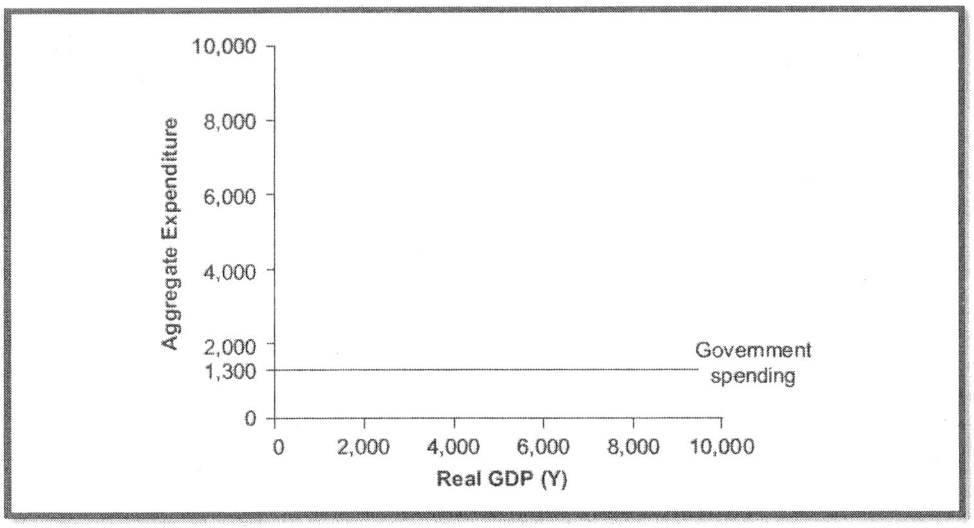

Exhibit 27-11 The Government Spending Function

The level of government spending is determined by political factors, not by the level of real GDP in a given year. Thus, government spending is drawn as a horizontal line. In this example, government spending is at a level of 1,300. Political decisions to increase government spending will cause this horizontal line to shift up, while political decisions to reduce spending would caus it to shift down.

would be consumed even if income was zero. When taxes are included, each additional dollar of income results in a smaller increase in consumption—because some of that income is now paid as taxes. For this reason, the consumption function with taxes included is flatter than the consumption function without taxes.

Exports and Imports as a Function of National Income

The export function, which shows how exports change with the level of a country's own real GDP, is drawn as a horizontal line, as in the example in Exhibit 27-13*a* where exports are drawn at a level of 840. Again, as in the case of investment spending and government spending, drawing the export function as horizontal does not imply that exports never change. It just means that they don't change because of what is on the horizontal axis—that is, a country's own level of domestic production—and instead are shaped by the level of aggregate demand in other countries. More demand for exports from other countries would cause the export function to shift up; less demand for exports from other countries would cause it to shift down.

Imports are drawn in the Keynesian cross diagram as a downward-sloping line, with the downward slope determined by the **marginal propensity to import, or MPI,** out of national income. In Exhibit 27-13*b*, the marginal propensity to import is .1. Thus, if real GDP is 5,000, imports are 500; if national income is 6,000, imports are 600, and so on. The import function is drawn as downward sloping and negative, because it represents a subtraction from the aggregate expenditures in the domestic economy. A change in the marginal propensity to import, perhaps as a result of changes in preferences or because of a change in relative prices of imported goods, would alter the slope of the import function.

marginal propensity to import (MPI): The share of an additional dollar of income that goes to imports.

Exhibit 27-12 The Consumption Function Before and After Taxes

The upper line repeats the consumption function from Exhibit 27-9. The lower line shows the consumption function if taxes must first be paid on income, and then consumption is based on after-tax income. The first column of the table shows income. The second column shows taxes, which in this example are 30% of income. The third column takes income and subtracts taxes to calculate after-tax income. The fourth column calculates consumption based on after-tax income, by multiplying after tax income by the MPC of .8 and adding 600. The final column calculates saving, given that consumption plus saving plus taxes must equal income. When taxes are included, each additional rise of income results in a smaller increase in consumption, which is why the consumption function with taxes included is flatter than when taxes are not included. In this example, taxes are .3 of income, MPC is .8 of after-tax income, and MPS is .2 of after-tax income.

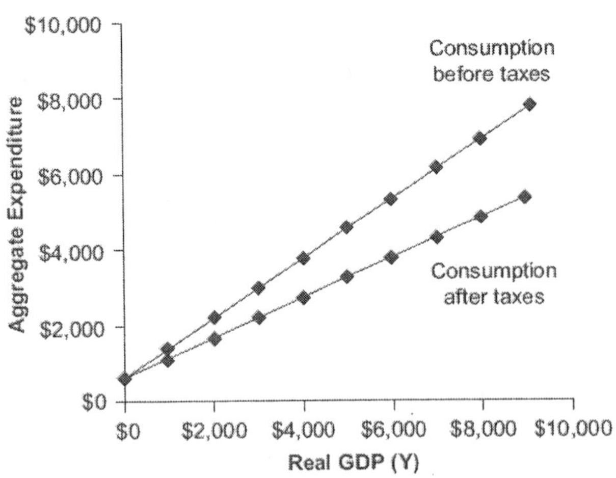

Income	Taxes	After-Tax Income	Consumption	Savings
0	0	0	600	–600
1,000	300	700	1,160	–460
2,000	600	1,400	1,720	–320
3,000	900	2,100	2,280	–180
4,000	1,200	2,800	2,840	–40
5,000	1,500	3,500	3,400	100
6,000	1,800	4,200	3,960	240
7,000	2,100	4,900	4,520	380
8,000	2,400	5,600	5,080	520
9,000	2,700	6,300	5,640	660

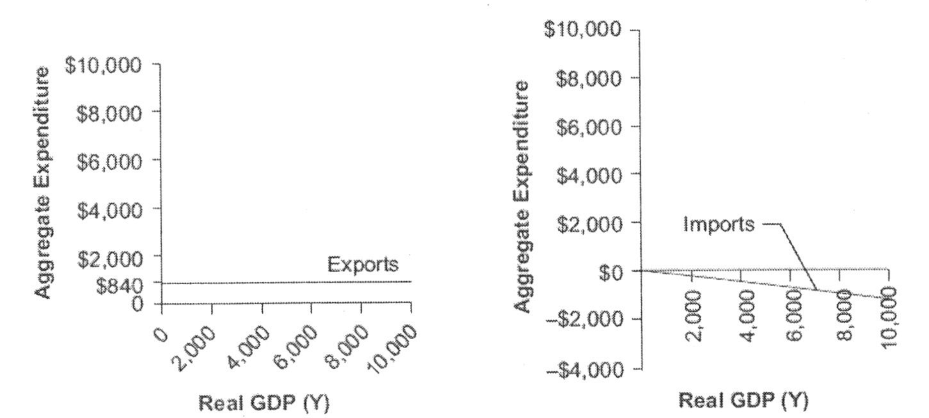

(a) The export function

(b) The import function

Exhibit 27-13 The Export and Import Functions

(a) The export function is drawn as a horizontal line because exports are determined by the buying power of other countries and thus do not change with the size of the domestic economy. In this example, exports are set at 840. However, exports can shift up or down, depending on buying patterns in other countries.

(b) The import function is drawn in negative territory because expenditures on imported products are a subtraction from expenditures in the domestic economy. In this example, the marginal propensity to import is .1, so imports are calculated by multiplying the level of income by –0.1.

Building the Combined Aggregate Expenditure Function

All the components of aggregate demand—consumption, investment, government spending, and the trade balance—are now in plaçe to build the Keynesian cross diagram. Exhibit 27-14 builds up an aggregate expenditure function, based on the numerical illustrations of C, I, G, X, and M that have been used throughout this section. The first three columns under Exhibit 27-14 are lifted from the earlier Exhibit 27-12, which showed how to bring taxes into the consumption function. The first column is real GDP or national income, which is what appears on the horizontal axis of the income-expenditure diagram. The second column calculates after-tax income, based on the assumption in this case that 30% of real GDP is collected in taxes. The third column is based on an MPC of .8, so that as after-tax income rises by 700 from one row to the next, consumption rises by 560 (700 × .8) from one row to the next. Investment, government spending, and exports do not change with the level of current national income. In the previous discussion, investment was 500, government spending was 1,300, and exports were 840, for a total of 2,640. This total is shown in the fourth column. Imports are .1 of real GDP in this example, and the level of imports is calculated in the fifth column. The final column, aggregate expenditures, sums up C + I + G + X – M. This aggregate expenditure line is illustrated in Exhibit 27-14.

The aggregate expenditure function is conceptually formed by stacking on top of each other the consumption function (with taxes included), the investment function, the government spending function, the export function, and the import function. The point at which the aggregate expenditure function intersects the vertical axis will be determined by the levels of investment, government, and export expenditures—which do not vary with national income. The upward slope of the aggregate expenditure function will be determined by the marginal propensity to save, the tax rate, and the marginal propensity to import. A higher marginal propensity to save, a higher tax rate, and a higher marginal propensity to import will all make the slope of the aggregate expenditure function flatter—because out of any extra income, more is going to savings or taxes or imports and less to spending on domestic goods and services.

The equilibrium occurs where national income is equal to aggregate expenditure, which is shown on the graph as the point where the aggregate expenditure schedule crosses the 45° line. In this example, the equilibrium occurs at 6,000. This equilibrium

Exhibit 27-14 A Keynesian Cross Diagram

The table starts with national income on the left, and then shows after-tax consumption, government spending, investment, exports, and imports, which combine to form aggregate expenditure. On the graph, each combination of national income and aggregate expenditure is graphed. The equilibrium occurs where aggregate expenditure is equal to national income; on the graph, this occurs where the aggregate expenditure schedule crosses the 45° line, at a level of $6,000. Potential GDP in this example is $7,000, so the equilibrium is occurring at a level of output or real GDP below the potential GDP level.

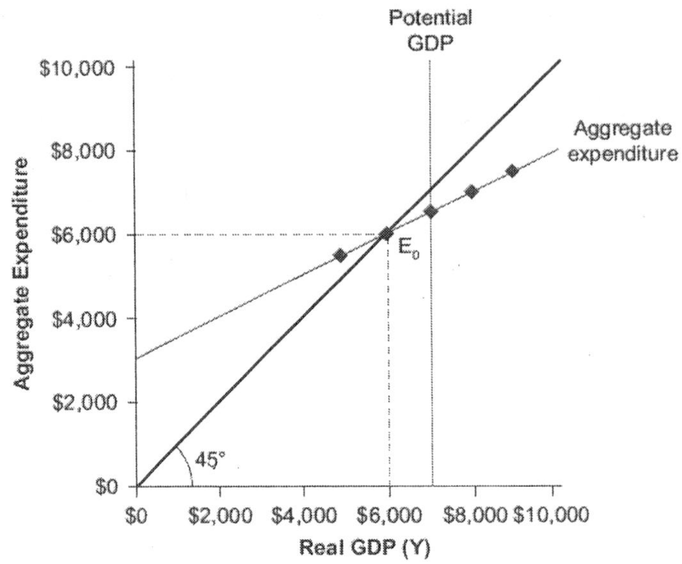

National Income	After-Tax Income	Consumption	Government Spending + Investment + Exports	Imports	Aggregate Expenditure
$3,000	$2,100	$2,280	$2,640	$300	$4,570
$4,000	$2,800	$2,840	$2,640	$400	$5,080
$5,000	$3,500	$3,400	$2,640	$500	$5,540
$6,000	$4,200	$3,960	$2,640	$600	$6,000
$7,000	$4,900	$4,520	$2,640	$700	$6,460
$8,000	$5,600	$5,080	$2,640	$800	$6,920
$9,000	$6,300	$5,640	$2,640	$900	$7,380

can also be read off the table under the figure; it's the level of national income where aggregate expenditure is equal to national income.

Equilibrium in the Keynesian Cross Model

With the aggregate expenditure line in place, the next step is to relate it to the two other elements of the Keynesian cross diagram. Thus, the first subsection interprets the intersection of the aggregate expenditure function and the 45° line, while the next subsection relates this point of intersection to the potential GDP line.

Where Equilibrium Occurs

The point where the aggregate expenditure line that is constructed from C + I + G + X – M crosses the 45-degree line will be the equilibrium for the economy. It is the only

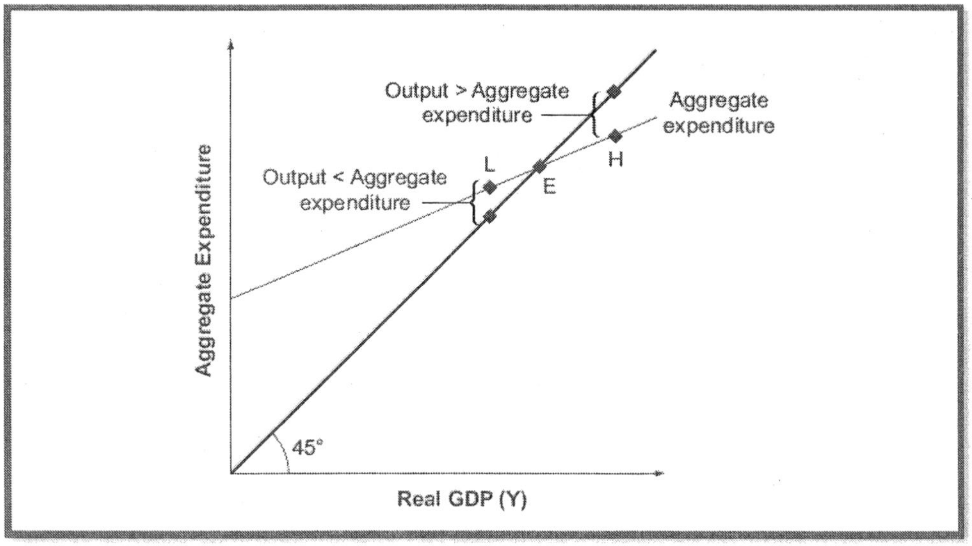

Exhibit 27-15
Equilibrium in the Keynesian Cross Diagram
If output was above the equilibrium level, at H, then the real output is greater than the aggregate expenditure in the economy. This pattern cannot hold in the long term, because it would mean that goods are produced but piling up unsold. If output was below the equilibrium level at L, then aggregate expenditure would be greater than output. This pattern cannot hold in the long-run, either, because it would mean that spending exceeds the number of goods being produced. Only point E can be an equilibrium, where output or national income and aggregate expenditure are equal. The equilibrium E must lie on the 45° line, which is the set of points where national income and aggregate expenditure are equal to each other.

point on the aggregate expenditure line where the total amount being spent on aggregate demand is in balance with the total level of production. In Exhibit 27-14, this point of equilibrium E happens at 6,000, which can be read off the table or seen in the figure.

The meaning of "equilibrium" remains the same; that is, equilibrium is a point of balance where no incentive exists to shift away from that outcome. To understand why the point of intersection between the aggregate expenditure function and the 45-degree line is a macroeconomic equilibrium, consider what would happen if an economy found itself to the right of the equilibrium point E, say point H in Exhibit 27-15 where output is higher than the equilibrium. At point H, the level of aggregate expenditure is below the 45-degree line, so that the level of aggregate expenditure in the economy is less than the level of output. As a result, at point H output is piling up unsold—not a sustainable state of affairs in the long run.

Conversely, consider the situation where the level of output is at point L, where real output is lower than the equilibrium. In that case, the level of aggregate demand in the economy is above the 45-degree line, indicating that the level of aggregate expenditure in the economy is greater than the level of output. When the level of aggregate demand has emptied the store shelves, it cannot be sustained in the long run, either. Thus, the equilibrium must be the point where the amount produced and the amount spent are in balance, at the intersection of the aggregate expenditure function and the 45-degree line.

Recessionary and Inflationary Gaps

In the Keynesian cross diagram, if the aggregate expenditure line intersects the 45-degree line at the level of potential GDP, then the economy is in sound shape. There is no recession, and unemployment is low. But there's no guarantee that the equilibrium will occur at the potential GDP level of output. The equilibrium might be either higher or lower.

For example, Exhibit 27-16*a* illustrates a situation where the aggregate expenditure line intersects the 45-degree line at point E_0, which is a real GDP of 6,000, which is below the potential GDP of 7,000. In this situation, the level of aggregate expenditure is too low for GDP to reach its full employment level, and unemployment will occur. The distance between an output level like E_0 that is below potential GDP and the level

Exhibit 27-16 Addressing Recessionary and Inflationary Gaps

(a) If the equilibrium occurs at an output below potential GDP, then a recessionary gap exists. The policy solution to a recessionary gap is to shift the aggregate expenditure schedule up from AE_0 to AE_1, using policies like tax cuts or government spending increases. Then the new equilibrium E_1 occurs at potential GDP.

(b) If the equilibrium occurs at an output above potential GDP, then an inflationary gap exists. The policy solution to an inflationary gap is to shift the aggregate expenditure schedule down from AE_0 to AE_1, using policies like tax increases or spending cuts. Then, the new equilibrium E_1 occurs at potential GDP.

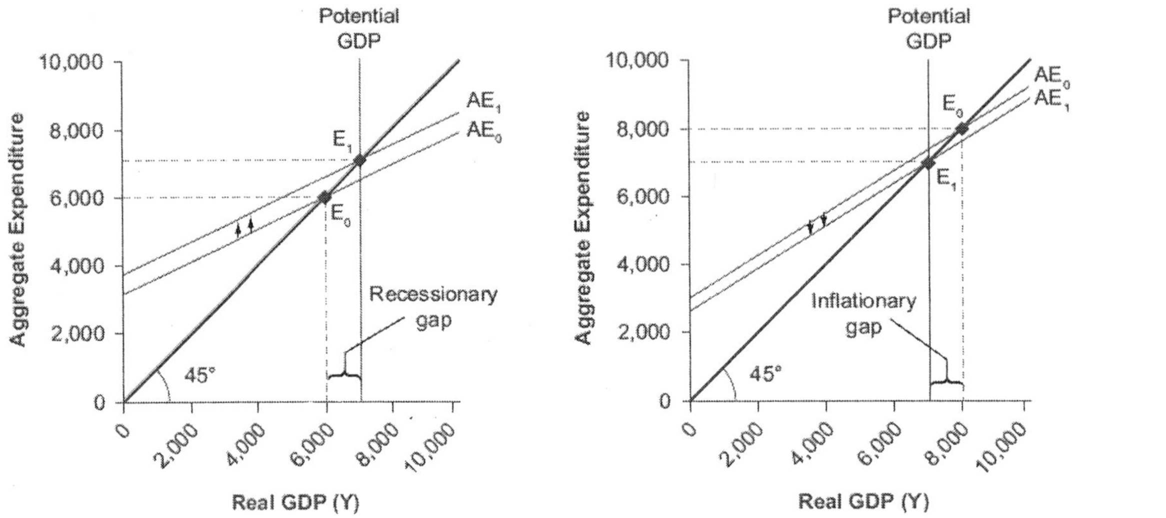

(a) Policy to address a recessionary gap.

(b) Policy to address an inflationary gap.

of potential GDP is called a **recessionary gap.** Because the equilibrium level of real GDP is so low, firms will not wish to hire the full employment number of workers.

recessionary gap: The gap in output between an economy in recession and potential GDP.

Unemployment will be high. What might cause a recessionary gap? Anything that shifts the aggregate expenditure line down is a potential cause of recession, including a decline in consumption, a rise in savings, a fall in investment, a drop in government spending or a rise in taxes, or a fall in exports or a rise in imports. Moreover, an economy that is at equilibrium with a recessionary gap may just stay there and suffer high unemployment for a long time; remember, the meaning of equilibrium is that there is no particular adjustment of prices or quantities in the economy to chase the recession away.

The appropriate response to a recessionary gap is for the government to reduce taxes or increase spending so that the aggregate expenditure function shifts up from AE_0 to AE_1. When this shift occurs, the new equilibrium E_1 now occurs at potential GDP as shown in Exhibit 27-16*a*.

Conversely, Exhibit 27-16*b* shows a situation where the aggregate expenditure schedule AE_0 intersects the 45-degree line above potential GDP. The gap between the level of real GDP at the equilibrium E_0 and potential GDP is called an **inflationary gap.** The inflationary gap also requires a bit of interpreting. After all, a naïve reading of the Keynesian cross figure might suggest that if the aggregate expenditure function is just pushed up high enough, real GDP can be as large as desired—even doubling or tripling the potential GDP level of the economy! This implication is clearly wrong. An economy faces some supply-side limits on how much it can produce at a given time with its existing quantities of workers, physical and human capital, technology, and market institutions.

inflationary gap: When an economy has output above potential GDP, the gap from that level of output to potential GDP.

The inflationary gap should be interpreted not as a literal prediction of how large real GDP will be, but as a statement of how much extra aggregate expenditure is in the economy beyond what is needed to reach potential GDP. An inflationary gap suggests that because the economy can't produce enough goods and services to absorb this level of aggregate expenditures, the spending will instead cause an inflationary increase in the price level. In this way, even though changes in the price level do not appear explicitly in the Keynesian cross equation, the notion of inflation is implicit in the concept of the inflationary gap.

The appropriate Keynesian response to an inflationary gap is shown in Exhibit 27-16*b*. The original intersection of aggregate expenditure line AE_0 and the 45-degree line occurs at 8,000, which is above the level of potential GDP at 7,000. If AE_0 shifts down to AE_1, so that the new equilibrium is at E_1, then the economy will be at potential GDP without pressures for inflationary price increases. The government can achieve a downward shift in aggregate expenditure by increasing taxes on consumers or firms, or by reducing government expenditures.

The Multiplier Effect

The Keynesian policy prescription has one final twist. Assume that for a certain economy, the intersection of the aggregate expenditure function and the 45-degree line is at a GDP of 700, while the level of potential GDP for this economy is 800. By how much does government spending need to be increased so that the economy reaches the full employment GDP? The obvious answer might seem to be 800–700 = 100, so raise government spending by 100. But that answer is incorrect. A change of say, 100 in government expenditures will have an effect of more than 100 on the equilibrium level of real GDP. The reason is that a change in aggregate expenditures circles through the economy: households buy from firms, firms pay workers and suppliers, workers and suppliers buy goods from other firms, those firms pay their workers and suppliers, and so on. In this way, the original change in aggregate expenditures is actually spent more than once.

How Does the Multiplier Work?

The process in which an original increase in aggregate expenditure cycles repeatedly through the economy and thus has a larger impact is called the **multiplier effect.** To understand how the multiplier effect works, return to the example in which the current equilibrium in the Keynesian cross diagram is a real GDP of 700 but the government, seeking to raise the equilibrium to a potential GDP of 800, increases government spending by 100. When the government first spends 100, it does indeed add 100 to aggregate expenditures—but this increase is only the first step. When the government increases spending by 100, someone in the economy receives that spending and can treat it as income. Assume that those who receive this income pay 30% in taxes, save 10% of after-tax income, spend 10% of total income on imports, and then spend the rest on domestically produced goods and services. As shown in the calculations in Exhibit 27-17, out of the original 100 in government spending in the first round, 53 is then cycled back into purchases of domestically produced goods and services in the spent second round. Moreover, a pattern begins. That 53 which was cycled back into additional expenditures is also income to someone, somewhere in the economy.

multiplier effect: How a given change in expenditure cycles repeatedly through the economy, and thus has a larger final impact than the initial change.

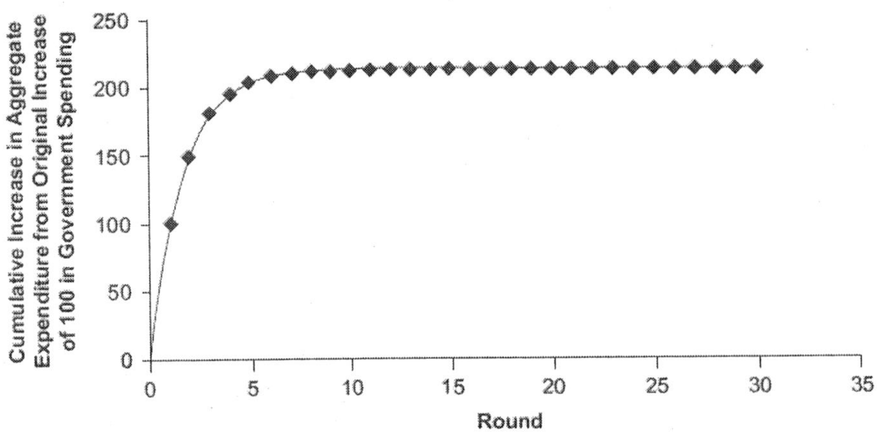

Original increase in aggregate expenditure from government spending	100
Which is income to people throughout the economy:	
Pay 30% in taxes. Save 10% of after-tax income. Spend 10% of income on imports. Second-round increase of . . .	70 – 7 – 10 = 53
Which is 53 of income to people through the economy:	
Pay 30% in taxes. Save 10% of after-tax income. Spend 10% of income on imports. Third-round increase of . . .	37.1 – 3.71 – 5.3 = 28.09
Which is 28.09 of income to people through the economy:	
Pay 30% in taxes. Save 10% of after-tax income. Spend 10% of income on imports. Fourth-round increase of . . .	19.663 – 1.96633 – 2.809 = 14.8877

Exhibit 27-17 The Multiplier Effect

An original increase of government spending of 100 causes a rise in aggregate expenditure of 100. But that 100 is income to others in the economy, and after they save, pay taxes, and buy imports, they spend 53 of that 100 in a second round. In turn, that 53 is income to others. Thus, the original government spending of 100 is multiplied by these cycles of spending, but the impact of each successive cycle gets smaller and smaller. Given the numbers in this example, the original government spending increase of 100 raises aggregate expenditure by 213; therefore, the multiplier in this example is 213/100 = 2.13.

Those who receive that income also pay 30% in taxes, save 10% of after-tax income, and spend 10% of total income on imports, as shown in Exhibit 27-18, so that an additional 28.09 (that is, 0.53 × 53) is spent in the third round. The people who receive that income then pay taxes, save, and buy imports, and the amount spent in the fourth round is 14.8877 (that is, .53 × 28.09).

Thus, over the first four rounds of aggregate expenditures, the impact of the original increase in government spending of 100 creates a rise in aggregate expenditures of 100 + 53 + 28.09 + 14.8877 = 195.9777. Exhibit 27-17 shows these total aggregate expenditures after these first four rounds, and then the figure shows the total aggregate expenditures after 30 rounds. The additional boost to aggregate expenditures is shrinking in each round of consumption. After about 10 rounds, the additional increments are very small indeed—nearly invisible to the naked eye. After 30 rounds, the additional increments in each round are so small that they have no practical consequence. After 30 periods, the cumulative value of the initial boost in aggregate expenditure is approximately 213. Thus, the government spending increase of 100 eventually, after many cycles, produced an increase of 213 in aggregate expenditure and real GDP. The definition of the **multiplier** is:

multiplier: Total increase in aggregate expenditures divided by the original increase in expenditures.

$$\text{Multiplier} = \frac{\text{Total increase in aggregate expenditures}}{\text{Original increase in expenditures}}$$

In this example, the multiplier is 213/100 = 2.13.

Calculating the Multiplier

Fortunately for everyone who isn't carrying around a computer with a spreadsheet program to project the impact of an original increase in expenditures over 20 or 50 or 100 cycles of spending, there is a formula for calculating the multiplier. The formula begins by calculating what fraction F of expenditures is recycled at each stage. To calculate this fraction, start off with a marginal dollar of income, and then adjust for how much money that flows into taxes, savings, and imports and thus doesn't become expenditures in the next round. In the example just presented,

Fraction of expenditures recycled = 1 – What goes into taxes – What goes into savings – What goes into imports

$$F = (1 - .3) - .1(1 - .3) - .1$$

$$F = .7 - .07 - .1 = .53$$

Deriving the Multiplier Formula

Say that the original change in aggregate expenditures is N. The fractional amount of how much expenditure is cycled back into the economy in the next stage—determined by tax rates, savings, and imports—is F. Then, the total aggregate expenditure T that is triggered by the original change N as it cycles through the economy will be

$$N + NF^1 + NF^2 + NF^3 + NF^4 + \ldots = T$$

If the N term is factored out, then the formula for the total expenditure T can be rewritten as

$$N(1 + F^1 + F^2 + F^3 + F^4 + \ldots) = T$$

The term in the parentheses is equal to the multiplier; it's the amount by which the original change in aggregate expenditures N is multiplied to get the change in equilibrium output T. Set the multiplier equal to M:

$$M = 1 + F^1 + F^2 + F^3 + F^4 + \ldots$$

This multiplier is an "infinite geometric series," a term you may have heard in a mathematics class. We want to express the multiplier in a simpler form that doesn't involve an infinite series. To accomplish this, we'll use a computational trick. Multiply both sides of the multiplier formula by F.

$$FM = F(1 + F^1 + F^2 + F^3 + F^4 + \ldots)$$

$$FM = F^1 + F^2 + F^3 + F^4 + \ldots$$

Then take the original equation for the multiplier and subtract the equation for the multiplier multiplied by F; that is, subtract the left-hand side of one equation from the other and the right-hand side of one equation from the other. In this calculation, the infinite series portion of one equation subtracts from the infinite series portion of the other equation and disappears, leaving only a value of 1 behind. Then manipulate the algebra so that the multiplier M is alone on the left-hand side.

$$M - FM = (1 + F^1 + F^2 + F^3 + F^4 + \ldots) - (F^1 + F^2 + F^3 + F^4 + \ldots) = 1$$

$$M - FM = 1$$

$$M(1 - F) = 1$$

$$M = 1/(1 - F)$$

This formula is the multiplier equation used in the text.

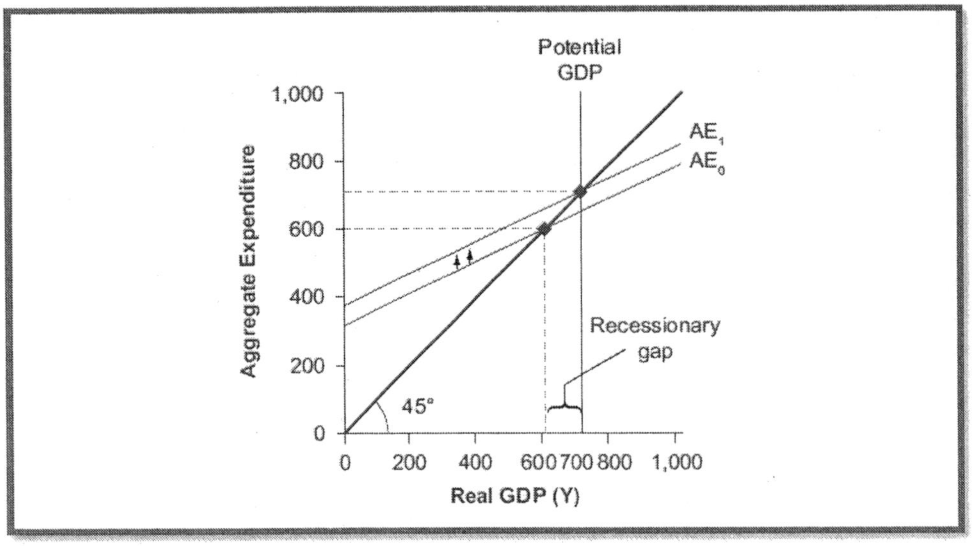

Exhibit 27-18 The Multiplier Effect in an Expenditure-Output Model

The power of the multiplier effect is that an increase in expenditure has a larger increase on the equilibrium output. The increase in expenditure is the vertical increase from AE_0 to AE_1. However, the increase in equilibrium output, shown on the horizontal axis, is clearly larger.

Given this fraction F, the equation for the multiplier (which is derived algebraically in the box) is:

$$\text{Multiplier} = \frac{1}{1 - F}$$

If F = .53, then the multiplier would be 1/(1 – .53) = 1/.47 = 2.13. Thus, an original increase in expenditures of 100, when multiplied by 2.13, will lead to an increase in aggregate expenditure of 213. Not coincidentally, this result is exactly what was calculated in Exhibit 27-18 after many rounds of expenditures cycling through the economy.

The size of the multiplier is determined by what proportion of the marginal dollar of income goes into taxes, saving, and imports. These three factors are known as "leakages," because they determine how much demand "leaks out" in each round of the multiplier effect. If the leakages are relatively small, then each successive rounds of the multiplier effect will have larger amounts of demand, and the multiplier will be high. Conversely, if the leakages are relatively large, then any initial change in demand will diminish more quickly in the second, third, and later rounds, and the multiplier will be small. Changes in the size of the leakages—a change in the marginal propensity to save, the tax rate, or the marginal propensity to import—will change the size of the multiplier.

Calculating Keynesian Policy Interventions

Now return yet again to the original question of this section: What if the intersection of the aggregate expenditure function and the 45-degree line in a Keynesian cross diagram was happening at 700, but potential GDP were 800. How much should government spending be increased to produce a total increase in real GDP of 100? If the goal is to increase aggregate demand by 100, and the multiplier is 2.13, then the increase in government spending that would be necessary to achieve that goal would be 100/2.13 = 47. That is, an increase in government spending of approximately 47, when combined with a multiplier of 2.13 (which is, remember, based on the specific assumptions about tax, saving, and import rates), produces an overall increase in real GDP of 100.

Using the Multiplier to Analyze the Economic Impact of Professional Sports

What effect does a professional sports team have on a local economy? John Siegfried of Vanderbilt University and Andrew Zimbalist of Smith College used the multiplier to analyze this issue. Most professional athletes and owners of sports teams are rich enough to owe a lot of taxes, so let's say that 40% of any marginal income they earn is paid in taxes. Because athletes are often high earners with short careers, let's assume that they save one-third of their after-tax income. However, many professional athletes don't live year-round in the city in which they play, so let's say that one-half of the money that they do spend is spent outside the local area. One can think of spending outside a local economy, in this example, as the equivalent of imported goods for the national economy.

Now consider the impact of money spent at local entertainment venues other than professional sports. While the owners of these other businesses may be comfortably middle-income, few of them are in the economic stratosphere of professional athletes. Because their incomes are lower, so are their taxes; say that they pay only 35% of their marginal income in taxes. They don't have the same ability, or need, to save as much as professional athletes, so let's assume their MPC is just 0.8. Finally, because more of them live locally, they will spend a higher proportion of their income on local goods—say, 65%.

If these general assumptions hold true, then money spent on professional sports will have less local economic impact than money spent on other forms of entertainment. For professional athletes, out of a dollar earned, 40% goes to taxes, leaving 60 cents. Of that 60 cents, one-third is saved, leaving 40 cents, and half is spent outside the area, leaving 20 cents. Only 20 cents of each dollar is cycled into the local economy in the first round. For locally owned entertainment, out of a dollar earned, 35 cents goes to taxes, leaving 65 cents. Of the rest, .2 is saved, leaving 52 cents, and of that amount, 65% is spent in the local area, so that 33.8 cents of each dollar of income is recycled into the local economy.

Siegfried and Zimbalist make the plausible argument that within their household budgets, people have a fixed amount to spend on entertainment. If this assumption holds true, then money spent attending professional sports events is money that was not spent on other entertainment options in a given metropolitan area. Since the multiplier is lower for professional sports than for other local entertainment options, the arrival of professional sports to a city would reallocate entertainment spending in a way that causes the local economy to shrink, rather than to grow.

The multiplier does not just affect government spending, but applies to any change in the economy. Say that business confidence declines and investment falls off, or that the economy of a leading trading partner slows down so that export sales decline. These changes will reduce aggregate expenditures, and then will have an even larger effect on real GDP because of the multiplier effect.

The multiplier effect is also visible on the Keynesian cross diagram. Exhibit 27-18 shows the example we have been discussing: a recessionary gap with an equilibrium of 600, potential GDP of 700, the slope of the aggregate expenditure function AE_1 determined by the assumptions that taxes are .3 of income, savings are .1 of after-tax income, and imports are .1 of before-tax income. At AE_2, the aggregate expenditure function is moved up to reach potential GDP. Now compare the vertical shift upwards in the aggregate expenditure function, which is 47, with the horizontal shift outward in real GDP, which is 100 (as these numbers were calculated earlier). The rise in real GDP is more than double the rise in the aggregate expenditure function. (Similarly, if you look back at Exhibit 27-16, you will see that the vertical movements in the aggregate expenditure functions are smaller than the change in equilibrium output that is produced on the horizontal axis. Again, this is the multiplier effect at work.) In this way, the power of the multiplier is apparent in the income-expenditure graph, as well as in the arithmetic calculation.

Multiplier Trade-offs: Stability vs. the Power of Macroeconomic Policy

Is an economy healthier with a high multiplier or a low one? With a high multiplier, any change in aggregate demand will tend to be substantially magnified, and so the economy will be more unstable. With a low multiplier, by contrast, changes in aggregate demand will not be multiplied much, so the economy will tend to be more stable.

However, with a low multiplier, government policy changes in taxes or spending will tend to have less impact on the equilibrium level of real output. With a higher multiplier, government policies to raise or reduce aggregate expenditures will have a larger effect. Thus, a low multiplier means a more stable economy, but also weaker government macroeconomic policy, while a high multiplier means a more volatile economy, but also an economy in which government macroeconomic policy is more powerful.

Is Keynesian Economics Pro-Market or Anti-Market?

Ever since the birth of Keynesian economics in the 1930s, controversy has simmered over the extent to which government should play an active role in managing the economy. In the aftermath of the human devastation and misery of the Great Depression, many people—including many economists—lost their confidence in a market-oriented economic system. Some supporters of Keynesian economics advocated a high degree of government planning in all parts of the economy.

However, John Maynard Keynes himself was careful to separate the issue of aggregate demand from the issue of how well individual markets worked. He argued that individual markets for goods and services were appropriate and useful, but that sometimes that level of aggregate demand was just too low. For example, Keynes argued that when 10 million people are willing and able to work, but one million of them are unemployed, individual markets may be doing a perfectly good job of allocating the efforts of the 9 million workers—the problem is that insufficient aggregate demand exists to support jobs for all 10 million. Thus, Keynes believed that while government should assure that overall level of aggregate demand is sufficient for an economy to reach full employment, this task did not imply that the government should attempt to set prices and wages throughout the economy, nor to take over and manage large corporations or entire industries directly.

Even if one accepts the Keynesian economic theory, a number of practical questions remain. In the real world, can government economists identify potential GDP accurately? Is a desired increase in aggregate demand better accomplished by a tax cut or by an increase in government spending? Given the inevitable delays and uncertainties as policies are enacted into law, is it reasonable to expect that the government can implement Keynesian economics? Can fixing a recession really be just as simple as pumping up aggregate demand? Chapters 32–33 on government tax and spending policy will probe these issues. The Keynesian approach, with its focus on aggregate demand and sticky prices, has proved useful in understanding how the economy fluctuates in the short run and why recessions and cyclical unemployment occur. In the next chapter, we'll consider some of the shortcomings of the Keynesian approach and why it is not especially well-suited for long-run macroeconomic analysis.

The Multiplier Process

by Bagher Modjtahedi

Assume that the marginal propensity to consume is 0.80, as before. When business firms increase their purchase of equipment by 100 units, the equipment producers experience 100 units of reductions in their inventories, and thus, increase production by 100 units to meet the new demand. This increases GDP by 100 units (the production aspect of GDP), resulting in 100 units of increase in the incomes of factors producing the equipment (income aspect of GDP). Since there is no change in taxes or transfer payments, this increase of 100 units in factor income translates into 100 units of increase in real disposable income.

Households that experience the 100-unit increase in their disposable income spend 80% of it on goods and services. As a result, a new round of demand and income equal to $0.80 \times 100 = 80$ units is generated in the economy. The recipients of these 80 units of income in turn spend 80% of it on goods and services, so a third round of demand equal to $0.80 \times 80 = 64$ units is generated. The process continues. Let's add up all these additional units of real GDP produced:

First round increase in $Y = 100$

Second round increase in $Y = 0.80 \times 100 = 80$

Third round increase in $Y = 0.80 \times 80 = 0.80 \times (0.80 \times 100) = 0.80^2 \times 100 = 64$

Etc.

So the overall increase in real GDP equals:

$$\Delta Y = 100 + 0.80 \times 100 + 0.80^2 \times 100 + 0.80^3 \times 100 + \cdots$$
$$= (1 + 0.80 + 0.80^2 + 0.80^3 + \cdots) \times 100$$

Using the results of the geometric progression from high school for the expression inside the parentheses we get:

$$\Delta Y = (1/1 - 0.80) \times 100 = 5 \times 100 = 500$$

Expenditure multiplier: A factor by which GDP would increase as a result of an increase in aggregate expenditure.

The term $1/(1 - 0.80) = 5$ is called the ***expenditure multiplier***. Note that a higher MPC results in a higher expenditure multiplier. For example, if the MPC were 0.90, the multiplier would equal $1/(1 - 0.90) = 10$, and the increase in the real GDP would equal 1,000 units. So in general:

$$\Delta Y = (1/1 - MPC) \times (\text{Initial Change in Aggregate Demand})$$

Note an important aspect of this story. In each and every round in the multiplier process, the increase in real GDP equals the increase in aggregate demand. (See the following chart.) This is because in each round, producers increase production to meet the increase in demand. So during the whole process, the goods market remains in equilibrium. Keep in mind, however, that these results were obtained under the assumption of fixed prices. Later we will see how things will change when we assume flexible prices.

The same result applies to the case of an increase in consumption spending (C) by households. For instance, suppose that households increase their consumption by 100 units for some reason other than an increase in disposable income. Then, applying the same multiplier formula, the real GDP will increase by 500 units. How about government spending (G)?

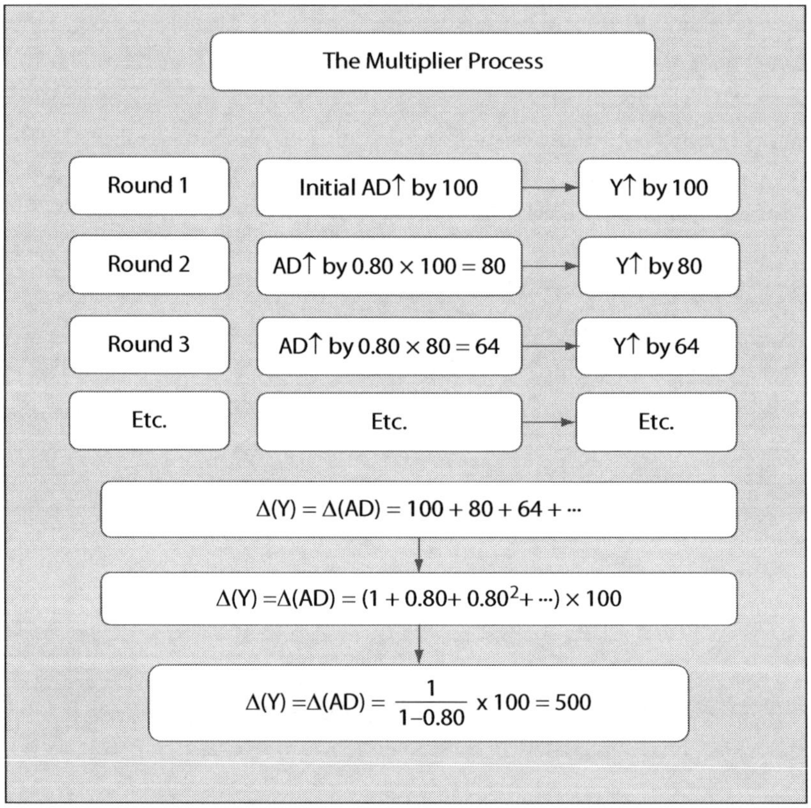

Fiscal Policy

Fiscal policy:
A change in government spending (G), taxes (TX), or transfer payments (TR) to change the state of the economy; especially, the real GDP or the unemployment rate.

Fiscal policy refers to changes in government spending, taxes, or transfer payments aiming to achieve a macroeconomic objective. On a yearly basis, every government buys certain amounts of goods and services, collects some taxes, and makes some transfer payments. Not all of these tax-expenditure programs qualify as fiscal policy. For example, every year the government spends money to repair roads and pay for the services of government employees, such as teachers and law enforcement officers. Moreover, every year people routinely pay taxes to the government out of their incomes. These ongoing tax and expenditure activities are necessary to "run the country."

Finally, the government provides social security payments and food stamps to help low-income families, and unemployment benefits to help the unemployed. These transfer payments are for humanitarian reasons and have nothing to do with fiscal policy.

We call a change in any of these variables fiscal policy if the sole purpose of the change is to affect the level of aggregate demand in order to achieve a macroeconomic goal. A policy to boost aggregate demand is called ***expansionary***; the one that aims to reduce it is called ***contractionary***. The goal is generally to increase the level of aggregate demand to fight a recession and increase employment, or to reduce it to fight inflation. At the same time, a change in G, TR, or TX will have the same effect on the real GDP, whether it is the result of an active fiscal policy or not.

The government budget is a record of the government's tax revenue and expenditure for a particular year.* If the expenditure (G + TR) exceeds the tax revenue (TX), we say that the government is running a ***budget deficit***. In the opposite case, the government would be running a ***budget surplus***. If the two are equal, we say that the government's budget is balanced. A government has three options to finance an increase in its expenditure:

a. It can raise taxes of an equal amount to leave the budget deficit or surplus unchanged. This is called a *balanced budget increase in spending*.
b. It can leave the amount of taxes collected unchanged, and instead borrow from the public. In this case, the budget deficit will increase; hence, this method of financing government expenditure is called *deficit spending (or deficit financing)*.
c. Finally, the government can print money to finance its expenditure if it does not want to increase taxes or borrow from the public. A version of this procedure is called *monetizing the debt*. This method of financing will also lead to an increase in budget deficit.

To understand the last two options, we need to know something about the financial markets and monetary policy. In this chapter, we talk about the first option.

Expansionary fiscal policy:
An increase in government spending and/or a decrease in taxes, aimed at increasing the level of aggregate demand for goods and services (in order to reduce unemployment).

Contractionary fiscal policy:
A reduction in government spending and/or an increase in taxes aimed at reducing the level of aggregate demand for goods and services (in order to reduce inflationary pressures).

Budget deficit:
The amount by which a government's expenditures exceed its tax revenues during a certain period of time.

Budget surplus:
The amount by which a government's tax revenues exceed its expenditures during a certain period of time.

Balanced Budget Increase in Spending

Suppose that the government wants to increase its spending (G) by 1,000 units and to finance it through an equal amount of taxes (TX). This will leave the budget deficit or surplus unchanged, but will it affect the aggregate demand? The increase in government spending of 1,000 units will directly increase aggregate demand by 1,000 units, because G is a component of aggregate demand—look at equation (1) above. On the other hand, the increase in taxes will reduce disposable income by 1,000 units. Assuming that

* Let us use the term "government spending" for the government's purchase of goods (G), and "government expenditure" for its total outlays (G + TR).

MPC equals 0.80, households will reduce their consumption expenditures by 800 units. So the net result will be an increase in aggregate demand of 200 units.

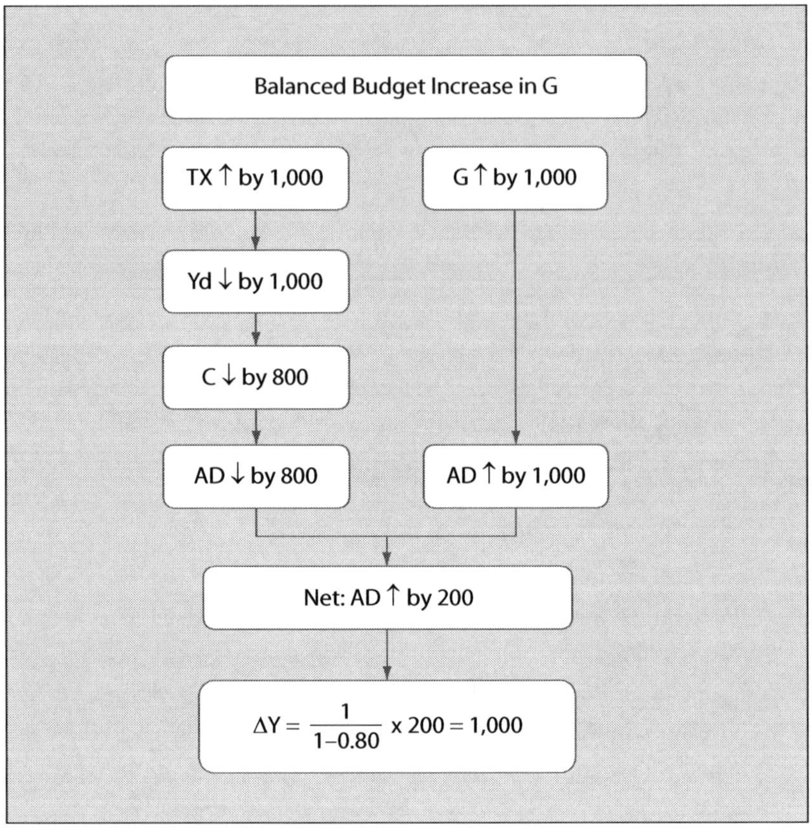

What will be the effect of this expansionary fiscal policy on the economy? Since the initial increase in aggregate demand is 200 units, the real GDP will increase by 1,000 units through the multiplier process as described above. This result is worth remembering. If the government increases spending and finances it by raising an equal amount of taxes, the real GDP will increase by the amount of the increase in government spending. This is called the ***unit multiplier*** result. Interestingly enough, it does not depend on the size of the multiplier. Suppose, for example, that MPC was 0.90 instead. Then the net increase in the aggregate demand would be $(1{,}000 - 0.90 \times 1{,}000) = 100$ and the real GDP would increase by 1,000:

Unit multiplier:
When the government increases spending and raises an equal amount of tax to finance it, the increase in GDP will equal the increase in spending.

$$\Delta Y = (1/1 - 0.90) \times 10 = 10 \times 100 = 1{,}000$$

Balanced Budget Increase in Transfer Payments

What if the government wants to increase the transfer payments (TR) by 1,000 units and finance it by an equal increase in taxes (TX)? Increases in TR and TX of an equal amount will leave the real disposable income unchanged. This policy, then, will have no effect on aggregate demand.

One reason why some governments conduct such a policy in a recession is the belief that those who are taxed generally have lower MPCs than those who receive transfer payments, such as the poor and unemployed. That is because, being poor, this group will spend most the income received on food and other necessities of life. So such an income transfer will increase aggregate demand.

Household Saving

What is not consumed is saved. Saving and consumption must therefore add up to disposable income.

$$Y_d = C + S \tag{4}$$

where S stands for saving. This simple concept has two important implications. First, given the level of income, consumption and saving must move in opposite directions and by the same amount. That is, an increase in consumption must be accompanied by an equal decrease in saving, and vice versa. Second, if disposable income increases, both consumption and saving will increase, and vice versa once again. Moreover, there will be a relationship between the increases in these two variables.

Suppose the marginal propensity to consume is MPC = 0.80. Then, if disposable income increases by 1,000 units, consumption will increase by 800 units. What will happen to the remaining 200 units? It will be saved. So if 80% of the increase in disposable income is consumed, the remaining 20% will be saved. The fraction of the increase in disposable income that is saved is called the ***marginal propensity to save (MPS).*** In our case MPS = 0.20. We see then that

Marginal propensity to save:
The fraction of the additional real disposable income that households save, rather than spending on goods and services. It is one minus MPC.

$$MPC + MPS = 1 \tag{5}$$

Conversely, if disposable income decreases by 1,000 units and MPC = 0.80, then consumption will decrease by 800 units and saving by 200 units. We will see in later chapters that this simple concept has important implications for the effectiveness of fiscal policy.

Key Concepts and Summary

1. Keynesian economics is based on two main ideas: a) aggregate demand is more likely than aggregate supply to be the primary cause of a short-run economic event like a recession, because aggregate supply usually moves slowly; b) wages and prices can be sticky, and so in an economic downturn unemployment can result.

2. **Menu costs** are the costs of changing prices. They include internal costs a business faces in changing prices in terms of labeling, record keeping, and accounting, and also the costs of communicating the price change to (possibly unhappy) customers.

3. The aggregate demand curve will shift based on movements in consumption, investment, government spending or taxes, exports, and imports. Consumption will change for a number of reasons, including movements in income, taxes, expectations about future incomes, and changes in wealth levels. Investment will change in response to its expected rate of return, which in turn is shaped by the real interest rate, the creation of new technologies, expectations about future economic growth, the price of key inputs, and tax incentives for investment. Government spending and taxes are determined by political considerations. Exports and imports change according to relative growth rates and prices between two economies.

4. A **Phillips curve** shows the trade-off between unemployment and inflation in an economy. From a Keynesian viewpoint, the Phillips curve should slope down so that higher unemployment means lower inflation, and vice versa. However, a downward-sloping Phillips curve is a short-term relationship that may shift after a few years.

5. Keynesian macroeconomic policy suggests that aggregate demand should be increased (shifted to the right) when the economy is in recession, and decreased (shifted to the left) when the economy faces a situation of high inflation.

6. The **expenditure-output model** or "Keynesian cross diagram" shows how the level of aggregate expenditure (on the vertical axis) varies with the level of economic output (shown on the horizontal axis). Since the value of all macroeconomic output also represents income to someone somewhere else in the economy, the horizontal axis can also be interpreted as **national income (Y).** The equilibrium in the diagram will occur where the aggregate expenditure line crosses the 45-degree line, which represents the set of points where aggregate expenditure in the economy is equal to output (or national income). Equilibrium in a Keynesian cross diagram can happen at potential GDP, or below or above that level.

7. The **consumption function** shows the upward-sloping relationship between national income and consumption. The **marginal propensity to consume (MPC)** is the amount consumed out of an additional dollar of income. A higher marginal propensity to consume means a steeper consumption function; a lower marginal propensity to consume means a flatter consumption function. The **marginal propensity to save (MPS)** is the amount saved out of an additional dollar of income. It is necessarily true that MPC + MPS = 1.

8. The investment function is drawn as a flat line, showing that investment in the current year doesn't change with regard to the current level of national income. However, the investment function will move up and down based on the expected rate of return in the future.

9. Government spending is drawn as a horizontal line in the Keynesian cross diagram, because its level is determined by political considerations, not by the current level of income in the economy. Taxes in the basic Keynesian cross model are taken into account by adjusting the consumption function.

10. The export function is drawn as a horizontal line in the Keynesian cross diagram, because exports don't change as a result of changes in domestic income, but they move as a result of changes in foreign income, as well as changes in exchange rates. The import function is drawn as a downward-sloping line, because imports rise with national income, but imports are a subtraction from aggregate demand. Thus, a higher level of imports means a lower level of expenditure on domestic goods. The **marginal propensity to import (MPI)** can be changed by movements in exchange rates.

11. In a Keynesian cross diagram, the equilibrium may be at a level below potential GDP, which is called a **recessionary gap,** or at a level above potential GDP, which is called an **inflationary gap.**

12. The **multiplier effect** describes how the impact of an original change in aggregate demand is multiplied as it cycles repeatedly through the economy. The size of the **multiplier** is determined by three leakages: spending on savings, taxes, and imports. The multiplier is defined as:

$$\text{Multiplier} = \frac{\text{Total increase in aggregate expenditures}}{\text{Original increase in expenditures}}$$

13. An economy with a lower multiplier is more stable—it is less affected either by economic events or by government policy than an economy with a higher multiplier.

14. The Keynesian macroeconomic prescription for adjusting aggregate demand higher or lower, as needed, need not imply that the government should be passing laws or regulations that set prices and quantities in microeconomic markets.

Unlocking the Mystery of Real-World Multipliers: Bang for the Buck

By David Moglen

As you have just read, the real-world expenditure multiplier is estimated to be much lower than textbook questions might imply. Major leakages that reduce the real multiplier are:

- Savings
- Taxes
- Imports
- Hiding assets offshore
- Holding assets as cash or in foreign investments
- Money diverted to the informal economy

Imports are the most severe diminishing factor, which explains why we seem to spend so much of our income, implying a large multiplier, while the real-world multiplier is quite small. The money is not re-spent inside the country because every step of the way, from the first round of spending to the last, so much of what we buy is imported. Even "Made in America" goods have significant components that are imported, and domestic firms have bought capital goods (factory equipment) that was imported. So there are numerous ways that studies tracking additional GDP from any injection of funds is much less than our high marginal propensity to consume (MPC) would imply. The money is being spent, but the large percentage that leaves the country can't circulate as additional domestic spending.

Further, some studies giving estimates of the multiplier look at impacts within one to two years, causing later rounds of spending to be ignored when they occur outside the study's time limit. Limited as the real-world multiplier may be, economists regularly forecast the GDP impact of a given fluctuation in spending; in other words, they are estimating an appropriate multiplier for that initial change.

As the vital equation in the text showed:

Amount of Initial Injection * Multiplier = total change in income after all rounds of spending are complete.

And: Income=Output=GDP=Y

Here are estimates by Moody's Economy.com and the Congressional Budget Office of the multiplier economists would apply to a variety of specific initial injections. This data is a guide for what would be the most effective fiscal policies in response to a recession.

The following estimates of the multiplier are from Moody's Economy.com.

Job Creation Policies' Bang for the Buck

Estimated one-year dollar change in GDP for each dollar reduction in federal tax revenue or increase in spending.

Tax Cuts	Bang for the Buck
Nonrefundable lump-sum tax rebate	1.01
Refundable lump-sum tax rebate	1.22
Temporary Tax Cuts	
Payroll tax holiday	1.24
Job tax credit	1.30
Across-the-board tax cut	1.02
Accelerated depreciation	0.25.
Loss carryback	0.22
Housing tax credit	0.90
Permanent Tax Cuts	
Extending alternative minimum tax patch	0.51
Making Bush income tax cuts permanent	0.32
Making dividend and capital gains tax cuts permanent	0.37
Cut in corporate tax rate	0.32
Spending Increases	
Extending unemployment insurance benefits	1.61
Temporary federal financing of work-share programs	1.69
Temporary increase in food stamps	1.74
General aid to state governments	1.41
Increased infrastructure spending	1.57

Source: Moody's Economy.com.

"For example, we estimate that each dollar spent on additional unemployment insurance benefits increases GDP over the following year by $1.61. It's important to note that most of the stimulus does not show up in the government component of national gross domestic product. One argument voiced by stimulus opponents, including some economists who should know better, is that federal government consumption and investment added less than 1 percentage point to annualized GDP growth in both the second and third quarters of 2009. This overlooks the fact that most stimulus spending ends up in other categories in the GDP numbers. Aid to state governments, for example, is why state and local government spending has been a plus for GDP growth, not a negative. And income support programs in the stimulus such as tax cuts and transfer payments are boosting consumer spending, which accounts for more than 70% of GDP."

—Augustine Faucher for Dismal Scientist[*]

The next two tables show estimates of the multiplier by the Congressional Budget Office (CBO)[2].

[3]http://www.economy.com/dismal/article_free.asp? cid=119925&src=nytimes.

Table 1. The Estimated Impact of the American Recovery and Reinvestment Act of 2009 on Output and the Budgetary Costs, 2009 to 2019

Category	Estimated Policy Multiplier		Major Provisions	11-Year Budgetary Cost of Provisions[a]
	High	Low		
Purchases of Goods and Services by the Federal Government	2.5	1	Division A, Title II: Other; Title IV: Energy Efficiency and Renewable Energy; Title IV: Innovative Technology Loan Guarantee Program; Title IV: Other Energy Programs; Title V: Federal Buildings Fund; Title VIII: National Institutes of Health; Title VIII: Other Department of Health and Human Services	$88 billion
Transfers to State and Local Governments for Infrastructure	2.5	1	Division A, Title VII: Clean Water and Drinking Water State Revolving Funds; Title XII: Highway Construction; Title XII: Other Transportation; Title XII: Other Housing Assistance	$44 billion
Transfers to State and Local Governments Not for Infrastructure	1.9	0.7	Division A, Title VIII: Education for the Disadvantaged; Title VIII: Special Education; Title XIV: State Fiscal Stabilization Fund; Division B, Title V: State Fiscal Relief Fund	$215 billion
Transfers to Persons	2.2	0.8	Division A, Title I: Supplemental Nutrition Assistance Program; Title VIII: Student Financial Assistance; Division B, Title II: Unemployment Compensation; Title III: Health Insurance Assistance	$100 billion
One-Time Payments to Retirees	1.2	0.2	Division B, Title II: Economic Recovery Payments, Temporary Aid to Needy Families, and Child Support[b]	$18 billion
Two-Year Tax Cuts for Lower- and Middle-Income People	1.7	0.5	Division B, Title I: Refundable Tax Credits; Making Work Pay Credit[c]; American Opportunity Tax Credit[c]	$168 billion
One-Year Tax Cuts for Higher-Income People	0.5	0.1	Increase in Individual AMT Exemption Amount[c]	$70 billion
Extension of First-Time Homebuyer Credit	1	0.2	Extension of First-Time Homebuyer Credit[c]	$7 billion

(continued)

(Continued)

Category	Estimated Policy Multiplier		Major Provisions	11-Year Budgetary Cost of Provisions[a]
	High	Low		
Tax Provisions for Business Primarily Affecting Cash Flow	0.4	0	Deferral and Ratable Inclusion of Income Arising from Business Indebtedness Discharged by the Reacquisition of a Debt Instrument[c]; Clarification of Regulations Related to Limitations on Certain Built-In Losses Following an Ownership Change[c]; Recovery Zone Bonds[c]; Qualified School Construction Bonds[c]	$21 billion

Notes: The policy multiplier is the cumulative impact on GDP over several quarters of various policy options. This table includes provisions scored by the Congressional Budget Office (CBO) or the Joint Committee on Taxation (JCT) as totaling $5 billion or more in budgetary costs over the 2009–2019 period. Selected provisions with lower total budgetary costs were included if the cost in the 2009–2011 period was large.

The economic impact of three tax provisions with budgetary costs over $5 billion—as titled in JCT's estimate, "Extend by Three Years the Placed-In-Service Date for Each Section 45 Qualified Facility," "One-Year Extension of Special Allowance for Certain Property Acquired During 2009," and in CBO's estimate, "Health Information Technology"—was analyzed using a different methodology, and their effects cannot easily be summarized by a multiplier.

Provisions affecting outlays (including refundable tax provisions) are identified by the same names used in CBO's cost estimate for the conference report on H.R. 1 (see Table 2). Provisions affecting revenues—all included in Title I—are identified by the names used in JCT's estimate (see www.house.gov/jct/x-19-09.pdf).

Some provisions include individual elements that have different multipliers, by CBO's estimate; in those cases, the provisions are listed with the multiplier used for the majority of the 11-year budgetary cost.

[a] Costs do not add up to the total budgetary cost of $787 billion presented in CBO's cost estimate because several provisions are excluded (because CBO's analysis of those provisions cannot easily be summarized by a single multiplier) and because the costs listed are translations of the budgetary costs to categories of the national income and product accounts.

[b] Most of the payments in this category go to retirees.

[c] Estimated by JCT.

APPLY YOUR SKILLS

The Expenditure Multiplier

By David Moglen

Useful Equations:

1. The Expenditure Multiplier Equation: (this is the most important one out of the following)

Change in AE * M = Change in GDP

Where Change in AE (Aggregate Expenditures) is the **initial** increase or decrease in some component of AE, either spending by C (Consumption), G (Government), I (Businesses) or NX (Net Exports, equal to Exports minus Imports). This starts the multiplier process. You multiply that initial change by the Multiplier, M, to get the Change in GDP **after all rounds of spending are complete**.

$M = 1/(1-MPE)$

MPE is interchangeable with MPC for this formula.

Y is another symbol for total income, so GDP = Y.

2. Autonomous Expenditures + (MPE*Y) = Y

3. Change in Taxes * (-MPE) = Change in Consumption Spending = Change in C When you are given a Change in Taxes to start the problem, this equation translates it into the **Change in C** so you have something to start the multiplier equation (eqn. 1, above). That equation has to start with Change in AE, which means some component of AE (C, I, G, or NX) has changed. Change in Taxes is not one of those four choices.

4. Okun's Rule of Thumb (aka Okun's Law): For a 1% increase in unemployment above the natural rate, estimate a 2% decrease in GDP (relative to GDP* aka potential GDP), and the same 1%:2% inverse relationship had unemployment fallen by 1%.

Directions: Half of the groups answer even-numbered questions and the other half will do the odds. Be sure your answer shows clearly whether it is negative or positive. Any number with decimal places can be rounded to two decimals.

Questions:

1. MPE=0.7, Autonomous C = 5000, Autonomous I = 800, Autonomous G = 600, and Autonomous NX = -300. What is GDP?

2. Imports Rise by 50 million dollars. MPE = 0.8. What is the change in GDP?

3. The government seeks to close a 500 billion dollar inflationary gap. MPE = 0.75. What should be the change in government spending?

4. The government seeks to close an 800 billion dollar recessionary gap, using incentives to increase business spending. MPE = 0.5. What should be the change in business spending (I) that the government needs to seek?

5. For a 70 billion dollar tax cut in an economy with an MPE = .8, what is the change in GDP?

6. For a 90 billion dollar tax increase in an economy with an MPE = .6, what is the change in GDP?

7. GDP = 10.8 trillion dollars. GDP*=10 trillion dollars.

A.) Use Okun's Law to find the new unemployment rate, using a natural rate of unemployment of 5%.

B.) MPE=0.75. What should be the Change in G to restore potential GDP (i.e. so that current GDP=GDP*).

8. GDP = 9.4 trillion dollars. GDP*=10 trillion dollars.

A.) Use Okun's Law to find the new unemployment rate, using a natural rate of unemployment of 5%.

B.) MPE=0.75. What should be the Change in G to restore potential GDP (i.e. so that current GDP=GDP*).

-6.66 trillion

CHAPTER 11

Money, Banking, and the Federal Reserve System

11 Money, Banking, and the Federal Reserve System

By Timothy Taylor

Money is not an end in itself. You can't eat dollar bills or wear your bank account. Ultimately, the usefulness of money rests in exchanging it for goods or services. As the American writer and humorist Ambrose Bierce (1842–1914) wrote in 1911, money is a "blessing that is of no advantage to us excepting when we part with it."

Here's a trivia question: In the history of the world, what item was used for money over the broadest geographic area and the longest period of time? The answer isn't gold or silver, or any precious metal. It's the cowrie, a mollusk shell found mainly off the Maldive Islands in the Indian Ocean. Cowries served as money as early as 700 B.C. in China. By the 1500s, they were in widespread use across India and Africa. For several centuries after that, cowries were used in markets including southern Europe, western Africa, India and China for a wide range of purchases: everything from buying lunch or a ferry ride to paying for a shipload of silk or rice. Cowries were still acceptable as a way of paying taxes in certain African nations in the early twentieth century.

What made cowries work so well as money? First, they are extremely durable and last a century or more. As one writer put it, they can be "poured, sacked, shoveled, hoarded in heaps" while remaining "clean, dainty, stainless, polished, and milk-white." Second, parties could use cowries either by counting shells of a certain size, or—for large purchases—by measuring the weight or volume of the total shells to be exchanged. Third, it was impossible to counterfeit a cowrie shell, but gold or silver coins could be counterfeited by making copies with cheaper metals. Finally, in the heyday of cowrie money from the 1500s into the 1800s, the collection of cowries was tightly controlled, first by the Portuguese and later by the Dutch and the English. As a result, the supply of cowries was allowed to grow quickly enough to serve the needs of commerce, but not so quickly that they were no longer scarce.

The discussion of money and banking in this chapter begins a new main section in the study of macroeconomics. At this point, you should have firmly in mind the four main goals of macroeconomics: economic growth, low unemployment, low inflation, and a sustainable balance of trade. You should also understand Keynesian and neoclassical frameworks for macroeconomic analysis and how these frameworks can be embodied in the aggregate demand-aggregate supply (AD-AS) model. With the goals and frameworks for macroeconomic analysis in mind, the final step is to discuss the two main categories of macroeconomic policy: monetary policy, which focuses on money, banking and interest rates; and fiscal policy, which focuses on government spending, taxes, and borrowing. This chapter discusses what economists mean by money, and how money is closely interrelated with the banking system. Chapter 30 discusses how central banks, such as the U.S. Federal Reserve, can affect the money supply in the economy. Chapter 31 discusses the international dimensions of money, including the economic and policy factors that determine exchange rates between the money from different countries.

Defining Money by Its Functions

Money is what people in a society regularly use when purchasing or selling goods and services, and thus money must be widely accepted by both buyers and sellers. This concept of money is intentionally flexible, because money has taken a wide variety of forms in different cultures. Money has been made of gold, silver, and paper. Native Americans and early American settlers used strings of beads called wampum as money. In the islands of Fiji in the southern Pacific Ocean, islanders once exchanged the teeth of the sperm whale as money. People have used cattle as money over the centuries; in certain areas of what was then Russia, horses were the main form of money well into the twentieth century, with sheep and lambskins used for small change. Metal forms of money have included not only coins, but metal anklets and bracelets have been used as a type of wearable money, especially in western Africa. In prisons and prisoner-of-war camps in the twentieth century, cigarettes have sometimes served as money. Modern examples of money include U.S. dollars, European euros, the Chinese yuan, India's rupee, Japanese yen, Nigerian naira, Brazilian reals, Polish zlotys, and the coins and bills of every country.

BARTER AND THE DOUBLE COINCIDENCE OF WANTS

barter:
Literally, trading one good or service for another, without using money.

double coincidence of wants:
A situation in which both of two people each wants some good or service that the other person can provide.

To understand the usefulness of money, consider the inconvenience of exchange without money. **Barter**—literally trading one good or service for another—is a completely inadequate mechanism for trying to coordinate the trades in a modern advanced economy. In an economy without money, an exchange between two people would involve a **double coincidence of wants**, a situation in which both of two people each wants some good or service that the other person can provide. For example, if an accountant wants a pair of shoes, this accountant must find someone who has a pair of shoes in the correct size and who is willing to exchange the shoes for some hours of accounting services. Such a trade is likely to be difficult to arrange. Think about the complexity of such trades in a modern economy, with its extensive division of labor that involves thousands upon thousands of different jobs and goods.

Mademoiselle Zelie's Problems with Barter

In 1875, famous British economist William Stanley Jevons (1835–1882) wrote a book called Money and the Mechanics of Exchange, in which he illustrated the problems of barter with the following example:

Some years since, Mademoiselle Zelie, a singer of the Theatre Lyrique at Paris, made a professional tour around the world, and gave a concert in the Society Islands. In exchange for an air from Norma and a few other songs, she was to receive a third part of the receipts. When counted, her share was found to consist of three pigs, twentythree turkeys, forty-four chickens, five thousand cocoa-nuts, besides considerable quantities of bananas, lemons, and oranges. At the Halle in Paris, as the prima donna remarks in her lively letter, printed by M. Wolowski, this amount of live stock and vegetables might have brought four thousand francs, which would have been good remuneration for five songs. In the Society Islands, however, pieces of money were very scarce; and as Mademoiselle could not consume any considerable portion of the receipts herself, it became necessary in the mean time to feed the pigs and poultry with the fruit. . . .

In modern civilized society the inconveniences of the primitive method of exchange are wholly unknown, and might almost seem to be imaginary. Accustomed as we are to the use of money, we are unconscious of the inestimable benefits which it confers upon us; and only when we recur to altogether different states of society can we realize the difficulties which arise in its absence.

Money greases the social machinery of exchange. In an economy with money, an accountant doesn't need to seek out people who sell shoes and find out if they want to exchange them for a few hours of accounting services. Instead, the accountant works for a company and receives money wages, which can then be used to purchase shoes or other goods. Employers don't need to pay their workers in apartments, food, or clothing; instead, employers pay money. People don't need to save for their retirement by piling up canned food in their basements; they save money in the bank instead. Money is a marvelous invention that makes the division of labor and other complex economic activities possible.

THREE FUNCTIONS FOR MONEY

Economists have identified three specific functions of money. First, money serves as a **medium of exchange**, which means that money must be very widely accepted as a method of payment in the markets for goods, labor, and financial capital. U.S. paper money, for example, carries the statement: "THIS NOTE IS LEGAL TENDER FOR ALL DEBTS, PUBLIC AND PRIVATE." In other words, if you owe a debt, then legally speaking, you can pay that debt with currency.

medium of exchange: Whatever is widely accepted as a method of payment.

unit of account: The common way in which market values are measured in an economy.

Second, money serves as a **unit of account**, which means that it is the ruler by which other values are measured. Without money, you would have to carry around list of all the possible opportunity costs in your head: for example, a loaf of bread will have an opportunity cost of 10 minutes of work or a rental movie. Money acts as a common denominator, an accounting method that simplifies thinking about trade-offs. At a supermarket, the unit of account function of money allows the cashier to add the values of many individual items into a single value. A

store of value:
Something that serves as a way of preserving economic value that can be spent or consumed in the future.

money:
Whatever serves society in three functions: medium of exchange, unit of account, and store of value.

common unit of account allows government statisticians to add up the value of cars, haircuts, Internet service providers and all other goods and services into a single money value to calculate GDP. Third, money serves as a **store of value**; that is, when you receive money, you know that you don't need to spend it immediately because it will still hold its value the next day, or the next year. Holding money is a much easier and less wasteful way of storing value than trying to purchase physical goods, such as apples or refrigerators, storing those goods, and then trying to exchange them in the future. This function of money does not require that money is a perfect store of value. In an economy with inflation, money loses some buying power each year, but it remains money.

Money needs to serve all three of these functions—medium of exchange, unit of account, and store of value. Serving only one of these functions is not enough. For example, a house may serve as a store of value, in the sense that it can be sold later. But houses do not serve as mediums of exchange or units of account, and so they are not money.

Measuring Money: Currency, M1, and M2

Cash in your pocket certainly serves as a medium of exchange, unit of account, and a store of value. But what about checks or credit cards? Are

The Case of the Missing Currency

Here is a puzzle. The Federal Reserve reported that about $862 billion in currency—that is, paper money and coins—was in circulation in 2009. Dividing the total currency by roughly 220 million U.S. adults 20 or older works out to an average of approximately $3,900 in currency for every man and woman.

This average seems ridiculously high. Survey results suggest that the average holdings of currency for each adult are more like $350—and that number takes into account well-off people who hold large amounts of cash in safes and safety deposit boxes. If 220 million adults are each holding $350, then total holdings of U.S. currency by individuals is about $77 billion. Businesses traditionally hold about 3% of all currency, or about $26 billion. After all, most businesses try not to hold currency, but instead quickly get money to the bank where it can earn some interest.

So if households and firms together hold about $103 billion in currency, where is the other $759 billion? No one is quite sure. There are three possible answers: it may be held by children; as part of the unmeasured "underground" economy; or by foreigners. Even if one believes that teenage buying power is important to certain sectors of the economy, and that underground, unreported businesses are everywhere, it is very hard to believe that these two components are larger than the uses of money by adults and legal businesses. As a result, it seems likely that hundreds of billions of dollars of U.S. currency is circulating in the hands of foreigners.

When a country's own currency is plagued with uncertainty, perhaps because of a high inflation rate, people in that country may start carrying out transactions and saving money by using U.S. dollars. But this explanation is not completely satisfactory either. In high-income economies like those of the European nations, Japan, and Canada, people have relatively little need to use U.S. currency for transactions or saving. People may invest in the United States, but they can do so with electronic money; they don't need actual currency in the form of paper and coins. In the middle and low-income countries of the world, the average families are too poor to account for hundreds of billions of dollars of U.S. currency.

The case of the missing currency remains unsolved.

Exhibit 29-1 Defining Money with M1 and M2

The money stock has several definitions, ranging from narrow to broad. M1 is mainly currency and checking accounts. M2 is everything in M1, plus savings accounts, small time deposits, and money market funds.

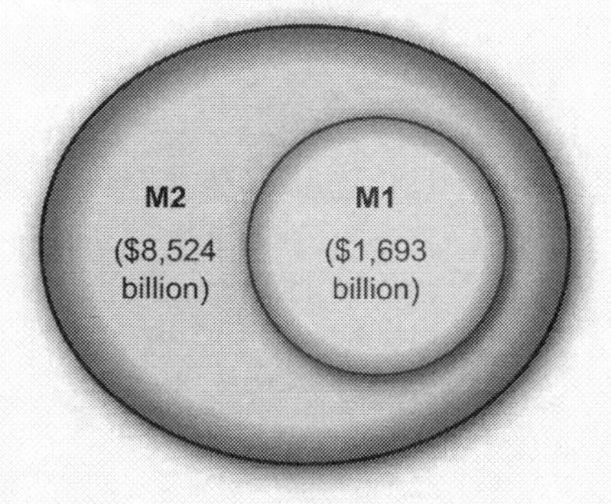

Currency	$862 billion
Traveler's checks	$5 billion
Demand deposits and other checking accounts	$826 billion
Total M1	**$1,693 billion**
Savings accounts	$4,849 billion
Small time deposits	$1,168 billion
Individual money market mutual fund balances	$814 billion
Total M2	**$8,524 billion**

they money, too? Rather than trying to state a single way of measuring money, economists offer a series of ever-broader definitions of money.

Money certainly includes **currency**, the coins and bills that circulate in an economy. Closely related to currency are two items that you can use, in most circumstances, almost as easily as cash. One of them is *traveler's checks*, which you purchase from a bank or financial company, sign, and then redeem with an additional signature when you want to spend them. Traveler's checks have the advantage of being accepted almost as widely as currency, and, if they are lost or stolen, the company that issued them will replace them. Cash offers no such protection. The other item closely related to currency is personal checks, also known to economists as **demand deposits,** because they are deposits in banks that are available by making a cash withdrawal or writing a check. These three items together—currency, traveler's checks, and checking accounts in banks—make up the definition of money known as **M1**.

A broader definition of money, known as **M2**, includes everything in M1, but also adds the bank accounts on which money can be withdrawn fairly easily, but not as easily as with personal checks. For example, M2 includes **savings deposits** in banks, which are bank accounts on which you can't write a check directly, but you can easily withdraw the money at an automatic teller machine or bank. Many banks and other financial institutions offer a chance to invest in **money market funds**, where the deposits of many individual investors are pooled together and invested in a safe way like short-term government bonds. Another ingredient of M2 are the relatively small (that is, less than about $100,000) **certificates of deposit** or **time deposits**, which are accounts that the depositor has committed to leaving in the bank for a certain period of time, ranging from a few months to a few years, in exchange for a higher interest rate. In short, these ingredients of M2 are money that you can withdraw and spend, but with a greater effort than the items in M1.

Exhibit 29-1 should help in visualizing the relationship between M1 and M2. Note that M1 is nested in M2. In 2009, M1 was $1,693 billion,

currency:
Coins and paper bills.

demand deposits:
Deposits in banks that are available by making a cash withdrawal or writing a check.

M1:
A narrow definition of the money supply that includes currency, traveler's checks, and checking accounts in banks.

M2:
A definition of the money supply that includes everything in M1, but also adds savings deposits, money market funds, and certificates of deposit.

savings deposits:
Bank accounts where you can't withdraw money by writing a check, but can withdraw the money at a bank—or can transfer it easily to a checking account.

money market funds:
Where the deposits of many investors are pooled together and invested in a safe way like short-term government bonds.

certificate of deposit (CD): A mechanism for a saver to deposit funds at a bank and promise to leave them at the bank for a time, in exchange for a higher rate of interest.

time deposits: Accounts that the depositor has committed to leaving in the bank for a certain period of time, in exchange for a higher rate of interest; also called certificates of deposit.

while M2 was $8,524 billion. For comparison, the size of the U.S. GDP in 2009 was $14.2 trillion.

The lines between separating M1 and M2 can become a little blurry. Sometimes elements of M1 are not treated alike; for example, some businesses won't accept personal checks for large amounts, but will accept traveler's checks or cash. Changes in banking practices and technology have made the savings accounts in M2 more similar to the checking accounts in M1. For example, some savings accounts will allow depositors to write checks, use automatic teller machines, and pay bills over the Internet, which has made it easier to access savings accounts. As with many other economic terms and statistics, the important point is to know the strengths and limitations of the various definitions of money, not to believe that such definitions are as clear-cut to economists as, say, the definition of nitrogen is to chemists.

Where does "plastic money" like credit cards fit into this picture? When you make a purchase with a credit card, the credit card company immediately transfers money from its checking account to the seller, and at the end of the month, the credit card company sends you a bill for what you have charged that month. Until you pay the credit card bill, you have effectively borrowed money from the credit card company, although typically no interest is charged on the loan if you pay your credit card bill on time. When you make a purchase with a debit card, another kind of plastic money, the funds are transferred directly and immediately from your bank account to the seller. With a *smart card*, you can store a certain value of money on the card and then use the card to make purchases. Some "smart cards" used for specific purposes, like long-distance phone calls or making purchases at a campus bookstore and cafeteria, aren't really all that smart, because they can only be used for certain purchases or in certain places. However, in the Netherlands, millions of smart cards that are good for small purchases in many stores have been in circulation since the late 1990s. In short, credit cards, debit cards, and smart cards are different ways to move money when a purchase is made. But having more credit cards or debit cards doesn't change the quantity of money in the economy, any more than having more checks printed increases the amount of money in your checking account.

One key message underlying this discussion of M1 and M2 is that money in a modern economy is not just paper bills and coins; instead, money is closely linked to bank accounts. Indeed, the macroeconomic policies concerning money are largely conducted through the banking system. The next section explains how banks function and how a nation's banking system has the power to create money.

How Banks Work

An old-time bank robber named Willie Sutton (1901–1980) was once asked why he robbed banks. He answered: "That's where the money is." From the perspective of modern economists, Sutton is both right and wrong. He is wrong because the overwhelming majority of money in

Banks, Savings and Loans, and Credit Unions

Banks have a couple of close cousins: savings institutions and *credit unions*. Banks, as explained in the text, receive deposits from individuals and businesses and make loans with the money.

Savings institutions are also sometimes called "savings and loans" or "thrifts." They also take loans and make deposits. However, from the 1930s until the 1980s, federal law limited how much interest savings institutions were allowed to pay to depositors. They were also required to make most of their loans in the form of housing-related loans, either to homebuyers or to real-estate developers and builders.

A *credit union* is a nonprofit financial institution that its members own and run. Members of each credit union decide who is eligible to be a member. Usually, potential members would be everyone in a certain community, or groups of employees, or members of a certain organization. The credit union accepts deposits from members and focuses on making loans back to its members. While there are more credit unions than banks and more banks than savings and loans, the total assets of credit unions are relatively small.

In 2008, the U.S. economy had 7,085 banks, 1,220 thrifts, and 7,806 credit unions. The banks and savings and loans tend to be roughly the same size. In 2008, on average, these institutions held $1.6 billion in assets each. Credit unions are much smaller. In 2009, they averaged about $100 million in assets each.

Exhibit 29-2 Banks as Financial Intermediaries

Banks act as financial intermediaries because they stand between savers and borrowers. Savers place deposits with banks, and then receive interest payments and withdraw money. Borrowers receive loans from banks, and repay the loans with interest. In turn, banks return money to savers in the form of withdrawals, which also include interest payments from banks to savers.

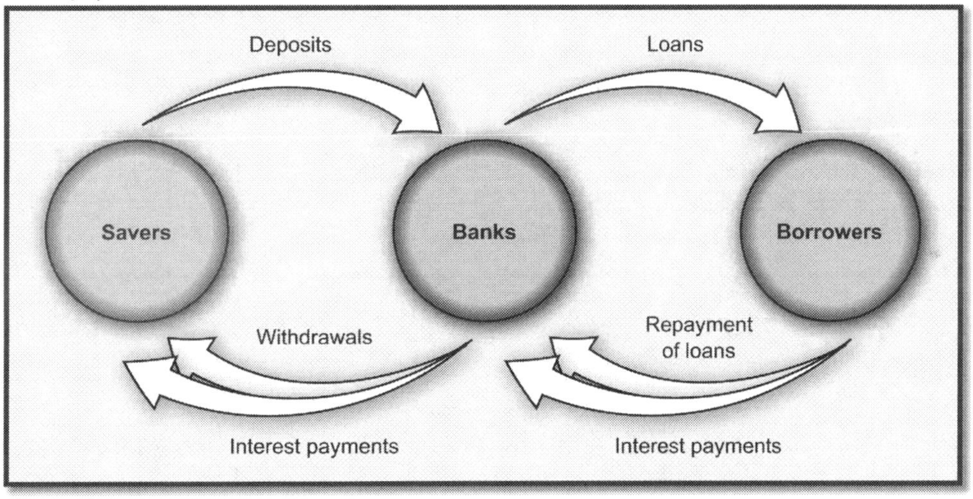

the economy is not in the form of currency sitting in vaults or drawers at banks, waiting for a robber to appear. Most money is in the form of bank accounts, which exist only as electronic records on computers. From a broader perspective, however, the bank robber was more right than he may have known. Banking is intimately tied up with money and consequently, with the broader economy.

Banks make it far easier for a complex economy to carry out the extraordinary range of transactions that occur in goods, labor, and financial capital markets. Imagine for a moment what the economy would be like if all payments had to be made in cash. When shopping for a large purchase or going on vacation you might need to carry hundreds

Exhibit 29-3 Revenues, Expenses, and Profits for the U.S. Banking Industry in 2008

Total Revenues		Total Costs	
Interest income	$603 billion	Interest payments	$246 billion
Other income (fees and charges)	$208 billion	Cost of loans that are not repaid	$174 billion
		Operating expenses (salaries, office space, equipment)	$365 billion
		Taxes	$6 billion
Total revenues	$811 billion	Total costs	$791 billion
Accounting profits = Total revenues – Total costs = $20 billion			

Exhibit 29-4 A Balance Sheet for the Safe and Secure Bank

The "T" in a T-account separates the assets of a firm on the left from its liabilities on the right. All firms use (much more complex) T-accounts. But for a bank, the assets are the financial instruments that either the bank is holding—its reserves—or those instruments where other parties owe money to the bank—like loans made by the bank and bonds purchased by the bank. Liabilities are what the bank owes to others: specifically, the bank owes any deposits made in the bank to those who have made them. The net worth of the bank is the total assets minus total liabilities. For a healthy business, net worth will be positive. For a bankrupt firm, net worth will be negative.

Assets		Liabilities	
Loans	$5 million	Deposits	$10 million
Bonds	$4 million		
Reserves	$2 million		

Net worth = Assets – Liabilities
$1 million = $11 million – $10 million

of dollars in a pocket or purse. Even small businesses would need stockpiles of cash to pay workers and to purchase supplies. In a world where large quantities of cash are common, burglars and pickpockets would be rampant. But along with making transactions much safer and easier, banks play a key role in the saving and borrowing that takes place in financial capital markets.

BANKS AS FINANCIAL INTERMEDIARIES

financial intermediary: An institution that operates between a saver with financial assets to invest and an entity who will receive those assets and pay a rate of return.

An "intermediary" is one who stands between two other parties; for example, a person who arranges a blind date between two friends is one kind of intermediary. Banks are a financial intermediary—that is, an institution that operates between a saver who deposits money in a bank and a borrower who receives a loan from that bank. But when a bank serves as a **financial intermediary**, unlike the situation with a couple on a blind date, the saver and the borrower never meet. All the funds deposited are mingled in one big pool, which is then loaned out. Exhibit

29-2 illustrates the position of banks as financial intermediaries, with deposits flowing into a bank and loans flowing out. Of course, when banks make loans to firms, the banks will try to funnel financial capital to healthy businesses that have good prospects for repaying the loans, not to firms that are suffering losses and may be unable to repay.

A bank receives revenue from two sources: interest payments to the bank from those who have received bank loans, and other fees and charges imposed by the bank. Conversely, banks have four main categories of expenses: interest payments to depositors; loans that are not repaid; operating costs of employees, office space and equipment; and taxes. Exhibit 29-3 shows the combined statistics for revenues and expenses for the roughly 8,000 U.S. banks and savings institutions. The U.S. banking industry as a whole earned $20 billion in accounting profits in 2008. Of course, just because the overall banking industry earned a profit doesn't mean that every individual bank did so; in fact, during the recession of 2007–2009, many banks experienced high costs of loans that were not repaid as expected, and lost money as a result.

A BANK'S BALANCE SHEET

Banks calculate their profits at the end of each quarter or year. But banks also evaluate their financial condition by comparing their **assets**, which are defined as items of value owned by the firm, with their **liabilities**, which are any amounts or debts owed by the firm. A **balance sheet** is an accounting tool that lists assets and liabilities. Exhibit 29-4 illustrates a hypothetical balance sheet for the Safe and Secure Bank. Because of the two-column format of the balance sheet, with the T-shape formed by the vertical line down the middle and the horizontal line under "Assets" and "Liabilities," it is sometimes called a **T-account**.

When bank customers deposit money into a checking account, savings account, or a certificate of deposit, the bank views these deposits as liabilities. After all, the bank owes these deposits to its customers, when the customers wish to withdraw their money. The Safe and Secure Bank holds $10 million in deposits.

Loans are the first category of bank assets shown in Exhibit 29-4. Say that a family takes out a 30-year mortgage loan to purchase a house, which means that the borrower will repay the loan over the next 30 years. This loan is clearly an asset from the bank's perspective, because the borrower has a legal obligation to make payments to the bank over time. But in practical terms, how can the value of the mortgage loan that is being paid over 30 years be measured in the present? One way of measuring the value of something—whether a loan or anything else—is by estimating what another party in the market is willing to pay for it. Many banks issue home loans, and charge various handling and processing fees for doing so, but then sell the loans to other banks or financial institutions who collect the loan payments. The market where loans are made to borrowers is called the *primary loan market*, while the market in which these loans are bought and sold by financial institutions is the *secondary loan market*.

assets:
Items of value owned by a firm or an individual.

liabilities:
Any amounts or debts owed by a firm or an individual.

balance sheet:
An accounting tool that lists assets and liabilities.

T-account:
A balance sheet with two-column format, with the T-shape formed by the vertical line down the middle and the horizontal line under the column headings for "Assets" and "Liabilities."

Clearing It Up: Is a Bank Account a "Liability"?

The way in which a bank views its "assets" and "liabilities" may seem backward at first. How can a bank account be a liability? The issue is that banks look at assets and liabilities in the opposite way from individuals. As a bank customer, you consider your bank deposit as an asset, while if you borrow money from a bank, you view it as a liability. But from the bank's point of view, it owes the bank deposit to you, which makes the deposit a liability, and the bank plans to receive loan payments from you, which makes the loan an asset to the bank. So when drawing up a list of bank assets and liabilities, think as if you are managing a bank!

One key factor that affects what financial institutions are willing to pay for a loan, when they buy it in the secondary loan market, is the perceived riskiness of the loan: that is, given the characteristics of the borrower like income level and whether the local economy is performing strongly, what proportion of loans of this type will be repaid? The greater the risk that a loan will not be repaid, the less that any financial institution will pay to acquire the loan. Another key factor is to compare the interest rate charged on the original loan with the current interest rate in the economy. If the original loan made at some point in the past requires the borrower to pay a low interest rate, but current interest rates are relatively high, then a financial institution will pay less to acquire the loan. In contrast, if the original loan requires the borrower to pay a high interest rate, while current interest rates are relatively low, then a financial institution will pay more to acquire the loan. For the Safe and Secure Bank in this example, the total value of its loans if they were sold to other financial institutions in the secondary market is $5 million.

bond:
A financial contract through which a borrower like a corporation, a city or state, or the federal government agrees to repay the amount that was borrowed and also a rate of interest over a period of time in the future.

reserves:
Funds that a bank keeps on hand and that are not loaned out or invested in bonds.

net worth:
Total assets minus total liabilities.

The second category of bank asset is **bonds**, which are a contract that works this way: when someone buys a bond, the party that issued the bond receives money in the present and promises to repay with interest in the future. Bonds are a common mechanism for borrowing, used not only by the federal government but also by state governments, private companies, and nonprofit organizations. A bank takes some of the money it has received in deposits and uses the money to buy bonds—typically bonds issued by the government. Government bonds are low-risk because the government is virtually certain to pay off the bond, albeit at a low rate of interest. These bonds are an asset for banks in the same way that loans are an asset; that is, the bank will receive a stream of payments in the future. The Safe and Secure Banks holds bonds with a total value of $4 million.

The final entry under assets is **reserves**, which is money that the bank keeps on hand, and that is not loaned out or invested in bonds—and thus does not lead to interest payments. The Safe and Secure Bank is holding $2 million in reserves. Government regulators typically set minimum reserve levels that banks must hold. The next chapter will explain how the level of these required reserves are one policy tool that governments have to influence bank behavior.

The **net worth** of a bank is defined as its total assets minus its total liabilities. For the Safe and Secure Bank shown in Exhibit 29-4, net worth

Securitized Subprime Loans and the Financial Crisis of 2007–2009

Many banks make mortgage loans so that people can buy a home, but then don't keep the loans on their books as an asset. Instead, the bank sells the loan. These loans are commonly "securitized," which means that they are bundled together into a financial security, which is sold to investors. Investors in these mortgage-backed securities receive a rate of return based on level of payments that people make on all the mortgages that stand behind the security.

Securitization offers certain advantages. If a bank makes most of its loans in a local area, then the bank may be financially vulnerable if the local economy declines, so that many people are unable to make their payments. But if a bank sells its local loans, and then buys a mortgage-backed security based on home loans in many parts of the country, it can avoid being exposed to local financial risks. (In the simple example in the text, banks just own "bonds." In reality, banks can own a number of financial instruments, as long as these financial investments are safe enough to satisfy the government bank regulators.) From the standpoint of a local home-buyer, securitization offers the benefit that a local bank doesn't need to have lots of extra funds to make a loan, because the bank is only planning to hold that loan for a short time, before selling the loan so that it can be pooled into a financial security.

But securitization also offers one potentially large disadvantage. If a bank is going to hold a mortgage loan as an asset, the bank has an incentive to scrutinize the borrower carefully to ensure that the loan is likely to be repaid. However, a bank that is going to sell the loan may be less careful in making the loan in the first place. The bank will be more willing to make what are called "subprime loans," which are loans which have characteristics like low or zero down-payment, little scrutiny of whether the borrower has a reliable income, and sometimes low payments for the next year or two that will be followed by much higher payments after that. Some subprime loans made in the mid-2000s were later dubbed NINJA loans: that is, loans made even though the borrower had demonstrated No Income, No Job, or Assets.

These subprime loans were typically sold and turned into financial securities—but with a twist. The idea was that if losses occurred on these mortgage-backed securities, certain investors would agree to take the first, say, 5% of such losses. Other investors would agree to take, say, the next 5% of losses. By this approach, still other investors would not need to take any losses unless these mortgage-backed financial securities lost 25% or 30% or more of their total value. These complex securities, along with other economic factors, encourages a large expansion of subprime loans in the mid-2000s.

The economic stage was now set for a banking crisis. Banks thought they were buying only ultra-safe securities, because even though the securities were ultimately backed by risky subprime mortgages, the banks only invested in the part of those securities where they were protected from small or moderate levels of losses. But as housing prices fell after 2007, and the deepening recession made it harder for many people to make their mortgage payments, many banks found that their mortgage-backed financial assets could end up being worth much less than they had expected—and so the banks were staring bankruptcy in the face.

is equal to $1 million; that is, $11 million in assets minus $10 million in liabilities. For a financially healthy bank, the net worth will be positive. If a bank has negative net worth, and depositors tried to withdraw their money, the bank would not be able to give all depositors their money.

HOW BANKS GO BANKRUPT

A bank that is bankrupt will have a negative net worth; that is, its assets will be worth less than its liabilities. How can this happen? The balance sheet helps to explain. A well-run bank will assume that a small percentage of borrowers do not repay their loans on time, or at all, and factor these missing payments into its planning. Remember, the calculations of the expenses of banks every year includes a factor for loans that are not repaid, and the value of a bank's loans on its balance sheet assumes a certain level of riskiness because some loans will not be repaid. But even if a bank expects a certain number of loan defaults, it will suffer if the number of loan defaults is much greater than expected, as can happen during a recession. For example, if the Safe and Secure Bank in Exhibit 29-4 experienced a wave of unexpected defaults, so that its loans declined in value from $5 million to $3 million, then the assets of the Safe and Secure Bank would decline so that the bank had negative net worth.

The risk of an unexpectedly high level of loan defaults can be especially difficult for banks because of a bank's liabilities, namely the deposits of its customers, can be withdrawn quickly, but many of the bank's assets like loans and bonds will only be repaid over years or even decades. This **asset-liability time mismatch**—a bank's liabilities can be withdrawn in the short term while its assets are repaid in the long term—can cause severe problems for a bank. For example, imagine a bank that has loaned a substantial amount of money at a certain interest rate, but then sees interest rates rise substantially. The bank can find itself in a precarious situation. If it doesn't raise the interest rate it pays to depositors, then deposits will flow to other institutions that offer the higher interest rates that are now prevailing. However, if the bank raises the interest rates that it pays to depositors, it may end up in a situation where it is paying a higher interest rate to depositors than it is collecting from those past loans that were made at lower interest rates. Clearly, the bank can't survive in the long term if it is paying out more in interest to depositors than it is receiving from borrowers.

asset-liability time mismatch:
A bank's liabilities can be withdrawn in the short term while its assets are repaid in the long term.

How can banks protect themselves against an unexpectedly high rate of loan defaults and against the risk of an asset-liability time mismatch? One strategy is for a bank to **diversify** its loans, which means lending to a variety of customers. For example, suppose a bank specialized in lending to a niche market—say, making a high proportion of its loans to construction companies that build offices in one downtown area. If that one area suffers an unexpected economic downturn, the bank will suffer large losses. However, if a bank loans both to consumers who are buying homes and cars and also to a wide range of firms in many industries and geographic areas, the bank is less exposed to risk. When a bank diversifies its loans, those categories of borrowers who have an unexpectedly large number of defaults will tend to be balanced out, according to random chance, by other borrowers who have an unexpectedly low number of defaults. Thus, diversification of loans can help banks to keep a positive net worth. However, if a widespread recession occurs that touches many industries and geographic areas, diversification won't help.

diversify:
Making loans or investments with a variety of firms, to reduce the risk of being adversely affected by events at one or a few firms.

Along with diversifying their loans, banks have several other strategies to reduce the risk of an unexpectedly large number of loan defaults. For example, banks can sell some of the loans they make in the secondary loan market, as described earlier, and instead hold a greater share of

Exhibit 29-5 System Bank's Balance Sheet, 100% Reserves

A bank with 100% reserves would hold all of its deposits as reserves, and not make any loans.

Assets		Liabilities	
Reserves	$10 million	Deposits	$10 million

Exhibit 29-6 System Bank's Balance Sheet: 10% Reserves, One Round of Loans I

magine that System Bank starts with the situation in Exhibit 29-5, but then decides to hold only 10% of its original $10 million in deposits as reserves and to loan out the remaining $9 million. However, since System Bank is the only bank in this economy, the $9 million that is loaned out also ends up being deposited in the bank by the recipients of the loan. Thus, bank deposits rise from the original $10 million to $19 million. With deposits of $19 million and loans of $9 million, the remaining reserves are still $10 million.

Assets		Liabilities	
Loans	$9 million	Deposits	$19 million
Reserves	$10 million		

assets in the form of government bonds or reserves. Nevertheless, in a lengthy recession, most banks will see their net worth decline because a higher share of loans will not be repaid in tough economic times.

HOW BANKS CREATE MONEY

Banks and money are intertwined. It's not just that most money is in the form of bank accounts. In addition, the banking system can literally create money through the process of making loans. This section describes how banks create money.

THE STORY OF SYSTEM BANK

Let's start with a hypothetical example. The people in an economy have $10 million in money, and they all deposit all of their money in a single bank, called System Bank. System Bank starts off with a simple business plan: It keeps the depositor's money safe by holding all money in the form of reserves. The T-account balance sheet for System Bank with 100% reserves is shown in Exhibit 29-5. Obviously, System Bank can't afford to pay interest to depositors, because it isn't earning any interest by making loans. In this form, System Bank is basically just a big piggy bank for keeping money safe.

However, the owners of System Bank notice that from month to month, the inflows of deposits from some people are pretty much counterbalanced by the withdrawals of others. Thus, in some months the deposits and reserves of System Bank grow a little higher than $10 million, and sometimes they fall a little below $10 million, but there is always at least $9.5 million in the bank. So the owners of System Bank come up with a new business plan. They will hold reserves of only 10%, rather than 100%, and they will loan out the remaining $9 million. By loaning out the $9 million and charging interest, they reason, they will be able to make interest payments to depositors. Instead of becoming just a storage place for deposits, System Bank can become a financial intermediary between savers and borrowers.

This change in business plan alters System Bank's balance sheet, as shown in Exhibit 29-6. In this economy, remember, people either deposit all of their money in System Bank, or they buy something from a firm that deposits the money in the firm's account at System Bank. So the total deposits in this economy—that is, the liabilities for System Bank—now total $19 million; that is, the original $10 million in deposits plus the additional $9 million in deposits resulting from the loans. The assets of System Bank also total $19 million. Although the bank loaned out $9 million, thus reducing its original reserves from $10 million to $1 million, the bank also received $9 million in additional deposits to put back into reserves, raising its reserves back to the original $10 million. In addition, System Bank now has $9 million in loan assets.

Before discussing further the situation of System Bank, pause for a moment and notice a remarkable fact: when System Bank decided to stop holding all money in reserves and instead to hold only a portion in reserves and loan out the rest, the quantity of money in the economy expanded. By making loans, System Bank created money.

Of course, the assumption that an economy has only one bank is a gross oversimplification, but the banking system as a whole will work to create money, just like in the example of System Bank. When banks start making loans, and people and firms start redepositing the loans in other bank accounts, money is created in the economy. System Bank uses the metaphor of a single bank for the entire economy to describe the process of money creation for the banking system as a whole.

THE MONEY MULTIPLIER

The owners of System Bank now notice another intriguing fact. They had originally decided that holding reserves equal to 10% of deposits was a sufficient margin for safety, to assure that System Bank would have enough cash on hand for those who are withdrawing money. But after making one round of loans, System Bank has $19 million in deposits. If the bank wishes to hold 10% of that amount in reserves, it need hold only $1.9 million in reserves. But if System Bank has $10 million in reserves, and wishes to hold only $1.9 million in reserves, then the bank can make a second round of loans, this time of $8.1 million.

Again, those people who receive the loans either deposit the money in System Bank themselves, or spend the money with a business that deposits the money in System Bank. The new balance sheet of System

Exhibit 29-7 System Bank's Balance Sheet: 10% Reserves, Second Round of Loans Imagine that System Bank starts off with the situation in Exhibit 29-6, but still wishes to hold only 10% of its deposits as reserves. Thus, starting with $19 million in deposits, it wishes to hold $1.9 million in reserves. Since the bank currently has $10 million in reserves, it can loan out $8.1 million. Total loans increase from $9 million to $17.1 million. However, since System Bank is the only bank in this economy, the $8.1 million that is loaned out also ends up being deposited in the bank by the recipients of the loan. Thus, bank deposits rise from $19 million to $27.1 million. With deposits of $27.1 million and loans of $17.1 million, the remaining reserves are still at $10 million.

Assets		Liabilities	
Loans	$17.1 million	Deposits	$27.1 million
Reserves	$10 million		

Bank appears in Exhibit 29-7. The liabilities of System Bank—that is, its deposits—now total $27.1 million, which is the previous $19 million in deposits plus $8.1 million. The total loans of the bank are now $17.1 million; that is, the $9 million in loans from the first round plus $8.1 million in loans from the second round. Finally, the reserves of the bank remain at $10 million. System Bank loaned out $8.1 million of its reserves, but it also received deposits of $8.1 million, which it is holding in its reserves.

But now System Bank is holding $27.1 million in deposits, and for a 10% margin of safety, it wishes to hold only $2.71 million in reserves. Since the bank is holding $10 million in reserves, it can now make a third round of loans, this time of $10 million – $2.71 million = $7.29 million. A pattern is forming here. System Bank is making cycle after cycle of loans, but each cycle is less than the previous one.

Exactly how much money will exist in this economy as System Bank (or the banking system) makes all of these successive rounds of loans? The original quantity of money in this economy was $10 million. In the first round of lending, System Bank kept 10% of that $10 million in reserves and loaned out the remaining $9 million, which then came back to the bank in the form of deposits. In the second round of lending, System Bank kept 10% of that additional $9 million in reserve, and loaned out the remaining $8.1 million. In a third round, System Bank would keep 10% of that $8.1 million in reserve, and loan out the remaining $7.29 million. These rounds of lending will continue through a fourth, fifth, sixth, and indeed an infinite number of rounds. Each round of lending will create additional money, but the marginal additions become smaller and smaller.

reserve ratio: The proportion of deposits that the bank holds in the form of reserves.

Fortunately, a formula exists for calculating the total of these many rounds of lending in a banking system. If the **reserve ratio** is the proportion of deposits that the bank wished to hold in reserves, then the formula is:

$$\text{Total quantity of money} = \text{Original quantity of reserves} \times \frac{1}{\text{Reserve ratio}}$$

$$= \$10 \text{ million} \times \frac{1}{0.1}$$

$$= \$10 \text{ million} \times 10 = \$100 \text{ million}$$

money multiplier: Total money in the economy divided by the original quantity of money, or change in the total money in the economy divided by a change in the original quantity of money.

Thus, in this example, the total quantity of money generated in this economy after all rounds of lending are completed will be $100 million. The **money multiplier** is equal to the total money in the economy divided by the original quantity of money. The formula to calculate the money multiplier is 1/reserve ratio. In this example, the reserve ratio is 10% or 0.1, and the money multiplier is 10. The money multiplier also shows how much the total supply of money in the economy would be altered if the original quantity of reserves was increased or decreased by $1.

CAUTIONS ABOUT THE MONEY MULTIPLIER

The money multiplier will depend on the proportion of reserves that banks choose to hold. System Bank chose to hold reserves equal to 10% of deposits, leading to a money multiplier of 10. But if System Bank had chosen to hold reserves of 20% of deposits, then the money multiplier would fall to 5. Banks may decide to vary how much they hold in reserves for two reasons: macroeconomic conditions and government rules. When an economy is in recession, banks are likely to hold a higher proportion of reserves because they fear that loans are less likely to be repaid when the economy is slow. The government may also raise or lower the required reserves held by banks as a policy move to affect the quantity of money in an economy, as the next chapter will discuss.

The process of how banks create money shows how the quantity of money in an economy is closely linked to the quantity of lending or credit in the economy. Indeed, all of the money in the economy, except for the original reserves, is a result of bank loans that are redeposited and loaned out, again and again. T

he additional creation of money in this economy isn't making anyone rich. Sure, the total quantity of bank deposits gets larger as the money multiplier operates, but so does the total quantity of loans. If you borrow $5,000 and put the money in your bank account, you haven't made yourself any richer, because the money in your bank account is exactly equal to the money you owe. The money multiplier reflects an increase in lending and borrowing in the economy, but lending and borrowing by themselves don't mean that real goods and services have been produced.

Finally, the money multiplier depends on people redepositing the money that they receive in the banking system. If people instead store their cash in safe-deposit boxes or in shoeboxes hidden in their closets, then banks cannot recirculate the money in the form of loans. Indeed, governments have an incentive to assure that bank deposits are safe because if people worry that they may lose their bank deposits, they may start holding more money in cash, instead of depositing it in banks, and the quantity of loans in an economy will decline. In low-income countries, economists sometimes refer to "mattress savings," by which they mean money that people are hiding in their homes, because they don't trust banks. When mattress savings in an economy are substantial, then banks cannot lend out those funds and the money multiplier cannot operate as effectively, the overall quantity of money and loans in such an economy will therefore be reduced.

Conclusion

Money and banks are marvelous social inventions that help a modern economy to function. Compared with the alternative of barter, money makes market exchanges vastly easier in goods, labor, and financial markets. Banking makes money still more effective in facilitating exchanges in goods and labor markets. Moreover, the process of banks making loans in financial capital markets is intimately tied to the creation of money.

But the extraordinary economic gains that are possible through money and banking also suggest some possible corresponding dangers. If banks aren't working well, it sets off a decline in convenience and safety of transactions throughout the economy. If the banks are under financial stress, because of a widespread decline in the value of their assets, loans may become far less available, which can deal a crushing blow to sectors of the economy that depend on borrowed money like business investment, home construction, and car manufacturing. The recession of 2007–2009 illustrated this pattern. Given the macroeconomic dangers of a malfunctioning banking system, the next chapter will discuss government policies for controlling the money supply and for keeping the banking system safe.

Key Concepts and Summary

1. **Money** is what people in a society regularly use when purchasing or selling goods and services.
2. If money were not available, people would need to barter with each other, meaning that each person would need to identify others with whom they have a **double coincidence of wants**—that is, each party has a specific good or service that the other desires.
3. Money serves three functions: **a medium of exchange, a unit of account and as a store of value**.

4. Money is measured with several definitions: **M1** includes currency, traveler's checks, and money in checking accounts (**demand deposits**). **M2** includes all of M1, plus **savings deposits**, small time deposits like **certificates of deposit**, and **money market funds**.
5. Banks facilitate the use of money for transactions in the economy, since people and firms can use bank accounts when selling or buying goods and services, when paying a worker or being paid, and when saving money or receiving a loan. In the financial capital market, banks are **financial intermediaries**; that is, they operate between savers who supply financial capital and borrowers who demand loans.
6. A **balance sheet** (sometimes called a **T-account**) is an accounting tool which lists assets in one column and **liabilities** in another column. The liabilities of a bank are its deposits. The assets of a bank include its loans, its ownership of **bonds**, and its **reserves** (which are not loaned out). The net worth of a bank is calculated by subtracting the bank's liabilities from its assets.
7. Banks run a risk of negative net worth if the value of their assets declines. The value of assets can decline because of an unexpectedly high number of defaults on loans, or if interest rates rise and the bank suffers an **asset-liability time mismatch** in which the bank is receiving a low rate of interest on its long-term loans but must pay the currently higher market rate of interest to attract depositors. Banks can protect themselves against these risks by choosing to diversify their loans or to hold a greater proportion of their assets in bonds and reserves.
8. If banks hold only a fraction of their deposits as reserves, then the process of banks lending money, those loans being redeposited in banks, and the banks making additional loans will create money in the economy.
9. The **money multiplier** is defined as the quantity of money that the banking system can generate from each $1 of bank reserves. The formula for calculating the multiplier is 1/reserve ratio, where the reserve ratio is the fraction of deposits that the bank wishes to hold as reserves.
10. The quantity of money in an economy and the quantity of credit for loans are inextricably intertwined. Much of the money in an economy is created by the network of banks making loans, people making deposits, and banks making more loans.

Review Questions

1. What are the three functions served by money?
2. How does the existence of money simplify the process of buying and selling?
3. What is the double-coincidence of wants?
4. Define M1 and M2.
5. Why is a bank called a financial intermediary?
6. How do banks help money to work better as a medium of exchange?

7. What does a balance sheet show?
8. What are the assets of a bank? What are its liabilities?
9. How do you calculate the net worth of a bank?
10. How can a bank end up with negative net worth?
11. What is the asset-liability time mismatch that all banks face?
12. What is the risk if a bank does not diversify its loans?
13. How do banks create money?
14. What is the formula for the money multiplier?

IN-CLASS PROJECT

Functions of Money

By David Moglen

Directions: Once you are in your groups, half the class will be assigned questions A and B below, and half will answer C and D.

The Functions of Money are:

1. Medium of exchange
2. Standard of value
3. Store of value
4. Means of deferred payment

Notes on these:

1. Means money can be used to buy consumer goods, services, *financial instruments*, and capital goods
2. Means money has one known value for purposes of exchanged that is known to actors in the economy
3. Refers to how well the currency retains its value over time
4. Refers to lending/borrowing/banking system

Think about how the dollar fulfills each function in our economy. Describe the effects each of the following (A–D) would have on money's ability to fulfill *each* function. If it appears that the function is unaffected by the shock (below), include *people's reliance on money for that use* as part of the concept of that function.

It may be useful to refer to the equation: (Real Interest)= (Nominal Interest)-(Inflation)

INTEREST RATE:

A. How is that function of money (first answer for #1, then for #2) affected when the interest rate fluctuates a lot—e.g. the population has mortgage loans with variable rates (they will have to pay much more per month as time goes on), student loans, credit card debt, and savings accounts all with highly variable interest rates?

B. How is that function of money (3 and 4) affected differently when the interest rate is persistently high?

INFLATION:

C. How is that function of money (first answer for #1, then for #2) affected when the inflation rate is persistently high?

D. Difference in impact on that function of money (3 and 4) when a high inflation rate is
   i. expected, anticipated (as opposed to …)
   ii. unexpected, unanticipated

IN-CLASS PROJECT

The Dollar Market

By David Moglen

Directions: At instructor's specification, either answer all questions or Group 1 can do Part A, question 1 and Part B Question 1. Similarly, Group 4 would answer question 4 in Parts A and B.

Part A:

Questions where appreciation or depreciation of the currency is the endogenous effect—the result:

All of these three questions **will be answered by your graph** showing the shift in the market for the U.S. Dollar. This means you do not need a statement in response to these questions, just keep in mind that your graph is demonstrating the following: What will shift (Demand or Supply), will Demand or Supply increase or decrease in the Market for the U.S. Dollar and is the result appreciation or depreciation of the dollar?

For all of these, draw the fully-labeled graph showing the **one** shift in that question. Make sure the graph you are drawing is the Dollar Market, where the vertical axis measures **E/1\$.** E stands for either Euro or Exchange, meaning a basket of major currencies other than the U.S. Dollar.

1. U.S. households buy fewer textiles and clothing from Latin America.
2. An American-made car is a big hit abroad resulting in skyrocketing export sales.
3. Investors all over the world increased their holdings of U.S. T-bills (i.e. loan money to the U.S. government) to reduce their investment risk in response to the recession/financial crisis.
4. In June 2009, Russia and China recently agreed to "use the (Russian) ruble and (Chinese) Yuan in bilateral trade to lessen dependence on the U.S. dollar."

http://www.bloomberg.com/apps/news?pid=20601087&sid=aSTmuCr.RD88.

Part B:

Questions where appreciation or depreciation of the currency is the exogenous shock:
(No graph is needed here. Just write a few words in response, as to whether the specified item is being bought more or less)

1. How will depreciation of the dollar affect purchases (quantity) of U.S. financial instruments e.g. stocks bonds and mutual funds? Investors view the currency change as an ongoing trend into the foreseeable future.
2. How will depreciation of the dollar affect purchases (quantity) of foreign financial instruments e.g. stocks bonds and mutual funds? Investors view the currency change as an ongoing trend into the foreseeable future.
3. How will appreciation of the dollar affect (quantity of) U.S. imports?
4. How will appreciation of the dollar affect (quantity of) U.S. exports?

CHAPTER 12
Monetary Policy

12 Monetary Policy

By Timothy Taylor

Money, loans, and banks are all tied together. Money is held in bank accounts. A banking system creates money when loans made by one bank are deposited and thus counted as money in other banks. When interlocking system of money, loans, and banks works well, economic transactions are made smoothly in goods and labor markets and savers are connected with borrowers. But if the money and banking system doesn't operate smoothly, the economy can tumble into recession.

The government of every country has public policies that attempt to assure that the system of money, loans, and banking functions well. But these policies don't always work perfectly, and the result can either be recession or a prolonged inflation. This chapter begins by discussing the policies that can affect the quantity of money in the economy. These monetary policy decisions are made by an institution called a central bank. In the United States, the central bank is called the Federal Reserve. In making decisions about the money supply, a central bank decides to raise or lower interest rates, and in this way, to affect some goals of macroeconomic policy like low unemployment and inflation. Another set of policies related to the money and banking system involves reinforcing the stability of a nation's banking system with a combination of protections for bank depositors and regular government inspections of the balance sheets of banks. In the U.S. economy, these policies to assure stability of the banking system involve both the Federal Reserve and several other regulatory institutions within the U.S. Department of the Treasury.

Monetary Policy and the Central Bank

Monetary policy involves altering the quantity of money (and the quantity of loans) in the economy. The **central bank** is the institution designed to control the quantity of money in the economy and also to oversee the safety and stability of the banking system. This section introduces the U.S. Federal Reserve and some other examples of central banks, while the next section discusses how central banks conduct monetary policy.

monetary policy:
Policy that involves altering the quantity of money and thus affecting the level of interest rates and the extent of borrowing.

central bank:
An institution to conduct monetary policy and regulate the banking system.

THE FEDERAL RESERVE

The most important task of a central bank is to determine the quantity of money in the economy. Article I, Section 8 of the U.S. Constitution gives Congress the power "to coin money" and "to regulate the value thereof." As part of the 1913 legislation that created the Federal Reserve, Congress delegated these powers to the Fed.

The Federal Reserve is a peculiar organization, because it mixes government appointees with representation from private-sector banks. The Federal Reserve at the national level is run by a Board of Governors, which consists of seven members who the President of the United States appoints and the U.S. Senate must confirm. Board of Governor appointments are for 14-year terms and they are arranged so that one term expires January 31 of every even-numbered year. A person may serve only one full term on the Board of Governors. However, the 14-year terms are so long that board members often leave before their term is completed. If a person is appointed to fill out the remainder of someone else's term, that person can still be appointed to a full 14-year term of their own. One member of the Board of Governors is designated as the Chairman. For example, from 1987 until the early 2006, the Fed Chairman was Alan Greenspan. Greenspan was appointed in 1987 to fill out someone else's term, but then he was appointed to his own 14-year term in 1992. Since 2006, the Federal Reserve chairman has been Ben Bernanke.

The Federal Reserve System is set up in 12 districts, which are headquartered in the cities shown in Exhibit 30-1. The commercial banks in each district elect a Board of Directors for each regional Fed bank, and that board chooses a president for each regional Federal Reserve district. In turn, on certain key policy-making committees, as explained below, members of the politically appointed Board of Governors are combined with presidents of the regional Fed banks.

OTHER TASKS AND FUNDING OF CENTRAL BANKS

Along with its glamorous task of managing the money supply, the Federal Reserve has a number of everyday responsibilities. For example, a central bank must ensure that enough currency and coins are circulating through the financial system to meet public demands. Thus, each year the Federal Reserve increases the amount of currency available in banks around the Christmas shopping season and reduces it again in January.

The Federal Reserve is also responsible for assuring that banks are in compliance with a wide variety of consumer protection laws. For example, banks are forbidden from discriminating on the basis of age, race, sex, or marital status. Banks are also required to disclose publicly information about the loans they make for buying houses and how those loans are distributed geographically, as well as by sex and race of the loan applicants. Banks are required to disclose certain information to

Exhibit 30-1 The Twelve Federal Reserve Districts

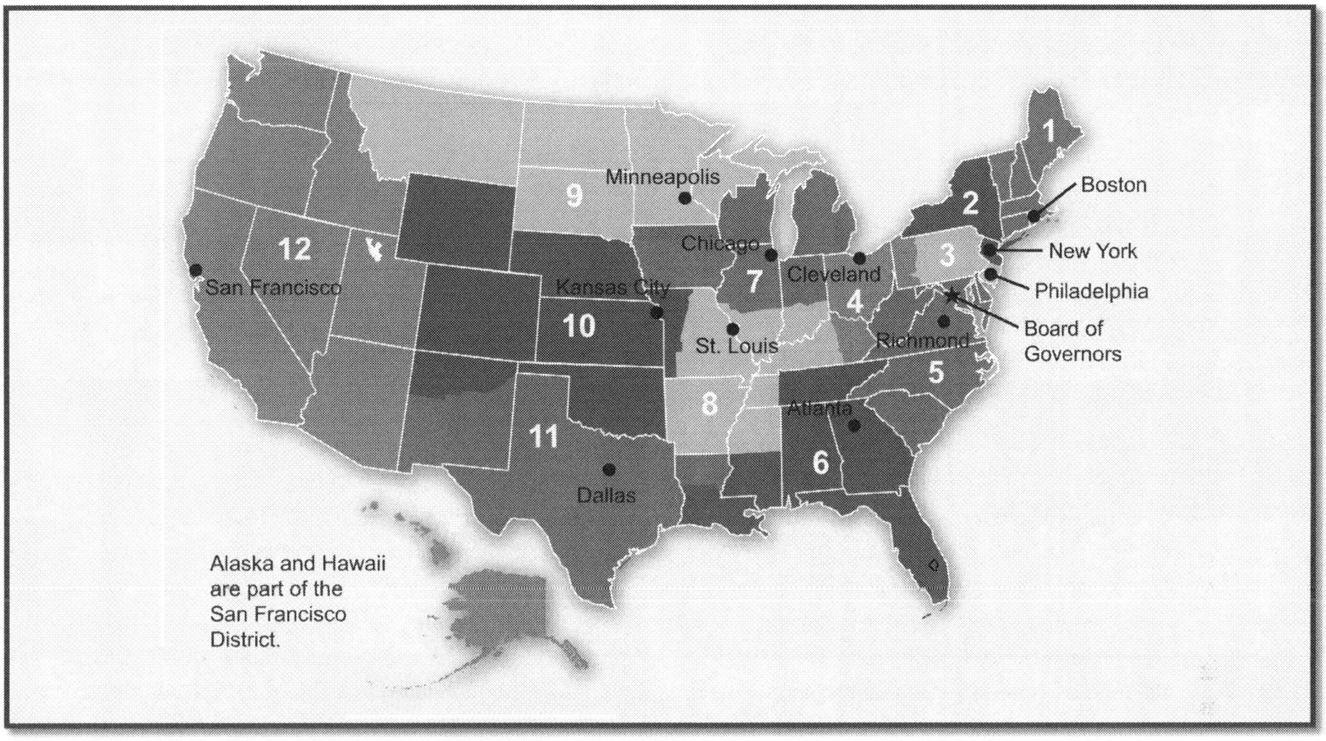

customers about interest rates and fees, but also required to protect the privacy of bank customers unless government authorities follow specific procedures. Most banks are examined on these matters about every 18 months, although those with a poor record of past performance are examined more frequently.

The Fed is also responsible for check processing. When you write a check, say, to buy a pizza, the pizza restaurant deposits the check in its bank. Then, the physical check (or an image of that actual check) needs to be returned to your bank. The Fed contracts out a substantial amount of this work of collecting, sorting, and transmitting checks to private firms. In addition, money needs to be transferred from your bank account to the account of the pizza restaurant. The Fed acts as a bank for the banks and transfers funds as needed between banks to reflect the flows of checks.

The Federal Reserve is financially self-supporting. The Fed holds reserves from member banks, and uses that money to purchase government bonds, which then pay interest to the Fed. The Fed also makes some money from charging banks about 2 cents per check for helping to send checks back from the bank that receives the check to the bank on which the check was written. If the Fed has any extra money left over after paying its expenses, it goes to the U.S. Treasury. Typically, about 90% of the total money received by the Federal Reserve—most of it in the form of interest payments on U.S. government bonds—is returned to the U.S. government. Thus, even though the Federal Reserve

Money at the Millennium

As January 1, 2000, approached, fears abounded of a great computer crash. One fear was that certain computer software might not be able to handle the change from 1999 to 2000. Another concern was that a hidden computer virus that had already spread secretly to many computers might be triggered by the change in date. No one knew quite how seriously to take the threat; after all, the financial and accounting systems of the world hadn't been running on computers in 1900. But U.S. firms spent roughly $150 billion to protect themselves against Y2K, as the change to the year 2000 was called.

With regard to the nation's banking system, the fear was that people might make especially large cash withdrawals in the days leading up to January 1. If credit card networks and check-clearing systems failed to function after Y2K, then people might flock to banks for even larger cash withdrawals. At worst, a financial panic could set in. Thus, by October 1, 1999, the Fed announced that it had stockpiled $200 billion in cash in Federal Reserve banks and commercial banks all around the country.

After New Year's Day in the year 2000, a number of minor computer mishaps occurred. For example, the U.S. government lost touch with a set of spy satellites for four days. A number of airports experienced short-term glitches in the computers that run their air traffic control systems. Seven nuclear power plants experienced problems with their computer systems. About 4,000 small businesses found that their systems for processing credit cards didn't work.

In the banking system, people's demand for currency did surge right around January 1, 2000, but the increase was only about $20 billion—far less than the Fed had on hand. By the end of January, that extra $20 billion in cash had been deposited back into the banking system. By having cash readily on hand, and by letting everyone know that cash would be readily available, the Federal Reserve fulfilled its function of helping to assure the stability in the nation's financial system.

In the end, January 1, 2000, brought only some minor computer hitches. But for the Fed, having extra currency on hand, just in case, was a relatively cheap form of insurance against the risk that something might have gone badly wrong.

is self-supporting, it is only allowed to keep enough money to cover its own funding needs.

Each currency is managed by a different central bank. These central banks share the common task of determining the money supply for their currencies. Thus, a European Central Bank determines the quantity of euros, the Bank of Japan determines the quantity of the Japanese yen, and the Bank of England determines the quantity of the British pound. In some nations, almost all of the bank supervision and regulation happens through the central bank. In other nations, like the United States, bank supervision and regulation are shared with other government agencies.

How a Central Bank Affects the Money Supply

A central bank has three traditional tools to affect the quantity of money in the economy: open market operations, reserve requirements, and the discount rate. In discussing how these three tools work, it's useful to think of the central bank as a "bank for banks"—that is, each private-sector bank has its own account at the central bank. Let's discuss these monetary policy tools in turn. In the recession of 2007–2009, these three traditional tools proved too weak, and so the Federal Reserve turned to an innovative set of monetary policies that are often summarized as "quantitative easing."

OPEN MARKET OPERATIONS

Open market operations involve the central bank buying or selling U.S. Treasury bonds in such a way as to influence the quantity of money and the level of interest rates. To understand how open market operations affect the money supply, consider the balance sheet of Happy Bank shown in Exhibit 30-2. Exhibit 30-2a shows that Happy Bank starts with $460 million in assets, divided among reserves, bonds and loans, and $400 million in liabilities in the form of deposits, with a net worth of $60 million. Now the central bank purchases $20 million in bonds from Happy Bank, so that the bond holdings of Happy Bank fall by $20 million and the bank's reserves rise by $20 million, as shown in Exhibit 30-2b. However, Happy Bank only wants to hold $40 million in reserves (the quantity of reserves that it started with in Exhibit 30-2a), so the bank now decides to loan out the extra $20 million in reserves, and its loans rise by $20 million as shown in Exhibit 30-2c. The open market operation by the central bank causes Happy Bank to make loans instead of holding its assets in the form of government bonds, which expands the money supply. As the new loans are deposited in banks throughout the economy, these banks will in turn loan out some of the deposits they receive, triggering the money multiplier discussed in the previous chapter.

open market operations: The central bank buying or selling bonds to influence the quantity of money and the level of interest rates.

Where did the Federal Reserve get the $20 million that it used to purchase the bonds? A central bank has the power to create money. In practical terms, the Federal Reserve would write a check to Happy Bank, so that Happy Bank can have that money credited to its bank account at the Federal Reserve. To be blunt about it, the Federal Reserve created the money to purchase the bonds out of thin air—or with a few clicks on some computer keys.

Open market operations can also reduce the quantity of money and loans in an economy. Exhibit 30-3a shows the balance sheet of Happy Bank before the central bank sells bonds in the open market. When Happy Bank purchases $30 million in bonds, Happy Bank sends $30 million of its reserves to the central bank, but now holds an additional $30 million in bonds, as shown in Exhibit 30-3b. However, Happy Bank wants to hold $40 million in reserves, as in Exhibit 30-3a, so it will adjust down the quantity of its loans by $30 million, to bring its reserves back to the desired level, as shown in Exhibit 30-3c. In practical terms, a bank can easily reduce its quantity of loans. At any given time, a bank is receiving payments on loans that it made previously and also making new loans. If the bank just slows down or briefly halts making new loans, and instead adds those funds to its reserves, then its overall quantity of loans will decrease. A decrease in the quantity of loans also means fewer deposits in other banks, and other banks reducing their lending as well, as the money multiplier discussed in the previous chapter takes effect.

Exhibit 30-2 Tracing an Open Market Operation through the Happy Bank's Balance Sheets

(a) Original balance sheet of Happy Bank.

(b) The central bank buys 20 in bonds from Happy Bank; Happy Bank receives money, and the central bank gets bonds.

(c) Happy Bank now has more reserves than it wants, so will lend out extra assets. Notice that total assets, total liabilities, and net worth of the bank don't change. All that changes is that because of the open market operation, the bank now holds its assets in a different form.

Assets		Liabilities	
Loans	300	Deposits	400
Reserves	40		
Bonds	120		

Net worth is 60

(a) The original balance sheet

Assets		Liabilities	
Loans	300	Deposits	400
Reserves	40 + 20 = 60		
Bonds	120 – 20 = 100		

Net worth is 60

(b) The central bank buys bonds

Assets		Liabilities	
Loans	300 + 20 = 320	Deposits	400
Reserves	60 – 20 = 40		
Bonds	100		

Net worth is 60

(c) The bank makes additional loans

Clearing It Up: Does Selling or Buying Bonds Increase the Money Supply?

Should a central bank buy bonds or sell bonds to increase the money supply? To avoid confusion, keep track of whether money is flowing in or out of the central bank. When a central bank buys bonds, money is flowing out of the central bank to individual banks in the economy, and thus increasing the money supply. When a central bank sells bonds, then money from individual banks in the economy is flowing into the central bank—reducing the quantity of money in the economy.

Exhibit 30-3 An Open Market Operation to Contract the Money Supply

(a) Balance sheet of Happy Bank at start.

(b) The central bank sells 30 in bonds to Happy Bank. Happy Bank receives the bonds, and the central bank gets money from the reserves of Happy Bank.

(c) Happy Bank now has less reserves than it wants, so it will build up its reserves by making fewer loans, which decreases the money supply. Because of the open market operation, Happy Bank now holds its assets in a different form—that is, more bonds and fewer loans—which decreases the money supply.

Assets		Liabilities	
Loans	300	Deposits	400
Reserves	40		
Bonds	120		

Net worth is 60

(a) The original balance sheet

Assets		Liabilities	
Loans	300	Deposits	400
Reserves	40 – 30 = 10		
Bonds	120 + 30 = 150		

Net worth is 60

(b) The central bank sells bonds to the bank

Assets		Liabilities	
Loans	300 – 30 = 270	Deposits	400
Reserves	10 + 30 = 40		
Bonds	150		

Net worth is 60

(c) The bank makes fewer loans

Within the Federal Reserve, the 12-member Federal Open Market Committee (FOMC) is responsible for making decisions about when to buy U.S. government bonds and increase the quantity of money and loans in the economy, or to sell government bonds and decrease the quantity of money and loans in the economy. The FOMC includes the seven members of the Fed's Board of Governors who are appointed by the president. It also includes five voting members who are drawn from the 12 regional Federal Reserve Banks—although all of the regional bank presidents typically attend the meetings and participate in the discussions of the FOMC. Thus, while the Board of Governors members hold a majority on the FOMC, the representatives of banks from different regions participate in the decision, too. The FOMC typically meets every six weeks. The FOMC tries to act by consensus; however, the chairman of the Fed has traditionally played a very powerful role in defining and shaping that consensus. For the Federal Reserve, and for most central banks, open market operations have over the last few decades been the most commonly used tool of monetary policy. For example, the Federal Reserve announced 78 separate open market operations from 1990 to 2009.

RESERVE REQUIREMENTS

reserve requirement: The proportion of its deposits that a bank is legally required to deposit with the central bank.

A second method of conducting monetary policy is for the central bank to raise or lower the **reserve requirement**, which is the proportion of its deposits that a bank is legally required to deposit with the central bank. If banks are required to hold a greater amount in reserves, they have less money available to lend out. If banks are allowed to hold a smaller amount in reserves, they will have a greater amount of money available to lend out.

At the end of 2009, the Federal Reserve required banks to hold reserves equal to 0% of the first $10.7 million in deposits, then to hold reserves equal to 3% of the deposits up to $55.2 million in checking and savings accounts, and 10% of any amount above $55.2 million. Small changes in the reserve requirements are made almost every year: for example, the $55.2 million dividing line is sometimes bumped up or down by a few million dollars or rulings are issued to clarify definitions of certain financial accounts. But changes in reserve requirements that have a large effect on bank reserves are rare. One exception was during the recession of 1990–91 when the Federal Reserve used changes in reserve requirements in a more dramatic way. In December 1990, the reserves that banks needed to hold on deposits that could not be immediately accessed, like certificates of deposit, were reduced to zero, which decreased the reserves that banks needed to hold by $13.2 billion. In April 1992, the reserve requirements on larger amounts of deposits was cut from 12% to their current level of 10%, which decreased the reserves that banks needed to hold by another $8.9 billion.

THE DISCOUNT RATE

discount rate: The interest rate charged by the central bank when it makes loans to commercial banks.

A third traditional method for conducting monetary policy is to raise or lower the **discount rate**, which is the interest rate charged by the central bank when it makes loans to commercial banks. If a bank finds that it is not holding enough in reserves to meet the reserve requirements, it needs to borrow at least for the short term from the central bank. If the central bank raises the discount rate, then banks will hold a higher level of reserves to reduce the chance of needing to borrow at that higher interest rate. When banks hold these higher reserves, it reduces the money supply in the economy as a whole. If the central bank lowers the discount rate it charges to banks, then banks will be less concerned about the prospect of needing a short-term loan to fill out their reserves. In turn, the bank will be more willing to lend aggressively, which will increase the money supply.

As it turns out, the Federal Reserve has traditionally loaned relatively little money at the discount rate. Before a bank borrows from the Federal Reserve to fill out its needed reserves, the bank is expected to first borrow from other available sources, like other banks. When banks ended up turning to the Federal Reserve for a discount rate loan, it was often taken as a sign that the bank was in financial trouble, and no other bank was willing to lend to it. Given that most banks borrowed little at the discount rate, changing the discount rate up or down has little impact on their behavior. Consequently, altering the discount rate is a relatively weak tool of monetary policy.

QUANTITATIVE EASING

The most powerful and commonly used of the three traditional tools of monetary policy—open market operations—works by expanding or contracting the money supply in a way that influences the interest rate. But in late 2008, as the U.S. economy struggled with recession, the Federal Reserve had already reduced the interest rate to near-zero. With the recession still ongoing, the Fed decided to take innovative and nontraditional steps to expand the quantity of money and credit. One method of quantitative easing was that the Federal Reserve began to make discount rate loans broadly available to many financial firms like those who buy and sell financial securities or even insurance companies, not just to banks. In addition, the Fed figured out a way so that firms which wanted to receive these loans could bid to receive the loans anonymously, so that firms didn't need to worry about whether receiving a loan from the Fed was a signal of being weak financially. Another method was that in the recessionary period from 2007–2009, the Federal Reserve bought some financial securities directly, including several hundred billion dollars of bonds issued by the U.S. Treasury and also more than a trillion dollars worth of private sector financial securities that were backed by mortgage loans. In these cases, the Fed expanded the supply of money and credit in the economy simply by creating the money and credit outright.

The quantitative easing policies adopted by the Federal Reserve (and by other central banks around the world) are usually thought of as temporary emergency measures. But if these steps are indeed to be temporary, then the Federal Reserve will need to stop making these additional loans and sell off the financial securities it has accumulated—and the process of quantitative easing may prove more difficult to reverse than it was to enact.

A central bank that desires to increase the quantity of money in the economy can buy bonds in an open market operation, reduce the reserve requirement, lower the discount rate, or engage in quantitative easing. Conversely, a central bank that desires to reduce the quantity of money in the economy can sell bonds in an open market operation, raise the reserve requirement, raise the discount rate, or reverse its past practices of quantitative easing.

Monetary Policy and Economic Outcomes

expansionary monetary policy: A monetary policy that increases the supply of money and the quantity of loans; also called a "loose" monetary policy.

A monetary policy that expands the quantity of money and loans is known as an **expansionary monetary policy** or a "loose" monetary policy. Conversely, a monetary policy which reduces the amount of money and loans in the economy is a **contractionary monetary policy** or a "tight" monetary policy. This section will discuss how expansionary and contractionary monetary policies affect interest rates and aggregate demand, and thus how such policies will affect macroeconomic goals like unemployment and inflation.

contractionary monetary policy: A monetary policy that reduces the supply of money and loans; also called a "tight" monetary policy.

THE EFFECT OF MONETARY POLICY ON INTEREST RATES

Consider the market for loanable bank funds, shown in Exhibit 30-4. The original equilibrium E_0 occurs at an interest rate of 8% and a quantity of funds loaned and borrowed of $10 billion. An expansionary monetary policy will shift the supply of loanable funds to the right from the original supply curve S_0 to S_1, leading to an equilibrium E_1 with a lower interest rate of 6% and a quantity of funds loaned of $14 billion. Conversely, a contractionary monetary policy will shift the supply of loanable funds to the left from the original supply curve S_0 to S_2, leading to an equilibrium E_2 with a higher interest rate of 10% and a quantity of funds loaned of $8 billion.

When describing the monetary policy actions taken by a central bank, it's common to hear that the central bank "raised interest rates" or "lowered interest rates." Such statements are potentially misleading if they are taken to imply that the central bank is a dictator that can force banks to charge a certain interest rate. Instead, the central bank alters the quantity of money in a way which affects the supply curve in the market for loanable funds, and in that way can move the interest rate higher or lower.

Since 1995, when the Federal Reserve carries out open market operations, it has announced in advance what effect it wishes to have on one particular interest rate—the **federal funds rate**, which is the interest rate at which one bank lends funds to another bank overnight.

federal funds rate: The interest rate at which one bank lends funds to another bank overnight.

For example, an overnight loan might occur when a bank needs money to meet its legal reserve requirement, and so it borrows the money from another bank. By selling and buying U.S. government bonds through open market operations, the Federal Reserve can move the federal funds interest rate that banks charge each other higher or lower.

Of course, financial capital markets display a wide range of interest rates, representing borrowers with different risk premiums and loans that are to be repaid over different periods of time. In general, when the federal funds rate drops substantially, other interest rates drop, too, and when the federal funds rate rises, other interest rates rise. But a fall or rise of 1 percentage point in the federal funds rate—which remember is for borrowing overnight!—will typically have an effect of less than 1 percentage point on a 30-year loan to purchase a house or a three-year

Exhibit 30-4 Monetary Policy and Interest Rates

The original equilibrium occurs at E_0. A expansionary monetary policy will shift the supply of loanable funds to the right from the original supply curve S_0 to the new supply curve S_1 and to a new equilibrium of E_1, reducing the interest rate from 8% to 6%. A contractionary monetary policy will shift the supply of loanable funds to the left from the original supply curve S_0 to the new supply S_2, and raise the interest rate from 8% to 10%.

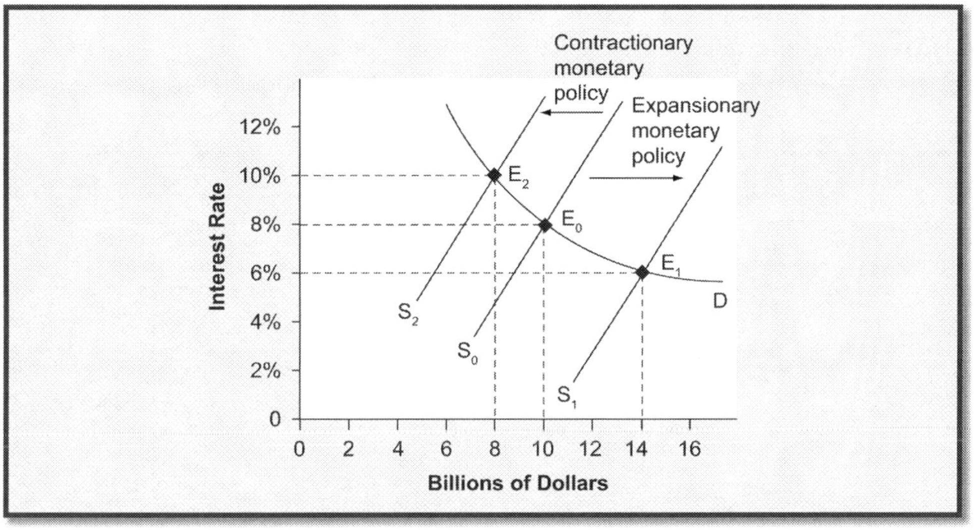

loan to purchase a car. Monetary policy can push the entire spectrum of interest rates higher or lower, but the specific interest rates are set by the forces of supply and demand in those specific markets for lending and borrowing.

THE EFFECT OF MONETARY POLICY ON AGGREGATE DEMAND

Monetary policy affects interest rates and the available quantity of loanable funds, which in turn affects several components of aggregate demand. Tight or contractionary monetary policy that leads to higher interest rates and a reduced quantity of loanable funds will reduce two components of aggregate demand. Business investment will decline because it is less attractive for firms to borrow money, and even firms that have money will notice that with higher interest rates, it is relatively more attractive to put those funds in a financial investment than to make an investment in physical capital. In addition, higher interest rates will discourage consumer borrowing for big-ticket items like houses and cars. Conversely, loose or expansionary monetary policy that leads to lower interest rates and a higher quantity of loanable funds will tend to increase business investment and consumer borrowing for big-ticket items.

If the economy is suffering a recession and high unemployment, with output below potential GDP, loose monetary policy can help the economy return to potential GDP. Exhibit 30-5a illustrates this situation. This example uses a short-run upward-sloping Keynesian aggregate supply curve AS. The original equilibrium during a recession of ER

Exhibit 30-5 Expansionary or Contractionary Monetary Policy

(a) The economy is originally in a recession with the equilibrium output and price level shown at ER. Expansionary monetary policy will reduce interest rates and shift aggregate demand to the right from AD_0 to AD_1, leading to the new equilibrium EP at the potential GDP level of output with a relatively small rise in the price level.

(b) The economy is originally producing above the potential GDP level of output at the equilibrium EI and is experiencing pressures for an inflationary rise in the price level. Contractionary monetary policy will shift aggregate demand to the left from AD_0 to AD_1, thus leading to a new equilibrium EP at the potential GDP level of output.

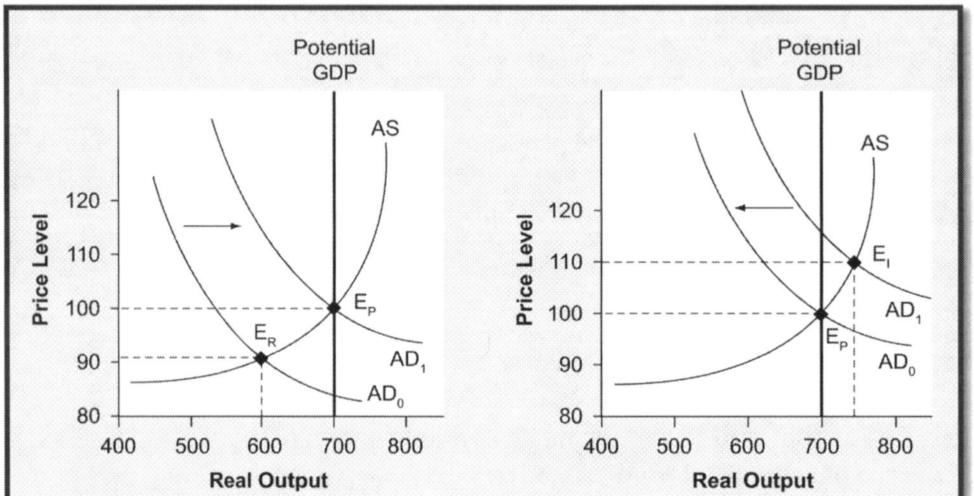

(a) Expansionary monetary policy (b) Contractionary monetary policy

occurs at an output level of 600. An expansionary monetary policy will reduce interest rates and stimulate investment and consumption spending, causing the original aggregate demand curve AD_0 to shift right to AD_1, so that the new equilibrium EP occurs at the potential GDP level of 700.

Conversely, if an economy is producing at a quantity of output above its potential GDP, a tight or contractionary monetary policy can reduce the inflationary pressures for a rising price level. In Exhibit 30-5b, the original equilibrium E_I occurs at an output of 750, which is above potential GDP. A contractionary monetary policy will raise interest rates, discourage borrowing for investment and consumption spending, and cause the original demand curve AD_0 to shift left to AD_1, so that the new equilibrium E_P occurs at the potential GDP level of 700.

countercyclical: Moving in the opposite direction of the business cycle of economic downturns and upswings.

These examples suggest that monetary policy should be **countercyclical**; that is, it should act to counterbalance the business cycles of economic downturns and upswings. Monetary policy should be loosened when a recession has caused unemployment to increase and tightened when inflation threatens. Of course, countercylical policy does pose a danger of overreaction. If loose monetary policy seeking to end a recession goes too far, it may push aggregate demand so far to the right that it triggers inflation. If tight monetary policy seeking to reduce inflation goes too far, it may push aggregate demand so far to the left that a recession begins. Exhibit 30-6 summarizes the chain of effects that connect loose and tight monetary policy to changes in output and the price level.

APPLY YOUR SKILLS

Deposit Multiplier Questions

By David Moglen

Useful Equations:

Use of the word "shock" below is the same as cause—every question has a cause and an effect.

1. Required Reserves + Excess Reserves = Total Reserves

RR + ER = TR

2. The Money Creation Equation

Initial Injection*DM = Change in Money Supply = Change in M1

The Initial Injection shock can come in any one of the following forms in a given question:

- Money is newly deposited into banks
- The Fed buys bonds
- Banks are holding Excess Reserves (ER)

The first number in the above equation would be negative, and would be called an Initial Withdrawal if a question has any one of these as the shock:

- Money is newly withdrawn from the banks
- The Fed sells bonds
- Banks are holding negative Excess Reserves—banks are not meeting their reserve requirement

DM is the Deposit Multiplier, equal to: 1/r. This is the same as the Money Multiplier. r = RRR = Required Reserve Ratio = Required Reserves/Deposits

Real-World Deposit Multiplier, aka Leakage-Adjusted DM = 1/(r+e+c), where r is still Required Reserves/Deposits, e = Excess Reserves/Deposits, and c=cash held by the public/Required Reserves/Deposits.

The effect, the total amount of new money in cash and checking accounts that eventually results (after all rounds of lending are complete) from one of the injections or leakages (bullet points) listed above, is the change in Money Supply as measured by M1.

Directions: Half of the groups answer even-numbered questions and the other half will do the or odds. Be sure your answer shows clearly whether it is negative or positive. **For all questions, assume RRR=10% unless the question says it is a different number.** Any number with decimal places can be rounded to two decimals.

Questions:

1. What is the change in M1 if $50 is newly deposited into a bank?

2. Banks have $5,000 in TR. Total deposits are $100,000. What will be the change in M1 (after all rounds of lending are complete)?

3. What is the change in M1 if $80 is newly withdrawn from a bank?

4. Banks have $20,000 in TR. Total deposits are $100,000. What will be the change in M1 (after all rounds of lending are complete)?

5. The Fed sells $20 billion in bonds. The banks are going to continue holding 15% of deposits in ER, and the public will continue holding 20% of the total amount deposited in cash in their wallet.

What is the eventual impact of the Fed's sale on M1?

6. The Fed buys $60 billion in bonds. The banks are going to continue holding 20% of deposits in ER, and the public will continue holding 5% of the total amount deposited in cash in

their wallet. What is the eventual impact of the Fed's sale on M1?

7. Deposits total: $1 million.

Banks actually have in reserves (TR): $150,000

What is the eventual impact on M1?

8. Deposits total: $1 million.

Banks actually have in reserves (TR): $20,000

What is the eventual impact on M1?

9. Banks hold no excess reserves. Banks start with $100,000 in reserves for the $1 million in Deposits. Now the Fed changes RRR from 10% to 15%. What is the eventual impact on M1?

10. Banks hold no excess reserves. Banks start with $100,000 in reserves for the $1 million in Deposits. Now the Fed changes RRR from 10% to 2%. What is the eventual impact on M1?

CHAPTER 13

Monetarism and Institutional Theories of Money

13 Monetarism and Institutional Theories of Money

By Timothy Taylor

What the Federal Reserve Has Done

For the period from the mid-1970s up through the end of 2007, Federal Reserve monetary policy can largely be summed up by looking at how it targeted the federal funds interest rate using open market operations. But in the Great Recession of 2007–2009, Fed policy began to use creative policies of quantitative easing.

Of course, telling the story of the U.S. economy since 1975 in terms of Federal Reserve actions leaves out many other macroeconomic factors that were influencing unemployment, recession, economic growth, and inflation over this time. But the nine episodes quickly sketched here also demonstrate that when telling the story of a macroeconomy, the central bank must be treated as one of the leading characters. Indeed, the single person with the greatest power to influence the U.S. economy is probably the chairman of the Federal Reserve, who has considerable power over the monetary policies of the Fed, rather than the President of the United States, who can only act through laws that must first be passed by Congress.

Exhibit 30-7 shows how the Federal Reserve has carried out monetary policy by targeting the federal funds interest rate in the last few decades. The graph shows the federal funds interest rate (remember, this interest rate is set through open market operations), the unemployment rate, and the inflation rate since 1975. Different episodes of monetary policy during this period are indicated on the exhibit.

Consider Episode 1 in the late 1970s. The rate of inflation was very high, exceeding 10% in 1979 and 1980, so the Fed used a tight monetary policy to raise interest rates, with the federal funds rate rising from 5.5% in 1977 to 16.4% in 1981. By 1983, inflation was down to 3.2%, but aggregate demand contracted sharply enough that back-to-back recessions occurred in 1980 and in 1981–82, and the unemployment rate rose from 5.8% in 1979 to 9.7% in 1982.

In Episode 2, when the Federal Reserve was persuaded in the early 1980s that inflation was declining, the Fed began slashing interest rates to reduce unemployment. The federal funds interest rate fell from 16.4%

Timothy Taylor, "Monetary Policy and Bank Regulation," *Principles of Macroeconomics*, pp. 573–585.

Exhibit 30-6 The Pathways of Monetary Policy

(a) The story of expansionary monetary policy is that the central bank causes the supply of money and loanable funds in the economy to increase, which causes the interest rate to fall. The lower interest rate stimulates additional borrowing for investment and consumption, causing AD to shift right. The result is both a higher price level and, at least in the short run, higher real GDP.

(b) The story of contractionary monetary policy is that the central bank causes the supply of money and credit in the economy to decrease, which causes the interest rate to rise. The higher interest rate discourages borrowing for investment and consumption, causing AD to shift to the left. The result is a lower price level and, at least in the short run, lower real GDP.

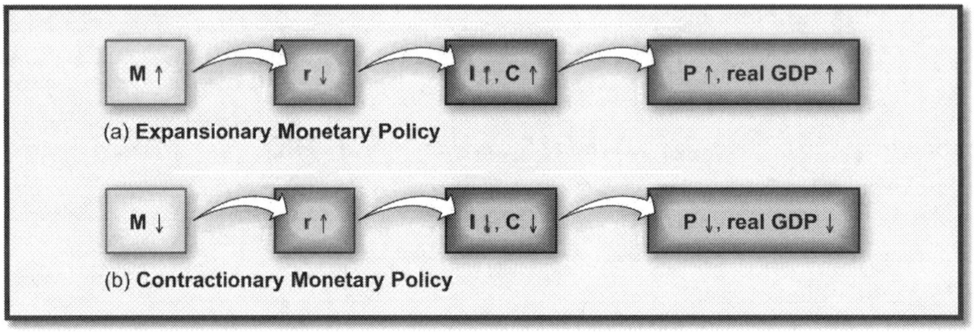

in 1981 to 6.8% in 1986. By 1986 or so, inflation had fallen to about 2% and the unemployment rate had come down to 7%, and was still falling.

However, in Episode 3 in the late 1980s, inflation appeared to be creeping up again, rising from 2% in 1986 up toward 5% by 1989. In response, the Fed used contractionary monetary policy to raise the federal funds rates from 6.6% in 1987 to 9.2% in 1989. The tighter monetary policy stopped inflation, which fell from above 5% in 1990 to under 3% in 1992, but it also helped to cause the recession of 1990–91, and the unemployment rate rose from 5.3% in 1989 to 7.5% by 1992.

In Episode 4 in the early 1990s, when the Fed was confident that inflation was back under control, it then reduced interest rates, with the federal funds interest rate falling from 8.1% in 1990 to 3.5% in 1992. As the economy expanded, the unemployment rated declined from 7.5% in 1992 to less than 5% by 1997.

In Episode 5, the Fed perceived a risk of inflation in 1994 and raised the federal funds rate from 3% in 1993 to 5.8% in 1995. Inflation didn't rise, and the period of economic growth during the 1990s continued. The federal funds rate changed little for several years.

In Episode 6, in 1999 and 2000, the Fed was concerned that inflation seemed to be creeping up from 1.6% in 1998 to 3.4% by 2000, and so it raised the federal funds interest rate from 4.6% in December 1998 to 6.5% in June 2000. By early 2001, inflation was declining again, headed for a rate of just 1.6% in 2002, but a recession occurred in 2001 and the unemployment rate rose from 4.0% in 2000 to 5.8% in 2002.

In Episode 7, the Federal Reserve conducted a loose monetary policy and slashed the federal funds rate from 6.2% in 2000 to just 1.7% in 2002. The recession ended, but just as it had taken some years for

Exhibit 30-7 Monetary Policy, Unemployment, and Inflation

Through the episodes shown here, the Federal Reserve typically reacted to higher inflation with a contractionary monetary policy and a higher interest rate, and reacted to higher unemployment with an expansionary monetary policy and a lower interest rate.

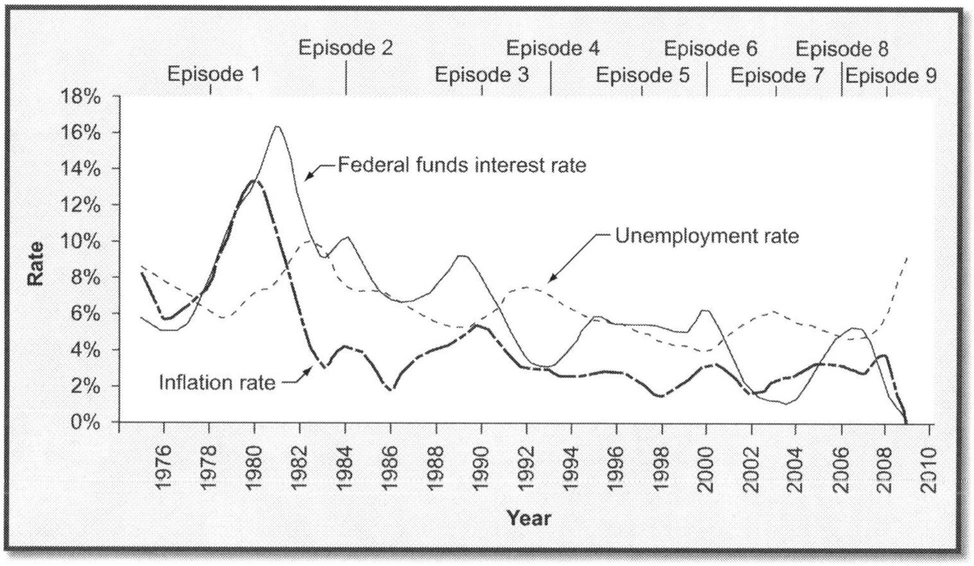

unemployment rates to decline after the recessions of the early 1980s and the early 1990s, unemployment rates were slow to decline in the early 2000s.

In Episode 8, the federal funds interest rate bottomed out at about 1% in late 2003 and early 2004. The unemployment rate had stayed low and declining, but inflation had perked up just a bit, and so the Federal Reserve began to raise the federal funds rate until it reached 5% by 2007.

In Episode 9, as the Great Recession took hold in 2008, the Federal Reserve was quick to slash interest rates, taking them down to 2% in 2008 and to nearly 0% in 2009. But when the Fed had taken interest rates down to near-zero by December 2008, the economy was still deep in recession. Open market operations could not make the interest rate turn negative! Thus, the Federal Reserve turned to the alternative policies of quantitative easing, greatly expanding the direct loans that it made and also creating money to purchase some financial securities directly.

Pitfalls for Monetary Policy

Monetary policy may seem straightforward. If the economy is in a recession, substantially below potential GDP, then the central bank should raise the supply of money and credit, first by reducing interest rates, and then by considering the use of "quantitative easing" and direct loans. If the economy is producing in overdrive above potential GDP, experiencing high inflation, then the central bank should raise interest rates by holding down growth of the money supply. However, in the real world, matters are more complicated than they may at first appear.

LONG AND VARIABLE TIME LAGS

Monetary policy affects the economy only after a time lag that is typically long and of variable length. Remember, monetary policy involves a chain of events: the central bank must perceive a situation in the economy, hold a meeting, and make a decision to react by tightening or loosening monetary policy. The change in monetary policy must percolate through the banking system, changing the quantity of loans and affecting interest rates. When interest rates changes, businesses must change their investment levels and consumers must change their borrowing patterns when purchasing homes or cars. Then it takes time for these changes to filter through the rest of the economy.

As a result of this chain of events, monetary policy has little effect in the immediate future; instead, its primary effects are felt perhaps 1–3 years in the future. Monetary policy is like steering a car down a twisting, turning road, where you can see the road behind you, but you have to turn the steering wheel to match the curves you cannot yet see that are ahead. For example, when a central bank decides to loosen monetary policy, it must consider the possibility that by the time the policy actually takes effect in 1–3 years, it will wish it had actually decided to tighten or to take no action at all. The reality of long and variable time lags doesn't mean that a central bank should refuse to make decisions—after all, refusing to make a decision is, in itself, a decision. But it does mean that central banks should be humble about taking action, because of the risk that their actions can create as much or more economic instability as they resolve.

EXCESS RESERVES

excess reserves: Reserves that banks hold above the legally mandated limit.

Banks are legally required to hold a minimum level of reserves, but no rule prohibits them from holding additional **excess reserves** above the legally mandated limit. For example, during a recession banks may be hesitant to lend, because they fear that when the economy is contracting, a high proportion of loan applicants become less likely to repay their loans.

When many banks are choosing to hold excess reserves, expansionary monetary policy may not work well. For example, consider an economy in the throes of a recession, with output substantially below potential GDP. The central bank diagnoses the situation and decides to use an open market operation to conduct an expansionary monetary policy. The hope and intention of the open market operation is that when the central bank buys bonds from banks, the banks will find themselves holding more money and will choose to make additional loans. But there's an old proverb that says, "You can lead a horse to water, but you can't make him drink." Similarly, a central bank can buy bonds from individual banks, but if the banks prefer to hold excess reserves above the legally required level, the central bank can't force individual banks to make loans. Similarly, sensible businesses and consumers may be reluctant to borrow substantial amounts of money in a recession,

Should Monetary Policy Decisions Be Made More Democratically?

Should monetary policy be conducted by a nation's Congress or legislature made up of elected representatives? Or should it be conducted by a politically appointed central bank that is more independent of voters? Here are some of the arguments made by each side.

The Case for Greater Democratic Control of Monetary Policy

Elected representatives conduct fiscal policy by passing tax and spending bills. They could handle monetary policy in the same way. Sure, they will sometimes make mistakes, but in a democracy, it's better to have mistakes made by elected officials accountable to voters than by political appointees. After all, the people appointed to the top governing positions at the Federal Reserve—and to most central banks around the world—are typically bankers and economists. They aren't representatives of borrowers like small businesses or farmers, or representatives of labor unions. Central banks might not be so quick to raise interest rates if they had to pay more attention to firms and people in the real economy.

The Case for an Independent Central Bank

America's judicial system is governed by judges who are presidential appointees. These judges interpret the laws made by elected officials. Few people believe that the legislature should vote on legal cases, and many of the same arguments apply to the central bank. Because the central bank has some insulation from day-to-day politics, its members can take a nonpartisan look at specific economic situations and make tough, immediate decisions when necessary. The idea of giving a legislature the ability to create money and hand out loans is likely to end up badly, sooner or later. Also, a central bank, acting according to the laws passed by elected officials, can respond far more quickly than a legislature. For example, the U.S. budget takes months to debate, pass, and be signed into law, but monetary policy decisions can be made much more rapidly. Day-to-day democratic control of monetary policy is impractical and seems likely to lead to an overly expansionary monetary policy and higher inflation.

Who Wins This Debate?

This debate isn't going away. Nevertheless, the trend in the 2000s has been that countries around the world are moving toward writing specific rules for the central bank to follow—like targeting a certain rate of inflation—and then leaving it up to the central bank to achieve that goal, rather than moving toward greater day-to-day democratic control of the central bank.

because they recognize that firms' sales and employees' jobs are more insecure in a recession, and they don't want to face the unrelenting need to make interest payments. The result is that during an especially deep recession, an expansionary monetary policy may have little effect on either the price level or the real GDP.

Japan experienced this situation in the 1990s and early 2000s. Japan's economy entered a period of very slow growth, dipping in and out of recession, in the early 1990s. By February 1999, the Bank of Japan had lowered the equivalent of its federal funds rate to 0% and kept it there most of the time through 2003. Moreover, in the two years from March 2001 to March 2003, the Bank of Japan also expanded the money supply of the country by about 50%—an enormous increase. But even this highly expansionary monetary policy had no substantial effect on stimulating aggregate demand. Japan's economy continued to experience extremely slow growth into the mid 2000s.

The problem of excess reserves does not affect contractionary policy. Central bankers have an old saying that monetary policy can be like pulling and pushing on a string: when the central bank pulls on the string and uses contractionary monetary policy, it can definitely raise interest rates and reduce aggregate demand. However, when the central bank tries to push on the string of expansionary monetary policy, the string may sometimes just fold up limp and have little effect, because banks decide not to loan out their excess reserves. This analogy shouldn't be taken too literally—expansionary monetary policy usually does have real effects, after that inconveniently long and variable lag. But there are also times, like Japan's economy in the late 1990s and early 2000s, when expansionary monetary policy has been insufficient to lift a recession-prone economy.

UNPREDICTABLE MOVEMENTS OF VELOCITY

velocity:
The speed with which money circulates through the economy, calculated as the nominal GDP divided by the money supply.

Velocity is a term that economists use to describe how quickly money circulates through the economy. The velocity of money in a year is defined as:

$$\text{Velocity} = \frac{\text{nominal GDP}}{\text{money supply}}.$$

In 2009, for example, M1 was \$1.7 trillion and nominal GDP was \$14.3 trillion, so the velocity of M1 was \$14.3 trillion/\$1.7 trillion = 8.4. A higher velocity of money means that the average dollar circulates more times in a year; a lower velocity means that the average dollar circulates fewer times in a year. Velocity can also be measured using other definitions of the money supply, like M2. Changes in velocity can cause problems for monetary policy. To understand why, rewrite the definition of velocity so that the money supply is on the left- hand side of the equation. That is,

$$\text{Money supply} \times \text{Velocity} = \text{Nominal GDP}$$

basic quantity equation of money:
Money supply × Velocity = Nominal GDP.

This equation is sometimes called the **basic quantity equation of money,** but as you can see, it's just the definition of velocity written in a different form. This equation must hold true, by definition. If velocity is constant over time, then a certain percentage rise in the money supply on the left-hand side of the basic quantity equation of money will inevitably lead to the same percentage rise in nominal GDP—although this change could happen through an increase in inflation, or an increase in real GDP, or some combination of the two.

If velocity is changing over time but in a constant and predictable way, then changes in the money supply will continue to have a predictable effect on nominal GDP. But if velocity changes unpredictably over

Episodes of Deflation

Deflation occurs when the rate of inflation is negative; that is, instead of money having less purchasing power over time, as occurs with inflation, money is worth more. Having money be worth more may not sound so bad! But when deflation interacts with interest rates, it can cause recessions that are difficult for monetary policy to address.

Remember that the real interest rate is the nominal interest rate minus the rate of inflation. If the nominal interest rate is 7% and the rate of inflation is 3%, then the borrower is effectively paying a 4% real interest rate. But if the nominal interest rate is 7% and there is deflation of 2%, then the real interest rate is actually 9%. In this way, an unexpected deflation raises the real interest payments for borrowers. It can lead to a situation where an unexpectedly high number of loans are not repaid and banks find that their net worth is decreasing or negative. When banks are suffering losses, they become less able and eager to make new loans. Aggregate demand declines, which can lead to recession.

Then comes the double-whammy: After causing a recession, deflation can make it difficult for monetary policy to work. Say that the central bank uses expansionary monetary policy to reduce the nominal interest rate all the way to zero—but the economy has 5% deflation. As a result, the real interest rate is 5%, and because a central bank can't make the nominal interest rate negative, expansionary policy can't reduce the real interest rate further.

In the U.S. economy during the early 1930s, deflation was 6.7% per year from 1930–33, which caused many borrowers to default on their loans and many banks to end up bankrupt, which in turn contributed substantially to the Great Depression. But not all episodes of deflation end in Depression. Japan experienced deflation of slightly less than 1% per year from 1999–2002, and while Japan's economy was mired in slow growth, it did grow by about 0.9% per year over this period. Indeed, there is at least one historical example of deflation coexisting with rapid growth. The U.S. economy experienced deflation of about 1.1% per year over the quarter-century from 1876–1900, but real GDP also expanded at a rapid clip of 4% per year over this time, despite some occasional severe recessions.

The central bank should be on guard against deflation, and if necessary use expansionary monetary policy to prevent any long-lasting or extreme deflation from occurring. But except in severe cases like the Great Depression, deflation does not guarantee economic disaster.

time, then the affect of changes in the money supply on nominal GDP becomes unpredictable.

The actual velocity of money in the U.S. economy as measured by using M1, the most common definition of the money supply, is illustrated in Exhibit 30-8. From 1960 up to about 1980, velocity appears fairly predictable; that is, it is increasing at a fairly constant rate. In the early 1980s, however, velocity as calculated with M1 becomes more variable. The reasons for these sharp changes in velocity remain a puzzle. Economists suspect that the changes in velocity are related to innovations in banking and finance which have changed how money is used in making economic transactions: for example, the growth of electronic payments; a rise in personal borrowing and credit card usage; and accounts that make it easier for people to hold money in savings accounts, where it is counted as M2, right up to the moment that they want to write a check on the money and transfer it to M1. But at least so far, it has proven difficult to draw clear links between these kinds of factors and the specific up-and-down fluctuations in M1.

Exhibit 30-8 Velocity

Velocity is the nominal GDP divided by the money supply for a given year. Different measures of velocity can be calculated by using different measures of the money supply. Velocity as calculated by using M1 has lacked a steady trend since the 1980s, instead bouncing up and down.

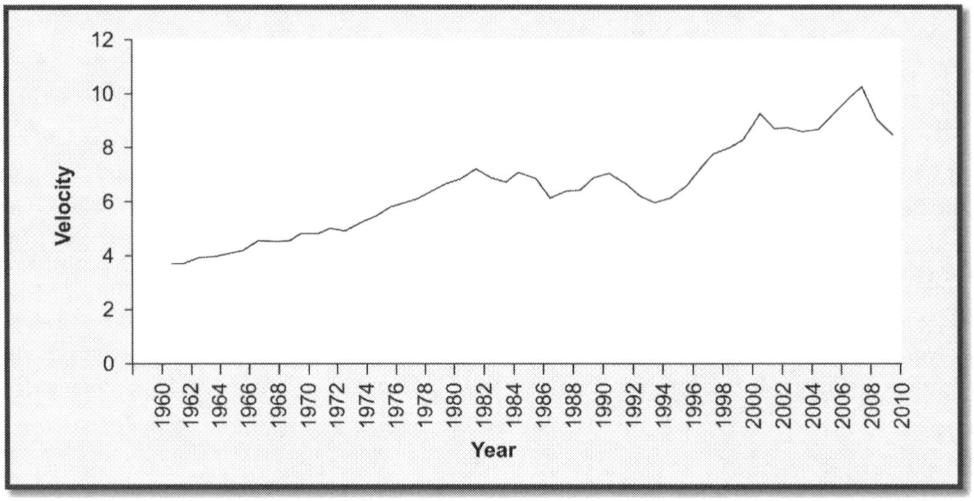

In the 1970s, when velocity as measured by M1 seemed predictable, a number of economists, led by Nobel laureate Milton Friedman (1912–2006), argued that the best monetary policy was for the central bank to increase the money supply slowly and steadily over time. These economists argued that with the long and variable lags of monetary policy, and the political pressures on central bankers, central bank monetary policies were as likely to have undesirable as to have desirable effects. Thus, these economists believed that the monetary policy should seek steady growth in the money supply of 3% per year. They argued that a steady rate of monetary growth would be correct over longer time periods, since it would roughly match the growth of the real economy. In addition, they argued that giving the central bank less discretion to conduct monetary policy would prevent an overly activist central bank from becoming a source of economic instability and uncertainty. In this spirit, Friedman wrote in 1967: "The first and most important lesson that history teaches about what monetary policy can do—and it is a lesson of the most profound importance—is that monetary policy can prevent money itself from being a major source of economic disturbance."

But as the velocity of M1 began to fluctuate in the 1980s, having the money supply grow at a predetermined and unchanging rate seemed less desirable, because as the quantity theory of money shows, the combination of constant growth in the money supply and fluctuating velocity would cause nominal GDP to rise and fall in unpredictable ways. The jumpiness of velocity in the 1980s caused many central banks to focus less on the rate at which the quantity of money in the economy was increasing, and instead to set monetary policy by reacting to whether the economy was experiencing or in danger of higher inflation or unemployment.

IS UNEMPLOYMENT OR INFLATION MORE IMPORTANT?

If you were to survey central bankers around the world and ask them what they believe should be the primary task of monetary policy, the most popular answer by far would be fighting inflation. Most central bankers believe that the neoclassical model of economics accurately represents the economy over the medium and long term. Remember that in the neoclassical model of the economy, the aggregate supply curve is drawn as a vertical line at the level of potential GDP, as shown in Exhibit 30-9. In the neoclassical model, the level of potential GDP (and the natural rate of unemployment that exists when the economy is producing at potential GDP) is determined by real economic factors. If the original level of aggregate demand is AD0, then an expansionary monetary policy that shifts aggregate demand to AD1 only creates an inflationary increase in the price level, but it does not alter GDP or unemployment. From this perspective, all that monetary policy can do is to lead to low inflation or high inflation—and low inflation provides a better climate for a healthy and growing economy. After all, low inflation means that businesses making investments can focus on real economic issues, not on figuring out ways to protecting themselves from the costs and risks of inflation. In this way, a consistent pattern of low inflation can contribute to long-term growth.

This vision of focusing monetary policy on a low rate of inflation is so attractive that many countries have rewritten their central banking laws since in the 1990s to have their bank practice **inflation-targeting,** which means that the central bank is legally required to focus only on keeping inflation low. By 2010, central banks in 26 countries from all over the world faced a legal requirement to target the inflation rate, including Austria, Brazil, Canada, Israel, Korea, Mexico, New Zealand, Spain, Sweden, Thailand, and the United Kingdom. The legislation establishing the European Central Bank, which controls the quantity of euros, sets "price stability" as its primary goal, which it defines as an inflation rate of 2% per year or less. However, the Federal Reserve in the United States does not practice inflation-targeting. Instead, the law governing the Federal Reserve requires it to take both unemployment and inflation into account.

inflation-targeting: A rule that the central bank is required to focus only on keeping inflation low.

Economists have no final consensus on whether a central bank should be required to focus only on inflation or should have greater discretion. For those who subscribe to the inflation-targeting philosophy, the fear is that when politicians who are worried about slow economic growth and unemployment will constantly pressure the central bank to conduct a loose monetary policy—even if the economy is already producing at potential GDP. In some countries, the central bank may lack the political power to resist such pressures, with the result of higher inflation but no long-term reduction in unemployment. The U.S. Federal Reserve has a tradition of independence, but central banks in other countries may be under greater political pressure. Or in another scenario, central bankers may be tempted to tinker continually with the interest rate, pushing it up and down from month to month in a way

Exhibit 30-9 Monetary Policy in a Neoclassical Model

In a neoclassical view, monetary policy affects only the price level, not the level of output in the economy. For example, an expansionary monetary policy causes aggregate demand to shift from the original AD_0 to AD_1. However, the adjustment of the economy from the original equilibrium E_0 to the new equilibrium E_1 represents an inflationary increase in the price level from P_0 to P_1, but has no effect in the long run on output or the unemployment rate. In fact, no shift in AD will affect the equilibrium quantity of output in this model.

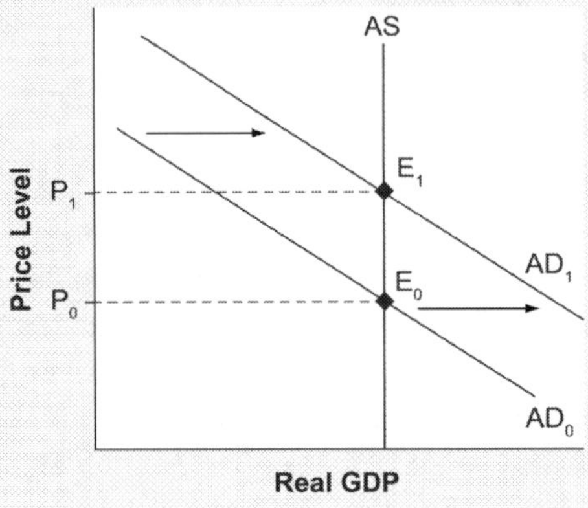

that creates uncertainty and risk in the economy. However, inflation-targeting has its risks, too. A central bank that focuses only on inflation will not use expansionary monetary policy to fight a recession. In the early 2000s, for example, unemployment rates rose in many European countries, but the European Central Bank focused only on keeping inflation rates low, not on whether it might have been wise to run a more expansionary monetary policy.

For all of these reasons—long and variable lags, excess reserves, unstable velocity, and controversy over economic goals—monetary policy in the real world is often difficult. But the basic message remains that central banks can affect aggregate demand through the conduct of monetary policy, and in that way influence macroeconomic outcomes.

SHOULD THE CENTRAL BANK TACKLE ASSET BUBBLES AND LEVERAGE CYCLES?

One long-standing concern about having the central bank focus on inflation and unemployment is that it may be overlooking certain other economic problems that are coming in the future. For example, in the late 1990s during what was known as the "dot-com" boom, the U.S. stock market as measured by the Dow Jones Industrial Index, which includes 30 very large companies from across the U.S. economy, nearly tripled in value from 1994 to 2000. The Nasdaq index, which includes many smaller technology companies, increased in value by a multiple of five from 1994 to 2000. These rates of increase were clearly not sustainable. Indeed, stock values as measured by the Dow Jones were almost 20% lower in 2009 than they had been in 2000. Stock values in the Nasdaq index were 50% lower in 2009 than they had been in 2000. The drop-off in stock market values contributed to the recession of 2001 and the higher unemployment that followed.

A similar story can be told about housing prices in the mid-2000s. During the 1970s, 1980s, and 1990s, housing prices increased at about 6% per year on average. But during what came to be known as the "housing bubble" from 2003 to 2005, housing prices increased at almost double this annual rate. These rates of increase were clearly not sustainable. When the price of housing fell in 2007 and 2008, many banks and households found that their assets were worth less than they expected, which contributed to the recession that started in 2007. At a broader level, some economists worry about a "leverage cycle," where "leverage" is a term used by financial economists to mean "borrowing." When economic times are good, banks and the financial sector are eager to lend, and people and firms are eager to borrow. Remember that the amount of money and credit in an economy is determined by a money multiplier—a process of loans being made, money being deposited, and more loans being made. In good economic times, this surge of lending exaggerates the episode of economic growth. It can even be part of what lead prices of certain assets—like stock prices or housing prices—to rise at unsustainably high annual rates. At some point, when economic times turn bad, then banks and the financial sector become much less willing to lend, and credit becomes expensive or unavailable to many potential borrowers. The sharp reduction in credit, perhaps combined with the deflating prices a dot-com stock price bubble or a housing bubble, makes the economic downturn worse than it would otherwise be.

Thus, some economists have suggested that the central bank should not just look at economic growth, inflation, and unemployment rates, but should also keep an eye on asset prices and leverage cycles. Such proposals are quite controversial. If a central bank had announced in 1997 that stock prices were rising "too fast" or in 2004 that housing prices were rising "too fast," and then taken action to hold down price increases, many people and their elected political representatives would have been outraged. Neither the Federal Reserve nor any other central banks want to the responsibility of deciding when stock prices and housing prices are too high, too low, or just right. But as further research explores how asset price bubbles and leverage cycles can affect an economy, central banks may need to think about whether they should conduct monetary policy in a way that would seek to moderate these effects.

Bank Regulation

The safety and stability of a nation's banking system is a matter of macroeconomic concern. If banks falter at their tasks of collecting deposits and making loans, the effect can be similar to a contractionary monetary policy enacted by the central bank: that is, a lower quantity of loans, a reduction in aggregate demand, and a recession. This section begins by discussing two scenarios in which weaknesses in the banking system have caused macroeconomic harm: (1) when households lose confidence in banks and rush to withdraw their money; and (2) when a large proportion of the banks in an economy have extremely low or negative net worth and decide not to make many loans. The discussion then turns to three government policies for assuring safe and stable banking systems: (1) the provision of deposit insurance to reassure households that their bank deposits are safe; (2) examining the financial records of banks to ensure that they have positive net worth; and (3) making emergency short-term loans to banks in times of financial chaos.

BANK RUNS

Back in the nineteenth century and during the first few decades of the twentieth century, putting your money in a bank could be nerve-wracking. Imagine that the net worth of your bank became negative, so that the bank's assets weren't enough to cover its liabilities. In this situation, whoever withdrew their deposits first received all of their money, and those who didn't rush to the bank quickly enough lost their money. This scenario, in which depositors raced to the bank to withdraw their deposits for fear that otherwise they would be lost, is called a **bank run.** The drama of bank runs has even entered the plot of some well-known movies. In Mary Poppins, the little boy Michael wants his tuppence back, and when someone overhears that the bank director played by Dick Van Dyke won't give back his money, a comic bank run results. In It's a Wonderful Life, the bank manager played by Jimmy Stewart faces a mob of worried bank depositors who want to withdraw their money, but manages to allay their fears by allowing some of them to withdraw a portion of their deposits—using the money from his own pocket that was supposed to pay for his honeymoon.

bank run:
When depositors race to the bank to withdraw their deposits for fear that otherwise they would be lost.

The risk of bank runs created instability in the banking system. Even a rumor that a bank might experience negative net worth could trigger a bank run, and in a bank run, even healthy banks could be destroyed. Because a bank loans out most of the money it receives, and because it keeps only limited reserves on hand, a bank run of any size would quickly drain any of the bank's available cash. When the bank had no cash remaining, it only intensified the fears of remaining depositors that they could lose their money. Moreover, a bank run at one bank often triggered a chain reaction of runs on other banks. In the late nineteenth and early twentieth century, bank runs were typically not the original cause of a recession—but bank runs could make a recession much worse.

A WEAKENED BANKING SECTOR

In a nation with many banks, the failure of any one bank probably won't affect the macroeconomy much. But if many banks are simultaneously close to failing, and as a result the bank system substantially reduces the quantity of loans, the result can be slow growth or recession.

Japan's economy offers a vivid connection from insolvent banks to a weak economy over the last decade or so. Japanese banks (unlike U.S. banks) are allowed to hold some of their assets in the form of real estate and company stock. But from late 1989 to late 1992, real estate and stock prices in Japan fell, on average, by about 60%. Many Japanese banks suffered a dramatic decline in the value of their assets and faced negative net worth. As a result, Japan's banks became extremely reluctant to make loans. This is one reason why Japan's economy was sleepwalking from the early 1990s to the early 2000s, dipping in and out of recession with an average real growth rate of less than 1% per year.

The U.S. economy during the Great Recession of 2007–2009 also experienced the link from a weakened financial sector to an economic slowdown. Over 160 U.S. banks failed in 2008 and 2009; many others were on the verge of failing. Again, a cycle can begin in which a weakened economy means that fewer people repay their loans, thus weakening many banks; then banks that are financially weak become reluctant to lend, which makes the economy weaker.

Given the macroeconomic dangers from an unstable banking system, government laws and regulations have sought to reassure households that their bank deposits are safe and also to supervise banks to make sure that their balance sheets show positive net worth and a moderate level of risk. The following sections describe the government policies to address these goals.

DEPOSIT INSURANCE

Deposit insurance is an insurance system that makes sure depositors in a bank do not lose their money, even if the bank goes bankrupt. About 70 countries around the world, including all of the major economies, have deposit insurance programs. In the United States, the Federal Deposit Insurance Corporation (FDIC) is responsible for deposit insurance. Banks pay an insurance premium to the FDIC. The insurance premium is based on the bank's level of deposits, and then adjusted according to the riskiness of a bank's financial situation. In 2009, for example, a fairly safe bank with a high net worth might have paid 10–20 cents in insurance premiums for every $100 in bank deposits, while a risky bank with very low net worth might have paid 50–60 cents for every $100 in bank deposits. Bank examiners from the FDIC evaluate the balance sheets of banks, looking at the value of assets and liabilities, to determine the level of riskiness. The FDIC provides deposit insurance for about 8,200 banks. Even if a bank has negative net worth and the executives of the bank lose their jobs, the government guarantees that depositors will receive their money up to $250,000, which is enough for almost all individuals, although not for some businesses.

deposit insurance: An insurance system that makes sure depositors in a bank do not lose their money, even if the bank goes bankrupt.

Since the United States enacted deposit insurance in the 1930s, no one has lost any of their insured deposits. Bank runs no longer happen at insured banks. But the costs to government of providing deposit insurance can be substantial. One study found that from 1976–1996, 59 banking crises occurred in low- and middle-income countries around the world. The average cost of these bank crises to the government because of deposit insurance was a whopping 9% of one year's GDP.

BANK SUPERVISION

Several government agencies also check the balance sheets of banks to make sure they have positive net worth and are not taking too high a level of risk. Within the U.S. Department of the Treasury, the Office of the Comptroller of the Currency has a national staff of bank examiners who conduct on-site reviews of the 1,500 or so largest national banks. The bank examiners also review any foreign banks that have branches in the United States. Also within the Treasury, the Office of Thrift Supervision monitors and regulates about 800 savings and loan institutions. The National Credit Union Administration (NCUA) supervises credit unions, which are nonprofit banks owned and run by their members. There are over 10,000 credit unions in the U.S. economy, but the typical credit union is small compared to most banks. The Federal Reserve also has some responsibility for supervising financial institutions. For example, there are firms that own banks and other businesses called "bank holding companies." While other regulators like the Office of the Comptroller of the Currency supervises the banks, the Federal Reserve supervises the holding companies.

When the supervision of banks (and bank-like institutions such as savings and loans and credit unions) works well, most banks will remain financially healthy most of the time. If the bank supervisors find that a bank has low or negative net worth, or is making too high a proportion of risky loans, they can require that the bank change its behavior—or in extreme cases even force the bank to be closed or sold to a financially healthy bank.

But bank supervision can run into both practical and political questions. The practical question is that measuring the value of a bank's assets is not always straightforward. As discussed in the previous chapter, a bank's assets are its loans, and the value of these assets depends on estimates about the risk that these loans will not be repaid. These issues can become even more complex when a bank makes loans to banks or firms in other countries, or arranges financial deals that are much more complex than a basic loan. The political question arises because the decision by a bank supervisor to require a bank to close or to change its financial investments is often controversial, and the bank supervisor often comes under political pressure from the owners of the bank and the local politicians where the bank is located to shut up and back off. For example, many observers have pointed out that Japan's banks were in deep financial trouble through most of the 1990s; however, nothing substantial had been done about it by the early 2000s. A similar unwillingness to confront problems with struggling banks is visible across the rest of the world, in East Asia, Latin America, eastern Europe and Russia and elsewhere.

In the United States, laws were passed in the 1990s requiring that bank supervisors make their findings open and public, and that they act as soon as a problem is identified. But as many U.S. banks were staggered by the recession of 2007–2009, critics of the bank regulators asked pointed questions about why the regulators hadn't foreseen the financial

The Emancipation of U.S. Banks

During the Great Depression of the 1930s, the banking system crashed along with the economy. Politicians at that time believed the solution was to pass the Glass-Steagall Act of 1933, which restricted the types of business in which banks could become involved. For example, the Glass-Steagall Act restricted banks to making loans only to businesses and individuals. Banks were not allowed to own companies, own stock in companies, sell stock, or offer other financial products such as insurance. A few years earlier, the McFadden Act of 1927 had placed geographic limits on banks, prohibiting such institutions from establishing branches across state lines. Many state laws also restricted the number of branches that a bank could have per state.

The idea behind these restrictions was that if banks were limited in what they could do, they were less likely to get into financial trouble. But as economists pointed out, such legislation limited banks' ability to diversify their risks, and in that way made it more likely that they would be financially shaky, rather than less likely. Banks in other high-income countries around the world did not face these kinds of restrictions.

In the 1990s, banking laws began to change. In 1994, the Riegle-Neal Act allowed banks to set up as many branches as they wished, both within states and across state lines. In 1999, the Gramm-Leach-Bliley Act allowed banks to set up overall companies ("financial holding companies") that contained banks within them, as well as insurance companies and companies that sell stocks and bonds. However, unlike the situation in any other high-income economies, except for Japan, U.S. banks are still prohibited from owning commercial businesses, and commercial businesses are prohibited from owning banks. Some in the banking industry would like to eliminate these restrictions, too.

But in the aftermath of the 2007–2009 recession, there was a widespread sense that many U.S. banks had borrowed and loaned unwisely. Perhaps returning to the laws of the 1930s was not the correct response, but banks seemed likely to face new restrictions and limitations on their risk-taking.

shakiness of the banks earlier, before such large losses had a chance to accumulate.

LENDER OF LAST RESORT

When a panic spreads in financial markets, a situation can arise in which a financial institution needs a short-term emergency loan. In the old days of bank runs, for example, a healthy bank could have positive net worth, but not enough cash on hand so that a flock of depositors could withdraw their money. In such cases, the central bank can step in as **a lender of last resort**, which involves providing short-term emergency loans when a financial crisis occurs. For banks, the central bank acting as a lender of last resort helps to reinforce the effect of deposit insurance and thus to reassure bank customers that they won't lose their money. But the lender of last resort task can come up in other financial crises. During the panic of the stock market crash in 1987, when the value of U.S. stocks fell by 25% in a single day, the Federal Reserve made a number of short-term emergency loans so that the financial system could keep functioning. When fears were expressed late in 1999 that bank computers might malfunction on January 1, 2000, the Federal Reserve loudly announced that if any problems occurred, it was standing by to act as a lender of last resort until the problems were sorted out. During the recession of 2007–2009, the "quantitative easing" policies of the Federal

lender of last resort: An institution that provides short-term emergency loans in conditions of financial crisis.

Reserve can be interpreted as a willingness to make short-term credit available as needed in a time when the banking and financial system was under stress.

SUMMARY

Overall, bank regulation in the United States is coordinated by the Federal Financial Institutions Examination Council (FFIEC), which in turn draws its membership from the agencies mentioned in this section: the Federal Deposit Insurance Corporation (FDIC), the National Credit Union Administration (NCUA), the Office of the Comptroller of the Currency (OCC), and the Office of Thrift Supervision (OTS), and the Federal Reserve. The task of the FFIEC is to assure that this alphabet soup of bank regulators all communicate with each other and use similar standards when evaluating the riskiness of banks.

The failure of a single bank can be treated like any other business failure. Yet if many banks fail, it can reduce aggregate demand in a way that can bring on or deepen a recession. The combination of deposit insurance, bank supervision, and lender of last resort policies help to prevent weaknesses in the banking system from causing recessions.

Conclusion

Through expansionary monetary policy, a central bank can reduce interest rates and increase the quantity of loans, increase aggregate demand to the right, and help a recession-stricken economy return to potential GDP. Through contractionary monetary policy, a central bank can raise interest rates and decrease the quantity of loans, shift aggregate demand to the left, and reduce inflation. The appropriate timing and direction of monetary policy isn't always clear, because of issues like long and variable lags, banks that hold excess reserves, movements in velocity, and disagreements over whether reducing inflation or unemployment should take higher priority. Moreover, in the long run the neoclassical model shows that economic output and unemployment are determined by real factors in markets, while monetary policy determines only the inflation rate. But during the ups and downs of the business cycle, when recessions and inflations occur, monetary policy can play some role in stabilizing the swings of the economy.

The discussion in this chapter has focused on domestic monetary policy; that is, the view of monetary policy within an economy. The next chapter explores the international dimension of monetary policy, and how monetary policy becomes involved with exchange rates and international flows of financial capital.

Key Concepts and Summary

1. The most prominent task of a **central bank** is to conduct **monetary policy**, which involves controlling the quantity of money (and loans) in the economy. Some prominent central banks around the world include the U.S. Federal Reserve, the European Central Bank, the Bank of Japan, and the Bank of England.
2. A central bank has three traditional tools to conduct monetary policy: **open market operations**, which involves buying and selling government bonds with banks; **reserve requirements**, which determine what level of reserves a bank is legally required to hold; and **discount rates**, which is the interest rate at which a central bank makes loans to individual banks. The most commonly used tool is open market operations. During the 2007–2009 recession, central banks around the world also used quantitative easing to expand the supply of money and credit.
3. A loose or **expansionary monetary policy** raises the quantity of money and credit above what it otherwise would have been and reduces interest rates.
4. A **contractionary monetary policy**, also called a tight monetary policy, reduces the quantity of money and credit below what it otherwise would have been and raises interest rates, seeking to hold down inflation. An expansionary monetary policy, also called a loose monetary policy, seeks to boost aggregate demand, and thus to counter recession.
5. Monetary policy is inevitably imprecise, for a number of reasons: (a) the effects occur only after **long and variable lags**; (b) if banks decide to hold excess reserves, monetary policy cannot force them to lend; and (c) **velocity** may shift in unpredictable ways.
6. The basic **quantity equation of money** is MV = PQ, where M is the money supply, V is the velocity of money, P is the price level, and Q is the real output of the economy.
7. Some central banks like the European Central Bank practice **inflation-targeting**, which means that the only goal of the central bank is to keep inflation within a low target range. Other central banks like the U.S. Federal Reserve are free to focus on either reducing inflation or stimulating an economy that is in recession, whichever goal seems most important at the time.
8. A **bank run** occurs when there are rumors (possibly true, possibly false) that a bank is at financial risk of having negative net worth. As a result, depositors rush to the bank to withdraw their money and put it someplace safer. Even false rumors, if they cause a bank run, can force a healthy bank to lose its deposits and be forced to close.
9. **Deposit insurance** guarantees bank depositors that even if the bank has negative net worth, their deposits will be protected. In the United States, the Federal Deposit Insurance Corporation (FDIC) collects deposit insurance premiums from banks and guarantees bank deposits up to $100,000.

10. Bank supervision involves inspecting the balance sheets of banks to make sure that they have positive net worth and that their assets are not too risky. In the United States, the Office of the Comptroller of the Currency (OCC) is responsible for supervising banks, the Office of Thrift Supervision (OTS) is responsible for inspecting savings and loans, and the National Credit Union Administration (NCUA) is responsible for inspecting credit unions. The FDIC and the Federal Reserve also play a role in bank supervision. These agencies coordinate their efforts through the Federal Financial Institutions Examination Council (FFIEC).
11. When a central bank acts as a lender of last resort, it makes short-term loans available in situations of sever financial panic or stress.

Review Questions

1. How is a central bank different from a typical commercial bank?
2. List the three traditional tools that a central bank has for controlling the money supply.
3. Explain how to use an open market operation to expand the money supply.
4. Explain how to use the reserve requirement to expand the money supply.
5. Explain how to use the discount rate to expand the money supply.
6. Explain how to use quantitative easing to expand the money supply.
7. How do the following types of monetary policy affect the quantity of money: expansionary or contractionary?
8. How do the following types of monetary policy affect interest rates: tight or loose?
9. How do the following types of monetary policy affect aggregate demand: expansionary, tight, contractionary, and loose?
10. Which kind of monetary policy would you expect in response to high inflation: expansionary or contractionary? Why?
11. Which kind of monetary policy would you expect in response to recession: expansionary or contractionary? Why?
12. How might each of the following factors complicate the implementation of monetary policy: long and variable lags, excess reserves, and movements in velocity?
13. Define the velocity of the money supply.
14. What is the basic quantity equation of money?
15. How does a monetary policy of inflation targeting work?
16. How is bank regulation linked to the conduct of monetary policy?
17. What is a bank run?
18. In a program of deposit insurance as it is operated in the United States, what is being insured and who pays the insurance premiums?
19. In government programs of bank supervision, what is being supervised?
20. What is the lender of last resort?
21. Name and briefly describe the responsibilities of each of the following agencies: FFIEC, FDIC, NCUA, OCC, and OTS.

CHAPTER 14
The Financial Crisis

14 The Financial Crisis

By David Moglen

INTRODUCTION: THE CREDIT CRUNCH AS AN OBJECT LESSON FOR FINANCIAL CRISES

Rather than brief summaries of an array of historical financial crises, the focus of this chapter is an in-depth presentation of the Banking Crisis that is still ravaging the economy at this writing in 2010 through the ongoing Credit Crunch, widespread foreclosures, and lingering effects of the directly induced Great Recession which officially began in December of 2007. This approach will cover key elements of the Credit Crunch, and provide insights into financial crises past and future and how they impact your life. You will have to do your own research to learn about other crashes, but if you do, you may find their similarities to this crisis are striking. You could investigate the gas price bubble of 2004–2008, the Electric Power (Enron) bubble in California of 2000–2001, the Dot-Com Internet bubble of the 1990's, the Savings & Loan crisis of the 1980's, the bursting of the Japanese Real Estate bubble of the 1990's, or the Asian Financial Crisis in that same decade.

UNLOCKING THE MYSTERIES

The Subprime Crisis

It's not surprising that people who were offered mortgage loans with low payments, often by brokers who concealed the downside of the loans and the real estate market, would go ahead and sign such a mortgage to own a home and live the American Dream. A valid debate can occur regarding how much of the blame for the mortgage meltdown should be placed on these subprime borrowers. But regardless how much we decide the borrower is to blame, it should not hide the fact that a loan requires not only a borrower but also a willing lender. So why did lenders make these loans which in many cases had little to no chance of being fully repaid?

To illustrate the point, just look at what mortgage brokers and lenders like CountryWide and Ameriquist called their loans: No-Doc loans (no documentation of the borrower's qualifications), Liar loans, NINA loans (No Income, No Assets), or NINJA loans (No Income, No Job, No Assets). Now, if you were going to lend someone $300,000 for thirty years, wouldn't you want to verify some things about that borrower first? Sure, you would want to check their income, assets, job stability, and credit rating. It's called "underwriting." In the entire history of mortgage lending, anyone offering such a loan would carefully check all these vital statistics before they hand over the $300,000 loan. But, quite suddenly, banks, mortgage brokers, and lenders stopped checking this information and simply made the loan. Something quite fundamental changed in the mortgage industry.

That something was the rapid, widespread introduction of private-label MBS (Mortgage Backed Securities), also called CDOs (Collateralized Debt Obligations). This mortgage derivative is simply a large number of subprime loans pooled together, and then sliced into thousands of shares to be sold off to investors. While in the basic concept of a mortgage loan, a lender has to diligently screen all borrowers to be quite certain that person can and will repay this loan for the next thirty years, now we have entered a whole new world. Why should the lender care if the borrower can't pay for thirty years? The lender doesn't need to care if the borrower will fail to make even the first month's mortgage payment. The lender is repaid the entire loan amount (let's say, $300,000) immediately, or within a week of making the loan. That's because the loan was sold (by way of an Investment Bank's CDO) to an investor. It's their problem now. The only incentive for banks, lenders, and brokers became to earn fees and create volumes of subprime loans. Just make as many of these bad loans as possible, because the full amount is repaid immediately as far as they are concerned.

This goes towards explaining why about 55—61% of all subprime borrowers actually qualified for a "prime rate" loan, with lower interest rates, fees and risk. A large percentage of subprime borrowers actually had credit that wasn't that bad, and qualified for a lower-priced loan they could have paid off, but instead they were steered by brokers into the subprime loan which they would not be able to pay off. Why? Because a high-interest rate loan looked better in the CDO than trying to sell investors a CDO with a low-interest prime rate loan for that same borrower.

And why did lenders provide loans to people with little to no chance of fully repaying such a treacherous loan? Because the derivative, the CDO, allowed lenders to have literally no skin in the game. They were repaid the whole entire loan amount not in thirty years, the way it's supposed to work, but by the end of the week.

Now, in this transaction where brokers and bankers have much more knowledge and information about the Real Estate market and the fine print in these subprime loans than the borrower, it is not surprising that the borrower winds up belly-up: bankrupt and in foreclosure. But why did the titans of Wall Street also find themselves on the bullet train to bankruptcy, what with all their access to the most sophisticated financial experts on the planet? To understand why even the most established investment banks, from Bear Stearns to Lehman Brothers, Citigroup to JP Morgan Chase all found themselves on a fast track to extinction (only to survive due to government bailouts, if at all), one must disaggregate, one must separate, the company from the individual people who ran it.

Sure, these century-old companies were on the brink of bankruptcy, but the executives who should have known better probably did know better and they made off like bandits, made very wealthy by their firms as they retired with their golden parachutes and left their storied company to die or grab the life raft of a government bailout.

THE MYTH OF THE SUBPRIME BORROWER

subprime
— ***adj***
(of a loan) made to a borrower with a poor credit rating, usually at a high rate of interest (Collins English Dictionary)

> In finance, **subprime lending** (also referred to as **near-prime**, **non-prime**, and **second-chance lending**) means making loans that are in the riskiest category of consumer loans and are typically sold in a separate market from prime loans. The standards for determining risk categories refer to the size of the loan, "traditional" or "nontraditional" structure of the loan, borrower credit rating, ratio of borrower debt to income or assets, ratio of loan to value or collateral, and documentation provided on those loans which do not meet Fannie Mae or Freddie Mac underwriting guidelines for prime mortgages (are "non-conforming"). Although there is no single, standard definition, in the United States subprime loans are usually classified as those where the borrower has a FICO score below 640. Subprime lending encompasses a variety of credit types, including mortgages, auto loans, and credit cards. The term was popularized by the media during the "credit crunch" of 2007.[1]

A subprime loan has higher a interest rate over the life (the term) of the loan. That interest rate might start low, but will increase—causing monthly mortgage payments to skyrocket. This variable rate is referred to as the loan's rate "reset." Subprime loans regularly have fees such as prepayment penalties. It is generally the loan—not the borrower—that is classified as subprime.

The widespread public belief is that subprime loans are so obviously worse than the prime rate loans that well-qualified borrowers receive due to the subprime borrowers' poor credit rating. In one of the most shocking findings in the subprime crisis, several sources and researchers (given below) cite evidence that 55–61% of subprime borrowers qualified for the more affordable prime rate loan. Had the broker been incentivized or compelled to get them the best loan for which they qualified, millions of households in foreclosure would have had a much better chance of avoiding losing their homes.

One explanation of the broker incentives leading to such an outcome is the yield-spread premium explained in the CNN Money article in Group 2 of the In-Class Project.

---

[1]http://en.wikipedia.org/wiki/Subprime_lending.

"In 2005, the peak year of the subprime boom, the study says that borrowers with such credit scores got more than half—55%—of all subprime mortgages that were ultimately packaged into securities for sale to investors, as most subprime loans are. The study by First American LoanPerformance, a San Francisco research firm, says the proportion rose even higher by the end of 2006, to 61%. The figure was just 41% in 2000, according to the study. Even a significant number of borrowers with top-notch credit signed up for expensive subprime loans, the firm's analysis found." ("Subprime Debacle Traps Even Very Credit-Worthy" by Rick Brooks and Ruth Simon in the *Wall Street Journal*, December 3, 2007)[†]

"Economic and housing experts have estimated that 55 percent of subprime borrowers qualified for a prime loan with lower interest rates and no resets in the first place."

("Majority of Minnesotans with Subprime Loans had 'Good' Credit" by Molly Priesmeyer in the Minnesota Independent, April 7, 2008)[‡]

"It's estimated that fully 55% of current subprime borrowers—particularly African Americans and Latinos—could have qualified for a prime loan at better rates and with better terms in the first place. Had these borrowers not been offered faulty products destined to fail, the subprime meltdown would not be the massive debacle that it is." ("Relief or a raw deal?" by Paul Leonard in the LA Times, March 27, 2008.)[§]

> "**Yield-spread premiums** (Ed. Note: see 2nd article under Group 2 in the In-class Project at the end of this chapter re: YSPs) ... YSPs distort competitive market forces by creating a reverse competition effect with brokers incented to shop for the best deal for them, not the best deal for the borrower. YSPs not only encouraged the steering of subprime borrowers into more costly and riskier loans, but also the steering of prime credit borrowers into subprime loans. **It is estimated that up to 60% of subprime borrowers could have qualified for prime loans** (emphasis added) or loans through FHA, Fannie Mae, or Freddie Mac that would have given them interest rates that were lower by 3% or more. Steering borrowers into worse and riskier loans than those for which they qualify is intrinsically linked to the issue of YSPs. As noted previously, compensation based on the terms or conditions of a credit transaction places the interests of brokers and borrowers at odds. Due to an informational asymmetry inherent in the broker-borrower relationship, the practice of steering is on its face an unfair and deceptive practice." ("Advanced Notice of Proposed Rule-Making: Mortgage

---

[2]http://online.wsj.com/article/NA_WSJ_PUB: SB119662974358911035.html.

[3]http://minnesotaindependent.com/3570/
majority-of-minnesotans-with-subprime-loans-had-good-credit.

[4]http://www.latimes.com/business/investing/la-op-leonard-thornberg-27mar27,0,187810.story.

Acts and Practices" by The Center for Responsible Lending July 30, 2009)[5]

In addition to steering borrowers into unaffordable subprime loans when so many qualified for prime rate loans, borrower lawsuits allege that they were told their loan had a fixed rate when in fact it had a rate that would later increase. "McCollum's complaint alleges many of the same things cited in Bennett's suit: Countrywide told customers interest rates were fixed when they were adjustable, misrepresented the length of teaser rates and long-term higher rates."[6]

("Saying They Were Tricked, Borrowers Fight Back With Lawsuits" by John Pacenti in the *Daily Business Review* July 10, 2008)

UNLOCKING THE MYSTERIES

Financial Derivatives

What are financial derivatives? A financial derivative is a bet that an underlying asset will go *up* or *down*.

The underlying asset involves real production, and a real asset in the real economy. In other words, the underlying asset is on the "Main Street" side. The derivative, on the other hand, is largely meant to aid the Main Street economic activity, but it is a financial product (or security), so it is on the "Wall Street" side.

For example, a potato farmer would like to get a high price for his crop when he brings his potatoes to market, but he knows there is some possibility that the market price of potatoes at the time he is ready to sell may be low. So to protect himself from making too little revenue, he buys a large number of Short Potato Futures Contracts, which, as you see above (in the "any commodity" row), are simply bets that the price per pound of Potatoes will fall. So if the bad scenario occurs, and the potato price is low, while his main business of selling potatoes will receive a dismally low amount of revenue, his bets that this was going to happen will pay off big time, putting his total revenue (and profit) at a reasonable level. If, on the other hand, the price of potatoes is high, then his main business of selling potatoes will make plenty of money, and he will not be too worried that his side bet (the Futures Contract) did not pay off.

This is called hedging. Our potato farmer has hedged his main business of selling potatoes by owning a large number of bets that the price of potatoes will fall. The Futures Contract, like all derivatives, is meant to aid activity on the Main Street side (a farmer is considered Main Street, not Wall Street).

Another example is that of company employees who typically have a lot of their personal investment portfolio in their company's stock. They own a lot of their own company's stock because that, in part, is how they are paid, and the stock they own for their company has restrictions

[5]http://www.ftc.gov/os/comments/map/542308-00048.pdf.

[6]http://www.law.com/jsp/article.jsp?id=1202422873307.

Underlying Asset:	The Derivative for that Asset is Called:	To Bet it will go Up (+), one would buy a:	To Bet it will go Down (-), one would buy a:
Any Commodity, e.g. Rice, Sugar, Steel, Oil, Cotton, Milk, Electricity etc.	The (oil) Futures Contract	Long (oil) Futures Contract	Short (oil) Futures Contract
Any economic indicator, e.g. the Interest Rate or a Currency	The (dollar) Futures Contract	Long (dollar) Futures Contract	Short (dollar) Futures Contract
Any Stock	Stock Option	Call Option	Put Option
Subprime Loans	**Mortgage Backed Security (MBS)**	**MBS or Collateralized Debt Obligation (CDO)**	**Credit Default Swap (CDS) or Short MBS**

preventing them from selling it for years. So, to protect their retirement portfolio from losing value, our company employee buys a lot of put options on their own company's stock. If the stock goes up, they are happy, even though their bet the stock would go down (the put option) is not worth anything. If, on the other hand, the stock falls in value, or the company even goes bankrupt (the stock price falls to zero) then at least they have this side bet (the put option) which will now be worth a lot of money, so their retirement account is not completely financially destroyed.

This is another example of hedging, and exemplifies how the derivative aids activity on the Main Street side. Unlike "genuine hedgers" who buy the appropriate derivative to offset what they fear will happen to the underlying asset they need or sell for their Main Street business activities, "speculators" only buy the derivative and have no role in the real economy, Main Street underlying asset related to that financial derivative.

Visualize a dog wagging its tail. The dog is the Main Street side, the underlying asset, and the tail is the Wall Street side, the derivative. The activity on the Main Street side is supposed to dictate what happens with the derivative—the dog is supposed to wag the tail. That is what happens in our examples of hedging. But what often happens—some would say, what *inevitably* happens—is that at some point the *tail wags the dog.* Wall Street investors—speculators—buy or sell the derivative in overwhelming numbers, and the Main Street underlying asset is severely impacted.

This is what happened in the oil market. In 2008 when gasoline was over four dollars per gallon, oil analysts like Fadel Gheit and Antonia Juhasz, and hedge fund managers like Michael Masters (not to mention the airlines, oil refineries, and trucking companies who set up the web site www.StopOilSpeculationNow.com) provide evidence that 50% or more of the price you were paying at the pump for gasoline was caused by speculators running up the price of the Oil Futures Contract. A bubble in the derivative due to Wall Street Investment activity severely impacted Main Street: how much you paid for gas at the gas station.

Something similar happened in the mortgage market: the sudden emergence of massive trading in Collateralized Debt Obligations (CDOs) created a massive increase in banks making subprime mortgage loans. Then the sudden near-total unwillingness on the part of investors to buy any CDOs starting in August 2007 brought an immediate end to banks making any more subprime loans. The tail wagged the dog. The activity with the derivatives (the CDOs) almost completely dictated the Main Street activity for the underlying asset—both the sudden, widespread availability of these new subprime loans, and the even more sudden almost complete disappearance of subprime loans from the mortgage market.

Note that the terms CDO and MBS are often, and quite rightly, used interchangeably. But you should also be aware that when one says MBS or "mortgage securities," they could be referring either to CDOs or credit default swaps (CDS: insurance against the failure of subprime mortgage derivatives) so you have to pay attention to the context and may want to use the terms CDO or CDS *only*, in order to avoid confusion when describing the mortgage meltdown.

Financial Crisis Timeline[††]

Don't feel like you need to know every detail from this timeline. Just try to get the main ideas about the events and actions taking place at the time, and any specifics your teacher mentions.

November 12, 1999: Key Deregulation—the Gramm-Leach-Bliley Act (GLB), also known as the Financial Services Modernization Act (FSMA) overturns the 1933 Glass-Steagall Act (GSA). The GSA was a law to keep Wall Street firms and activities such as securitizing, gambling and speculating separate from Main Street firms and activities such as deposits and home loans. While the 1999 GLB Act tore down that firewall between Wall Street and Main Street, which stood to protect the latter from the former for 66 Depression-free years, it did leave intact the GSA's other creation, the FDIC.

December 21, 2000: Key Deregulation—he Commodity Futures Modernization Act of 2000 ensured that derivatives (including CDS) would not be regulated by any direct federal or state rules, which included the elimination of capital requirements, transparency, and preemption of state laws that prohibited derivatives transactions as gambling or otherwise illegal. Part of the CFMA included the "Enron Loophole" deregulation which helped enable Enron's electricity speculating that caused blackouts and Californians' electric bills to multiply in the summers of 2000 and 2001.

August 2007: The market for mortgage derivatives dries up and becomes illiquid, meaning almost no one will buy the CDOs. New CDOs cannot be issued since existing CDOs are of unknown value or sharply reduced values. So the huge volume of subprime loans that had been issued abruptly slows to a trickle. With no investors to sell mortgage

[7]Some timeline information is from http://money.cnn.com/news/storysupplement/economy/bailouttracker/.

derivatives comprised of subprime loans, there was no more reason for Wall Street to continue subprime lending.

Dec. 31, 2007: By the end of 2007, 1.3 million homes are in foreclosure proceedings.

March 11, 2008: The Federal Reserve (the "Fed") makes an early foray into backing major investment banks in what ultimately would represent their lending, guaranteeing, or buying assets in amounts that total several trillion. Most of that was loaned or guaranteed against possible losses and never had to be spent, but the Fed has expanded its balance sheet by a few trillion, most of which it should recover. The Term Securities Lending Facility (TSLF) program started in 2008 committed up to $200 billion in T-bills in a temporary swap for mortgage securities.

March 16, 2008: JP Morgan Chase agrees to buy Bear Stearns, one of the half-dozen major Wall Street investment banks (founded 1923) for about a billion dollars. The Fed provided a $29 billion loan to cover the deal. Bear Stearns collapsed when "hedge funds" it owned were heavily invested in suddenly illiquid (thus temporarily worthless) CDOs.

July 11, 2008: FDIC seizes and shuts down insolvent bank IndyMac, supplying $10 billion to cover insured depositors. It is one of the first of about 80–100 banks per year over the next three years that the FDIC seizes and shuts down before the bank completely plunges into bankruptcy.

July 30, 2008: Help For Homeowners Act housing bill authorizing up to $300 billion in loan guarantees for a selected group of borrowers, at lender's option. Predicted actual cost at the time: $68 billion. (See footnote #6) To date: $20 billion actually spent.

Sept. 7, 2008: Treasury takes ownership of the GSEs (founded 1938, privatized in 1969 and 1984), committing up to $200 billion to back up their losses and ensure Fannie and Freddie bondholders will be paid off.

Sept. 13, 2008: Lehman Brothers, a major investment bank (founded 1850) is bankrupt due to credit default swaps and subprime investments. It is the one example in this crisis where a "Too Big to Fail" firm actually was allowed to fail, and many or most analysts say that inaction accelerated and needlessly worsened the crisis.

Sept. 14, 2008: After having already acquired ailing subprime lender CountryWide, Bank of America doubles down and buys Merill Lynch (founded 1914) for $50 billion before their eminent collapse due to investments in mortgage securities. Merill Lynch simultaneously pays executives $3.6 billion in bonuses.

Sept. 16, 2008: The Fed takes ownership of the collapsing insurance giant AIG (founded 1919) as it buckled under the payout demands required as a major provider of credit-default swaps. The $85 billion backstop at the time was later increased, when combined with other programs, to guarantee up to $182 billion, of which $127.4 billion was actually spent.

Sept. 26, 2008: Washington Mutual (founded 1889) is acquired by JP Morgan for about two billion dollars, despite the major deposit-taking bank having net assets with a nominal value of $240 billion on paper. Again, bad mortgage investments were the cause. The sixth largest bank in the country, WaMu saw over $16 billion withdrawn by depositors over a ten day period, amounting to almost 10% of its deposits before the FDIC blew the whistle and shut it down.

Oct. 3, 2008: The Treasury's TARP (Troubled Asset Relief Program) passes into law and offers up to $700 Billion to buy toxic mortgage securities. About half of that would be actually spent.

Oct. 3, 2008: Wachovia (founded 1906), the fourth-largest bank holding company in the nation, is bought by Wells Fargo for $15.1 billion as mounting mortgage losses were forcing them into bankruptcy.

Oct. 14, 2008: Treasury announces that instead of buying toxic assets, the TARP funds will be used to buy new stock shares (equity) in all major banks. Buying or temporarily swapping safe assets for toxic mortgage derivatives is mostly left to the Fed.

Nov. 23, 2008: Treasury increases its investment in Citigroup to $45 billion, to own about a third of the company, and Fed and FDIC agree to cover up to 90% of $306 billion in potential losses (Citigroup itself is responsible for the first $29 billion in losses), although the government has not had to pay on any of that. Government's ownership of the firm decreases to 18% by August 2010.

Dec. 31, 2008: By the end of 2008, 2.3 million homes are in foreclosure proceedings

Feb. 18, 2009: Making Home Affordable Program is launched, which includes four programs to help borrowers[‡‡]. The primary vehicle is called the Home Affordable Modification Program through which qualified borrowers have mortgage payments reduced to 31% of their income. While still offering a loan modification at the lender's option, the program reverses the incentive some middlemen (called loan servicers) had to collect more fees by pursuing foreclosure. The program pays $500, $1000, and $1,500 amounts to the loan servicers, lenders, or investors who make the loan modification happen. Initially stated cost: up to $75 billion. Amount actually invested, loaned, or spent as of late 2009: $350 million[§§]. Permanent loan modifications completed through the program as of April 2010: 300,000[¶¶].

Dec. 31, 2009: By the end of 2009, 2.8 million homes are in foreclosure proceedings. 870,000 foreclosure were finalized and the homes repossessed, about the same number as in 2008.

July 1, 2010: In the first six moths of 2010, 1.7 million homes are in foreclosure proceedings. Banks have repossessed about 528,000 homes over the period.

As I implied at the start of this timeline, this is information for your reference and to deepen your understanding of the Subprime Crisis and Credit Crunch, not something you need to memorize in detail.

Nevertheless, if you feel this is getting to be a bit too much information or too many numbers, you can skip the next two sections and go straight to the In-Class Project and Discussion Question Sets at the end

---

[8]http://makinghomeaffordable.gov/about.html.

[9]http://bailout.propublica.org/programs/ 6-making-home-affordable.

[10]http://makinghomeaffordable.gov/pr_05172010.html.

of this chapter. You already have read enough to complete those activities. If you are ready for more context, read the last two segments.

Fannie Mae and Freddie Mac

The commonly used nickname for the Federal National Mortgage Association is Fannie Mae and the nickname for the Federal Home Loan Mortgage Corporation is Freddie Mac.

The two mortgage giants (also referred to as the GSEs—government sponsored enterprises) started by the Federal Government with specific "charters" directions as to how to operate and parameters around the loans they can own or insure, now totaling about half of all U.S. mortgages. In other words, they have unique regulations that do not apply to other private sector financial institutions. Fannie Mae and Freddie Mac were privatized, with their shares traded in the stock market until they were re-nationalized and taken over by the Federal Government in September of 2008. It was widely perceived that these two shareholder-owned private sector firms retained the implicit backing of the government. The perception was that the government would rescue them if they got in trouble. Before their nationalization, July 30, 2008[***] legislation added some confirmation to this perception.

That law authorized "the government until the end of 2009, to lend them emergency money or buy" stock in Fannie and Freddie. Without specific limits, this unlimited cushion rendered them even more quasi-public in an attempt to shore up the dwindling investor confidence that had cost both GSEs the majority of their stock's share value. The Treasury worked out a deal to cover up to $200 Billion in Fannie and Freddie losses in return for 80% ownership of the two mortgage giants[†††].

This summary of the early history of Fannie Mae and Freddie Mac describes what mortgage lending was like before the GSEs existed.[‡‡‡]

Mortgages in the Depression Era

> Fannie and Freddie are the products of an earlier and larger mortgage meltdown. During the Great Depression, 50% of borrowers were late or in default on their mortgages (sound familiar?) and banks became dangerously strapped for cash. So President Franklin D. Roosevelt and Congress created the Federal National Mortgage Association (Fannie Mae) in 1938. The agency's mission was to buy mortgages from lenders, providing liquidity that could be used to make more loans.
>
> Fannie Mae's creation allowed lenders to loan money to low- and middle-income buyers who otherwise might not have been considered creditworthy. According to the St. Louis Federal

---

[11]http://money.cnn.com/2008/07/30/news/economy/housing_bill_Bush/index.htm?postversion=2008073010 and http://money.cnn.com/2008/07/26/news/economy/housing_bill_Senate/.

[12]http://money.cnn.com/2008/09/07/news/companies/fannie_freddie/index.htm?postversion=2008090711.

[13]http://library.hsh.com/articles/government-programs/fannie-mae-freddie-mac-and-you.html.

Reserve[§§§], mortgage lending before Fannie Mae was very different from the way it is done today. Lenders typically required 50% down payments. Moreover, they usually structured their home loans with short terms—terms as brief as five years, after which the borrower had to come up with a "balloon payment" for the remaining balance. As a result, homeownership was out of reach for most American households.

Fannie Mae and Freddie Mac's charters specify roles that they should take in promoting homeownership affordability. If your parents own their homes, chances are it's because of Fannie Mae that they were able to finance their purchases.

Freddie Mac: Fannie Mae's Younger Brother

Fannie Mae grew so large over the years that in 1968, with the pressures of the Vietnam War straining the national budget, President Lyndon Johnson took Fannie Mae's debt portfolio off the government's balance sheet. Fannie Mae was converted into a publicly traded company owned by investors. Two years later, the Federal Home Loan Mortgage Corporation (Freddie Mac) was launched, mainly to keep Fannie Mae from functioning as a monopoly. Freddie went public in 1989. Freddie Mac's guidelines and pricing structure are almost identical to Fannie Mae's.

Also note that the GSEs "went public," meaning they now were owned *not* by the government but by shareholders who own their publicly traded shares. In other words, Fannie Mae was privatized in 1969 as was Freddie Mac in 1984, and both were re-nationalized in 2008.

Standard & Poor's (S&P) is a U.S. financial services company with a 150-plus year history. An S&P study[¶¶¶] shows only 4% of GSE loans outstanding in late 2009 were to borrowers with credit scores below 620. Their research also shows that even for the lowest credit score loans (under 620), the default rate is 13–16% in late 2009, deep into the mortgage crisis. This rate, while historically high, is far lower than the rates for private-label securitized subprime loans.

A Chicago Federal Reserve study[****] shows that, after controlling for credit scores and many other variables, GSE loans defaulted at lower rates than non-GSE loans. While Fannie and Freddie had 13–16% default rates for sub-620 borrowers, 40–60% of subprime loans held outside of the GSEs were in default, a number that only increases as this crisis goes on.

More specifically, the Chicago Fed study shows that from 2004–2006, Lender Processing Servicing data (a lending research service) indicates that less than 5% of subprime loans were purchased by the GSEs. A higher percentage in 2007 is largely due to the shutdown of the subprime

---

[14]http://www.stlouisfed.org/publications/cb/articles/ ?id=797.

[15]http://www2.standardandpoors.com/spf/pdf/fixedincome/Housing_GSEs.pdf. (Ed. note: see Page 9, Table 3.)

[16](http://papers.ssrn.com/sol3/papers.cfm? abstract_id=1406594).

market; so the portion that GSEs purchased became a third of all subprime loans purchased, but the total number of subprime loans being made had sharply fallen. While some of these statistics may be cherrypicked data based on the dates, the totality of the evidence shows that the GSEs at most enabled the crisis and were clearly not the sole cause.

Finally, in an article[††††] for McClatchy Newspapers on October 12, 2008 headlined "Private sector loans, not Fannie or Freddie, triggered crisis," David Goldstein and Kevin G. Hall write: "More than 84 percent of the subprime mortgages in 2006 were issued by private lending institutions." And: "In 2005 and 2006, the private sector securitized almost two thirds of all U.S. mortgages, supplanting Fannie and Freddie, according to a number of specialty publications that track this data." And: "Fueled by low interest rates and cheap credit, home prices between 2001 and 2007 galloped beyond anything ever seen, and that fueled demand for mortgage-backed securities, the technical term for mortgages that are sold to a company, usually an investment bank, which then pools and sells them into the secondary mortgage market. About 70 percent of all U.S. mortgages are in this secondary mortgage market, according to the Federal Reserve."

In essence, a major cause (many would argue, the main cause) of the mortgage crisis was mortgage securities, aka derivatives, in this case known as the MBS, CDOs, and CDS. Yet the GSEs were essentially giant securitizers. So isn't the whole thing their fault? The question then becomes, how exactly did GSE-based government assistance in the mortgage market, which began in 1938, cause a subprime bubble from 2003–2007 and subsequent financial meltdown from 2007 to the date of this writing in 2010?

Did Government Cause the Crisis?

It is insightful to include the reasoning that government intervention caused the subprime bubble and mortgage crisis. As expressed in the flagship conservative magazine, *National Review*, the GSEs are secondarily responsible but the primary fault is with the mortgage interest tax exemption and other misplaced tax incentives to own and/or "flip" properties.

The following is excerpted from the *National Review* article, "The Committee to Reinflate the Bubble" by Kevin D. Williamson published June 8, 2009:[‡‡‡‡]

> Policies that encourage and reward homeownership are deeply embedded into our government and financial institutions, from the mortgage-interest deduction to the FHA loan. It's a case of the best of intentions producing the worst of economics.

---

[17]http://www.mcclatchydc.com/2008/ 10/12/53802/private-sector-loans-not-fannie.html.

[18]http://nrd.nationalreview.com/article/?q=YjU3ZTIyYjI5MTRkNjRiYWVhNTkzODU2NjVlYTMyMjc=.

Consider the case of the government-sponsored enterprises (GSEs), Fannie Mae and Freddie Mac, which are at the center of the current meltdown. The GSEs created a market for poorly assessed real-estate securities based on mortgages implicitly guaranteed by the U.S. government, but doing this made it easier and cheaper for people to get mortgages, so nobody much bothered. Their mission was encouraged, and sometimes distorted, by political forces left and right. There was tremendous political pressure from Barack Obama's community-organizing gang to get banks and institutions to loosen lending standards. The most frequently cited example of this is the Community Reinvestment Act, the effects of which probably have been overstated, but there is no denying that for a decade Barney Frank labored furiously against Republican efforts at tightening Fannie oversight. At the same time, tax-cutting Republicans zealously defended the mortgage-interest deduction, which did much to encourage interest-only loans during the boom—and added a new tax break, the capital-gains tax exemption for home sales, the effects of which are only now becoming clear.

The Taxpayer Relief Act of 1997 might well have been called the House Flippers' Enabling Act, and it put a lot of money into the pockets of a lot of realtors: The law exempts most home sellers from paying capital-gains taxes on houses, without requiring them to invest the profits in new houses. It created what might be called a literal tax shelter: an investment you could live in while escaping the 20 percent tax on capital gains. When the dot-com bubble burst, the lure of tax-free real assets attracted a lot of investors looking to ride out market turbulence in the comfort of their new, highly leveraged homes. Republicans love a capital-gains tax cut, and they should, but creating special tax breaks for particular investments inevitably will warp the market. Predictably, capital gushed out of dot-bomb and into the housing bubble.

The result was the sort of thing that should offend every conservative's inner Puritan: Buyers stopped calculating whether they could afford the house, and instead calculated whether they could afford the mortgage. The more daring buyers took out interest-only mortgages, placing a counterintuitive bet that buying a house they couldn't afford would make them rich enough to afford it. That bet was hedged up by what is probably the most popular item in the U.S. tax code: the mortgage-interest deduction. That made interest-only loans a sweet deal indeed for the investors with good timing, which set off a rodeo of speculation: borrow the whole nut, pay nothing but interest (which, thanks to the work of Alan Greenspan, might be less than rent would have run), get a huge income-tax benefit in return thanks to the mortgage-interest deduction, sell the house at a profit, and pay

> no taxes on the capital gain. Place a losing bet and you end up bankrupt or in foreclosure.

So certain misplaced tax incentives and the GSEs, Fannie Mae and Freddie Mac, were to blame for the bubble. There is some causality between Mr. Williamson's targets and the crisis, but it is limited and, more importantly, presents some vital questions about what exactly are the policy implications of this narrative?

Regarding the GSEs, recall from the section on Fannie Mae and Freddie Mac above that they bought a minority percent of subprime loans, made only a tiny percentage (4%) of their loans to people with very poor credit, and have a much lower loan default rate than loans made or owned by private banks and investors.

Additionally, the loans they did buy from private investment banks had agreements that if the loans are found to have fraudulent borrower information, the banks have to repurchase (buy back) these bad loans from the GSEs. So, as always, much depends on enforcement, which in this case means how aggressively the court cases are prosecuted to force banks to make good on their repurchase obligations. "Fannie and Freddie require lenders or loan servicers to sign contracts requiring those firms to repurchase loans that don't meet certain standards relating to borrower incomes, job status or assets. Loans that were extended fraudulently, or deemed to have been predatory, are also candidates for buybacks."[§§§§]

But if we accept for argument's sake that the GSEs were to blame, recall what life was like before the GSE (see the section on Fannie Mae and Freddie Mac). Borrowers faced five or ten years to pay the mortgage off, a fifty percent down payment, huge balloon payments, and a reality where middle-class homeownership is virtually nonexistent and impossible under those conditions. If the policy proposal is removing the GSEs from the picture, where are borrowers to turn? Williamson's promotion of "tightening Fannie oversight"—increasing regulation of the GSEs—seems to make more sense than calls for their total elimination.

Regarding the mortgage interest tax deduction, which allows homeowners to receive thousands of dollars in tax refunds for interest paid each year on their home loan, Williamson may be right that it played a role in the crisis. But the policy implication to eliminate this fundamental tax benefit for homeowners would face an uphill battle finding political support or passing legislatively, to put it mildly. The Taxpayer Relief Act of 1997 which he criticizes may be easier politically to do something about, and even repeal, but it is striking to hear a generally anti-tax magazine argue convincingly against these two tax cuts.

CONCLUSION

Many different groups (homeowners, brokers, banks, etc.) and even social phenomena (greed, groupthink, deregulation, etc.) had a hand in the subprime crisis which induced the Great Recession, the longest

[19]http://topics.nytimes.com/top/news/business/columns/fair_game/index.html?scp=1-spot&sq=fair%20game&st=cse.

and deepest downturn since the Great Depression. If any of the links in this chain had acted more prudently, the catastrophe could have been lessened or even stopped cold in its evolution. To most people, grasping the significance of this crisis requires new concepts and buzzwords like derivatives, mortgage securities, credit default swaps, and securitization. For economists, this crisis provides countless case studies of old concepts like bubbles, moral hazard, and too big to fail. It became a sounding board and test case for policy prescription. Forward-thinking economists like Robert Shiller and Dean Baker saw the crisis coming and proposed policies to proactively deal with the crash that was coming soon. Time will tell if policymakers and their advisors have learned enough that they can deal better with the next disaster that may threaten the communities, neighborhoods, and cities that comprise this nation.

DISCUSSION QUESTIONS: (SET 1)

1. Who is to blame?

There is plenty of blame to go around in the subprime/financial/banking/mortgage crisis.

Explain how each of these groups were to blame, and specify which were primarily to blame (can you argue for a number one, most at-fault group?) and which groups were more peripheral (only blameworthy in a narrow or limited sense) or fairly blameless.

The groups to analyze (in no particular order) are:

1. Mortgage borrowers
2. Lenders
3. Brokers
4. Mortgage derivative investors/ derivatives themselves
5. Investment banks ("securitizers")
6. Ratings Agencies
7. Banking and other Regulators including the Fed, SEC, OTS, Congress, and others
8. Politicians
9. Appraisers
10. Fannie Mae and Freddie Mac (the GSEs)
11. Anyone or anything else to blame?

2. To what extent is assigning blame simply a time-wasting blame-game, and to what extent does it give us useful insights in dealing with the current crisis and preventing future financial meltdowns?

3. Once the banks have received bailouts and other assistance from the federal government and the Federal Reserve, name several things taxpayers would like the banks to do with that money? What are several uses of that money taxpayers would least like for the banks to select? How can the government's response be designed so that taxpayers get what they want out of the banks in terms of how the bailout money is spent?

IN-CLASS PROJECT

Subprime Mortgage Meltdown/Banking Crisis Group Work

By David Moglen

Directions:

Once you are assigned a group number from (from Group 1–7 below), take five to ten minutes to meet with your group, and begin planning how you will coordinate your responses. Then everyone should go read the links (articles) assigned to your group, and type your rough draft answers to the questions. When your group emails their rough answers to each other, start to synthesize the best parts of your members' contributions into one answer you are happy with for each question. **Alternatively**, you may want to lessen your workload by coordinating with your group so that question 1 assigned to your group (let's say you are Group 3 below, for instance) is done by person A, person B is responsible for question 2, etcetera. Your group should determine what is the most fair distribution of the questions for your members.

When you have your answers finalized, put all your names on the top of the first page and staple all your pages together. Your teacher will pick whatever questions they feel are most pertinent for your group to answer verbally, explaining your group's response to that question.

Group 1

http://www.counterpunch.org/toussaint01122008.html.

1. What are the roots of the financial crisis according to the article?
2. What is a CDO and what is a CDS? How do CDOs figure into the current crisis? To answer this, you might want to think about what happened to subprime lending when the CDO market dried up (meaning the CDO became something no one would buy) as described in paragraph 15:

> The SIVs mentioned previously specialize in selling CDOs (Collateralized debt obligations) that many investors have been trying to get rid of since August 2007. As of mid-December 2007, default repayments of CDOs had reached a sum of 45 billion dollars . Since August 2007, the issuing of new CDOs has stopped as a result of the severity of the crisis.

3. How does the author describe risks and costs of the crisis will be shifted, i.e. who will bear the burden, and who should bear the burden?
4. Describe at least 2 of the financial "time bombs" for the economy mentioned in paragraph 20.

http://blogs.wsj.com/economics/2008/10/23/greenspan-testimony-on-sources-offinancialcrisis/.

1. Why does Greenspan say, "I see no choice but to require that all securitizers retain a meaningful part of the securities they issue." Explain in terms that would make sense to someone who has never taken an economics class.

Group 2

The own-to-rent solution:

http://tpmcafe.talkingpointsmemo.com/2007/08/19/own_to_rent_the_way_to_save_su/.

1. What is the own-to-rent solution? Who elects the option, and at what point? What if the bank sells the house?
2. How does this plan affect neighbor homeowners?
3. How is the current crisis a Wall Street vs. Main Street conflict?

http://money.cnn.com/2008/07/14/news/economy/fedrules/index.htm?cnn=yes.

1. What did you think of the fact that a rule had to be passed against mortgage brokers "saying a rate is fixed when it can change"? How do mortgage brokers gain from the situation where they have been allowed to call a variable, adjustable rate mortgage "fixed"? How is the borrower impacted?
2. What did you think of the fact that "In a nod to the brokerage industry, the Fed withdrew a proposal requiring additional disclosure of the 'yield-spread premium,' which allows banks to pay brokers for steering homeowners into higher-priced loans"? What incentives do these payments create for brokers? Why should these payments be legal or illegal?

Group 3

http://www.nytimes.com/2007/12/06/washington/06cnd-debt.html.

1. "Secretary Henry M. Paulson Jr. argued that lenders should try to work out new terms on a case-by-case basis. But Mr. Paulson and federal banking regulators became increasingly impatient with the industry's failure to produce a systematic, rapid approach to evaluating borrowers." Why is there a "but" in this quote? Is there a conflict between Sec. Paulson's desire for a systematic resolution and his reluctance to regulate?
2. Explain why this is or is not a problem in the mortgage (home loan) market: "Some analysts say that more than a third of all subprime borrowers could have qualified for cheaper conventional loans at the outset."
3. President Bush said: "Some borrowers took out loans they knew they could not afford. And to compound the problem, many mortgages are packaged into securities and sold to investors around the world." It's clear enough how the first sentence says borrowers are partly to blame. Explain how the second sentence says someone else is also to blame.

Critique of Dec. '07 plan:

http://www.illinoisattorneygeneral.gov/pressroom/2007_12/20071206b.html.

1. Illinois Attorney General Lisa Madigan on the Dec. 07 law is critical of the White House Plan—why is she critical?
2. Analyze how effective at least two of her proposals will be to address the crises.

Group 4

http://www.rollingstone.com/politics/story/29127316/the_great_american_bubble_machine. (Editor's note: make sure you click "next" to read all pages of the article.)

1. What are the bubbles that occurred and what was Goldman Sachs role in each (describe separately)?

2. How are these bubbles similar?
3. What is the next bubble Taibbi foresees and what is Goldman's role in that?
4. How did Goldman make money when the housing market collapsed and other financial institutions were taking massive losses?
5. Which activities during the Internet IPO craze and subprime housing boom were illegal enough that Goldman paid a fine or settled litigation with the claimants? What was the impact of these legal cases on Goldman's behavior?
6. What tax rate did Goldman pay and how does that compare to its CEO's pay and other employee compensation statistics?

Group 5

http://www.propublica.org/article/banks-favorite-toothless-regulator-1125. Esp. photograph, even just photo and caption if rights too much/too show.

1. What is the significance of this article's 2003 photo to banks and non-bank financial institutions like AIG and Countrywide?

Be sure to describe the relevance of the following people (A and B specified below) to be posing in such a photo-op:

> This photo from 2003 shows two regulators: (A) James Gilleran of the Office of Thrift Supervision (holding the chainsaw) and John Reich (then Vice Chairman of the FDIC and later at the OTS, second from right), along with (B) representatives of three banker trade associations. (FDIC/OTS file photo)

2. What is regulator shopping?

3. Explain how two specific actions by the Office of Thrift Supervision contributed to the subprime bubble. The two specific actions mentioned in the article were (1) with regard to appraisers and (2) when the "Office of the Comptroller of the Currency (OCC) ... made a move to ... make sure that borrowers could afford their monthly payments on adjustable rate loans after the rate reset".

Opinion Survey:

http://www.gallup.com/poll/106114/Six-Oppose-Wall-Street-Bailouts.aspx.

1. Do Americans lean toward helping banks or struggling homeowners? How is this poll asking a Wall Street vs. Main Street question?

2. What questions were asked in the poll? How would you respond to these questions, and why?

3. What is the "too big to fail" concept?

*4. What does this mean? "In fact, swooping in to rescue struggling homeowners could be crucial in offsetting consumer resentment toward the Fed over its Wall Street bailout."

Group 6

Fannie Mae bailout suggested by (Treasury Secretary) Paulson:
www.businessweek.com/bwdaily/dnflash/content/jul2008/db20080715_178267.htm.

1. What are Paulson's proposals and what is the argument for why they would help?

2. What does this mean? "If you have a squirt gun in your pocket, you may have to take it out," he said. "But if you've got a bazooka in your pocket, you may not have to take it out."

3. What is naked short selling, why do some consider it a problem, and who temporarily banned the practice?

The Financial Reform Bill of 2010, a.k.a. the Dodd-Frank Act.

http://www.nytimes.com/2010/06/27/business/27gret.html?_r=1&ref=fair_game.

http://www.economist.com/node/16481494.

1. What are the three best parts of the Dodd-Frank Act and what are its three worst aspects? Use quotes and reasoning in your own words to support your answer.

2. "Much depends on how American regulators implement its provisions." What will be the main factors determining the effectiveness and enforcement of provisions in the Dodd-Frank Wall Street reform bill?

*3. Explain why you predict it will be effective reform or why/where do you think it will be (in the article's description) on the spectrum between "interpret(ing) the new rules in the friendliest possible way to Wall Street" and regulatory "overreach—stifling innovation"?

4. Which of these did the new Dodd-Frank Act do something to address (pick the best answer):

A. Fannie Mae and Freddie Mac

B. Too big to fail

C. Exact implementation guidelines for affected agencies

D. Securitizers are required to retain part of the securities they issue

5. Which of these did the new Dodd-Frank Act **fail** to address:

A. Creating a Consumer Financial Protection Agency

B. Creating a resolution authority—a system of orderly "winding down" of troubled financial firms

C. GSEs

D. Rules about banks' involvement in derivatives

Group 7

http://www.forbes.com/2008/09/26/wamu-morgan-deposits-oped-cx_lw_0926white.html.

1. What accounts for the huge gap between "The net assets acquired by JP Morgan Chase had a nominal value of around $240 billion" and the $1.9 billion JP Morgan paid for WaMu's Assets?

2. How does having JP Morgan Chase take over WaMu have benefits and also pose threats to the economy? Hint: you might include how this and similar takeovers can worsen and improve the "too big to fail" problem. Propose another solution for Washington Mutual that would have been more ideal than the JP Morgan takeover.

http://www.bis.org/publ/work163.pdf. (See pages 10–12.)

A report about the Bond Rating Agencies including the concept of "Ratings Shopping,"

1. What is ratings shopping?

2. What is the concern or fear about what can happen when investment banks who create CDOs are allowed to decide which agency will rate the instrument?

3. Why isn't there the same fear (induced by the possibility of ratings shopping) you see with derivatives such as CDOs when it comes to the same agencies rating typical corporate bonds?

*4. Who are the three major credit rating agencies for Personal Credit—the ones who determine your credit rating?

*5. Why isn't there a possibility for rating shopping in the personal credit market? What would be the effects if there was that possibility?

*6. How would such a standard (the same one as for personal credit) work for rating derivatives such as CDOs?

DISCUSSION QUESTIONS

All group questions with an * above can be omitted from the small-group assignment and posed to the whole class, in addition to the overall queries listed below.

1. What insights can we learn from the subprime crisis/financial meltdown that apply to other crises, and can help avoid future catastrophes?

2. Are there some ways in which the subprime crisis/financial meltdown are so unique that fixing the flaws that led to it will not prevent future crises?

3. In what ways is the Financial Crisis of 2007 macroeconomic and how is it microeconomic?

1. What insights can we learn from the subprime crisis/financial meltdown that apply to other crises, and can help avoid future catastrophes?

2. Are there some ways in which the subprime crisis/financial meltdown are so unique that fixing the flaws that led to it will not prevent future crises?

3. In what ways is the Financial Crisis of 2007 macroeconomic and how is it microeconomic?

CHAPTER 15
Fiscal Policy and Deficits

15 Fiscal Policy and Deficits

By Neva Goodwin, Julie Nelson, and Johnathan Harris

What happens when economic conditions are not good—when the economy enters a slowdown or recession? We often hear of the need to "stimulate" the economy. Sometimes political leaders advocate tax cuts or a variety of specific government spending programs. The common-sense idea behind this is that more spending, either by individuals and families who receive tax cuts, or by government, will create demand for goods and thereby expand employment and output. In terms of the macroeconomic theory sketched out in Chapter 9, these policies are intended to *increase aggregate demand,* generating positive *multiplier effects.* That sounds good. But critics sometimes argue that such policies will create other problems, such as large government deficits or inflation. The analysis of such issues is the subject of this and the next two chapters.

1. THE ROLE OF GOVERNMENT SPENDING AND TAXES

Economists often disagree about what tax and spending policies are best in different economic situations. These debates are about **fiscal policy**—what government spends, how it gets the money it spends, and the effects of these activities on GDP levels. To understand these issues, we need to extend the simple macroeconomic model of Chapter 9 to include the role of government.

fiscal policy: government spending and tax policy

In Section 3 of this chapter, we will also introduce another step toward realism in our model of the economy by adding the international sector—exports and imports.

Bringing in the role of the government, the equation for aggregate demand used in previous chapters becomes:

$$AD = C + II + G$$

Government spending by federal, state, and local governments (G) is added to aggregate demand since it represents additional goods and

Neva Goodwin, Julie Nelson, and Johnathan Harris, *Macroeconomics in Context*, pp. 234–254.

services purchased. Taxes do not appear directly in this equation, but, as we will see, they have an impact through their effect on consumption spending.

We will examine the effects of these changes to our model one at a time, starting with the impact of a change in government spending.

1.1 A CHANGE IN GOVERNMENT SPENDING

Government spending (*G*) has a direct impact on the level of GDP. When the government purchases goods and services, this adds to aggregate demand, boosting equilibrium output. In Chapter 9 we showed how a decline in intended investment lowered the *AD* line, leading to equilibrium at a lower level of income. This suggests that government spending might be used as an antidote to low investment spending.

Suppose we start with the macroeconomic equilibrium that we showed in Chapter 9, Table 9.5 and Figure 9.14. Remember that this was an unemployment equilibrium. If we start at an unemployment equilibrium, additional aggregate demand will be needed to get back to full employment. Our first model assumed no government role; hence initial government spending (*G*) is equal to zero. Thus a simple policy would be to increase government spending on goods and services from 0 to 80. As you can see in Table 10.1 and Figure 10.1, the addition of 80 units of government spending causes the equilibrium to shift up by 400, to the full employment Y^* of 800. Why does this happen?

Let's look at a simple example—a new building construction program. Government money is spent to purchase goods such as concrete and steel, as well as to pay workers. This directly creates new aggregate demand. In addition, there are multiplier effects—construction workers will spend their paychecks to buy all kinds of consumer goods and services. The multiplier effects add to the original economic stimulus resulting from the government spending.

The effect is exactly the same as the multiplier for intended investment that we discussed in Chapter 9. The initial change in government spending ΔG becomes income to individuals (ΔY), which leads to a round of consumer spending ΔC equal to *mpc* ΔY, which in turn becomes income to other in individuals, leading to another round of consumer spending, and so forth. The whole process can be summarized using the same formula as in Chapter 9, but now applied to government spending rather than intended investment:

$$\Delta Y = \frac{1}{1 - mpc}\Delta G$$

or

$$\Delta Y = mult\ \Delta G$$

Using the same *mpc* and multiplier as before (we had chosen the example where $mpc = 0.8$, resulting in $mult = 5$), this allows us to predict the impact of government spending on economic equilibrium. The multiplier applies to government spending in exactly the same way that it does to changes in intended investment. Therefore an increase in government spending of 80 leads to an equilibrium shift of 80 × 5 = 400. Looking at it the other way, if we start with the goal of an increase of 400 in Y, we can divide 400 by 5 to find the needed quantity of ΔG: 400/5 = 80.

Note that at the original AD level, there is an equilibrium at 400, where $AD = Y$, and there is significant unemployment. After the addition of 80 in government spending (G), the new equilibrium is at the full-employment level of 800, where $AD_1 = Y$. (You can check other levels in the table to make sure that this is the only level at which $AD_1 = Y$) Figure 10.1 shows the same thing graphically. The aggregate demand schedule moves up by 80 at each level of income, so that the horizontal intercept of the AD line moves up from 80 to 160. The slope of the AD line remains the same, since there has been no change in the *mpc*. The change in equilibrium income is equal to the change in government spending times the multiplier.

Using the multiplier, we can easily calculate the effect of further changes in government spending. For example, suppose government spending were reduced from 80 to 60. This negative change of 20 in G would lead to a change of 5 × (−20) = −100 in equilibrium Y. Income would fall from 800 to 700.

So we can see that an increase in government spending will raise the level of economic equilibrium, while a decrease in government spending will lower it. The multiplier effect, which is the same size in both directions, gives the policy extra "bang for the buck"—in this case, a change in government spending leads to five times as great a change in national income. In real life the multiplier is rarely this large (see Appendices A2 and A3 for an algebraic treatment of some reasons why real-world multipliers tend to be lower), but there will usually be some multiplier effects from a change in government spending. Econometric studies of the U.S. economy generally indicate a multiplier effect of 2.0 or less.

1.2 TAXES AND TRANSFER PAYMENTS

To complete the picture of fiscal policies, we need to include the role of taxes and transfer payments. If voters and government officials do not want to raise government spending, they have another option. To raise GDP, the government could cut taxes and/or increase **transfer payments.** Transfer payments are government grants, subsidies, or gifts to individuals or firms.

Examples of transfer payments include Social Security payments and payments of interest to holders of government bonds.

---

transfer payments: payments by government to individuals or firms, including Social Security payments, unemployment compensation, and interest payments

---

In recent decades the fiscal tool most often chosen by policymakers has been tax reductions. (Tax reductions, of course, tend to be politically popular in addition to providing economic stimulus.) Increases in

Table 10.1 An Increase in Government Spending

(1) Income (Y)	(2) Consumption (C)	(3) Intended Investment (II)	(4) Original Aggregate Demand ($AD = C + II$)	(5) Government Spending (G)	(6) New Aggregate Demand ($AD_1 = C + II + G$)
300	260	60	320	80	400
400	340	60	400	80	480
500	420	60	480	80	560
600	500	60	560	80	640
700	580	60	640	80	720
800	660	60	720	80	800

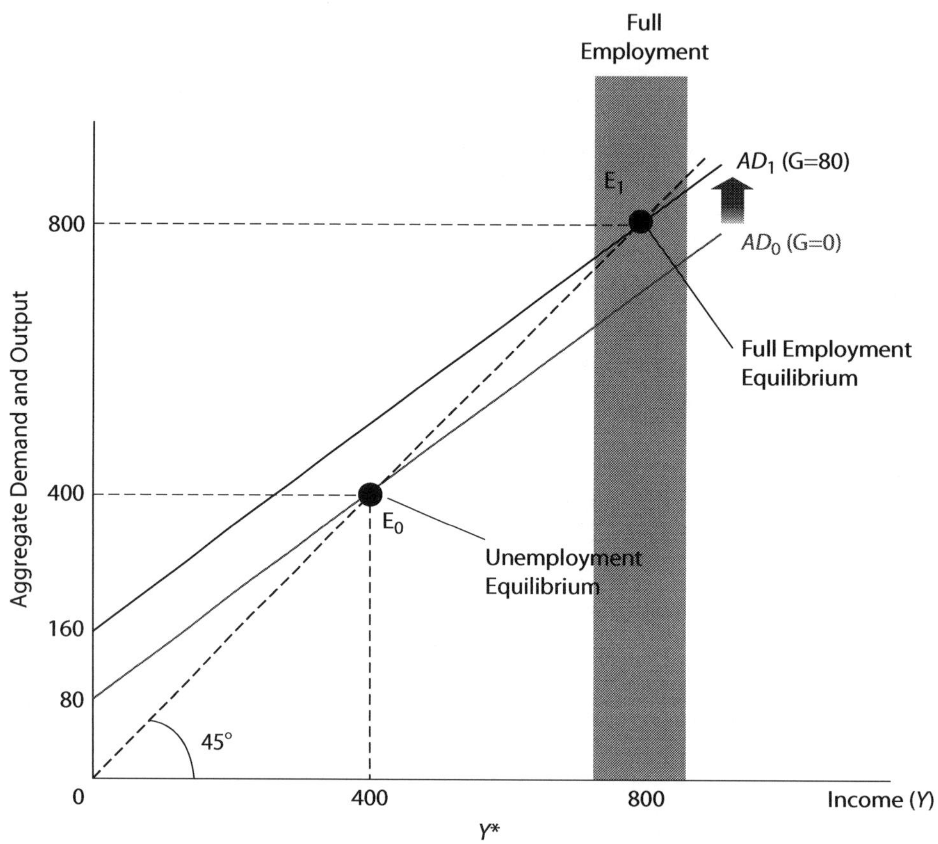

FIGURE 10.1

Increased Government Spending

An increase in government spending has a similar effect to an increase in private fixed investment. It shifts the AD line upward, as government spending rises. This increases the equilibrium levels of income and output.

transfer payments would have the same general positive effect on aggregate demand. The opposite policies—increasing taxes or decreasing transfer payments—would have a negative effect on economic equilibrium, similar to a reduction in government spending.

Changes in taxes and transfer payments, however, are not exactly similar to changes in government spending. The mechanism by which tax and transfer changes affect output differs from the process discussed above for government spending. While government spending *directly* affects aggregate demand and GDP, the effect of taxes and transfer payments is *indirect,* based on their effect on consumption or investment. There are many kinds of taxes and transfers, including corporate taxes, tariffs, and inheritance taxes, but we will focus here on the effects of changes in personal income taxes and transfers to individuals.

For example, let's say consumers receive a tax cut of 50. If they spent it all, that would add 50 to aggregate demand. But according to the "marginal propensity to consume" *(mpc)* principle, consumers are likely to use some portion of the tax cut to increase saving or reduce debt. With the *mpc* of 0.8 that we used for our basic model in Chapter 9, the portion saved will be $0.2 \times 50 = 10$, leaving 40 for increased consumption. Thus the effect on aggregate demand would be only 40, not 50 (since saving is not part of aggregate demand).

The same logic would hold if consumers received extra transfer income of 50. They would spend only 40, and save 10. The reverse would be true for a tax increase or a cut in transfer payments. With a tax increase or benefit cut of 50, individuals and families would have less to spend, and would reduce their consumption by 40.

Economists define **disposable income** (Y_d) as the income available to consumers after paying taxes and receiving transfers:

$$Y_d = Y - T + TR$$

where T is the total of taxes paid in the economy and *TR* is the total of transfer payments from governments to individuals.

---

disposable income: income remaining for consumption or saving after subtracting taxes and adding transfer payments

---

Changes in taxes (T) or transfer payments directly affect disposable income, but only indirectly affect consumption and aggregate demand. Hence their impact on economic equilibrium is less than that of government spending, which affects aggregate demand directly.

For this reason, the multiplier effects of changes in taxes and transfer payments are less than the multiplier impacts of government spending. If taxes are "lump sum"—that is, set at a fixed level that does not change with income, then we can write $T = T$. The **tax multiplier** for a lump sum tax works in two stages. In the first stage, consumption is reduced by *mpc* (ΔT), which can be expressed as:

$$\Delta C = -(mpc)\, \Delta T$$

In the second stage, this reduction in consumption has the regular multiplier effect on equilibrium income. The combined effect can be expressed as:

$$\Delta Y = (mult)\ \Delta C = -(mult)\ (mpc)\ \Delta T$$

The tax multiplier is equal to $\Delta Y / \Delta T = -(mult)\ (mpc)$. Mathematically, *(mult)(mpc)* always works out to exactly 1.0 less than the regular multiplier. (You can use the multiplier formula from Chapter 9 to work out why this is true.) Using the figures from our previous example, where *mpc* = 0.8 and *mult* = 5, the tax multiplier would be –(0.8)(5) = –4. (For a more detailed algebraic account of the tax multiplier for a lump sum tax, see Appendix Al.)

tax multiplier: the impact of a change in a lump sum tax on economic equilibrium, expressed mathematically as $\Delta Y / \Delta T = -(mult)\ (mpc)$

Just as a tax increase has a contractionary effect, a tax cut will have an expansionary effect. Historically, tax cuts played an important role in U.S. economic policy in the 1960s, 1980s, and 2000s. In all cases, the effect on GDP was expansionary (though there is debate about the exact mechanism through which this occurred—not all economists accept the simple tax multiplier process that we have discussed).

Transfer payments, which as we noted are a kind of "negative tax," affect the level of output through a similar logic. An increase in transfer payments, like a tax cut, will give people more money that they can spend. But the expansionary effect only occurs when they actually do spend—so, according to the *mpc* logic, the impact of an increase in transfer payments is reduced by whatever portion of the extra income people decide to save. The multiplier impact of a change in transfer payments is therefore the same as that of a change in taxes, except in the opposite direction. A cut in transfer payments, like an increase in taxes, will be contractionary, tending to lower economic equilibrium.

In the real economy, income taxes are generally proportional or progressive—that is, they increase with income levels (as discussed in Chapter 3). In our model, the effect of a proportional tax would be to *flatten* the aggregate demand curve, since it has a larger effect at higher income levels. (See Appendix A2 for a more detailed treatment of the impact of a proportional tax—we omit analysis of progressive taxes, which is a bit more complex.) This in turn will affect the multiplier, reducing it somewhat.

How can we explain the effect of a proportional tax on the multiplier? Taxes that rise with income will tend to lower the proportion consumed out of each dollar increase in income. For example, with a 15 percent tax each extra dollar of income will be reduced to 85 cents of disposable income. Applying our original *mpc* of 0.80 to the remaining 85 cents, we get $0.8 \times 0.85 = 0.68$, indicating that 68 cents will be devoted to consumption (and 17 cents to saving). The result is similar to having a lower *mpc,* which also means a lower multiplier. This will damp down the effect of income changes on aggregate demand and economic equilibrium.

You might wonder what would be the effect of an increase in government spending that is exactly balanced by an increase in taxes (a balanced budget)? Since we have shown that the multiplier effect of taxes goes in the opposite direction from that of government spending, it might appear that the effects would cancel out. But this is not the case. Because the tax multiplier is less than the government spending multiplier, there is a net positive effect on aggregate demand and equilibrium. The difference between the two multipliers is equal to one, so the net multiplier effect will also be equal to one. In the example we have used, the government policy multiplier is 5, and the tax multiplier is 4, so the **balanced budget multiplier** = 5 – 4 = 1. Thus the impact on economic equilibrium is exactly equal to the original change in government spending (and taxes). So we can say that $\Delta Y = \Delta G$.

For example, an increase of $50 billion in government spending, balanced by an equal increase of $50 billion in taxes, would be expected to lead to a net increase in equilibrium output of $50 billion. One way of thinking about this is to consider that the original government spending boosts GDP, but its multiplier effects are cancelled out by the negative multiplier effects generated by the tax increase. This results in a weaker net effect than government spending of $50 billion alone, which would lead to $\Delta Y = (mult)\ \Delta G = 5\ \Delta G$, or $250 billion in this example.

balanced budget multiplier: the impact on equilibrium output of simultaneous increases of equal size in government spending and taxes. The multiplier is equal to positive l, showing that the effect on GDP is equal in size to the original change in government spending and taxes.

1 .3 EXPANSIONARY AND CONTRACTIONARY FISCAL POLICY

These three fiscal policy tools—changes in government spending, changes in tax levels, and changes in transfer payments—will affect income and employment levels, as well as inflation rates. They will also, of course, affect the government's budgetary position. The budget could be balanced, in surplus, or in deficit, depending on the combinations of spending and tax policies that are employed.

Increasing government spending is an example of what economists refer to as **expansionary fiscal policy.** Another expansionary fiscal policy would be to increase transfer payments or to lower taxes. Whether through a direct impact on aggregate demand, or through giving consumers more money to spend, these policies will increase aggregate demand and equilibrium.

expansionary fiscal policy: the use of government spending, transfer payments, or tax cuts to stimulate a higher level of economic activity

If that was the whole story, macroeconomic policy would be simple—just use sufficient government spending or tax cuts to maintain the economy at full employment. But there are complications. One problem is that in order to spend more, the government either has to raise taxes, borrow, or "print money." (Issues of how government finances its expenditures will be discussed later in this chapter and in Chapter 11.) Raising taxes would tend to counteract the expansionary effects of increased spending. Borrowing money creates deficits and raises long-term government debt, which may or may not be a problem—we'll discuss this in Section 2 of this chapter.

Another problem is that too much government spending may lead to inflation. The goal of expansionary fiscal policy is to bring the economic activity up to its full-employment level. But what if fiscal policy overshoots this level? It's easy to see how this might occur. Government spending on popular programs is easy for politicians, and raising taxes to pay for them is hard. This can lead to budget deficits (discussed in Section 2 below), but it can also cause excessive aggregate demand in the economy. Excessive demand could also, in theory, arise from high consumer or business spending, but usually government spending, alone or in combination with high consumer and business expenditures, is partially to blame when the economy "overheats." The result is likely to be inflation.

According to our basic analysis, the cure for inflation should be fairly straightforward. If the problem is too much aggregate demand, the solution is to reduce aggregate demand. This could be done by reversing the process discussed in the previous section, and lowering government spending on goods and services. A similar effect can be obtained by reducing transfer payments or by increasing taxes. With lower transfer payments and/or higher taxes, businesses and consumers will have less spending power. Lower spending by government, businesses, and consumers will result in a lower equilibrium output level, and there will no longer be excess demand pressures creating inflation.

Thus we have identified another important economic policy tool—**contractionary fiscal policy.** This is a weapon that can be used against inflation, though it would generally be unwise to use it at times of high unemployment. (The problem of what to do if unemployment and inflation occur at the same time—something that isn't shown in our simple model—will be discussed in Chapter 12.) Of course, too large a spending reduction could overshoot in a downward direction, leading to excessive unemployment and possibly a recession.

---

contractionary fiscal policy: reductions in government spending or transfer payments, or increases in taxes, leading to a lower level of economic activity

---

Although the effects of contractionary fiscal policy can be painful, it would be wrong to assume that expansionary fiscal policy is always beneficial, and contractionary policy always harmful. Contractionary policy can be essential when previous policies have "overshot" the goal, or when the economy is suffering from inflation. We'll discuss this issue of policy choice a lot more in this and the following chapters.

Discussion Questions

1. What recent changes in government spending or tax policy have been in the news? How would you expect these to affect GDP and employment levels?
2. Tax increases are generally politically unpopular. Would you ever be likely to favor a tax increase? Under what circumstances, if any, might a tax increase be beneficial to the economy?

2. BUDGETS, DEFICITS, AND POLICY ISSUES

The federal government budget includes spending on goods and services, transfer payments and taxes. (This is also true of state and local government budgets, but our focus for purposes of fiscal policy analysis is mainly on the federal budget.) Thus we can break down total government expenditures, or **government outlays,** into two categories. Total government outlays include not only government spending on goods and services (*G*) but also government transfer payments:

$$\textit{Government Outlays} = G + TR$$

government outlays: total government expenditures including spending on goods and services and transfer payments.

On the revenue side, government income comes from taxes (*T*). When revenues are not sufficient to cover outlays, the government borrows to cover the difference. The actual financing of a deficit is accomplished through the sale by the United States Treasury of **government bonds**—interest-bearing securities that can be bought by firms, individuals, or foreign governments. In effect, a government bond is a promise to pay back, with interest, the amount borrowed at a specific time in the future.

government bond: an interest-bearing security constituting a promise to pay at a specified future time

Current federal sources of revenue and outlays are shown in Figure 10.2. The major sources of federal revenue are personal income and Social Security taxes. In fiscal 2006, the federal government also borrowed an amount equal to 9 percent of the total budget. Government borrowing varies from year to year, but deficits are more common than surpluses. The major categories of government spending are Social Security, defense spending, and social programs. Interest payments on the debt amounted to 8 percent of federal spending in fiscal 2006.

Clearly, government borrowing and interest payments on the debt will have economic impacts. What is the nature of these impacts? To answer this question, we need to look more carefully at the nature of government deficits.

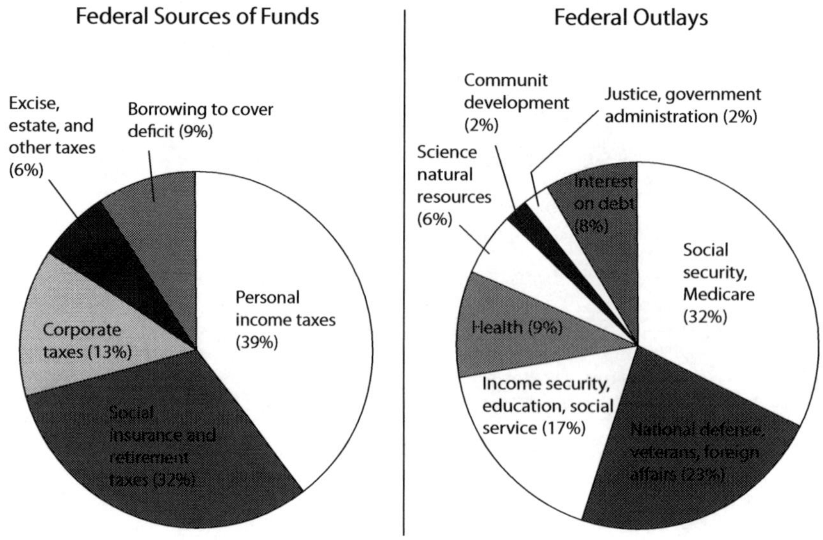

FIGURE 10.2

U.S. Federal Government Source of Funds and Outlays, Fiscal 2006

The largest sources of federal revenues are personal income and Social Security taxes. Part of the budget—in 2006, 9 percent—is covered by borrowing (issuing government bonds). Net interest on the debt represented 8 percent of federal outlays. (Source: *Economic Report of the President,* 2007, Table B-81.)

2.1 THE GOVERNMENT BUDGET: SURPLUS AND DEFICIT

First, we need to define what we mean by the *government budget surplus or deficit.* This can be calculated by subtracting total government outlays from total government tax revenues. A positive result indicates a surplus; a negative one, a deficit.

Budget Surplus (+) or Deficit (–)
= T – Government Outlays
= T – (G + TR)

Showing the government's deficit as a percentage of nominal GDP is a simple way to correct the numbers for the effects of both inflation and the ability of the economy to handle the deficit. The larger the economy—as measured by GDP—the easier it is to manage a given deficit, since both the fiscal and budgetary impacts of the deficit will be smaller relative to the size of the economy. A bigger economy means that people will have higher incomes, and are likely to be willing to purchase more government bonds, making it easier for the government to borrow.

State and local governments are generally required to separate their current spending and capital budgets. Current spending must be paid for out of current taxes, but money can be borrowed for investment ("capital") projects such as new schools, bridges, and transit systems. The federal budget, however, makes no such distinction between current and capital spending.

During the period 1992–2001, the U.S. federal government budget went from a large deficit to a surplus (Figure 10.3). Then in 2002 the government budget went back into deficit. Since 2004 the deficit has moderated a bit, but it is projected to continue in future years. This has

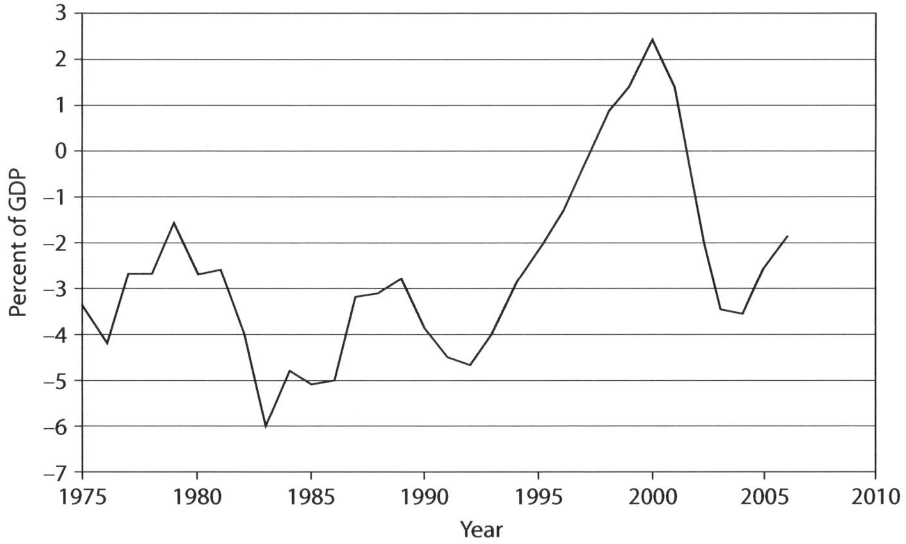

FIGURE 10.3

Federal Surplus or Deficit as a Percentage of GDP

The federal deficit—as measured by its borrowing—reached 6 percent of GDP in 1983, a year of deep recession. The deficit was reduced as a percent of GDP from the early 1990s until 1998, when the budget went into surplus. From 1998 to 2001, the government actually had a surplus in its budget (so that it retired some of its debt). After 2000, a recession combined with the Bush administration tax cuts put the budget back into deficit. (Source: *Economic Report of the President,* 2007, Table B-79.)

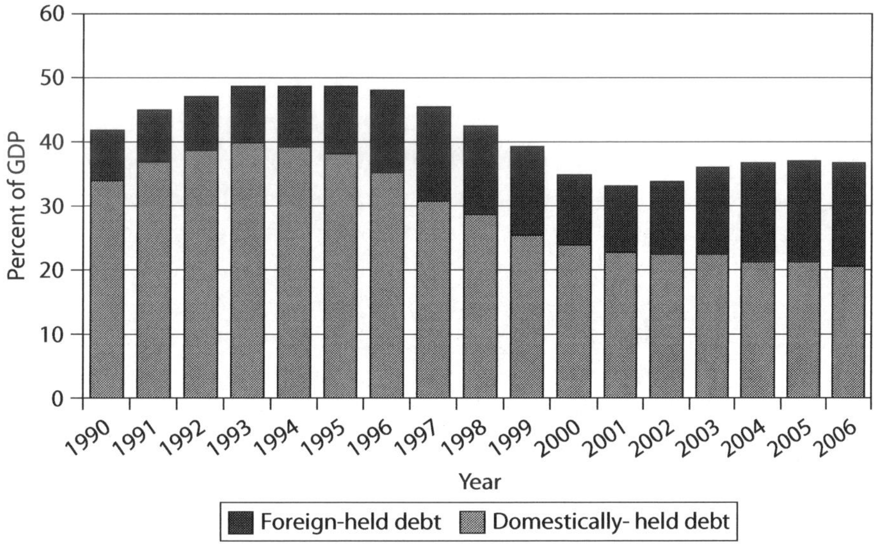

FIGURE 10.4

Government Debt Held by the Public as a Percentage of GDP

In the second half of the 1990s government debt (the tall line) fell as a percentage of GDP, as a result of government budget surpluses and strong GDP growth during that period. In 2002, it began to rise, as a result of the rising deficits of that period along with slower growth of *GDP. Throughout, the fraction of the government debt that was owed to foreign citizens and governments (the shorter segment of each tall line) has increased significantly as a proportion of total debt in recent years, amounting to 44 percent of all federal debt in 2006.* (Source: *Analytical Perspectives, Budget of the United States Government, Fiscal Year 2008,* Table 16-6.)

led to an extensive debate about the impact of deficits on the economy. In this section, we examine this question and other issues related to the government budget and fiscal policy. As we will see, there is much continuing controversy, both among economists and the general public, about the significance of budgetary policy and deficits, and many different ideas about the best way to handle issues of government spending, taxes, and transfer payments.

Perhaps because the two terms sound so much alike, many people confuse the government's deficit with the *government debt.* But these two "D words" are very different. The deficit totaled about $248 billion during 2006, while federal debt owed to the public equaled about $8 *trillion* at the end of 2006. The reason why the second number is more than thirty times as large as the first is that the debt represents deficits accumulated over many years. In economists' terms, we can say that the government deficit is a *flow variable* while its debt is a *stock variable.* (See Chapter 3 for this distinction.)

The government's debt *rises* when the government runs a deficit and *falls* when it runs a surplus. Figure 10.4 shows some recent data on the government's debt, again measured as a percentage of GDP. This percentage was fairly steady during the period 1993–1996. After 1996, growth in GDP, combined with a government budget that moved from deficit into surplus, reduced debt as a percent of GDP from nearly 50 percent down to about 33 percent. The government debt started rising again as GDP growth slowed and as deficits became positive in the 2000s.

What is the impact of government debt on the economy? One commonly expressed view of the government's debt is that it represents a burden on future generations of citizens. There is some truth to this assertion, but it is also somewhat misleading. It implicitly compares the government debt to the debt of a private citizen. Certainly, if you personally ran up a huge debt, this would not be a good thing for your financial future. But government debt is different in some important ways.

First, most of the government debt is owed to U.S. citizens. When people own Treasury bills (T-bills), Treasury notes, or Treasury bonds, they own government IOUs. From their point of view, the government debt is an asset, a form of wealth. If your grandmother gives you a U.S. Savings Bond, she is giving you a benefit, not a burden. These assets are some of the safest ones you can own.

Second, the government debt does not have to be paid off. Old debt can be "rolled over," i.e., replaced by new debt. Provided that the size of the debt does not grow too much, the government's credit is good—there will always be people interested in buying and holding government bonds. Most economists use the rule of thumb that as long as the government's debt does not rise significantly faster than GDP for several years in a row, it does not represent a severe problem for the economy. The government debt is currently a smaller percentage of GDP (less than 40 percent) than it was immediately after World War II (when it was more than 100 percent). The fact that this debt was not a severe burden is indicated by the relative economic prosperity of the 1950s and 1960s.

Third, the U.S. government pays interest in U.S. dollars. A country such as Argentina that owes money to other countries and must pay interest in a foreign currency (the U.S. dollar) can get into big trouble and go bankrupt. But it is much easier to manage a debt that is denominated in your own currency. Even if some of the debt is owed to foreigners we do not have to obtain foreign currency to pay it. And so long as foreigners are willing to continue holding U.S. government bonds, it will not be necessary to pay it at all—instead, the debt can be rolled over as new bonds replace old ones.

But this should not encourage us to believe that government debt is never a concern. Rising debt creates several significant problems. First, interest must be paid on the debt. This means that a larger share of future budgets must be devoted to paying interest, leaving less for other needs. It is true that most of this interest goes to U.S. citizens who hold government bonds. But it is also true that the largest holders of government bonds tend to be wealthier people, so that most of the interest paid by the government goes to better-off individuals. If this payment is not counteracted by changes in the tax system, it encourages growing income inequality. It also creates a problem of generational equity—future taxpayers will have to pay more interest because of government borrowing today.

A second problem is that in recent years an increasing proportion of the debt has been borrowed from foreign governments, corporations, and individuals (Figure 10.4). The interest payments on this portion of the debt must be made to those outside the country. That means that the United States must earn enough income from exports and other sources to pay not only for imports, but also for interest payments to the rest of the world. Alternatively, the country could borrow more, but it is best to avoid this solution in the long run. It also poses another problem—what if those foreign debt holders decided to sell the U.S. bonds they hold? In that case the government might have trouble finding enough people who are willing to hold government bonds (that is, lend money to the government). As we will see in Chapter 13, this could cause interest rates to rise sharply, which in turn would push the government budget further into deficit. Some painful belt-tightening would be needed as a result.

The question "is government debt worth it?" can only be answered if we consider what that debt was used to finance. In this respect, an analogy to personal or business debt is appropriate. Most people—including economists—do not reject consumer and corporate debt—rather, our judgment about debt depends on the benefits received.

For example, if debt is accumulated for gambling, it is a bad idea. If the bet doesn't pay off, then it is very difficult to pay the interest on the debt (not to mention the principal). But if borrowing is done to pay for intelligently planned investment, it can be very beneficial. If the investment leads to economic growth, this raises the ability of the government to collect tax revenue, so this kind of borrowing can pay for itself, as long as the investment is not for wasteful "pork barrel" spending, poorly planned or unnecessary projects, etc. Even if the debt finances current spending, it can be justifiable if it is seen as necessary to maintain or protect valuable aspects of life. Most people would not be opposed to borrowing to pay for clean up after a natural disaster or to contain a deadly pandemic. How about for military spending? Opinions will differ about whether particular defense expenditures are necessary to maintain or protect valuable aspects of life. But wasteful spending, or spending on unwise defense policies, would constitute a drag on more productive economic activity (as suggested by the production-possibilities curve "guns-versus-butter" analysis introduced in Chapter 2).

The management of debt involves standard principles of wise stewardship of finances. When we apply them to government deficits and debt, we will need to weigh the economic benefits of different spending and tax policies. In the following sections, we will look at some of the issues involved in the evaluation of fiscal policy.

2.2 AUTOMATIC STABILIZERS

Since the 1950s, government spending has been a major part of the U.S. economy. As we have seen, this was partly a result of the Keynesian idea that government spending was needed to prevent recession. In recent decades, the use of expansionary fiscal policy has been controversial, partly as a result of issues such as deficits and inflation. During this period, however, total government outlays (including transfers and spending on goods and services) have not gone down, either in money terms or as a percent of GDP.

As Figure 10.5 shows, government receipts and outlays tend to fluctuate over time. For example, during the period from 1992 to 2000, when the economy was generally expanding, government receipts rose and outlays fell. Economists refer to this as the **automatic stabilization** effect of government spending and taxes. This refers to the way in which the government budget moderates fluctuations of aggregate demand even without any active decision-making or legislating by the government.

automatic stabilizers: tax and spending institutions that tend to increase government revenues and lower government spending during economic expansions, but lower revenues and raise government spending during economic recessions

Even if no specific budgetary action is taken, the government's budget will vary over the business cycle. Suppose the economy is entering a recession. As aggregate demand falls, the government deficit generally rises. Tax revenues fall as falling GDP reduces people's incomes. In addition, more people receive unemployment insurance and "welfare" payments. If the agricultural sector declines, more farmers receive farm-support payments. This limits the fall in personal disposable income—and thus the fall in consumer spending.

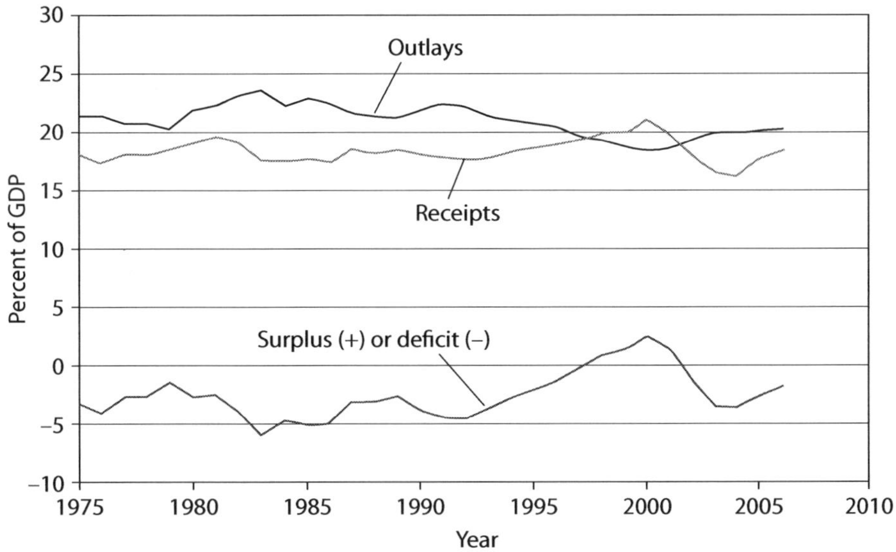

FIGURE 10.5

Federal Government Outlays, Receipts, and Surplus/Deficit as a Percentage of GDP

Federal government outlays as a percent of GDP have not changed much over the last thirty years. Tax receipts tend to rise during economic expansions and fall during recessions, leading to higher federal deficits in recession years such as 1975–76, 1982–83, 1991–92, and 2001–2. The Reagan tax cuts in the 1980s and the Bush tax cuts in the 2000s further lowered tax receipts and increased deficits. (Source: *Economic Report of the President,* 2007, Table B-79.)

If the federal government does not actively move to balance its budget, these automatic changes in spending and taxes tend to moderate the recession. In effect, the recession creates an automatic response of expansionary fiscal impacts—increased spending and lower taxes. It will also, of course, tend to increase the government deficit (or reduce any surplus).

Similarly, if aggregate demand is rising during an economic expansion, tax revenues rise. Fewer people receive unemployment or "welfare" payments, and farmers receive fewer subsidies if demand for agricultural products increases. This means that personal disposable income does not rise as quickly as national income. This in turn puts a damper on increases in consumer spending—and limits the inflationary over-heating that can arise from increased aggregate demand.

This phenomenon helps explain why the U.S. government was able to enjoy budgetary surpluses in the late 1990s. It is true that the policies of the Clinton administration, which included raising tax rates to try to balance the budget, contributed. But as private investment and consumer demand soared, this allowed the government's coffers to fill.

In addition to the automatic stabilizers, the federal budget has another aspect that levels the fluctuations of output. This is the steadiness of government spending. Unlike investment, consumer spending, net exports, and to some extent state and local government spending, most areas of federal spending do not change drastically from year to year. This adds an element of stability to the economy's aggregate demand.

Economics in the Real World: Fiscal Policy and the 2001–2007 Expansion

It is well known that, starting in 2001, federal policies in the United States have emphasized tax cuts. What is less well known is that during the same period federal spending has risen significantly. Between 2001 and 2006, total federal outlays rose from $1,863 billion to $2,655 billion, an increase of 43 percent. As a proportion of GDP, federal outlays rose from 18.5 percent to 20.3 percent during these years, while total federal revenues fell from 19.8 percent to 18.4 percent of GDP (see Figure 10.5). These combined changes in outlays and revenues led to a significant increase in the federal deficit (Figure 10.3).

Both tax cuts and spending increases are expansionary policies. Since the economy entered a recession in March 2001, it is reasonable to suggest that these expansionary policies contributed to the recovery that started in 2002 (see Figure 9.1 in the previous chapter); Real GDP grew at annual rates of between 2.5 percent and 3.6 percent per year from 2003 through 2006, and continued strong through the third quarter of 2007 (the last period for which data are available as of this writing).

Was this expansion partly a result of fiscal policy? Certainly government spending played an important role in increasing employment. Between 2001 and November 2007, total employment in the United States rose 4.5 percent, gaining about six million jobs. Of these new jobs, about 1.5 million jobs were created in the government sector—about 25 percent of the total gain in employment. Thus increased government spending directly accounted for a large proportion of the net gain in lobs over this four-year period.

According to the analysis of fiscal policy developed in this chapter, we would expect that both increased government spending and lower tax levels would have positive multiplier effects on GDP The pattern of recovery and expansion in the economy during 2001–7 is consistent with this analysis. Classical economists would generally reject the idea that increased government spending can be beneficial to the economy, arguing that the Incentive effects of lower taxes were the key factor in promoting recovery. Keynesian economists would suggest that both increased spending and tax cuts contributed to the recovery, but that tax cuts would have been more effective if targeted to middle- and lower-income families, who tend to have a higher marginal propensity to consume.

Whether the impact of government policies is felt more on the "demand side" (as Keynesian economists would suggest) or on the "supply side" (consistent with classical views), it seems that fiscal policies of increased spending and reduced taxes under the Bush administration had an expansionary effect on the economy—whether or not that was the deliberate intent.

Sources: *Economic Report of the President*, 2007; U.S. Department of Labor, Bureau of Labor Statistics; and the U.S. Bureau of Economic Analysis.

2.3 DISCRETIONARY POLICY

Sometimes the automatic stabilization effect of government spending and taxes cannot smooth economic ups and downs as much as is desired. Relatively severe problems of recession or inflation often give rise to proposals to use an active fiscal policy to remedy the situation. This issue is one that arouses more controversy among economists. Some economists, as we will see, believe that the government should *never* use activist fiscal policy—that it is likely to do more harm than good.

Others believe that it should be used, but with caution. Regardless of economists' advice, the fact is that governments are making fiscal policy all the time, whether in a planned or unplanned manner. Each year the government revises its budget, including levels of spending and taxation. These spending and tax levels have effects on the economy, and it is important to try to understand them.

Historically, the first major experience with expansionary fiscal policy was during World War II. Prior to the war, President Franklin D. Roosevelt's New Deal had initiated some government spending programs intended to put the unemployed to work during the Great Depression. But these programs were dwarfed by the size of war spending in the 1940s. As a result, unemployment, which had been as high as 25 percent in 1933 and 19 percent in 1938, fell to about 2 percent by 1943.[*] The fall in unemployment was a beneficial side-effect of the onset of World War II and the war-induced spending.

After World War II, government spending never returned to prewar levels, and it seemed that the beneficial effects of the expanded government role—steady economic growth with relatively low unemployment levels—justified this. In the 1960s, economists became even more optimistic about the benefits of fiscal policy. At that time, it was suggested that it would be possible for the government to "fine-tune" the economic system using fiscal policy, to ratchet aggregate demand up or down in response to changes in the business climate.

"Fine-tuning" was largely discredited in the 1970s and 1980s, as the economy struggled with inflationary problems that were partly a result of sharp increases in oil prices, but were also seen as having been worsened by excessive government spending (we'll look at this in more detail in Chapter 12). In addition, many economists argued that problems of **time lags** made fiscal policy unwieldy and often counterproductive.

---

time lags: the time elapsing between the formulation of an economic policy and its actual effects on the economy

---

To understand the problems with fine-tuning and time lags, we can use a common-sense example. Imagine that your apartment is too cold, so that you turn up the temperature on the thermostat. It might take so much time for the apartment to warm up that you do not get the benefits before you leave for work. You then might become impatient, raising the temperature again. In that case, it could easily happen that the apartment gets too hot, so when you return home you have to turn the thermostat down again. Thus delayed responses make your management of the apartment's temperature less effective. The best strategy is to set the thermostat at a single temperature and then to resist fiddling with it.

[*]Employment figures for that era covered a labor force in which a much lower proportion of women were seeking jobs than is the case today. During World War II, an unusually large number of women were employed, filling jobs left vacant by men who were serving in the armed forces.

Similarly, time lags can make active fiscal policy less effective as a way to stabilize the economy. There are two types of lags: *inside* and *outside* lags. Inside lags refer to delays that occur within the government, while outside lags refer to the delayed effects of government policies. There are four major types of inside lags:

1. A *data lag*: It may take some time for the government to collect information about economic problems such as unemployment.
2. A *recognition lag*: Government decision-makers may not see an event as a problem right away.
3. A *legislative lag*: Discretionary fiscal policy must be instituted in the form of legal changes in the government's budget. The government's economists may want to increase spending or decrease taxes, but they have to convince both the president and Congress to act to solve the problem.
4. A *transmission lag*: These legal changes take time to show up in actual tax forms and government spending budgets. One solution is that changes can be made retroactive to speed up their implementation—for instance, a tax cut legislated now may apply to income received during the last year. However, this is not always done.

In addition, even if all these lags have been overcome, it takes time for the new policies actually to affect the economy (the "outside lag"). Suppose, for example, that the government responds to a rise in unemployment with increased government spending or a tax cut. By the time these policies are in place and create an economic stimulus, the economy may have recovered on its own. In that case, the extra aggregate demand will not be needed, and is likely to create inflationary pressures.

Despite these problems with discretionary fiscal policy, governments have continued to use it, with mixed results. Government fiscal stimulus, with or without a formal economic justification, was applied during the periods 1964–68, 1975–77, 1980–87, and in the early 2000s. An especially popular form of expansionary policy has been tax cuts, implemented under Presidents Kennedy, Reagan, and George W. Bush. In recent years overt policies of increased government spending have not been viewed favorably, but as Figure 10.5 shows, even conservative presidents have tended to maintain or increase the level of government spending. So while increasing spending is less often advocated as a desirable expansionary policy, it has frequently been practiced.

Proponents of tax cuts sometimes appeal to **supply-side economics** (first introduced during the Reagan administration) to support their policies. The supply-side argument for tax cuts is essentially that lower tax rates encourage more work, saving, and investment, thereby creating a more dynamic economy. According to the most enthusiastic advocates of supply-side economics, output will grow so rapidly in response to a cut in tax rates that total tax revenues will actually increase, not decrease. This is different from the logic of increased aggregate demand that we have discussed, which implies that tax cuts will create an economic stimulus, but are likely to raise the government deficit. The economic record seems to show that tax cuts do indeed create an economic stimulus—but debate continues among economists as to whether this effect is demand-led (as implied by our fiscal policy model) or based on supply-side effects. And in general, tax cuts have usually led to lower revenues and higher deficits (this was true both of the Reagan tax cuts in the 1980s and the Bush tax cuts in the 2000s).

supply-side economics: an economic theory that emphasizes policies to stimulate production, such as lower taxes. The theory predicts that such incentives stimulate greater economic effort, saving, and investment, thereby increasing overall economic output and tax revenues.

2.4 BALANCED BUDGETS AND DEFICIT SPENDING

The long history of federal deficits has led some critics to call for legislation requiring a federal balanced budget. Under this proposal, the U.S. government would be subject to a "balanced budget amendment," compelling it to keep spending equal to tax revenues. Thus the U.S. government's budget would be like the current expenditure budgets of most state and local governments, which are generally required to be balanced.

To many people, a balanced budget amendment sounds good. It would prevent deficit spending and the accumulation of more federal debt. But our discussion of fiscal policy and automatic stabilizers suggests that there are three major problems with this idea:

1. A rule requiring a balanced budget at all times would make it difficult to respond to emergencies such as natural disasters and wars.
2. Every time the economy went into a recession, the automatic increase in the deficit would have to be counteracted by an increase in taxes, a cut in transfer payments, or decreased government spending. This would make the recession worse, since each of these policies decreases aggregate demand. In other words, this kind of rule would destroy the role of the automatic stabilizers.
3. The federal government would not be able to respond to severe recessions such as the Great Depression. Discretionary fiscal policy would be ruled out. Monetary policy (discussed in the next chapter) would still be possible, but many economists argue that monetary policy alone would be insufficient in the case of severe recession.

The theory of fiscal policy presented in this chapter suggests that deficit spending is sometimes necessary, and indeed can be beneficial to the economy. As we have noted, problems may arise when deficits are too large and continue for too long, pushing the government debt up significantly as a proportion of GDP. For this reason, economic judgment is required concerning what level of deficit is "too high." Economists often differ in their opinions on this issue. It is unlikely, however, that the problem can be solved with a single, inflexible rule.

Before we move on to other elements of economic analysis that are relevant to this debate—in particular a consideration of money, monetary policies, and inflation—we need to add one more element to our macroeconomic model—the international sector. In today's economy, it is impossible to get a complete picture of issues of fiscal policy, unemployment, and inflation, without considering the role of international trade and investment flows. We will go into these in greater detail in Chapter 14. But first, we can take some simple steps to add international trade to our basic model, which we will do in the next section.

Discussion Questions

1. "The national debt is a huge burden on our economy." How would you evaluate this statement?
2. Would you favor a federal balanced budget amendment? Why or why not?

3. THE INTERNATIONAL SECTOR

How does trade affect the economy? It is certainly an important factor. Consumers who go to any U.S. shopping mall can't help but notice that a large proportion of the goods are imported. Many U.S. jobs are in industries that depend on export markets. We often hear concern expressed about the **trade deficit.** In 2006, as in many previous years, the U.S. trade deficit equaled about 5.5 percent of gross domestic product. This meant that people in the United States were spending much more on foreign goods and services (importing) than the United States was selling to foreign buyers (exporting). In other words, U.S. net exports (exports minus imports) were negative. In other countries, such as China, the situation is reversed—they are large net exporters. Clearly, it is important to examine how trade, trade deficits, and trade surpluses are related to macroeconomic issues of income, unemployment, and inflation. Here we will look at the relationship of trade to employment and equilibrium income levels; in Chapter 12 we will deal with the question of inflation.

trade deficit: an excess of imports over exports, causing net exports to be negative

3.1 EXPORTS AND IMPORTS

We can introduce trade into our macroeconomic model by adding Net Exports (NX) into the equation for aggregate demand:

$$AD = C + II + G + NX$$

As discussed in Chapter 5, Net Exports (NX) equals Exports minus Imports $(X - IM)$. Exports, like intended investment and government spending, represent a positive contribution to aggregate demand. More exports mean more demand for domestically produced goods and services. Imports, on the other hand, are a negative in the equation. That means they represent a *leakage* from U.S. aggregate demand—a portion of income that is not spent on U.S. goods and services.

Negative net exports (when $X < IM$) therefore represent a net subtraction from demand for the output of U.S. businesses, and a net leakage from the circular flow. A decrease in exports (or increase in imports) tends to reduce the circular flow of domestic income, spending, and output—unless injections such as intended investment and government spending counteract this contraction. On the other hand, an increase in net exports encourages a rise in GDP and employment. For example, if Americans increase their purchases of foreign cars while buying fewer domestic cars, this will lower aggregate demand in the United States (and raise it in other car-exporting countries). On the other hand, if the U.S. computer software industry increases foreign sales, this will raise U.S. aggregate demand and employment.

The multiplier effect for an increase in exports is essentially the same as that for an increase in *II* or *G*. In our model (with a multiplier of 5), an increase of exports of 40, for example, would lead to an increase of 200 in economic equilibrium.

$$\Delta Y = mult\ \Delta X$$

We can use exactly the same logic for a lump-sum increase in imports—the effect on equilibrium income just goes in the opposite direction. An increase in imports of 40 would lower the equilibrium level of income by 200, and a decrease in imports of 40 would raise the equilibrium by 200.

The multiplier logic becomes a little more complicated, however, when we consider how import levels are determined. In general, when people receive more income in an economy that is open to trade, they spend some of it on domestically produced goods and some on imports. The proportion spent on imports, as we noted above, is a "leakage" that does not add to domestic demand. If we want to account for this fully, we need to modify our multiplier logic. The effect is similar to that of a proportional tax on consumption: It will, tend to flatten the aggregate demand curve, and for the same reason. When people receive extra income, some portion of it "leaks" away into imports. This portion does not stimulate the domestic economy, so multiplier effects are smaller and the economic response a bit less dynamic. (For a full treatment of this effect, see Appendix A3.)

In effect, a portion of any aggregate demand increase goes to stimulate *someone else's economy* via imports. Thus American consumers who buy imported goods from Canada are creating jobs and income in Canada, not the United States. Does this mean that imports are bad for the United States? Not necessarily. Two other factors are important to consider. One is that U.S. consumers and U.S. industry benefit from cheaper imported goods and services, raw materials, and other industrial inputs. Another is that at least some of the money spent on imports is likely to return to the United States as demand for exports, which as we have seen stimulates an increase in GDP and employment. Problems can arise, however, when trade deficits (negative net exports) are too large for too long. We will explore this issue further in Chapter 13.

3.2 A Complete Macroeconomic Model with Trade

We have now completed our basic macroeconomic model. We started with a very simple economy, with just consumers and business, then added government spending, taxes, and the international sector. We can sum things up by referring back to the macroeconomic circular flow diagram show in Chapter 9, Figure 9.6. In that simple model, there was one "leakage" from the macroeconomic circular flow (saving), and one "injection" back into the flow (intended investment). As we discussed, the process of macroeconomic equilibrium essentially concerns balancing these leakages and injections.

Now we have a more complex model, with three leakages (saving, taxes, and imports) and three injections (intended investment, government spending, and exports). Taxes and imports are considered leakages because, like saving, they draw funds away from the domestic income-spending flow. Government spending and exports add funds to the flow. We can modify our original circular flow diagram to show all these flows (Figure 10.6).

Macroeconomic equilibrium involves balancing the three types of leakage with the three types of injection. A change in any one will alter the equilibrium level of output. The model we have constructed allows

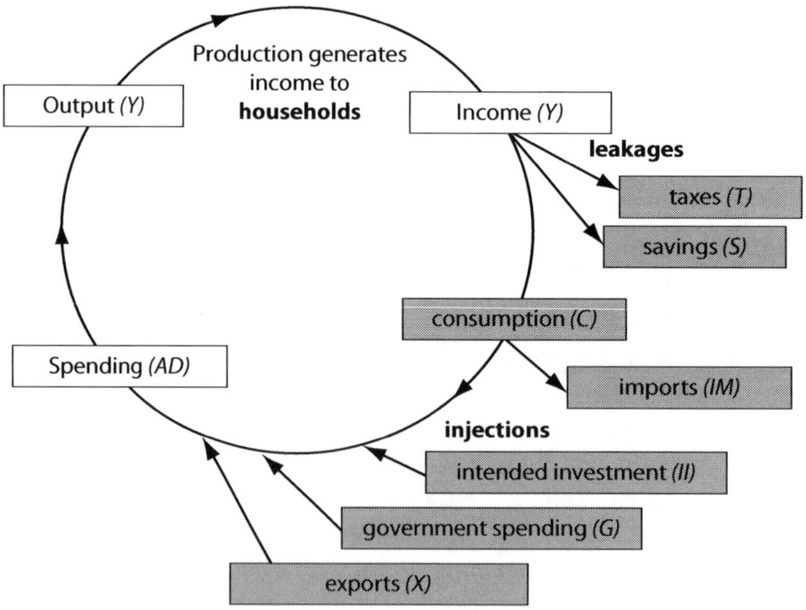

FIGURE 10.6

Leakages and Injection in a Complete Macroeconomic Model

Leakages from the circular flow include taxes, saving, and imports. Injections include intended investment, government spending, and exports. *The level of macroeconomic equilibrium will depend on the balance of all these flows as well as consumption levels.*

us to understand how all these factors are related to levels of income and employment.

Does this complete our study of macroeconomic theory? No, for two major reasons. One reason is that, as we noted in Chapter 9, economists differ about how the economy works at the macro level. Economists in the classical school tend to believe that the leakages, and injections will balance themselves automatically at the full-employment level of output, provided that government does not adversely affect the situation with excessive government spending. Economists of the Keynesian school believe that government policy is essential to achieve acceptable levels of income and employment. We will have a lot more to say about these economic policy debates in the next chapters.

The other reason is that we have yet to consider a very important aspect of the economy: the money supply and monetary policy. The supply of money in the economy is very important factor affecting, among other things, interest rates and inflation. We need to understand how the money supply is created and regulated, and how this relates to other macroeconomic factors. This is the topic of Chapter 11. After we have covered the topics of money and monetary policy, we will return to a consideration of the issues of unemployment and inflation, and appropriate policies to respond to them, in Chapter 12.

Discussion Questions

1. What will be the likely effect of increased imports on U.S. GDP? Do imported goods undercut employment in the United States? What other developments in the economy might counteract this effect?
2. Savings, imports, and taxes are all considered to be "leakages" from aggregate demand. Are they bad for the economy? Or is there an important function for each? How are their levels related to equilibrium GDP, income, and employment?

REVIEW QUESTIONS

1. What is the impact of a change in government spending on aggregate demand and economic equilibrium?
2. What is the impact of a lump-sum change in taxes on aggregate demand and economic equilibrium? How does it differ from a change in government spending?
3. Give some examples of expansionary and contractionary fiscal policy.
4. How is the federal budget surplus or deficit defined? How has the federal budget position varied in recent years?
5. How is the federal debt different from the deficit? How has the federal debt varied in recent years?
6. What is meant by an automatic stabilizer? Give some examples of economic institutions that function as automatic stabilizers.

7. What are some of the advantages and disadvantages of discretionary fiscal policy? Give some examples of the use of discretionary fiscal policy.
8. How would a balanced budget amendment work? What are some of the arguments for and against it?
9. How does an increase in exports affect economic equilibrium?
10. How would an increase in the trade deficit affect economic equilibrium?
11. What are the three leakages and three injections in a complete macroeconomic model? How do they affect the level of economic equilibrium?

EXERCISES

1. Using the figures given in Table 10.1, determine the economic equilibrium for a government spending level of 60.
2. Using Table 10.1 and the formulas and figures given in the text for the multiplier and tax multiplier, calculate the effect on equilibrium GDP of a government spending level of 100 combined with a tax level of 100. What does this imply about the impact of a balanced government budget on GDP, as compared to government spending alone?
3. Go to the *Economic Report of the President* at http://www.gpoaccess.gov/eop/. Consult the most recent *Report's* table on "Gross Domestic Product." For the last year, with final rather than preliminary figures, find the values of gross domestic product personal consumption expenditures, and gross private domestic investment. Now find the value for fixed investment (which is the same thing as what we have called intended investment). You will notice that the column on the right titled "Change in Private Inventories" is equal to the difference between total and fixed investment (just as we have noted that total investment equals intended investment plus change in inventories). Calculate personal consumption expenditures (C) and fixed investment (II) as percentages of gross domestic product (Y). Calculate a simple measure of aggregate demand ($C + II$) without government spending.
4. Continuing from the question above, go to the table "Government Consumption Expenditures and Gross Investment." Find the total for the same year. This is what we have referred to as G (government spending on goods and services). Approximately what percentage is G of gross domestic product? Calculate aggregate demand including government spending ($C + II + G$). Now go to the table "U.S. International Transactions" and look at the column entitled "Balance on Goods and Services" for the same year. This is what we have identified as ($X - IM$). Finally, calculate aggregate demand ($C + II + G + X - IM$). This final figure for aggregate demand should be very close to the gross domestic product (Y)—the difference will be change in inventories and a statistical discrepancy.

5. Which of the following are examples of automatic stabilizers, and which are examples of discretionary policy? Could some be both? Explain.
   a. Tax revenues rise during an economic expansion
   b. Personal tax rates are reduced
   c. Government spending on highways is increased
   d. Farm support payments increase
   e. Unemployment payments rise during a recession
6. Suppose exports (*X*) rise by 120 billion and imports (*IM*) rise by 200 billion, resulting in an increase of 80 billion in the trade deficit. In an economy with an *mpc* of 0.75, what will be the effect of these changes on economic equilibrium? (Calculate the multiplier for this economy using the formula given in Chapter 9, Section 3.7 and repeated on page 235 of this chapter. Then apply this multiplier to the changes in *X* and *IM*.)
7. Match each concept in Column A with a definition or example in Column B.

Column A	Column B
a. Tax multiplier	1. Reduction in income
b. Disposable income	2. Unemployment compensation
c. Expansionary fiscal policy	3. $Y - T + TR$
d. Contractionary fiscal policy	4. Imports
e. Government outlays	5. $G + TR$
f. Automatic stabilizer	6. Reduction in government spending
g. Trade deficit	7. $X < IM$
h. Leakage from circular flow	8. Intended investment
i. Injection into circular flow	9. – *(mult) (mpc)*

APPLY YOUR SKILLS

Deficit and Debt

Useful Equations:

1. G – T= Deficit

   Where G is (total) Government Spending and T is (total) Tax Revenue.

   If T is greater than G, Deficit will be negative. Remove the negative side and call the remaining positive number the Surplus. In other words, **your answer is always stated as a positive number.**

2. Nominal Deficit – Inflation*(Debt) = Real Deficit
3. Structural Deficit + Passive Deficit = Actual Deficit

   (Actual Deficit = Nominal Deficit = Reported Deficit. These three terms all mean the same thing.)

   Passive deficit is that portion of your current, actual total deficit that is caused by your current GDP not being equal to Full-Employment Potential GDP.

   Passive Deficit = t*(Potential GDP – Actual GDP)

   Where t = the overall tax rate in the economy.

   Remember, GDP = Y = Output = Income

4. The National Debt is the sum of all previous deficits, minus any past surpluses.

Directions: Half of the groups answer even-numbered questions and the other half will do the or odds. Your answer must be positive. If you have a negative answer when you solve for any type of deficit, remove the negative sign and change the word deficit to surplus. Any number with decimal places can be rounded to two decimals.

Questions:

1. The Deficit is $800 billion. Deflation is 2%. Debt is $5 trillion. What is the Real Deficit?
2. The Deficit is $800 billion. Inflation is 10%. Debt is $5 trillion. What is the Real Deficit?
3. Output is currently $12 trillion. GDP* is $10 trillion. The deficit is $300 billion. Calculate Passive and Structural Deficits. (Tax rate = 19%)
4. Output is currently $7 trillion. GDP* is $10 trillion. The deficit is $300 billion. Calculate Passive and Structural Deficits. (Tax rate = 19%)
5. There is an $800 billion inflationary gap. The tax rate is 25%. Structural Surplus=$100 billion. Debt=$2 trillion. Inflation=3%. What is the Real Deficit? (Hint—you have to find Passive Deficit first, in order to find Actual aka Nominal Deficit, and use that to get the Real Deficit.)
6. There is a $1 trillion recessionary gap. The tax rate is 20%. Structural deficit=$200 billion. Debt=$5 trillion. Deflation=4%. What is the Real Deficit? (Hint—you have to find Passive Deficit first, in order

to find Actual aka Nominal Deficit, and use that to get the Real Deficit.)

7. Potential Output is $8 trillion, and GDP is currently $8 trillion. The tax rate is 25%. How much is the passive deficit?
8. Calculate the national debt at the end of year 2013 for Richoslovakia, a (fictional) country founded in 2008:

2008	G=500, T=200
2009	G=500, T=600
2010	G=600, T=700
2011	G=600, T=400
2012	G=700, T=600

IN-CLASS PROJECT

Deficit Reduction Proposals

Directions:

Each Group will get a number from 1–5. That number corresponds with the Deficit Reduction Proposal below that group will analyze. All groups should ensure their analysis answers questions A, B and C.

Questions:

A. Explain the proposal in your own words.

B. What are the obstacles to passing this proposal into law and getting it fully implemented so it can greatly reduce the deficit? Conversely, if you think it will pass and be executed quite easily, explain why you think this is the case. This question can deal with social, political and economic obstacles (or lack thereof).

C. If you haven't already, explain why you think this proposal will make a big dent in the deficit or, conversely, why it will be ineffective in reducing the deficit.

Deficit Reduction Proposals 1–5 (the name of the proposal is in "quotes"):

1. The proposal to add a "Balanced Budget Amendment" to the Constitution narrowly failed to pass the U.S. Senate in 1995. Those in favor argued it was the only way to reduce deficits significantly, while those opposed argued that this would constrict the flexibility required for active fiscal policy. It would prevent Compensatory Fiscal Policy. Imagine that in the year 2008 AD shifts down and the economy is in a recession. This could have been caused by a crash in the stock market, or plummeting home values, which would reduce C. The balanced budget amendment would prevent the government from any new spending to restore the economy at Y* (Full-employment GDP). The only way it could increase G is if there was an equal increase in T, which would reverse the positive intended effect on Consumption. To make fiscal matters worse, falling incomes decreases revenue from taxes.

2. The "line-item veto" would enable the President to cut certain sections out of newly passed legislation, as opposed to the standard all-or-nothing veto. Sections could be eliminated to reduce increases in G or tax cuts that often arrive packaged in bills resulting from compromises during the legislative process. Line-item veto power existed briefly when Clinton was president, but in 1998, the "Line-Item Veto (was) Outlawed … In a 6–3 decision, justices rule Constitution prohibits president from rewriting legislation by striking out single items of spending or specific tax breaks passed by Congress" (Infoplease.com "Major decisions of the Supreme Court" June 25, 1998).

3. "Privatization" is the migration of public services to private sector business owners. The operation of services like Military, Police, Fire Department, Amtrak, , Buses, K-12 education, regulatory functions,

elections, Medicare, Medicaid, Social Security, the Post Office or (California references) Caltrain, BART, could be contracted to firms. Motivated by profits, it is argued that firms will produce more efficiently than the government.

In another form of privatization, government assets can be simply sold ("Asset Selling"), such as oil reserves, public land, buildings, city power plants, water treatment facilities. Governors in several states have sold roads, highways, bridges, and toll roads to private companies, which almost inevitably means a toll booth or other fee-collection system will be installed if there is not one on that road already.[†]

4. The proposal that government should reform the way the budget is accounted is called "Current account—Capital account budgeting" and is the procedure private firms must use. "Current revenues" (tax dollars collected this year) could balance the "current expenditures" of salaries for government workers and transfer payments (which pay for services or benefits enjoyed this year). "Capital expenditures" which expand the potential output for future generations, like building roads, dams, bridges, and power sources (i.e. infrastructure) could be financed by deficit spending. This addresses the problem inherent in the current "cash-flow accounting system."

5. Another solution to layoffs (unemployment) in a recession (explain why this relates to the deficit) is called the Share Economy, a.k.a. the "Two-Wage Economy". Wages would be partially tied to profits. A majority of a worker's salary would be stable, in economist Martin Weitzman's proposal, while 15–20% would be variable and directly tied to the profits of the firm. The result, Weitzman argues, is that in recessions, when firms can not sell as much of their output, profits decrease, and the variable (or "bonus") portion of salaries will decrease. Layoffs will decrease since firms' payroll expenditures—the input costs of labor—have decreased.

Major opposition to the Two-Wage Economy would come from senior union leaders who have enough seniority that the threat of layoff is not a risk, eliminating benefits for them from the proposal while they still would face the cost of a variable paycheck.

Former U.S. Dept. of Labor Secretary Larry Summers also notes the *fellow worker problem* that could arise. Any newly hired workers means more people with whom to split the workers' share of the profits through bonuses, making those with seniority likely to resist new hiring and welcome layoffs of less efficient and newer hires so their own share profit pie can grow. Also there could be an investment problem when stockholders see there is another claimant to profits.

[1] http://motherjones.com/politics/2007/01/highwaymen.

Notes